REPORTAGE PRESS

ABOUT THE AUTHORS

Sergei Golitsyn was born on a small family estate south-east of Moscow in 1909, and lived through the social, political and industrial upheavals that created the Soviet Union. Growing to manhood, struggling to find employment with the terrible handicap of coming from a noble family, he endured the hunger, injustice and cruelties of the times. In 1941 he joined the army as an engineer, advancing with the Red Army all the way to victory in Berlin. After demobilisation in 1946, and until his death in 1989, he wrote many articles and stories, mostly for a young audience. His love of his homeland and its history, and his sense of the spiritual and cultural losses caused by the transformation of Old Russia, drove him to share something of the past with his young listeners and readers. It was during these years that he worked on his memoirs, and the manuscript was published in Russia in 1990. He wrote of his childhood and his years in the army, but most dear to him was the massive manuscript describing his life and times between 1918 and the end of the 1930s. Conditioned by the terrible years of Stalin's reign, Sergei believed that his manuscript would only be read in the twenty-first, or even twenty-second centuries. Thanks to perestroika, his pessimism was unfounded. Though he died on the eve of publication, his *Memoirs of a Survivor* will stand as a memorial to all the victims – but also survivors – of those tragic times.

Nicholas Witter is related to the late Sergei Golitsyn through his maternal grandmother, Countess Bobrinsky (born Princess Vera Golitsyna), who was Sergei's aunt. Born in 1930, he has led a peripatetic life, partly thanks to his upbringing, when his father served as a Cunard Line manager in several European countries, and partly to his own restlessness. In the course of nearly sixty working years he has been employed, inter alia, as a young executive in London, a timekeeper on Canadian construction sites in Labrador and an

English language teacher in Greece and Cambridge. Knowledge of languages, especially French and Russian, eventually led to his working for twenty-six years as a simultaneous conference interpreter at the International Atomic Energy Agency in Vienna, a profession he still practises freelance from Highbury in London. He is married to Tania (who, despite her name, is not Russian). They have three children and seven grandchildren.

Dominic Lieven is Professor of Russian Government at LSE and a Fellow of the British Academy. He has written many books on Russian history, including Russia's Rulers under the Old Regime and Empire: the Russian Empire and its Rivals. His next book, War and Peace: Russia against Napoleon 1807–14 will be published in 2010. His family were influential members of the aristocracy under the Tsars.

MEMOIRS
OF A SURVIVOR

SERGEI GOLITSYN

Translated by Nicholas Witter
Introduction by Professor Dominic Lieven

REPORTAGE PRESS

REPORTAGE PRESS
Published by Reportage Press
26 Richmond Way, London W12 8LY United Kingdom
Tel: 0044 (0)7971 461 935
E-mail: info@reportagepress.com
www.reportagepress.com

Memoirs of a Survivor was produced under the editorial direction
of Ellen Hardy.

Sergei Golitsyn © 2008
Introduction Copyright © Dominic Lieven 2008
Translation Copyright © Nicholas Witter 2008
Foreword Copyright © Nicholas Witter 2008
First published in Russia in 1990

British Library Cataloguing in Publication Data
A catalogue record for this book is available from the British Library.

ISBN-13: 978-1-9067020-1-4

Cover design by Sheridan Wall
www.wallwideweb.com.
Layout by Florence Production Ltd
www.florenceproduction.co.uk.

Maps by Phil Kenny.

Printed and bound in Great Britain by
CPI Antony Rowe, Chippenham, Wiltshire.
www.antonyrowe.co.uk

Introduction

BY DOMINIC LIEVEN

Prince Sergei Golitsyn was eight-years-old in 1917, the year when the Russian revolution transformed his family's life. His memoirs cover the years from 1918 until the outbreak of the Second World War. They are a rich and vivid everyday account of people, events and feelings but in a context in which every day could bring arrest, imprisonment and death. On a personal level they are a moving tale of courage, struggle, humour and tragedy. Since few such memoirs of members of the old aristocracy who lived on in the Soviet Union exist even in Russian, they are also a fascinating insight into Soviet history and society from an unexpected angle. Their translation and publication in English is very welcome.

Sergei Golitsyn came from the heart of the Russian aristocracy. His memoirs are packed with aunts, cousins and relatives by marriage from the grandest families in old Russia. After the revolution for a time his extended family lived on the estate of his aunt, Countess Vera Bobrinsky, in Tula province. Though almost all their land was taken, they grew their own food in an impromptu kitchen garden and lived reasonably. The local peasantry disliked the Bobrinskys but they were more or less left in peace until one of Sergei's uncles bagged a number of ducks for dinner. Denunciations followed and the family found itself first squeezed into a single floor of one wing of their mansion and then evicted totally. Of course, even without the ducks eviction could only have been postponed.

After being removed from the manor house they moved into the nearby town of Bogoroditsk. There his father worked as an official in the local public health administration. One of Sergei's uncles had admired Leo Tolstoy in his youth and had bought all the tools needed for cobbling. His mother now took up this trade, as well as rearing chickens and gathering food and firewood to keep her family alive. One uncle was shot in Moscow and other relatives fought for the Whites and emigrated. But when Sergei's grandfather was arrested he was released and given a safe conduct by one of the most senior Bolsheviks, Kamenev, on the grounds that Vladimir Golitsyn had always treated political prisoners well during the pre-revolutionary era. The safe conduct was counter-signed by Zinoviev, another of Lenin's closest associates. The Golitsyns kept the document until 1938 when both leaders fell victim to Stalin and it was safer to burn it. On the other hand, Ekaterina Peshkova, the wife of Maxim Gorky, was to remain a vital intermediary for the family with the Soviet authorities throughout the 1920s and 1930s.

In 1923 the family moved back to Moscow, where Sergei Golitsyn spent his adolescence. During the years of the so-called New Economic Policy Sergei Golitsyn was at school in Moscow. These were not easy times. There was very little money to go round – not enough for instance to supply him with underwear. A number of relatives were arrested. One of his Bobrinsky cousins turned informer – merely one particularly bitter element in a world of suspicion, distrust and insecurity. His own chances of a higher education and worthwhile career were compromised by his background. On the other hand, cultural life flourished and some of his relatives earned reasonable wages from private and even foreign employers. Very faint whispers of the old world survived. He recalls a dance at the home of his relatives, the counts Sheremetev, at which an old general who had served as an aide to the Grand Duke Sergei conducted proceedings in French, beginning with the command: "*Les cavaliers, engagez vos dames pour la première contredance.*"

Sergei Golitsyn describes his family at the beginning of 1929 as "contented, hard-working and fortunate" but life soon worsened dramatically. Many of Sergei's relatives disappeared into the camps. Some returned. He himself was arrested briefly and his survival hung by a thread on a number of occasions. With the end of NEP there were no private or foreign employers left and his aristocratic name and background made it very difficult to find and hold a job in an economy where all employment was a state monopoly. In the totally arbitrary world of Stalin's Russia nothing could guarantee Sergei Golitsyn from imprisonment or death, but it proved both somewhat safer and much easier to find a job outside Moscow. The memoirs therefore tell the story of his work in the forests of Siberia and on the construction of the Moscow-Volga canal. They also recount the fate of his family and that of his wife, Klavdia Bavykin, the daughter of a railway worker. The memoirs end with the outbreak of the Second World War, during which Sergei Golitsyn served as a military engineer, reaching Berlin in the ranks of the Soviet army in 1945.

Sergei Golitsyn emerges from the memoirs as a likeable and credible witness. He drew inner strength from religion, Russian literary and musical culture, and strong family loyalty and mutual support. Neither he nor his parents spent any time bewailing lost riches partly because they were too busy staying alive but also because their spiritual and cultural values went deep, as did their strong sense of Russian pride and identity, and their ethic of duty and honour. They never had been spoiled rich kids and this served them well in adversity. There was a naïve and honourable innocence about Sergei and his family. For example, he himself, his brother and father were virginally chaste when they married. This is about as far-removed from today's *jeunesse dorée* as it is possible to be, though to be fair it was also far-removed from the lives of some of Saint Petersburg's "fast set" in pre-revolutionary times. Sergei Golitsyn was very proud of his family's traditions and heritage but not too proud to marry a railway worker's daughter or appreciate her family's qualities. The only feeling that held him back was fear that her life and those of any children they might have would be ruined through associating with a former aristocrat.

His account of his wife's family is just one of the many fascinating insights into Soviet society and its values. Her relatives were if anything even more horrified than his own by their marriage. They were loyal Soviet citizens who believed everything the state's propaganda told them – until the moment when Stalin's purges ripped through the communist party itself in 1936–8. Many years before that, Stalin's error had already destroyed the world of the Russian peasantry. Some of the most moving and lyrical pages of the memoirs describe Sergei Golitsyn's journey to northern Russia on the eve of collectivisation, where he was one of the last witnesses to a society of sometimes quite well-off independent farmers, traditional north Russian peasant architecture, and a superb landscape dotted with churches and monasteries and still untouched by Soviet environmental vandalism. Above all, however, this book is a moving personal account of how one member of the former aristocracy perceived, suffered and survived the early Soviet era – and how so many of his relatives were less fortunate.

Dominic Lieven
London School of Economics
2008

Foreword

BY NICHOLAS WITTER

Like many parents, my mother, the "beautiful Sofia Bobrinskaya", as she is described in this book, did not abound in stories of her early years. In her case, given the place and time of her young years, this is not surprising. She was born in 1904 and so was just thirteen when the 1917 Russian revolution overturned her world and changed it forever. Eviction from home, hunger and fear were the new features of her life and that of her family. I remember that she talked of her happiness as a little girl sliding on an ice-hill in the park surrounding their house, of the walks she took with her father after the spring thaw when the ground was thick with flowers and of other simple domestic scenes; but only fleetingly did she touch on darker times. Once, looking at a photograph of ragged men and women shovelling snow in a Moscow street soon after the revolution, she said, "I did that, too. We were forced to," and then fell silent. Like so many children, I never pressed her to talk on.

So when this book came into my hands, this loving narrative by her cousin Sergei Golitsyn of the life of both my mother's family and many other related families of the old aristocracy, my pleasure was intense. Not only was it a gripping story of how these families were challenged, faced up to, or crushed by the events that followed 1917, but it was also a saga of the way Russia turned into the Soviet Union. What came alive as I read this book was not just the personal story of the troubles and joys of related families – it was even more a vivid account of the harsh realities of a country transformed by the new ideology.

Sergei Golitsyn was born in 1909 and lived a long life, dying in 1989. Born with the title *Knyaz* (Prince), and bearing the name of a famous family, he therefore belonged to one of the classes – nobles, officers and officials of the old order – explicitly condemned by the new regime. The fates suffered by these people in the first years of Soviet times varied greatly; uncounted numbers died in the civil war between Whites and Reds, thousands were summarily executed, huge numbers managed to flee the country, and of those who remained, death by starvation, cold, infection or imprisonment was all too common. This book describes how Sergei struggled to survive, without ever hiding his identity. First through the turbulent years of the 1920s and then in the bad years of Stalin's rule, from 1928 onwards. As he tells us, he was proud and glad to have remained in his own country. He writes, "If I had left Russia I would have become a translator at the United Nations and have enjoyed a comfortable life, but lost the beauty, colour and joy of my Motherland." After reading this book, one sees his point.

After serving in the army during the entire Second World War, he finally achieved his long-cherished ambition to become a professional writer. He wrote many articles and stories for children, but his main interest lay in recalling the people and places of Old Russia, the monasteries and churches that had made so many towns beautiful. Inevitably, he had to be careful how he tackled such subjects. In this book, he describes one incident when at a public function his outspoken views on the destruction of churches struck his audience silent and caused the cancellation of the newspaper report that was to have been made of his lecture.

Like other writers in the Soviet Union, it was only in secret that he could tell the truth, and this book owes its existence to his determination to get down on paper something of the reality of life after the revolution for future generations. As he says at the beginning of his memoir, many people wrote about life before the revolution, but very few people could face writing about the horrors that followed. This he did, writing, as it was expressed in those years of night time searches and arrests, "for his drawer"; the expression is evocative, though in reality I imagine he must have concealed his manuscript more securely than in a desk drawer.

Throughout the many years of Soviet rule it must have seemed to most people that there was little hope of change. There had of course, following the war, been short periods of slight and vague liberalization, periods referred to as "thaws". There had been the notorious Twentieth Congress of the Communist Party, at which the then Party Secretary, Khrushchev, had denounced Stalin's reign of terror. It was Khrushchev, too, who had allowed the publication of Solzhenitsyn's *One Day in the Life of Ivan Denisovich*. But these events were only tiny cracks in the massive grip on power of the *nomenklatura* – the ruling class of officials at whose apex stood the Central Committee and the Politburo. The prevailing demoralisation of the general public, the endless fruitless sloganeering, the material shortages endured by all but the most privileged – these factors, like the Soviet regime itself, seemed beyond change . And yet by the 1980s, change was gathering force, like the ice breaking up on Russia's great rivers in the spring (a sight described by Sergei towards the end of his book). In that decade, so momentous for the future of the country, the publication of truth-telling writing was suddenly possible.

In these years of milder repression, Sergei was able to write up the memoirs of both his earliest childhood and of his war years, aiming in this way to produce a trilogy of his life and times. Sadly, time was not on his side, and in 1989, having just put the finishing touches to his main manuscript, a heart attack carried him off. He died, however, knowing that his work was about to be published. Much earlier in his life he had expressed the thought that only in the very distant future would historians be able to read what he was writing. Thankfully, his prophecy was too pessimistic.

Nicholas Witter
London 2008

Translator's Note

Generally, if one is not too pedantic, Russian lends itself to relatively straightforward transliteration from the Cyrillic, though usually a choice has to be made between equally valid possibilities. Most readers will already be familiar with Russian transliteration through reading the great novelists, so they will find little difficulty in this book. Perhaps the way Russians address each other by name and patronymic – Nikolai Vladimirovich, Alexander Pavlovich – causes some unease, but the logic is simple as the father's name distinguishes one from the many other bearers of the same first name. (After all, in English we have often to say "John who? Or "Which Bill are you talking about?") It is also the way one addresses older people, new acquaintances, bosses and leaders. However, once intimacy or friendship is established, Russians drop the patronymic, formality no longer being required.

I have chosen to write "y" for the double Russian "i" in name endings such as Georgy, Yury etc. However, for names such as Sergei, Andrei and Nikolai, the "i" is more appropriate.

Then Russian has six sounds formed by single letters that require two letters in the Latin alphabet: Zh, Kh, TS, Ch, Sh, Shch. Hence names like Mikhail, Zhenia, Shchukin.

There are many memoirs of life in Russia before the revolution,
but few covering the years after 1917. The painter, M.V.
Nesterov, for example, confessed that he found it too terrible
to try to describe his experiences after October 1917. It is as
if some unknown force prevented pen being put to paper.
In the pages that follow, I shall try to convey the reality of the
lives of my family and related families of the Russian aristocracy
up to the outbreak of the Second World War. I shall try to
be as objective as possible and pray God give me the
strength to complete my task.

Sergei Golitsyn

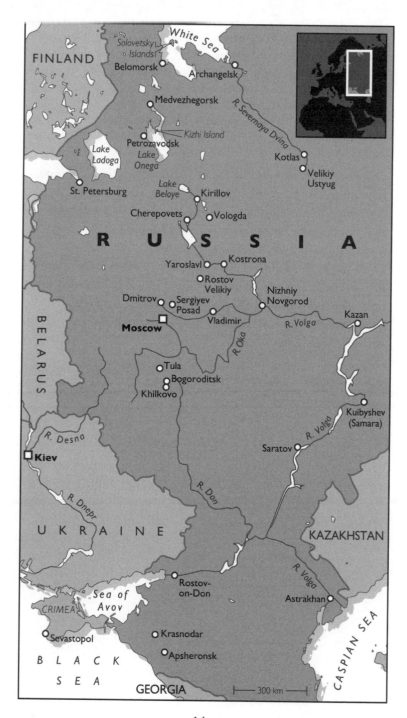

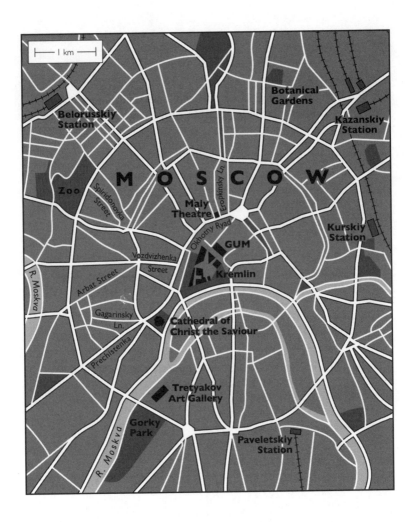

THE GOLITSYN FAMILY

The Bobrinsky family descends from an illegitimate son of the Empress Catherine II and Count Grigory Orlov

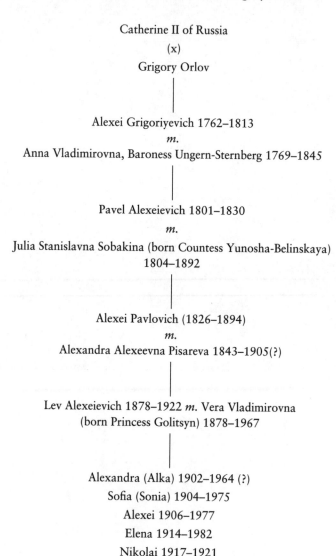

Catherine II of Russia

(x)

Grigory Orlov

Alexei Grigoriyevich 1762–1813

m.

Anna Vladimirovna, Baroness Ungern-Sternberg 1769–1845

Pavel Alexeievich 1801–1830

m.

Julia Stanislavna Sobakina (born Countess Yunosha-Belinskaya)
1804–1892

Alexei Pavlovich (1826–1894)

m.

Alexandra Alexeevna Pisareva 1843–1905(?)

Lev Alexeievich 1878–1922 *m.* Vera Vladimirovna
(born Princess Golitsyn) 1878–1967

Alexandra (Alka) 1902–1964 (?)
Sofia (Sonia) 1904–1975
Alexei 1906–1977
Elena 1914–1982
Nikolai 1917–1921

GOLITSYN FAMILY TREE

Great Uncle: Alexander Mikhailovich G. (1838–1919)
(owner of Petrovskoye estate)

|

Grandfather: Vladimir Mikhailovich G. (1847–1932)

m.

Sofia Nikolaevna (born Delianova) (1851–1925)

|

Father: Mikhail Vladimirovich (1873–1942)

m.

Anna Sergeevna (born Lopukhina) (1880–1972)

|

Alexandra (Lina)1900–1991

Vladimir 1902–1943

Sofia (Sonia)1903–1982

Sergei (Seryozha)1909–1989

Maria (Masha) 1911–1988

Ekaterina (Katia)1914–

Chronology

1917 The October Revolution. Hunger stalks the cities.

1918 January The Bolsheviks close the Constituent Assembly and move to seize absolute power.

Civil war between the Communists (Reds) and Conservatives and Monarchists (Whites) tears the country apart. The Bolsheviks pursue a policy of "war communism". Tsar Nicholas II and family murdered in Ekaterinberg.

1921 Civil war ends.

1918 July The Bolsheviks adopt limited market capitalism to revive the Russian economy – the New Economic Policy (NEP).

1922 March Lenin is struck down by a stroke.

1923 The Cheka take control of Solovki monastery and turn it into a concentration camp.

Sergei Golitsyn, then aged eight, is living with his family in Georgievsky Lane, Moscow.

The Golitsyn family moves to Bogoroditsk, driven by hunger. They are invited by their father's sister Vera, who is married to Count Leo Bobrinsky.

Execution of Uncle Mikhail Lopukhin for taking part in a plot to free the imprisoned Tsar.

Golitsyn and other family members manage to build a life in Bogoroditsk, despite eviction and persecution. Leo Bobrinsky dies in a Moscow prison.

Families in Bogoroditsk move back to Moscow. Sonia Bobrinskaya marries Reginald Witter. Georgy Osorgin is imprisoned in Butyrka Prison in Moscow.

1924 Death of Lenin. Stalin begins to take control of the Communist Party. Lenin's letter criticising Stalin is concealed.

Reports in newspapers of the trial and execution of prominent figures.

1926 The struggle for the leadership intensifies as Kamenev, Zinoviev and Trotsky join forces against Stalin.

Sergei fails to enter University. In 1927, Sergei and his sister Masha attend the State Higher Course in Literature.

1928 Stalin achieves total power. Trotsky expelled from the country. First Five Year Plan introduced.

Sergei and a friend travel to the northern lakes. Sergei is arrested and briefly imprisoned. Georgy Osorgin executed at Solovki.

The entire Golitsyn family is deprived of the vote and sent into internal exile. They settle in Kotovo, just outside Moscow.

1929 Millions die during the collectivisation of agriculture.

1932–33 Famine in the Ukraine. Millions die.

Sergei is employed as a surveyor on some of the country's major industrial sites.

1932–37 Construction of the Moscow-Volga canal by prisoners from the Gulag.

1936–38 Show trials of leading Bolsheviks.

1939 August Nazi-Soviet Pact.

1941 June Hitler invades USSR.

Sergei joins the Russian army as an engineer.

1. The Hard Years Begin

1

The scene is Georgiyevsky Lane, Moscow, at the beginning of 1918. Logs were being brought into our courtyard, several cubic metres of thick birch logs. Clearly my father had been able to use some of his former influence to get hold of such a load. My brother Vladimir, our manservant, Felix, and grandfather Alexander Mikhailovich's valet, Nikita, immediately began to cut up the logs and carry the pieces down into our cellar. Vladimir liked to claim that it was this experience that had given him a lifelong passion for cutting firewood. Soon fires were roaring all over the house and warmth began to spread. It made life begin to feel much better, though really only superficially, as in fact hunger, despite a year of good harvests, was already stalking the land. The whole country was in a state of breakdown and hardly any food was being brought into the cities, even though in the countryside supplies were abundant.

That winter many members of the former privileged classes fled south and east from Petersburg and Moscow, driven, not as the Bolsheviks claimed, by fear alone, but above all by hunger. In those early days after the revolution, the Bolshevik authorities acted indecisively, and their many decrees only succeeded in sowing fear. People fled so as to sit events out on their estates or in small towns, intending to return to their homes in the cities when the Bolsheviks disappeared. There was the general assumption that the Bolsheviks would not be defeated or driven out, but would somehow melt away of their own accord.

Uncle Kolya Lopukhin and Uncle Sasha Golitsyn went east with their families, while amongst those who went south were our uncles, Petya Lopukhin and Volodya Trubetskoi, together with many Gagarins, Obolenskys, Lermontovs, Chertkovys and Lvovs. They left with their numerous families, their nannies and governesses and a few faithful servants, taking with them their jewels and what possessions they could carry, leaving furniture and property to be looked after by other faithful servants left behind. Then when the Whites seized the border regions of Russia, they entered their service, until the White leaders, Denikin and Kolchak, were defeated. Then a new exodus began and tens of thousands found their way as refugees to Paris, Harbin, Serbia and other far away places.

At this time, there was in Nastasinsky Lane in Moscow a Savings and Loan Bank where people deposited not only their valuables and gold but also their stocks and shares, assuming that these would be held in absolute security. My father's parents, as well as his uncle, Prince Alexander Mikhailovich, all firmly announced that they would remain in Moscow, and since my own parents could not abandon them, they too decided to stay. Many of our relatives moved only within the Moscow area – to the estates of the Sheremetyevs, Samarins, Osorgins. My mother's sister, Ekaterina Sergeievna, with her husband, Alexander Vasilevich Davydov, our Uncle Alda, and their children went to his estate in the Tambov region. There the peasants accepted him into their community, granting him land which he began to cultivate for himself and his family.

Already, by the end of 1917, my father had taken a job in a bank, the Narodny Bank, as a department manager. What relationship this bank had to the Soviet authorities, I do not know. He also became a kind of intermediary between relatives who had left the country and the Savings and Loan Bank where they had deposited their valuables and other important papers. It goes without saying that none of these valuables were ever returned to their owners. Meanwhile, my father continued conscientiously to do his job at the Narodny Bank, receiving rations and a small salary. The rations were very meagre, but his salary rose every month; however, prices on the black market rose even faster. It soon became obvious to the employees that they were working for nothing but their allocation of rations, and these rations, too, kept shrinking, although they only sank to an "eighth", that is, fifty grams of bread per person per day, the following winter. As the transport was so bad my father was forced more and more to go about his business on foot and the meagre diet and long walks tired him out. Eventually, this led to enlargement of the heart, a condition he was to suffer from to the end of his days.

2

Sadly, very few of us are familiar with the best writings about those years. I am thinking of such works as *Doctor Zhivago* by Boris

Pasternak, *Dead End* by V. Veresayev and the short stories of Panteleymon Romanov. I hope that they will be published again one day and readers will have truthful accounts of these first years after the revolution.

Famine began to take hold in Moscow. Bread was rationed out in tiny pieces, and even these were full of chaff. Mikhail Mironich, our cook, learned to fry little balls of minced potato peelings. Two of our menservants, Anton and Nikita, still served at table as in the past, but another, Gleb, though still living in our basement, left our service and became a thief. We also heard that he had turned Bolshevik. We ate whatever was served at table. Our dog, Romochka, went on hunger strike due to the nature of the food and when grandmother tried to persuade her to eat, she simply looked up with her dark, expressive eyes and turned away from her bowl; after a week, though, she gave in and took to eating anything and everything.

I was moved into the nursery, already full of the beds and cots of my younger sisters, Masha and Katya, and of the children of Uncle Vladimir and Aunt Eli Trubetskoi, Grisha and Varya, and their nanny, Christina. My place was taken by my cousin Vladimir, nicknamed Boombook, the eldest child of the Lvov family, who was a cornet in the cavalry. Every morning he went off somewhere, leaving on the table a magnificent volume of the history of his brilliant regiment. I leafed eagerly through the pages with their portraits of dashing officers and brightly-coloured pictures of riders in white and gold uniforms and golden helmets, sabres raised as they galloped on their chestnut horses. In the early mornings, I watched with fascination as this slim and elegant cousin cleaned his nails, oiled his hair and dabbed himself with scent. He left us, and died in the ranks of the White Army. Much later, in a book published abroad, *The Cavalry Guards,* I read how somewhere in the south his squadron had driven the Reds out of a village and Vladimir had shot a commissar. But the commissar was still alive and as Vladimir walked away, the commissar shot him in the back, killing him, before himself being hacked to pieces.

I went back to sharing a bedroom with my brother, but not for long. This time my place was taken by my mother's youngest brother, Uncle Misha – Mikhail Sergeievich Lopukhin – and once more I was back in the nursery. I have not yet said anything about Uncle Misha, and yet he was of all my uncles the most distinguished. I do not recall whether he managed to finish his legal studies before volunteering for the front, but already before the war with Germany he had tried to persuade the peasants on the Lopukhin estate of Khilkovo to join together in something like a communal farm. It is unlikely that his efforts would have succeeded; the peasantry had too strong a sense of individual ownership. During the German War[1] he served in the Sumsk regiment of Hussars, and distinguished himself by his bravery. He was twice awarded the St George Cross and was promoted to lieutenant. But after the revolution he had to strip off his insignia and return to Moscow. A tall man with irreproachably groomed hair, wearing an English trench coat and tall boots, always moving at a rapid pace, he was very handsome, with dark hair, a short dark moustache and an eagle's gaze from under thick eyebrows. His looks were especially enhanced by a kind of yellowish flush of the brows, a feature that he shared with grandmother Lopukhin, my mother, my brother Vladimir and my sister Masha. My brother Vladimir was enormously proud of his resemblance to Uncle Misha and worshipped him, just as I in turn worshipped Vladimir. Naturally I also transferred these feelings to this brave, kind and handsome officer-uncle. Now there lay on the table a different splendid book, the *History of the Hussar Regiment of Sumsk*, and with the same fascination I drank in the pages with their portraits of officers and coloured pictures of riders in white uniforms and tall black shakos galloping on their bay horses and brandishing their swords.

Uncle Misha went off somewhere every day, but occasionally former officers visited him, and when that happened I was forbidden to enter the room. I was eaten up with curiosity but my pride forced me into silence and I made a show of not caring a bit. Now I know what the officers were talking about, and why they met – they were struggling over the decision as to whether to leave for the south or to stay in Moscow. Uncle Misha Lopukhin and Uncle Vladimir Trubetskoi soon made up their minds – they stayed.

3

At this time I was obsessed by one particular book. When much later I had to fill in a questionnaire asking me what book had made the greatest impression on me, I answered without hesitation: *The Knights of the Round Table*. It was a translation of a popular English book of legends about King Arthur and his knights. I cannot remember the author, and today I would not want to read it again so as to avoid disappointment. In childhood I would read a book once before putting it aside, but this one, though a long one, I read

---

1. *First World War.*

over and over, often opening it in the middle and reading again of the deeds of these legendary knights, Gawain, Owen, Parsifal, Galahad and King Arthur and his bearer Kay, of Merlin the wizard and Sir Lancelot of the Lake and his love for Queen Guinevere. Sir Lancelot was the bravest, the most daring, the most noble of the knights of the Round Table. In my mind, Uncle Misha was Sir Lancelot. He had done heroic deeds in the war, I knew, because now and again he would read us his wartime diary. I expected more acts of bravery.

The *Knights of the Round Table* made me think about myself. I genuinely felt I was "the most awful child in the world". My Aunt Sasha and our housekeeper Nasyenka constantly called me this. But now, under the influence of this book, my nine-year-old self resolutely decided to become better, so as to be like those brave knights. Knights are brave, but I was frightened of the dark, frightened of the neighbourhood children and strange dogs. Now I deliberately cooped myself up in a dark room and sat there daydreaming about the exploits of Lancelot and how Gawain, Parsifal and Galahad had set off to find the Holy Grail. And during the day I went to the gates of the house next door and watched the children playing in the street, though, in fact, they paid no attention to me. Later, in the country, I taught myself not to be frightened of geese, dogs and goats, and even bulls.

Knights are stoical, so I stoically endured hunger. And when I bruised myself, or cut my finger, or banged my knee I never cried. I tried, too, not to be capricious. Knights serve the ladies of their heart. After Lyubochka Obolenskaya left for the Caucasus, the only ladies left as targets for my service were my younger sisters. Now, I strove never to be the first to tease them, and set out to protect them as best I could. Knights never tell lies. I had got into the habit of lying, and found it very hard to change. From time to time I forgot my vows, but consoled myself by saying it was "excusable", as our Nanny Bush used to say. Knights never tell tales, but this was a law that I already respected. So this book, *The Knights of the Round Table* had a generally good influence on me. For a few years I lived through its heroes. Here was a world of fantasy into which I could escape in my dreams, reliving many of its episodes; I guarded it as a precious secret. Not even my mother knew about it. Once, however, the following incident happened: I was alone in my room, had put out the light and was huddled on a chair, dreaming, when suddenly Aunt Sasha came into the room and, switching on the light, caught sight of me.

25

"What are you doing here?" I was silent.

"What are you doing here, you awful boy?" she raised her voice.

"I'm thinking."

"What are you thinking about?"

"Shan't say."

The torments of hell would not have forced me to tell Aunt Sasha of the exploits of Lancelot. She went out, slamming the door, and complained about me to my mother. Mother scolded me a little but said nothing more.

4

When the spring came our principal food was still potato peelings in various guises. At meals we talked of nothing but food and of what the future might hold for us, and tried to guess how soon the Bolsheviks would go away. The famine in Moscow affected everyone. Soviet historians like to claim that the leadership also went hungry, but they fail to mention how, from 1918 onwards, workers, petty civil servants and those who still had the energy, had to travel out into the country to barter their possessions for flour and potatoes. You simply could not buy a train ticket; people just crowded into the goods wagons without them. Everywhere there were guards who confiscated food as fast as they could; some of it went to the government stores and the rest was sold secretly on the black market – or to put it more accurately, was traded for clothing, valuables, paintings and portraits of ancestors. The collections of paintings and china set up in this period – the Tropinin Museum founded by Vishnevsky, for example – were founded on this kind of barter. In her memoirs, printed in the monthly journal *Novy Mir*, Princess Ekaterina Meshcherskaya claims that ladies of her class stood in rows begging on Stoleshnikov Street. I never heard of this. And anyway to be given money would have meant nothing, nor would anyone have handed over even a fistful of flour.

In 1918 and the following year the peasants still had plenty of bread. The government organised armed parties that went out in all directions on special trains, stopped at the village stations and marched from house to house, demanding bread. They did not confiscate but actually offered thousand-rouble notes for what they took, although this money was already worthless. Illicit liquor was distilled in the villages, which was strictly forbidden. The special parties did what they liked, confiscating bread and flour, drinking the homebrew and fooling around with the women. In some places they were killed, and then punishment squads would be sent out, not to kill off the *kulaks* (richer peasants) but to kill anyone they met, at random, without any investigation or referral to the courts. The authorities set up so-called "committees of the poor", into which they enlisted the poorest peasantry so as to get them on their side and thus split the country up into three groups – *kulaks*, merchants and the poor.

Uprisings took place against these scavenging parties and against the authorities. As soon as they were put down in one place, they broke out in another. In 1918, in Svenigorod, an uprising was sparked by the desecration of the relics of St Savva. There was another in Rogachov against food squads. Soviet historians describe these as *kulak* rebellions, but they were in fact peasant uprisings. It was the patient Russian peasantry, bound together by the land, who rose up. The murder of a commissar led to the random execution of dozens of villagers, of anyone who fell into the hands of the authorities. Collective farms, *sovchozy*, were set up on the estates. The writer Mikhail Bulgakov has written vividly about just such a collective farm in his story *The Fatal Eggs*.

In 1918, the entire transport system fell to pieces, and was even worse the following year. Trains were only made up of freight cars normally used for animals and were supposed to be reserved for travellers with permits, but in fact they were packed out with the hungry, the persecuted and "bag people" hunting for food. These trains were given the nickname "Maxim Gorkys" – I have no idea why they were named after the founder of Soviet literature.

The newspapers of that time, unlike today's papers, did not hide the truth about uprisings and repression. They were filled with the names of those executed as well as the names of the dead from the special food parties. The latter were described as heroes who had died in the cause of the revolution. Memorials to them are still to be seen on many town squares; many streets were renamed after them. The papers were also filled with accounts of worrying events – that Soviet power had been overthrown on the river Don, beyond the Caucasus, or in Siberia. Mobilisation into the Red Army, the army that was to defend the revolution, began in the towns and villages. There was also plenty of foreign news, proclaiming, as Marx had predicted, the imminent outbreak of revolution in other countries where the working class was particularly strong – in Germany, France and England. After all, the proletariat had "nothing to lose but their chains". This faith in world revolution increased the enthusiasm of those who supported the revolution in our country.

5

Meanwhile, in Georgievsky Lane we went on living in a close-knit family, rather like the family in Bulgakov's novel *White Guard*, only there were a lot more of us. We ate extremely poorly and often sat in the dark without any light. Father continued to bring home his meagre rations. The adults read the newspapers, discussed, hoped, prayed, picked up all sorts of rumours – some hopeful, some threatening. Grandfather wrote his diary, the older children went to school, while I and my younger sisters were taught by Aunt Sasha. Our servants and housemaids continued to be in our service.

Grandmother spent her time bewailing the state of the world. Poor woman, she moaned and groaned because she could not understand what was happening. She was tormented by the continual disappearance of her comforts and the rising prices. Paintings of ours by famous artists such as Levitan and Polenov had to be bartered for food. Yet there was one ray of light in her existence; the disappearance of rich cooking and creamy French sauces achieved a cure for all her stomach ailments; suddenly she was a healthy woman.

During Holy Week the family fasted under the spiritual guidance of our old priest at the church of St George-on-Vspole, and once again I listened with wonder to the choral singing in the church. But we needed something special in the way of food to mark the end of our fast on Easter Sunday. Uncle Vladimir Trubetskoi, always a keen hunter, resolved to go duck shooting. If he could shoot a dozen duck, and even perhaps a passing goose – what a festive table we would have! With my brother Vladimir he set off for the Golitsyn estate, Petrovskoye, on the outskirts of Moscow. Our photo album in its grey oilcloth binding has survived. My brother took pictures of their hunt. In three days, they did not bag a single duck, but they did kill a badger and there is a picture of the triumphant hunters carrying the badger slung on a long pole. They brought their prize home and left it on the upper landing of the back stairs, where I rushed out to see it. What they did with it I cannot recall, and I do not remember if it was served at the Easter table. No doubt there were offerings from the peasants at the Golitsyn estates of Petrovskoye and Znamenskoye, and no doubt also some cured badger meat.

Spring came and with it growth. In our garden I collected the willow seeds and new buds, peeled and ate them. Aunt Sasha and the Trubetskoi's nanny took us children to Morozovsky Park and there we picked neat little bunches of dandelions and, putting on our gloves, tore up the young nettles. All this we handed over to Michael

Mironovich, who dressed the dandelions with vinegar to make a salad, and cooked vegetable soup out of the nettles. In those days the curative properties of vitamins were not known, but it was assumed that these dishes had to be healthy.

Uncle Vladimir Trubetskoi disappeared somewhere. It was only fifty years later, in Paris, that I eventually discovered where he had gone. Uncles Vladimir and Misha Lopukhin, along with a group of officers, had travelled beyond the Urals to free the Tsar and his family from captivity. How this plot was devised and why it failed has been recorded somewhere abroad, but I have never been able to trace any account.

At this moment, we had a letter from my father's sister, Aunt Vera Bobrinskaya, who was living on the estate of Count Bobrinsky at Bogoroditsk in the province of Tula. She wrote that they were managing well with their supplies of food and that she and her family were under the protection of the SRs (Socialist Revolutionaries), who were employees and workers at the local sugar factories. Most important of all, she said there were no Bolsheviks in the town. She invited us all to move to Bogoroditsk and take shelter in these troubled times under the Bobrinsky roof. As I write this, I realise, in comparison to the way people act now, what a fine and generous act this was, to invite such a large number of new mouths into her household.

The secondary school term had not yet finished, so it was decided to despatch the three youngest off first, along with Aunt Sasha, Nasenka and Lenya, the two Trubetskoi children with their nanny Christina and assistant nanny Polya, my mother and Aunt Eli Trubetskoi. My grandparents, as well as Grandfather Alexander Mikhailovich, refused to move.

Before our departure my mother handed over her responsibilities at the Society for the Protection of Mothers and Children to a communist woman, Lebedeva. Together they toured the orphanages and shelters for mothers and Lebedeva was able to see how, despite the shortages of food, everyone had been well cared for and everything was in order. Lebedeva could not help but notice how upset the staff were about my mother's decision to leave, so she begged her to remain and continue with her work, but my mother was adamant. She and Lebedeva parted on extremely good terms, and she assured my mother that if ever she needed help, she would be there to give it.

Later on, this woman became deputy commissar for social affairs. Some seven to eight years afterwards my mother sought her help, and was received in a friendly manner. They had a long conversation, during which Lebedeva complained that she was criticised for wearing nice clothes and using powder and lipstick. This was at a time when leading women were supposed to wear loose jumpers, wide skirts and red headscarves. A few years later she disappeared, liquidated.

We travelled to Bogoroditsk in far less comfort than we used to go to our estate at Buchalki, but at the time it was considered a great privilege to be allotted a private compartment where there were only two other ladies – even if they did have a mountain of luggage.

6

Now let me tell you something about the history of Bogoroditsk.

On the site of a seventeenth-century border fortress and military outpost, the Empress Catherine the Great commissioned the architect Starov to build her a fine mansion with two wings and an adjoining church. Starov redesigned the gates to the fortress creating a tall bell tower with an archway entrance. The main house and various other buildings were laid out in a large park of oak trees and limes. The river Uperta was dammed to form a lake; the mansion stood above on one bank, while on the other a town was built, its five streets laid out to radiate in such a way that the convergence point of these five radii was opposite the oval salon of the house, the mansion's main reception room. The salon had a five-angled window each of which had a view down the corresponding street on the far side of the lake. Each was given a name related in some way to Catherine, such as the names of her grandchildren, or to the court, and were crossed in turn by further geometrically laid out streets, also with significant names. Thus the town stretched away from the lake rather like a spider's web, although as time passed streets came into existence that did not obey the original strictly geometrical pattern. This ambitious project to build a mansion with its church, a town with its own church, and then park and farm lands, was entrusted to a typical eighteenth-century man of learning, Andrei Timofeyevich Bolotov, an agronomist, scientist and prolific writer all rolled into one. He was then put in charge of managing the estate.

Catherine gave birth to an illegitimate child fathered by her then favourite at court, Count Grigory Orlov. Immediately after his birth the baby was secretly whisked away from the Winter Palace and taken to Finland so that Catherine's husband, Tsar Peter, didn't find out what had been going on. Legend has it that he was wrapped in a beaver – *bobr* in Russian – mantle, which subsequently led to him being given the name of Bobrinsky. Gambling and dissipation marked his adult life, causing him to run up huge debts abroad. After the death of his mother, he was summoned home by his half brother, Tsar Paul, given the estate of Bogoroditsk and some other lands, and ordered to reside there permanently.

The youngest son of this first Bobrinsky, Vasily, was associated with the Decembrist plot to overthrow Tsar Nicholas I. He had set up a secret printing press at Bogoroditsk, but never managed to make use of it. He did not actually take part in the Decembrist uprising, as at the time he was abroad with his young wife on their honeymoon. Although his sympathies were known, as a cousin of the Tsar he was spared the ordeal of a trial. Another descendant, Alexei Pavlovich Bobrinsky, a grandson of the first Bobrinsky, was a minister under Tsar Alexander II and attempted to spread the religious ideas of Lord Radstock among his fellow aristocrats.[2] Occasionally, Leo Tolstoy would visit him to discuss religion. Later he used Bogoroditsk as a model for Vronsky's country estate in the novel *Anna Karenina*.

The Bobrinskys would have been very rich, if the debts run up by their ancestor had not hung over them, and much of their income was devoted to paying off just the interest on those debts. After the death of Alexei Pavlovich his four sons inherited Bogoroditsk, although the eldest, Alexei, took his inheritance in cash and left. The second son, Vladimir, managed the estate; in his youth he was energetic and liberal, but later become extremely right wing. In cooperation with his relatives in the senior line of the Bobrinskys, who had extensive lands in the Ukraine around the village of Smela, he tried to pay off all the ancestral debts.

Sugar factories were built both at Bogoroditsk, and also at Smela in the south. These began to generate income, but Smela enjoyed a warmer climate and the beet grew better there than further north. The new factory at Bogoroditsk was well equipped but the conservative peasantry refused to change their crops over to sugar beet, which caused the enterprise to fail. The situation was saved by the intervention of a Bobrinsky cousin from Smela who, together with the creditors and his Bogoroditsk cousins, devised a financial plan to save the estate. The brothers were to receive a relatively small income for life, whilst the estate was to be managed by an independent

---

2. *Baron Granville Walgrave, Lord Radstock (1833–1913) was a wealthy man who evangelised in Russia in the late nineteenth century during a period known as The Great Russian Awakening.*

representative of the creditors. This was the state of affairs for the Bobrinsky family just before the revolution. The Russian debts were to be paid off over ten years, leaving only the English debts. I discovered all these details in memoirs written by my father.

When we reached Bogoroditsk, I was struck by the grandiose scale of the estate; its great park, with a broad lake, and the massive house with two wings and a bell tower gateway. The Empire-style church was a little distance away from the house. What estates I had seen up till then seemed small in comparison with Bogoroditsk; it was on the scale of a palace such as Ostankino. Its land was reckoned to amount to twenty-seven thousand hectares: there were ten farms and nine mills (at Buchalki, our Golitsyn estate, there were only two). Use of the adjective of ownership, "the Count's" was widespread and can even be heard today. The banks of the lake on the town side were "the Town's", the opposite banks "the Count's". There were Town woods and Count's woods, and most of the contents of the mansion were marked with the family coat of arms.

The big house was closed up when we arrived, though the interior was intact, and it was referred to as "the Museum". Someone called Mitka or Mishka acted as a sort of guardian and carried a big bunch of keys for it. Only once did we, a bevy of youngsters, penetrate into the big house, where in the gloom of the shuttered interior we saw paintings in massive gold frames and furniture all in linen dust covers. Some of those paintings and furniture can now be seen in the city museum in Tula.

Aunt Vera and her family occupied the right wing of the building. Count Vladimir Alexeievich and his family had emigrated the year before; the twin bachelor brothers, Peter and Paul, were roaming the country; and I was happy to learn that the youngest brother, Leo, who had the reputation of being rather terrifying, was not at home. A Bobrinsky sister, Sophia Alexeievna – Auntie Misya – also lived at Bogoroditsk. At the age of sixteen she had suffered a hernia when lifting her overweight invalid father and for whatever reason had never had it operated on. She had grown abnormally fat, more of a mountain than a woman, and walked with difficulty, but was full of energy and keen to help – not with money, of which she had little, but through work. A small building was built for her down by the dam, and there she organised a nurses' training course. Her assistant was a similarly energetic spinster lady, Anna Vasiliyevna Bibikova, the daughter of a local landowner. They lived with their trainee nurses in this building, which was called the "Community House". The nurses went to work at the local hospital, until the war with Japan in the Far East, when the entire unit was despatched to that front in a medically equipped railway carriage. In the war with Germany they served on the Turkish front. Sophia Alexeievna used to tell the story of how she was travelling by car with a driver and two officers when they were stopped by a tiger lying across the road. The two officers dived under their seats, but she calmly seized a rifle and shot the beast.

In Bogoroditsk we sensed the lingering aura of the awesome respect that had surrounded the Bobrinskys for four generations. One was not allowed to run about the house or talk in loud voices. The servants went about in felt shoes. Apart from the cook, Stepan Egorovich, whom I had already met, there was a former serf, Ivan, who despite his very advanced years continued to lay and serve at table. He was constantly to be seen on the other side of the big house sitting lost in thought among the unweeded beds; it was said that he could see the ghost of the Count, his old master, whom he had served so long.

There was also a very ancient housekeeper, once housemaid to the old count's mother. In her youth, which was before the abolition of serfdom, she had been a great beauty, but then some drama had befallen her. Now quite deaf, but still very beautiful, she wandered about with her bunch of keys, opening and shutting the innumerable Bobrinsky cupboards and trunks and suitcases, poking about in them and then shutting them up. She was intensely interested in the goings on around her, and would thrust out her hand, palm upwards, and ask people to write on it with their fingers. These sign-words she could understand without difficulty, always replying briefly and to the point. I remember too a spritely barefoot girl, Natashka. She was the dishwasher and worked with tremendous energy, laughing to herself as she made the dishes clatter and clash in the sink. There were many other servants, who now I cannot remember.

7

Steadily the number of mouths to feed grew. When school was over in Moscow, Lina, Vladimir and Sonya arrived with a French couple – the Couesses. Our fourteen-year-old cousin, Kirill Golitsyn arrived from Petrograd. He was a handsome boy in his smart scout uniform with lots of badges on his chest and shoulders. His Bobrinsky cousins, Alka and Soynka, and my sister Sonya, clung to him and together played all kinds of games. In the evenings they went off in a gang to collect milk from the home farm.

My father finally convinced his parents to leave Moscow. They arrived with their dog, Romochka, and grandfather's valet, Felix. Father remained in Moscow, continuing to work at the Narodny bank, and living in the house on Georgievsky Lane with Grandfather Sasha, who refused to listen to any attempts to persuade him to leave Moscow, simply repeating that all he wanted was to be buried on his estate at Petrovskoye.

Uncle Vladimir Trubetskoi also arrived – I have already mentioned where he had been. And my mother, happy with the way everyone had settled in at Bogoroditsk, returned to Moscow to be with father. At meal times, we were joined by Zalzman, an Austrian prisoner of war who was a fine violinist. During the day he gave music lessons to the Bobrinsky children, and in the evenings arranged little concerts. Either Aunt Vera or grandmother played the piano, Zalzman the violin and Uncle Vladimir Trubetskoi the cello. People came from the town to listen to these concerts, among them singers who performed operatic arias and songs; others came from the nursing centre, or from the sugar factory, while the servants listened at the doors. Besides the classics, Uncle Vladimir's own compositions were performed. He was a man of many talents and later on I will write more about him, but as a composer he lacked technical skill, and my sister Sonya told me how hard he had to work before a performance to improve his playing and his composition, and how much Aunt Vera helped him with advice as they played. I was bored stiff by these concerts and could not understand why my cousin Alexei Bobrinsky did not want to go off and play, but just sat and listened. The paraffin lamps burned and it was dark outside as the grown-ups sat listening with closed eyes. These first two months at Bogoroditsk were a quiet oasis compared to our home in Moscow. Several times the employees of the sugar factory came to see Aunt Vera to assure her that we could continue to live without disturbance under their protection. They also brought us various provisions.

Alexei was three years older than me. I began to follow him everywhere. Aunt Sasha and Nasenka now stopped paying me any attention, and Alexei accepted me into his little band of friends. These children were the offspring of the former Bobrinsky house servants and of the local priesthood. They were called by the names of their parents' position – Mitka-priest, Mishka-deacon, Misha-coachman, etc. I followed this gang everywhere, fishing with them in the lake, imitating everything they did, although at football I was given the rather passive role of playing at the back. We discovered how to make bows and arrows. That winter the peach and apricot trees in the orangery had frozen. They were supported by wires, which we used as bowstrings on our maple shafts, and for arrow tips we melted down bullets, which were generally available in most homes in those times. We would have competitions under the bell tower to see who could shoot highest. My brother Vladimir cut me a special arrow, putting a chicken feather at one end and a pistol bullet on the other, and I shot it higher than anyone else. Time and time again we strung our bows, and every time it was my arrow that flew the highest. Then a jealous boy seized my arrow and broke it in two. I rushed off to Vladimir to show him the pieces; there was a lump in my throat, but I had sworn never to cry. He told me off and said he would never make me an arrow again. Deeply hurt, I turned away. I have described this incident with the arrow because years later I wrote a story about it. I showed it to many editors, but it was never accepted; the subtext was ideologically suspect. And yet it was, even though I say it myself, a good story.

My younger sisters were not really suitable as damsels. I found it difficult always to give way to them and we often quarrelled. And in Aunt Sasha's eyes I was invariably the guilty party. Yet as a knight of the Round Table I had to have a lady of my heart. Where could I find one? The family went to church regularly every Sunday. There I noticed a girl who kept staring at me. She was a little older than me, with long fair hair, blue eyes and a pointed little nose. She always stood with her mother on the left side. My sisters and I stood on the right. Every Sunday instead of praying we would turn to look at each other, blush, and then bow our heads in prayer. The girl's name was Zoyka Kormilitsin, and she was the daughter of the count's former storeman.

The first time I spoke to her we were both playing hide-and-seek and found ourselves hiding behind the same bush.

"I love you," I said.

"And I love you too," she replied.

I could not keep this to myself and told my sister Sonya. For ages after that she teased me about Zoyka, and that was the end of that romance.

I spent my days running about with the gang of boys. It did not take me long to become aware that among themselves they used all sorts of unfamiliar words and that these words were bad ones. But I could not understand what they meant, especially two of them that in Russian begin with the letters *zh* and *kh*.[3] I did after a while

---

3. *Zhopa (arse) and khui (prick).*

discover the meaning of about a dozen such words, but I was bewildered by the fact that the one used most often was the word "mother", which for me meant the most precious person in the world. Now there appeared on the estate a new character, Kovalevich, a healthy young soldier, who was allegedly a Bolshevik.[4] He did no work, lounged about from one wing of the house to the other, chewing and spitting out pumpkin seeds, and chatting with the menfolk; his language was peppered with swear words.

I asked Nasenka, "Can you swear m— f—?"

Her furious reaction bowled me over. She screamed and seized me by the shoulder. "How dare you! That's the worst sin. For every word like that the Mother of God renounces you for three years."

I was terrified. What of Kovalevich? I immediately set out to find him in the usual crowd of idlers and stood behind him. I began to count. Once, twice, three times . . . Kovalevich moved off with someone, I followed. Four, five . . . I spent the whole day stalking him and counting his "mother" oaths. In the evening, I wrote down the total and multiplied it by three. In general, much as I loved history, geography and the natural sciences, equally I loathed arithmetic. But I really enjoyed following Kovalevich for three days and then doing my multiplication sum. The result was staggering – not only would the Mother of God renounce him for his lifetime, but also his children, grandchildren, great-grandchildren, and so on, right down to the Day of Judgement.

8

Uncle Leo Bobrinsky spent the second half of the war serving as adjutant to the Governor of Galicia, his Bobrinsky relative from Smela. But as Galicia was only briefly captured by the Russians, the headquarters staff were posted to Kiev to await future victories that did not materialise, and were eventually reassigned. On his journey back to Bogoroditsk, Uncle Leo fell ill and was taken in by the Baryatinsky family in the province of Kursk. Even though he was only a teenager, my brother Vladimir set off to fetch him. We still have Vladimir's travel sketchbook, with its drawings of soldiers catching "bag people" and crowds storming the trains. Vladimir brought Uncle Leo home. He was very ill and weak, and turned out to be suffering

---

4. *Lenin's party followers were known as Bolsheviks (the majority) in contrast to Mensheviks (the minority). The Bolsheviks were more ruthless, and so greatly feared.*

from kidney disease. I discovered he was not at all as terrible as I had imagined. He walked with difficulty, using a stick, and at table talked loudly, vying with Uncle Vladimir Trubetskoi in a continual exchange of witticisms. Their spirited talk made all the younger members of the family roar with laughter.

The older children decided to put on a theatrical show, made up of scenes from Gogol's *The Government Inspector*, Griboyedov's *Woe from Wit* and Pushkin's *The Stone Guest*. Uncle Vladimir Trubetskoi was the director.

My sister Sonya took the parts of Marya Antonovna and Liza. Sonya Bobrinskaya was Anna Andreievna and Sophia. Alka Bobrinskaya, Dona Anna, and Alexei, Molchalin. My sister Lina played men's parts as Chatski and Don Juan, whilst Kirill played Chlestakov, Famusov and Leporello. Uncle Vladimir was the immobile Commendatore, clad in a sheet and standing on a chair. I was terribly proud also to be given a role as Famusov's manservant. With my arms crossed over my stomach and a big grin, I walked to the front of the stage and announced "Alexander Andreievich Chatski to see you!" The Bobrinsky family cupboards and trunks were full of all sorts of clothes dating back to the beginning of the last century and offered a wonderful supply of costumes. The stage was set up in the drawing room behind a curtain. There was a crowd of spectators. The town doctor, Alexei Nikolsky, came with his wife, Julia. Princess Ekaterina Miyshetskaya, whom the scholar and writer V.V. Veresayev wrote about as Katya Konopatsky in his memoirs and called his first love, came, as did a former head gardener of the estate, Baranov, and his wife, some employees from the sugar factory and the nurses from the dispensary. The room was packed. The show was a great success, and the audience were particularly impressed by Sonya and Kirill's fine acting.

We decided to put on a second show. But what? Well, we would write it ourselves. We all got together to do this, but the main scriptwriter was Uncle Vladimir. The comedy was given the title *Auntie on the Shelf*. An aged spinster (sister Lina) lives on her estate with three nieces (the Bobrinsky girls, Alka and Sonya, and our Sonya). Life is boring, but then along comes a young man, Coco Zavolevsky (Kirill) who at first does not know which of the nieces to court, and when he chooses one, the other two are furious. The conflict is resolved by the arrival of two more young men, a tall one, Count Kutilo-Zabaldausky in a red and blue Ulan uniform (brother Vladimir), and a short one, Baron Friedrich von der Hieraus (Alexei Bobrinsky) in a tailcoat, white trousers and high boots. The three gentlemen propose to the three nieces, and "auntie remains on the shelf", but at this point a neighbour enters armed with a bouquet, with puffed out cheeks and a pillow round his midriff. His name is Semyon Semyonovich (Uncle Vladimir). In silence, he hands the bouquet to Auntie, kisses her hand, and with that the play ends. I was due to play the part of Cupid, shooting an arrow at each of the lovers, but I do not think I would have agreed to play this role wearing only a maple leaf.

The play was a great success. There was long applause and demands to stage it again. Uncle Vladimir and Aunt Vera consulted together on writing music and songs for a new production. But a third show was never put on.

9

I do not remember which piece of terrible news came first – whether it was the telegram from my mother in Moscow, or the brief, five-line notice in the papers announcing the shooting, in Ekaterinburg, of the Tsar and his family and others close to them – eleven people in all. A few days before this news my father had arrived on leave from Moscow and the stories he told us, calmly and tersely, silenced our uncles' light-hearted badinage at table. The shock of the murder of the Tsar and his family was terrible. A requiem mass was sung in the church on the estate. Much later a family friend, D.V. Polenov, told me that a similar mass has been held in the village of Byokhovo on the river Oka where the peasants wept. I do not doubt that such secret and not-so-secret masses in memory of the martyrs were held all over our country. Without anyone knowing, I wept into my pillow. In those days many city and village houses were decorated, alongside their icons, with simple paper portraits of the Tsar and Tsarina, the pretty Princesses in their white dresses and the handsome young Tsarevich in his sailor costume. Millions of boys, myself included, worshipped the Tsarevich, who was only four years older than me. I was horrified. Death at war I knew about. But how could anyone raise their hand against the young man and his beautiful sisters? Everyone, young and old, was horrified and angry, or wept. Much later I learned that there were no ethnic Russians among the murder squad – they were either Latvians or Jews.

The second piece of terrible news came in a telegram from my mother; all it said was; "Brother Misha has died – arriving Tuesday." The telegram was brought to us when we were at table. Uncle Lev, standing, read it aloud. My sister Lina gave a shriek and ran out of the room. The rest of us sat in silence. Someone said that perhaps

Uncle Misha had died of a sudden illness, but we all knew he had been in prison for a month, and that he had met a different end. Father took Lina, Vladimir, Sonya and me aside, explaining that this was a great sorrow for our mother and that when she came we should be as considerate as possible and try to distract her from sad thoughts.

She arrived a few days later, wearing black, and with her turquoise brooch smeared with black ink. She walked about like someone lost, spoke to no one at table, and was even silent with us. If you went up to her, she would caress you, embrace you, and then push you away. And all this in silence. Night after night, I wept secretly into my pillow for her and uncle Misha. It was only a year later that she told me what had happened.

On his return to Moscow after the unsuccessful attempt to save the Tsar and his family, Uncle Misha became one of the leading members of an underground "Society for the Protection of the Homeland and its Freedom". It was mostly made up of former officers sworn to the deepest secrecy; each member only knew the names of five others and that of their leader. Uncle Misha himself knew five leaders. The Society was betrayed by an orderly. Some members were able to flee to the south; the rest, including Uncle Misha, were arrested.

A lot has been written about the exceptionally watchful eye of the Chekists (the secret police) and their ability to uncover plots. In fact, their methods were absurdly simple; they would arrest the first people to come their way, detain them and interrogate them in the hopes of picking up a thread of information. They would threaten these frightened people, saying, "We know about all these plots, we just wanted to clarify things with you". And their prisoners, sometimes quite innocent people, but having heard some rumours, would chatter away. Others, frightened to death, would confess to nonexistent misdoings. In those days open courts with timid defence lawyers and menacing prosecutors such as Krilenko, handing out sentences for predetermined numbers of years, were a rarity. The usual way out of prison was either up against a wall, or release to freedom. The majority, those like Stanislavsky, Moskvin, Nesterov and Vernadsky, were arrested but then set free.

They used a technique known as the "siege". The Chekists would select a suspicious apartment, install their people in it to keep watch and detain everyone who called there. Thus a visiting friend, the milkman, a priest with his communion vessels or the children's friends would all be detained in the apartment for a few days, then released, except for the ones the Chekists took away with them.

Active intervention was vital. You had to find some way of being received by an important communist and convince him or her of the innocence of the arrested person. And quite frequently, thanks to their authority, this sort of important person, or skilled intermediary or even the arrested person himself, could by a simple telephone call bring about a release. Communists like this were described as "tame". People would say, "Go to her, she knows a tame one. He'll get so-and-so released." This system of vigorous intervention worked from immediately after the revolution right into the middle of the 1930s. But it only worked for more or less innocent people. Uncle Misha's case was quite different. After all, from the Soviet point of view he was a real enemy. Nonetheless, my mother hurried to intervene for him. Years later I was gathering mushrooms with her in the woods when a hen grouse noisily broke cover from under our feet and flew around us, trying to draw us away from her nest.

"That's how I acted to save Uncle Misha," said my mother.

She did everything she could to save her younger brother, even risking her own imprisonment. In those days, access to the leadership was much easier than it is today. Mother did not manage to see either Lenin, or Trotsky or Sverdlov, but she did see Kamenev and Dzerzhinsky and the latter's immediate subordinates – Peters and Menzhinsky.[5] She got to see Bonch-Bruyevich. At first she took along with her Uncle Misha's fiancée, Princess Maria Turkestanova, the niece of Metropolitan[6] Trifon, but the Princess fainted in one of the offices and mother then continued her visits alone. She never forgot what venomous looks Dzerzhinsky gave her, and how the others turned glazed eyes away from her. Everywhere it was the same answer: "No".

She did find one humane member of the government – Pyotr Smidovich, whose brother had spent two winters in the country near Tula as tutor to the Lopukhin children. From this brother, Smidovich had heard of the close and warm relationships of our huge family. Mother paid him several visits and he took up her case quite energetically, saying, "If your brother swears an oath never to go against the Soviet state, I could vouch for him and he would be freed."

---

5. *Vyacheslav Menzhinsky (1874-1934), a leading Communist, succeeded Dzerzhinsky as head of the Ob'edinennoe Gosudarstvennoe Politicheskoe Upravlenie (OGPU) secret police in 1926. He died a natural death in 1934.*

6. *The Orthodox has a Patriarch (at Constantinople), then provincial Metropolitans, then Archbishops, then Bishops.*

I never knew whether Smidovich himself went to Butyrka prison, but my mother and Princess Turkestanova were allowed to visit Uncle Misha three times. My father, still in Moscow, wrote Uncle Misha a long letter in which he tried to convince him to agree to the conditions for his release. Uncle Misha was deeply offended that a close relative was urging him on the threshold of death to defile his soul. My mother found the strength in herself, and in her love of her brother, not to support my father's reasoning. She made the sign of the cross over her brother, and left. The next time she saw Smidovich, he said that under those circumstances he could do no more. As she left him, he assured her that if ever she needed help in the future she could come to him.

Somehow she found out that the prisoners were going to be shot at the Bratsky cemetery near the village of Vsesvatsky and would be taken there in trucks at intervals of several days, probably because they were short of armed escorts. The first batch was the officers, close friends of Uncle Misha's, including Volodya Belavsky and the son of a famous Moscow psychiatrist, Korotnev. The night before, Korotnev had a dream where he saw himself sitting on the tailboard of the truck and how, when the vehicle slowed at a corner, he jumped off and managed to escape. And this is indeed what happened in real life. He spent the entire civil war on various fronts and then got away to America, where he married Princess Turkestanova, who had left Moscow some time after the death of Uncle Misha. Korotnev's father, the doctor, lived unharmed in Moscow for ten years, continuing to treat patients. But one day someone who knew his son in America came to call on him after crossing the frontier illegally, and the past incident was remembered, including his son's last minute escape. The old doctor was arrested and disappeared.

When on her final visit my mother told her brother of Korotnev's escape, his face lit up and he said, "You can't imagine what good news you've brought me." Among Uncle Misha's belongings, given to her after his execution, was his English trench coat, which my brother Vladimir wore from then on.

Mother wanted to know where her brother had been buried. She went to the Bratsky cemetery and wandered about among the graves of Russian soldiers who had died in Moscow hospitals during the war with Germany. Standing under a tree and praying, she noticed a bird singing nearby; she followed it and ended up close to a long brick wall on one side of the cemetery. The wall was pitted with bullet holes, and at its foot was a long bed of sandy soil, one end of which looked freshly turned over, possibly even from the night before. Mother knew immediately what that wall and flowerbed signified. When we returned to Moscow, I went with my parents by tram to the village of Vsesvatsky and the cemetery. We saw the endless rows of identical white crosses, on all of which there was more or less the same inscription – "Here lies so and so, fallen for his motherland, may he rest in peace". We walked about the graveyard. The brick wall had been stuccoed over and beneath it were several rows of overgrown flowerbeds. Mother could not say where Uncle Misha lay. We said our prayers and left. Many years have passed since that cemetery disappeared under urban development. Now rows of buildings stand on that piece of land, cars and buses hurry along newly laid out roads, pedestrians walk the pavements, and no one knows, or thinks, of the thousands who lie buried there in the cold earth.

Mother brought her brother's clothing and a group photograph back to Bogoroditsk. It shows some twenty officers sitting and standing, all in uniform, and on each side, with revolvers in their belts, the armed escort. This picture was actually taken in Butyrka prison. And what fine faces they all have! In the front row is a young officer, his face all smiles, whilst next to him is an older officer with a serious expression. In the centre of the group is a figure who particularly stands out. Tall, with piercing eyes and a small moustache over tightly compressed lips, his head is held high. That's my uncle, Mikhail Sergeievich Lopukhin. I looked so often at this photograph during the years at Bogoroditsk that the faces became engraved in my memory. We only lost one bag when we moved back to Moscow, but it was the one full of many letters and that particular photograph. At the time mother was bitterly upset. Then, almost half a century later I saw a print of the same photo in Maria Sergeievna Trubetskoi's flat in Paris, and persuaded her to let me have it.

At the age I was, Uncle Misha's death made a tremendous impression on me. A great change came over me; I more or less stopped playing with the other boys, took to wandering alone in the park, began to read and think a great deal. I began to lead a double life. In the one I talked to people, played with my sisters, entertained myself; in the other I lived an inner, secret life, which I did not reveal even to my mother. This second, more important life continued throughout my childhood and into adulthood, and today is still part of me. There is nothing strange about it. Because of the way life is in our country, we all lead double lives. Perhaps, what is astonishing is that I was so young when Uncle Misha's death prompted me to start talking and behaving one way, while inside I was thinking something completely different.

My uncle's heroic figure still lives on in my heart. He became for me an unattainable ideal, someone who never compromised his principles, who gave his life for the freedom of his Motherland. I have never before spoken to anyone of the enormous influence his death had in the shaping of my character, personality and convictions. These convictions were implanted in me in my ninth year and have stayed with me ever since. And today, as I put them down on paper, they are still a vital part of me.

The book *The Knights of the Round Table* had been left behind in Moscow, but in my mind I relived their many adventures. I identified Uncle Misha with Sir Lancelot, and later with Andrei Bolkonsky in *War and Peace*.

10

I developed a passion for reading. After leafing through some dull books in the Count's library, I came across one by Fenimore Cooper and became a fan. The figure of Nathaniel Bumpo, the skilled tracker, delighted me, and I alternated between identifying myself with him or choosing to be an Indian chief. This new pleasure wooed me away from my recent, un-childlike grief. Though I have never read those stories again, I can still remember them clearly.

Life proceeded fairly normally on the estate. Father's leave came to an end, and he returned to Moscow. Then we discovered that on the other side of Bogoroditsk, on the property of the local agricultural institute, there lived a biology teacher, Vladimir Deters, who collected butterflies. Mother organised an outing to pay him a visit, which turned out to be far more interesting than I had expected. This delicate little man, with his pale eyes and a slightly damp moustache and goatee, whose students had nicknamed Tichinka, showed us a score of cases full of butterflies and moths. We gasped with delight and admiration. Deters then kitted me out with an outfit of net, boards, a box, pins and chloroform, and I turned into a collector, rushing about the park, catching, chloroforming and setting butterflies.

Our supplies of food at this time were more or less adequate. Uncle Leo had introduced the concept of a day's rations for one adult, which he termed "a man-day's food" – for people who sat down to three daily meals. This was for the Bobrinskys, Trubetskois and us, together with grandfather and grandmother. I felt proud to be counted as a full grown-up, whereas my younger sisters, Masha and Katya, were only halves. We bought and ate a foal, and then another, assuring grandmother that she was eating beef. Milk continued to come from the home farm. Led by Aunt Vera we worked all summer in the vegetable garden, growing cucumbers, carrots, turnips and some potatoes.

Uncle Vladimir Trubetskoi went hunting and occasionally came back with a hare. But a hare does not go far when there are twenty mouths! One day he did something awful. Returning from an unsuccessful day's hunting, he came across a flock of domestic ducks on the lake, and shot them all. Our dinner that evening was a feast, but unfortunately, these ducks had an owner, a former employee of the Bobrinskys by name of Dood. His family began an investigation, someone had witnessed the shooting, and they sent their young son, Vanka, to see me. "What did you have for dinner last night?" he asked me, and like a fool, I told him ducks, shot by my uncle.

The matter seriously damaged relations between us, the former landowners, and those living on the estate. Whereas earlier there had been compassion, now there was what Marxists call "class hatred". The Bobrinskys had never had the same close relationship with their peasants as we had had on our estate at Buchalki. They had never created handicraft workshops, or orphanages, or poorhouses. They kept a proud distance from the common folk, and although they did give help, this was done only through the estate office. There was even a saying, "as proud as Countess Bobrinskaya", which one heard well beyond the province of Tula.

The owners of the ducks complained to the local authorities, and demanded compensation. I do not know whether it was the result of this incident, or just the times, but an article appeared in the local paper, *The Red Voice*, under the heading "How long must we tolerate this?" In indignant language, the article talked of "languorous little countesses and plump-faced little counts in sailor suits dawdling about the park". In a similar tone the words "exploiters and bloodsuckers" were used. The countesses referred to were the Bobrinsky girls and my sisters; the plump-faced counts could only be one, Alexei Bobrinsky. Kirill always wore his scout's uniform – and I did not have a sailor suit and was very thin. Once again the representatives of the sugar factory came to us and reassured us that we were under their protection, but the very next day people came from the authorities with a piece of paper ordering us to vacate the whole second floor of the house within twenty-four hours.

Two incoming families with numerous children were installed there. They were timid, apathetic people, who came and went by the back door and with whom we had no contact. It was clear that they expected the old times to return, and then they would have to clear out fast. Our living conditions became very cramped. The dining room was made into the nursery. Uncle Leo and Aunt Vera turned the sitting room into their bedroom, but the room was also used as our dining room. My brother Vladimir moved into the pantry and the girls somewhere else. But still we managed to make music in the evenings; Aunt Vera at the piano, Uncle Vladimir on the cello, Zalzman on the violin. The music of Beethoven, Bach, Mozart and Chopin took our minds off the reality outside.

Soviet power was triumphant for a short time in the south, and we began to receive mail. A letter brought the news that Uncle Lev's nephew, Gavril, the youngest son of his brother Alexei, had been shot in the town of Kislovodsk. He was a midshipman, a tall and graceful youth of nineteen, and I remembered him well. They had caught him when he was in the marketplace. Some forty men were shot, including my mother's cousin, Count Alexei Kapnist, and a second cousin, Prince Obolensky. My Aunt Maria Sergeievna's husband, Prince Vladimir Petrovich Trubetskoi, was able to escape. In the Bogoroditsk area a local landowner Dimitri Dimitrievich (another Prince Obolensky but not related to us) was arrested and put in the local prison.

I listened in to the adults' worried conversation as they sat together, talking and reading the papers. An assassination attempt had just been made on Lenin by the Social Revolutionary Fanny Kaplan. Uritsky was shot in Petrograd.[7] In Yaroslavl, there was an uprising of Social Revolutionaries. The papers were screaming, "Against White terror we'll respond with Red terror!" For every assassinated Bolshevik, thousands were shot at random. I understood little of this, but the adults felt themselves to be utterly defenceless. The people from the sugar factory stopped coming, and that was the end of their contributions of foodstuffs. One or two of the local Social Revolutionaries were shot; others left the district in fear.

In Bogoroditsk, there were convinced communists who thought that world revolution was around the corner and that for the sake of the high ideals of the revolution any measures, however bloody, were justified. I can name one of these – Jacob Tarakanov. He was the father of a horde of ragged young children whom he took somewhere every morning, and he himself was also dressed in rags. He was tubercular and lived on nothing. But there were many other

---

7. *Moisei Uritsky (1873-1918), Bolshevik revolutionary leader, head of Petrograd Cheka, assassinated in revenge for executions ordered by him.*

predatory types who sensed easy prey – unsavoury people such as Kovalevich who wandered about the courtyard, glaring at us with greedy eyes.

Incidentally, as far as the attempt on Lenin's life goes, I know the following story. Brother Vladimir had a friend in the 1930s, a young literary researcher called Vladimir Goltsev, who told him how as a lad he had been an autograph collector. He had the autograph of the Tsar, tsarist ministers and generals. He also had the autographs of Kerensky and later Trotsky, Sverdlov, Zinoviev and Kamenev, but he had never managed to get Lenin's. When he found out that Lenin was to make a speech at the Michelson factory, Goltsev went there and picking his moment, thrust his paper out for Lenin to sign. Lenin mistook the gesture and told Goltsev where to send in his petition. Goltsev then explained what he wanted, so Lenin bent down to sign the paper. At this very moment, Fanny Kaplan fired her revolver at Lenin; he fell, and the frightened workers scattered, leaving only Fanny Kaplan and Goltsev next to Lenin. She ran one way, Goltsev another. The papers reported that Kaplan had had an accomplice with her, dressed up as a schoolboy, who had deliberately diverted Lenin's attention by handing him a paper. This "schoolboy" had managed to escape, but was being hunted.

Present-day writers deny this story. And the papers from of that time are locked up behind tightly sealed doors. But it is interesting that in the artist Pchelin's picture (a very poor one, by the way) there is a figure of a schoolboy beside Fanny Kaplan. I offer this as a puzzle for future historians to solve.

11

One evening, as usual, we were playing our music, when suddenly there was loud banging at the door. We opened it and in they burst. The first was a stocky sailor holding a machine gun and a whip, with two ammunition belts criss-crossed on his chest. Behind him came three or four soldiers with rifles at the ready and, bringing up the rear, an officer wearing a cloak.

The sailor was Commissar Kashafchev. I do not remember the other man's name. They held out their search warrant and then set to work, opening every trunk, slitting open the upholstery of the armchairs and sofas and climbing under the tables and beds. They were obviously looking for weapons. They examined Uncle Vladimir's shotgun, but did not take it. They took two other hunting guns as well as a pair of ancient duelling pistols with mother-of-pearl encrusted butts, probably dating back to the eighteenth century. They forced the children to get up, searching their beds and pillows. Little Varya Trubetskaya began to cry. They scoured the Cousesse's room with special care, turning out all their papers and demanding explanations of things written in French and German. Did they think they were spies?

The man in the cloak stood by, not taking any part. Kashafchev gave the orders, pointing with his whip to wherever they were to search. Once, at an exhibition of self-portraits in the Tretyakov gallery, I saw the picture *Little Brother*, painted by Fyodor Bogorodsky, and it immediately reminded me of Kashafchev. The same bestial face and eyes filled with hate, except that our Bogoroditsk sailor had two ammunition belts, whilst the subject of the portrait wore three.

The adults sat motionless and silent. There were so many belongings it took the searchers hour after hour. At some stage, Zalzman suggested to Alka Bobrinskaya that she should have her regular music lesson, and so they sat to one side, the search continuing to the accompaniment of a violin. Sitting there, some of us dozed off, but I was not sleepy and watched the search proceed. Dawn broke and we put out the lamps. A long cart drew up at the entrance. And at this point, Kashafchev announced that since the concealed weapons had not been found, he was arresting grandfather and Uncles Leo and Vladimir.

Grandmother screamed, rushed to the cloaked man, seized him by the shoulder and began to plead that grandfather was old and sick and totally innocent. The man had a pale, intelligent face. He had probably only just graduated, but grandmother had not yet understood what it was to encounter the cold, pitiless eyes of the secret police, the Cheka. There was hatred in the eyes of the sailor, but it was a human emotion and grandmother might just have persuaded him to leave grandfather alone. But the one in the cloak was immovable.

Aunt Vera rose from her chair, came over to grandmother and silently drew her away. They began to put together some things for those who had just been arrested. Poor grandmother was weeping as if her heart would break; someone else, too, was crying, and tears poured down the cheeks of the old chambermaid. Aunt Vera with her two daughters stood proudly and silently aside. They all went out onto the porch. Grandfather tried and failed to climb into the cart. Uncle Vladimir helped him in and sat down beside him. Despite the early hour a large crowd had gathered. It was a scene recalling the famous picture of Boyarin Morozova being sent into exile, only this was summer, not winter. Everyone who lived nearby had rushed over. Most of the adults looked on with compassion, but just as in Surikov's picture, there were gleeful faces, too. And unlike in Surikov's picture, where two lads sit on a fence, here there seemed to be dozens. That same evening, at my mother's request, Aunt Sasha wrote a long letter to my father. She wrote as usual in her even, clear hand, as she had been taught to at her school for young gentlewomen. I can recall one of the final sentences, "Prince Vladimir Mikhailovich, for the first time in his life, climbed into a peasant cart."

The arrested men were taken to the town prison. Mother and Aunt Vera went to see the local executive committee, who reassured them that they would contact Tula. But these were terrible times. The papers carried lists of people shot, and it was rumoured that even these lists were not complete. In other towns, for instance in Yurev-Polsky, the entire nobility had been arrested, taken away and shot.

A carriage was hired and grandmother, and Aunts Vera and Eli visited the men in prison. They came away not in the least reassured. From then on these became daily visits. I was taken along on one of them. The prison was a long way off, on the outskirts of the town, next to the cemetery. It was utterly unlike any prisons we have today; it was a large clapboard building with an ordinary front door, surrounded by a fence. There was not even any barbed wire along the top of it. The gaps between the fence planks were quite wide, and you could see what was going on in the inner courtyard. Just like flies in the fly-trap jars we used to set out in Bulchalki, the inmates were walking to and fro in their twos and threes, young and old, some in uniform, some in fine civilian clothes, some in soft peasant boots. Grandfather, Uncles Leo and Vladimir came up to the fence and chatted to us. We pushed clothing and food at them through the gaps. An elderly gentleman came up and spoke some words in French with grandmother before turning away; it was Prince D.D. Obolensky.

Grandfather had a philosophical attitude to this unusual residence. His only regret was that it interrupted his diary writing. They all slept on wooden bunks, telling each other all sorts of interesting stories, while at night the rats ran about leaping over their sleeping bodies. A week later, grandfather was released; who knows whether this was thanks to the steps taken by my father in Moscow, or to his great age? But both uncles remained in prison, visited on foot by Aunt Vera and the children, as Aunt Eli, being pregnant, could no longer go on such long excursions.

12

It is difficult to remember the order of events, so it could be that the following incident happened before the arrest and sealing up of the house. A group of commissars turned up one day, not the same ones. The head of the Cheka, Proligin, produced a paper authorising the requisitioning of clothes for the Red Army. We Golitsyns and the Trubetskois had come to Bogoroditsk lightly dressed, but the Bobrinskys had many chests and trunks of clothes, often dating back to the time of Catherine the Great. Uncle Leo was quite a dandy and they took some of his suits and many pairs of boots. They hardly touched the women's clothing, but piled up our beds and mattresses and blankets. They made a huge heap, and in it was probably the uniform once worn by the Bobrinsky with Decembrist sympathies and the morning suit worn by Uncle Lev's father, he who had propagated the ideas of Lord Radstock. When the men went off in search of further booty and the pile was left unguarded, Aunt Vera and her daughters quickly retrieved some of their things. I also wanted to take part in this tantalising game, but was held back.

They began to pile up the carts. The chief requisitioner was persuaded to leave behind enough beds, mattresses and blankets in proportion to the number of occupants of the house. At this very moment Nasenka and the Bobrinsky maid, Elizabeth, shouted at these guardians of the peace that they were "robbers and bandits". The men could not believe their ears and asked them to say it again, and the two women repeated their words, even adding a colourful epithet. They were immediately arrested and taken away on top of the carts. We were very worried about them. It all ended well, however, with their return that evening, very proud of their behaviour towards the Cheka. Nasenka told us how they were reproached with forgetting the class struggle, but they roundly replied, "My master and mistress have done us so many great kindnesses, we'll serve them faithfully to the end of our days."

Where were our belongings taken? I found the answer to this question in a letter I discovered in 1977, in the Bogoroditsk museum, in the personal file of Commissar Boris Rudnev. In this letter, dated 10 February 1966, the now retired Rudnev recorded how the then head of the Cheka in Bogoroditsk, Proligin, had to be sacked "for committing fraudulent acts and other disgraceful actions during the persecution of the Bobrinsky family. He also unlawfully pocketed monies belonging to the State." So it turned out that Nasenka, in calling Proligin a bandit, had been quite right. Two years later, Aunt Sasha set me an essay to write. I filled a whole copybook with the tale of our misfortunes that summer and autumn and showed it to all who knew Bogoroditsk. They were shocked by the events, but praised my writing. Modestly, I lowered my eyes.

I must tell another story of possible interest to future historians of Bogoroditsk. The entrance to the main courtyard was through an arch in a tall bell tower. Just above this archway there was a locked room, which the local officials demanded to have opened. The room contained the records of estate expenditure, plans and other books, many of them dating back to the time of Andrei Bolotov, who had developed and looked after the estate for Catherine the Great. The authorities dug about in all this material and, finding nothing useful, left the broken door open. My two uncles, Leo and Vladimir, collected all the old plans drawn on linen cloth and tore off the satin covers of the account books. The idea was to process the linen into useful handkerchiefs and diapers, and turn the satin into little pocketbooks, all of which could be sold or exchanged for food. We children went wild over all these coverless books and remnants of old accounts, chucking them out of the windows of the tower, watching them fly about and intending to make a huge bonfire, until finally the adults stopped us. I managed to appropriate a couple of old notebooks for myself.

Autumn was upon us, and Kirill went off to school in Petrograd. My brother Vladimir was accepted at the local secondary school. An art class was organised in the town, under Stepan Timofeyevich Rozhkov, which Vladimir attended. There are portraits of this teacher in Vladimir's notebooks, a thin man with a beard and long hair. Rozhkov was not himself a master of drawing but he persuaded Vladimir to work at drawing vases and flowers in order to improve his technique. About this time, a competition was organised in the town for the design of a monument to Karl Marx. My brother took part; his sketch is still extant. Attempting to emphasize the wisdom of the founder of such great revolutionary ideas, Vladimir had Marx holding out an enormous book. Had the monument been built, the weight of this extended book would have made the whole thing topple over. This scheme to erect a monument in Bogoroditsk fell through, but in many other towns at this time hastily made statues of Marx and others, mostly made of plaster, were put up, only to be discreetly removed, usually at night, and carted off to the rubbish dump as wind, rain and snow took their toll of them.

The first frosts arrived. Aunt Vera shared out amongst us the clothes her children had outgrown. I was given Alexei's coat, jacket and trousers. A great deal of remaking was needed to fit out my young sisters. We were organised to cut up cabbage into a long trough. The older children gathered under Nasenka's command. Chopping and slicing went on in a jolly atmosphere. We treated ourselves to bites of cabbage stalk. My job was to pull the cabbages out of their heaps, cut off the green leaves and throw them into the trough.

Then the younger children all came down with the mumps. With one exception, the illness was mild. The exception was Grisha Trubetskoi, who had such a terrible cough it looked like he would not survive. The illness was at its height when once more the commissars were at our door, with an order to re-house us within three days. At that time, re-housing was not what it became later, namely, "Go where you like!" The system then was to double up with other families. It was called "squeezing up", and was the authorities' way of trying to solve the housing crisis.

13

From the beginning of Soviet times, political jokes were common currency, their butt being our great leaders or our new style of life. These jokes travelled like wildfire and were repeated with tremendous relish, though always with a cautious glance sideways. It was a kind of satirical literary genre. My friend S.N. Durylin commented that the subject was truly worthy of a doctoral dissertation. The jokes had an impact because of the way they instantly responded to events, sometimes wordlessly, by a mere gesture. Witty, often scabrous, they were in full flow in the 1930s, but thereafter you could be imprisoned for telling them, so people began to hold their tongues. Who made them up? They were often attributed to Karl Radek.[8] Something that Durylin rejects. He maintained they were self-generating, invented in an elemental, anonymous way before being spread about by repetition. In these memoirs of mine I will try to include some of these jokes.

For instance, every institute or organisation was referred to by its initials or the first syllables of its name. The local executive committees all had sections that dealt with the housing crisis by doubling up families. So you were told to go to the *zhopa* (*zhilichniy otdel*) for your needs. This was exactly what they told Aunt Vera, my

---

8. *Karl Radek (Born Karol Sobelson in Galicia in 1885) was a leading revolutionary and member of the Comintern, liquidated in the Great Purges in 1939.*

mother and Madame Couesse when the three of them reported for re-housing. Aunt Vera received an order to occupy two rooms in the house of a certain Kobyakov, near the church in Pokrov. My mother was told to move to two rooms in the home of the director of the Agricultural Institute just outside the town. We moved there with Auntie Misya, who had been turned out of the Bobrinsky nurses' training building. The Couesse couple were ordered to move to the house of a gardener, Senyavin, near the village of Vyasovsky, and Uncle Vladimir went with them.

A massive sharing out of the Bobrinsky goods and chattels took place – clothes, kitchen utensils and furniture. Aunt Vera simply said, "Take what you want. In any event, it's all going to end up with strangers." The clothes we had been wearing these past few years all came out of the Bobrinsky cupboards and trunks. Most of the books ended up in the local library, where my sister Lina had started working. Brother Vladimir at first settled in with the Couesses, but old friends of his had been asking him for a long time to come to Bulchalki, and he soon set off accompanied by our under-nanny Lenya, whose married sister lived in the nearby village of Orlovka.

Our grandfather's valet, Felix, left our service. He somehow got hold of a carriage, a sledge and a skewbald horse and became a coachman in the town. He plied this trade for a couple of years. Whenever he saw any of us on foot he would invite us to climb in, even if he already had a passenger, and cheerfully take us where we were going. Later, he moved to Latvia. The old manservant, Ivan, and the Bobrinsky's old deaf and blind maid ended up in the poorhouse on Bazaar Square near the town church. There they were constantly hungry. Now and again we and the Bobrinskys were able to bring them little treats. But within two years they died, most probably of hunger.

What happened later to all that Bobrinsky furniture, the cupboards, beds and chairs, I do not know. A plain white table served me for years as a writing table, and went with our family wherever our nomadic life led us. Just recently I spotted it in a niece's home. Such a simple piece, and yet it has survived. Seeing this table from my childhood and youth made my heart leap. What has remained with us of the Bobrinsky family's china and cutlery are a few heavy copper saucepans and a couple of dozen silver-plated knives, forks and spoons. Engraved on all these items is the Bobrinsky crest, a bear walking across a crenulated wall, the symbol of the Anhalt-Zerbsts, Catherine the Great's parents. There is a two-headed eagle on the bottom left hand corner and the Bobrinsky beaver bottom right. Only one of these crested spoons is still in my possession; the crest has been almost totally worn away and if I put it in my mouth it tastes faintly of the underlying copper. I still cherish it for the memories it evokes.

14

Thus was broken the last link with our aristocratic past. We were resettled, despite the fact that the children were in the middle of the mumps, and Aunt Eli was about to give birth. The head of the local hospital, Dr Alexei Nikolsky, now acted, from today's perspective, in a most astonishing way. Learning of our imminent eviction, he announced that he would take Aunt Eli into the maternity ward of his hospital and that all the children, with their nannies, could occupy half of another ward. We moved into this separate building, with its entrance porch and corridor. We were seven children in all – Alexei and Elenka Bobrinsky, Grisha and Varya Trubetskoi, as well as me and my two younger sisters. Aunt Sasha together with Nasenka came with us, as did Christina, the Trubetskois' nanny, the under-nanny Polya and the Bobrinskys' nanny, Masha. We were in quarantine because of the mumps, so visitors were not allowed. Aunt Vera and my mother would come as far as the porch and we would run out to meet them, keeping our distance. Supplies of food, soups, bread and wheaten cakes were brought to us in covered dishes.

Aunt Sasha was my teacher. Her lessons struck me as impossibly difficult. Nor was she very good at explaining them. I would get frustrated, and her monotonous dictations and attempts to teach me grammar bored me stiff. The only interesting part of our time there was watching the peasants as they came to the hospital. Dressed in orange-coloured jackets and sheepskin coats they would ride in, tie up their horses, relieve themselves under our windows, and then carry their children over to Dr Nikolsky's consulting rooms, wrapped in heavy clothing. These figures in clothing dyed with onion extracts were far more colourful than our present dull jackets. There are some coloured drawings of these hospital courtyard scenes in Vladimir's sketchbooks.

Dr Nikolsky visited us now and again, bringing little presents the peasantry had given him – rolls of sweets or a pie, sometimes even smoked meat, which we shared out carefully. Grisha's cough, which seemed to tear him apart, greatly alarmed Dr Nikolsky. In fact, this was the beginning of Grisha's asthma, from which he suffered his whole life. He was terribly thin and pale. In the long run, though, his asthma saved him, as when doing time in the Gulag he was assigned to a sick man's brigade and was thus able to survive.

Alexei Bobrinsky was soon allowed to leave the hospital, which left me the eldest among the children. Dr Nikolsky asked me how I felt, and when I told him I was bored stiff without books, kindly brought me Korney Chukovsky's *Krokodil*. I got through it in a day, even though it was not my kind of book at all. I read it aloud to the other children, and then asked Dr Nikolsky whether he could bring me something a bit weightier and more serious. Finally, after more than a month I was allowed to leave the ward with a clean bill of health, to my great relief. Mother came for me with felt boots and a warm cap and scarf, and we set off along the misty streets of Bogoroditsk towards where the red brick buildings of the Agricultural Institute loomed up. Mother carried the bag with my things and told me about the people living in the same flat with us, and how lovely it was to walk in the snowy fields, and how she intended to teach me and read aloud to me.

2. Life with the Bobrinskys

1

In 1898, the government-funded Agricultural Institute in Bogoroditsk was built on lands belonging to the Bobrinskys. It consisted of a three-storey main building with the laboratories and auditoria, a two-storey building for the teachers and other staff, and a further two buildings of student accommodation. The institute trained middle-level agronomists. It owned a dairy farm, orchards and fish ponds, although after the revolution the ponds were neglected. The institute had a first class reputation thanks to its highly qualified teachers, ample laboratories and modern equipment. It is to the credit of these teachers and especially the director, Mikhail Fyodorovich Arnold, that its work was not affected by the famine and destruction of those years. He was the son of a well-known forester, the founder of forest conservation practices in Russia. Mikhail was an intelligent and liberal man in the true meaning of those words, with a clear sense of his mission in life which was, regardless of the revolution, simply to train honourable people to teach the peasantry how to cultivate the land better and reap more abundant harvests. He could see no connection between the growth of socialism and agriculture.

His wife was the daughter of another famous agronomist, I.A. Stebut. It would be impossible to call Natalya Ivanovna either a lady or a noblewoman. Imbued with the ideas of the intelligentsia, who wanted to bring enlightenment to the countryside, she went about in simple clothes with her hair cut short. Despite this unconventionality she was a fine, good woman, greatly esteemed. There were two daughters: the elder, Vera, worked with our Lina in the town library; the younger was Natasha. Later on, Vera was for many years the partner, though not the legal wife, of the writer Boris Zhitkov. The Arnolds dealt with the unexpected arrival of so many people coming to live with them with warmth and love. Our Sonya settled in with their younger daughter Natasha, and they quickly became good friends. In another room lived three or four students from the institute.

Quite a number of things had happened to my family while I was in quarantine in the hospital. Brother Vladimir returned from Bulchalki after only a week. He had been warned that the authorities were about to have him arrested. He told us how the big house at Bulchalki had burned down because of a faulty stove, and how last year's puppies had grown into handsome dogs. I do not remember any other details. He went to live with the Couesse couple on the far edge of the town. The other news was that Aunt Eli had given birth to a daughter, called Alexandra in honour of the Empress. Mother and daughter now moved into a tiny room in the Arnold's apartment. Because of the poor diet, Aunt Eli was very weak after the birth and could hardly move at all, so Sophia Alexeievna Bobrinskaya – Auntie Misya – looked after the infant. It was a good outlet for her energy.

The third piece of news was that once again they had arrested grandfather and Uncles Vladimir Trubetskoi and Leo Bobrinsky. They had been sent to Tula and then to Butyrka prison in Moscow. The arrest had taken place before I left the hospital, so I did not know the exact circumstances. Mother told me how, as the outer door of the Arnold's apartment was firmly locked at night, the police had had to shout and bang to get in and make their arrest. In Moscow, grandfather and Uncle Leo were soon freed; possibly the age of the one and the ill-health of the other had led to their release, or it could have been that someone spoke up for them. Uncle Vladimir, however, remained in prison for over a month.

Grandfather was summoned to see one of the leaders, Kamenev, the chairman of the Moscow City Council. He apologised for grandfather's arrest and said he remembered how humanely grandfather had treated political prisoners when he himself was Mayor of Moscow. Kamenev went on to assure grandfather that from then on he could be at peace, as no one would touch him. He gave grandfather a kind of *laissez-passer*, stating that without the permission of the authorities no one had the right to evict, search or arrest him. This paper was signed by both Kamenev and a close colleague of Lenin's, Zinovyev. We kept this document for a long time, although it served little purpose. When both leaders were arrested and accused of the most improbable crimes, Uncle Vladimir burnt it.

Poor historians of the twentieth century, how difficult things will be for you! Still, in an attempt to help you, I have to say that the most popular leader in those days among the general public was not Lenin, but the army commissar, Trotsky, that pitiless executioner and energetic organiser under whose leadership the Red Army came into being. He attracted many former tsarist officers into the ranks of the Reds; eventually the Whites were beaten, driven out or shot. Trotsky was a fine orator, travelling across the whole country, making speeches everywhere, ruthlessly putting down peasant uprisings, issuing stern decrees and in general promoting himself with the help of a servile press.

2

When I moved into the Arnold's apartment everyone, but especially grandmother, was waiting impatiently for the return of the released men and my father. If you wanted to travel, you could not just buy a rail ticket, you had to have a warrant, an imposing piece of paper signed by several higher authorities and stamped with their seals, and such authorisations were only given to the most trusted or influential people. I was put into the same room as Auntie Misya, Aunt Eli and her new baby, Alexandra, nicknamed Tatya. Mother taught me my school subjects and did the cooking, or more accurately, began learning to cook. I do not remember what we ate or how we obtained our provisions, but I do remember that the food was not tasty and certainly not very nutritious. To sweeten our carrot tea we used saccharine, as sugar was unobtainable.

The Couesses were getting ready to return home to Switzerland, via Finland and Sweden. They visited us to say farewell. Madame Couesse and our Sonya burst into tears as they parted. They left, but were delayed in Helsinki, where a daughter was born, called Sophia. I can imagine the colourful stories they told about their life in our country. Fifteen years later one of our relatives met them in Paris. Our former tutor was then working as an assistant in a bookshop; indeed, before coming to us he had been a tutor in Leo Tolstoy's family and even wrote a book in French about the great writer.

Vladimir moved in with us. He was found a room in one of the other buildings with the teacher of German, Herr Swikke, and was very happy there. Frau Swikke was fifteen years younger than her husband. She flirted with Vladimir and made him special little cakes and in general fed him better than the rest of us. Sadly, the album Vladimir used at that time has not survived; there were sketches of Herr Swikke, with his long nose and goatee – his nickname was "Goat" – as well as a sketch of his wife, a handsome lady with thick curls and a pert nose.

Vladimir, my sister Sonya and her friend Natasha Arnold attended the school in town, which had previously been the gymnasium, or secondary school. This was a time of sporadic schooling, a little of this, a little of that. Under the wise guidance of the People's Commissar for Education, Lunacharsky the elder, the old order in schools was abolished; marking was done away with, as were lessons and exams. In short, reliance was placed on the "socialist awareness" of the future builders of socialism. Religious education, Greek and Latin were all banned after the revolution. From time to time, inspectors checked these reforms were being carried out. The glib writings of Soviet authors, such as Leo Kassil and others, poured scorn on the teachers of tsarist times. In fact, they were dedicated and self-sacrificing people. Under the enormously difficult conditions of the civil war they continued to do their jobs, using their old curricula to continue teaching the eternal rules of mathematics, physics and chemistry, and to awake in their pupils a love of nature, the arts and literature, and above all a love of Russia. Let me mention here the names of some of these Bogoroditsk teachers, names remembered by my older sister, Sonya. Ivan Yegorovich Rusakov taught Russian language, Urivayev taught law, Alexander Ivanovich Nekrasov economics and politics, Alexei Pavlovich Burtsev psychology and literature, Matvey Matveyevich Krikshchunas physics. The school director was Alexander Alexandrovich Delectorsky.

One day, mother took me along with her into the forest to arrange for some firewood to be delivered. It was my first sight of the woods under snow. She showed me the crisscross tracks of hares and we saw tits and bullfinches and were overtaken by peasants on their sledges, all wrapped up in their yellow and orange sheepskins and jackets. We walked and walked along the Tula road past the dairy farm and then along the edge of the forest, called "the Town woods", and then struck deep into the forest that even today is still called "the Count's". Mother drew my attention to the colours of the forest, the blue shadows on the snow, the slanting branches of fallen oaks, the tracks of hares. I remember my joyful cries. It was four *versts*, or about four kilometres, to the forester's hut, where we left our order for firewood before retracing our steps.

I was now given the daily duty of fetching the milk from town. In one of the first houses on the right hand side of Voronezh Street there was a family who kept cows. The wife was the usual sort of elderly woman; the husband looked like Grandfather Frost with his long white beard. I handed over my money and walked home with the milk on my shoulder, like a soldier carrying his rifle. It was at this time that the first Soviet money began to appear, printed in the various languages – Georgian, Armenian, Arabic – with the most prolific but as yet unfulfilled slogan "Proletariat of the World, Unite!"

I once gave Grandfather Frost one of these new five hundred rouble notes. He took it, turned it round, even smelled it, then handed it back to me, saying, "Ask your mother to look again. She must have some Romanov roubles hidden somewhere. We don't want this Jewish money. And don't bring any Kerenskys either." From then on I paid for the milk with tsarist money, which was still accepted without question in the bazaar. "Kerensky" was the name given to the big twenty- and forty-rouble notes issued by the Provisional Government, which were equally despised by the Bolsheviks and the public. Poles, Latvians, Lithuanians and Estonians were being resettled into newly formed republics and they willingly took tsarist money with them, which was said to circulate freely there.

The term "Jewish money" was common over the entire country. A decree published at this time threatened punishment of anyone so lacking in "socialist awareness" as to refuse the new money. The next issue of paper money left off the foreign languages that the people could not understand. This money was now accepted, but people anyway avoided using paper money, preferring to barter goods, and exchange clothes for food. Tsarist money, however, continued to be accepted.

3

We children had by now recovered from our mumps and could no longer stay in the hospital ward. With some help, Dr Nikolsky obtained authorisation for a first floor flat on Constantinovsky Street. It was a stone house with a wooden upper storey. Aunt Eli and her newborn child and the other two children, Grisha and Varya, moved into the flat with their nanny, Christina, and the under-nanny Polya. In fact, very soon Christina left for Latvia. Ivan Ivanovich Rayevsky's wife had just died of typhus on the Rayevsky estate of Begichevka. He invited Auntie Misya – Sophia Alexeievna Bobrinskaya – to come and look after the household, and she gladly set off in a sledge, wrapped up to the eyebrows. Dr Nikolsky's brother fell victim to the typhus; he had been a doctor in the Sukhanovsky hospital close to Bulchalki. When his wife, too, died, Dr Nikolsky brought their teenage son and daughter to live in Bogoroditsk.

Instead of the Trubetskoi family, Aunt Sasha and Nasenka now occupied their small room. I moved into the big room. Unexpectedly, our old under-nanny Lyena reappeared with a shaven head and in a miserable state. Bursting into tears, she told us that her sister's husband had died of typhus and she had nowhere to go. She begged to be allowed to stay, and promised she would do whatever duties my mother required. My mother agreed, but that very night Lyena again fell ill and had to be taken to hospital. When she was discharged a month later, she was so weak she still needed to be looked after.

Typhus and typhoid fever were just as dangerous enemies for the new Soviet state as the White Army who were attacking on all fronts. Whether in town or country, front line or at the rear, thousands died of these diseases. The carriers were the fleas that abounded in unprecedented numbers. People told how when you walked through communal lodgings or railway stations, the fleas crunched under your feet. I remember seeing a man in the bazaar collecting them off his shirt by the handful and chucking them on the snow. Russian humour is a hardy plant, even under the worst circumstances. Recently, the *Literary Gazette* reported how citizens had called these spreaders of disease "tanks", and said how witty that was, but this is not the truth. Tanks were hardly used at all during the civil war, and in fact the fleas were give a much more witty name; they were called *semashkos* after the then Soviet commissar for health, Semashko. "Oh, what a lot of *semashkos* he's got," the nurses would exclaim as they took in a typhus sufferer. And when the managers of communal lodgings, or railway stations gave orders to their cleaners, the first thing they would say was "Get rid of all the *semashkos* first." Our family was saved from an invasion of fleas by Nasenka and Aunt Sasha's meticulousness. With her habitual punctilious accuracy she kept a very neat log of our daily ablutions. If anyone missed their turn, they were immediately reminded of it. We all bathed in a big tub behind a curtain. We did have fleas in our hair, but they were considered to be harmless. Regularly Aunt Sasha would carefully comb them out of my little sisters' curly hair.

Grandfather, Uncles Leo and Vladimir finally returned, together with my father. The two uncles went straight from the station to their respective families. Father and grandfather drove up to the house on a sledge and we rushed downstairs to greet them. When we all sat down to table, grandmother sat next to grandfather, weeping and stroking his hand. Every time she looked at him, her weeping intensified. The only person left living, or rather waiting for death, in our Moscow house was Grandfather Alexander Mikhailovich. He was nursed by his unloved nephew Vovik, who had come to Moscow to avoid the threat of arrest in Liven. Instead of him, they arrested Aunt Tanya, but did not detain her for long. In addition our former cook, Mikhail Mironovich, and his wife lived in the basement, promising to look after our furniture.

Father and grandfather had brought as many things with them as they could, mostly clothes and shoes, some of which we intended to barter for food. They also brought a box of cobbler's tools. Some years back, my mother's brother, Pyotr Sergeievich Lopukhin, had become a disciple of Leo Tolstoy's teachings and had decided to give up his career in the law to become a shoemaker. When he left Moscow, this box of tools had remained behind. Mother now decided to teach herself the same trade.

I must say some more about this uncle, Pyotr Sergeievich. He married the youngest of my father's sisters, Tatyana. In tsarist times, canon law forbade such marriages. Grandfather called on Metropolitan Makary to obtain his permission. The Metropolitan took his time in replying. On the one hand, it would be very awkward to say no to such an important person as grandfather, a former mayor of Moscow; on the other hand, it was impossible to say yes. He spread his fingers over his eyes and said to grandfather, "This is how I will regard such a union." The marriage took place in a church in the distant outskirts of Moscow and was not followed by a wedding feast. The couple had two children, Eli and Tanya, of whom I have no memory other than that they were constantly howling. At the beginning of the revolution they all left for the south.

Denikin appointed Pyotr Sergeievich governor of the city of Tambov, even though the Whites only controlled the southern suburbs. Then fate took him and his family on to Bulgaria, where his wife Tania died of measles. An odd coincidence occurred at this time. On the day of Tania's death, grandmother had a dream in which she saw her youngest daughter standing under a halo next to a long-dead man. On waking, grandmother told everyone that her daughter was dead and, however much they tried to talk her out of this, saying that one should never believe in dreams, all that grandmother would say was, "Be quiet. I know she has died." No news was reaching us from outside at this time and for more than a year, nothing was known of Aunt Tania's and her family's fate. When finally a letter from Uncle Pyotr reached us, announcing Tania's death, grandmother took it all very calmly.

"I've known for a long time that she was dead."

Pyotr Sergeievich settled in Yugoslavia and there married my cousin, Maria Constantinovna Lvova. He worked as secretary to Metropolitan Anthony, an outstanding figure in the church. After the war, they moved to France, where the Metropolitan died. Two of Pyotr Sergeievich's writings have been preserved; one is a religious piece, the other, entitled *Our Pushkin*, proves, in my opinion very convincingly and is backed by quotations from his poetry, that towards the end of his life Pushkin had become deeply religious and a monarchist. By his second marriage, Pyotr Sergeievich had no children. He was very popular in church circles and was considered a Biblical scholar. The major work of his life, which one comes across all over the world, was a three-volume interpretation of the Bible, the so-called "Lopukhin Bible" with its abundant commentaries.

4

Life in Bogoroditsk went on. Father started a job, recommended by Dr Nikolsky, that same doctor who was so good to our family. Father was made secretary of the regional health office, and with his usual thoroughness compiled case histories in files, stamped professional certificates and wrote reports. Grandfather also had a job; the authorities asked him to write a history of the town from its earliest days. He also catalogued the books in the library. So both father and grandfather were paid salaries, at first in the so-called "Jewish money", then in regular Soviet currency. But most important of all, they had the right to rations for themselves and their dependents.

Aunt Sasha kept an account of income and expenditure, noting the money she received from father and grandfather and how it was spent. In ten years, she accumulated a stack of account books, a priceless record for today's historians. A box of matches was eventually to reach a price of five hundred million roubles. The books contain successive entries of sums given to the poor; for example, five hundred roubles, then ten thousand, then four hundred thousand. There is a simple explanation of these apparent alms; when she could not balance her accounts, Aunt Sasha entered the difference as gifts to the poor. Unfortunately, all these books were burned in one of our moves.

Nasenka did most of the cooking. Mother baked pies for feast days; they were either undercooked or burnt. However, with their cabbage and carrot fillings they were considered to be very tasty and every Sunday Uncles Leo and Vladimir with their wives would come over on their sledges, bringing a bottle of pinkish home-brewed spirits, and afterwards we would crack a lot of jokes and there was a lot of laughter at the table, the recounting of funny stories and much drinking of carrot tea.

Grandmother taught me French, whilst Frau Swikke, not wishing to be considered idle, organised a German language class. She was a very good teacher and it was thanks to her efforts that I mastered the basics of the language. Her pupils were the children of some of the families at the Agricultural Institute, plus my sister Masha and I. Through these children, with whom we played, I learnt that on the same staircase where the Swikkes lived there also lived the Chetvertushkin family – the father was the Russian language teacher – and that their only son was a very studious little boy who had read a thousand books but was never let out by his mother. My curiosity was roused. One of the stories in *The Knights of the Round Table* was about a prince imprisoned from earliest childhood. Could it be that this mysterious Zhenya was just such a prisoner-prince? It was difficult to get up to the windows of their apartment because of the prickly bushes, and I did so want to see inside. None of the children could tell me anything.

The first signs of spring were in the air. For me this time is firmly linked to the book I now fell in love with in the same way as I had been in love with *The Knights of the Round Table*. From the time we moved into the institute, mother had been reading aloud to me from Gogol and Pushkin. She had also started *The Childhood of Bagrov's Grandson* by S.T. Aksakov. This book of Aksakov's captured my heart. The hero of the book was also a Sergei, like me, and I found all his thoughts and adventures totally understandable. Aksakov's Sergei loved his mother, the forest, the rivers and the flowers; he also loved being alone and reading. All his thoughts and feelings were mine; only his love of fishing left me cold. This book coincided with my first early spring in the countryside. The boy in the book played with the new buds and leaves opening on the trees. And I watched as well as the forest changed colour. Young Sergei knew about melting snow, and I saw how patches of brown earth began to show through the snow. He watched the butterflies appear and, delirious with joy, started collecting them. I too saw the first butterflies as they came out. My mother took me to visit Deters again, and he kitted me out with all the necessary equipment as he had the year before, and once again showed us his wonderful collection. Butterflies occupied a special place in my life in Bogoroditsk that spring. It is to this time that I owe my love of nature, which has never left me. I always feel at peace when I walk in the woods or along a stream. It was my mother's guiding and Aksakov's book that taught me this love. Grandfather was very fond of botany, but at his age could not walk any distance. He used to send me off to the marshes to find varieties of sedge, which were difficult to identify, and over which he would sit with his magnifying glass for hours. So, I learnt something about botany. One of the ways of identifying sedge is by the length of the tongue and ears in the depths of the leaf, and another is by the length of the stamen. I once deliberately pruned back the tongue, ear and stamen and watched how grandfather struggled to understand what he was looking at and, getting angry with himself, furiously licked his lips.

I became friendly with the four students who lodged with us. Other students would visit them and then they would go off to the lake to swim, taking me with them, and I would feel so proud when they deigned to speak to me. One of them was a tall young man called Kargopoltsev, who the following winter enrolled into one of the units that scavenged for food. On one of their expeditions the entire unit was killed as they lay sleeping. A punishment squad was then sent in on an armoured train; it blew to pieces the entire village that lay close to the railway. The squad also arrested many peasants, found them guilty and shot them. Meanwhile, the murdered food scavengers were buried with great pomp and ceremony in the town square. A monument was erected over their grave with the inscription "Here lie heroes dead in the cause of the revolution". Kargopoltsev is among them, and every spring the young pioneers lay a wreath at the monument. The square is still named after their leader, commissar Mikhailov.

Storm clouds hung over the country. The White armies were advancing on all fronts. The papers were full of frightful news about peasant uprisings. Decrees were constantly being published, threatening executions. Lists of those who had been executed were published. In these lists the adults kept finding their friends, familiar names in Moscow society. I can give some of my father's former employees – Shchepkin, Astrov, the Alferov couple, the head of the secondary school, Alexandra Samsonovna and her husband, Alexander.

Many peasant uprisings took place in the farmlands during 1919 and 1920. A decree laid down that the peasants were allowed a fixed amount of cereals per head, or per animal, all the surplus being handed over voluntarily. The food squads were sent out into the country to collect this surplus. The uprisings were not, as has been asserted, uprisings of the rich peasantry – the *kulaks* – but of the entire peasantry. These protests were ruthlessly crushed. Twelve parishes of the twenty in the area of Bogoroditsk went up in flames. And what terrible numbers of people were killed by these special squads! At the time the figures quoted were astronomical.

The students living with us behaved very quietly and we rarely heard a sound from them. In the morning, they crowded about the basin in the bathroom as they washed, and it was thanks to this bathroom that our lives changed radically. Grandmother's little dog, Romochka, gave birth to a litter of pups in a heap of rags close to the bathroom basin. Her attitude towards us was perfectly peaceful, whereas she bared her teeth and rushed snarling at the students. One of these was called Boris Rudnev, a Bolshevik and organiser in Bogoroditsk of the *Sokmol,* as the *Konsomol* was then called. He was also keen on my sister Sonya, even trying to recruit her into that youth organisation. As he went to wash one evening, Romochka flew at him; he kicked her, whereupon she bit him in the leg. Whether it was that, or the fact that Sonya had rejected him, or that his class consciousness was stirred, whatever the reason, Rudnev went to the management committee and complained that strangers were living in the director's apartment, preventing the students from studying; he very likely added something about class enemies as well.

Two men on horseback rode up to the house and told us to vacate the apartment within twenty-four hours. Mother rushed off to the housing office (whose name started with that indecent letter *zh*) and was given authorisation to occupy a house known locally as Vasiliyev's Inn. A carrier piled our belongings on his cart and we left the apartment where we had lived for about eight months. The Arnolds bid us farewell with great sadness; we had all become very close friends during our shared time there. I was also really sad to lose the woods, the lake, the fields, and the knowledge that my collection of butterflies would now stop growing upset me enormously. I felt wounded to the very quick of my soul. This feeling of hurt at being insulted, driven out, pushed about and not accepted, simply because you are the son of somebody, this feeling that was first born in me when we were thrown out of the Bobrinsky estate, was now reinforced by this second eviction and became a heavy burden that has weighed down on me most of my life.

5

Vasiliyev's Inn was on a wide square, Ekaterinskaya, which was crossed by Ekaterinskaya Street, and so was at the very centre of the geometric figure of streets laid down in Catherine the Great's town plan. Despite the regal name of the square, the houses were dilapidated wooden buildings, all overgrown with moss and grasses. Chickens ran about and calves grazed, tethered to stakes. The most dilapidated and sagging building was Vasiliyev's Inn. One of grandmother's drawings has been preserved; it shows a house with seven windows on one side, four on the other. The windows were nailed up, the roof full of yawing gaps. Even before the revolution the house stood abandoned because it was in such a bad state. It belonged to a family called Kuchurenko, who lived in a small white house just alongside. What the man did, I do not recall. His wife was very fat and gave birth to identical triplet boys. Other children ran all over the place, and there was also a brother of the owner who was mentally retarded. A pig was being fattened up in the barn for the wedding of this brother, but Kuchurenko complained that he could never find him a bride.

The only good thing about this building was that it consisted of four large rooms, although no one could occupy the first one, as half of it was taken up by a structure of huge shelves. I assume that in earlier times Kuchurenko's father had stood behind them as he dished out jugs of vodka to the peasants. And it was not at all easy to live in the other rooms, with their broken stoves and cracks and gaps in the walls. It also rained nearly every day and leaked through the moss-covered roof. We often woke up to find water dripping on our faces. We got to know where the leaks were, putting the Bobrinsky crested bowls and dishes to catch the drips.

Stove men and carpenters came, shook their heads and departed. Even if it were possible to rebuild the house, where could one find the money and materials? And the housing committee just said, "Find somewhere for yourselves." So from then on we spent day after day looking for accommodation. Eventually a room, due to be vacated in a month's time, was found for the grandparents, close to the Trubetskois. But our family found nothing.

In addition to the incessant typhus raging at that time, cholera and dysentery now began to spread. Thanks to the vigorous efforts of the doctors, the cholera was overcome. There were weeks when only my father sat in the health administration office whilst the rest of the staff was in the countryside fighting the outbreak. At the Agricultural Institute, the curly-haired four-year-old son of one of the teachers, Vilinsky, went down with dysentery. He was near death when Dr Nikolsky stated that only grape wine could now save him. His parents were ready to pay any price for a bottle. Aunt Sasha saved the day; she was the only person in the whole town to have a bottle of port. She gladly handed it over, the child was saved, and we received generous gifts of flour and oatmeal.

Aunt Sasha had also saved a piece of dark grey English cloth from before the revolution. I do not know how much there was, but it weighed a great deal. Aunt Sasha maintained that she was keeping it for the darkest of rainy days, when there would be nothing at all to eat. We faced many dark and rainy days, yet the cloth remained untouched. Aunt Sasha bequeathed it to her goddaughter, Masha, who carried it from place to place in her moves. It was only during the last war, when she was dying of hunger, that she decided to part with the cloth. When she unrolled it, it was completely mouldy. What a good story this would make.

Our cousin, Kirill Golitsyn, arrived now for "feeding up", and brought with him a friend, Misha Poletsky. At this time we were only able to feed ourselves with food from the market by bartering Bobrinsky goods and chattels. So mother had to say, "My dear ones, do come and visit us, but you must live elsewhere." Both young men found somewhere to live in the nearby village of Vyasovka, where they went to work in the offices of a coal mine, coming to visit us only occasionally before returning with the army to Petrograd.

There were a number of doctors in Bogoroditsk; Burtsev with the military commissary, Pospelov, head of the health administration and so my father's boss, Samorodskaya, the paediatrician, and Zharkovsky, a dentist. But the one doctor the whole town and district really loved was Alexei Ippolitovich Nikolsky. Grandfather fell ill and Dr Nikolsky carried out a prostate operation on him. We visited grandfather in hospital, which was quite close by. Grandfather got well, but Nikolsky advised him to stay on. Why? Dreadful times were approaching. When I remember Dr Nikolsky now, I truly believe, doctors like him no longer exist. Tall and lean, grey-haired with grey whiskers, looking out with dark eyes from behind his glasses, he walked with a rapid and firm step. What was his speciality? In those days, you did not ask. He was simply "The Doctor", in capital letters. He healed any and every illness, carried out difficult operations, managed the hospital administration, got up at night for serious cases and travelled about the district. In those days the hospital had no X-ray machine and could only do the simplest laboratory analyses, yet Nikolsky was famous for his diagnoses; only a hint was needed for him to understand what was wrong. He told the story of how a woman came to him saying a sheep was chewing her right side; he immediately understood the trouble and cured her. Patients trusted him, and this trust helped in their recovery. He was humane, in the best sense of that word. He helped, to the extent that he was able, both our family and many other people in our situation. When there was a death, he comforted the family; when someone was arrested, he intervened.

He was also a witty, gregarious man, who liked to invite and be invited. He was not above taking a glass or two on occasion, enjoyed hunting, taking part in the wolf hunts common in those days when many wolves still roamed the countryside. His wife, Julia Lvovna, the daughter of a small local landowner, was enthusiastic and lively but not greatly interested in social life; she preferred reading novels and poetry. The Nikolskys adored each other, but had no children. They lived in a fine house in a little street close to Mikhailovsky Square, together with their nephew and niece, the children of his brother who had died of typhus.

I was told that the whole town took part in Dr Nikolsky's funeral. His death was a real sorrow for the ordinary people, who truly loved him. His wife, Julia Lvovna, survived him only for a short time. She left no will and the authorities in Bogoroditsk took advantage of this to take away all the furniture, silver, china and books, and evict the nephew and niece. Where all these goods have ended up, I cannot say. All this was told me with much sadness in 1968. That was when I saw with satisfaction a brass seal in a case in the Bogoroditsk Museum marked "Dr Nikolsky's seal". When, nine years later, I visited the town museum again the seal was no longer on show. When I inquired after it, the museum officials could find neither it nor its nameplate in their storerooms. A few more years will pass and the very memory of this noble man will have faded.

6

Dr Nikolsky kept grandfather in the hospital because the worst times in the history of Bogoroditsk had now begun. Denikin was advancing from the south, while General Mamontov's army corps had broken through in the rear of the Reds and was moving from east to west, blowing up bridges, overturning trains and killing any commissars who could not get away. In Bogoroditsk a state of siege with a night-time curfew was declared. In the centuries when the Central Asian Khans occupied our land, they either let their hostages go, or held them in dungeons, or put them to death without trial. The example of the Khans was followed by the *communards* in Paris, who shot many thousands of hostages. In our country, it was Trotsky who instigated the shooting of innocent people. This senseless kind of bloodletting bedevilled our own civil war. As the Whites advanced to take a town, the Reds would round up merchants, civil servants and landowners, move them behind the lines and, when the Whites captured the town, shoot them all. So, retreating from Orel, the Reds shot many hostages. Historians will never discover the number of victims, as in the chaos of events no lists were kept. Among the dead of Orel were two of my mother's cousins, Boris and Yuria Alexandrovich Lopukhin. At this time, too, the husband of my grandmother's sister, Alexander Grigoryevich Buligin, a leading tsarist politician, was shot. Uncle Leo Bobrinsky, without being allowed to bid anyone farewell, was moved to Tula and from there to Moscow. News came from Uncle Vovik in Moscow that our grandfather Sasha had died in his arms at the age of eighty-two. There was so much bad news from all over the country that this death of the eldest Golitsyn barely evoked the appropriate response from us.

Amongst those commissars who were famous for their cruelty I can name two; the chairman of the Bogoroditsk city administration, Belolipetsky, and the head of the Tula Cheka, the Latvian Kaul. The following story about the latter was frequently told at the time; a prisoner returns home and his young son starts showing off his newly acquired knowledge. "You know, Daddy, Adam had two sons." "And can you name them?" asks the father. "They were Kaul and Abel," replies the son.

Were people waiting for the Whites? You dared not say this aloud. Infuriated by the requisitioning of their grain, the peasants were certainly waiting, and indeed the Whites, having taken Orel, were slowly advancing north. In Bogoroditsk a military headquarters was set up in the local school buildings. The schoolchildren had to make do with the cinema where they sat in groups and were addressed by the teachers, but not questioned. My education continued under Aunt Sasha and mother. In October the dark streets were barely lit by the light of the moon. It seemed to rain incessantly. One night a stray dog came to our house and was howling at the moon. My brother Vladimir went outside and threw a stone at the dog, which disappeared. He was no sooner back in bed when it was back again, howling mournfully.

"It bodes no good," moaned Nasenka.

The next night, and the one after, the same dog was back, howling under our windows. What was happening on the front lines no one knew. There were rumours, but no one believed them. In the district of Bogoroditsk two Cossacks were killed. Their fine horses, well fed and beautifully kitted out, were deliberately paraded through the streets.

The promise of some good fortune for our family was held out to us; a whole house, with supplies of wood and a plot of land, would become available for us on a street near the Agricultural Institute. The present occupiers were moving to a village called Tovarkovo. We began asking about a wagon to move our modest belongings.

But the move did not happen. One night there was loud knocking at the door. We lived in expectation of such knocking, knowing that, inevitably and inescapably, it would come, so we were ready for it. A back door led out of the room where my parents slept and from there a way through the garden and orchard led to the road out of town. My parents had scouted out this escape route; provisions of bread and potatoes were always at their bedside. I awoke to hear mother whispering to my father, "Quick, quick, they're knocking." Father dressed and slipped out into the night, Vladimir locking the door behind him. Meanwhile mother was deliberately making a long job of opening the front door, which they were still banging violently. Two Chekists burst in, revolvers at the ready, and a soldier with a rifle. They shouted for lights and went through all the rooms, looking under the beds. Mother demanded to see their warrant. They said something sharply in reply and asked where father was, but not just him, also about sister Lina. As it happened, she was spending the night with Anna Bibikova in the Community House. Despite their age difference, they were close friends.

Mother began to say that she herself was worried about her husband and why he had not returned from his work. Just then there was loud knocking at the back door. One of the men, revolver at the ready, ran to open it. It was the neighbour's mentally defective brother, the one who could attract no bride. Panting, he described how he had stepped out into the garden to relieve himself and seen a shadowy figure slip out of our back door and run off through the gate. He said he had run after him, but in vain.

"And who are these people?" he asked, looking about him.

"So that's it!" exclaimed one of the Chekists. "You push off to bed." Turning to the soldier with the rifle, he ordered him to go outside and hunt around. Then, exchanging a glance with his companion, he announced that they were going to carry out a search. Meanwhile, the soldier had gone out. Most of our things were already tied up in bundles for our move. At the order of the Chekists, we were beginning to untie these, when there was the sound of a shot. Only little Katya could fail to understand whom they were shooting at. Mother slumped onto a chair; Aunt Sasha began crossing herself. The soldier came back.

"Well?" the Chekists demanded.

"I just shot into the air," the soldier replied. "Not a thing to be seen."

The search took until dawn. They turned everything upside down, pulled up the rugs, read our letters, asked who wrote them, kept on searching. They found no weapons. We simply sat there, in silence. When the search was over the two men consulted in whispers, casting glances first at mother, then at Vladimir. Finally, the older one told my mother to get her things together, turned to Vladimir, and said, "When your father gets back he must come to the Cheka. Then we'll let your mother go."

And he added, "I give you my word, we'll let her go."

Mother put on her coat, slipped a piece of bread into her pocket, and said goodbye to us all, making the sign of the cross over us. My younger sisters were crying, as were Aunt Sasha, Nasenka and Lenya. I had to bite my lips to keep control of myself. They took mother away. I watched from the porch until their dark shapes had faded into the night. Aunt Sasha put the little girls to bed again. Vladimir also lay down. I went through to the end room to have a sleep and found sister Sonya on her knees in front of the icon in the corner; she was fervently praying and bowing to the ground. I knelt beside her and prayed to God to bring back my parents. We prayed like this until dawn's reddish light broke through the rain clouds.

Father soon returned. Aunt Sasha started to tell him everything that had happened in great detail. Before she was taken away, mother had managed to whisper to Aunt Sasha to tell father under no circumstances to give himself up by going to the police station. He stood listening in silence, drops of sweat standing out on his forehead.

"Put some things together for me," he told Aunt Sasha. "I'm going."

They tried to talk him out of it, but he simply repeated that he was going. To me, at that moment, he was like one of my fearless white knights. He set off accompanied by Sonya, and within an hour mother was back with us. I had never seen her in such a state. Probably, that day was the worst of many such dreadful days in her life. She reproached Aunt Sasha with failing to persuade my father to hide himself somewhere, anywhere; then she collapsed in a chair. And yet it was now as ever a time to act, to try to get something done at the police station, to send things to father, and to move the whole family to a new abode. Lina, too, had disappeared, and on top of all this, Nasenka announced there was nothing left to eat in the house. We had absolutely no food supplies left. Normally, it was mother who went to the bazaar to exchange bits of clothing for flour and potatoes. She had always been full of energy and her strength bolstered our morale. Now she sat hopeless, unable to get up.

Someone came to tell us they were taking the hostages to the station, and this news had an electrifying effect on mother. She leapt to her feet, saying "Quick, quick!" There were a few unpeeled boiled potatoes in a pan. She wrapped these up with a piece of bread and some salt, tied a pillow in a blanket and seized a bowl and a spoon. We set off – mother, sisters Sonya and Masha and I. Vladimir remained behind for fear that he too might be seized.

The station, Zhdanka, was a *verst* away beyond the cemetery. On the north side of the station stood a large, ugly grain elevator. Sitting on the grass or on their bundles were a motley crowd of men and women of all ages and social class. We saw our father, Uncle Vladimir, our Lina, and Sonya Bobrinskaya, who was just fifteen-years-old. We knew many of the other townsfolk there. In all there must have been about a hundred people. Tired sentries in ragged uniforms and bandages guarded the crowd. Twenty paces was the nearest any of the crowd of relatives who, like us, had hurried over, was allowed to approach the prisoners. A few passengers waiting at the station looked on with curiosity.

"They're hostages," a voice was heard. "When the train comes they'll all be taken to Tula."

And an angry voice added, "They'll all be put up against a wall there."

"What for, they're all innocent?" a woman's voice moaned.

More relatives of the prisoners kept arriving. Seeing us, father stood up and tried to speak to us, but in the general clamour of voices it was hard to hear him. I started to throw him potatoes, which he caught. It was just as if we were playing ball. One of the guards took our bundle and passed it to father. Now there approached a group of men in a mixture of leather jackets, civilian clothes and uniforms. Among them I recognised the two men from last night. A sorting process began. The hostages were told to come up in turn to the group of officials. Sonya pointed out the tall man who was the head of the Cheka – Belolipetsky. He ordered some to clear off entirely, and some to line up in special place. Most of the hostages were set free, including our Lina and Sonya Bobrinskaya, but twelve were told to wait with their bundles, including father and Uncle Vladimir.

When I visited the town museum of Bogoroditsk in 1968 I saw Belolipetsky's photo there. Staring out of the picture at me were the cold eyes of a relatively young man. "So that's the man who decided the fate of my father," I thought. His life had been the sort of life that was more or less normal for party members. He rose through the ranks, was transferred to Moscow to take up increasingly senior posts, and then in 1937 ended up in the same place to which he had sent so many thousands in the course of his career.

Lina came over and told us how she and Sonya Bobrinskaya had been picked up just as evening fell the day before. She and I did not wait for the despatch of the prisoners, but went home. Mother and Sonya stayed until they saw father off in a freight car to Tula. They returned in the evening with dreadful news. The Whites had advanced into Tula province and all hostages in the extreme southwest had been shot.

Mother returned from the station ready to act. She would move us to a new lodging as quickly as possible, would exchange goods for food and then set off for Tula. The next morning she took me with her to the bazaar. It was quite close, as Ekaterinskaya Street ran into Bazaar Square. But an enormous disappointment was waiting for us; normally there were peasant carts with potatoes, rye and wheat flour, sugar beet and milk. Today, however, the square in front of the town church was empty, save for a couple of old ladies selling seeds.

Vladimir had gone to hunt for transport for our move and for the trip to Tula. He found that the only transport to Tula was setting off in three days, and the carter for our move wanted eight kilos of oats as payment. Where on earth could we get hold of such wealth? Our situation was desperate. For several days now no bread had been issued against ration cards. We had no potatoes, and our flour bin was empty. I cannot remember what we ate that day. Someone had given my sister Katya a carrot, which she cut up in tiny pieces, saying "It looks more that way." In the evening mother called us together for prayers. She prayed with great fervour, bowing deeply as she did so. Earnestly, we crossed ourselves over and over.

7

Then, a miracle happened; it is the only way to describe it. That very day, or perhaps the next, there drove up to our house a large cart and out stepped Yegor Antonovich Sukhanov. In terms of psychology I find it hard to explain this event. Why did this former enemy of my mother, this *kulak* of Bulchalki, hearing that his masters were living poorly in Bogoroditsk, collect a whole cartload of provisions from the estate folk at Bulchalki, those who still remembered the earlier generosity of their masters, and drive them over to us? I can only think that he imagined the Bolsheviks would eventually be defeated and then the princes his masters would return to Bulchalki filled with such gratitude that they would from then on bring prosperity upon him.

Sukhanov unloaded two sacks of rye, two more of wheat, some smoked ham and butter, a couple of bottles of golden-green rapeseed oil, loaves of bread, doughnuts and a live chicken. Grandmother had moved into a room near the Trubetskois, where grandfather joined her on leaving the hospital. We shared all these provisions with the Trubetskois. Yegor Antonovich moved all our things to our new home and departed for Bulchalki, saying that once the winter snow-road had hardened off he would be back with more gifts from the peasants of Bulchalki.

Putting on my father's sheepskin coat and armed with a bag of provisions, mother set off for Tula. She had a very hard time on the way, as when the driver discovered where she was going and why, he was furious and uttered nothing but curses, saying that "there was freedom now" and "all the masters should be destroyed" and that it was pointless my mother going to Tula as "they had all been perforated by now." On her arrival in Tula mother went straight to her former governess, Ludmilla Tipolt, by profession a midwife, who was living in a small room in the house of a famous samovar manufacturer Batashchov. Alexandra Vasiliyeva Batashchova had been great friends with mother in their childhood. She now took her in and during mother's stay, made her more than welcome and helped her as much as she could.

Mother soon located father and Uncle Vladimir in prison. It was not at all certain whether the hostages were going to be shot or not. The papers were screaming about Red victories near Orel, which was a small comfort. On the other hand, could one believe the papers? There were hostages from all over the country, being fed a starvation diet. Every morning this endless line of prisoners was marched out under escort to work in the fields gathering in frozen cabbages. Their relatives would rush up to them with food. The escort closed their eyes to this infringement of regulations. My mother hired herself out as a hand on adjoining farmland and was able to see my father twice a day as he marched to and from work, and in this way was able to hold out to him a bowl of boiled cabbage that he could dip into as he walked. For a month and a half she managed to feed father and Uncle Vladimir like this. But prison food, even with the additional cabbage she was able to pass to them, was just not enough nourishment. The two men, and indeed all the hostages, were becoming weaker and weaker. Fleas and bedbugs and other creatures attacked them continually. Prisoners ended up in the prison hospital, or the morgue.

Thanks to the help of doctors who knew my father, both he and Uncle Vladimir were transferred to a brightly-lit ward and the snowy sheets of a hospital bed. Father told me later that one of the best moments in his life was when, after a hot bath and in clean hospital pyjamas, he lay down on a hospital cot and covered himself with the coarse prison blanket. Uncle Vladimir had started to suffer from tuberculosis and was running a temperature. My father did not have a temperature, but among the nurses there were some who had worked in Epifansky district and had heard a lot of good things about him.

Only one person was to be feared, and that was the commissar who was head of the hospital, a Bolshevik and former medical orderly. He kept a sharp eye out for anyone pretending to be ill. Father just could not fake his temperature, as schoolboys did, by rubbing the thermometer between the palms of his hands. The nurses brought him lukewarm tea and he was supposed to hold the thermometer in the tea just long enough to make the temperature rise, but not too high. Thus did these patients, the genuinely sick and the pretend sick, pass their time in the wards, telling each other stories, smoking, walking about and waiting for the rounds of watery soup. They were only reminded of the reality of their situation by the guard with his rifle standing at each doorway. Father came across many old acquaintances, from work, or who he had met at assemblies of the nobles and other social events and meetings.

Mother was allowed to visit every day, bring food parcels and talk to him in the presence of a guard. Denikin was beating a hasty retreat. The hostages would not be shot. It was rumoured that the Reds had won thanks to the reappearance of two companies of Latvian riflemen. During this time, we exchanged letters with mother and father.

8

How did we manage to exist in our new home without our parents in those last two months of 1919? The Lyubimovy house was a wooden building with a tin roof, a spacious entrance porch on one side and a large barn behind. In the first room stood a huge Russian stove with a small room behind the partition. A curtain divided the main room in two, so that in effect we could say we had a four-room house. Vladimir and I were allocated the little room behind the partition, Lenya slept in the kitchen behind the stove, my two older sisters took one half of the main room, where there was also a bed awaiting the return of my parents. Aunt Sasha, Nasenka and my two little sisters occupied the other half. Some of the Bobrinsky furniture that we had with us was very ordinary, but much of it was luxurious pieces made of mahogany and oak, so my parents had a fine bed and toilet table and two upholstered chairs.

Aunt Sasha continued to give lessons to me and my little sisters. Lina went on working at the town library. Sonya was still at school, but Vladimir had finished school and for a time had no occupation, though he was sometimes asked to paint placards. I can remember a large piece of plywood that he painted with a blacksmith striking an anvil with a massive hammer. I was delighted by the sparks flying off the anvil. This placard was hung in Bazaar Square on the second anniversary of the revolution, where it lasted a few days until the rains washed the picture away.

This was the first time I saw a demonstration with red flags and banners. On the square, opposite the town's main church, a wooden stand was put up and Vladimir's placard hung behind it. The speaker proclaimed world revolution, claimed that the wise prophecies of Karl Marx were being fulfilled in Bavaria and in Hungary, that the whole of Europe was in flames and that the proletariat would seize power all over the world. There was a silly joke circulating – that even the dogs were now growling "worrld rrrevolution". Later, the small groups that had seized power in Bavaria and Hungary were crushed. The headlines in the papers screamed "Bloody dog Noske! Socialist traitors Kautsky, Zeidman and their like!" Specially targeted were the German social democratic leaders, who were in fact leading their followers peacefully forward towards purely economic goals.

Lina and Sonya were usually out in the evenings with their friends and boyfriends. It was Vladimir who stayed at home. I would watch him for hours as he carefully spread out some of the old Bobrinsky paper in his usual pose, feet up on his bed and leaning on the table, choosing his paints, selecting his brushes and mixing and applying the colours with infinite delicacy as he painted. He always wore the English trench coat inherited from our late Uncle Misha, and big felt boots. I do not know where he read one of the most beautiful fairy tales of old Russia, *The Invisible City of Kityezh*, but he did a series of pictures of Prince Georgy on horseback with his falcon, of Grisha Kuterma leading the Tartars, of the battle at Kerzhents, the blue lake of Svetloyar surrounded by birch trees, and of the invisible city with its white walls and gilded churches hidden in the still waters of the lake. Vladimir was passionate then about the painter Bilibin and painted in solid colours, surrounding his paintings with decorative borders taken from various books or from his own imagination. This whole series of pictures was lost in one of our moves. It was from that time onwards that I began to dream of one day reaching the banks of that magical lake and seeing the invisible city of Kityezh.

We fed ourselves mostly thanks to the donations brought from Buchalki, the main item of which was rye. Nasenka did much of the cooking, though she had no great talent for it and never mastered the Russian stove. She soaked the rye for two days and then cooked it a further two days in an iron pot, but it still came out as hard as ever and was a torture for our digestion. We cherished our live hen, called her Lenya in honour of our under-nanny, and hoped for a daily egg from her when spring came.

I still remember the little pancakes of rye flour cooked on a griddle, and the potatoes that we ate boiled in their jackets. We were also allowed a teaspoonful of rapeseed oil, measured out by Aunt Sasha with the accuracy of a pharmacist. Our cabbage soup was meatless, cooked from rotten cabbage, grey in colour. In the morning we youngsters had a glass of milk. Bread was sold only against ration cards. Everyday I would go to the shop on Voronezh street where a red-haired Austrian former prisoner of war, Franz, would weigh out our five kilos; given our poor diet this was not a lot. Nasenka cut up the bread. My little sisters and I ate the crumbs. During the day I would go for milk to the former superintendent of the town prison, now empty, the prisoners now being held in former merchants' storerooms on Bazaar Square. After our meals we drank tea with saccharin or sugar. You could hold a lump of sugar in your cheek and let the carrot tea run over it; one lump did two cups.

Sukhanov arrived from Bulchalki again, bringing richer offerings, including a pair of felt boots, two or three pairs of socks, a live cockerel and three hens. Part of these supplies went to our grandparents and the Trubetskois, whilst we ate ourselves sick with the rest all in one day. I called the cockerel George, the hens Nasenka, Nanny Bush and Polya, in honour of the Trubetskois' under-nanny. We exulted over the eggs we would have in the spring.

Nearer spring Sukhanov came for the last time, bringing three more live hens. The next time we saw him was in Moscow in 1926. That was during the time when merchants were beginning to be heavily taxed. Sukhanov had opened a shop during the years of the so-called New Economic Policy, and was so heavily taxed that he protested. As a result, his entire stock was confiscated and his house threatened with seizure. He came to Moscow to try to do something about the situation and stayed with us, describing with bitterness the treatment he had received from his fellow villagers. My parents tried to help him, got some sort of paper for him, but when he was back in his village he wrote to say the paper had been no help at all and he had been ruined. In 1929, he reappeared on our doorstep in rags and covered with fleas. Mother fed him in the entrance hallway and in reply to her questions got only evasive replies. Suspecting the worst, she asked him, "Yegor Antonovich, you've escaped from prison, haven't you?"

"Yes, I've run away."

Mother was greatly alarmed. She let him sleep on a mat in the hallway, but in the morning told him he must go; we never learned of his subsequent fate. But in Bogoroditsk he literally saved our lives. His visits restored our spirits and bolstered our confidence.

9

Aunt Sasha and Nasenka began to be increasingly irritable, constantly scolding me. Nasenka shouted at me, but then immediately stroked my head, and I knew that she was good. Aunt Sasha said I paid no attention to my lessons and that I wrote messily in my copybooks. But how could I write neatly when instead of ink I had to dip my pen in a mixture of soot and water and my fingers were covered with festering sores? I tried not to quarrel with Masha and Katya, but when I did, they went straight off to tell tales about me. I thought how unhappy I was, and how much I missed my parents, particularly my mother. I took out books from the library where Lina worked, and these were my only consolation and joy. Reading one after another, I was carried away into a land of dreams.

One day, I was reading quietly by myself. In the next room, my little sisters were quarrelling. Then Masha hit Katya. Aunt Sasha rushed in, seized me and dragged me to stand in a corner. I shouted that I had not done a thing, and tried to resist but she continued to shout at me and push me into the corner, where I stood fuming and plotting revenge for this injustice. In the evenings, we lived by the light of an oil lamp, which you had to be careful not to walk past too quickly or it would blow out. By the light of that lamp I wrote mother a long letter begging her to let me join her in Tula and saying that I could no longer live with such an awful aunt. I had to cover the envelope with scores of Provisional Government one rouble stamps, which were still in circulation; the stamps covered back and front of my missive to Tula – today I imagine such a letter would be coveted by philatelists.

Mother later told me what an impression my clear and soul-searing letter had made on her, and how she showed it to father in hospital. She had in any case decided to return to Bogoroditsk to see how we were getting on. It was decided that Lina would replace mother in Tula, whilst Lina's job in the library could be done by Sonya. So mother returned to Bogoroditsk, found us all in a reasonable state, and was content. On learning that Frau Swikke had restarted her German lessons, she despatched Masha and me to attend her class twice a week. Walking past the windows of the Chetvertushkins, I tried to see if I could spot their secret prisoner-son, Zhenya.

We had no toilet in our house and had to use a bucket in the barn. One day, mother came rushing out, shouting "George has shit all over me!" Her hair and half her face were covered with the cockerel's droppings from his overhead perch. Nasenka rushed to heat water and washed mother's head over a basin, repeating over and over, "It brings happiness, it brings happiness." Less than an hour later, whilst her hair was still drying, the outside door swung open and there appeared a figure in a cloud of condensation, with ice on his whiskers and a bag under his arm – my father.

The next day he inspected the ground behind the house and announced that come the spring we would take it in hand to grow vegetables. From that very first evening he himself carried out the toilet bucket and carefully spread its contents over the ground as manure for our future garden. Father returned to his job in the health administration. Mother went a little distance to Voronezh Street, where Lyubov Bauman, the sister of Michael Volotsky, a close colleague of the world-famous eugenicist Professor N.K. Koltsov, was teaching her how to make shoes. I remember how Michael Volotsky visited us when we were living in Moscow, measured our heads, noses and hands and gave us a copy of his very interesting book about the Dostoyevsky family line. He had studied that family, starting in the middle of the eighteenth century and demonstrated that nearly all its members had been more or less abnormal. For his work in eugenics this talented man was arrested at the end of the 1920s and perished.

It was thanks to the enthusiasm of educated people for "going to the people" in the nineteenth century that Lyubov Bauman was able to teach cobbling.[9] Mother was soon able to sew soft shoes from the green baize that had once covered the floor of grandfather's study in our Moscow house. Her first effort was a pair of slippers for me,

---

9. *The most famous exponent of this striving to return to the simple life, including making your own shoes, is Tolstoy.*

which turned out to be of different sizes and rather shapeless. Mother's intention was to earn money by producing shoes, but there was such a big demand amongst our three families: Golitsyns, Trubetskois and Bobrinskys, that it was agreed that mother would shoe us all, in return for Aunt Vera clothing us all with Bobrinsky garments.

10

Uncle Vladimir's fate was not as happy as my father's. He was not released with all the other hostages, but sent off as a military conscript to a Moscow hospital. There he was more or less restored to health before being discharged with an order mobilizing him into the Red Army. He heard that General Brusilov, the former commander of the southwest front, was now one of Trotsky's deputies and inspector-general of the cavalry. Uncle decided to pay him a visit, especially as Brusilov knew him well from the German war, during which uncle had been an outstanding commander of the only motorized cavalry company on the entire front. A number of former officers were waiting in the reception room. Uncle went up to the adjutant and gave his name. His heart sank at the very thought that such a popular hero as Brusilov was now serving the Bolsheviks. He deliberately emphasized the word *tovarishch* when asking to see "Comrade" Brusilov. The adjutant went off and in a moment Brusilov came to the door of his office and beckoned Uncle Vladimir in. When they were alone, he said "Prince, I'm so pleased to see you!"

They had a long conversation. Brusilov told my uncle how much he valued every one of his officers and how Trotsky was whole-heartedly behind the army and that they would undoubtedly win. But he also described how difficult the situation was with some of the military commissars, who often did not trust the officers, and that there had been cases of completely loyal officers being executed. Uncle was a convinced monarchist, so much of what Brusilov told him upset him, but the former's sincerity and grace earned uncle's respect. After all uncle had three children to think of, which left him with little choice. He left the office with papers authorising him to travel to Orel to report to the commander of the southern front, and a note from Brusilov saying that he knew Trubetskoi to be a sensible and competent commander of a motorised company and should be given a responsible post either at headquarters or with the troops.

With such orders and – for those times – a generous parcel of rations, uncle first visited his few remaining relatives in Moscow and then set off for Tula. There he decided to take the risk of coming to see his family in Bogoroditsk, especially as he wanted to leave a large part of his rations with them. He knocked on our door very late in the evening. Alas, a policeman had noticed him as he walked through the town and raised the alarm. Neither uncle's impressive marching orders, nor his explanation as to why he had made a diversion to see his family, had any effect on Belolipetsky, who had him arrested for a fourth time and sent to prison in Tula. In prison uncle's tuberculosis flared up again and he was removed to hospital. Not long after, quite seriously ill, he returned to us in Bogoroditsk. It was there that he told me this whole story.

Here I bring to an end my account of a year so full of events in the history of Russia, Bogoroditsk and our family.

3. The Muses in Bogoroditsk

1

The reader may find it amazing, given all that was happening – civil war, peasant uprisings, searches, arrests, executions, hunger, unheated homes, poor clothing, wick lamps instead of real lights – that there could be an awakening of the arts. But such was the case. Ekaterina Vasilyevna Sakharova, daughter of the artist Polenov, wrote most interestingly in her collection of stories of just the same thing happening in the village of Tarus in the province of Kaluga, though without mentioning searches, arrests and executions. One of Tolstoy's family wrote of seeing Schiller's play *The Robbers*. In Fedin's novel *The Bonfire* there are also descriptions of artistic revival in those years. I remember hearing of amateur theatricals, of artists' studios and orchestras in many towns and villages, not to mention the flowering of all the arts in Moscow.

Psychologically speaking it is hard to explain how hungry and frightened people, suffering all kinds of hardships in those years, still talked, as they queued up for bread, of the theatres and cinemas they had been to, the books they were reading, the poets they had heard. But so it was. In Bogoroditsk this upsurge of artistic activity probably started with our play *Auntie on the Shelf*, with the musical evenings in the Bobrinsky house, and the shows put on in the Agricultural Institute and in the former boys' and girls' school.

Later the teachers put on Turgenev's *A Month in the Country*, Chekhov's *Jubilee* and Gogol's *The Marriage*. This latter was the first play I ever saw in the auditorium of the institute. The stage, the raising and lowering of the curtain and the acting of the players, stunned me, even though mother said the parts of Podkolesin and Kochkarev were poorly acted. She only praised the acting of Galia Derevyanko, the daughter of a former head of the institute, in the role of Agafyev Tikhonovna. Though still a schoolgirl, my sister Sonya very much wanted to act in these plays. There was another girl competing with Sonya for the part of Merchutkina in Chekhov's *Jubilee*, but

Sonya acted so well at the audition that they never even tried out the other girl.

That winter of 1919–20, the same auditorium saw the staging of *Tartuffe*, Gorky's *The Lower Depths*, and Tolstoy's *The Fruits of Enlightenment*. I never saw the Gorky play, but I remember the other two down to the tiniest detail. The English teacher, Chetvertushkin, directed the plays, but now it was not the institute's students who acted but teachers and members of the town's intelligentsia. Spectators poured into the theatre. They even drove in on their sledges from neighbouring villages.

Much later, I saw *The Fruits of Enlightenment* at the Arts Theatre in Moscow. Perhaps it was my childish impression, but the rapid speech of the Arts Theatre actor in the part of the professor was not at all comparable to the parodied pseudo-wisdom portrayed by the actor in Bogoroditsk, whilst the laconic gestures and quavering, capricious voice of Alexandra Lomakina, the former head of the girls' school, in the role of the noblewoman, put even the famous Olga Knipper's acting in the shade.

Our Sonya played a fat noblewoman, and Uncle Vladimir played Petrishev. Elegant in a starched shirt, bow tie and dark suit, he made the others sitting round the little table in the spiritualist scene quiver with laughter. I silently reproached him for playing the fool on the stage. Vovo was played wonderfully by Alexei Pavlovich Burtsev. I cannot recall what the local paper, *The Red Voice*, wrote about the plays, but I vividly remember how our many friends and family – and there were many of them who had somehow ended up in Bogoroditsk – talked endlessly about them, either praising or criticising them.

The auditorium at the institute was not large, and it was also quite a walk away from the town. Both the public and the authorities, who were in a sense the patrons, realised this, so that with the warmer weather a large building next to the town's primary school was done up as a theatre. Many plays were put on, some for a few nights, some for longer. The players were nearly all local teachers and officials who could only come for rehearsal in the evening; the plays were usually put on twice a week. As for rewards, before the New Economic Policy (NEP), was introduced, their sole reward was the applause they received, though occasionally people would pass up a little food. With the NEP, some kind of small salary began to be paid.

The best actors were undoubtedly Alexei Burtsev and Igor Rusakov, both of whom taught Russian and were popular both as teachers and actors. When Burtsev fell dangerously ill, the whole town hung on news of the progress of his illness, and there was widespread joy when he made a full recovery. There was a constant turnover among the actors, as they were sent to the front or left town. Only Chetvertushkin, Burtsev and Rusakov remained throughout this period. Chetvertushkin's brother, a minor actor at the Maly Theatre in Moscow, came for the summer to Bogoroditsk, probably to enjoy some proper food, and gave one or two lectures on the art of acting, as well as himself going on the stage.

In that first, or possibly, second season of the summer theatre, I saw *Revizor*, *The Cherry Orchard* and *Twelfth Night*. I was intensely proud of my sister Sonya who played some of the leading roles – for example, of Maria Antonovna and Olivia. I remember a silly episode during one production of *Twelfth Night*. It had already been on for four evenings and there was hardly anyone in the audience; after all, the town only had six thousand inhabitants. Masha and I were alone in the second row. The show seemed endless, with two long intervals, and round about the third act we were beginning to need to relieve ourselves. There was no such thing as a toilet in that old barn; there was not even a foyer. The only thing to do was to go outside and find a convenient bush. When we made to leave, we were stopped by a squad of soldiers who were checking documents at the doors, probably looking for deserters. Instead of pointing out that we were hardly of the age to be anything like that, we turned back in fear and resumed our seats. By the fourth act, however, we could no longer hold out; we relieved ourselves in that empty row and quietly slipped across into other seats.

Intervals were always very long while the scenery was changed. In 1977, an old accountant by name of Archangelsky told me in great detail how he had worked as prompter in the theatre in Bogoroditsk at that time. It seems that there was always a great fuss and bother between acts and the main actors such as Chetvertushkin, Burtsev et al. refused to let the secondary actors rest, but kept urging them into action. Nails were in very short supply and Chetvertushkin in particular pleaded with everyone to take great care of every nail, and if one was bent, to straighten it out rather than throw it away. My brother Vladimir painted the backdrops. An album has survived which shows the spring and autumn backdrops for *The Cherry Orchard*, the one with flowering cherry trees, the other with gnarled, leafless branches. I used to watch Vladimir laying out the huge canvas sheet and beginning to sketch in his subject, and I was often ordered to bring a brush, or the glue, or help him in some other errand. Chetvertushkin decided that the backdrop for *Revizor* should be the two ancient houses that stood near the town church of Pokrov. Vladimir sat in front of these houses and sketched them, whilst I stood by watching him and, if any children pressed in too close, I drove them away.

2

1920 was a terrible year. The civil war was raging, not a drop of rain fell during the summer and famine spread across the land. It was at this time that a permanent theatre was created in Bogoroditsk. A large two-storied stone house that had belonged to a merchant, Kuptsov, was rebuilt. The inner walls and floor were removed, a stage was put up and there was a pit for the orchestra, a gallery fitted in somehow and even a foyer. There were two toilets in the courtyard. In this way, the town acquired a genuine theatre with seats for three hundred, or even five hundred spectators – memories differ.

The first performance in the new theatre was *Hamlet*. It ran for ten performances. Sonya had no role in it. Chetvertushkin mercilessly cut the play, but it still lasted until midnight. Very likely many of the spectators – soldiers, peasants, the children of local townsfolk – failed to understand everything, but they must have had a vague awareness from the monologues and interplay of dialogue that here they were listening to the great art of Shakespeare, which the talented Bogoroditsk actors were trying to get across to them. The applause was fantastic; the spectators' hands were red from clapping; people shouted until they were hoarse.

Burtsev played Hamlet, Rusakov the king, and the queen was played by a professional actress called Chelnokova. Galia Derevanko played Ophelia, and the son of a local priest, Postinkov, played Laertes. I think the production of this play was the summit of theatrical achievement in that small provincial town. Some years later I went to see *Hamlet* at the second Moscow Arts Theatre. The hero was played by the great Michael Chekhov, Cheban played the king, Giatsintova the queen, Durasova, Ophelia. It is not right to compare the two events, yet I do feel that in Bogoroditsk everything was simpler, more accessible, more human. It is true that some of the spectators laughed when Hamlet came on stage with his stockings round his ankles, thinking this a slip, just like the occasion when a plywood panel behind which the ghost of Hamlet's father was hiding, fell over.

Chetvertushkin strove for historical accuracy with the costumes. There was a costume lady but she could not dress everyone, so the actors sewed for themselves or got their relatives to help. The Bobrinsky trunks and cupboards, as well as the velvet curtains from the windows of the big house, supplied pretty well the entire clothing needed by the cast. For a short time, a certain Baroness Friedrich came and stayed in the town. She donated an old silk dress to Sonya, which was turned into an elegant Renaissance costume for the part of Olivia. Chetvertushkin was in despair about the actors' stockings. Up until the revolution, skirts were long and stockings only went a little above the knee. In the age of Shakespeare, men wore hose much more like the pantyhose of today. Wetting the stockings and stretching them was tried, but they still looked wrong. In the end, he had to make a concession and let the men wear half-length trousers. No one seemed to notice this historical inaccuracy.

One of the reasons underlying this vigorous theatrical movement all over the country and in Moscow was that none of the commissars interfered with what was produced. Talented directors and enthusiastic actors put on what they chose. How often *Princess Turandot*, an ideologically liberal play, ran at the Vachtangov Theatre, without being taken off as a result of official interference. In Bogoroditsk, the plays were chosen by Chetvertushkin and the two actors, Burtsev and Rusakov. And the local authorities came along to see these plays just like the rest of the people. The authorities even helped the theatres, getting hold of glue and wood and paints and even those nails that were in such short supply. They sometimes provided food, and there was one occasion when they arranged for all the actors to travel in a heated freight car to Moscow, where they were able to see a number of plays and collect clothing and other materials to bring back to Bogoroditsk. Sonya told us with excitement the story of this journey that took three days each way, and the fun they all had.

3

It was not only the theatre that flourished in Bogoroditsk. Music did too. At first the musicians met at the Bobrinsky house before moving to the town. The Shchedrin brothers, exiled from their estate in Aleksinsky province and all four of them talented musicians, arrived in town. They were joined by Uncle Vladimir and the dentist Israel Zharkovsky, both violinists, and Aunt Vera as pianist. A full orchestra was established with wind and horn sections, and the great music of Bach, Beethoven, Mozart and Russian composers played. Rehearsals and concerts were held in the fairly large auditorium of the girls' school, attracting a select company of listeners. Uncle

Vladimir was their first conductor, but was soon replaced by Evgeny Shchedrin. Uncle also taught musical theory. During the day he worked in the town's military commissariat, where he accepted or rejected the horses mobilised from the peasantry. He was still a passionate hunter, of which more later. His wife, Aunt Eli, the mother of their three, later four children, played the drum so as to collect extra rations. She was a pale, emaciated woman, worn out by lack of sleep and proper food. The big drum was not at all the right instrument for her slender figure. She sat to one side of the orchestra, holding her sticks and trying not to miss her cue, and when the time came, striking the drums with as much strength as she could muster. Sometimes she would bring the children with her and they would sit like little angels, without moving, just waiting for mother to lead them home.

In 1921, the actors began to be paid a small salary. Uncle Vladimir resolved to earn some extra money, but it was grandmother who created the opportunity. She translated one of Boccaccio's stories, *The Pear Tree*, and when Uncle Vladimir read it he was suddenly inspired. He sat down at the piano and began to compose an operetta. Aunt Vera helped him. I can remember some of the lines later sung by Khomyakov:

> *Tricked here, fooled there,*
> *Our eyes burn with passion.*
> *Our wives betray us*
> *With any kind of fool,*
> *And often fit us out*
> *With huge horns*

Grandmother painted two identical posters of a pear tree with the jealous husband sitting in its branches and the wife and lover kissing below. The operetta was performed early in 1922 and made a great impression on me. It had several performances and Uncle received a modest fee. Encouraged by this relative success, he decided to write another work, this time aimed at the Moscow stage. For more than a year he struggled with this project, called *The Magician's Pill*. The story was very light; a Spanish king suffers from impotence and is unable to produce an heir to the throne. Along comes a magician and gives him a box of magic pills. But the pills are distributed around the court by mistake, and soon aged ladies-in-waiting are launching themselves at all the young men, whilst the young maidens sing lustful songs.

I cannot remember whether the work was put on in Bogoroditsk. Uncle took it to Moscow and managed to get an audition with Yaron, then the ruling figure in the operatic world. Uncle played and sang his operetta to Yaron and a committee of four surly men. Yaron laughed a lot and said he liked it very much, but the four sour-looking members of the committee said, "No". There was nothing in it about the class struggle, nor a single member of the hereditary working class. Uncle Vladimir's trip was failure, but he was an optimist by nature and returned to Bogoroditsk to his beloved hunting and his job accepting and rejecting horses for the army.

This was a time when a desire to study was sweeping through the country. Young people, provided they had graduated from secondary school, could enter the universities without taking examinations. Soon my sister Lina and Alka Bobrinskaya were to leave for Moscow to study in the faculty of history and letters. The commissars were much closer to the ordinary people in those days than our present "bosses". The then military commissar, Golev, not only organised a class for classical wrestling but, baring himself to the waist, regularly took part in the contests. Today, such a combination of the active sportsman and the political leader is absolutely unthinkable.

One day a startling piece of news was broadcast around the town. An unknown wrestler, calling himself "Grey Mask", had challenged Golev to combat. Who he was, and where he came from no one knew. The town was agog with curiosity. On the day of the fight the theatre was packed out. Golev later told his staff that he had accepted the challenge expecting to be beaten, but wanting to popularise the sport, had resolved to stay in the fight as long as he could. "Grey Mask" came into the ring and silently bowed to the public. He was taller and thinner than Golev, and less muscular. The first round ended in a draw, and in the second round Golev was still in the fight. The public was in an uproar. In round three, Golev decided to launch an attack and without much difficulty soon had his opponent on his back. The man now got to his feet and took off his mask. There was a roar of disappointment, even anger. He was no mysterious stranger, but the actor Postnikov, who had played Duke Orsino to great effect in *Twelfth Night*. He was booed as a fraud.

A circus came to town. The huge tent rose up at the end of Uspensky Street on an open piece of land. How well I remember the clown BimBoom, the jugglers, the tightrope walkers, the trained dogs. The public particularly loved a ten-year-old boy trapeze artist. High up in the crown of the tent he performed his graceful swings and swoops and when he finally climbed down the rope ladder, bowed with exquisite grace on all sides to the wildly applauding audience. I dreamed – admittedly only for an evening – of becoming a circus artist for the sake of such wonderful applause.

4

In those years, I thought seriously of becoming an artist. Brother Vladimir was pursuing his career as a painter of scenery and posters. Stepan Rozhkov and another artist, Boris Yurev, were painting landscapes and teaching art classes. Imitating my brother, I too spent those years painting watercolours of battle scenes, historical events and fairy tales. Yurev took an interest in me and asked me to show him some of my work. He was not at home and so I left the folder there for him and went away. Imagine my delight when I discovered that at the exhibition of children's art a whole stand was devoted to my work. What especially pleased me was the notice on the stand, which read "Seryozha Golitsyn, thirteen-years-old" – I was actually only eleven. Since then my pictures have never been on any stand. Though I undoubtedly had some talent I knew I would never be the equal of brother Vladimir, and in my pride preferred not always to be second best. I gave up pencil and brush.

My life was not just a time of enjoyment and painting and drawing. There were also some unpleasant incidents. Running down to the lake was a steep slope, which for generations had been the favourite toboggan run for the local children when the winter snows turned it into an icy, slippery run. Using benches and baskets, the children spent the entire day sliding past the windows of our house, but as I did not know any of them, I was shy of joining in their fun. My sister Lina more or less dragged me away from my reading and forced me out into the street, assuming that any one of the single children would call me over to share his bench. These benches were simply two planks held together by a couple of struts, the underside of one of the planks having been splashed with water and left out to freeze. They went faster and were easier to haul back up if manned by two boys.

When a crowd of boys were coming back up the hill I went boldly towards them. One of the boys was turning to call me when another, a tow-haired lad, shouted out at the top of his lungs, "Don't give him a seat. He's a prince." The blood rushed to my face. I even staggered back. The girls jumped into their baskets, the lads onto their benches, and the whole herd whizzed off down the slope, leaving me standing like a pillar of salt. And from that time on, for three winters, I never once went out to toboggan on that slope and for three winters never even talked to the neighbourhood children, even though we often stood side by side in bread queues. What a funny character was mine.

I suffered not a whit from boredom; books were my friends. Thanks to the fact that Lina worked in the library, I could go there even when it was closed and change my books. It was astonishing how much reading I got through. Nor did I race through these books; I read carefully, savouring certain passages, learning dialogue and special extracts by heart. Many of these books I have never since come across, but I can still remember their contents. I read the complete works of Jules Verne, Mayne Reed, Brett Hart, Stevenson, Scott; novels by Solovyov, Lazhechkin, Zagoskin; the works of Tolstoy, Shakespeare, Schiller, Zhukovsky, Rostand; Merezhkovsky's trilogy, Greek and Roman myths. I was only defeated when it came to Solovyov's *History of Russia*, stopping at the accession to the throne of Michail Fyodorovich. In addition, my mother read aloud to me from the classics.

Shakespeare and Schiller were in the magnificent Brockhaus editions, with lots of pictures. I was enraptured by the plays of Shakespeare, living in a dream world inspired by their imagery and poetry, and very far from our hungry reality. I dreamed of writing plays like his – in verse, of course. Paper from the Bobrinsky stores and ink made of soot were to hand, but what would I write about? Well, historical subjects, of course, full of duelling, murders and suicides. I began to compose plays in secret, in blank verse without rhyme, about Romulus and Remus, Brave Mistislav, Sir Lancelot, Savonarola. I dreamed of future fame; my plays would be produced in Bogoroditsk and I would be applauded as Uncle Vladimir had been for *The Pear Tree*. Just like my sister Sonya, I would come home with thousands of roubles and baskets of food. It goes without saying that everything I wrote was rubbish. But that is what I think now. Then I thought I was only slightly inferior to Shakespeare.

One day, Sonya came home and told me Chetvertushkin had invited me to visit his son, Zhenya, the following Sunday. I was going to visit the man I considered a theatrical god and magician. I would, of course, make great friends with his son, the mysterious prisoner who was never let out of the house. My clothes were in a terrible state; my trousers were all patches, my coat was torn, my felt boots were too big for me. Aunt Sasha tried to make me look a little more presentable, and told me how to hold my knife and fork, and not to throw myself on the food. My little sisters saw me off with envy in their eyes. I flew to the institute as if on wings. I was full of the thought of how I would make friends with the son, and so be able to show my plays to his all-powerful father.

The door opened to reveal, behind a curly-haired lady, a tall boy in a velvet suit. His face was as white as ghost, touched with bluish tones. I thought he looked like a sprouting potato. Why did his parents keep him locked in, I wondered. I soon discovered that his parents had had a daughter, the apple of their eyes, who had died of scarlet fever at the age of eight. When their son was born they resolved never to let him out where he might catch an infectious disease. So he grew up, seeing the trees and fields and sunshine through the windows of their house and never going out, living only through his books. I was the first child ever to have played with him. We hit it off right from the start, not playing with his soldiers, of which he had hundreds, but sitting side by side talking; by our second meeting we were close enough to embrace each other.

I had always concealed from my mother my dream world of knights and beautiful ladies. From Zhenya I hid nothing. I confessed to him the feelings of terrible sadness I had suffered at the murder of the young Tsarevich Alexei. Only the execution of our beloved Uncle Misha did I keep to myself. Zhenya admitted that he still suffered the same agonies over the Tsarevich's murder. He showed me portraits of him and he also told me something he had never told his mother, which was that his room was populated by invisible creatures, "wallers" in the walls, and "carpetters" in the carpet, and I forgot what the people in the ceiling were called. He carried on conversations with all these beings. We also described to each other all the books we had read, and here my pride was hurt, as Zhenya had read far more books than I had, even philosophers such as Kant and Nietzsche. He was only eleven-years-old.

They fed me royally. At home Nasenka made a thin wheaten gruel, only sometimes seasoned with rape oil. Here Zhenya's mother produced thick, milky porridge, with added sugar. There was as much bread as I could eat. I only caught glimpses of his father, who came home, swallowed his meal and vanished into his study. It must have been at my third visit that I brought my plays to show him. On my next visit, he called me into his study and with the greatest delicacy and tact tore my work to pieces, but in such a nice way that far from being downcast I was encouraged. Most important of all, and for this I am still grateful to this day, he urged me not to be dispirited about my writing and not to give up, but to keep at it.

My visits continued for a number of Sundays. Then one day his mother did not let me in, saying Zhenya was not too well. It transpired that there was a case of scarlet fever two streets away from our house. I was offended, and Aunt Sasha was also angry on my behalf. A couple of months later I was allowed to visit again, but our relationship gradually grew cooler. One day, I used a namesday or birthday as an excuse not to pay my usual Sunday visit. Eventually, however, Zhenya's mother was persuaded to let her son live a normal life. He was let out into God's world and was happily welcomed by the neighbourhood children – I became superfluous, and so our friendship came to an end.

There was another lad, very like my peculiar self, who clung to me. His name was Yura, the son of Lyubov Bauman, the lady who had taught my mother how to make shoes. About two years before I made friends with him, he had badly damaged one of his eyes when dancing around a Christmas tree and it had left the eye sticking out of its socket in very noticeable and ugly way. The other children never left him alone when he went out into the street, shouting "Hey, squinty, look at squinty!" Until we met, he was never sent out on errands and avoided going out at all. His only outings were when he came to our house. Masha and I used to play cards with him, but his excessive self-confidence got under my skin. For instance, he used to say that the earth was bigger than the sun, and you could not persuade him otherwise. He often distracted me from my reading, while himself not liking to read. Mother, however, said that I had to be polite to my visitor, and I also discovered that Yura's mother greatly valued our relationship, as I never even mentioned his physical disfigurement.

Let me go back now to the subject of the theatre in Bogoroditsk. I have written about it in detail because I believe it to be of general social interest, and without my memory of it, it would vanish into oblivion. The manuscript of A.P. Burtsev's memoirs of the theatre is preserved in the town museum, but it consists of only a few pages. He lists the seventy-four plays in which he acted. These are Western and Russian classics, various second-rate pre-revolutionary playwrights and a lot of not-very-talented imitative plays that the authorities promoted at the time. My knowledge of the theatre in Bogoroditsk derives from what I heard from the former prompter, a teacher called Golovskaya, from my sister, Sonya, and my own vivid memories.

From 1923 onwards, the theatre began to lose impetus. Actors gradually dropped out until only Rusakov and Burtsev remained. In 1926 the theatre burned down, and there were neither the enthusiasm nor the means to restart it, nor did the authorities step in to support it. Some acting continued to take place in various locations: for instance, the schools put on one or two plays. Troupes from Tula also passed through and gave performances. But the public lost interest, very likely because only dull Soviet plays were staged.

Gradually, Burtsev and Rusakov reverted to being only schoolteachers. Rusakov died just after the Second World War. Burtsev was awarded the title of "Meritorious Teacher" of the Russian Federation, retired and died in advanced old age, in 1975. Chetvertushkin's fate was a sad one. Some clever officials decided that future agronomists did not need to learn Russian and sacked him. He was forced to move to Podolsk for work. One day he visited us in Moscow, but it just happened to be when we were in the middle of a mad evening of dancing. Seated between grandmother and Aunt Sasha, he spent a few minutes abstractedly watching couples swinging crazily past, then quietly left without a word. I never saw him again.

When I visited Bogoroditsk in 1977, I learned of his subsequent fate. He was arrested in Podolsk. His son Zhenya, by then an adolescent, came to Bogoroditsk to collect information about his father. What he managed to find, I do not know, nor whether his father was freed or died in the camps. May this chapter serve as a kind of memorial to the memory of the man who in those distant years inspired finer feelings in the people of Bogoroditsk.

4. Life in Bogoroditsk – The Prosaic Side

1

Whereas in the last chapter I wrote about the Muses, in this one I shall concentrate on the prosaic side of life in 1920 and 1921. In 1920, my parents received a letter from Petrograd written by the servants of a deceased cousin of my father's, Nadezhda Mikhailovna Golitsyna. She was the only daughter of grandfather's elder brother, Mikhail Mikhailovich, who had been a general, a *bon vivant* and a great spendthrift in his youth. Aunt Nadya had never married and had no direct descendants. She had left all her valuables to my father, and it was the servants, whom she had informed of her last will, who now communicated the news to my father. It was decided that Lina should travel to Petrograd, and for that purpose a highly official-looking travel permit, with all kinds of seals, was obtained from the director of the library. It stated "the holder of this . . . is authorised to . . ." but I do not recall what it was she was authorised to do.

Lina travelled via Moscow, visiting the old people's home where Nanny Bush was living. She was appalled at what she found; Nanny Bush was gradually dying of hunger. In Petrograd, Lina was given a small but rather heavy suitcase and on her return journey she collected Nanny Bush and, together with the suitcase, returned to Bogoroditsk. I remember how the contents of this suitcase were turned out on our table. There was first some table silver, and then several long strings of pearls, and an exceptionally beautiful gold diadem in three parts, covered with large emeralds, a gift to great-uncle Mikhail Mikhailovich from the Emir of Bokhara. This treasure was all poured back into the suitcase and I was very strictly ordered not to breathe a word of it to anyone.

We were delighted by the return of our beloved Nanny Bush. She began to knit us mittens and socks and stockings, and also to help out in the kitchen.

2

The time had now come for Vladimir to be called up for military service, a prospect that he did not relish at all. We had some friends in the town, the Zadulskys, a mother and two daughters. A relative of theirs, a young biologist called Zenkevich, later to become a world-famous oceanographer and member of the Academy of Sciences, visited them from Moscow. He was recruiting staff for an expedition to establish a biological station on the shores of the bay of Kolsk, near the town of Alexandrovsk, and needed an artist.

How my brother managed to obtain a birth certificate attesting to his birth in Bogoroditsk and not in Bulchalki, I have no idea. Nor do I know how he proved that he was a sailor from the cruiser *Askold* and was to go as a highly qualified artist on the Zenkevich expedition. That cruiser had been sent into the Mediterranean to take part in the Dardanelles campaign during the First World War and had then been interned by the French in the Tunisian port of Bizerta. No sailor from that ship could have been in Bogoroditsk in 1920. Whatever the case, we saw Vladimir off to the ends of the earth, to those polar regions where they were just about to found the city of Murmansk and from which British interventionist troops had only just withdrawn. There he painted pictures of many different animals, shared with the others the hard physical conditions of the expedition and also drew pictures in his own albums, which have survived. He composed landscapes of the Murmansk region in pencil and watercolour, genre pictures and caricatures of his companions. These varied subjects clearly demonstrate the awakening of a great artistic talent. Sometimes we received letters illustrated by sketches from him, letters that were always read out aloud. I also took them off on my own and pored over them. How proud I felt when once mother read out a few lines directly addressed to me. The letter started "Hey, Seryozhka!" Sadly, these letters are all lost.

Within a year, the expedition returned to Moscow from the Kolsk peninsula. Preparations for the next venture, to be based in Archangelsk, were underway, but in the meantime Vladimir wrote that he would be allowed to spend a few days in Bogoroditsk. With what impatience we awaited him! That winter our only talk around the table was when Vladimir would come. Occasionally, hopeful letters arrived from him, saying he would soon be arriving. Every day Sonya and I went off to the station to wait for the afternoon train, although it was nearly always late so we would have to wait in the freezing cold, then go back home until the next day, when once again we would walk to the station. One day, the weather was so bad we knew the train would be terribly late; we did not even leave the house, and the storm was whistling around the house as we went to bed. Then in the middle of the night came a loud knocking. Later mother said she had been sure it was the police coming to search the house again.

I was woken by Sonya's and my mother's joyful cries and immediately knew who had come. I jumped out of bed and, wearing only my little nightshirt, threw myself into the arms of my snow-covered, beloved brother, my bare legs banging against the cold snow on his fur coat. Hugs and embraces were showered on him. The entire household got out of bed. Nanny Bush lit the samovar, Nasenka started the stove, and my parents sat on either side of Vladimir. I curled up at his feet. It was morning before we went back to bed.

In the morning, Vladimir and I went to visit the grandparents. His striking fur clothing from the expedition would have been a rare sight in Moscow, let alone Tula, and was even more so in our little town. He was not wearing a normal fur coat but a Lapp reindeer skin without buttons with bright coloured patterns on the sleeves and skirts and a deep hood. What his trousers were I cannot remember as the reindeer skin was so long, but I remember his boots, which were called "shackletons" after the British Antarctic explorer: fur-lined felt boots with thick soles and broad laces that had been left behind by the British intervention forces.

Our way to the grandparents went through the town from our street, Uspenskaya, to Konstantinovskaya Street. I was bursting with pride as I walked along beside Vladimir, just as, I am sure, younger brothers of astronauts feel today. And yet those astronauts are probably either in civvies or uniform, whereas Vladimir was dressed like the king of explorers. He was a tall man, and the thick soles of his "shackletons" made him even taller; even the horses shied as we passed. His rosy, slightly yellow cheeks were made more vivid by the cold, whilst his blue eyes were full of smiles. As we walked the passers-by stopped and stared, and those who knew him engaged him in conversation as I stood by, hopping from foot to foot, in my delight with this romantic brother.

Three days later, to our great sadness, he left again. On the second Polar expedition he sailed from Archangelsk to Novaya Zemlya and took part in the construction of the *Perseus*, the ship that became a polar legend. All this is described in the articles written by his comrade, V.A.Vasnetsov, the son of the famous artist, in a collection dedicated to "V. Golitsyn, the life of the artist, sailor and explorer", as well as in Vasnetsov's book, *Sailing on the Perseus*. There is also a plaque to V.M. Golitsyn on the house in Archangelsk where he once lived.

3

I go back now to the beginning of 1920 and to a very humdrum topic, namely food. The rations issued by the authorities were really and truly pathetic. Sukhanov's offerings from Buchalki, as described earlier, had been a marvellous supplement, but by the spring of 1920 these had stopped coming, and bartering with bits of Bobrinsky clothing was getting ever harder. The peasants' stores were running out. Mother took up shoemaking again and was quite successful in sewing uppers and soles, working not for money but for flour and other foodstuffs. She also made rope-soled shoes for all of us as well as for the Bobrinskys and Trubetskois for free, using tow combed out of flax by father, who had somehow got hold of this raw material. Strangers, of course, had to pay for these rope-soled shoes with food.

We had difficulties with potatoes in our first year in the Lyubimov house as we had not been able to build up a stock in the autumn. In the spring, we had heard that we could collect frozen potatoes from the silo near the station. Mother, my sisters and I went to the station and found at the foot of the gigantic silo a mass of rotten, soggy potato mush on the ground. Here and there long sprouts stuck out, so that in this mountain of rotten potatoes one could pick out a few handfuls of the crop. In this way we managed to collect a couple of buckets full of soggy potatoes – but Nasenka rejected the lot and threw them out.

There was a man, a victim of syphilis, who lived just outside the town and who slaughtered old and sick horses. He sold their flesh as horsemeat, but we could not afford it. We could only afford to buy their heads and hooves, which Nasenka then boiled down to make soups and brawn. These quivering, light brown liquids and jellies had a dreadful taste. In the spring, under my father's guidance, we dug over the plot of land that had been fertilised by our own waste. We planted potatoes and pumpkins and other vegetables and laid out a little path to a platform where we set up a table and chairs. Another bed we planted with flowers. The potatoes and pumpkins were a major addition to our food supplies, although 1920 was a year of drought and we had to carry water from the well to keep our crops healthy. Pumpkins do not mind the drought, so they produced big globes, out of which Nasenka made rather tasteless dishes. The dried pumpkin seeds we chewed without much enjoyment.

We also made a big effort to gather young nettles and sorrel for our vegetable soup, and young buds for tea. The drought meant that there were hardly any mushrooms, and in any event we did not know those secret places where mushrooms grew. Occasionally we found some *Russula Foetens* mushrooms which the local people did not collect because they were extremely bitter. After Nasenka had cooked them we swallowed them, holding our breath.

Sugar was unobtainable, and salt cost a fortune. The managers of the sugar factory had promised to supply these valuable products as well as flour, but in the event only offered anyone plots of land that they could cultivate. We took one. When we came up to the furrows allotted to us, we were horrified to find the area covered with a thick layer of prickly weeds, through which, here and there, there poked up a sickly sugar beet plant. We began to pull the weeds. Every day, we walked the three *versts* to spend the whole day in the blazing heat weeding, returning home with swollen hands and feet. That done, we hoed the ground, lifted, split and replanted the beets. In the autumn, as the wind howled and wet snow fell we began to pull up our beets. We had no choice but to keep at it out of fear of the frost that would kill the fruits of this immense labour.

A couple of old peasant ladies kindly offered to help us. In no time the beets were dug out, cleaned and piled in a small heap. This harvest was taken away in a cart, and we were due to receive a proportion of the products. Later that winter mother and I went with our sledge to collect our due and were given about eight kilos of sugar, the same of salt, a bucket of treacle as black as tar and sixteen kilos of flour. It was very difficult to drag this precious load back over the snow; the sledge kept tipping over and some of the treacle spilled out and our bags fell in the snow. I had to clench my teeth not to cry. Mother tried to cheer me up.

Next year, 1921, we again took a strip of land, this time six *versts* away. Once again the drought was pitiless, the whole summer passed without a drop of rain and the sugar beet plants withered, so that in the end it was not just we who abandoned the work, but everyone else as well. The foreman who supervised them and lived nearby, a former employee of the Bobrinskys, felt sorry for us and he and his wife invited us to a meal from time to time, along with Aunt Vera and her family, Uncle Vladimir and Aunt Eli, and our whole crowd, some twelve of us, would pile into their house where they treated us to all kinds of good foods that we ate till we could eat no more. The other way to have something to eat was to be invited out. Our parents were often invited by their new friends to namesdays and birthdays, where they ate their fill and were given treats to take back "for the children".

4

We children were really saved by the hens that Sukhanov had brought us. It was with utter delight that we greeted the first egg laid by the one we had nicknamed Nanny Bush. As the youngest in the family, this was given to Katya. As she peeled and ate it, the six members of the family looked on in silence. Then the remaining hens began to lay, and we three youngest children enjoyed these eggs every day. Even today I can describe those fowl, the sounds they made, the colour of their feathers, their way of walking. And the cockerel, George, deserves half a page for himself. He was prince of the farm-yard fowl. I called him George after Yegor Kamayev, a young fellow with ginger whiskers who went about in white slippers and lived at the crossing of Uspensky and Voronezhsky Streets. I had overheard Lyena telling Nasenka that she liked this Yegor and had nicknamed him George. I am sure that nothing romantic happened between Lyena and Yegor since she was much too modest a girl, but that is how George the cockerel got his name.

He was wonderfully handsome with white and yellow and black feathers shot with glinting green, a thick tail, a deep scarlet comb, and talons as sharp as daggers. He was always the first to crow in the early mornings, singing like Chanticleer, and won every fight with the neighbouring cocks, thus attracting their hens into our barn. Nasenka had many a quarrel with our neighbours, but she knew every egg that our hens laid and stoutly defended the truth.

We had a neighbour who was a widow with a daughter a year older than me, and a single hen who had become the unwed wife of our George. In 1968, when I returned for the first time to Bogoroditsk and walked down Uspenskaya Street, I saw that a new house stood where ours had once been. An old lady, very like the neighbouring widow I remembered, came out of a nearby house, and I realized that this was the daughter who had now grown old. I got into conversation with her and found out that the Germans had burned down all the houses in that street. I was able to show her where the well had been, where there had been two lime trees and where the willow used to be. She confirmed what I was telling her, but when I asked her if she remembered the family who had lived next door for three years, she shook her head. Then I asked whether she remembered the cockerel that had flirted with all the local hens. Her face lit up and she exclaimed, "You're talking about George. Of course I remember, who could forget a fellow like that."

Both the summers of 1920 and 1921 I spent collecting butterflies with the intensity of oblivion. As soon as spring set in I was off into the woods with my bottle of ether and my net. The shortest way would have been along Voronezh Street, but that way I ran the risk of meeting other boys who would certainly jeer at me when they saw what I was doing. So I went a roundabout way along Selichevsky Street. There was just one house at the end, the home of a very large, poverty-stricken family who had a blind son. One day I was walking past them with my net and bag. All the children were sitting on the verandah, and they shouted out in chorus:

Hey, Prince, fell in the mud on his tum,
Tumbled in a hole, cried for his Mum

The blind boy laughed raucously. I was angered and humiliated and hurried past. From that day on I chose an even more circuitous way to the woods. I must have covered mile upon mile as I hunted butterflies, returning in the evening to eat my supper, drink a big glass of water and then get down to setting out and pinning my day's trophies.

5

When September came round, lessons with mother and Aunt Sasha began again. In winter there were week-long holidays for Christmas, Lent and Easter. Sundays, and the name days and birthdays of all family members were also holidays. All in all, only about half the time was study time. I detested mathematics. I would sit next to my mother as she worked at her shoe-making staring dumbly at my textbook. With infinite patience she would say, "No, that's wrong. Think again." I could only sigh and blink my eyes. Mathematics is connected in my mind with the family of Dr Pyotr Ivanovich Rayevsky, distant relatives of ours. The family moved from Tula to Baryatino, a village near Bogoroditsk, and they would sometimes all come over to visit us. Dr Rayevsky caught typhus and was admitted by Dr Nikolsky to our local hospital. Mother sat by the patient's bedside until he died. He was buried in the local cemetery with our whole family at the graveside. The Rayevskys stayed with us for a few days and mother ordered me to entertain the children as best I could. Eventually they returned to Baryatino, occasionally coming to visit us, and finally moving to Sergiyev Posad. Both mother and Aunt Sasha invariably compared me to those children, saying how clever and kind and well behaved they were, and how they loved their school books. I just could not believe any child could enjoy sums and problems to do with bathwater running out.

Aunt Sasha taught me all other subjects. On natural history, geography and history I had to read certain texts and then repeat them to her in my own words. As I knew these subjects better than she did, she had to follow me in the text. I had no particular difficulty learning grammar by heart, and I loved writing out the texts of the classics we were reading, as well as doing my own compositions on all sorts of topics. Aunt Sasha would correct and polish my writing, in my opinion usually for the worse, but I had to hold my tongue. Once she asked me what I would like to write about. I said I would like to write how I had caught a particularly rare butterfly that had somehow come as far north as Bogoroditsk from its southern habitat. I had spotted it one evening on our bushes but had not had my net. I had then watched for it for two more evenings, only catching it on the third. In my essay I wrote "A swipe of the net . . . and I caught her!!!" Aunt Sasha changed it to this – "When she settled on a flower, I swung my net and caught her." My own feelings told me that three dots and three exclamation marks properly described my triumph and the swiftness of the action. But she was merciless in stamping on my feelings. It was she, too, who gave me religious instruction, making me learn the communion service by heart, together with all the Orthodox prayers and intercessions, and even the words of the evening and night services. I swotted away, but was bored stiff. We used to go to the Uspensky cemetery church for our evening services. Since I had been forced to learn the liturgy by heart, I began to feel indifferent to church and the primitive choral singing, and only groaned "How long, O Lord, how long," and thought of the interesting book waiting for me at home. I saw no similarity to the ancient church fathers in Father Evgeny and, while not at all losing my faith, I began to feel disenchanted with the external trappings of religion. All this I attribute to Aunt Sasha's teaching. It was only Holy Week, with its wonderful singing, the fasting, confession and communion and the late evening service on the eve of Easter Sunday that brought me close to God again. It was with light hearts that we came out of the church into the exhilarating air of early spring. After the Maundy Thursday service we would return home bearing lighted candles; it was always a challenge to be able to keep them alight the whole way home.

Aunt Sasha started to teach two of the children of the priest, who lived in Lomovky, a nearby village. During the week they boarded in an adjoining street, then on Saturday a peasant would come with his horse to take them home. Masha and I sometimes went on visits to that family, and during our holidays spent long periods of time there. How clearly I remember the track running beside snowy fields, the steaming horse dragging the country sledge, the evenings of good food followed by card games, and in the morning, after mass, exhilarating toboggan runs down a long, though not very steep slope. They were a large and friendly family.

After our departure from Bogoroditsk, Aunt Sasha corresponded for a long time with the priest's wife. Then one day two young village men beat up the priest outside his church. He died of the trauma. The family moved to another district and the correspondence ceased.

6

I remember the visit of the Archbishop of Tula. He did not arrive by train but in a huge carriage drawn by three pairs of horses. A great crowd, including our family, met him in the open area between the town and the Agricultural Institute. As he passed, everyone bowed from the waist. My parents went off to the service in the main church but soon came back, disappointed, as there had been such a huge crowd they could not even get into the church. We decided the whole family would go to the Uspensky church service instead.

This was the first time I had been to such a magnificent service. The archbishop stood on a raised platform, a tall man with a long grey beard who spoke the prayers with great sincerity and clarity. I was moved to pray and cross myself just as sincerely. His golden vestments and mitre, and the gold in the vestments of the priests surrounding him, could not but inspire our souls with worshipful feelings. When he began to preach – not in the monotonous voice of our Father Evgeny but with rising and falling tones – and quoted in a declamatory voice long verse passages from Pushkin and Lermontov, the entire congregation, men, women and children could not contain their tears. Whenever I open either of these poets and begin to read those verses, I am taken back to that striking and moving service.

During the drought of 1921, the miraculous icon of the Virgin was brought to Bogoroditsk from the village of Gretsov, which was near the railway station at Uslov. The icon was very large, about four foot square. It was carried around the whole town by pairs of men who took it in turns to carry it. People fell on their faces before it and allowed it to pass over them as they lay. Mother and I did likewise as the Virgin and Child came towards us, her large, sad eyes looking down on us. A crowd of thousands had gathered in a field where the icon was placed on a bench and a service was held, the crowd calling out their prayers that included the words "Grant rain to our thirsty earth. Save us." But no rains came.

Massed gatherings of such crowds in the name of God were still tolerated by the authorities. Religious persecution was only just starting. The authorities had just ordered the requisitioning of church valuables as famine spread across the country. The churches owned a large amount of silver in the form of icon frames, covers and various vessels, donated by the devout over the centuries, and this treasure was all confiscated on the pretext that it would pay to help feed the hungry. The papers assured us it would all be melted down to pay for imported wheat. People still believed the press, as they had before the revolution, and so the requisitioning took place quietly, without disturbance. "Of course we must give it up for the hungry," was the sentiment. Future historians will doubtless discover where the proceeds actually went.

Contemporary historians have written of the famine along the Volga and of the cases of cannibalism there, but there was also famine in central Russia, and in the region of Tula. By the autumn of 1921 many granaries were empty, though not all. The markets were empty, there were poor folk from the country everywhere, even townsfolk were afflicted by famine. As for our family, by the end of 1921 a new source of food had opened up.

7

Alka Bobrinskaya and my sister Lina had taken themselves away to become students at Moscow University, but whether their studies were too much for them, or necessity forced them to it, they took jobs with the American Relief Agency (ARA). When news of the famine in our country reached Europe and America, people, whether capitalists or from the churches, made their voices heard. They wanted to help the people, of course, not the communists. In our country we tend to paint capitalists as only thinking of profit, but the huge sums of money raised, particularly in the USA, prove that there was a genuinely disinterested response. Three international organisations were created. The first, the ARA, was headed by President Hoover, whom our historians now refer to with special hatred. The second was led by the famous polar explorer Nansen, who unlike Hoover is remembered in our country with sympathy and called a humanist. Pius XI, also a hated figure, was patron of the third body. Future historians will certainly be able to give exact figures for the amount of grain shipped to Russia. Some of these supplies remained in Moscow, while the rest was sent to the Volga region. A number of Americans went with these supplies to the Volga, but after a couple of them had been eaten, they preferred to remain in Moscow to oversee the transfer of supplies to our authorities and also to set up and run free food kitchens. Russians who lived abroad could subscribe ten dollars and then food parcels worth six dollars were sent to their relatives still in the country.

Lina and Alka, as they could speak foreign languages, were taken on by the ARA. In addition to money, they also received food parcels that they were able to send on to Bogoroditsk. Rich relatives of the Trubetskois, the Counts Khrebtovich-Butyenev, also made their ten dollar contribution and so Uncle Vladimir's family began to receive generous food parcels. It was a former employee of the Bobrinsky family, now a railway despatcher, who sent these parcels on to us all. Sofia Alexeievna Bobrinskaya – Auntie Misya – also received similar parcels, the contents of which she distributed to needy people in the town.

The first parcel to arrive at the post office, triumphantly brought home on a sledge by mother and me, caused a sensation. It weighed about twenty kilos and was in a box made of fine, planed wood, with English words printed on its sides and a bright American flag pinned to its cover. Nasenka broke open the case with pincers and a hammer, and we all gasped with pleasure. There were tins of condensed milk with pictures of grazing cows on their labels as well as many other bags and packages also covered with pictures. We pulled out slabs of cured pork bearing the thrilling name "bacon", bags of flour, macaroni a couple of feet long, rice, and sugar in long cubes.

After Lina's departure, our grandparents moved in with us, occupying the space behind the curtain. Nanny Bush and I slept in the kitchen, she in Vladimir's bed, I on the top of a trunk. Grandfather was still writing synopses of books for the local library, sometimes with my help; I would read the books and then describe their contents for him to write out. Grandmother did a great deal of moaning and groaning – when prices rose, or when the authorities did things she considered stupid or criminal. She rejected everything. So it really surprised me when once, in 1921 or 1922, she undertook to organise our New Year's celebrations. In the evenings either mother or father read aloud to us, or one of our grandparents told us tales of their youth. What a lot of interesting stories we heard that we never noted down.

8

The so-called New Economic Policy, or NEP, came into being in 1921.[10] Frightened by the peasants' uprisings, workers' strikes and the Kronstadt rebellion,[11] the authorities had to make concessions. Private trading and small enterprises were allowed, and the slogan – "Enrich Yourselves!" – became the catchphrase of the day. The onset of the famine, however, somewhat held back the initiatives of those energetic people who could see the benefits for themselves, and who, not giving a fig for world revolution, wanted to take advantage of these new freedoms. The shop on Voronezh Street which used to distribute rationed bread now became a cooperative. I could go there and order as much bread as Nasenka needed, and it was good black bread, sometimes mixed with a few oats.

My sister Masha and I were learning French from grandmother and English from Auntie Misya, who lived in Pavlovsk Street. Twice a week we went there to read and translate a short history of England, every paragraph of which seemed to contain the word "beheaded", and so I thought these lessons were fascinating. Since then, and thanks also to Shakespeare's historical plays, I have always had a good grasp of English history. Opposite Sofia Alexeievna's house a private confectionery shop opened up, one of the first in town. After the arrival of a food parcel, or when mother received a

---

10. *The New Economic Policy was proposed by Lenin and approved at the tenth Party Congress in 1921. In order to stop the Russian economy collapsing some private ownership was restored to small parts of the economy, especially farming and small businesses were allowed to re-open. The commercial instincts unleashed by the NEP were seen by many as a betrayal of "socialism".*

11. *Kronstadt, the home of the Russian Baltic Fleet on a fortified island close to St Petersberg, was a centre of political anarchism. In 1921 the sailors rose up in support of strikers in the city who were protesting against the dire economic situation brought about by the civil war and the policy of war communism, under which private industry and trade were proscribed. The uprising was ruthlessly suppressed.*

new order for shoes, Masha and I would be given a little money and on our way home could buy a few brightly coloured little cakes. We would eat one each and keep one for Katya.

Mother's order book for shoes grew all the time. Sitting on her bed, her tools laid out around her, she worked the whole day through. Her hammer with its broad head is still in existence; such items, despite several removals, seem not to perish. Father spent the evenings preparing lengths of string for the soles of the shoes. However, his attempts to make wooden shoemaker's nails were pronounced below standard by mother, so their production was contracted out to an old man in the neighbourhood. Grandmother painted a small watercolour of mother; she is depicted wearing a faded cotton gown, sitting on the old mahogany bed and working with her shoemaker's hammer, while in the background, on the log wall, you can see a picture by Moravov of a little boy fishing, and under it a few photographs. Both grandmother's watercolour and Moravov's picture now hang in my room.

The nineteenth of September 1921 was my grandparents golden wedding anniversary. It was a day of great celebration. Lina, Vladimir and Alka Bobrinskaya came from Moscow, and there were many congratulatory telegrams from relatives. In the morning, we went in a crowd to have our photograph taken as the only photographer in the town did not want to haul his heavy equipment over to our house. The picture, rather a poor one, was reprinted and a copy has been preserved. It shows how badly we were dressed in those days; Uncle Vladimir is wearing an old army coat, my father has on a speckled jacket, my sisters and the Bobrinsky girls are wearing plain dresses; only brother Vladimir looks smart in his new seaman's uniform. I sit in front with Alexei Bobrinsky and Grisha Trubetskoi, all of us in rope-soled shoes. We look sickly and scraggy, and Grisha's fingers are like sticks. I do remember that I had been suffering from a bad stomach all summer, a condition not then regarded as an illness.

From the session at the photographers we all, except for the youngest Bobrinsky, Nikolai, and the two youngest Trubetskoi children, went over to the home of the Bobrinskys' former head gardener, Baranov, who was also a friend, on Pavlovsky street. His wife had prepared a grand feast of some kind of Ukrainian soup and delicious savoury pies. In the evening we drank tea at home and received many guests, who sat on chairs that spread out into the kitchen and the porch. The food offered was not sophisticated, but thanks to the provisions brought by Vladimir from his polar expedition, and Lina from Moscow, it could be described as a luxurious meal. Doctor Nikolsky made an emotional speech and presented my grandparents with six gold spoons.

I cannot recall whether it was before or after the celebration that I heard a conversation that aroused my interest. It revealed that my brother Vladimir was in love. He did not confide this in a whisper to my mother, but announced it in a fairly loud voice to both our parents and our grandparents. Grandmother's exclamation, "Oh, what a beauty. She really is lovely," told me they were looking at a photograph. In Tatiana Tolstaya's memoirs she quotes her father, the great writer, exclaiming with admiration, of the way Homer describes the first appearance of Helen, "When she entered and they saw her beauty, the old men rose to their feet." Just those words, nothing more. For me, a twelve-year-old boy, who had never seen such a beautiful woman, she seemed beyond compare. I mention here only her large, shining eyes, a feature of all the members of her family. We were sincerely delighted, but the age of the couple was a concern; Vladimir was twenty, she was only seventeen. Nevertheless it was felt that God would provide. She was a member of one of the most famous Russian families, the Counts Sheremetyev, and bore the same name as the wife of King Menelaus, Helen. Had it not been for the revolution, the union of two of the most famous Russian names would have been considered a great event.

Vladimir, Lina and Alka Bobrinskaya returned to Moscow. My sister Sonya, without finishing her second year at the Agricultural Institute, also went to Moscow to enter the university. The rest of us went back to our occupations. Then, suddenly, little two-year-old Nikolai Bobrinsky died. No one had noticed when he had picked up an apple lying on the ground and ate it – but he caught dysentery. The death of this sweet little boy so soon after the great celebration shook everyone. His funeral service was held in the church of Kazan in the Bobrinsky park and he was laid to rest with his ancestors. The priest who took the service several times misquoted his name in the prayers, calling the boy Leo. Each time he was corrected and each time he again used the wrong name. It was a slip of the tongue that added to the sense of doom and gloom, especially as we were all aware that Uncle Leo was very ill in prison in Moscow.

His illness continued all through the winter. Aunt Vera was able to visit, taking her two other daughters with her, Sonya and Helena. Alexei had to stay behind so as not to miss school. Then in the spring a telegram arrived announcing the death of Uncle Leo; he was only forty-four-years old. He was buried in the Novodevichy cemetery, where five years later I visited his grave with its plain wooden cross.

It has long since disappeared.

Alexei brought over the telegram with the news of his father's death. For a long while he wept into grandmother's lap, and then asked if I could come over to be with him for three days. I felt much pride and joy at this; I would be comforting my cousin and also not doing any lessons for three days. As we all lived at different ends of the town and Alexei was three years my senior, we normally only met at family gatherings. He had his own circle of school friends, too. Yet many years later he told my brother Vladimir how grateful he would always be that I had not left him alone in his time of grief. For three days, we played pirates and other games, but the subject of his sorrow never crossed our lips.

I hope the reader will remember this episode, as later on it may have played a vital part in determining my fate.

5. The End of My Childhood

1

Our relatives, now scattered all over the globe in France, America, Austria, China or Yugoslavia, gradually discovered our whereabouts, thanks to the letters they wrote to each other. In those early years of Soviet rule it would never have occurred to anyone that private correspondence with relatives about purely family matters, even if the correspondent had been a White officer, would have been treated as espionage. Letters came, were read aloud, and I collected the envelopes and stamps.

My mother's elder brother, Nikolai Sergeievich Lopukhin – Uncle Kolya – was married to a niece once removed, Sofia Mikhailovna Osorgina. He was a lawyer, and until the revolution also a successful businessman, dealing in property in Moscow. At the beginning of 1918 he went east, taking his wife, three children, his mother-in-law, two sisters who were still girls, and an aunt, Evgeniya Pavlovna Pisareva – Aunt Zhenya. Their inseparable governess and part of the family, Lydia Kurdyumova, also went with them. They ended up in Tyumen and there a fourth child was born, a son. The family of Uncle Sasha, Alexander Vladimirovich Golitsyn, joined them there and they retreated with Kolchak's army, reaching Omsk, then Irkutsk and finally settling in Harbin. Uncle Kolya was made mayor of the town there and spent ten years living off the salary that went with the office. Two more daughters were born there. In 1929, the Chinese general Shan Doalin drove out the Russian administration and Uncle Kolya received nothing for his pains. The entire family set off on their travels via Hong Kong, Singapore and the Suez Canal, ending up in Marseilles and from there going on to Paris, where relatives were able to help them and find a good job for Uncle Kolya. Grandmother Alexandra Pavlovna died in 1934. Uncle Kolya brought up his daughters as decent young ladies. He died soon after the war. I was able to visit Aunt Sonya on my two visits to France and had long conversations with her about the past.

2

One of the last of our relatives to discover our whereabouts was my mother's other brother, Alexei Sergeievich – Uncle Alyosha. He was a dreamer and an idealist, a very nice man, but paralysed by inertia. He was likened to Oblomov, the idle dreamer in Goncharov's novel of that name. In contrast to his energetic and enterprising brother, Nikolya, Uncle Alyosha was feeble and little fitted for life. In his youth he was for ever falling in love.

After university he found a job in Kiev and there fell in love with a girl from a very good Ukrainian family, Gudim-Levkovich. The day of the wedding was settled and the relatives arrived in Kiev. The night before the wedding, Uncle Alyosha had a terrible dream. Later, on waking, he was told that his bride had in fact run away with a previous lover, whom her parents had refused to accept. Uncle Alyosha was almost out of his mind with grief. His brothers, fearing he would try to take his own life, took him to the Lopukhin estate, Khilkovo, and left him there. The house was unheated except for the kitchen, which had a small stove. Next to it was a tiny room, in which Uncle Alyosha spent several months, only once in a while taking himself out into the grounds with a gun, though never managing to kill anything, and lying on his bed reading the newspaper cuttings that were glued to the walls. I remember how, many years later, he was able to quote from them from memory. When he recovered he went to work in Vladimir, where he met a somewhat older lady and married her. My mother was sent off to scout out the situation and was horrified by the wife. Nonetheless, the young people came to Moscow, where they received a frosty reception from the family. Not long after, Uncle Alyosha divorced his wife and left Vladimir.

When the German war started he was sent to Turkey, where he served behind the lines. Later, when thousands of people were retreating with the defeated White army through Turkey, making for the Balkans and then further west, Uncle Alyosha did not move but stayed in a town called Nalchik. Since he was a lawyer he was appointed a magistrate, even continuing to hold this post after the Reds arrived. He also got married. He used to tell the story that he had married thanks to his trousers. Living a bachelor's life, he just did not notice that his leather trousers had become worn to the point of indecency. There happened to be two nurses, sisters, living nearby. They asked a friend of Uncle Alyosha's to extract his trousers from his room after he had gone to bed, mended them during the night and returned them by morning to the foot of his bed. Uncle went to thank them, they invited him in to tea, and a week later he proposed to the older sister and soon married her.

In a letter to us he wrote that his wife's name was a little unusual, Fyokla Bogdanovna, and that he had finally found happiness. He described his wife's good looks and great qualities, and only at the end of the letter mentioned that she was a Baltic German, Baroness Meindorf, and that before she became a nurse during the war she had lived in Petersburg and moved in the highest circles, even on occasion attending balls in the Winter Palace in the presence of the Tsar. My parents were very surprised by his letter, knowing how unwillingly Uncle Alyosha undertook anything new. In a further letter he announced the birth of their first son, whom he named Sergei in honour of his father, but he added that he had been forced out of his magistrate's job and was facing hard times, and wondered whether he could settle in Bogoroditsk.

Later, he told me why he had fallen foul of the Soviet authorities. In the first years after the revolution neither civil nor criminal laws were in force, which meant that judges had to be guided by common sense and existing Tsarist laws. At the same time so-called revolutionary law, when people were executed or pardoned without trial, was practised. Lawyers with integrity, such as Uncle Alyosha, accustomed to Roman law and the principles of justice, could not go along with arbitrary rule and lawlessness. One day two arrested men were brought before him, one accused of being a "former Count", the other of "collusion". Uncle Alyosha could discover no crime that they had committed, nor was either of them a count. He therefore ordered their release, and as a result was driven out of his job.

Mother set about helping her brother energetically. The Lopukhin estate of Khilkovo was only twenty-five kilometres south of Bogoroditsk, in the district of Krapivensky. We heard that the authorities in the province of Tula were renting out abandoned estates, where the fruit and vegetable gardens were going to waste, and very often renting them to their former owners. Today such a policy would be totally inconceivable – building socialism and yet returning land to the class enemy. But common sense persuaded the government to try to reap the benefits of these productive market gardens, and they were right. Mother went to Tula, and there had a meeting with a former merchant of Bogoroditsk, Chistozvonov, and in three days she was back home with an impressive warrant from the provincial agricultural department. The paper said that citizens Lopukhin and Chistozvonov were to have a three year lease on the fruit orchard, extending to fourteen hectares, in the village of Khilkovo in the district of Krapivensky.

Travelling in a heated goods wagon and with all their belongings, Uncle Alyosha, with his wife and small son, arrived in Moscow in the spring 1922. After a short stay, and leaving behind some of their unwanted possessions, they finally made it to Bogoroditsk. There was great joy at their arrival. Our new aunt, Fyokla Bogdanovna – Aunt Tyosa – was a lovely lady and captivated us all. She was tiny and fragile, with the big Meindorf eyes, but very lively. Her only defect was her missing front teeth. For three days the adults sat engrossed in conversation, going over the stories of their lives. Now and again, Uncle Alyosha would go out into the kitchen to smoke *mahorka*, the cheap, strong tobacco of those years, usually giving a pinch or two to Nanny Bush. Driven by Andrei, one of the Khilkovo peasants and a childhood friend of our uncle's, a cart arrived from the estate. Andrei had lost a leg in the war. He and Uncle Alyosha stood clasped in an embrace for a very long time, and to my surprise, were in floods of tears. Then they tied their things onto the cart and, sitting on top of them, all set off for Khilkovo.

3

Three weeks later, Uncle Alyosha reappeared on the same cart. He had rented a small cottage in Khilkovo and needed cutlery and crockery, various provisions and agricultural tools. Just as he was getting ready to leave, he suggested to my parents that I might go with him.

"Would you like to go with Uncle Alyosha?" asked my mother.

I was always very unhappy to part with my mother, but now it was I who could choose to be away from her; and I also thought, well, now I'm thirteen-years-old. I agreed to go, but I set off with conflicting feelings in my heart – pleasure at the thought of a new place, sadness at the separation from my mother. In my excitement I completely forgot my butterfly equipment. The road was magical. We crossed open fields past little lakes, rumbled along the edges of copses and saw, here and there, rising from the little hamlets, the silhouettes of church belfries. White summer clouds drifted across a blue sky out of which the sun shone brightly, and the ears of the rye were already swelling up, promising a fine harvest. We reached our destination late in the evening, ate a quick supper, and then Aunt Tyosa showed me a shelf in the entrance hall of the little cottage. It took me only a moment to fall fast asleep.

In the morning, Uncle Alyosha led me out into the orchard. In those days there were thousands of fruit orchards, and above all, apple orchards, not only in the province of Tula, but all over central Russia. That spring the blossoming trees were particularly fine; the countryside was dappled white. The civil war was nearly at an end and people were returning to a life of peace. In a novel written about that time, the author describes how blossoming apple trees gave everyone new hope. Other novels wrote of the building of socialism, but what the peasants were really thinking was that there were better times ahead.

In addition to the Lopukhin's fourteen hectares, there was a ten-hectare orchard belonging to a prosperous peasant, as well as a couple of hectares around the church and smallholdings around each home. And what is left of all this now? Either it has all been ploughed over or is now overgrown in weeds. Apples, and to some extent pears and cherries, had become the daily food of all those emaciated people who had gone hungry during the years of civil war. If there was a surplus, it was fed to the pigs, or distilled into homebrew.

Uncle Alyosha showed me the broad pastures along the river Uperta, the same river that flowed past Bogoroditsk. Some ten hectares of this had belonged to the Lopukhins, producing a small income. The orchard itself began quite close to the church, and had been planted by grandfather Sergei Alexeievich. We climbed up a little overgrown hill. On the opposite side of the river there stretched an alley of lime trees. On this rise had once stood the Lopukhin house, buzzing with the life and vigour of a numerous and close family and their many guests. That lively family life had now died. The house had burned to the ground. Uncle Alyosha pointed out the pieces of tiled stove that lay about, pulling some of them out, stacking them to one side. We moved on through an older part of the orchard planted by the people who had owned the place before the Lopukhins. The trees were massive and gnarled; some of them had dried out. There was clearly a lot of work needed here; pruning, uprooting, re-planting. Uncle Alyosha talked repeatedly about the work to be done, marked the trees to be removed, but more than that, did nothing. We came to an open place and sat down on a bench which was called the Bogoroditsk bench. The big house at Bogoroditsk could just be made out in the distance along the valley of the Uperta, the tip of its belltower just visible above the trees.

Only a few hundred metres away from us there lay a village of new houses with bright yellow thatched roofs and a new red brick church. The history of this village, Kolichev, is fascinating. In the days

113

when there was still serfdom, the then owner of the estate of Khilkovo was greatly disturbed by the proximity of the villagers with their singing, their barking dogs and their crowing cockerels. He forcibly resettled them some *versts* away. The new location did not suit them at all; the water was brackish and hard to pump and the fields themselves very poor. For sixty years they endured their hard lives, yearning for their old home, telling stories to their children and grandchildren of their former rich fields and sweet water. In 1917, without asking anyone's permission, they left their unloved settlement in a body and returned to Kolichev, commemorating the event by building a new church in only a few months.

Uncle Alyosha managed his orchard rather as he had earlier managed his estate. He rose late, ate the breakfast prepared by Aunt Tyosa, then appeared in the orchard. Lame Andrei and another old man organised everything, directing several women where to dig and what else to do, whilst they pruned the trees and propped up branches beginning to be heavy with fruit. Uncle Alyosha sat nearby smoking his pipe, listened to their reports, and offering advice, always very businesslike but not necessarily practical. Then he would go to the hill where the big house had once been, stand there in thought for a while, and continue his way to the Bogoroditsk bench, where he would once again light his pipe and contemplate the view. If the weather was warm, he would go down to the river, undress and plunge into the water, swim to the other bank and back, then sit naked on the grass, smoking another pipe. Returning home for lunch he would follow this with a nap, then sit outside on a bench. The old men of the village would come over and there would be endless talk until supper, when he would go over to the priest's house, or the schoolteacher's, to play cards late into the night. The other lessee of an orchard, Chistozvonov, only once appeared at Khilkovo while I was there. He was making preparations to harvest, first the summer apples, then the winter ones. The crops that year were expected to be especially abundant.

Unlike her husband, Aunt Tyosa was a dynamo of energy. Her spirits were never low, and despite being pregnant she bustled about doing the housework and catching her little son, who like all the village children ran about without any knickers and was invariably dirty. She worked in the orchard and although there were no medicines available, did her best to cure the ills of the local people. All that Uncle Alyosha did was to advise her; what she should plant in the vegetable garden, what she should cook for dinner, how to heal somebody. In general, he handed out very good advice; his theories were sound. I remember I had to chop wood one day. He sat down with his pipe near me and began to explain how to do the work, how to place the log, at what angle to strike and where. In a word, he gave me a detailed lesson in how to cut wood. I was rather weak and puffed and panted as I struggled to make an impression on the wood but he never got up to chop even one piece – he much preferred to sit there, giving advice. Still, nowadays, if ever I have to chop wood, I do it according to Uncle Alyosha's theory.

4

Many kinds of fish lived in the river Uperta. My uncle could tell countless stories of fish caught in his childhood. In the hay barn, which was the only building not to have burned down when the house was torched, there hung a long freshly cut branch with a stone attached to its thin end. The idea was that when the wood dried out it would be a very flexible rod and Uncle Alyosha would then go fishing for carp, using bread soaked in rapeseed oil as bait. The rod hung there unused for the whole time I stayed at Khilkovo. I imagine it ended up as firewood. In fact, there were masses of fish in the river. Everyday I went with the other children to a spot just below the dam by the mill run, where we caught baskets full of little river fish – mostly perch and roach. I swelled with pride when Aunt Tyosa told me what an important contribution I was making to our diet.

What engineering wonders those Russian watermills, now all gone, seemed to us. Two big paddle wheels driven by the river's current turned the grinding stones through a series of gears; grain went in on one side, flour came pouring out on the other. Now and again the miller, white-faced from the flour, would come out and adjust the paddles on the wheels, whilst we lads, unable to speak because of the noise of the mill, sat watching our floats and hauling out our catch. When the cherries were ripe I gave up fishing, instead climbing from tree to tree and eating so much of the fruit that I could hardly touch my food.

The apples began to ripen. I ate so many that I was unable to eat a mouthful of my meals. These apples replaced every other food – bread, water, vegetables and milk. At first Aunt Tyosa worried about my lack of appetite, then shrugged her shoulders and left me alone. The Hilkovo apples were of many different kinds in shape, colour and taste. The summer apples had many names, but the economically important apples were the winter variety, that ripened a little later and could be stored through the winter. And what wonderful fruit they were. Nowadays all kinds of apples are sold in Moscow, but they are imported, tasteless, soggy things. It is only on private market stalls, and then rarely, that one can find real Russian apples.

One day, lame Andrei filled a country cart with apples and went from village to village, selling or bartering them. By evening he was back without any apples, but bringing wheat and eggs and some money. He complained that it was very difficult for him to do all this alone as in every village his cart was surrounded by children who tried every trick to pinch his apples, whilst he had to weigh and exchange goods or money, and also hold the horse.

"Would you like to go?" Uncle asked me.

I was proud to be asked to do such an important job, but modestly casting down my eyes, muttered, "Yes, please."

We set off at dawn, though it was not with lame Andrei, but the old man who also worked for Uncle Alyosha. On arrival in a village, he started to shout in his deep voice "Aa-ap-ples!" And I, prompted by the memory of how I used to echo the chanting of prayers, began to repeat his call in my thin little voice. When we came to a stop, at once we were surrounded by women of all ages and a crowd of little boys. I could not fall asleep on this job! I had to brandish a little whip to frighten off the boys. My duties were to weigh the apples, pass them to the old man, who tipped them into the women's skirts or into the lads' caps, collected whatever bartered provisions he was given and passed any money to me. We covered a great distance, all the way back into the district of Bogoroditsk, so that it was already dark when we made our way back home, weary from the long day and the heat, but our apples all sold. I was too tired to eat even a mouthful of food. I handed over a bundle of money to Uncle Alyosha and fell on my bed. When much later he woke me, I waved him away and again fell asleep; in all I slept for twenty-two hours.

5

It was at this point that Aunt Tyosa's nephew, Petrusha Sheremetyev, the brother of Vladimir's future bride, came to Khilkovo on holiday. He was six months older than me, adventurous, quick moving, cheerful, never downcast, though only average at his studies – a kind of Tom Sawyer. I liked him from the very first, though we had rather different characters. He wore short pants whilst mine were down to the ankle, but the similarity of our destinies brought us close. Both of us ran about in bare feet, were proud of our ancestors and grieved over our lost estates. We both mourned the death of the young

Tsarevich Alexei. Petrusha declared himself to be a monarchist, I equally firmly said I thought Russia needed to be a republic. Two of his uncles had been shot, one of mine. We both adored our older brothers and were proud of them. After the revolution his eldest brother Boris fought in the ranks of the White army. Both of us unceasingly boasted to each other.

"And my brother Boris . . ." he would say.

"And my brother Vladimir . . ." I would interrupt, "my brother Vladimir is an artist and is sailing across the Arctic seas, and your brother has gone to America and is raising chickens."

We were both delighted at the prospect of Vladimir marrying his sister Helena. Petrusha's father, an officer in the Guards, had died of tuberculosis before the German war. His son hardly referred to him at all and I tactfully refrained from mentioning my own father. We talked a lot about ourselves. Petrusha invariably won these exchanges. His grandfather, Count Sergei Dimitriyevich Sheremetyev, had been the senior nobleman at court, had known the Tsar when he was still a little boy, and was the only courtier who had the right to call the Tsar "Nicky" and use the familiar form of the personal pronoun to him. In short, Petrusha and I had enough in common to keep us talking and arguing as we ran in the fields, or lay fishing on the river bank, or eating apples, or just getting ready to go to sleep.

The only thing that saddened me was that he laughed at my love of reading. There were hardly any books at Khilkovo, and Petrusha kept me from any reading for a long while. And, fearful of his scorn, I never told him I wanted to be a writer. My musical taste was quite undeveloped, whereas he was very musical – he had perfect pitch and was learning to play the violin. His instrument, back in Moscow, had been made by the famous violin maker, Amati. He was shorter than me, and had the large, bright Sheremetyev eyes, but his face was somewhat spoiled by a broad, upturned nose and too large a chin. Petrusha is no longer alive. I write about him in such detail because I truly loved him. He had a certain influence on me, both good and bad.

Late one evening, I was woken by the sound of excited cries and recognised my parents' voices. I leapt to my feet and rushed to embrace them. They had come from Bogoroditsk on foot. In the morning, we went out together to the churchyard to visit the grave of my mother's youngest brother, Pavlik. Then we continued through the orchard to the little rise where the house had stood, where mother's whole childhood had been spent. The hill was bright with purple rosebay willow herb. We stood there in silence for a while, as I showed mother the little pile of tiles, and she bent down and took two of them as a memento of the house. Then we moved on to the Bogoroditsk bench. That day she wrote a very long letter to her mother, now in Harbin, in which she described the hill as being a beautiful memorial. This letter was copied by my grandmother and sent on to all her brothers and sisters and their children now living abroad, where they all read it out aloud. Everyone agreed what a sad but beautifully poetic letter mother had written.

Leaving the bench, we went along the path my parents had taken on that memorable day when father proposed to mother. "Here," she said, "he announced that he must speak to me seriously. And here," we went on a little, "we sat down under this birch tree and for the very first time, he said the words, 'I love you'."

6

After lunch, my parents set off again on foot to return to Bogoroditsk. Quite soon after that Uncle Alyosha had some business to do and drove over in the cart, taking me with him.

"I've only come for the day," I shouted joyously as I rushed into our house.

Mother announced that soon our lives were going to change radically. We were going to move back to Moscow, where sister Lina had found us a flat and my father had been promised a good job. He would be first to set off. Mother also told me that I would be going to a new school and would need to pass some difficult exams, for which I was poorly prepared. I went cold all over. Was I not going to go back to Khilkovo? Such a harsh decision was felt to be too abrupt, so my parents said I could go back for a short time on condition that I took my schoolbooks with me and did some studying. Uncle Alyosha offered to coach me in maths, and as for the rest, I promised I would revise everything that I had learned with Aunt Sasha, though leaving out religious instruction. So they let me return to Khilkovo.

Petrusha burst out laughing when he saw my books. "Only idiots study in summer," he jeered.

Still, I did leaf through my books and decided that I had forgotten nothing. Petrusha dragged me off into the orchard and down to the river to fish. Under my breath I repeated the rules of Russian grammar as he pulled my arm. For a few days, Uncle Alyosha tried to teach me my maths, but he too was confused by pools of water that emptied at a certain rate and groups of pedestrians dividing up. On top of that, there was only enough paper in Khilkovo for essential letter writing and scoring at cards, and then every evening a boy, the son of the priest, would poke his head over the window sill, summoning Uncle Alyosha to play cards or offering some other distraction. Soon a letter arrived, addressed to Uncle Alyosha, telling him to send me back to Bogoroditsk as soon as possible. Within the week, it so happened that one of the priest's sons, a youth with a fine but untrained baritone voice, was setting off for Moscow to enter the music conservatory. At the same time, we heard that Aunt Tyosa's younger sister, Alexandra, together with Petrusha's younger sister, Marika, were coming to Bogoroditsk from Moscow on their way to Khilkovo. I had heard from my sister Sonya, who had been in Moscow, that Marika was a really lovely little girl and that when Sonya had shown her my picture as an eight-year-old in a sailor suit, she had been much taken with it. So I was very keen to meet Marika.

After fond farewells to Uncle Alyosha, Aunt Tyosa and Petrusha, we set off in the peasant cart. As it was very hot our departure was in the late evening, under a full moon. The young man sang softly in his fine baritone as we rolled along in the silvery light. Today, when I hear those same songs, I am taken back to that night and the young man setting off for Moscow in search of fame. He did in fact enter the conservatory, but was dismissed after six months, at which point he came to us to borrow money for the journey home. Whether he was expelled because he was failing to meet the required standard, or because he was a priest's son, I never knew, nor do I know what became of him in later life.

We reached Bogoroditsk just before dawn. Opening the door to me, mother announced that father and Sonya had already left for Moscow. I fell into bed and only woke at midday to the sound of excited voices. Dressing quickly, I went to where my sisters were in the company of a girl who immediately struck me as being a fairy-tale princess. Marika was the same age as my sister Masha, but petite and much livelier. Her large, bright Sheremetyev eyes looked at me furtively, then were lowered. I found that she was very like her older sister, whose photo Vladimir had shown us the year before, but much more beautiful. There was no chance to get to know her, as that very evening she, her Aunt Sandra and also, to my great envy, my sister Masha, all left for Khilkovo. So this beautiful girl flashed momentarily before my eyes like a vision, and vanished. But my heart beat faster when I thought of her.

In the morning mother took me to Ivan Yegorovich Rusakov, the Russian teacher, in Konstantinovskaya Street. I felt flattered at being seated next to this famous local actor, who had played so many major roles. After questioning me carefully, he reported to mother that I was an excellent student. Mathematics, however, was a different story. Mother kept me by her side as she worked at her shoemaking, and I just stared at my textbooks and hung my head. Every now and again she would stop, put her head in her hands and cry out, "Dear God, what am I going to do with you?" She taught me a prayer, which I was supposed to repeat all day, "Prophet Nahum, be in my brain-um!"

One day I was told that Deters wished to see me at the Institute, where he asked me what I intended to do with my butterfly collection. I admitted I did not know.

"Then sell it to our institute," he suggested, and immediately sat me down to write out an invoice. This was the first time I had ever written out that sort of paper – "Please pay me, Sergei Golitsyn, etc." I handed over my four boxes of butterflies and was sent to the former treasury building which now housed the financial department of the town's Executive Committee. There a surly man wrote out a slip of paper for me to take to the treasurer. An even surlier clerk grumbled "Don't you know how to sign things?" but in the end passed over a thick bundle of notes, quite a large sum in fact.

When, almost fifty years later, I walked past this same building, with its peeling façade and gloomy windows, I felt a flush of pride on remembering that it was here that I earned my first roubles. Mother urged me to hold on to the money until we were in Moscow. There I could not make up my mind what to buy for a long while, during which time the value of money dropped like a stone, so that in the end all I could buy was a huge watermelon, which the whole family solemnly ate as dessert one lunch. Now, after my sixtieth birthday, I have gone back to my butterfly collecting and find that the skill and art of it have not deserted me, nor the enjoyment.

It was already the end of August by the time mother and I were ready to make the move to Moscow. We were leaving behind my grandparents, the Trubetskoi family, Aunt Vera with her two youngest children, Aunt Sasha and Nasenka, my two little sisters, Nanny Bush and Lenya, but little by little they also began to collect together their things. Our four year stay in Bogoroditsk was coming to an end. When mother and I were ready, Aunt Vera came to see us off at the station. The train conductor was a former Bobrinsky servant, so I was put in a seat in his compartment, while mother bought an unreserved ticket. As the train began to move I gazed out of the window, feeling both pleasure and anxiety. My childhood was over.

6. Moscow and the Beginning of the New Economic Policy

1

Historians and writers, after reading my father's memoirs, usually commented that the most interesting chapters were his descriptions of Moscow in the 1880s and 90s, as well as the chapter entitled "Nine Hundred Years of Moscow". On coming to Moscow, I spent quite a lot of time wandering the streets, looking into churches and shops and idling through the markets. So, like my father, I also have a store of impressions of the city, though now dating from the 1920s.

Everywhere you could see the effects of the NEP. Even the name of the secret police, the Cheka, had been changed to OGPU (Joint State Political Directorate). The harshness of authority had lessened; there were fewer arrests, and those mostly of actual criminals. People sensed that the age of promised freedoms had arrived; they felt they were free to choose their jobs, or become small entrepreneurs, making and selling things, in other words, making as much money as they could. Bukharin's famous slogan "Work and become rich!" was all the rage. This encouraged energetic and inventive people to leap into action, trusting in the new order. Moscow was seething with activity.

In those days, only the main streets and central areas of the city were paved with asphalt. Most streets were laid with irregular cobblestones packed into sand, and only a few were edged with kerbstones. Along these rough streets, from early morning to late at night, there trundled and rumbled all manner of carts, driven at a walking pace when loaded and at a gallop when empty, as their drivers whipped their horses along in their hurry to make as many trips as possible. Every extra trip meant greater earnings. The biggest concentrations of carts and drivers was at the railway stations, the markets and on the highways into Moscow. In those years, few Moscow institutions owned motor vehicles – what they had was a stable of horses and carts. The population of Moscow was growing rapidly, which meant goods were constantly moving in and around the city. This was a time when the system of internal passports and residence qualifications was not as strict as it is now. Anyone with even a cubby hole could be registered to live in Moscow. Many of the people who had fled the city in the face of famine were now returning, just like us. Also, young people from all over the country were coming to the city in search of fame and fortune. Merchants and businessmen were arriving in pursuit of wealth. All these returnees and newcomers naturally brought their possessions with them, and these had to be transported from the stations to their homes. All sorts of merchandise was also being brought in, not least by the peasants who carted in their country produce, most of which was sold in the markets.

The most fascinating spectacles in Moscow were the markets. There was Okhotny Ryad (Hunter's Row), Tishinsky, Zazapsky and Pereyaslavsky. But the biggest market was the Sukharevsky, running for over a mile along the Sadovoye Koltso (Garden Ring) from Tsvetnoy Boulevard. A huge structure, Sukharev Tower, divided the market in two. This tower of fine red brick with white stone embellishments and decorations, was in the Moscow baroque style. The market dealt in every sort of produce, though it had started out originally as a flea market. On sale here was every sort of bits and bobs going right back to the time of Ryurik, legendary founder of Russia: there were clothes and shoes and paintings and furniture and all the medley of things that are the lifeblood of a flea market. And the so-called *bwyvshy lyudyi* ("former people"), brought their redundant evening clothes, ball dresses and perfume flasks to try and sell them here. You could see them standing in rows, talking French to each other and hoping for a sale.

Sukharevsky market also traded in the cheapest goods, in rags and worn out furs, moulting caps and battered articles of every kind. As had been the case with the Bobrinskys in Bogoroditsk, people had trunks full of stuff and as families were crammed into smaller and smaller accommodation, so housewives brought along these old things, rusty objects and unfashionable clothing, which they could no longer store, and which in any case would help provide the food that was in such short supply and becoming more expensive by the day.

The crowds were immense. Sellers, buyers, traders, porters, petty thieves and pickpockets all jostled together, arguing and quarrelling, shouting and gesticulating. On a bit of pavement a Chinese magician sat doing a disappearing act with apples. Nearby was a Roma lady telling fortunes. Both of them were surrounded by crowds of gaping observers. Homeless and orphaned children slipped through the crowd looking for the chance of stealing any unguarded items. And through this churning mass the trams moved at walking pace, frantically ringing their warning bells. Thousands and millions of roubles changed hands every day. Some people became very rich; some very poor.

Another famous market was the Smolensky. It ran from Novinsky Boulevard at the corner of Krechetnikovsky Street, and before it reached Arbat was blocked by a big building that straddled Sadovaya, after which it continued to the beginning of Smolensk Boulevard. This end of the market was called the Sennaya (Haymarket). Smolensky also had a small flea market section, but mostly it consisted of stalls heaped with foodstuffs. I shall not try to describe it; the reader has only to recall or read Zola's *The Guts of Paris* to get the right impression. As for the section in Sennaya, I do not believe any hay was sold there any longer, as by this time cows and goats were no longer kept in central Moscow. There were, however, many carts full of firewood. Mother and I once dragged a load from there on our sledge. In those days Moscow had no central heating; it was entirely heated by wood stoves.

Most of all I remember the market in winter, when the choking dust of summer was replaced by deep snow and each stall was surrounded by piled up snowdrifts. The rivers, lakes and seas of Russia had scarcely been fished since the year 1914, so the waters were teeming with fish and massive catches could be hauled in. In those days, there were no collective fisheries; instead the fishermen organised themselves into guilds or cooperatives, sharing the profits amongst themselves. The best quality fish, sturgeon and salmon and trout, as well as caviar, were sent for sale in Okhotny Ryad, Moscow's most expensive market, the remainder finding their way to the Haymarket section of Smolensky market. I remember the huge frozen, open-mouthed carp, so beloved by the Jews. There were pike lying in frozen heaps like birch logs; today only honoured foreign guests in the Kremlin are privileged enough to eat such delicacies. Then there was the *vobla* (Capsian roach), so common that it was offered for free on tavern tables, the innkeepers well aware that a free mouthful of this fish would cause a raging thirst for their beer. In fact, this roach was not even considered to be a fish. Although mother was always struggling with the cost of our food, she never used roach as a base, instead buying eel. It was only in old people's homes, orphanages and prisons that it was used to make soup.

The market called Okhotny Ryad was beyond our means. The most expensive of all, it actually consisted of rows of proper shops. Old things, such as clothes and shoes, were never to be found there. It did not cover a large area, starting near the tallest building in Moscow, the Assembly of Nobles, now the House of the Soviets, and ending at the bottom of Tverskaya street. The middle of the market was graced by a beautiful church in the Moscow baroque style – Paraskeva Pyatnitsa, the patroness of trade and commerce. Its ornate belfry with its white stone filigree decorations and elaborate architecture had the finest peal of bells, soft and melodious, in all Moscow.

Behind this church, where there now stands the cold, grey building of the Council of Ministers, there once stood a row of plain two-storey houses. It was only at the end of the 1920s that historians realised that one of these dated back to the seventeenth century. When restored, it revealed itself as being a fine red brick mansion decorated with a dainty frieze, its windows framed in white limestone. It had once belonged to the Empress Sophia's favourite, Prince Vasily Vasilivich Golitsyn. Anyone who loved Moscow considered it a sight to be seen. Sadly, this restored gem only survived two years; collectors now treasure the picture postcards of it.

Still standing, however, is Boyarina Troyekurova's house, with its restored window sills and lintels, but it is no match for the lost elegance of the Golitsyn house. On the other side of the square, where the Hotel Moskva now stands, there used to be a row of two- and three-storey houses. One of these was a vast fish shop that sold only the best – salmon and sturgeon and lobsters and caviar – the sort of fish ordinary people can only dream about. Above its doorway and window were huge pictures of improbable fish. Next came a game shop. Its counters were heaped with piles of hare and pheasant, grouse and snipe. Once I found myself transfixed by the sight of a bear's paw, very like a human hand, but I had no time to study it as I was angrily told to move on.

A stretch of Tverskaya Street that no longer exists housed a few more shops next to the large Lowenbrau beer hall. In one of these houses the editorial offices of the satirical magazine *Krokodil* used to be located; the sign outside showed a crocodile holding a fork. And here, running parallel with Alexander Gardens, were two scruffy alleys, Lebyazhy and Loskutny, where the Okhotny Ryad shops had their storerooms. Behind the church of Paraskeva Pyatnitsa were buildings where food was salted. Sweet, rotting smells filled the air. Barrels of salted cabbage and cucumbers and various kinds of mushrooms – milk agaric and milk caps, that one only finds now in the homes of old ladies in the dying north country – stood about. This was Okhotny Ryad; not a stone of it now remains, not a single brick. Even its name, a very ancient one, has disappeared into oblivion.

There was another market, Bolotny, known simply as Boloto. I only went there once and that was with Uncle Alyosha. He and the merchant Chistozvonov had in some rather backhanded way got hold of a couple of railway freight cars. The station nearest to Khilkovo was called Lazarevo and was on the Kursk to Moscow line. Here they loaded the wagons with winter apples, not in boxes as is now done, but in heaps. Chistozvonov now took charge of the operation, leaving Uncle Alyosha to be a not-very-energetic sleeping partner, as the perishable fruit had to be delivered as quickly as possible. In those days, the railways were not the epitome of efficiency, so Chistozvonov indulged in some liberal bribes all round and managed to have the wagons hooked onto a direct Moscow passenger train. He also saw to it that willing lads were waiting at Kursk station to take the apples to Boloto market, and so within twenty-four hours the whole lot was delivered in good condition. Boloto was purely a wholesale fruit and vegetable market, and was by the relief canal in Zamoskvarechye, near the Tretyakov gallery. Today there is only a rather dull square there and a mediocre monument to the painter Repin. The apples were sold without delay, so fortune smiled on the two men. But whereas the profit was just another business deal for Chistozvonov, Uncle Alyosha counted on living off this money until the following apple season.

I walked about the market with my mouth hanging open. The mountains of apples made one's imagination boggle. This was a strictly wholesale market; no one here would bother to sell just a few kilos. Rows of laden rickshaws set off in all directions, the fruit being sold on to young lads and old ladies camped on boards or stools by the roadside, who now traded the fruit and vegetables by weight or by the piece. At some crossings it was not just one or two old ladies and lads, but entire groups of them angling for sales. These same old ladies and young lads also sold sunflower seeds, brought from Boloto market. Somewhere or other these were grilled and loaded into baskets and then sold by the cupful at the street crossings. All Moscow filled its pockets with these seeds, chewing and spitting out their shells everywhere and anywhere – in the cinema, on the tram, in the streets, at home. The whole city, indeed the whole of Russia, seemed to be chewing and spitting out sunflower seeds in those days.

2

There were only a few expensive restaurants. In the centre you had the Metropole and the National, and on the street called Arbat you had the Prague. There were Caucasian eateries in basements, and very cheap "workers" eateries. Beer halls, with their green and yellow signs, were everywhere. Ice cream was sold on the streets; the cheapest portion was a single scoop, an ice cream sandwiched between two biscuits was more expensive. In the autumn, melons and watermelons could be bought off roaming barrows. Tartars wearing their little caps wandered up and down calling for any old things in their muffled Asiatic voices, and all kinds of repair men with various kinds of instruments offered to mend or sharpen or fix things, though some of these did not call out their wares but could be seen going busily on their way to already arranged appointments.

In the state shops, the Moscow Union of Consumer Associations (MSPO) prices were cheaper. We had to shop there, even though goods could sometimes be rotten and the salespeople were often very rude, whereas in the private shops you were greeted with smiles and the goods were attractively laid out and nicely packed. The assistants were mostly members of the former merchant families; for instance, Smeshnikov's fur shop in the Okhotny Ryad and in other shops in that market. But the majority of business people and traders, christened "NEPmen" under the new dispensation, were recent arrivals and former salesmen. Very many of them were Jews. The revolution had done away with the "Pale Settlement" whereby Jews could only live in designated areas in certain towns, so that once the civil war was over they abandoned these settlements, so colourfully described by Sholom-Alekhim, Gomel, Berdichev and Krasilovka. Most Jews headed for Moscow, a few for other towns. They were enterprising people who took easily to trade, and it was not distant Palestine that became their promised land, but Moscow with its many golden churches and – at this stage of the NEP – still-spacious apartments with people hungering to buy new clothes and rebuild their lives and have the good time so long denied them by war and revolution. Despite the revolution and the civil war, many people had managed to conceal their gold and other valuables.

It was not only in commerce, medicine and journalism that the Jews occupied leading positions. Important positions in the party and state organisations, including the OGPU, were filled by representatives of this race. Russians have a character trait not shared by the Jews, which is that they are capable of being indifferent to the fate of their fellow men, even their own brothers. Russians not only do not help each other, they actually encourage the downfall of others. Whereas Jews help anyone in their family, they would also help a second cousin once removed, and even the friend of the cousin. Once established in Moscow, hordes of relatives, and relatives of relatives, followed in their wake.

In Moscow, two Jewish theatres were opened, Jewish language newspapers came into existence, as well as publishers, and a great number of shops and businesses owned by Jews sprang up. On Arbat, a watchmaker, Kishinevsky, opened. On Myasnitsky, three Jews opened a plumbing and piping business. In the streets one would often see black vans with the inscription "Jacov Ratser – Charcoal" painted on their sides; tea was invariably made with samovars that burned charcoal. Both before the revolution and during the years of the NEP there was Verein's pharmacy on Nikolsky Street, Rubanovsky's where Sadovaya street crossed with Zhivodvorky, and other Jewish shops on every corner. Jewish doctors, mostly venereologists and dentists, had their signs out everywhere. I also remember Jewish restaurants with their signs written in two languages. In my third year in Moscow I happened to go into one, just an ordinary apartment off the street. I was met by a smiling elderly lady and was served by her daughter, Rebecca, with an excellent three course meal. Together with Georgian and Armenian cooking, Jewish cooking was considered the best in the world, and their smiling and polite service would have been the envy of any French restaurateur.

Some of the NEPmen earned enormous profits, often beyond calculation. As it would have been madness to hold on to cash with the dizzying fall in the value of the currency, at that time called *sovznaki* (soviet notes), these NEPmen were always in a hurry to convert the money into something durable. Here they were helped by "former people" who had possessions to sell; pictures, gold, jewels and property. There was a law forbidding the transfer of such goods and property, and although during the years of the NEP it was rarely enforced, nonetheless most transactions were done in secret for fear of the possible consequences.

3

"Former people" sold, "NEPmen" bought. Collectors such as Vishnevsky, like vampires, would descend upon some needy old lady, with her portraits of ancestors, her china and glass, her *objets d'art*, and having given her miserable sums of money, walk off in triumph with all her possessions. (In fairness, I should add that we have now to thank Vishnevsky for the huge collection he left to the state, which became the basis on which the Tropinin Museum collection was started.) Businessmen preferred gold, which led to the rise of intermediaries, or brokers. One such broker was my second cousin, Georgy Mikhailovich Osorgin. He was completely honest, took a fixed percentage as his commission, and "former people" trusted him, believing in his honour as a nobleman when they handed over their brooches and gold cutlery and gold five rouble coins to him. He rarely dealt directly with purchasers, working mostly through two or three Jewish brokers, about whose honesty I know nothing. How did some members of the nobility come to work in what was for them such an unusual business?

"Well," they would explain, "we took the oath of service to the Tsar. We do not serve Soviet power."

In addition to gold and other valuables, the NEPmen also traded in foreign currencies, above all in the hardest currency of all, the US dollar. More and more foreigners were coming to Moscow – the ARA, Nansen and Pope Pius XI famine relief missions, diplomats, businessmen, trade representatives. The state began to allow foreign-owned concessions, such as the Lena Goldfields in Yakutia owned by the British, manganese deposits in Chiatura in the Caucasus owned by the Americans, Armand Hammer's pencil factory in Moscow, and so forth. Foreigners were immediately recognisable by their round glasses and the thick, pale-coloured soles of their shoes. They dressed much more elegantly than Muscovites and had a proud look. They arrived with bulging pocketbooks and very quickly discovered that there was no point in changing money at the official rate when outside every bank there would be someone standing unobtrusively in the shade, prepared to offer five times the official rate of exchange. In the small square on Ilinka street shadowy figures went to and fro, some whispering "I change dollars," others saying "I change roubles." One wondered why they did not simply get together and exchange with each other. They were called "currency guys" and were often picked up and taken off to Butyrka prison. Total honesty was the hallmark of my father throughout his life; when his brother Alexander Vladimirovich started to send him ten dollars a month, father changed them in the bank, flatly refusing to be involved in illegal dealing. It was with great difficulty that he was persuaded that everyone did this, but even then, he himself never went down to Ilinka street, leaving it to Georgy Osorgin to handle these operations.

In addition to the Jews, many Chinese came to Moscow. They not only set themselves up as conjurors in the markets, but also opened little laundries all over the city, as well as trading in those same markets and by the Pervopechatnik monument over by the walls of Kitaygorod. Here you would find them standing in rows offering homemade buttons, combs, watch-straps and other small goods. The government was paying special attention to China, hoping to enlist the support of that huge country, suffering from its own terrible civil war, in the cause of world revolution. A special Chinese communist university was established on Volhonkaya Street and another one, behind Strastny Monastery, called "Workers of the East", also a communist one. The students at those two establishments went about in cheap blue-grey uniforms; after learning the fundamentals of Marxism-Leninism they were sent home to their countries to spread the ideas of communism. Among the students were Ho Chi Min, Chiang Kai Shek and other contemporaries of Mao Tse Tung. The future was to show how mistaken were our government's hopes.

4

What did Moscow look like in those years? There were many churches, some built in the seventeenth century, a few in the sixteenth, most of them heavily restored. There were particularly many in the district of Kitaygorod and in or around Prechistenky, Arbat and Bolshoy Nikitsky streets, and in the district of Zamoskvorechy. Buildings and churches were pockmarked with bullet holes and had been damaged in the fighting that had followed the October Revolution. Near Nikitsky Gate, an old house that had been particularly badly damaged was pulled down and in its place a statue of the communist Timeryasev erected, but nearly all the houses kept their peeling and pockmarked appearance for years, until finally the city council was able to carry out repairs.

Most people went about their business on foot, since trams were few and far between and during rush hours were so full that passengers hung off them like clusters of grapes, young lads even clinging on to the buffers. Today, the terms "A ring" and "B ring" are still in use, but people are unaware of their origin. The A tram, that Muscovites fondly called "Annushka", ran along the inner Boulevard Ring – as there was a very steep stretch of line along Pozhdestvenny Boulevard, this A tram could only be a single car. The B tram, nick-named *bukashka* (beetle), pulled a second car and ran along Sadovoye

Ring, the outer ring. And whatever earth-shattering events, such as the October Revolution, took place, trams A and B still continued their screechy, jolting rounds along routes that had been laid down in the so-called "era of despotism".

Once upon a time there had been a sandy track, which was already covered over in the eighteenth century, which followed the line of Sadovoye Koltso. From Kudrinsky Square, interrupted by Smolensky market, ran the boulevards called Novinsky, Smolensky and Zubovsky. They were lined with ancient lime trees and lawns where grannies and nannies watched their young charges while they gossiped on nearby benches. These green areas were the delight of Muscovites; people loved to walk along the pathways where the air was fresh. Then in the 1930s these boulevards with their two-hundred-year-old lime trees were barbarously wiped from the face of the earth.

In winter the markets emptied and trading was much quieter. By night the gangs of orphaned *bezprizorniki* (homeless children) kept themselves warm around burning pieces of asphalt in metal drums and huddled for shelter in the foundations of the unfinished buildings of Kazansky Station. Clad in rags, with wind-burned faces and shining eyes, they wandered about the streets in search of prey, slipped through the crowd in shops or on the trams, or stood in groups beating time on old spoons as they intoned songs and collected coins in their caps. Once about a hundred of these *bezprizorniki* launched an attack on a kiosk on Lyubyanka Square where an old woman was selling sausage and other meats. In a flash the kiosk, with the woman still in it, was overturned and cleaned out and the children had fled in all directions. Rumour had it that Dzerzhinsky himself (head of the OGPU) watched this incident from his office, and that from that day he befriended these homeless children. By chance my brother Vladimir arrived on the scene at the very end of this attack and so was able to tell us what had happened. The next day there was a full account in the papers.

At the time, incidents like these were widely reported, uncensored, in the newspapers. There were fewer papers then and circulation figures were much lower. *Pravda*, *Izvestia*, *Rabochaya Gazeta*, *Krestyanskaya Gazeta* and *Bednota* were some of the titles. The last three were of a smaller format and had larger circulations. There was also the railway workers' paper, *Gudok*. The most interesting and weighty of the papers was the eight-page daily, *Izvestia*. The editor was the elderly and much respected Bolshevik I.I. Skvortsov-Stepanov, who had a tolerant attitude towards "former people".

His death came early on and so his name was not erased from the record. As there were few kiosks, the streets were always full of lads shouting the titles of the papers they were trying to sell. Unfortunately, all the papers of that time are now tightly locked up behind closed doors; I can only write about them from memory. In *Izvestia*, apart from foreign and home news, that was quite openly reported, there were scientific articles and racy serials by people such as Ryklin and Lvovich, as well as other articles and poetry. The accounts of court cases and street incidents that one now never finds in the papers were very popular. There was almost never anything about the leaders, not even Lenin, nor were any workers mentioned, and the concept of "socialist competition" had not yet been invented.

Here are some examples. A street incident; two trams collided at a crossing because neither driver wanted to give way. This first appeared as an incident, and later as a court case. Thanks to the sincere repentance of the two drivers, their lack of a criminal record and their proletarian origins they received only a "social reprimand" as punishment. Or the mountain goat that escaped from the zoo. He galloped along Bolshoy Gruzinsky Street, knocking people over and causing panic before running into a barbershop where, on catching sight of himself, he smashed the mirror, ran back out into the street and, still at full charge, dashed off in the direction of Tishinsky market. There he knocked over a couple of floats before being caught and put into a cage. The account of this event took up as much space as an instalment in a serial story; the names of all the victims were given, there was an interview with the barber, and a discursive article by the then very popular zoologist, Professor Manteufel.

Readers tend now to ignore three quarters of what is published in the papers. I, then a fourteen-year-old boy, read practically everything, believing it all. The saying "There's no *pravda* (truth) in *Izvestia* (news) and no news in *Pravda*" had not yet been invented. A publication somehow came into my hands, the sort of thing that is now kept behind locked doors. It was a collection of articles on the history of the Russian Communist Party, dated 1923. Nearly every article asserted the imminent arrival of world revolution and that capitalism was living through its last hours. The most strident of these prophets was Grigory Zinovyev, the closest of Lenin's collaborators, who on one occasion had shared Lenin's hiding place. His article pulled no punches in asserting, without a shred of evidence, that the world was on the brink of revolution, which could happen within months or even weeks. In general all the papers, as well as meetings and conferences, were obsessed with the expectation that world revolution was inevitable and that one should have no mercy for capitalists.

5

I come now to the arts. I have already described how in the first years after the revolution the authorities rarely interfered with the arts. Discussion was completely open and posters urged people to take part in these frank exchanges of opinion. The atmosphere of those days encouraged people to be controversial, and yet despite the many disputes, people remained friends. I want to mention the names of some talented writers. Pantaleymon Romanov was very successful with his comic stories, although his unfinished novel *Rus* was on the heavy side; the author had obviously hoped to write a kind of *War and Peace*, but was just not up to the challenge. He disappeared from society, died in poverty, and the hundredth anniversary of his birth passed unnoticed. Sergei Sergeievich Zayaitsky wrote a fine and cleverly malicious satirical novel, *The Beauty from the Island of Lyu-Lyu* which satirized both capitalism and the Soviet system. Perhaps this reference to him will encourage someone to reprint the work of this talented, prematurely deceased author.

I saw Leonid Leonov three times. With his slightly puffy face and bright eyes, he was an energetic and enchanting person. His best work, *Tyoitamur*, and *Petushihinsky Prolom* were written when he was still young. Boris Pilnyak was a difficult author for me as a youngster, but I could see that others loved his manneristic writings. When Mikhail Bulgakov's slender little books, printed on cheap paper, came out, they were worn to pieces by the many readers who laughed over their stories and appreciated their satirical picture of life. I read *The Fateful Eggs*, *Dyavoliada*, and *Chichikov's Adventure* when I was still very young and have never forgotten them. Only the first part of the novel *White Guard* was printed in a journal; the government became alarmed, shut down the publication and this first part continued to circulate from hand to hand until its pages fell apart.

One of the most popular writers was Mikhail Zoshchenko. His short, comic tales made the whole country laugh and were read out aloud at many an evening gathering. But in comparison with Bulgakov his satire was pretty toothless and today he seems very dated. I can name two more writers, Ilya Erenburg and Marietta Shaginyan, who were very popular, although their quasi-detective novels had no attraction for me. Mayakovsky and Esenin were the kings of poetry. People flocked to hear them declaim their work, but I leave it to others to write about them. I shall say nothing of Anna Akhmatova. Then there was a poet who was also a painter, Maximilian Voloshin, who was legendary. He lived in the Crimea, and when the Whites were in the ascendant he sheltered the Reds, and when the Reds were on top, he sheltered the Whites. He painted landscapes that he gave to his friends, and also wrote poetry that was never printed. Over the door of his house was painted, "My house is open to the invited and the uninvited". In the twenties, friends came to stay with him and to listen to his poetry and his words of wisdom, but as the years went by, fewer and fewer came to see him. He went on living there, solitary and independent, painting his pictures and writing his poetry in the certainty that one day fame would descend upon him. His deeply religious poems about the hermetic, isolated Moscow Kremlin, the monastery town of Suzdal, the restored icon of the Virgin Mary of Vladimir, and Russia in the image of a peasant girl, were copied out by hand or on the typewriter and circulated from person to person. He was the first *samizdat* writer.[12] The poems were declaimed or communicated in a whisper, and I know that there were the people who wept over them. Then came a time when simply keeping a copy of these poems was enough to send you to the camps. The poet himself was left untouched.

I now come to a writer who was glorified by the press and servile critics, but who was one of the most disgusting people ever to disgrace the name of literature. He is now totally forgotten. His name was Demyan Bedny. He wrote twenty volumes of fables and serial stories and dared to blaspheme the Gospels. In 1925, *Pravda* printed his *New Testament Without Mistakes According to the Apostle Demyan*. I can only remember lines such as "You only grunted, Christ, you pig." I also recall the story of how a proletarian poet said to Mikhail Koltsov, "I've just been reading something by Demyan Bedny and find him better than our earlier poets." At which Koltsov pointed to a heap of dog dirt and asked, "Which is better, that or a real sausage?" A bitter denunciation of Bedny, allegedly made by the poet Esenin, also circulated widely.

In the twenties, there were many poets writing futuristic, religious and abstract poetry, who read out their work to gatherings and small groups of listeners but were never printed. I listened to them with

---

12. *The abbreviation samizdat (samo-izdatel'stvo) means 'self-published' and refers to the clandestine copying and distribution of government surpressed literature.*

glowing admiration, even to the point of feeling a lump in my throat and wanting to cry. In the twenties, too, it was fashionable not just to scorn the art of earlier ages, but to mock it with sadistic vehemence. Even Pushkin and Tolstoy were abused. The poets who now moved into the front rank were "factory" and "farmhand" people. Men of proletarian origin with a couple of years schooling proclaimed themselves major poets and were backed up in articles in papers such as *Bednota* or *The Workers' Daily*, publicly declaiming their work in factories and all over the countryside. Later many of them realised they were not poets at all and lost themselves amongst the *Konsomol* and Party faithful. The best known of these – Zharov and Utkin – did go on writing, though Mayakovsky considered them both worthless. Utkin died in a plane crash; Zharov gave up poetry and, fat and unkempt, turned up from time to time as chairman of some conference or other.

6

I am not qualified to write about music and painting at this time. I leave that to others. But I must say something about the cinema, both private and state-owned. On Arbat there were the *Pervy Sovkino* (First Sovkino) and two others, *Carnival* and *Ars*; the latter was the cheapest and the tickets were unnumbered; when the doors opened everyone rushed forward to get the best seats. Zoshchenko wrote a funny story about these stampedes. On Strastnaya Square, there was the *Chat Noir*, on Triumfalnaya Street, the *Aquarium*. On Bolshoy Nikitskaya, the main hall of the Conservatory was turned into a cinema, the *Collosus*, where the portraits of great composers seemed to look down on the cinema audience with disapproval. Classical concerts were relegated to the small hall.

Pre-revolutionary films starring Moszhukhin and Vera Kholodnaya were shown, as well as crude, boring propaganda films featuring enraged White guards and vicious capitalists. American films, with their cowboys and kidnapped beauties or detective stories, were the most popular – every seat would be taken. These were always in six instalments, and each instalment broke off at its most exciting point. One such film I remember clearly; a girl is running along the top of a moving train pursued by gangsters shooting at her; she reaches the very last coach; there is no saving her. At that point a title appears "End of instalment two. Instalment three such and such a date". On go the lights in the hall. Then the whole week is spent wondering how on earth the girl is going to be saved. The answer is that a scientist just happens to fly past in his balloon, lowers a rope and rescues the girl. Then in instalment four she has been caught again by the bandits, lowered into a well, tied to a metal stanchion. The water rises up to her chin – and again the title "End of instalment four". And again you have to hunt about for the money to come back the following week. The age of the great silent films, both Russian and foreign, came later on.

Let me end this chapter with some words about religion. At this period, many people not only lost their faith but also actively reviled it, becoming virulent atheists. It was fashionable to pour scorn on all believers. In the revolution countless people lost their homes, their work, their very future, and lived in fear of the terror unleashed by both Whites and Reds – yet there was a return to thinking about the fate of Russia, and a return to faith in God as the salvation of their country and their souls. The churches not only continued with their regular services, but also celebrated the calendar of saints and the seasons of fasting. They were packed with praying people. In later chapters, I shall come back to the subject of religion and the destruction of the monasteries and churches. I was a personal witness to the terrible and tragic fate of the Orthodox church and the persecution of the priesthood.

7. Our Life in Moscow

At first, as the flat we were supposed to have was not yet free, we went to live in an old house on Spiridinovka Street, No. 18, that had previously belonged to distant relatives of ours, the Samarins. This two-story house, instead of housing a single family, was now packed to the eaves with residents who ranged from being on good terms with each other to being at daggers drawn. From the hall a creaking staircase with broken banisters led up to a landing on which stood kitchen tables full of crockery and pans, and that indispensable instrument of all Moscow apartments, the primus stove, which seemed to be on the go all day long. Three doors opened off this landing. In a tiny room there lived an old bachelor, a retired Captain Polozov, whom Aunt Sasha had once fancied. Since the revolution he had lost weight and his beard and whiskers were sparse. His later fate was sad; in the mid-1920s he was arrested and exiled to the Komi Republic, where he died. Behind the second door lived a quiet medical student, a girl who now and again brought home pieces of human bodies, which gave off a sharpish odour that blended with the cooking smells and the stink of the primus stove. The toilet was on the ground floor, and seemed always to be occupied. The third door opened onto a large room which had an ottoman big enough for four people and a variety of furniture, both intact and broken, filled the available space. There were also pieces of china and bronze and faded portraits of Samarin ancestors. The roof of the ground floor was outside the window, so that in good weather you could step out on to it.

Two doors led out of this room. Through one there was a small room with two beds, a chest of drawers and a cupboard, and everything neat and clean. The other door opened onto a larger room, also with two beds, but covered by messy blankets and filthy pillowcases and sheets. This room was filled with dilapidated old furniture and piles of all sorts of antiques that had been brought in here from the rest of the Samarin house. There was a layer of dust on everything and the room stank of tobacco smoke and urine. This latter smell came from a sculptured bust of the Empress Volkhova by Vrubel that was jammed upside down in an old armchair and served – antiquarians will be horrified – as a pisspot.

The small, neatly kept bedroom was where my sister Lina and the Bobrinsky girls slept, was nicknamed "Paradise". The first room through which one passed was called "Purgatory" and was occupied by my sister Lina and brother Vladimir, who had left his post after the last expedition to the Sea of Karsk. Any male guests who spent the night also slept in that room. The smelly room was "Hell", and belonged to two eighteen-year-old friends, Yusha Samarin and Misha Olsufyev, who was the son of a country neighbour of ours, Count Yuri Alexandrovich Olsufyev.

The house was a peculiar community, of which there were many in Moscow in those years, bringing together people whose ideas ranged from the far left to the most ascetic or religious. This Spiridonovka community was famous for its fairly wild hospitality. Lina and both the Bobrinsky sisters were working at the ARA, whose office was also on Spiridonovka Street. Yusha and Misha were studying at the university in the faculty of history and philosophy. My sister Sonya had just failed her political knowledge exam in the natural history department of the university, so now father was desperately trying to find somewhere else where she could continue her studies.

We all ate together. The girls brought home American rations. A helpful nearby baker would exchange a pound of flour for a three-quarter-pound loaf of white bread. Yusha, recognised as in a sense the owner of the house, now and again pulled out some statue or other *objet d'art*, took it to the antiquarian shops and donated the proceeds to the common housekeeping funds. Lina was both cook and a kind of prefect. Yusha ran errands to the baker's, but Misha Olsyufev played the idle gentleman, although he did now and again bring provisions from Sergiyev Posad, where his parents were then living.

There were many visitors, mostly men. Our second cousin, Georgy Osorgin, just freed from Butyrka prison and living quite near, was one of them. Following a successful financial transaction he got hold of some wine, there being no vodka available, and organised a lively party. He even took guests out to the pub and to the Prague restaurant, paying for them to ride on the notorious fast sleighs, *likhachi*, probably to impress Lina, who he was courting. Someone made up an amusing bit of doggerel:

> *Spiridonovsky Lina*
> *Struck by Cupid's arrow*
> *Truly loves Georgy*
> *And his tunic so snowy*
> *Officer's boots so shiny*
> *And his golden whiskers*

Mika Morozov also visited us; he had graduated from university but had not yet made his name as a Shakespearean scholar. Paying no attention to his surroundings, he spent all his time writing complicated poetry. Once he read us a poem he had written about the Archangel Michael; none of us understood a word. He, too, was courting Lina. One of the university lecturers, Fedya Petrovsky, also used to come round, a kindly, gregarious and witty man who had once upon a time courted both Aunts Eli and Tania Golitsyn, and had now turned his attention to Lina, Alka Bobrinskaya and the other girls. His advances were spurned by one and all.

My second cousin once removed, Artemi Rayevsky, was also a visitor to Spiridonovka Street, but he was too shy and reserved to flirt with any of the girls. He had a rich baritone voice and used to sing romantic songs to the accompaniment of the harmonica. The house was filled with such a powerful atmosphere of tender sensuality that it seemed impossible not to be attracted to the pretty girls living there. Someone composed this couplet about Artemi:

> *Artamon, Artamosh*
> *Who is your love here?*

An elderly painter who lived quite near us on Sadovo-Kudrinsky Street, Pyotr Petrovich Konchalovsky, appeared on the scene. He was a very talented painter of still lives, portraits and flowers, and also a charming man, full of life, who loved mixing with young people. His pleasure in their company was wholehearted and genuine, but he also had his eye on Vladimir as a possible husband for his daughter Natalya. Vladimir, however, had already pledged his heart elsewhere.

My parents were living elsewhere at this point. Lina arranged for me to sleep in "Hell" on two armchairs and a chair pushed together. Misha Olsufyev totally ignored me, which made me dislike him intensely. Yusha Samarin, however, immediately took me under his wing, asked me all about my life and accompanied me on walks around the local streets. He told me that I reminded him of his younger brother, also called Seryozha, who had died in childhood. I loved everything about Yusha, his smile, his lively, rather small eyes and his wonderful voice. Everyone who met him invariably said the same thing, "What a nice young man!"

Then mother announced that I would be accepted in the sixth class in the former Alferov Girls' School provided that I passed some rather difficult exams, particularly in maths. The atmosphere in "Hell" was not conducive to study, and mother was busy with other matters, including visiting her parents, whom she had not seen for a long time, so I had to sort all this out by myself. Yusha cleared an old marble table for me to lay out my books and tried to help me with the maths, but he too had difficulty solving the problems. My sisters were far too busy to be of any help. It meant all I had to fall back on was prayer. I went on repeating the line "Prophet Nahum, Sit on my brain-um!" Mother also took me to the Iversk Chapel next to the History Museum where rows of beggars lined up on either side of the entrance and the queue waiting before the miraculous icon of the Virgin Mary moved only slowly forward. The Virgin's eyes looked down on me with reproachful sadness, as if saying, "I'll try to help you". We knelt, bowed low and went out past the beggars, handing out thousand rouble notes, then worth a fraction of a kopek. My spirits were somewhat raised, and I continued to repeat "Prophet Nahum, sit on my brain-um".

My sisters were madly busy preparing for a grand ball, to which all the young ladies had been told to come wearing white. Where and how they managed to find tulle curtains, old lace and even plain white cloth, I have no idea, but find these they did, and while I sat cudgelling my brains in "Hell", they were busily cutting and sewing in "Purgatory". On the eve of the ball I heard Lina come in and call me "Seryozha, come here." Shoving aside my books, I came out of my room and saw a lady with greying hair, wearing a plain dress and white panama-style hat. She also worked with the ARA and had accompanied Lina home. Her figure, stance and appearance were very grand, and I instantly described her to myself as regal. She looked at me with her large eyes, long-lashed and smiling. I had never before kissed a lady's hand and this lady who was looking at me in such a welcoming way was holding out her hand, not to shake mine, but to receive the touch of my lips. With a shock, I realised I would have to bow low and plant my lips at the base of her fingers.

"So this is Seryozha!" she exclaimed. "I do hope you'll come to the ball?"

I quivered with happiness. I had of course realised that this gracious and queenly lady was Countess Elena Bogdanovna Sheremetyeva, the mother of Vladimir's betrothed and of my new friend, Petrusha, and of his sister Marika, who had been much more on my mind than my forthcoming exams. Countess Sheremetyeva was the older sister of Aunt Tyosa Lopukhina. I was overjoyed to know that now I would be able to watch the dancing at the ball; it was also a triumph over my sisters, who had kept on telling me that a youth like me would never be invited. I could stick my tongue out at them. Yusha, too, was triumphant as for days he had being saying I should be invited to the ball.

2

Before the revolution, the Sheremetyev family owned all the houses in the street where they lived. Apart from the big eighteenth-century house on the corner of Vozdvizhenskaya Street, these houses were divided into elegant apartments, which were let. In later years, disgraced leaders such as Molotov, Khrushchev, Semashko and Krizhanovsky lived there. In the big corner house, in a set of rooms on the third floor, lived three widows and their families: Countess Elena Bogdanovna Sheremetyeva, otherwise known as Aunt Lilya, and two of her sisters-in-law: Anna Sergeievna Saburova and Countess Maria Sergeievna Gudovicha, otherwise known as Aunts Anna and Maria. These two sisters-in-law, however, behaved very humbly. Their husbands, Alexander Saburov, formerly governor of St Petersburg, and Count Alexander Gudovich, a former provincial governor, had been arrested. The family had tried in vain to discover where they were being held; their wives were convinced they were still alive. Deeply religious, they were constantly in church, praying for the well-being of their two Alexanders. Rarely did they receive anyone. Like Aunt Lilya, they were regal in appearance, but there the resemblance ended. Their complexions were pale, like fine china, and they were silent and sad, aloof from the busy world around them. Only occasionally would you bump into them in a corridor, but even then they would pass you by in silence.

There were also plenty of young people around, as the many sons and daughters all had friends and the apartments were large and roomy. Yet whereas the fun and games at our place in Spiridonovsky were spontaneous and lighthearted, at Vosdvizhenskaya youthful high spirits were restrained by an awareness of etiquette and also by the premonition that these high spirits were doomed, as if we were all participating in the "feast before famine".

The Sheremetyev house had a fine oval room from which one could see the walls of the Kremlin and the faded gilt cupolas of the churches with their towers still decorated with two-headed eagles. Once Aunt Lilya took me to the window, pointed at the cupolas and towers and said, "Look, they're the only things the Bolsheviks haven't soiled. Just remember that." In our flat we had a number of antiques, some of them even valuable. At the Sheremetyev house, however, there were some real masterpieces. I remember a large painting by Rembrandt, *Jesus with Mary and Martha*. Now it is in the museum of figurative art, which was then called the Alexander III Museum, though today the experts attribute it to the studio of Rembrandt. There were two Dutch still-life paintings, one of them of a goblet of red wine, a dagger and a dead bird, which I used in my story *Forty Explorers*. There were precious carpets and tapestries, fine mahogany furniture and a great deal of valuable china and glass.

One room remained permanently locked up. It was assumed to be full of treasures and the key was held by Aunt Lilya's brother-in-law, Count Pavel Sergeievich Sheremetyev. Until the revolution he had been a man of leftish convictions, who lived alone and did not receive an allowance from the family. Eventually he became the director of the museum in the former Sheremetyev palace of Ostafyev close to Moscow, which since the eighteenth century had housed family furniture and ancestral portraits, as well as the papers of a grandfather of Pavel Sergeievich, the poet Vyazemsky. Among them were letters from Pushkin as well as the waistcoat, pierced with a bullet hole, worn by the poet in his fatal duel with d'Antes. In 1929, after the abolition of the Ostafyev Museum, Pavel Sergeievich joined the staff of the museum at Ostankino, living out the rest of his life in a tower of the Novodevichy monastery. He survived thanks to his hermetic style of life and to the protection of Commissar Lunacharsky, who had known him for many years.

3

I was at my first ever ball. Entering the huge ballroom, lit by a massive bronze chandelier, I hid myself away on the corner of a long divan. Mother and Aunt Lilya, together with some other ladies, all clutching their lorgnettes, were nearby. The young people were clustered in groups, moving about, sometimes going outside to smoke, chattering and telling each other jokes. When a new arrival came through the door they rushed over to greet him or kiss her hand. If she was an old maid, they just bowed to her. None of the young men wore evening clothes or dinner jackets, indeed virtually none of them even wore jackets or white shirts and ties. Since most young men did not own such items it had been agreed that they would all come in their everyday clothes. Some wore trenchcoats, some hunting jackets, there were Russian shirts and military jackets, velvet coats and plain cotton shirts. There was also a wide range of footwear, from top boots to oriental slippers. My brother Vladimir had donned his sailor's uniform.

The young ladies, chattering and giggling, were crowded together along the walls in their white dresses, though none of the dresses were as low-cut as in Pushkin's time. Three more young ladies now came in. Two of them were very alike, the one older and taller, the other younger and petite; the third lady was less striking. Suddenly the atmosphere in the ballroom brightened up with the arrival of these Sheremetyev eyes and smiling lips. The old men did not stand up, as in Homer – there were in any case only two or three old men – but the young broke off their chatter and rushed forward to greet the newcomers. These were the two Sheremetyev sisters, Elena and Natalya, and their Gudovich cousin, Marinka. It took me a moment to know which was Elena – until Vladimir went forward to her, and she turned an adoring smile on him.

The room was filling up quickly. The music master, the only man in full evening dress, sat down to the piano and played a waltz, and the couples started to whirl and spin about so fast that even I began to feel giddy. Suddenly the music stopped. Into the middle of the room there stepped a tiny, pink-faced and extremely elegant little gentleman with a delicate white goatee, who wore a military dress jacket with the faded marks of torn-off epaulettes, baggy blue trousers whose gold braid had also been ripped off, and shining patent leather shoes. This old gentleman looked over at Aunt Lilya and she made a sign with her handkerchief which he acknowledged by a little bow, then lifted his hand high in the air. In a surprisingly loud voice for such a small man he cried out, "*Les cavaliers, engagez vos dames pour la première contredance!*" This old man, General Vladimir Sergeievich Gadon, adjutant to Grand Prince Sergei Alexandrovich, was the famous master of ceremonies of the grandest balls in St Petersburg and Moscow. Already famous in the late nineteenth century, my grandmother could remember how she had danced to his orders.

The dance he had called was a quadrille. It has long been out of fashion, so I will try to describe it. Three quadrilles always had to be danced. For the first, the son of the house was obliged to invite the least attractive of, say, his sister's girl friends. For the second he could invite someone like a cousin. It was only in the third that he could dance with his beloved. This was the usual, but not invariable order; sometimes the order was only agreed at the beginning of the ball. Elena Sheremetyev always danced her second quadrille with Yusha Samarin, who was madly in love with her but obviously took second place to his more fortunate friend, my brother Vladimir, who had the third quadrille.

The dancers drew up in two long lines facing each other. At a signal from General Gadon the pianist played a march, or a waltz, or a galop and then again a march, but more slowly. A lot of different figures were danced, all called out in French, "*Les cavaliers, avancez, les cavaliers reculez, les cavaliers changez vos dames, chaine chinoise, figure corbeille, chaine simple, valse, galop par toute la salle!*" Everyone changed places, the men lost their ladies, a dress got torn or someone fell, and Gadon would shout out, "*A vos places et à vos dames!*" So once again the whole melee would burst into life and the dance would get faster and faster until all were more or less back in their places. Then came Gadon's cry, "*Cavaliers, remerciez vos dames!*" at which the men bowed low to their partners.

After each quadrille there was a rush for the tables with their plates of cheese and sausage sandwiches and bowls full of apples. Homemade fruit drink was there in quantity, as well as jugs of a white wine punch, sweetened with sugar and pieces of fruit. The men tended to disappear into a mysterious little room where a bottle or two of spirits were sampled. In those days, neither vodka or cognac were on sale; the newspapers were always full of accusations of how tsarist Russia had made drunkards of the people. Waltzes followed the quadrilles, and then there were more quadrilles. No foxtrot was played. The Americans who had come to Russia had brought the foxtrot with them and Russian girls had learned it in secret, but all respectable mothers shuddered at the thought of it. They agreed with the newspapers that saw in the foxtrot a sick manifestation of degenerate capitalism. Sitting in my corner I was overwhelmed by all these new sensations, but there was also a tiny voice that whispered to me – "And what about that calculation about water flowing out of a pool?" After the second quadrille I was overcome with drowsiness. Mother took me home.

How did all these people who were at the ball, all these "former people", get by in life? Some of them lived by selling off their remaining antiques. So as to be able to come to this sort of ball, bringing a contribution of food or wine, they would have taken a Sèvres dish or a bronze chandelier to the dealers in Sukharovka. But as for everyday life, most of them had jobs or were students at the university or some other academic institution. Some of their jobs were quite unusual; for instance, the four Lvov brothers rented a pottery kiln in the village of Gzhel, eighty kilometres along the road to Kazan, and ran a successful business. Elena Sheremetyeva set off daily to a flat in Nikolo-Pevskov Street where she picked up a tray of bakeries for delivery to a confectioner's shop in Stoleshnikov Street. I have already described the way Georgy Osorgin earned a living. Many of those with foreign languages worked for foreigners, as did Aunt Lilya, my sister Lina and both Bobrinsky girls. Artemi Rayevsky worked for an English shipping company. Oleg Volkov worked for the Lenya Goldfields concession. Petya Istomin had a job at the Nansen Misson and many ladies taught French to the children of NEP businessmen. Elena's elder brother, Nikolai, was a student at the Conservatory and later became a member of the orchestra at the Vakhtangov Theatre. In short, everyone had something to do.

What fate awaited the dancers at the ball? I once made a list and was horrified by the story it told. The majority of those young men and women, but especially the young men, who had enjoyed themselves in such a carefree way at the ball, later ended up in the camps. Some died, some came back after the torments of hell, some left the country. At this stage I shall not mention all their names, but will describe the fate of some of these in later chapters. Many were arrested just because of their titles. Avenir Vadbolsky, for example, was a madcap, poetaster youth, who came from one of the oldest princely lines, the Belozorsky-Ryurikoviches. His father was just a junior officer, however, and owned nothing more than a tiny estate – yet his son, inheriting his title, suffered for it.

There were titled people who escaped imprisonment or death. How Nikolai Sheremetyev survived I will come to in due course. All the Counts Tolstoy, whether relatives of the great writer or not, survived. Many were saved because they did not show themselves too much in public or at the sort of ball I have described, and did not associate with foreigners. My uncle, Vladimir Vladimirovich Golitsyn, was never arrested. Nor did Count Nikolai Alexeievich Bobrinsky, a professor at Moscow University, ever serve a term in the camps; but then he spent the most terrible years of the 1930s in Tashkent. Vasily Alexeievich Golitsyn, cousin of the Gudoviches, who lived in Tbilisi, was never touched – the authorities were too busy arresting the entire Georgian nobility. Prince Vladimir Nokolayevich Dolgorukov survived; he became a writer under the pseudonym of Vladimir Vladimirov. He was protected by Gorky and published several books about Captain Cook and others. After Gorky's death he was blacklisted, like Bulgakov, only writing "for my desk drawer" (i.e. in secret), earning a living by typing the work of other writers. When the blacklist was abolished, he was published once more, writing two very good historical novels. Yusha Samarin, a member of one of the oldest families, also survived, in part because he left Moscow in good time.

I have written enough for the time being on this blood-spattered subject.

4

Two days after the ball mother took me to Leo Tolstoy School No. 11 in Khamovnichesky district, abbreviated to "Khamraiyon", which before the revolution was the Alferov Girls Gymnasium. It was at 7 Rostov Street near Plyushchika and was the school that my older sisters had attended. They had left behind them a reputation for good work and behaviour, but when I went to take my exams I did not see how this would help me and I arrived, still repeating to myself those words about the prophet Nahum sitting in my brain-um. I was well prepared in Russian, history, geography, French and German. Regardless of my sisters' reputation, I would have passed in those subjects. Actually, the teachers all began happily to reminisce about Lina and Sonya, to praise them and to ask what they were doing now. After this I was asked only a few questions. The stumbling block here was my knowledge of natural science, which I had not studied at all. I said that humans had twenty ribs and that they were joined both back and front by two vertebrae. And when I was asked for the two types of blood group, to the teacher's surprise I said black and righteous, and when I was asked to explain this I quoted a well-known line from Pushkin – "You cannot wash away your black blood with the righteous blood of the poet." I was accepted for this subject on condition that I passed a further test in a month's time, which is what happened.

Now it was time for the final exam, the dreaded maths. I was shaking with fear. I had heard that the maths teacher was new and so would not have known my sisters. He came in, a tall man with a goatee and glinting spectacles. As one by one boys and girls went in for their interviews, I visualized him in the role of executioner. Finally, it was my turn. I was so nervous I was hardly able walk in and place my exam paper on the table in front of him.

"Sit down," he said without looking up.

I sat on the edge of the chair. He read my paper and looked over at me. I wanted to sink through the floor. But the question he asked me was the last question I was expecting.

"Tell me, the Vladimir Golitsyn who was at the school on Starokonyushny, is he a relative of yours?"

"My older brother!" I cried out in delight.

"He was a good boy, although not always sure of his maths, and his behaviour was . . . Tell me, what's he doing now?"

And now I saw that his eyes were not at all vicious – they were shining with kindness. I poured out an account of my brother; that he was a talented artist and had sailed with a polar expedition, and had helped build the famous ship *Perseus*. I told him about the ice floes and the "shackleton" boots.

The teacher, whose name was Andrei Isakov, punctuated my description with the occasional, "How interesting."

I was just about to start on Vladimir's coming wedding when a lady teacher came in and said, "Andrei Konstantinovich, you're tormenting the boy, and there's a huge queue outside."

"Yes, yes," he said hastily, "I'm just coming to the last question." And turning to me he asked, "Give me a definition of compound concrete numbers."

I happened to have swotted up on just that question and so was able to reply without hesitation.

"Excellent," he said, and ticked my exam paper.

I rushed out of the room and, paying no attention to the crowd of children with their mothers and aunties, I ran over to my mother shouting out, in a deliberately loud voice, "I've passed!"

Even before the revolution the Alferov Gymnasium for Girls was one of the best schools in Moscow. My sisters had been there, as well as our second cousins, the three Gagarin daughters, the daughters of the singer Shalyapin and the painter Nesterov. Marina Tsvetaeva, the poet, had been a pupil. The gymnasium's teachers were also famous. The pupils not only respected and loved them, but actually worshipped them. Despite the many years that have passed since I was a pupil there, I still remember the teachers who devoted their time and energy to us, not just teaching us, but also helping us to become decent people.

There was Olga Nikolaievna Maslova, our Russian teacher. She was no beauty – she wore a plain steel pince-nez, and had an overly large chin. Day in day out, wearing an old fashioned hat over her piled-up hair, striding along with a masculine gait, she would walk all the way from Antipevsky Street. As she went along, children would come alongside her and engage her in conversation so that by the time she reached school there would be a whole crowd around her. Taking off her coat, she would reveal her invariable old-fashioned dress with wide sleeves. I never had her as a teacher in my class, but if one of our teachers fell ill she willingly took their place. I remember in one of those sessions how she captured our attention by telling us about Maeterlinck, and since then I have always loved his writings.

There were the three Zolotaryovy sisters – Margarita, Lydia and Lyudmilla. The first was the headmistress when I entered the school and directed the plays in which I had a part; the second taught drawing and constantly praised my work; the third I hardly knew as she taught the youngest classes. Antonia Nikolaievna Pashkova also taught the little ones. She was what is now called the deputy director of education – she lived in the school on the first floor and often talked to me about my sisters, which made me swell with pride. Elena Yegorevna Becker was the geography teacher, a clever and lively German with a long nose; this feature made her the butt of many a caricature. She too lived in the school and would often speak to me. Then there was Julia Fedorovna Gertner, the German teacher, who was terrifyingly strict, but at the same time much loved.

There were some teachers like Andrei Konstantinovich, the maths teacher, who had only just joined the staff, but the majority of the staff consisted of "Alferovians" who had known and been loyal to the couple who were the founders of the gymnasium, Alexandra Samsanova and her husband, Alexander Danilovich Alferov. She was the director of the school and he was literature teacher. Today, their names are not to be found in any of the literature devoted to teaching. Nor does one find the name of Vasily Porfirievich Vakhterov (1853–1924), long-time president of the Union of Russian Teachers and author of several anthologies and other school books. When he was invited by Lunacharsky to work in the Narkompros (People's Commission on Education) he refused, saying he could not sit down to work with people whose hands were covered in blood.

This mention of blood undoubtedly referred to the Alferovs, his close colleagues in the field of education. Armed guards came for them in the winter of 1918, and only a few days later horrified Muscovites read their names on a list of people who had been shot – without any investigation or trial. On that same list of victims were the names of many other members of the intelligentsia. A few years later the memory of those others had faded away, whereas the aureola of martyrdom continued to shine brightly around the names of Alexandra Samsonovna and Alexander Danilovich Alferov inside the walls of the gymnasium they had founded. Their spirit was everywhere in the building. I entered the school after their deaths, but I had already heard stories about that noble and innocent couple from my sisters. This posthumous homage was passed on to later generations of students, making a strong bond between old schoolfellows, even of different generations.

The execution of the Alferovs generated a hatred of Soviet rule and methods. Opposition to Soviet rule also came from the Scouts. This movement only reached Russia just before the German war, but it survived through the revolution, attracting adolescents by its romantic image and the exotic names of its companies and platoons, by its badges and emblems, its khaki tunics with big pockets and shorts and the broad hats. The Alferov gymnasium had one such detachment of Scouts. I was hoping to join, but was too late. In my first year, the authorities, on the pretext that the Scouts were a bourgeois organisation, disbanded it. The senior Scouts were greatly angered by this decision. They were deeply imbued with the spirit of Scouting; namely, to do good, help the needy, keep fit and organise interesting gatherings where they practised quasi-military exercises and sporting events.

"How can our organisation be called bourgeois?" they cried indignantly. "We salute with our left hands because our right hands are hard at work!"

They began to meet in secret. In the woods, somewhere along the Kazan road, several hundred Scouts, both boys and girls, would gather together, but the organisers and many of the older Scouts were arrested, including the elder brothers of two of my classmates, Petya Burman and Vasia Ganeshin. They behaved admirably at their interrogation and refused to betray anyone. Many of them were sentenced to terms of imprisonment. There is no record of their numbers; some said two hundred, others four hundred.

5

I only had to go the long way to school from Spiridonovskaya Street for about ten days, as soon we had moved to 16 Eropkinsky Street, where we had five rooms and a hall. This flat belonged to a prominent Moscow intellectual, Vladimir Egorovich Giatsintov, who was director of the Alexander III Museum of the Figurative Arts. He had been allocated a flat in the museum, which meant we could buy his old one. Today, this kind of transaction would be considered illegal, swamped as we are by all kinds of regulations and prohibitions, but in those early days after the revolution, if you had the money you could still buy property.

Our income was very little, but we did have the inheritance my father had received from his cousin, Nadya Golitsyna, in the shape of the Emir of Bokhara's diadem, the strings of pearls, and so on. Not all this treasure was used to purchase the flat; part if it was kept aside for a rainy day. So the Giatsintov family moved out – Vladimir Egorovich, his wife, his son-in-law the artist Mikhail Semyonovich Rodionov, two grandchildren – both girls, Elena and Sofia – and an unmarried daughter, a future "Meritorious Artist of the USSR" Sofia Giatsintova, together with all their furniture – and we moved in. My grandparents' old cook, Mikhail Mironovich Kryuchkov and his wife Pelagea Trofimovna had managed to save some of our furniture from Georgyyevskaya Street; a dining table and chairs, some armchairs and a few pictures, including *The Circumcision of Christ* from the studio of Rembrandt.

It was at this time that, on the basis of a list written, it was said, by Trotsky himself, some seventy professors and their families from Moscow and Petersburg were driven into exile abroad. Among the names on the list were the philosopher Berdyaev, S. Bulgakov, Professors Kizevetter and Novikov of Moscow University, and Professor Ugrimov, President of the Russian Agricultural Society. The flower of the Russian intelligentsia was being expelled. One of the names on the list was a young lecturer at Moscow University, Prince Sergei Evgeniyevich Trubetskoi, our second cousin and son of the well-known philosopher Prince Evgeny Nikolaievich Trubetskoi. Sergei Trubetskoi was in fact in prison and was deported together with his mother, Vera Alexandrovna, and his young sister, Sofia, directly from the prison. They had no time to arrange anything about their possessions, so we took in their furniture and a very fine library, as well as some trunks. We did not know what was in those trunks, though we did have the keys. The library was a large one. There were finely bound editions of the classics, Herzen's complete works, printed abroad, works by the writers now referred to in the Soviet encyclopaedias as "idealists", as well as *Das Kapital* by Marx.[13] There were books with dedications by their authors, such as the writings of Vladimir Solovyov, Sergei Nikolaevich Trubetskoi and other philosophers. Today these books would be very valuable.

Once we had installed this furniture in our new flat, brother Vladimir and I went to 38 Pokrovka Street, which had been our Golitsyn home, and collected the portraits of our ancestors and Tsars, together with oil paintings and watercolours from the eighteenth and nineteenth centuries, all of which had been brought here in 1917 from the Golitsyn estate of Petrovskoye, just outside Moscow, by Uncle Alexander Vladimirovich, and had been looked after for five years by a former family estate manager, a certain Korneyev. We hired a cart, piled all these paintings into it and cheerfully set off for our new home across Moscow.

Vladimir took charge of hanging these pictures in our two best rooms. Since then, over the years, these ancestral portraits have been silent witnesses of many events in the lives of their descendants, both joyful and sad. They have survived ten moves and seen six searches and arrests, one death, six weddings, several baptisms, innumerable festivities, birthday parties, name days, not forgetting just plain drinking sessions.

6

The organisation where my father now worked was called Moskust, an association of various enterprises; two shoe factories and two textile companies based in Moscow, two glassworks in Bryansk, a knitware firm in Tver, a metal workshop in Vladimir and several others. At this stage of the NEP, the government was attempting to organise these nationalised firms into a flexible management structure. Moskust was the brainchild of Trotsky, and therefore under his special protection. It was headed by Kolegayev, formerly a leading Socialist Revolutionary, and the first people's commissar for agriculture, who had joined the Communist Party. He was under the direct patronage of Comrade Trotsky, who even favoured the

---

13. *Alexander Herzen (1812-1870) a major Russian figure in nineteenth century socialist theory and a prolific political writer. Today, his memoirs are probably his most interesting work.*

Moskut offices with a visit. Sadly, the term *tovarishch* (comrade) had lost its noble connotations after the revolution, and began to be coupled with aggressive verbs. More and more one heard phrases such as "the comrades robbed", "the comrades drove out", "the comrades arrested", and so forth. In the press all the leaders had to be referred to by this devalued and now colourless epithet. In our circles we used quite different forms of address; Mr and Mrs, and Ladies and Gentlemen. I remember how proud I felt when I called on someone and the lad who opened the door ran in to his father saying, "Daddy, there's a gentleman here to see you!"

At Moskust my father was employed as an economist and planner, doing the job in his usual meticulous and conscientious way, and was able to suggest ways to improve how the firms were run. His chiefs appreciated his work, but his salary was extremely low. Nominally it seemed huge, increasing steadily from millions to billions, but this was worthless money, and as more than ten people depended on his earnings, we had no choice but to stick to a very strict programme of austerity regarding food, clothing, transport and firewood.

Up from Bogoroditsk came my grandparents, together with Aunt Sasha, Nasenka, Nanny Bush, Lyena and my young sisters Masha and Katya. They brought with them a lot of provisions that cost less in Bogoroditsk, but they also brought the dead bodies of our faithful fowl. It was with a sad heart that I touched the sharp spurs of our cockerel George. We had to eat the birds up quickly, although they were already tasting gamey; it was years before I could eat chicken again.

Father's salary was just not enough for us all. Black bread and carrot tea were our staples; butter and white bread were beyond our means. Sugar was carefully rationed out, soup we made only with the cheapest bones, and for our main course we ate potatoes in their jackets or thin millet gruel seasoned with a teaspoonful of rape oil. Every month, Lina brought home a food parcel from the ARA, but it was not as good as it used to be; instead of good quality bacon there was some sort of fatty substance, instead of rice, maize flour, instead of rich condensed milk, a sort of white liquid. At the gymnasium, lunch was a couple of slices of black bread and one or two boiled potatoes. Only in exceptional circumstances was I allowed money for a tram fare. In church, we were allowed to make a minimal offering – a handful of useless millions. Our money was controlled by Aunt Sasha, who wrote down everything we spent. Father occasionally went over these accounts, usually with a frown on his face.

Mother was able to buy cloth to make clothes at a discount from Moskut's textile factory. The cloth was invariably white, so mother had to dye it herself in a bucket; it usually came out all unevenly coloured or blotchy. An inexpensive seamstress made up the women's dresses. Nowadays, parents try to dress their children as smartly as possible. We children wore a strange variety of clothes. Sister Katya was proud of a pair of soft boots over which she turned down her socks, so that she looked as if she were wearing skates. I wore dancing shoes bought from Moskut at a huge discount, and a blue jacket with brass buttons passed on to me by Alexei Bobrinsky, and which I slowly grew out of over a period of three years. I did not have any underwear at all, simply putting on my jacket and the trousers inherited from brother Vladimir on my bare skin, so that my clothes scratched me.

These trousers were responsible for a humiliating experience. I was running about during one of our school breaks when a boy grabbed me by the seat of my trousers. There was the sound of ripping cloth, and a large part of the garment was torn open. The girls screamed at the sight of something round and pink as I rushed away to the lavatories, where a group of sympathetic boys surrounded me. One of them lent me his overcoat and I made my way home through the streets of Moscow with a burning face. In the evening, mother covered the rent with a big patch of a different colour; I sat by her, doing my homework, wrapped in a blanket.

When the weather turned cold I could no longer wear my dancing shoes and instead had a pair of much-patched *valenky* (felt boots) that were too big for me. These *valenky* caused me all kinds of humiliation. On arrival at school one had to wipe one's footwear completely dry, which meant that for those pupils who were lucky enough to have galoshes, they simply slipped them off and went about in dry shoes. Children wearing felt boots had to wipe the felt soles on a special mat and then, watched by two eagle-eyed janitors, walk across a piece of linoleum at the foot of the stairs. If there was the slightest damp still on our soles, back we would have to go for more lengthy wiping before being allowed upstairs, by which time the school bell would certainly have rung. One consolation was that there was another lad with even worse boots than mine and the son of the school boilerman was dressed even worse than me.

Yusha Samarin passed on to me his old gymnasium overcoat and, instead of the regulation school cap, a huge dark-blue French beret with a red pompom. I immediately tore off the pompom, but still my appearance, even for those times, was pretty awful. In addition to that there were passers-by who treated me as a class enemy, shouting out "Little whippersnapper Lord!" or "Pencil!" Before the revolution gymnasium pupils were nicknamed "pencils" because of their narrow, tapering uniform coats. I thought this nickname very offensive. I was also ashamed of the linen bag with blue edging that my mother had sewn for me to carry my schoolbooks. My classmates said it looked as though I had found it in a toilet. One day, I begged mother to buy me a proper rucksack. Very seriously, she told me that she could buy me one, but then we would not eat for two days.

Where I felt no shame at all was with my school nickname. Teachers and pupils alike all had these, and our school artists drew caricatures of everyone, picking on their salient features – a long nose, bushy hair or their social origins – but all in a charitable spirit. There was a special album for these drawings. My nickname was "Prince" and I was drawn wearing a crown and sitting on a commode with my long legs sticking out. But apart from me there were other titled boys, Count Rostopchin, Prince Kropotkin and Prince Gedroyts, which spared me from feeling that only I stood out because of my origins.

My awful clothes did, however, cause me a lot of pain. When I was in year 8, I was approached by a group of fellow pupils who suggested, very tactfully, that I should ask my parents to buy me some better clothes. When the girls looked at me they tended to frown. Everyone agreed that Shura Karinsky was worse dressed, but then his drunkard father earned very little. I found it very bitter to listen to my friends' comments, and said nothing, but I did talk to my parents. Mother sold some silver spoons, and bought me a more or less decent jacket, trousers and overcoat. To keep their crease, I folded the trousers under my mattress every night.

In a separate room in our flat we had a lodger, a respected widow and former landowner, Elizaveta Alexandrovna Babynina, who had made friends with us from the day we moved in. She would come out of her room, bringing her own sugar, to drink tea with my grandparents and their guests, and they would all talk about the good old days. I got on very well with her and in return for a few million roubles would cart up sacks of wood for her stove. It was Nanny Bush who usually organised the samovar, but now and again she would forget to fill it with water and its metal casing would crack. Nanny Bush also roasted the rye for our 'coffee', though she sometimes forgot the griddle on the stove and then an awful smell would spread around the flat.

We celebrated all birthdays and namesdays, usually inviting friends. For these occasions Nanny Bush always baked a pie made of wetted black bread and raisins which she called a "charlotte". Days before a festivity, she would go to mother and in a trembling voice beg her to ask Aunt Sasha to give her some money out of the family housekeeping funds so that she could buy half a pound of raisins. These "charlottes" tasted heavenly to us. Three years later, when Nanny Bush had yet again caused the samovar to crack, my father, normally a very restrained man, angrily scolded her. She broke into tears, crying out "I'm just a burden to you all." Not long after she announced that she had found a place in an old people's home. Father begged for her forgiveness and we all pleaded with her to stay, but she had made up her mind and left us. She died in 1928. Our whole family attended her funeral.

7

Generally, the same people visited us as had come to Georgyyevskaya Street during "the times of despotism"; pallid-faced old gentlemen and ladies who had lost a lot of weight and whose fur coats looked worn and scraggy. One of these was Prince Volkonsky, a university contemporary of my grandfather's, who taught chemistry at the former Flyorovsky Gymnasium for boys in Merslyokovsky Lane. He had been a simple teacher all his life. Grandfather was very fond of him and the two of them would chat for hours on end. One day somebody complained, saying "A Soviet school and one of the teachers is a prince?" Volkonsky was called in and asked, but in a gentle tone, whether he was a relative of the Decembrist Volkonsky. He need only have answered, "Yes, a relative, he was a cousin twice removed of my grandfather," and he would have been saved. But the foolish, unfortunate man muttered, "Oh, no, I'm of a quite different branch." He was sacked, in spite of close on fifty years of teaching, and died in 1930, probably of hunger.

There was Pyotr Petrovich Konchalovsky, a well-known painter, a big broad-shouldered man with a permanent smile, whose presence would fill our flat with laughter and witty repartee. Grandmother always accompanied him on the piano to the Neapolitan songs he sang in Italian; old and young, we loved to hear him.

Another visitor was Elena Sergeievna Petukhova, the widow of the owner of some ready-made dress shops. She was nicknamed "the Moscow Semiramis" and even in old age kept her great beauty. She lived in her own house in Maly Ekaterinsky lane between Orlinka and Polyanka streets, had four married daughters and a bachelor son, and was a very lively companion. She would always bring my grandparents some sort of confectionery. I could write a great deal about her and her descendants; they were all colourful characters. I must record here that her four sons-in-law, children of the merchant class – Noev, Vishnyakov, Sveshnikov and the fourth, an officer in the Guards, Bulfert – all died in prison camps. Her own son, Nikolai Grigoryevich, remained owner of his home for the rest of his life, though this brought him nothing but worries and financial hardship. After the war he gave shelter to the well-known collector of china and paintings, Vishnevsky. The Petukhov house is now the Tropinin Museum, though today's art historians are silent about the key role played by Nikolai Petukhov in its creation.

There was Countess Anastasia Mikhailovna Baranova – Aunt Nastenka – born Baratynskaya, the granddaughter of the poet Baratynsky's brother. She lived near us in Obukhov Lane. In 1918, her husband Alexander Pavlovich, my mother's uncle, died, and her two sons were arrested; Misha, who was an officer, and Kolya, still at school. They were led away and she never found out what had happened to them. Just like the two Sheremetyev sisters, A. S. Saburov and M.S. Gudovich, she was convinced that her sons were still alive, languishing in some secret prison. She was very affectionate with me, saying that I reminded her of her younger son. She carefully concealed her grief and was both lively and witty, combining two seemingly opposite qualities, piety – she went to church every day – and a love of indecent stories. Whenever she visited us my brother Vladimir would tell her the sort of stories that made her cover her face with her hands and exclaim, "Oh, God, no!"

The supervisor of the house where she had a little room made every effort to drive her out; he claimed she was the widow of an ex-governor of Nizhny Novgorod, although her husband had only been a minor official. The case was continually brought to court. Her great friend, the barrister Orlovsky, always defended her and won, but the supervisor would not give up. Even when Aunt Nastenka agreed a truce with him, he would break his word and return to the attack. Oddly enough, the one thing about her that he never knew was that she was a Countess. In 1934, she emigrated, led a materially difficult life and ended up living in an old people's home. This need not have happened; already in the 1920s literary societies were inviting her along to their meetings as the descendant of the great poet and she would have been assured of a reasonable life.

I could go on and on with this list of our many interesting guests. Some lived out their lives more or less well, many others ended up in exile or the Gulag – for instance, General Gadon, the Imperial "master of the ball" died in the far north, on the banks of the river Vychegda.

The only visits grandfather made were to a merchant's widow, Bakhrushina, in Denezhny Lane; otherwise he only left the flat to walk their dog, Romochka. Grandmother, by contrast, made frequent visits to her friends, either on foot or, if any distance, by tram. As she did not like going out alone, I usually accompanied her. I enjoyed these outings. The people she visited always treated me to food and drink, and I was proud of being given charge of the money for the tram tickets and guiding grandmother around. Once she called on the poet Valery Bryusov, but there I simply sat outside in the hall, so I never got to see this famous poet, who died a little later. I remember a visit to the famous actress, Fedotova, in a street near Pokrovka. She was sitting in a chair, her legs paralysed, surrounded by cats, the walls hung with icons and photographs. I was used to the Soviets being criticised, but Fedotova was filled with deep hatred of them. One of her cats unravelled the wool of grandmother's dress, and Fedotova remarked, "You see, with the Bolsheviks even the cats have become uncontrollable!"

My parents rarely paid visits, and then only at two addresses. They went to Sergei Lvovich Tolstoy's in Bolshoy Levshinsky Lane, to listen to concerts played by well-known musicians. Sergei Lvovich himself was a fine pianist. Their other visit was to Maria Nikolaievna Yuzhina (born Korf) in Palashovsky lane. She was the wife of the actor Alexander Ivanovich; father had been associated with her in his work before the revolution. Yuzhin himself rarely put in an appearance. After his death in 1927, his wife marked each anniversary of his death by holding an evening reception, to which my parents were always invited.

Mother suddenly found herself saddled with a vital job – she had to become the cook for our large family. Our beloved Nasenka was summoned to Tula to look after her brother, Sergei Akimovich, who had been storeman on our estate at Bulchalki. Nasenka said she could see how hard it was for us to make ends meet, and anyway the children were now grown up. She was unshakeable in her decision to go, however much we tried to persuade her to stay. Her departure caused us all great sadness. From Tula she did, however, keep up a regular correspondence with Aunt Sasha. Unexpectedly, she reappeared in our lives in the 1930s.

Her sister's husband, a country schoolteacher, had been arrested. Nasenka had heard that Lenin's widow (known only by her surname, Krupskaya) might help. She got as far as Krupskaya's secretary in the Narkompros (People's Commissariat for Education) but when the secretary heard what Nasenka wanted, she refused to let her get any further. Nasenka threw herself at the woman's feet begging to be allowed to see Lenin's widow; she was convinced Krupskaya was all-powerful. They had to turn her out by force. It was very unlikely that Krupskaya could have helped her at that stage, as her own colleagues were already being sent to the camps, and she herself was probably wondering about her own skin. One day, when I was already a writer, I happened to be in the House of Literature and noticed a pompous and overweight woman, a model of classic Soviet womanhood; it was Krupskaya's former secretary, who had been made a member of the Union of Writers because of her volume of memoirs of Krupskaya. I would surmise that the memoirs made no mention of the many distressed people that woman had turned away from her office.

Our whole family went to church every Sunday. Our parish church was actually Troitsa-on-Zubov, the tallest tent-roofed church in Moscow, but we preferred to go to the eighteenth-century church of Pokrov-on-Levshin, with its white walls and gleaming blue domes, on the corner of Bolshoy and Maly Levshinsky Lanes, even though it was further away. The singing there was better and grandmother knew many of the congregation and could use the opportunity to talk to them after the service. One of these ladies was Madame Naryshkina, a former lady-in-waiting and once considered the most important noblewoman in Moscow. Although eighty-years-old, she walked as straight as a rod, not turning aside for anyone. The whole of old Moscow society went to her funeral.

There was also Princess Sofia Alexandrovna Golitsyna, born Princess Vyazemskaya, the former owner of the estate of Simi in Vladimir province. Her husband, who was of a different branch of the family to ours, had already died before the revolution. Two of her sons had been shot, and the third was to end up in the camps in the 1930s. She survived thanks to gifts of provisions from the peasants on her estate. When in the 1960s I was at a gathering of tourists in Vladimir I met a young girl who had been on a visit to Simi. In her diary of that trip she had written – "Two old women were telling me about Sofia Alexandrovna, their former mistress, how she was not at all an exploiting landowner, had built a school with her own money and if a peasant lost a cow she would give them a new one from her own herd."

At the church of Pokrov there was an unusual young deacon, who had deliberately chosen this lowly rank – Sergei Sergeievich Tolstoy. He sang the responses in a rather light but expressive voice. Later he gave up the diaconate, becoming a teacher of English. Tolstoy's descendants and the staff of the Tolstoy Museum are notably reluctant to mention those years in the life of the great writer's grandson.

8

Let me now come back to our family. About two months after we had moved in to Eropkinsky we were visited by the building management committee. After carefully measuring every nook and cranny of our flat they announced that we had too much space and must give up a room. My father protested against this decision and wrote a complaint, but he was then threatened with more drastic steps, even being warned that they might bring up our right to be here at all. My grandparents' room was now taken over by a young man called Adamovich. At first we took him to be a Bolshevik. He worked as an accountant somewhere, had sheep-like eyes and behaved very quietly, but then one day he hung over his bed a large portrait of a beautiful woman in a ball-gown, explaining that she was his grandmother, a Polish lady, Countess Yablonovskaya. Immediately, we realised he was no Bolshevik, but one of us, and began to invite him to tea in the evenings.

My father's younger brother, Vladimir Vladimirovich (Uncle Vovik) also came from Liven to move in with us, with his wife and three children – their son Sasha, a year and a half older than me, daughter Elena, who was my age, and little Olya. It was a very tight squeeze. I was moved into the women's room and, under Aunt Sasha's watchful eye, had to sleep in a cupboard, which was wide enough for me though my feet stuck out. During the night, the door of the cupboard was kept open so that I did not suffocate. I must have slept like this, under hanging skirts and dresses, for about three months. Then Uncle Vovik and his family found a flat in the basement of a house on Khlebnoy Lane, which they bought with the remains of Aunt Nadya Golitsyna's legacy of valuables. Living with us they had, of course, paid nothing for their food, but on leaving they gave us two sacks of millet they had brought from Liven. Not long after they left, mother read us her story *A Cook's Grief, or A Tale of Millet*. It described how she had cooked millet for the family for a whole year, racking her brains to invent new ways of cooking it, and how she dreamed of cooking some other grain – any grain, just not millet. But people kept on giving her sacks of millet . . . Sadly this story was lost in one of our many moves.

Modestly though we all lived, my parents, together with the parents of other children, decided that we must all learn to dance. Where else but in our one big room! So every Saturday around twenty young people, mostly children and grandchildren of relatives, gathered together and were taught to dance by a real ballerina who had failed to get into the Bolshoy ballet company because she was not pretty enough. She taught to the accompaniment of a piano in a dull and rather bored manner. But when she and the pianist had left, merriment and laughter broke out. Grandmother went to the piano and sister Sonya took upon herself the role of mistress of the quadrille, closely imitating General Gadon. *"Les cavaliers, engagez vos dames pour la première dance!"*

Our quadrilles in no way resembled the grand and elegant dances on Vozdvizhenka. Grandmother played nothing slowly. Her galop was so fast our legs ended up shaking with the effort. I have never since heard anything like grandmother's playing for that particular dance. *"Galopant en toutes les directions!"* Sonya would shout out, and the most extraordinary scene would unfold. To quote a poet:

> *The whole hall was shaking*
> *Heels all over banging*

Pairs of dancers raced in every direction, bumping into each other. The girls screamed with excitement. As prescribed by the rules, in the first quadrille I had to ask the person whom my sisters, Sonya and Masha, ordered me to invite. They would come over to me and in an angry whisper, tell me to ask so and so. For the second quadrille, I invited my cousin, Elena Golitsyna. But for the third, I could ask Marika Sheremetyeva.

When our young guests arrived, father and grandfather would slip off to their bedroom. Aunt Nadya Rayevskaya made up a little verse:

> *Sadly grandpa slinks away*
> *Now it's not his place to stay*
> *Daddy also hurries after*
> *Silently from the laughter*

159

And about me she wrote:

> *Be quick and start now*
> *Watch our Sergei mop his brow*
> *As our host's young son*
> *He must dance with everyone*

There were times when our neighbours from below banged loudly on our door and begged us to bounce around less, as they feared for the plaster on their ceiling.

It was this winter that Uncle Vladimir Trubetskoi arrived from Bogoroditsk to try to start a life in Moscow. There were now five children and his job as a kind of repair man in the army was far from enough to keep the family. I suppose it was on this occasion that he brought his music and the libretto of *The Magic Pills* to try and have the musical performed. This was a total failure, as I mentioned earlier.

In spite of the difficulties of life, the increasing cost of living, and the many problems we faced in our school lives, the thoughts of our family, and of the family of Aunt Lilya, the Sheremetyevs, young and old, were very much focused on the romantic engagement and forthcoming marriage of our two young family members, Vladimir and Elena. Their relationship had something poetic about it, which was a delight to us all, but at the same time the older members of the family were seriously worried by their youth and the complete uncertainty as to how they could start an independent life. Vladimir was studying at the institute of art and technology, known by the acronym VHYTEMAS (Union Art Institute), a place typical of the times, which was in fact a collection of studios where established artists taught classes. Vladimir worked in Konchalovsky's studio, even though he was not officially registered there; it was by personal invitation of the master. Konchalovsky favoured Vladimir with more of his time than the other students, correcting and advising him and using his work as an example to the others. In due course some of the young men and women were formally accepted as students, while others were dismissed as incompetent. Vladimir was one of the latter. Konchalovsky protested, saying that Golitsyn was his best student. He was not the only one to make a fuss; so too did the artist Apollolinary Mihailovich Vasnetsov. Father, too, appealed to some of his old friends, hoping they would help him gain access to the important people.

"Well, even if he's super-talented, the fact is, he's the son of a prince," was all the reply they got from the various authorities. "There's no place for princes among Soviet artists."

Vladimir enlisted in the art class at a private studio on Prechistenkaya Street, but this was soon closed down. He now faced a serious dilemma. There was unemployment everywhere and the papers repeatedly urged people to move to the provinces. But Vladimir went daily to the house on Vozdvizhenka where he spent all his time with Elena. He did not want to abandon Moscow, nor did his parents want him to leave. The expulsion of Vladimir from Konchalovsky's studio was the greatest blow our family had suffered. It was the first interdiction placed on us due, as the phrase then went, to our "social origins". I cannot remember how Vladimir took this setback, as he always kept his feelings to himself. My parents, however, were deeply upset. It was a new development for them, this punishment of people for the supposed sins of their fathers.

Vladimir and Elena's love for each other was deepened and strengthened by these challenging circumstances. On the other hand, our parents, together with Elena's mother, Aunt Lilya Sheremetyeva, were trying to postpone the wedding for as long as possible on the pretext of the couple's youth. This state of affairs continued through the winter of 1922. Vladimir's uncertain status meant that he had no income. Someone recommended him to the owner of a confectionery shop who asked my brother to design and paint a cover for boxes of candy. Vladimir worked hard, designing a number of different covers that were all rejected. After a while, Vladimir abandoned the commission; it was obvious the man himself did not know what he wanted. In the spring, the young couple issued their ultimatum; the wedding must take place at the latest by the week after Easter. The parents accepted this in the spirit of "God will help", and "We'll see what happens", and "After all, one can be happy in a hovel." The thirtieth of April was agreed.

The Sheremetyev's parish church was the baroque seventeenth-century Znamenya Bogoroditsy (Sign of the Virgin) still standing behind the University building. It was too small for the number of guests expected however, so instead they chose the Bolshoy Voznesenye (Ascension) between the two Nikitsky streets, where Shalyapin's daughter had been wed, and where the singer himself once read the Gospel. Some people still believe that Pushkin was married there, but the present church was built by Bovais only in 1840 after the old church, where Pushkin was indeed married nine years earlier, had been pulled down.

The wedding of Vladimir and Elena remains one of the most romantic memories of my early youth. My parents and Aunt Lilya had to have several meetings to decide on the guest lists; who was to be invited to the church only, or to the church and the later standing buffet in our flat, or to the church and to the grand dinner in Vozdvizhenka Street in the evening. The organiser of the wedding was an elder of the Sheremetyev parish church and a longtime admirer of Aunt Lilya, Sergei Georgyyevich Pribytkov. At that time he was still a wealthy man, although later, in 1929, he was arrested and exiled. He undertook to cover half the costs of the wedding. The marriage ceremony was conducted by the Sheremetyev family priest, Father Pavel Levashov, who was priest of the church of the Nikitsky Monastery (although the monastery itself had been abolished in the reign of Catherine the Great).

There were ten best men, or grooms, for each of the couple. By rights I should have been first best man for Vladimir, but I was too short to hold the crown above his head when he walked around the analoy. Elena's first best man was her older brother. The one who had dreamed of being first best man was Yusha Samarin, who had always been in love with Elena. His cup of happiness would overflow if he could drive over to her house from the church in a fast sledge, announce the triumphant words "The groom is in the church", hand over her flowers, and then race back with her in the wedding car. So I was paired in fourth place with Petrusha Sheremetyev.

The church was filling up with guests. Grandfather and Nanny Bush arrived by cab, while others came by tram. I had walked. Vladimir, in his sailor jacket and bell-bottomed trousers, his face pale, stood tall and strikingly handsome. The bride arrived, looking beautiful beyond belief. Her appearance, in a long white dress and white jacket decorated with orange flowers, and her huge, dark Sheremetyev eyes shining with happiness, made everyone feel joyful. She came forward on the arm of her surrogate father, the heavily-built, bewhiskered Pribytkov, who looked very like Taras Bulba, Gogol's fictional Cossack leader. Ahead of her stepped a child bursting with the importance of the occasion, her youngest brother Pavlusha, bearing the holy icon. There followed her sisters Natalya and Marika, and Yusha Samarin.

This was my first experience of that most beautiful of church liturgies, the wedding service. The crowd was huge, not only relatives and friends, but also quite a few strangers. I cannot remember all who were present, but I do remember Nanny Bush, her face streaming with tears and quite unable to look at her "incomparable tsar and master" – Vladimir. The crowns were lifted above the heads of bride and groom and the priest led them around the analoy. These were ancient crowns that had belonged to the old church of the Ascension, and had almost certainly been held above the heads of Pushkin and his bride. One by one the crowns were passed on to the second and third best men; then the couple knelt and it was Petrusha's and my turn to lift and hold the crowns above their heads. I was surprised by the weight, and standing on tiptoe had to exert all my strength to keep it up; it felt as though any minute I might let it drop. Finally, the fifth best man took it from me.

The crowd outside in the street trying to get into the church was so big that they were forced to close the doors. At the end of the service, the guests pressed forward to congratulate the couple. I was rewarded by a kiss on the forehead from Elena. The best men opened the church doors and by dint of vigorous pushing through the ever-growing crowd formed a double line to open the way for Vladimir and Elena to pass and reach their car. The crowd gasped in wonder as the couple appeared on the steps and moved slowly forward. This church of the Ascension, much restored, is still there today, and whenever I happen to walk down the alley between the Bolshaya and Malaya Nikitsky streets, I remember that day when the happy couple walked between the great crowd pressing in on either side.

The wedding guests now arrived at Eropkinsky street by car, tram or on foot. As the happy couple climbed the main staircase, dry oat flakes showered down on their heads. Inside everyone had glasses of punch and were tucking into canapés and sandwiches. Every few minutes there would come the cry of "*Gor'ko!*" (bitter), the call that forces the young couple to kiss. The wedding, however, did not pass entirely without incident; someone had forgotten to send an invitation to a very important and pious old lady, a cousin of grandmother Lopukhina, Ekaterina Petrovan Vasilchikova. She was greatly offended and insisted that the young couple should visit her to apologise. They utterly refused to do this, and could not be persuaded to change their minds, so in the end it was mother who went to visit her and took all the blame upon herself.

A selected number of guests moved on to Vozdvizhenka Street. There, in the Sheremetyev house, a long table had been set out for the adults, with a smaller table alongside for the children. There were many toasts. Elena's cousin, Boris Saburov, read out some verses he had composed, and having drunk from his crystal glass, hurled it to the floor where it broke into a thousand pieces. I cannot remember what food we ate, I only remember that suddenly the chatter, louder and livelier with every passing minute, came suddenly to a stop. There was total silence.

Rising to his feet was Vladimir's great friend from Archangelsk, Boris Shergin, son of the shipbuilder and seafarer, who had moved to Moscow to make his way in the world of literature and so had been able to come to Vladimir's wedding as one of the best men. He was young and full of youth's hopes and was certainly much affected by the beauty and poetry of the wedding. Raising his glass, he began –

"Prince Volodimir and Princess Dove-Olena!"

In his slightly rough northern accent he continued with allusions from fairy tales and songs. I can only approximately render his inspiring words. He talked of sailing to Spitzbergen and the Far North, of reaching the great rivers of Siberia and the remote islands of the Arctic, and never meeting anyone so beautiful as "lovely swan Olena". He talked of the happiness of the young couple that lay ahead, and predicted for his friend a hard but successful life as an artist. Finishing, he drank the toast and he, too, smashed his glass on the floor.

At the end of the meal many of us went with the young couple to see them off at Nikolaievsky station in their train to Petrograd, as St Petersburg was now named, where Uncle Nikolai Vladimirovich Golitsyn had offered them the use of a couple of rooms in his flat on Baseyn street. At least for the duration of their honeymoon they intended to set aside any thoughts for the future as they explored the streets, museums and palaces of that beautiful city. Elena's surrogate father had done them splendidly; he had booked them a twin-berth sleeper in the international coach. I was enchanted by its luxury, feeling all the brass handles and nobs and wondering at its fine furniture and tapestry walls. It was like a tiny palace. Elena wore a light grey costume, a gift from our family, Vladimir his dark blue sailor's uniform. The third warning bell rang, final embraces were exchanged, handkerchiefs waved. As the train gathered speed, Petrusha and I raced with it along the platform.

8. Life Continues in Moscow

1

At the end of May 1923, my parents and Aunt Lilya decided to rent a *dacha* (summer cottage). They found that rents in villages close to the city, like Kuntsevo, Krylatsokoe, Kuskovo and Malakhovka, were too high, so they thought of Petrovskoye, once the property of the Golitsyn family. They got to the station at Yudino – now called Perkhushkovo – on the Belorusskaya railway line, and then walked a further eight *versts* through the forest to the village of Znamenskoye, which had also once belonged to our ancestors. There they came to a stop, tired out; there were still three *versts* to go, and then a ferry ride across the river Moskva. It seemed too far to go, but by a stroke of luck, they were offered *dachas* in this very village of Znamenskoye. The grandparents were offered accommodation in the local furniture-maker's house for nothing; he wanted to repay the favours he had received from the family in the past. They had commissioned furniture from him for the Golitsyn house in Georgievsky Lane (some of these pieces are now in the possession of my sisters and my nephew Illarion). Thanks to these orders he had received a lot more work from other gentry in Moscow.

Aunt Lilya's sister, Aunt Nadya – Nadezhda Bogdanov Rayevskaya – also settled in Znamenskoye with her two daughters. Her husband, Alexander Alexandrovich, Uncle Shurik, a bank employee, now came with my father for the weekends, bringing various provisions with them from the city. Milk, potatoes and bread we could buy locally, though to economise we rarely bought eggs. The water supply was a problem, as the village wells, which were very deep, had been spoiled and the villagers could not agree to share the cost of repairs. The richer peasants who owned horses could fill up their barrels in the River Moskva, but the rest had to carry water in buckets on a yoke. We bought two buckets of water a day for a million roubles. The shortage of water made our ablution-loving Aunt Sasha very unhappy.

165

At that time the water of the river Moscow was crystal clear, clearer than anything found on earth today. Fish abounded. The village lads caught hundreds of gudgeon a day, whilst experienced fishermen, using live bait, were able to catch pike and perch, and sometimes even rarer fish. These fish, though, were far too dear for us; they were taken to Archangelskoye for Comrade Trotsky's kitchen, as well as to Zubalovo, the former estate of an Armenian millionaire that was protected by a brick wall not much lower than the Kremlin's walls. Stalin was to live here later on but at this point, Kamenev was in residence.

Petrusha Sheremetyev and I tried our hand at fishing but without the proper hook, line and sinker we could never catch a thing, and soon gave up. It was also a very wet summer, which often made it impossible to think of playing or swimming. Mother read *War and Peace* aloud to my sister Masha and me. I can remember listening enthralled. When I think back over our time in Znamenskoye, I can still feel the delight as every single page of that great book was turned and we followed the destinies of its many characters. Crucial to that memory is the sound and tone of mother's voice.

2

I remember a visit to Izmalkovo, the estate of the Samarin family, not far from station No. 20 – which was just a platform on the Belorusskaya line. It is now called Bakovko. There on the banks of a lake, formed by damming the river Setun, stood a very stylish old house with two wings and a colonnaded porch. At that time, three families were living there. Two of them were related, the Osorgins and Komarovskys, and the third were the Istomins. Petrusha and I had been invited there to celebrate the birthday of Sergei Istomin, who was our age. It was our first ever journey alone, though I had been at the Istomin's in Izmalkovo the winter before. The family had heard the no doubt exaggerated report that I was a very well-read and sensible lad and had wanted me to get to know their son.

The house is still standing and is now a children's sanatorium. There were a couple of stone lions in front of the columned porch. The three families in occupation created a kind of miraculous community at this period, already five years after the revolution. Later, I will write about the Osorgins, whose friendship and shared destiny linked our families closely together. The second family in Izmalkovo were the Counts Komarovsky. There was Vladimir Alexeievich, a talented painter with his own style of portrait painting, who also decorated churches. He perished in the camps in the 1930s. His wife, Varvara Fyodorovna, born Samarin, was our second cousin.

The third family were the Istomins – Pyotr Vladimirovich, his wife Sofia Ivanovna and their two children, Sergei and Ksana. The father had served as adjutant to Grand Prince Nikolai Nikolaievich and struck me as being a man with very firm principles. Just like my second cousin, Georgy Osorgin, he had refused to work for Soviet organisations, instead becoming a broker who, for a fixed percentage, sold valuables and fine objects to the newly rich NEPmen and their families. I immediately became friends with his son Sergei and, apparently meeting with his parents' approval, I began to spend a lot of time with him.

The atmosphere at Izmalkovo was imbued with a sense of poetry, inner well-being and memories of the past. All three families were deeply pious, attending long church services to their very end and keeping all the fast days. Their children were also taken to church, made to fast, and were educated by their parents at home rather than being sent to Soviet schools. So they finished their schooling without any official certificates. There were quite a few such families, whose children were to suffer many vicissitudes thanks to this absence of official graduation papers.

Sergei Istomin resembled his father in being a person of principle. He was devout and in his own way honourable and I saw him as a true knight. At the same time he had a scabrous turn of mind, over-whelming me with a string of dirty stories, songs and poems, which I learned by heart, soaking them up like a sponge. His parents never for a moment knew of this side of their son's character. On that summer day, Petrusha and I found ourselves amongst friends and relatives of all ages and had a wonderful time, singing and eating and playing all kinds of games.

The three families in that house were protected by their "tame" communist, a certain Muranov, the grandson of one of the Samarin's former serfs, who before the revolution had been a deputy in the first Duma (National Assembly) and after the revolution was director of the Moscow Land office. Then an article appeared in the *Workers' Gazette* under the heading 'They do not fear heavenly thunder, and earthly thunder is in their hands', angrily denouncing the former 'exploiting landowners' who, under someone's protection and five years after the revolution, were still attending church, teaching their children religion and living in half the house, while orphaned and homeless children were crowded together in the other half. Within two months all three families had been evicted. The Osorgins and Komarovskys moved to somewhere in the neighbourhood; the Istomins settled in the monastery town of Sergiyev Posad.

3

Quite unexpectedly, Uncle Vladimir Sergeievich Trubetskoi arrived in Znamenskoye. That summer he had been trying to find a post as a musician in one of the Moscow orchestras, but without success, not because of his title or officer's rank but simply because there was no position open. He was not a man to be cast down by failure and spent his time with us in a very cheerful mood. He was in funds, having sold a sculpture, *Boys*, by his uncle Paolo Trubetskoi, for a fair sum of money. This piece, the joined curly heads of two boys – himself and his elder brother Nikolai – is now in the Russian Museum in Leningrad.

Some organisation or other had been clearing tree stumps by blasting in an area near the village. The dynamiters had carelessly left tubes of dark brown explosive and coils of fuses lying around. Petrusha and I noticed this careless oversight and mentioned it to Uncle Vladimir, which led him to plot something which would be utterly unbelievable today. Having collected some of these materials, he made five home-made little bombs similar to the ones the anarchists used to assassinate Alexander II – old tins stuffed with the explosive, and with a length of fuse sticking out through a hole, the hole being sealed with church candlewax. We then discussed our plans, biding our time whilst rain kept us indoors. Then, with our deadly devices in a sack, we headed for the river Moskva to try our luck at stunning fish, gloriously imagining staggering home with bags full of pike and perch and other rare fish.

Uncle Vladimir tied a stone to one of the bombs, lit the fuse and, holding the device above his head whilst the fuse consumed itself, threw it as far as he could into the river. Holding our breaths we watched the bubbles and smoke rising to the surface before there came a muffled explosion and a column of water shot up. We leaped into the water and collected three stunned little bleak. We threw the other bombs into different places with the same result. Had we carried out this operation ten years later, what a juicy case it would have made for the OGPU. Not only would they have locked us up, but also all our relatives, as well as the dynamiters, their bosses and families. Many would have been the fairy-tale confessions, too.

Whereas on that day, our exploit only evoked the mocking laughter of the villagers.

Petrusha and I followed Uncle Vladimir everywhere. We swam with him, collected mushrooms with him, and followed the tracks of grouse and other wild fowl. He adored nature and infected us with his passion for the countryside. He was a wonderful storyteller, entertaining us with sea stories, tales of hunting and memories of his childhood, which were sometimes slightly obscene, always full of humour or tinged with mystery, overwhelming us with the vividly colourful variety of his experiences. He also told us dirty stories and verse, declaiming the whole of *Luka M**va* (a lascivious tale in verse), the *The Guards' Alphabet* and *A Watermelon Likes to Ripen*. For us boys he became an idol. I thought about how I would astonish my school friends and Sergei Istomin and felt no sense of shame, instead thinking "What a lad I am, eh!"

Yet that summer I was also filled with a sense of purity and adoration of my brother Vladimir and his young wife. Their honeymoon over, they returned to the flat in Eropkinsky and stayed there rather than coming to us in Znamenskoye. On their own in Moscow, they must have been enjoying the absence of the usual family crowd. Eventually, after a few false alarms, occasions when we went down to the station at Usovo to meet them but they failed to arrive, they did finally come, staying in the attic above our grandparents lodgings. The owner of the house probably saw in Vladimir the eventual master of the Golitsyn estate. But Vladimir and Elena did not stay long; perhaps they found the adoring attentions of their younger brothers and sisters too difficult to take.

Uncle Vladimir and his family also left us, settling in a flat in a private home in the Krasyukovka district of Sergiyev Posad. He took a job as a cinema pianist; in the days of the silent film all cinemas had a musical accompaniment to their films and no special talent was needed other than to suit the music to the mood of the film. He was fortunately receiving small transfers of money from abroad from his sister Maria Sergeievna, the wife of the Polish magnate, Khreptovich-Butyenev, and from his brother Nikolai Sergeievich, a world famous academic linguist and member of the Austrian Academy of Sciences. In his free time, Uncle Vladimir would take his gun and go out hunting, his great passion ever since childhood. In the fields and woods with a gun under his arm he could forget the cares and worries of life and the constant lack of money.

At the end of the summer, my cousin Alka Bobrinskaya married Philip Baldwin, her American boss at the ARA. The wedding was in the now-destroyed church of Spiridoniya, and my parents, older sisters and brother Vladimir and his wife were among the guests. Within a few months the ARA was disbanded and the young couple went to live in Florence with Philip's wealthy mother. They had two boys, and lived out their lives in Florence on the income from the mother's capital. This was a time when many aristocratic young ladies married foreigners and left the country for good. It was in a sense how the young, feeling themselves bypassed by events, expressed their feelings. There were more and more frequent cases of young wives seeing their men arrested, then standing endlessly in line at the prisons to pass on provisions, or following their men into exile where they suffered deprivation and inconsolable loneliness, or were themselves arrested, exiled and sent to the camps to die.

4

Father had a fortnight's holiday. The two of us went mushroom picking and he showed me how to find the Boletus mushroom, which did not grow in the Tula district. In the area around Znamenskoye, where later a *dacha* was built for the writer Maxim Gorky, these mushrooms, particularly that wet summer, were abundant. Father took me to see Petrovskoye, crossing the river Moskva by ferry to visit his sister Masha. In the park around the Empire-style house, now well known to all tourists, he showed me the oak tree planted to mark his birth. There were herons' nests in the tops of the trees. The herons have now been completely exterminated. Once upon a time, Tsar Alexei Mikhailovich (who reigned between 1645–76) hunted on this estate. One wing of the house was being used as an orphanage. In the other, a laboratory had been set up to work on developing a smallpox vaccine from horses' blood, and a herd of the creatures wandered freely about the park. Close to the church there was a modest wooden cross over the grave of the last owner of Petrovskoye, Prince Alexander Mikhailovich Golitsyn – Grandfather Sasha.

An ancient doorman, bowing deeply to my father, let us into the cool interior of the church. The beauty of the delicately carved eighteenth century wooden icon frames was very striking. Golden doves in flight, similar to those in one of the side chapels, were painted above the pictures in the iconostasis. Father showed me the dark, almost black Tykhvinsky icon of the Mother of God, dating from the sixteenth century, that was carried by the Lord of Petrovskoye, Ivan Petrovich Prozorovsky, on his military campaigns. Beyond the chapel stood a fine marble sarcophagus on a richly decorated plinth, the last resting place of my great-great-grandfather, Prince Fyodor Nikolaievich Golitsyn, and in the wall behind, under a marble slab, his son, Prince Ivan Fyodorovich.

The sole extant picture of the exterior of the church is to be found in the book *Petrovskoye*, by M.M. Golitsyn. Built in the seventeenth century, with dome and bell chamber, decoratively carved window casings and an external ambulatory, the church was greatly altered in the eighteenth century when the ambulatory was removed, the carved windows planed smooth and the whole building stuccoed over and painted. Today, art historians believe that the original church served as the model for the famous baroque churches, in the style known as "Naryshkin baroque", of Filya and Ubora. This lovely church, with its delicate and beautiful icons and priceless manuscript books, was ruthlessly pulled down – and in just three days, at that – simply because Stalin, hiding away in his Zubalov fortress nearby, happened to mention that he was sick and tired of seeing its dome sticking up through the trees.

5

One day, my sister Lina arrived at Znamenskoye, clearly over-excited. Normally, she rarely visited us while she was still working with the ARA and spent her evenings having a good time with her boyfriends and others. Her sudden arrival put me on the alert, especially as mother began to urge us into bed on the pretext that it was raining and we needed to economise our consumption of paraffin. Aunt Sasha went off to sleep in her quarters and my young sisters and I dutifully lay down to sleep. I pulled the blanket over my head and waited. After a while, mother asked:

"Children, are you asleep?"

I kept silent, as did Masha and Katya.

"They're asleep," mother said. "So tell us, what's happened?"

"Georgy Osorgin has proposed to me, and I've said yes," said Lina.

"A-a-h!" I shouted, as did Masha, who had also sensed that something exciting was in the air; only Katya was actually asleep. The grown-ups hushed us and swore us to secrecy. Later Vladimir told us how Georgy had proposed to Lina when he and Elena were sitting with them in a bar. He described how he had sensed that Georgy was on the point of his declaration of love for Lina, and so Elena and he had pulled away their chairs and turned their attention to the gypsy music.

This former Horse Guards officer, Georgy Osorgin, was our second cousin. The Osorgin family at first reacted coldly to the engagement, considering Lina to be too frivolous. She was religious, but only moderately so, not often going to church, failing to observe fast days, and liking to amuse herself in the evenings at the cinema or the theatre. The Osorgins considered religion to be the most important thing in life. There was also the fact that Georgy's sisters were passionately fond of him and saw his future withdrawal from the family circle as a great sadness. Georgy himself was also very devout. He regularly attended early morning services at the church of St John the Baptist in Starokonyushnaya Street, where he donned a vestment, read the canonical hours and was leader of the choir. Not a trace of this church remains.

Often he would arrive at the church after a night of merrymaking with friends, being entertained by the gypsies and driving about in fast sleighs. His earnings from his percentage of the sales of the *objets d'art* and valuables of "former people" varied greatly. Half would go to his parents and relatives, the other half he squandered just as the officers of the Guards had done in the age of Pushkin. He seemed to me to be a mixture of Prince Andrei in *War and Peace* and Denis Davydov. Lively, impetuous and restless, he was always wanting to be up and away, to be doing something. With his energy, and as a thoroughly honourable man, in another age he would have gone far. What was really astonishing was his combination of deep religiosity with riotous living. No one could remain indifferent to this vivid personality; he was loved by many.

My parents also reacted coldly to the prospect of Lina's marriage. They were apprehensive about Georgy's love of dissipation and his careless attitude to money. He might earn a lot, but he squandered it much too light-heartedly. Georgy swore to my parents that once married he would behave with restraint, and he kept his word. His final spree – the so-called "boys' night out" – took place in his flat on Spiridonov on the eve of the wedding. I do not know whether there were any other girls there, but Lina and two or three girl friends were allowed to come, at the very least. From what Vladimir told me, I know that there were dozens of bottles of wine, a huge bowl of hot punch and other drinks. A gypsy band played for some hours and when they had gone, everyone sang to the accompaniment of a guitar until seven in the morning.

Georgy and Lina were married in the Church of Boris and Gleb on Povarskaya Street on St Pokrov's day. The weather was unusually sunny and clement; no one wore coats. There was a big crowd. I had the honour of being number one groom to the bride, and so the first to raise the crown above her head and follow her round the analoy. Everyone noticed that the bridegroom was much shorter than his bride. Nothing remains of this church either.

A big crowd assembled for the wedding feast at Spiridonov Street. It was not a sit-down meal, but a buffet of sandwiches, snacks, and all sorts of fruit. I quickly stuffed my pockets with juicy pears as a result of which my trousers were soon soaking wet. I tried in vain to get myself a drink, but could only find empty glasses. Then Sergei Istomin showed me the trick. Standing behind the punchbowl and bottles of wine, with a ladle in his hand, was one of the former footmen of the Osorgin family. All you had to do was to go up to him, hold out a glass and tell him the name of the person to whom you were taking the drink. I had just been reading Griboyedov's famous play *Woe from Wit*, and so every time I went up I quoted a different character's name and each time the footman duly filled my glass. Then I slipped off into a dark corridor and there tossed back the wine. I have Yusha Samarin to thank for helping me out into the courtyard and making me stick two fingers down my throat. After I had been thoroughly sick, I went off home, long before the feast was over. When mother scolded me, I promised I would not do it again, but in my heart I felt very proud of myself – had I not roistered just like Georgy?

For their honeymoon the young couple went to Byokhovo, the Polenov's estate on the river Oka. Georgy's best friend and once a fellow-officer in the Guards, Dimitri Vasilyevich Polenov, the son of the famous landscape artist, met them with a carriage and personally drove them the fifteen *versts* from the station of Tarusskaya. Dimitri was madly in love with Georgy's sister Maria, but she thought he was not handsome and, worse than that, came of an inferior family; she turned him down. In fact, he was one of the finest and noblest people I have ever known.

6

Sasha, the son of Uncle Vladimir Vladimirovich Golitsyn, was a year and a half older than me. Handsome, self-assured and bold, he immediately became the dominant figure in our group. The idea arose of putting on theatrical shows for the children in the Sheremetyev home. Scenes from *Woe from Wit* by Griboyedov, Gogol's *Revizor* and Pushkin's *Boris Godunov* were chosen. Sasha, who certainly had a talent for acting, played Khlestakov, Chatsky and the Pretender at the Fountain (in *Boris Godunov*). I played Gorodnichy and Skalozub; Marika Sheremetyeva was Maria Antonovna, Sofia and Marina Mnishek. Our directors were my sister Sonya and her then-boyfriend, Vladimir Nikolaievich Dolgorukov.

I soon realised to my horror and confusion that Sasha was flirting with Marika and that she was responding to his advances. I was in love with her, and considered that she was in love with me. I felt deeply wounded and at our next ball I deliberately did not invite her for the third quadrille, instead inviting a friend of Sonya's. Sasha invited Marika. That winter I suffered greatly from this break and avoided talking to her, and she in turn pretended not to notice our estrangement. Come the spring I was delighted to discover that Sasha had started to flirt with another girl, leaving Marika with her nose out of joint.

Uncle Vladimir Vladimirovich (Uncle Vovik) worked in the foreign trade department of a bank and used to bring me foreign stamps for my collection. That winter his wife, Aunt Tania, a peasant by birth, died on the operating table from an overdose of chloroform. Her funeral service was held in the church of Nikola Plotnik on the Arbat. In her coffin she looked amazingly beautiful, just like a young girl. She was buried in Dorogomilovsky cemetery. Neither the church nor the cemetery still stand. From then on Uncle Vovik lived as a widower on Khlebnoy Street. His daughter Elena, although still a girl, became his housekeeper. Once a week he would visit us at Eropkinsky Street, sit in silence the whole evening next to grandfather and when nine o'clock struck, my brother Vladimir would emerge from his room and suggest a game of bridge. If a fourth were needed, I would have that honour, but if two guests arrived – often that would be Artemi Rayevsky and Yusha Samarin – I would be disregarded, which hurt me a lot. I loved playing bridge and was good at it, except that I tended to become over-excited. In my brother's memoirs, which have miraculously been preserved, he mentions my bridge playing.

7

That autumn, after more than a year's interval of relative peace, the arrests started up again. What were referred to in the press as "gangs" were being liquidated; these were the last remnants of Whites and Greens and Nationalists in the Caucasus, the Ukraine and Siberia. The anti-Soviet elements in Central Asia – the so-called *basmachi* – still held out. It was certainly very unlikely that conspiracies and the recruiting of spies took place among "former people".

For the most part, such people were superficially loyal to the Soviet regime, although there were many who in their thinking and convictions remained implacable foes. Some of the Russians who were in contact with foreign missions passed on stories about the life they led and reported on conditions in the country and, of course, these accounts were vastly different from the triumphant articles that filled the newspapers. The secret police, the OGPU, were alert to the alienation and scepticism of such people, to their deep religious feelings and their lack of faith in socialism. The arrest of titled people, of important officials and of former officers was intensified. Under questioning the one and same question was invariably asked, "What are your political views?" Some would answer without hesitation, "I'm a monarchist". Others would say, "I'm loyal". The former would be sentenced to five years or longer in the camps; the latter would be sent into exile or released. These were times that were considered to be humane – relatively, that is. The minimum penalty was what was called "minus six" – which was applied to those who showed at their interrogation that they were not very committed to socialism. This meant exile to any town in the country except for Moscow, Petrograd, Kiev, Kharkov, Sverdlovsk or Tbilisi, as well as all frontier regions. In the archives in the Lubyanka prison in Moscow the files from this period were carefully preserved, and when, in the 1930s, those files were pulled out again, those who had somehow had the good fortune not to be sent to the camps now found themselves less fortunate.

The first person in our family to be arrested was my twenty-year-old cousin, Kirill Golitsyn, who lived in Petrograd. As I write these words I know that he is alive and is writing his own account of how he was arrested and spent more than twenty years in two stages in prison, in the camps and in exile.[14] It is better that I say nothing here so as not to confuse things. When he was arrested he was living with his father, my Uncle Nikolai Vladimirovich (Uncle Niksom), his mother having just died. The father baked a pie in which he concealed a note telling his son how to answer questions at the interrogation. He did not realise that all parcels were thoroughly searched. The note was discovered and the father also arrested for the supposed crime (which his great-great-grandmother had been arrested for under Peter the Great) of "not reporting certain words". The family in Moscow rushed to try and do something about their

---

14. *Kirill's memoirs were published in Moscow in 1997.*

arrest. Mother went to see her "tame" communist, Smidovich. My beautiful cousin, Son'ka Bobrinskaya, went to see the secretary of Commissar Enukidze, and my father went to the Political Red Cross, which was headed by that remarkable woman, Ekaterina Pavlovna Peshkova, wife of the founder of Soviet literature, Maxim Gorky.

Let me try and describe her extraordinary office in some detail. It was in a modest building on Kuznetsky Most, No. 26, now demolished and replaced by a tall building occupied by the KGB. There were no signs on the entrance save for a small notice that read "Berlitz Courses". You went up the stairs to a long corridor at the end of which, under a dim electric light, you could read on a half-glazed door the notice "Political Red Cross" and the hours of reception for lawyers and others. Opening the door you would face two secretaries who wrote down the purpose of your visit. Against one wall was a bench for visitors. In the next room sat Peshkova's deputy, a lawyer who had been a prominent Menshevik and in tsarist times had been sent into exile, an intelligent-looking Jew with a short beard and pince-nez called Mikhail Lvovich Vinaver. Behind a desk in that same room sat a tall, fair-haired young woman who received the visitors and whose duty it was to inform them as to what convictions their men had received and the length of their sentences. A door led out of this room into Ekaterina Pavlovna's office, but special permission was required for admission. My parents were on familiar terms with Peshkova through their joint management of maternity homes and orphanages, and were always allowed in without waiting their turn.

When was this Political Red Cross founded? It did not exist right after the revolution; it must have come into being when the Cheka was renamed OGPU in 1922. It was a kind of information office, but above all, it was a place where some degree of comfort was on offer. Distraught, shattered, or just bewildered people came there to try to understand why the sudden, inexplicable and unjustified nightmare of arrest and imprisonment had fallen out of the sky on to their relatives. Word of the existence of the Political Red Cross spread. The number of visitors increased. After the cold indifference and harshness of the Prosecutor's Office, after the misery of queuing to hand over food parcels at the prisons, here they heard words of comfort, even of hope. Did they also receive any kind of help? In some cases sentences were reduced. In cases of clearly arbitrary injustice, Peshakova intervened vigorously and saved people; yes, she really did save people. And there were some families, our own included, whom she made a great effort to help for many years.

The first time I saw her, she was stepping out of the doorway marked "Berlitz Courses", a tall, strikingly graceful figure in a long leather coat and leather pilot's helmet, with a bulging briefcase under her arm, who then climbed into the sidecar of the motorcycle that was waiting to take her over to the Lubyanka prison. This was the mode of transport she invariably used. I know from many accounts that the whole Peshkov family were friends of the heads of the OGPU and that Yagoda, the supreme head, was a regular visitor to the house on Malaya Nikitskaya Street and to Gorky's *dacha* in the country. Ekaterina Pavlovna could get past all the guards and secretaries straight to Yagoda's office. She did not plead for people, but when she felt it was right, demanded their release or mitigation of their sentences. When Ezhov replaced Yagoda as head of the secret service, he liquidated the PRC and its staff, with the exception of Peshkova. Until World War II she was in charge of sorting out the archives of the PRC, as well as those of her husband. During the war she was in Tashkent, dealing with refugees, a period described by Tamara Vladimirovna, wife of the writer Vsevolod Ivanov. I have dwelt at some length on this remarkable woman, as little is known of her abroad, and even in Solzhenitsyn's *Gulag Archipelago* she is only mentioned in a couple of lines.

8

One day in the spring of 1924, Aunt Lilya Sheremetyeva came to us, her eyes full of anxiety.

"What's happened?" my mother asked.

Aunt Lilya, once she had ascertained that we were all well, told us that they had searched her house throughout the night and arrested her son Nikolai and her nephews, Boris Saburov and Dimitri Gudovich. Later, we learned that the very same night they had arrested others who had been at the ball on Vozdvizhenka Street – General Gadon, two of the four Lvov brothers, Lina Levashova and Avenir Vadbolsky. None of our family had been touched. Nikolai Sheremetyev was released after three days; the rest were exiled to various remote northern towns. Nikolai owed his release to his wife. I am not sure whether at that time his marriage had been formalised, as up till then his relationship with Cecilia Lvovna Mansurova had remained a secret. She was a talented actress, a favourite of Vakhtangov's, an incomparable Princess Turandot, but also the wife of Nikolai, then a modest violinist in the Vakhtangov orchestra. Not surprisingly, people were excited to learn of a Count Sheremetyev's secret marriage. The story was that Cecilia had gone to see the entire leadership – Rykov, Kalinin, Bukharin and Kamenev – and after a dramatic and emotional performance worthy of Shakespeare, they eventually agreed to release Nikolai for the sake of her great talent. When he asked what his crime was, they replied, "You yourself should know."

There is a very fine description of Nikolai in the memoirs of a Vakhtangov actor, Elagin, who fled to Germany during the Second World War. Everyone in the theatre, from the humblest to the highest, loved Nikolai for his open and cheerful character and sensitive wit. But Elagin is wrong to write that Nikolai was arrested ten times and ten times released. If my memory is right, he was only arrested once more, in 1932, when internal passports were being introduced. The policeman who gave him that supremely valuable Soviet document, his passport, said, "Your Excellency, sign here and say thank you to your wife."

At the beginning of the summer of that year, 1924, the Sheremtyev, Saburov and Gudovich families were evicted from their flats. They were given only three days notice. Everyone in the world of antiques and old clothes in Moscow, most of them Tartars, gathered in Vozdvizhenka Street. In front of the Tartars, Nikolai Sheremtyev, Andrei Gudovich and Yuri Saburov opened up chests and trunks that were full of things dating back to the time of Parasha Zhemchugova in the sixteenth century, and sold them all off at knock-down prices. Pavel Sergeievich Sheremetyev collected all the pictures, books and bronzes and stored them in his quarters in a tower of the Novodevichy monastery. On a visit after the war, I saw these priceless books in disorderly heaps littering the floor of his room.

The efforts made to intervene on behalf of Uncle Nikolai Vladimirovich Golitsyn and his son Kirill met with failure. Kirill was sentenced to five years in the northern monastery-prison of Solovki, his father three years, and their friends various terms. The only result achieved by high-level intervention on their behalf was that they were transferred from Solovki to Butyrka prison in Moscow. In Butyrka, there was the so-called "workers' corridor" where a certain number of prisoners served their sentences working in the kitchen, the washrooms, the library and so on.

For two whole winters, once a week, I would set off with a heavy basket of provisions for delivery to the special parcel reception area of the prison in Novoslobodskaya Street. Usually there was an enormous crowd of mothers, wives and other relatives, who had to wait for hours before they were allowed into an inner hall, where again they might wait and wait until a little window would open, their name would be called, and they could hand over their parcel. They had to announce the name of the prisoner, upon which any previous packaging, marked "Received, contents intact" and signed, would be given back to them. Any other words on the wrapping, such as "I embrace you" would have been heavily crossed out.

As I was bringing parcels for prisoners in the workers' corridor, I was allowed to go to the head of the line. Holding my parcel above my head and shouting, "For the workers' corridor!" I would force my way through the crowd to the little window. I soon got to know the Red Army soldier receptionist and he would quickly pass over the signed packaging, so my deliveries only took a matter of minutes. However, getting there and back by tram, with two changes, took three hours. These trips were sometimes undertaken by my cousin, Sasha Golitsyn.

Sunday was visiting day. Grandmother went every Sunday, and the rest of the family took turns. Only those in the "corridor" were allowed visits, and then only for forty minutes. I saw Kirill several times. The visiting room was divided by two parallel rows of upright rails with facing benches on either side of each row. In between, one at each end, sat two warders, there to make sure nothing was thrown across the divide. Grandmother was slightly deaf and found it very difficult to hear her son across the wide gap. In general, she suffered terribly for him, every evening praying fervently in front of the holy icon and bowing low to the ground as her tears fell.

Other prisoners on that "corridor" were the ancient General Kazakevich, a young engineer, Vladimir Kisel-Zagoryansky, the philologist Anatoly Mihailovich Fokin, and others I cannot now remember. And later on many of our friends and relatives were to serve their time or await their despatch to the camps in that "worker's corridor". Two years later, instead of parcels of provisions, only money was accepted. My weekly trips ceased. Money was being sent by Uncle Alexander Vladimirovich Golitsyn from America, but most of all, it came from a lady in Italy. Her name was Moina, her maiden name Demidova, and she was the widow of grandmother's cousin, Semyon Semyonovich Abamelek-Lazerev. They had owned several factories in the Urals until the revolution and had capital invested abroad. Every month, through her secretary, Moina sent money to around fifty relatives in the USSR, some more, some less. She included my grandparents on her list after Alka Bobrinskaya, now living in Florence, visited her in her palazzo and described the grandparents' desperate situation.

9

In 1923, the currency was reformed. Over a period of two or three months the *sovznak* was replaced by the new *chervonets*, a hard currency backed by gold. My father no longer brought home bundles of multicoloured notes, but instead a monthly salary of seventeen *chervontsi*, which in those days was considered a reasonable income, although not for such an enormous family as ours. The new currency was printed on one side with its denomination, a pattern of whorls and scrolls and the signatures of the members of the Board of the National Bank. The other side was completely blank. One day, on leaving for the office, father left a folded banknote for household expenses on a table by the door. Some time later it had vanished. What had happened to it? People had been coming and going all morning. However, the mystery was very quickly solved. Nanny Bush, seeing what she thought was a blank piece of paper, had pushed it into the stove as fire-lighting paper. Luckily, the stove had not yet been lit. Father considered this currency reform to have been totally successful and praised its author, who had been a senior member of the Ministry of Finance before the revolution. His name was Kutler. Twelve years later in Dmitrov I had pointed out to me an unprepossessing-looking old man – he was the "father" of the *chervonets*. He had been arrested for sabotage and, after serving his term, was working as a volunteer on the construction of the Moscow-Volga canal.

This monetary reform particularly pleased grandmother. Up till now she had constantly moaned about the high prices of everything, not surprisingly, as a box of matches cost five hundred million roubles. Now she could go shopping and for only one *chervonets* buy a whole heap of nice things. Father had to warn her, however, that although things seemed cheaper, his income was also much lower.

10

Early in 1924, with a friend of mine, I attended a public debate. At this time, the Orthodox Church was headed by Patriarch Tikhon. As a kind of counterbalance to the patriarchate, a new religious movement had come into existence, calling itself "The Living Church", founded by the priest of a church in Dolgorukovskaya Street, a powerful and intelligent person, Father Alexander Vvedensky. The Soviet authorities saw a chance to split the church and supported Father Vvedensky, but neither the general public nor the ecclesiastical authorities followed him, and his church remained empty. The public debates in which he took part, however, were very popular. The one I attended had a portly Comrade Lunacharsky facing Father Vvedensky across a little table. After bowing to each other, they spoke in turn. Vvedensky's voice was shrill and piercing and he gesticulated a lot, so that he looked like a black crow in flight. Lunacharsky quite deliberately expressed his ideas clearly and calmly. No doubt they both spoke intelligently and convincingly but I personally, and probably many others, could not understand a thing. After about an hour and half, both rose, once more bowed to each other and made their exit. The public left the hall, the religious remaining religious, the atheists, atheists. These public debates have long been out of favour with the authorities. There are religious thinkers now amongst Marxists, and in any debate these theologians would certainly win against anti-religious opponents.

On the seventh of January, and so, strange as it may seem, on Christmas day,[15] our school holidays began. I was invited by the Istomin family to Sergiyev Posad. I made the journey with Uncle Vladimir Trubetskoi and spent my first night in his home. I was woken up in the morning by my little curly-headed cousins, some dark, some fair, all still in their nightshirts, standing in a ring round my bed and urging a beautiful English setter dog on to my bed. The Trubetskoi apartment was like so many of the homes of "former people". The furniture was simple – a cupboard, a table, stools and benches – mixed in with fine mahogany pieces, mostly rather damaged. On the walls there was a beautiful oval mirror, a shotgun in an elegantly decorated holster and an oil portrait of a great-grandmother, the daughter of Field Marshal Wittgenstein, in its heavy gold frame.

After breakfast the older cousins, Sasha and Grisha, took me over to the Istomins, who lived in the same district of Krasyukovka, but in a different street. I had already made friends with Sergei Istomin and loved this lively, dark-eyed, exotic-looking boy with his knightly nobility of character. With him and his younger sister Ksana we played games all day and then in the evening the father, Pyotr Vladimirovich, in an even voice, almost without intonation, told us stories of his life and of all the people he had known. He was a highly intelligent man. I was totally absorbed by his stories, and felt great respect for him.

---

15. *The Julian calendar, followed by the Orthodox church, is thirteen days behind the Gregorian, which was adopted by the State.*

Sergei Istomin had made friends with Uncle Vladimir. When the latter was playing the piano in the local cinema, Sergei would take advantage of this family connection to sit through several shows at a time. I, too, went to this same cinema during my stay. Sergei also went hunting with Uncle Vladimir, and so one day we all set off, Uncle, Sergei, the English setter Oryel and I. This was my first time in an evergreen forest in winter. Uncle showed us fox, hare and dog tracks. He pointed out the droppings of blackcock and grouse, and how the bullfinches were pecking at piles of horse manure. The forest then was full of life – today it stands empty with only the white snow and no bird droppings anywhere. I do not remember whether he shot anything that day. There were no hares and he did not shoot grouse. It was the beauty of the forest that captivated me, with its spruce trees all in white, the blue shadows mantling the snow and all the magic that my uncle felt and which he somehow passed on to us.

We visited the Monastery of the Trinity, my first view of that wonderful architectural complex founded by the most holy saint of Old Russia, the Venerable Sergei, he who had blessed Dimitri Donskoy at the battle of Kulikovo Field in 1380 against the Mongol hordes. The historian Klyuchevsky wrote that so long as a lamp burns in the saint's shrine, Russia would survive. In the first years after the revolution the lamp was extinguished, the monks driven out, and the remains of St Sergei were opened up and desecrated. These and the famous iconostasis painted by Daniil Chorny and Andrei Rublyov were kept locked up in the main church, inaccessible to the public. The rest of the monastery was turned into a museum.

We were met by the scientific curator, Count Yuri Alexandrovich Olsyufev, a short, bearded man, with bright eyes and a lively manner. Sergei introduced me and he shook our hands just like adults. Then he led us on a tour. I walked round under arched vaults gazing at the collections of gilt and gem-incrusted church implements and objects. Most of the valuables had at that time been taken away, supposedly to "help the hungry". Vestments and hangings and other linen articles were still untouched. But the objects and articles one sees today are far, far less in number – so much of that treasure found its way abroad in the thirties and after the war. Not all the monks had been driven out. In each room there sat a monk-guardian, completely trusted by the museum staff. As the whole place was unheated, these rooms were icy cold. Sergei and I had removed our caps out of respect, and kept them in our hands until one of the monks pointed out that we would catch cold if we did not put them on. I felt like something sacred had been driven out.

Several times we went to church services in the district of Krasyukovka. Once we went to an all-night service in the small monastic building known as the Gethsemane hermitage, which was still active. There were four hermitages and apart from Gethsemane, the only other one still in use was the most distant and the strictest, that did not allow women, the hermitage of the Paraclete, eight *versts* away. The two nearer ones, three *versts* away, were Kinovia with its white-hipped roof tower and Chernigovsky, with five cupolas and a massive red brick bell tower. Both are now old people's homes.

The hermitage of Gethsemane was surrounded by forest. A pink and white single-domed tower rose behind high walls. It was evening and we went in through the heavy metal gates and into the church. There were many worshippers, as that year permission had been given to the public to enter the hermitage, so crowds flocked there. The monks stood to one side, some very old with long beards, others quite young with black or fair beards. The choir sang the service standing on both sides of the church. Hundreds of candles and varicoloured lamps shone their light on the congregation. Sergei pointed out to me the monk who had taken the *schema* and stood alone to one side; I could only see a long grey beard under his lowered cowl. His black vestment was decorated in silver with a skull and cross-bones and the words, "Holy Lord, strong and immortal, have mercy upon us!"

This was the first time I had been in a monastery. The service was extremely long and tiring because of the many candles and oil lamps and the heat emanating from the congregation, but I managed to stick it out, listening patiently to the drawn-out singing of the monks. Everything superfluous was relegated to the outside world, leaving only the monks standing as they intoned their prayers in witness of Jesus Christ, ready to endure whatever tribulations came their way. The service was led by the abbot himself, Father Israel, a sturdy, full-bodied old man with a thick beard, wearing a black vestment picked out in gold. He spoke with great force, enunciating the prayers with great clarity, and you could sense the weight of responsibility that lay on his shoulders – to protect his flock of monks from worldly temptations, to negotiate with the authorities and to raise high the banner of Orthodoxy, knowing all the while that terrible trials lay ahead.

11

My holidays came to an end, and it was time to return to Moscow. The Istomins went with me to the station – a small wooden building

– and put me into a freezing carriage. A monk of their acquaintance was travelling too. We sat on opposite benches, talking about spiritual and religious subjects, until we arrived in Pushkin where other passengers joined us. At the Yaroslavl station in Moscow where we parted company, the monk said something very encouraging and I left him in a really good mood. Then immediately, on Kalanchevskaya Square, I saw the newspaper boys running to and fro, shouting, "The death of Lenin! Special edition! Lenin dead!"

Those newspapers, and since then novels and poems and stories and memoirs, have described the grief that overwhelmed the whole nation, young and old. I cannot recall such grief. On the day of his burial, sirens were sounded from town halls and factories all over the country, whipping up people's misery. But the ordinary people remained indifferent and silent. It was only later, when the authorities had begun to promote the idea of frantic dancing and the wild playing of music on the communal farms, that the peasants remembered Lenin and muttered – "If he were still alive, they would not be taking the piss out of us this way."

His death had been long awaited; frequent medical bulletins had appeared in the press. There were many reports of how he had periods of sanity, interspersed with times of total insanity. An old friend of my father and grandfather, the Moscow doctor Fyodor Alexandrovich Gyotye, was caring for Lenin. When asked if the rumours of his mental health were correct, he answered in the affirmative. In the pages of an anthology, *The Fifth Anniversary of the Russian Communist Party*, there is a group photo and it is clear that Lenin is quite definitely a sick man. In the two years before his death he was sidelined from power, others ruling in his stead. In those days he had not yet been turned into a sort of divine figure. I must repeat, when he died there was not the widespread grief that has been described. But the papers were full of sad obituaries and mournful poems. Black flags hung everywhere, and a song was constantly sung to the tune of a popular melody:

Ilich, Ilich, Ilich!
Hear our cries and sorrow!

For three whole days I had nothing to do and wandered around the streets in the company of a school friend, Yuri Nevedomsky, a dirty-minded and dissolute boy. Like us, many people were out and about. In Okhotny Ryad, we saw a long line of people waiting to pay their last respects to Lenin as his body lay in state in the Pillared

Room of the Palace of the Soviets. We joined the line. The frost was bitter and bonfires had been lit on the streets – long, uncut logs burning fiercely. Yuri and I frequently left the line to get warm. We were wearing felt boots, but those who had come in their ordinary boots had to keep dancing about to stop from freezing. We were controlled by surly, frozen militiamen who moved to and fro along the line. When we got into the building it was immediately much warmer. The place was hung with black banners and a hidden orchestra was playing funeral music. The guards kept hurrying us along – "Quicker, quicker!" The guard of honour, four Red Army soldiers in trenchcoats, stood to attention around the open coffin, which rested on a bed of artificial flowers on a high stand. I was just able to see Lenin's face, very round and pink, and totally bald. When at midnight I arrived home, frozen and hungry, Georgy was furious – "What happened to you? Where've you been? If Uncle Misha were alive he'd box your ears!" And he turned away from me in anger. I was particularly hurt by his reference to Uncle Misha, whose name was sacred for me.

It took only three days to build the first wooden mausoleum for Lenin's embalmed body, based on a design by the architect Shchusev. This building, with its gilt wooden walls, was quite attractive as its clean lines looked well against the background of the Kremlin walls. Eighteen months later I stood in an even longer line, a quiet and orderly one where the people stood with bowed heads and revealed real grief on their faces as they moved slowly forward. This line began at Kaluzhskaya Square, went along Donskaya Street to the beautiful little church in Donskoy monastery. The people had come to pay their last tribute to the recently deceased Patriarch, Tikhon, a great father of the Russian church. My brother Vladimir told me later how Pavel Dimitriyevich Korin, the painter, had been so impressed by the funeral of the Patriarch that he had conceived a vast canvas which, however, he was never allowed to execute.

12

One evening, at the height of a riotous children's ball, a short, balding, lively man, bearing a remarkable resemblance to Shakespeare, came into the room, accompanied by a girl of the same age as our sister Masha. He was Igor Vladimirovich Ilyinsky, a member of a minor landowning family from the district of Chernsky in the province of Tula. At university he had been a fellow student and close friend of my mother's brother, Nikolai Sergeievich Lopukhin. He was the talented author of a poem entitled *Marxiada,* the manuscript of which had been passed from hand to hand. The authorities had failed to discover who the author was. The poem described how Karl Marx rose from the grave, travelled to Russia, was arrested and locked up in Butyrka prison, was released and sent to a communal farm on a former landowner's estate, then returned to Moscow. He went about, astonished at the country he was in, its character and its people, and then suddenly discovered that the authorities were acting in his name, writing slogans using quotations from his writings, and had even erected statues of him.

I knew Igor Vladimirovich only for a year but I remember this entrancing man so well. He was a wonderful story-teller, who had no fear of telling slanderous, often indecent anecdotes, but they were always very funny. Before the revolution he was the kind of liberal who denounced tsarist rule, was an atheist, on occasion served time in prison or exile, and only after the revolution did he begin to understand that the previous regime had been incomparably better than what followed after 1917. His appearance amongst us we owed to the fact that he had heard of our lively and friendly gatherings and wanted his daughter Lyalya, an only child, to meet some young people. Lyalya was extremely attractive and dressed far more smartly than any of our girls. She declined to take part in our wild dances, simply observing us from her seat with obvious disdain. Nonetheless, Igor Vladimirovich invited half of our crowd to his daughter's birthday party at their fifth floor flat at No. 6 Povarskaya Street. The food was excellent and the party a success. From that time on we children became regular visitors to this hospitable home where Lyalya's mother, a full-bosomed lady, always welcomed us with unfeigned pleasure.

A crowd of people lived in that same flat. There was Nikolai Alexeievich Pusheshnikov, a nephew of the writer Bunin, and a very kindly old lady, Igor's mother, who had relapsed into childhood and went about in an old fashioned gown, smiling at everyone. Lyalya was not only beautiful but also clever and talented, and very well aware of her gifts. She wrote verse, some of it political, and liked to read it aloud in a voice full of pathos. I recall a couple of lines she wrote:

> *When one day the two-headed eagle*
> *Will return to fight the red star . . .*

The boys were all crazy about her. Sasha Golitsyn jilted Marika Sheremetyeva so as to run after Lyalya. According to Lyala, I was the only one not to succumb to her charms, though we became good friends and often discussed "serious" topics together.

It was Igor Vladimirovich who conceived and launched the scheme for a class of girls of more or less the same age to be educated outside the Soviet system. A man and wife who were qualified teachers, the Efimovs, began to teach this group of eight girls, including Lyalya and my sister Masha. All these pupils eventually passed their secondary school examinations successfully as external students.

13

That winter two elderly people turned up at our house. They were a former footman and a chambermaid of the Counts Khreptovich-Butyenev. My mother's aunt, Ekaterina Pavlovna Baranova, was married to a member of the family, Konstantin Apollinarionovich. The Butyenevs had all gone abroad at the time of the revolution, leaving their property in the care of this old couple. Now a rascal of a house superintendent had ordered them to vacate their basement flat, and they had come to us to ask us to look after the removal of the Butyenevs' possessions. There was no time to be lost, so that very Sunday father, Vladimir and I took a big sledge and went to the Butyenevs' home at 18 Povarskaya Street.

So as not to alert the other tenants of the house, we went down into the basement on tiptoe, lighting our way with a couple of candles. We were greeted by the sight of some huge metal trunks, but were disappointed, when we broke these open, to discover only a mass of linen and cotton articles, the Butyenevs' table and bed linen, all completely rotten, with the family crest only faintly visible. At the bottom of one of these trunks we found a few small pictures and portraits, and a thick book, which we bundled together and took away with us. The watercolours Vladimir hung up in his room, while I chose a pastel portrait of two young ladies – the older in a blue dress, the younger in apricot yellow. This I hung by my bed so that when I woke up I could admire the young ladies. A note on the back told me that these were the Vasilchikov sisters. One of them, Anna Alexeievna, was my great grandmother, the other my great-great aunt Ekaterina Alexeievna. The former had married Count Pavel Trofimovich Baranov, the governor of the city of Tver, and the latter Prince Vladimir Alexandrovich Cherkasky, who had played an active part in the repeal of serfdom. This portrait hung by my bedside for a few years, during which time I told myself that I was in love with the older sister – the only difficulty was that she was my great-grandmother. Much later I gave it as a present to my sister Sonya on her wedding day. Whenever I visited Sonya, I would feel a flutter when I looked at it. A sad fate awaited this picture; a nanny accidentally broke the glass and, noticing that the picture was dusty, took a wet cloth to wipe it. The two beauties were gone for ever.

As a young woman, my great-grandmother had known Dostoyevsky. In a letter to his friend Baron Vrangel he writes that "she pleased him". After his time in a forced labour camp and in the army, Dostoyevsky was allowed to return to Russia and to live anywhere except in the two capitals. He chose Tver and was a guest at the governor's table. After four months Anna Alexeievna managed to get permission for him to return to live in Petersburg. I wrote a novelette around this story, but was told by the editors that while Dostoyevsky was a subject of interest to readers, my old great-grandmother was not. Finally, it was not a novelette that appeared but a very much shortened documentary article about Dostoyevsky (in No. 52 of the journal *Ogonyok*, 1977) with just a passing reference to Anna Alexeievna. The editors also struck out the mention of my relationship to her.

The thick book we had found in the Butyenev trunk turned out to be a collection of autographs collected by the younger sister, Ekaterina. This album was studied carefully by a number of literary critics and scholars; the director of the Tyutchev literary archive at the Muranovsky Museum, the brothers B.I. and G.I. Yarkho (the elder was later to be sent to the Gulag); the brothers M.A. and F.A. Petrovsky (the elder was later to die in the Gulag). They were all bowled over by the collection, declaring it to be priceless. There were the signatures of tsars and kings, generals and ministers, but above all writers, including Schiller and Goethe, many French writers, and a letter from Pushkin to his wife, although scholars already knew of this letter. There were the signatures of men of letters and poets, such as Karamzin, Zhukovsky and Baratynsky; there was an envelope with a cutting of Gogol's hair, and a copybook with the autograph manuscript of Lermontov's tale *Ashik-Kerib*, which had only ever been printed from a copyist's version, and which revealed a number of variant readings that made the find doubly valuable.

Later on, when our family was going through a particularly difficult time, the director of the Literary Museum, Bonch-Bruyevich, who had once been Lenin's secretary, bought the album from us. It was immediately taken apart and the writers' autographs distributed to their respective literary archives. The autographs of tsars and kings, generals and ministers, were sent to the State Central Archives.

14

At the beginning of 1924, a law came into force that led to the eviction of the last remaining landowners from their estates. Mother had an elderly aunt, Julia Pavlovna Mukhanova, the childless widow of Sergei Ilyicha Mukhanov, a former cavalry officer and distant relative of the Decembrist Mukhanov. Up until the revolution, Grandmother Julia lived on her estate of Ishakovo, now renamed Mukhanov in honour of its earlier owners, some twenty *versts* northeast of Sergiyev Posad. In the winter holidays she was very fond of inviting her nephews and nieces and their children, and this included my brother Vladimir. She was on friendly terms with her neighbours, went frequently to her husband's grave, was very fond of her housekeeper, who was the same age as herself, and devoted much time to the affairs of the local old people's home that she had established and supported out of her own income. She was a small woman, not at all attractive, covered with warts and very talkative. Vladimir called her "God's dandelion", a nickname that seemed to suit her.

Some time after the revolution she was evicted from the main house with her housekeeper and moved into the old people's home, where as their benefactor and mistress she was privileged with a room of her own. She was treated with the greatest deference not only by the residents but also by the peasants, and lived there more or less decently for seven years. The worst blow she suffered was when the authorities, in search of valuables, dug up her husband's grave and scattered his remains; she managed to reinter these with the help of her peasant friends. Not long after she was turned out of this home too. She and her companion now went to live with the housekeeper's brother, a priest in the village of Glinkovo, four *versts* south of Sergiyev Posad. Grandmother Julia wrote to my parents, complaining that she was now being treated less well than in the old people's home.

My parents made the journey to Glinkovo. They discovered that the surroundings were beautiful and arranged to rent, rather cheaply, the priest's second, now empty house as a summer cottage. Grandmother Julia was brought back to Moscow where she went to live with her brother's widow, Aunt Nastenka Baranova, whom I have mentioned. Aunt Nastenka, after the death of her husband and the brutal execution of her two sons, had become quite used to living on her own and found it very hard to put up with her sister-in-law's garrulousness. So my parents then wrote to Grandmother Julia's younger sister in Paris – Countess Ekaterina Khreptovich-Butyenev – asking her to give a home to the poor old lady.

My sister Masha and I were taking English lessons at this time with Sofia Alexeievna Bobrinskaya – Aunty Misya – who was living in Bolshaya Vlasyevskaya street, opposite the church of Uspenye na Mogiltsach, a church now much defaced, but still standing. She suddenly made it known that she must speak urgently to my mother. Mother called on her, returning home looking quite serious. Later that evening I was summoned by my parents, to have an astounding question put to me: "Would you like to go abroad? For ever?" I did not need to reflect for even an instant. "No," I answered decisively. My parents said nothing to make me change my mind. I then learned that Aunty Misya had vigorously tried to persuade my mother that I should accompany Grandmother Julia to Paris and that if I stayed in Russia I would certainly perish. Clearly, I have survived. Had I left, I would have lost my roots in Russia, would doubtless have become a translator in the United Nations, would not have become a writer, but have lived a comfortable life without troubles in the West. I am grateful to my mother that she ignored Sofia Alexeievna's advice, even though that seemed to be acting against common sense. I know that mother put her trust in the power of prayer and the mercy of God.

Grandmother Julia left behind her a mahogany casket decorated with mother-of-pearl inlay. Inside were old letters and photographs of relatives, mainly of her husband, as well as an album of poems from the 1830s written in various hands. The album, which also had some pressed flowers between its pages, had belonged to a young lady, an aunt of Grandmother Julia's husband. Her friends had written verses to her in the album; one of these was entitled *To a Dusky Beauty* and signed A. Pushkin. The casket is now in the possession of my sister Katya, while my nephew Illarion has the album. He wrote to our *Literary Gazette* about the supposed poem by Pushkin. In a capitalist country there is no doubt that this would have caused a sensation, with a reporter instantly at his door, but the *Literary Gazette* took a month to reply and then only to say that any consultation in connection with Pushkin should be arranged with the Pushkin Museum, whose address and phone number they gave. Eventually, the Pushkin scholar who looked at the poem, S.M. Bondi, concluded that it was, in fact, the work of a second-rate poet of the period.

15

The priest who owned the *dacha* we rented at Glinkovo, Father Alexei Zagorsky, was an uncle of the Bolshevik V.M. Zagorsky who was killed in an explosion in Leontyevsky Street in 1919, and in whose honour the monastery town of Sergiyev Posad was renamed Zagorsk. Our family rented this *dacha* for six years in a row. I think I am right in saying that my younger sisters and I developed a great deal in the summer months we spent there. We could not but be captivated by the surrounding countryside with its fauna and flora, its boundless horizons, the church towers or domes that poked their tops just above the trees, the little river Torgosha that wound its way between banks covered with bushes, and the many little villages, all of which created that magical poetic landscape that painters such as Vasnetsov, Nesterov and others, who loved Old Russia, tried to capture on canvas. I wandered around the countryside in a mood of heightened sensitivity, and believe it's thanks to Glinkovo that I became a writer on Old Russia, its glorious history and natural beauty.

The Trinity-Sergei monastery was closed, but the little isolated monasteries of Gethsemane, close to Glinkovo, and Paraclete, rather further away, have survived. On the road to Sergiyev Posad or in the forest you might meet a monk in his skullcap, with dusty patched boots, walking along head bowed and lips moving as he said his prayers. Against the background of the fir forest and wild flowers he would seem to come straight out of a picture by Nesterov or a drawing by Korin. The spirit of Holy Sergei had left the big monastery, but here in the hermitage-monasteries, in the forest and along the flowing streams, his spirit was still alive.

The priest, Father Alexei, was a simple country priest who had for many years christened, married and buried the people of Glinkovo and the two neighbouring villages. In appearance he resembled the writer Aksakov when he was an old man. With a mass on Sunday, an evening service on Saturday, the services for the local patron saints and additional services on major saints' days, he was a busy man in his Russian Empire-style church of the Holy Mother of Korsun. Vladimir drew a picture of this church in an album dedicated to Father Alexei. Today, the church stands despoiled and abandoned.

We, together with the Ilyinsky family, had the second of the priest's empty houses. Vladimir and Elena, who had just had their first child, also named Elena, occupied a separate house but came to us for dinner. Aunt Lilya Sheremetyeva, evicted from the family house in Moscow together with her three children, also found a *dacha* to rent near us in Glinkovo. She was joined by her sister, Nadya Rayevskaya, with her husband Alexander Alexandrovich and their three daughters, who rented yet another *dacha*. Then, in the late summer, when my sister Lina had given birth to her daughter Marina, she and her husband Georgy likewise moved to Glinkovo. Thus a crowd of close friends and relatives were gathered together. The men travelled out from Moscow on Saturday evenings and had to return to their jobs at dawn on Monday, so it was only on the Sunday that we could all play all sorts of games – bowls, ball games, tag and suchlike.

Uncle Vladimir Trubetskoi and his family were now living permanently in Sergiyev Posad. He regularly came over to Glinkovo to visit my brother Vladimir, to whom he was particularly attached. The Trubetskois now had six children. Grandmother received an amusing note in verse from him on the occasion of a yet another birth, written partly in French, partly in Russian, which, whilst announcing that mother and child were well, also versified the family's total lack of money. All the Trubetskoi children were given names that had the letter "r" in them, the parents feeling this letter guaranteed their staying alive.

Quite a number of "former people" had come to live in Sergiyev Posad. The Olsyufevs had already bought a house there in 1917. The priest-philosopher Pavel Florensky and his family moved there. Natalya Ivanovna Goncharova, an old maid who was also the niece of Pushkin's wife and so a most important figure, also arrived. I have already written about the Istomins and Trubetskois. In addition, many professional people, not strictly speaking "former people", but who felt they could not work for the Bolsheviks, settled in the town. I can name those who were friends of the Trubetskoi family and so through him our friends too: Ivan Florovich Ognev, the family of the painter Vladimir Andreievich Favorsky, the family of David Ivanovich Ilovaysky who was a professor at the Institute of Mining, and the forestry specialist Obrecht. There were many others. Mikhail Mikhailovich Prishvin, the writer, with his wife Efrosinya Pavlovna and two sons, bought a house in that same district of Sergiyev Posad, Krasyukovka. The hunters who lived in Sergiyev Posad, including Uncle Vladimir, soon got to know him. Efrosinya Pavlovna, with her good nature and hospitable spirit, was friendly with this crowd.

That first summer in Glinkovo our wanderings were confined to the little stream, Torgosha, and to visiting a spring that rose in a thicket of alders on the slopes of the steep valley where the monks collected water they considered to be holy water. An icon was nailed to a nearby tree. We also visited Vifany (Bethany), a former monastery two *versts* from the village on the banks of a large lake, where five monks were still in residence. The monastery was founded in the late eighteenth century by the Metropolitan of Moscow,

Platon, who loved to relax there, but now the main building was used as teachers' institute and his residence was a museum. It survived into the 1930s.

We also picked mushrooms. The boletus mushroom grew in great abundance. Lyalya and I walked together, discussing "serious" topics as we went along and competing in the number of books we had read and mushrooms gathered. That summer the mosquitoes were terrible. A school friend, Yuri Nevedomsky, had initiated me into smoking and, like so many children, I took to secretly indulging the habit in that inevitable place, the lavatory. Now, because of the clouds of mosquitoes everywhere, mother and Aunt Lilya allowed Petrusha and me to smoke, so that we went about puffing away at the cheapest cigarettes we could find – "Trezvon", costing six *kopeks* a pack, and "Chervonets", ten *kopeks*.

A newspaper campaign was under way that spring, calling for a purge of the universities and institutions of higher learning of the children of "former people", NEPmen and priests, who were "soiling the purity of these fountains of learning". Only the children of factory workers should be allowed to do higher studies. The actual names of class enemies in such institutions were quoted. This bitter cup did not pass by my sister Sonya, who had been studying, attending lectures and conscientiously doing her laboratory work at the university. She was purged along with others. They put their case to the professors, who listened sympathetically and wrote warm recommendations on the work of their pupils, but all to no avail. My father also turned to former friends and tried, in vain, to exert some influence. Sonya was quite deeply affected by this end to her dreams. She lost no time trying to find a job, but here again, due to the level of unemployment in the country, nothing came up for some months. Stuck in this situation, she took to helping me with my algebra and geometry. Thanks to my poor marks in these subjects, I had only been moved up into class 8 provisionally. Nor was my situation helped by the fact that the maths teacher had earlier been my brother Vladimir's tutor. Sonya's way of teaching me was rather peculiar. The moment I got anything wrong she would shout out "Idiot!" and hit me on my forehead. So she literally beat these subjects into my head, and quite soon I was coping with them more or less competently.

Uncle Alyosha was arrested in Khilkovo that summer. He had gone to Moscow to sell a harvest of apples, not large, but also carrying a message from a group of priests in the district of Krapivensky to the Patriarch, Tikhon. The message professed their submission to the

Patriarch but declared that they could not join the "Living Church" movement. On his return from Moscow, Uncle Alyosha was arrested. I do not know what happened to the priests. Sonya immediately hurried to Khilkovo, where Aunt Tyosa was about to give birth to a third child. After the birth, Sonya brought them all to our flat on Eropkinsky, where we found a corner for them in one of our rooms. Mother went to see Smidovich about Uncle Alyosha, and he was released from the prison in Tula. Smidovich, however, told mother that it would be very unwise of Uncle Alyosha to return to Khilkovo and that he should make himself scarce somewhere else. But where? Where else but in God's own town of Sergiyev Posad! The Trubetskois found him a flat in a little house in their district of Krasyukovka and the family were reunited.

Sonya now faced a major difficulty; she had been thrown out of the university and had tried to find work without success. What was she to do now? A solution soon came from another direction – Petrograd. There Sofia Vladimirovna, the widow of father's cousin, Pyotr Abramovich Khvoshchinsky, had been arrested with a group of people who had taken part in a church service celebrating the feast day of a particularly saintly nun. The widow's arrest left three children without a parent. Sonya went to take care of them and in due course returned, bringing with her the youngest to live with us – nine-year-old Kolya, a spoiled and badly brought up child. A few months later Sofia Vladimirovna was freed and, with her children, managed to leave the country.

In the end, Sonya found work thanks to Sofia Grigoryevna Ilyinskaya, Igor Ilyinsky's wife, who was a medical doctor. She was paid to compile medical statistics. Great stacks of charts arrived from the various city hospitals, data from thousands of cases over many years. Sonya's job was to make tables of the statistics of patients' weight, breast size, number of children, number of abortions, when menstruation had started, when finished, whether the patients drank and if so, how much and how often. All this data had to be entered in both vertical and horizontal columns and in the bottom right hand corner the totals had to agree. The doctors were delighted with this valuable information, and I believe the tables are in use to this very day. Nor was it only Sonya who earned money in this way; other "former people", for instance the Osorgins, also drank from this inexhaustible spring of data.

In the meantime, we continued to enjoy our life in Glinkovo. The Trubetskois visited us from Sergiyev Posad, as did Sergei Istomin and the middle of the three Rayevsky brothers, Mikhail. The eldest

Rayevsky brother, Sergei, was working as a photographer in the electrical laboratory in Moscow directed by that exceptional man and scientist, Father Pavel Florensky, who, being under the personal protection of the Commissar for economics, Dzerzhinsky, was tolerated by the authorities on his occasional appearance at committee meetings wearing a cassock.

One day Pyotr Vladimirovich Istomin arrived in Glinkovo and had a long talk with Igor Ilyinsky as they both sat on a log. We then learned that the latter was going to be the defending lawyer for the monks of Gethsemane monastery, who were threatened with eviction. New regulations on eviction made it mandatory to first have a ruling from a court. Appeals to a higher court were also, in theory, possible. In practice, court decisions were nearly always quite arbitrary, but the appearance of correct procedure was preserved. Ilyinsky absolutely refused to take any payment from the monks, even though he was a convinced atheist. He saw how hard they worked in their fields and orchards and felt they had right on their side. He was, however, so energetic in pleading the defence that he himself was arrested. His case went on for a long time and in the course of it the secret police unearthed the fact that he was the author of the *Marxiad*. There was a danger that he would be sent to Solovki in the far north, but Peshkova intervened and instead he was exiled to a distant part of the region of Perm. Eventually, he managed to get himself to Tolstoy's estate of Yasnaya Polyana, where as he himself put it, he became yet one more of the many researcher-worms feeding off the body of the great writer. His searches in the archives in Tula were published under other people's names since, as an internal exile, he could not print under his own name. In the 1930s he was arrested again and disappeared for good. The monks' case dragged on for a couple of years, but in the end they were evicted from Gethsemane.

16

We were back in Moscow in the autumn. I was now in Year 8 in school – I have now to refer to it that way, and not as a "gymnasium". People, probably Party activists, appeared amongst us to find out how many of the pupils were of working class origin. In our class that meant only Shura Karinsky, son of the school boilerman. At a general assembly a census was taken on which of us were Pioneers or *Konsomol*s (National Youth Organisation). There were two Pioneers in Year 7 and only one *Konsomol*, in Year 9. The local education people began to keep a watchful eye on the school. A new director was appointed, Anatoly Sergeievich Darsky. He had a resemblance to Lenin, and before the revolution had been a teacher of maths at the Adolf gymnasium on Malaya Nikitskaya Street. Once installed, he did nothing to change the style and traditions established by the Alferovs.

Just before the anniversary celebrations of the October Revolution, Darsky and Olga Nikoleyevna Maslova went round the senior classrooms, calling everyone to assemble together at a certain hour and then, with red banners and flags, to march to Red Square and see the leaders there. They said that, for the sake of the school, we should make a show of our "class consciousness". In our break time, many of us began whispering to each other –"Will you go?" "Not on your life!" I said, as also did others. We did not go. It is true, though, that the weather was very wet. Later, Darsky and Olga Nikolaievna went round the classrooms and held us up to shame, saying that we had betrayed the school. Any who had failed to go was to bring a justificatory note from their parents. My father wrote that I had stayed at home because of the rainy weather and illness. In brackets he added – "a light cold". Darsky was satisfied with this.

We learned we were to be taught a new and interesting subject – political literacy. The whole of Year 8 came together for the first of these lessons. Olga Nikolaievna led in a stout, bearded gentleman in a trench coat and patent leather shoes. When she had gone, the man announced that in order to get to know us, he wanted us to answer a question. He turned to a girl in the front row.

"If a girlfriend of yours came to Moscow who had never been here before, where would be the first place you would take her to?"

"I'd take her to the Kremlin," she girl answered in a low voice, "but they don't let you in."

The man frowned, then put the same question to a boy.

"The Tretyakov picture gallery," answered the lad.

Again there came a frown. The question was put to another girl. "The Alexander Third Museum," came the answer.

The fat man groaned and banged his hands together.

A boy who had understood the situation now said, "Lenin's Mausoleum". At this the man looked happy and began to tell us what a great man Lenin had been. He took only one more lesson with us, never to reappear, obviously disillusioned by our lack of class-consciousness. His replacement was a handsome young man with sweeping moustaches, Konstantin Vasiliyevich Basilevich. The girls swooned over him. The subject he was supposed to teach us was not political literacy but sociology. In fact, it should have been called

Russian history, but Basilevich, a historian at a time when this subject was beginning to be frowned upon, had the sense to put on a mask. He did not teach us a lesson so much as read us lectures on the history of our country, and I can really say that I owe my love of history to him. Later on he rose to great heights, becoming, after the purge of the most famous historians, professor at a higher Party school and a corresponding member of the Academy of Sciences.

Political clouds still hung over our school, partly because of two clever but not so exemplary students. Andrei Kiselev and Kostya Krasilnikov, both pupils in my class, had rigged up a sort of home laboratory where they did all kinds of experiments. Just before a school assembly they put together a phial with sulphuric acid at one end, and at the other, separated by a thin divider, a particular kind of powder. They passed it round the rows of assembled pupils until one of them, accidentally dropped it. The tube smashed and a most terrible smell of rotten eggs spread through the hall just as a visiting activist was passionately lecturing us about the future of communism. The lecture had to be broken off, the room ventilated, and it was some time before we all reassembled. All this excitement put us in no mood to listen to the prophetic utterances of the speaker. The immediate reaction of the administration had to be "the class enemy is aiming to wreck things". When an investigation revealed that some of the best pupils were implicated in the affair, an attempt was made to hush things up. Had this same incident occurred a few years later the pupils, their parents and their teachers would all have been arrested.

I became friends with Andrei Kiselev and his friend Alyosha, the son of the great Russian painter Nesterov. We decided to publish our own magazine, which we called *Salamander*, and enlisted two other boys from Year 7. Alyosha submitted some poetry, I wrote a story and Andrei provided a serious article – he wrote that if the institutions of higher learning were only accepting workers' sons and poor peasants, then there was nothing left for us sinners to do but to take up self-education. We also received articles and stories from some of the girls, and our caricaturists supplied the cover. Andrei was bursting with energy and enterprise. He had read in an old copy of *Niva* how to make a printing press, and this led to a secret printing press being set up in Kostya Krasilnikov's flat in Ruzheyny Street. By inking up a sheet of plywood covered with letterpress, we managed after great efforts to print off ten copies of our magazine. Two copies were given to the teaching staff, the remainder distributed about the classes. This happened on a day when Basilevich was teaching us. He poured considerable praise on our initiative and recalled how in his youth at the gymnasium he had helped to produce a similar journal. The whole class looked at me, a member of the editorial group; modestly, I kept my eyes lowered. There was already, however, an official magazine, edited by the one and only *Konsomol* in the school – a rather pimply lad called Albov. He quickly recognised the danger of a rival paper. As the official magazine printed articles about Lenin and about world revolution, it was hardly surprising that most of the pupils preferred our *Salamander*. Albov and his colleagues spread the rumour that not long ago in another school an identical domestic printing press had been discovered, and that it had been printing anti-Soviet material

Andrei Kiselev and Alyosha Nesterov were called in by Darsky, who frightened them enough to have them abandon the magazine. After lessons our editorial group met; there was a proposal to go on printing in secret, but in the end reason prevailed and we decided to heed the school director's advice. We four – Kiselev, Nesterov, Krasilnikov and I – left school in a gloomy mood, but vowing to consecrate our friendship. Mingling our blood would be unsanitary, so we settled on beer. We knew of a private pub on Zubovsky Square, the "Zubok". Between us we had enough small change for four beers. Thus, for the first time in my life, I penetrated, shamefaced, through a little door into a smoky and overheated room, crowded with suspicious-looking men. I think I must have felt how a young man would feel going for the first time into a brothel. Andrei and Alyosha were tall, Kostya Krasilnikov rather short. The barman poured out three glasses, but said that he did not serve anyone under-age. We found a table covered with pools of beer and ashtrays full of fag-ends, and taking an empty glass, shared out the three measures. After we had drunk to our friendship, we all went home. From then on I sometimes revisited this bar with either Andrei or Alyosha. Kostya declined to come again. Once I bumped into my brother Vladimir there and we were both quite embarrassed; it turned out that he occasionally came here, probably without telling his wife. Three years later the "Zubok" was closed and to our annoyance the building was turned into a public toilet. Not long after that, however, on the grounds that it interfered with the line of the Sadovoye Koltso, it was pulled down.

I was invited to Alyosha Nesterov's birthday party. He and his sister lived with their parents on the street called Sitsevoye Vrazhko. Knowing that I was going to see his father, the famous artist, my mother asked me to try to convey to the painter what a lasting joy his paintings of Holy Sergei, the patron saint of Sergiyev Posad, had made on her as a fourteen-year-old girl. I was the first to arrive at Alyosha's party. I was met by a short, strongly built, bearded man with sharp eyes and a slightly asymmetrical bald head. I quickly stammered out mother's words; he was clearly very pleased and asked me to thank her for them.

For the conditions of the time, the Nesterov flat was luxurious. There were fine pieces of furniture, good china, plenty of books, and many paintings by well-known artists. In a second room, which was not open to just anybody, there hung two pictures by Nesterov himself. One was a big canvas of three monks resting under a pine tree with a fox cub coming up to them and a valley stretching out in the background. The other canvas was called *The Philosophers* and showed two figures walking along a forest track in deep thought – one was the philosopher S.N. Bulgakov, the other the priest, Father Pavel Florensky.

As far as school went I was an average pupil and, except for maths, would have got fair marks in my other subjects. But in those days the Soviet authorities had decided that marking was a survival of the old, discredited system, so subjects were not marked other than by the word "satisfactory". The only subject for which I did homework was maths, which led my mother one day to ask me, in an anxious way, "Why don't you ever do any other homework?"

"Only idiots do homework," was my reply. My classmates would have given the same reply, adding, "Now if we got marks, then we'd study quite differently."

In the autumn of 1927, my cousin Lelya Davydova joined my class. She was brought to Moscow by her parents, Ekaterina Sergeievna and Alexander Vasiliyevich Davydov – Aunt Katya and Uncle Alda – from their home in the province of Tambov. The family lived in the Davydov family home, a fine mansion with a columned portico, but in every other respect they shared the lives of the peasants of their village, Kulevatovo, into whose communal life they had been welcomed. Uncle Alda ploughed and sowed and reaped along with all the other peasants. Lelya settled in with us, but was at first very homesick and for that reason found it difficult to make friends at school. However, when our friends visited us at the weekends and we played crazy games, such as pillow fights, Lelya would join in with as much spirit as anyone else. Ever since those days, with the exception of the war years, we have kept up a close friendship.

The summer of that year a little man, dressed neatly in a grey suit, arrived at Glinkovo with Aunt Lilya Sheremtyeva and her four children. We discovered that she had made plans to leave Russia, and that the man was a relative of hers who was a member of the Estonian embassy. They had contracted a fictitious marriage, though how her four children were recognised as his, remains a mystery. They were with us for quite a long time as the formalities, as is always the case in our country, dragged on and on. One evening Petrusha and I found a young man sitting eavesdropping under one of our windows. We tried to catch him, but he ran away too fast. He had certainly been sent to spy on us. It was already November when finally the Sheremetyevs were able to leave. No less than fifty people saw them off at Belorussky station, including two snoopers. I shall not write about their subsequent life. Had the two boys, Petrusha and Pavlusha, stayed in Russia, it is almost certain they would not have survived.

9. The Light and the Dark

1

Father's salary was nowhere near enough to feed his family and dependants – something like twelve people in all, so we had to be extremely careful about what food and clothes we bought. There was in those days a paper called the *Financial Gazette* and one of father's friends, who was on the editorial staff, encouraged father to write some articles. Father wrote to his brother, Alexander Golitsyn, in America, and began to receive copies of American financial journals, which helped him to write on subjects such as "Belgium's Budget", or "The Financial Situation in Canada". He was careful only to sign these with his initials, M.G.

Mother used to say that when father came back from work she could always tell whether an article had been published and exactly how much he had been paid for it – three roubles, five roubles, or even more. Meanwhile in Sergiyev Posad the families of Uncle Vladimir Trubetskoi and Uncle Alyosha Lopukhin were finding it almost impossible to make ends meet. Attracted by the prospect of decent earnings, Uncle Vladimir joined the band that played in a local restaurant, where the drunken diners often sent gifts of money or bottles of wine and vodka over to the musicians. Vodka had just begun to come onto the market again. The commissar for economics was Comrade Rykov, and so it was called *rykovka*. The work was hard on Uncle Vladimir and also led him, unwittingly, into acquiring a taste for wine. My grandparents helped his family by handing over most of the money they were sent from abroad, and Uncle Vladimir's own nearest relatives who were abroad also sent some, though not at all generous, sums of money. He bought a cow, which soon died. Nor was Aunt Eli a frugal housekeeper. Yet despite these worries, Uncle Vladimir never seemed to be downcast; whenever he had any free time he would go off into the forest with his gun.

Uncle Alyosha and his family were in an even worse situation. They had settled in Sergiyev Posad and, along with the Istomin family, had tried to set up a church candle business, which quickly failed. But then someone suggested that they buy a knitting machine to make socks. Uncle Alyosha was a born mechanic and by removing certain pins he soon adapted the machine to make vari-patterned socks and stockings. He also worked out how to make the heels out of two layers so that the socks would last much longer, and named this feature "the steel heel". For four years my mother was commissioned to buy brown and beige wool from some Chinese merchants in Moscow. At regular intervals Uncle Alyosha would arrive in Moscow with his batches of finished socks which mother, together with my sisters Lina, Sonya and Masha, would sell to their friends and their friends' friends. There was no lack of market for these elegant and relatively cheap products; Sergiyev Posad was full of people wearing them. Uncle Alyosha was even nicknamed "Sockman". On his visits to us in Moscow, he would invariably spend the evening playing bridge before setting off back home with his earnings.

Turning the handle of a sock-making machine was an activity that he found very boring; he much preferred gossiping and smoking his pipe, or indulging in his favourite reading, Elena Molokhovets' book *A Gift for Young Housewives*.[16] Fortunately his wife, Aunt Tyosa, was an energetic and capable mother and housekeeper, who not only managed all their domestic affairs, but even found time to turn the handle of the sock-making machine. Nonetheless, the earnings from this machine were minimal, whilst Uncle Alyosha's family kept on growing, eventually reaching a total of seven children. The family was helped by Aunt Tyosa's unmarried younger sister, Alexandra Bogdanovna Meyerdorf – Sandra, or Sandrishka. She had a job as secretary to a certain Speed Elliot, representative of the American millionaire Harrison, who owned a manganese concession in Chituary in the Caucasus. Sandra was a wonderfully spirited young lady. She lived in a single room in a communal apartment in Serebranaya Street and shocked her elderly neighbours by keeping company with young, similarly high-spirited, people.

2

It was about this time that Russians who had "relations with foreigners" (employees of embassies, missions and trading firms, or who just knew foreigners) began to be arrested. It was certainly why Oleg Volkov was arrested. A joke did the rounds: a lady is arrested

---

16. *The Russian Mrs Beeton.*

and asked, "Have you had relations with any foreigner?" Blushing, she replies, "Only once, with a Greek, in Odessa." Sandra Meyerdorf was repeatedly warned by her sister, Nadezhda, and husband Alexander Rayevsky – Aunt Nadya and Uncle Shurik – to change the way she behaved towards foreigners, but she loved the carefree life she was leading and did not heed their wise advice. Uncle Shurik's particular characteristic was his great caution. He had laid down a rule for his nearest and dearest, that when they visited him they should always ring three times. He and his wife both loved music and often went to concerts in the evening. If they were out, Sandra would bring her foreign friends to their large flat on Arbat street and spend the evening dancing to the gramophone.

Uncle Shurik received his education at the Moscow Lyceum – the building on Ostozhenka that now houses the Institute of Foreign Affairs – and then became an officer in the artillery. It so happened that a group of former pupils of the Lyceum, living as emigrants in Paris, were celebrating an anniversary and in their dinner-table speeches remembered their contemporaries with the words, "living in servitude under the Bolsheviks, though undoubtedly still loyal to their oath to the Tsar". These speeches were printed in an emigrant paper and as a result the OGPU arrested all former Lyceum pupils, not just in Moscow but also in Petersburg. Those arrested included our cautious Uncle Shurik Rayevsky. His case ought to have been mitigated by his circumstances; he had no title, before the revolution had owned no property, and was now a Soviet employee, if only a minor one. Former officers were not necessarily persecuted at this period, and in any case, at his interrogation he replied that he was "loyal". But against that was the fact that foreigners visited his flat and worse than that, he could not explain to the interrogator why his nearest and dearest visitors always pressed the doorbell three times. Such odd behaviour smacked of an anti-Soviet conspiracy. Under articles 58(10) and 58(11) of the Penal Code, Uncle Shurik was sentenced to five years in the Gulag.

When Aunt Nadya, visiting him in prison, learned what her husband had been accused of, she began to wonder who could have revealed to the secret police the fact of the three rings and the names of their visitors. By the simple process of elimination, she guessed who was the betrayer. Whilst Uncle Shurik was still locked up in the Lyubyanka prison, his sister-in-law, Sandra, had had her flat officially searched. They did not dare arrest her; she was, after all, the secretary of a favoured American businessman. But on that fateful evening there just happened to be visiting her my brother-in-law, Georgy

Osorgin, and my cousin Alexei Bobrinsky. Both were arrested. Normally, Georgy avoided Sandra's company and I cannot imagine why he had turned up at her flat at all. However, as a man of enormous integrity he would anyway hardly have been left free for long. Alexei Bobrinsky, who was then living in Uncle Vladimir Golitsyn's flat on Khlebnoy Street, was still a mere youth. I do not remember where he was working at that time, but I know that he was very proud of the fact that he was received into the circles of older and fast-living adults where he, too, could let himself go. Anyway, after some ten days he was released, whilst Georgy was transferred to Butyrka prison. Sister Lina now went with provisions for her husband every week. There she would receive the previous week's wrapping back, with the words "received and complete" written on the outside, and her husband's signature. Once she discovered on a dirty towel the two letters NX written in pencil. What could they mean – do not intervene, or hopes are good? I have to say that in those days we all lived in hope. However bleak our present was, we lived in the hope of better times, of a brighter future.

Energetic steps were taken on Georgy's behalf. My beautiful cousin, Sonya Bobrinskaya, went to plead on his behalf with Commissar Yenukidze. My mother went to see Smidovich, whilst my father turned for help in two directions – to Doctor Gyotye, who was physician to the Party leaders and their wives, and to Peshkova at the PRC. He introduced the unhappy Lina to Ekaterina Pavlovna Peshkova, who allowed Lina to come and see her without making an appointment or waiting endlessly outside her office with all the other petitioners. Peshkova questioned Lina closely about our families and what we all were doing and was obviously very concerned about our situation. These acts of intervention were of no help to Georgy, who at his interrogation, when asked for his political views, unhesitatingly replied, "Monarchist", and even added more about his views, which the interrogator gleefully wrote down in his statement. Georgy was sentenced to ten years forced labour. Peshkova told Lina that he might have been sentenced to be shot, as Yagoda had told her that Georgy had been excessively "challenging" at his interrogation.

The only effect of all our efforts was to save Georgy from being sent to Solovki; instead he ended up on the "workers' corridor" in Butyrka together with Uncle Shurik, Uncle Nikolai Vladimirovich Golitsyn and his son Kirill, and many other friends, who all formed a fairly jolly company of prisoners. In addition to her weekly deliveries of provisions, Lina was now allowed a forty minute visit with her husband every Sunday. Georgy was even privileged to receive a second visit on the same day from either his parents or one of his sisters.

3

Many people wondered out loud about casting pearls before swine in front of the interrogators, and in return for their bold and sincere words were given long sentences in the camps, leaving behind wives and children and other dependants to struggle to keep alive, or even without any support at all. When Uncle Vladimir Trubetskoi was arrested (for the fifth time), he was soon released, whereas Georgy remained locked up, even though both were monarchists. Georgy refused to go back on his convictions, but Uncle Vladimir at that time had six children and so answered the interrogator with the word "loyal". I think both were right to act as they did, in their own ways.

At their interrogation it became obvious to our relatives and friends that the OGPU knew their relations and friends very well. How did they know all this, who was the informant? It was soon obvious to all who the only possible betrayer could be: Alexei Bobrinsky, who had also been arrested, but then set free after only ten days. My father warned me sternly to be very careful in my conversations with Alexei. I was truly shattered by this piece of news. A Count Bobrinsky, the descendant of the Empress Catherine, and my close friend – could he really be a traitor? Someone who goes to the secret police and tells them all about us and our affairs, and then moves amongst us, listening to our talk? I believed that if any of us, "knights without fear or reproach", found a traitor amongst us, he must be put to death without mercy. I began to wonder how I could kill Alexei. This was, however, only in theory. It was quite different in practice. Greeting him, I shook his hand, talked to him and shared cigarettes with him. Others shook his hand also and conversed with him, and the girls willingly danced with him. But when he approached, conversations either stopped or went into a neutral mode. An invisible barrier rose between him and us. I do not think that he was very perceptive and for two or three years was unaware of these invisible barriers.

We "former people" clung very closely together as misfortune struck us. We were ready with material help even for cousins three times removed, if their brothers or husbands were arrested. Our togetherness gave us strength, and this close relationship between brothers and sisters and distant cousins meant that having a betrayer in our midst was like having a Judas. From now on, we met any newcomer with suspicion, pondered the exact meaning of his or her questions, watched their behaviour, and only after some years of friendship could any doubts be dissipated. In the course of the coming years other traitors appeared in our ranks, while some were perhaps wrongly suspected. In this context, I shall later mention three men and one woman. Others are still alive as I write these lines; yet others lie in the earth at Kolyma or Vorkuta.[17] I shall not mention their names as they have family and descendants still alive who loved and respected them. May the stain on their lives go to the grave with me.

Was there no pleasant side to life? Unfortunately, those were our lives, the dark side dominating. Yet we were young and carefree, and every Saturday in our spacious apartment on Eropkinsky Street my guests and my sister Masha's guests, our various cousins, the Rayevsky brothers – Sergei, Mikhail and Andrei – and other youths attracted by Masha's charms – would all get together. Lilya Ilyinskaya came, too, as did the man we felt was regularly betraying us, my cousin Alexei Bobrinsky. We would start up our crazy game, the "mad pillow", and if Sonya was at home she would lead a quadrille whilst Grandmother played her famous galop on the piano and we dashed about in the dance.

Not far off, in Starokonushnaya Street, in a damp little room, the library that had belonged to Anna Vladimirovna Belyavsky, Uncle Alexander Vladimirovich Davydov's cousin, was slowly mouldering away. At the beginning of the revolution her husband had died and her only son, an officer, had been shot. Left all alone, she moved with the Davydovs to Kulevatovo. We transported bundles of these books by sledge to our flat. Today many of them would be of enormous value. It is thanks to them that I acquired my knowledge of history. I can name some of them – Oscar Jaeger's *A General History* in four volumes, Elise Reclus's *The Universe and Mankind*, Schilder's *Alexander I* and Catherine II's *Memoirs*.

Those were times when publishing the memoirs of some of the White Guards, for example Denikin's, or Shulgin's *Days* and *1920*, was not dangerous. Many foreign authors were translated – some are still available, others prohibited and so vanished. The writings of Hemingway, Galsworthy, the two Sinclairs and Romain Rolland

---

17. *Vorkuta, north of the Arctic Circle and Kolyma in the Siberian Far East, were notorious Gulags.*

were permitted, Claude Farrere's and André Gide's forbidden. The *Adventures of Tarzan* came out in instalments eagerly passed from hand to hand. All this writing I swallowed whole, without distinction, sometimes sitting up until late in the night.

4

Our cousin, Sonya Bobrinskaya, married her boss, the representative of a British shipping company, Reginald Witter. At that time many distressed NEPmen, mostly Jewish, were able to emigrate without obstacles, above all to South America, so the shipping companies were doing good business. Reginald – Reg for short – won everyone over with his simplicity, kindness, considerate behaviour and intelligence.

"Lucky you, you'll be a subject of His Majesty!" grandmother said to her granddaughter when the engaged couple came to see her before their wedding. They were married in the church of Spas on Peskakh near the Arbat. Thanks to Polenov's picture *A Moscow Courtyard*, this church is the only one of a dozen neighbouring churches to have survived to this day. The bride went into the church on my father's arm. The first groom was her brother Alexei, the second her cousin, Sasha Golitsyn, and I was very happy to be her third groom. I was very proud of this, and looked condescendingly on the fourth groom, Yusha Samarin. The bridegroom's best men were all foreigners; the first a friend of Reginald's, Mr Burberry. The others I cannot remember. The priest's words, "We here marry this servant of God, Reginald, and this servant of God, Sofia" for some reason made everyone smile, and this was followed by a bit of confusion – the groom's best men started to follow the couple around the analoy, and had to be pulled back by their coat-tails.

As we had a spacious flat on Eropkinsky, the wedding feast was held there, with a great number of guests from both sides. There was food in abundance and the wine flowed in torrents. A snooping spy was discovered to have infiltrated himself among the guests, but made himself scarce when a dozen pairs of eyes swivelled on him. The young couple moved into an old house that had belonged to the Geyre family on Gagarinskaya Street, taking with them Aunt Vera Bobrinskaya and Sonya's younger sister, Elena. Other tenants had now moved into "Hell", "Purgatory" and "Paradise" on Spiridonovka Street.

The Witters occasionally organised lively parties. An invariable guest was the tall, well-built, moustached figure of Mr Burberry, a former officer who had taken part in the English intervention in Archangelsk and spoke excellent Russian. I was delighted when one day Sonya Witter, visiting us with her husband, said, "Why don't you ever come and see us?" From then on I was a regular visitor in Gagarinskaya Street, where one always ate very well. On one occasion, Burberry sat down next to my sister Lina and asked her about the fate of her husband, why he had been arrested and about her visits to him in prison. People began to say that one had to be careful with Burberry because he seemed to be interested in all those people whose husbands or brothers had been arrested. One winter evening, when there had been a thaw, all the Witters' guests came out into the courtyard and began to play snowballs. I threw a snowball that hit Burberry's wife in the face and brought tears to her eyes. The couple made to leave, muttering angry words in English as they did so. As he helped his wife on with her coat, Burberry shook his fist at me. From that time on I was no longer invited to the Witters. I was hurt and humiliated, but now I think, "Thank goodness I stopped going there," as many of the Witters' guests ended up in prison. If I had hit Burberry's wife on the shoulder instead of the nose, I might have continued to visit them and finished up the same way.

5

One of the pleasures of those times was the theatre. Alexander Ivanovich Yuzhin was not only a great actor, but also the director of the Maly Theatre. I have already written about his wife, Maria Nikolaievna, who was an old friend of my father's. She had use of the director's box until the death of her husband in 1927, and would often ring up my father and offer it to him for a particular evening. Father would announce this happy news and we would cast around for our friends. There was a special, separate entrance to this box, which is why later on our leaders took to using it as they could shield themselves from the wider public behind a curtain. The box would be packed with all of us from Eropkinsky, cousins from Khlebnaya Street and, on occasion, grandfather. What a wonderful place the Maly Theatre was. In those dark days of my youth, what evenings of beauty and magic we enjoyed, jammed together, two to a chair, elbow to elbow, watching the inspirational scenes unfolding on its stage. I still have some of the notebooks in which I wrote up my impressions of the plays we saw.

We only rarely went to the Arts Theatre. Alexander Alexandrovich Rayevsky had a cousin, Countess Anna Petrovna Uvarova, who for a time ran an orphanage on her estate. One of these children became administrator of the Arts Theatre, Fyodor Nikolaievich Mikhalsky – later portrayed in great detail as Fili Tulumbasov in Bulgakov's book *A Theatrical Novel*. Anna Petrovna would write out little notes – "Dear Fedya, my nephew, cousin, or friend would like to have – ". I would call on this Mikhalsky, a stout man rather like the capitalists depicted in the humorous journal *Krokodil*. Once he gave me a keen look and asked – "Do you have a girlfriend?" I blushed and said nothing. He handed me a slip authorizing entrance for two; he never gave such slips for only one person. Taking with us a newspaper, we would lay this on the steps in the amphitheatre, sit ourselves down and be lost to the world as the curtain with its famous and beloved seagull rose before us.

I went to other theatres, again after getting hold of special vouchers. This way my friends and I got into every theatre, so brilliantly described by the comic writers, Ilf and Petrov, in their book *The Twelve Chairs*. There was no point in queuing at the box office, but only at the administrator's door. As for girlfriends, well, for the time being I shall stay silent on that subject.

6

At the beginning of 1925, the school curriculum was reorganised. We were told that now we were not studying in school number 11, Leo Tolstoy Khamraion, but that in the Years 8 and 9 we would be studying land-surveying and assessment, which meant that geodesics, draughting and mapping would be added to our usual studies. We protested against this reorganisation and followed the new course without any interest in it. An ancient military surveyor, a heavy drinker, taught draughting. For homework, he made us draw a large-scale plan, which I managed more or less, though spoilt by ink blots. When at our next lesson I handed over my paper, he laughed and asked me in front of the whole class, "What, did you scratch it out with a pair of scissors?" Annoyed, I replied "Anyway, I'm not going to be a draughtsman." I now acquired a new friend, Shura Sokolov, the son of a tsarist colonel. We shared the same desk, in the front row on the right. After my failure at draughting, Shura drew two copies, one for himself and one for me. In our desk we kept a piece of chalk and a slate and if I was in difficulties answering a problem when called up to the front of the class, Shura would write the answer on the slate and hold it up for me to see. Shura was poor at Russian, whereas I was considered one of the best, so I would write two different essays and all Shura had to do was copy one out in his own hand.

Once these double essays led to a nasty incident. The subject set by our teacher was "The Decadence of the Nobility in Chekhov's *Cherry Orchard*". For Shura, I wrote a piece describing the rotten state of the nobility, the way they exploited their servants, how their social roots were polluted and about their inherent melancholy. Then, remembering my childhood at Bulchalki, I wrote how the estates of the nobility flourished, how they helped the poor when in need and enjoyed close ties with their peasants. I said that only vegetables and meat can go rotten, not living people. I think my tone was rather harsh and I put my case without using much logic or skill. The next day the teacher came in with the huge stack of essays. First, she read out an exemplary essay by a model girl pupil, then mine, and immediately called on the class to discuss them both. This discussion was stormy. Yura Nevedomsky, with whom I had already quarrelled, attacked my work as that of a class enemy. In reply, I said I would say nothing in my defence. The bell rang, and before leaving, Vera Vladimirovna whispered to me to come to the teachers' room. There all she said was, "Don't ever write such awful things again!"

From then on, I only wrote essays full of the ideas of the time, and the teacher heaped praise on me. But it almost came to a break in our relations when she set us the task of writing the story of our lives. Before submitting my long piece on the ups and downs of our family life, I took the precaution of showing to my mother and sisters. They immediately told me to burn it, so I ended up writing nothing. Two other pupils also refused to write this essay. One was Petya Birman, who had had a very hard childhood. His father had been a major general in the engineers and had died of typhus in Butyrka prison. Only a few years later his mother also died, leaving Petya to be brought up by his two sisters, whilst their older brother had been sent into exile. The other was Leva Miklashkevsky, who came of an old and well-known Ukrainian family. There were five Miklashevksy children in the school, an older sister and four brothers, all very close. They had dark eyes and were very attractive, though rather short in stature. Leva was the second brother. Their mother was dead, and their father was constantly being arrested, released and then arrested again, finally dying in the Gulag. An old aunt brought up the family. It was obvious why Petya and Leva were not keen to write the story of their lives. Tactfully, Vera Vladimirovna suggested we choose another subject. I wrote a piece about the first time I had experienced spring in the countryside. She praised this composition in front of the whole class and said I had the makings of a real writer. For some time, I walked about with my nose in the air.

7

I was now sharing a bedroom with both my grandparents and my parents. As usual in Holy Week, we fasted, confessed and took communion with Father Vladimir Vorobev in the church of Nikola Plotnik on the Arbat. On Good Friday, I visited twelve churches and bowed to the images of the Passion. In those days there were so many churches between Prechistenkaya Street and the Arbat that it took more than a couple of hours to do this, even when one stopped for just a few minutes in each church. For Holy Week, mother sold some silver spoons and was able to prepare the Easter dish of *paskha* – cottage cheese, cream and egg whites – and *kulitch*, the dry Easter cake to eat with it. We had our usual argument as to where to go for the morning service – Trinity on Zubov, or Pokrov in Levshin. We never stayed for communion but walked home with our lit candles. Then began the exchange of the Easter greeting, *Khristos voscres* (Christ is Risen), at which point Lina fled, not wishing to exchange this greeting with our lodger, Adamovich, who was one of her admirers. We then sat down to break our fast.

Holy Week fell during school holidays, so my bedtime was late. On the Tuesday I went to bed about midnight and had barely laid my head on the pillow when the doorbell rang, and went on ringing insistently. I leapt out of bed, dressed quickly and looked out into the corridor. Standing at the other end was the tall figure of a Red Army soldier in his greatcoat and blue cap trimmed with red. I hurried into the sitting-room and saw there an official in a leather jacket holding out a paper to my brother Vladimir, who had his back to me, on which was written the word "Order" and in both print and handwriting the words "Search" and "Arrest of Golitsyn Mikhail Vladimirovich, and Golitsyn Vladimir Mikhailovich, the 'Young'." The word "young" was underlined, and the order was signed "G. Yagoda, Deputy Head, OGPU".

One by one, in their nightwear, the bewildered members of our family came into the room. Her nerves caused Nanny Bush to need the bathroom, but the official, whose name was Chernyavy, refused to let her go until, as she sat there groaning, he understood her problem and with an angry wave allowed her to leave the room.

Mother sat all hunched up and trembling by the table. Grandmother was moaning. The others sat in gloomy silence. A second Red Army soldier was called in from the back door; he had obviously been posted there to stop anyone escaping. The official witness was the house supervisor. Chernyavy checked with him the register of occupants to make sure everyone was present. Then he straightened up and pointed at a white-painted desk covered with schoolbooks and asked, "Whose is that?"

"Mine," I said, and stepped forward.

This desk had once been in the Bobrinsky's schoolroom, but in Moscow it became mine to use. It was to go with us in our many changes of address, and I last saw it in the home of my niece, Elena Trubetskoi, after the war. It's hard to believe that after more than fifty years it can have ended up on the rubbish heap. Chernyavy pulled out the desk drawer and began to shuffle about among my notebooks, after which he went over to Sonya's table where he found the health records she had been working on. She tried to explain what they meant – these columns of figures headed "drinks moderately", "does not drink", "used to drink", but he soon abandoned these and fixed his attention on a photograph of a young officer with an ensign's insignia of rank.

"Who's this?" he asked.

"I don't know," she answered.

"Who is it?" He showed all of us the picture, but we either shrugged our shoulders in silence or answered that we did not know, although we all knew perfectly well that it was Prince Vladimir Nikolaievich Dolgoruky, one of Sonya's admirers. Chernyavy put this clear piece of evidence on the dining table. The soldier then began to leaf through the books on their shelves, pulling a letter out of one of them. Chernyavy went through into the next room and found the foreign financial papers and journals lying on father's desk. Father explained their origins and showed his articles in the *Financial Gazette*. These papers were also laid on the dining table. Luckily, Chernyavy did not pay any attention to the rather massive volume of grandfather's diary. He did, however, take a thick sheaf of letters and other documents, and also a notebook bound in blue satin with the words *Letters from Tsarist Individuals* printed in silver on the cover. He also took our letters written from Bogoroditsk to our parents in Tula when father was in prison there, amongst which was a letter from six-year-old Katya, written in big letters in coloured pencil, "Dear Mama and Papa, come quickly, we have a hen. Katya."

In the years ahead, when massive arrests were taking place, such quantities of documents were seized, papers, letters, writings and books, that they began to burn all these in the basement of the Lyubyanka and similar places. What talented writings, philosophical tracts and scientific papers must have disappeared, just like their authors, known and unknown. That was how the papers of the writers Pilnyak and Babel, of Vavilov and Florensky went up in smoke, as did the millions of works of those whose name was "Only you, O Lord, know us". Yet all the papers taken from us in that search have survived intact. Where? In the Central State Archives for ancient papers! My little sister's letter is carefully preserved under its own catalogue number in the same place as seventeenth-century records and the testament of Dmitry Donskoy[18] (over which quarrelling broke out amongst his heirs, that lasted more than twenty years). I was able to have a look at the so-called Golitsyn archive, consisting of more than ten thousand items, beginning with a coarse letter from Peter the First to my great-great-great-grandmother and ending up with our scrawls. It seems unbelievable, but it's true.

The search continued. Taking a gold snuffbox decorated with black enamel that lay on grandfather's desk, Chernyavy said, "Surely it's gold?"

"Yes, it's gold," said my mother faintly. "But if my husband and son are sent far away, we shan't have any way of living, and will sell it. Please don't take it." There was urgent pleading in the way she said "please". Chernyavy turned the snuffbox round, weighed it in the palm of his hand and put it back in its place. There was a story behind this beautiful piece of work. When in 1717 Peter the First went abroad for the second time, he ordered the snuffbox and had it decorated with his portrait by the famous Parisian goldsmith, Charles Boitou, as a present for Philipe d'Orleans. Some fifty years later, Louis XV gave it to Ivan Ivanovich Shuvalov. Shuvalov died in 1797 and the box was inherited by his nephew, my great-great-grandfather, Fyodor Nikolaievich Golitsyn. It then passed, judging by the initials cut into its leather case, to his third son, Fyodor Fyodorovich, ambassador to Naples, whose portrait in watercolour by Bryulov was sold by us to the Tretyakov Gallery and is now to be found there in their storerooms. After Fyodor Fyodorovich's death the snuffbox went to his younger brother, my great-grandfather Mikhail Fyodorovich, and then to my grandfather, who took it with

---

18. *A major Russian warrior hero who defeated the Mongols at the battle of Kulikovo in 1380, on the river Don.*

him to Bogoroditsk, where in the course of two searches the Chekists paid no attention to it and he was able to bring it back to Moscow. At this third search its fate hung in the balance, but it remained in our family.

After finishing searching my grandparents' room, Chernyavy went into the room where my sisters, Aunt Sasha and Nanny Bush slept. He came across such a mass of baskets and bundles with all kinds of rags, not to mention the chamberpots under the beds, that he gave up any search and moved on into Vladimir and Elena's room. There on the writing desk were all kinds of artist's materials, a jar with pencils and paintbrushes, little bottles of ink and tubes of colour, surrounded by sketches and drawings. There was also the hand-written manuscript of a book that Vladimir was illustrating. Vladimir began to explain that he was an artist, that he illustrated books, and begged Chernyavy not to take anything away as this was the only clean copy of the author's work and he would be in despair if it were lost. Chernyavy put the things he had picked up back on the table, and said, "I see that all of you work somewhere." His words and the look in his eyes conveyed not exactly compassion, but at least a hint of compassion.

"Yes, everyone works," my mother confirmed.

It was almost light. The searchers were visibly tired. Chernyavy sent the sleepy house superintendent and a soldier off to telephone for the truck, while the other soldier went on slowly picking things over. We all wanted to sleep. Nanny Bush lit the samovar and we sat down to drink tea, inviting the searchers to join us.

"We are not allowed to," replied Chernyavy, although he clearly would have liked some tea. He sat down to write his report.

The terrible moment of separation was approaching. One of the soldiers went out onto the landing to have a smoke, then came back and whispered something to Chernyavy. Both went out and there came an exclamation of astonishment as Chernyavy saw the tower of suitcases and trunks standing on the landing. Mother pointed to the upper trunks and explained that only those belonged to us, the remainder belonging to relatives of ours who had emigrated. The reader will recall how we were entrusted with the furniture, books and pictures belonging to the family of my mother's cousin, Prince Evgeny Nikolaievich Trubetskoi, when they were exiled abroad in 1922. Mother told Chernyavy that we had no idea what was in any of their trunks. He demanded the keys, ordered a soldier to open up one of the trunks, pulled back the cloth covering the contents, and we all exclaimed in horror at what was revealed.

"I swear we had no idea what was in there," mother moaned. Lying on top were two large photographs in elaborate, encrusted mahogany frames. They showed Tsar Nicholas II wearing rows of medals, and Tsarina Alexandra Fyodorovna in a stately white dress. Mother repeated that we had never known what was in these trunks. Chernyavy gave a sarcastic laugh, laid the two frames on the table and added a line to his report.

The prison truck – the "black crow", as it was known – now arrived, with its tiny windows covered with steel mesh. Father and Vladimir with their bundles containing a change of underwear, a spoon, a bowl and a mug, were escorted down the back stairs, accompanied by all of us. They climbed into the back of the truck, where there were already other people who had been arrested.

We were shattered by the arrest of our nearest and dearest. I went to school, but did not tell a soul of our sorrow. I was not alone in this situation. Andrei Kiselev, swearing me to silence, whispered that Alyosha Nesterov's father had been arrested. It was awful to see Alyosha; his face dark with sorrow and his eyes wandering crazily. This fact, that the famous painter Nesterov was once arrested, is not known to historians, but I can attest to it. Thanks to the efforts of the architect Shchuchev, he was quickly released.

Mother rushed off to see Smidovich. He was very understanding, promised to intervene, but added. "if only those portraits . . .". When Lina told Peshkova about the arrests, Peshkova cried out, "Such a wonderful man, who has intervened for so many others, and now he's arrested too". She promised to speak to Yagoda, but also added, "if only those portraits . . .". At their next interviews with Smidovich and Peshkova it was obvious that all might have been well, as they had made a very good impression on their interrogator, were it not for the fateful portraits of the Tsar and Tsarina. The interrogator was implacable. "It's impossible to believe that they did not know about them. They were just waiting to hang them up again."

8

Despite the interrogator's thoughts on the matter, so much influence was exerted on Yagoda and his colleagues that father was released after two weeks and Vladimir a few days later. On the day of my father's release the cat gave birth to kittens on mother's bed. How can one not believe in good and bad omens? Father and Vladimir both told us how politely they had been treated by the interrogator. They were put in adjoining cells, and the interrogator showed interest in father's work and asked him his views. Both father and Vladimir made it clear why they were not monarchists. Father added that he approved of the monetary reforms, the introduction of the *chervonets*, and the government's policy of helping hard-working peasants to improve their methods of cultivation. As for the portraits, both men stoutly denied on oath that they had ever known about them. Vladimir was warned to fraternise less with foreigners, although this restriction did not apply to Mr Witter, who was now a relative. That year Vladimir and his wife and my sister Sonya, to my great envy, were quite often invited to the home of the Norwegian ambassador, Mr Urbi, whose residence was a few steps away in Mertvoy Lane. Urbi, an elderly, respectable man, also visited us with his wife. We were allowed to be friendly with them. But we kept our distance from Mr Witter's friend, Burberry, who was no lover of the Soviet Union and a spy.

Father and Vladimir were astonished by the detailed information the police had about us and our friends and relatives, information that could only have been given to the OGPU by Alexei Bobrinsky. On his return from prison, father resumed his work on Pokrovka Street in the enterprise now renamed "Kombinat Joint Stock Co.". The director, Kolebayev, called father into his office and at great length questioned him about his interrogation. He told father that he had intervened on his behalf with Yagoda. "Why on earth did you keep those portraits of the Tsars – ay, ay, ay?" he scolded father, and clearly only half-believed that father knew nothing about them.

9

Though it was now rather late in the season, mother set off to arrange the rental of a *dacha* in Glinkovo, as the local priest's second house had been turned into a club. In its place she found the front half of another house into which we settled with our cousins, Elena and Olya Golitsyn, and my sister Masha's friend Lyalya Ilinskaya, whose father was in prison. We all went about barefoot, as was then the custom. Vladimir and Elena and their little daughter, Elena or Elenka, moved into a large, newly built house, while our grandparents settled close to the Trubetskoi family in Sergiyev Posad. Glinkovo, like the rest of peasant Russia at that time, was prospering. Twice a day, kicking up the dust, the herds of cows and sheep were driven past our door. The shepherd played on a pipe and his lads ran about the herd with their whips. On all sides you could hear the thud of axes as new houses were built with their decorated eaves and carved window frames. Young couples wandered about the village from dusk to dawn, invariably singing the same song – *Hazbulat Udaloy* (bold and dashing Hasbulat).

Harvest time began on St Peter's day. First came the reaping, then the threshing. Everyone worked, from youngest to oldest, from dawn to dusk, regardless of how tired they were. I do not believe our country has ever since witnessed such hard work done on the land. Everyone was acutely aware that their food for the entire year depended on their work, so they reaped with their sickles, tied the wheat with their hands, hurried to stook the bundles, to thresh the rich harvest. Now, whenever I am in the countryside, I am carried back to the memories of that year; the mooing of cows, bleating of sheep, the shepherd's pipe, the crack of whips, the cries of lads riding in the night, the ringing of axes on wood, the hissing of sickles; sounds no longer heard in the countryside.

On the patronal feast day of the Twelve Disciples the church was full of smartly dressed peasants; the men in shiny shoes, beards carefully combed, their wives wearing white headscarves. After the mass, majestic in his golden vestments, Father Alexei went out on to the porch where he proclaimed the blessing in his deep bass voice, then held the cross for all his parishioners to kiss. By the feast day of the Dormition the intensity of harvest-time diminished. We sometimes went to mass at the monastery of Gethsemane, where the major feast day was the Burial of the Virgin, three days after the Dormition, and the church was so packed with worshippers that you could hardly make your way inside.

That year we made friends with a family of summer visitors, the Smirnovs, whose children, two daughters and a girl cousin, were the same age as us. We ran about with them for two summers, and then they stopped coming to Glinkovo: the father, an enthusiast for the propagation of Esperanto, was arrested. At first the papers wrote that under communism everyone should speak Esperanto, it was such a useful international language; then because of their correspondence with people abroad, all those connected with the language were arrested, accused of spying, and exiled into goodness knows what kind of poverty. The Society of Esperantists was closed down.

From that summer on more and more young people visited. We played endless and various games. On John the Baptist's Day, we had a tremendous water fight, boys against girls, showering each other mercilessly. Life was carefree, full of fun. But our only food was a watery wheaten gruel and jacket potatoes, and all we had to drink was carrot tea, sometimes with sugar. The girls slept in rows on the floor; the boys were sent off to the hay barn.

For her summer holidays, Lelya Davydova went to her parents at Kulevatovo. From there she wrote us a persuasive letter inviting Masha and I to join her. We refused, partly because of the cost of the tickets, but mostly because it was such fun in Glinkovo. This was a pity, as we would have seen a new part of the country, and it was the last year that the Davydovs were able to live in their big house. Soon after they were evicted and moved to a little shack in the village. Uncle Alda was now just like all the other villagers. It was suggested he rent a nearby windmill, and at that time it seemed to be a profitable move.

The villages around Sergiyev Posad were now threatened by a bandit who roamed about with a shotgun, killing or wounding solitary passers-by. Sentry posts were set up outside the villages. Young boys were encouraged to carry stout sticks. The Moscow and local papers wrote angrily about this threat and printed colourful accounts of the latest incident. An entire company of soldiers arrived and there were vivid stories written about the brave Red Army troops and how they had hunted down the criminal, stormed his hideout, seized the badly wounded man, treated his wounds and then sent him for trial. He was condemned for the murder of no less than seven people and executed.

Leaving the grandparents in Sergiyev Posad to enjoy that year's fine Indian summer, we returned to Moscow. Then a telegram arrived – grandmother was seriously ill. Mother immediately left to be with her, and then, a few days later, we received a telegram announcing grandmother's death. Father asked for leave and set off for Sergiyev Posad. The circumstances of grandmother's death were unusually special. She and grandfather lived next door to the Trubetskois, with whom they dined each day. In the Trubetskois' main room hung, in a heavy gilt frame, a portrait of their great-grandmother, Princess Elizaveta Ksaverevny Trubetskaya, born Sein-Wittgenstein, daughter of the field marshal who had defended the road to St Petersburg against Napoleon's army. It was the portrait of a lady with her hair in ringlets looking proudly down upon her descendants. The Trubetskois took it everywhere with them as she was in a way the epitome of their family's ancient line. One day, grandmother came up the narrow stairs to the first floor, banging the door behind her. The cord of the heavy picture broke and it crashed to the floor, giving grandmother a terrible shock and causing a sudden violent pain in her stomach. She was hardly able to drag herself to a chair, where Aunt Eli found her.

"It's death coming for me," grandmother said quite simply. When the doctor came the pain was so terrible she could not speak. He diagnosed that she had suffered an instantaneous cancer and within three days, in fearful agony, she died. The funeral rites took place in the church in the Krasyukovka district of Sergiyev Posad, after which her body, accompanied by Sasha Golitsyn, was brought to Moscow where she was buried close to her daughter-in-law, Tania Golitsyna, in the Dorogomilovsky cemetery. On a simple white wooden cross are written the words she herself chose – "Blessed are the pure in heart, for they shall see God." Grandmother Sofia Nikolaievna was indeed one of the pure in heart. We all loved her and I have tried to describe something of her for her descendants.

10

Left alone, grandfather was often plunged in gloom and lost in his private thoughts. He took consolation in reading and translating French and writing up the thirty-first volume of his diary. His favourite grandson was my brother Vladimir, who tried always to find a spare hour after supper to sit with him and help him lay out the very difficult "lady's patience" which he had played for decades. As he played, grandfather told stories of his distant youth. Much later, Vladimir was to regret having only written down one tenth of grandfather's stories.

Some two weeks after grandmother's funeral an old lady appeared on the scene. She sat with grandfather for about an hour and as she left, told mother that she would arrange for a cutlet to be sent in to him every day from the cafeteria of an organisation called Tsekubu, which had been set up to help scientists in their daily life. This cafeteria was just a short distance away in what is now the House of Scientists on Prechistenkaya Street, a building once owned by the industrialist Konshin of Serpukhovo. From that day on for several years another old lady would come to the door with a covered plate, one of us would transfer the cutlet and its garnish onto one of our plates and the old lady would bow low and leave. From time to time the first old lady came visiting, when grandfather would lead her into his room and they would talk together for an hour or so.

In Vladimir's diary there is a note written at the time. After the first visit of this mysterious lady, grandfather paced up and down the room, chewing his lips, always a sign that he was troubled or excited. Finally, he came over to where Vladimir was working on a picture, and told him that the lady had once been the lover of one of his friends. Vladimir muttered something in reply, and grandfather again walked up and down the room, chewing his lips. After a while he stopped behind Vladimir's back and asked, "Can you guess whose lover she was?"

"I can," said Vladimir.

Some three years later grandfather told Vladimir the whole story. When he was a young man and the Golitsyns lived in the family home on Pokrovka Street, there was a tailor's shop in a nearby basement where the window was usually open and a young woman sat sewing. Grandfather often passed by, she smiled at him and so they began to meet. It's a story that could be written in the style of Maupassant.

10. More Light and Dark

1

Eight years my senior, my brother Vladimir was a talented artist. From my earliest childhood I had always loved him, indeed worshipped him. In the years immediately after his marriage, he was quite unable to make his way in life. He undertook a commission to paint chocolate boxes for a NEPman, but that failed. He then tried something else, also unsuccessfully. Then he found an opening in the Arts and Crafts Museum on Leontyevskaya Street, to which, before the revolution, mother had donated some peasant dresses made in Bulchalki. His drawings were exhibited there, arousing some interest. He was given a commission to draw designs for wooden boxes to be manufactured in a Moscow workshop. Vladimir went to work with a will, even though payment was likely to be modest. During the winter of 1923–24 he worked intensively on designs for the sides and tops of these boxes. In 1925, some of them were sent to Paris to the International Exhibition of Decorative Arts, where Vladimir was awarded a gold medal along with the well-known artists Kravchenko, Kustodyev and Favorsky. He was very proud of his certificate, a lithograph decorated with figures of the Muses and signed by the French Minister of Culture. For years this diploma hung above his bed and is now owned by my nephew Illarion, even though during their many searches, agents of the OGPU turned it about in their hands, wondering whether to confiscate it or not.

I would not have known anything of this period of Vladimir's work had it not been for the writer, the late Yuri Arbat, who almost half a century later discovered these boxes in the basement of the Arts and Crafts Museum and went into raptures about them. His article on them, with pictures, was printed in the journal *Ogonyok*. In 1961, at the one-man exhibition in the House of Literature devoted to Vladimir's work, the public were able to see these beautiful boxes for the first time. Their compositions drew on the artistic traditions of peasant art, but the artist has infused them with the spirit of his

221

age, showing simple pairs of lovers and brave soldiers in their bright uniforms marching against the cast-iron railings of the Intendancy building on Krymskaya Square. In the thirties, the metal disks with the letters NI, which stood for Tsar Nicholas I, were removed, spoiling the harmony of these railings. Vladimir had painted them from life, as his workplace was nearby. I remember, too, how when he travelled in the region of Archangelsk, he had painted boxes with motifs that were drawn from the local artisan cultures of the Pinega and Mezen districts. They were all marvellous designs. After the exhibition these boxes were again immured in the basement store-rooms of the Arts and Crafts Museum. I can only hope that one day they will be properly exhibited for visitors to admire.

Sadly, Vladimir received little payment for this work. As he had a wife and child to support, he was forced to give it up. It was suggested he contact Meksin, the editor of the children's books section of the state publishing monopoly, Gosizdat. After seeing a portfolio of Vladimir's work, Meksin commissioned him to illustrate a book, handing him a text translated from English, V. Mitchell's *Song of a New Engine*, which was about railway engineering and the exploitation of the workers. The pictures Vladimir produced pleased Meksin. He commissioned a further book, and then yet another, and Vladimir was launched. The authors of these books appreciated the accuracy of Vladimir's illustrations. Novikov-Priboy was one of them. If in a story he wrote about a particular minesweeper, he could be sure Vladimir would draw precisely that vessel and not just any generalised minesweeper, as other artists might have done. Gradually, Vladimir built up a collection of photos and drawings of ships and aircraft, of animals and flowers, and of much else, from which he drew the images he needed. He stored this collection in his room on pine plank shelves, and knew exactly where every photo or drawing was stacked.

At first, in pencil, he would attempt various versions of his subject, working out the composition, altering it often; then with a piece of cotton wool in his hand he would use a sharpened quill and Indian ink to make the final drawing. He usually worked at night, to avoid any interruptions, and if I could not sleep I would sit huddled up by his side, barely drawing breath, delightedly following the movements of his pen. At midday, he would wake and go into the sitting-room with the drawing in his hand, followed by his proud and smiling wife and little Elenka, at first in her mother's arms, later led by the hand. Vladimir would lay the picture on the dining table in front of grandfather and we would all gather around to inspect it, with

Nanny Bush standing a little back, looking not at the picture, but at her "tsar-hero". We would all express our admiration; only mother would allow herself to make constructive comments. The next day we would all be in a state of excitement. Vladimir was taking the work to the editor – would the editor accept it, or reject it? Sometimes he was asked to re-do certain pictures, but gradually he received more and more commissions. He did illustrations for the magazines – *Pioneer, Science – Power, Friendly Lads, The Entertainer*, and others.

As regards his artistic talent, sufficient has been written on that subject in the book dedicated to his life and work. I liked everything he did, and that is that. Editors appreciated Vladimir not only for his talent but also because he was a conscientious man who never failed to produce his work on time. Having once been a sailor he loved to draw the sea, and these pictures were among his best work. He loved children and so many of his pictures were done for children's magazines. I remember a cover he did for the journal *Pioneer* of a Red Army frontier guard in his orange sheepskin standing tall against the background of a map of Russia. I remember too the many little pictures he drew for children's small-format magazines, such as *The Entertainer* and *Friendly Lads*. I remember his illustrations for the books of sailor-writers such as Novikov-Priboy, SudWest-Byvalov and Petrov-Grumant. But after the editor of the *Universal Pathfinder* asked Vladimir to work for him, that magazine became his main employer.

I wrote an essay on Vladimir Alexeievich Popov, the founder of the *Universal Pathfinder*, in volume three of *Detskaya Literatura* in 1965, and also wrote something about him in the anthology of recollections of my brother Vladimir, so I will not repeat that here. I only want to add something that, due to censorship, I could not say then. Before the revolution Popov was not only editor of a popular magazine *Around the World*, but also the founder and leader of the Moscow Scout movement. He was fortunate, however, in having left the Scouts and therefore surviving their liquidation and subsequent arrests. He was protected by Krylenko, who was both Prosecutor-General and a passionate tourist, the founder of the Association for Proletarian Tourism and Excursions (OPTE), and a man who had travelled in the Pamir mountains. It was thanks to Krylenko that Popov was able to found his magazine, which was read avidly by both young and old in the 1920s and early 1930s.

In those days, it was full of crude advertisements for proletarian writers who wrote about the horrors of serfdom, capitalist exploitation, the cruelty of the White Guards and, in contrast, the unblemished nobility of heroic Bolsheviks. But even so, in the *Universal Pathfinder* the reader could learn a lot about what was going on in the world. Travellers like V. Arsenyev, P. Kozlov, S. Obruchev, Rastambek-Tageyev and others simply came to the editorial office and handed in the accounts of their travels. Popov also printed translations of the best foreign travellers' tales, and attracted other talented writers; for instance, Alexander Belyaev, Alexander Grin and V. Yan. Popov, however, could not avoid being the target of envious people who wished his writers ill. Pressure was exerted on him from above. It was bandied about that he did not sufficiently denounce the capitalists, and was not revolutionary enough. His print run was cut back, but so long as Krylenko remained one of the leaders, the *Universal Pathfinder* flourished.

Vladimir became his principal artist. All stories and novels about the sea were illustrated by him. His innate humour helped him to become the illustrator of humorous works as well. Eventually Popov entrusted him with doing the covers of the magazine. The first was volume four in 1926. This cover was also reproduced in the book of recollections of my brother's life, but unfortunately not in colour. It was a full-page picture of the head of a Norwegian sailor with a pipe in his gleaming teeth against a background of the sea and cliffs and a lighthouse. Volume six of the magazine has a cover of a Martian with long worm-like fingers and a big pink head against a background of forest and a multi-coloured sky. From then on, Vladimir was responsible for half the magazine's cover pictures. He would have been capable of working from morning to night if he had been mercenary-minded, but he also liked going out and about in the evenings. Invariably good-tempered, he was always the heart and soul of any party. Elena and he were invited everywhere and were prized for their friendliness and, I must add, their great culture. Once he began to earn a proper wage he liked to spend time buying rare books, mostly French, from the booksellers who gathered close to Lyubyanka Square by the walls of Kitaygorod. His knowledge of French was excellent. The booksellers sold him the twelve volumes of Casanova's *Memoirs*, which he read from beginning to end. There are Casanova societies abroad, but in our country the memoirs are considered to be pornographic and so are not published, although attempts have been made to translate them.

Where did his culture and great knowledge come from? After all, his education had only been to Year 8 at the local school in the provincial town of Bogoroditsk. Yet he was able to talk about life in other countries, about the latest developments in technology and about the distant past. He had clear views and convictions. And he was not without literary talent, often writing short commentaries on his paintings and drawings for the magazines. His letters were always very witty. Thanks to being well read and having an excellent memory, he was able to scale greater heights than his friends. My own belief is that this culture somehow came down to him from the long line of ancestors, passing on to him their talents, their principles and, above all, their love of our homeland. Now, thanks to his work for the magazine, he and his family could eat on their own account and were even able to engage a nanny-cum-maid and welcome visitors, usually Yusha Samarin and Artemi Rayevsky.

Sitting about reading or doing my homework, I used to wait anxiously to find out whether I would be asked to make a fourth at bridge. If bridge was decided upon, Elena would set about preparing some supper, Vladimir would produce a flask of vodka and a bowl of marinaded mushrooms, mushrooms that I had collected especially for Elena in the summer. With what pleasure we would tip up our little glasses!

2

Masha and I had guests on Saturdays. Grandmother's death brought an end to the famous galop, the "mad pillow dance" and our childish quadrilles; instead we danced the foxtrot in a dignified way to the music of the gramophone. Once a week I would take my sledge and head over to No. 15 Zubovsky Boulevard, to the Lyuboshchinskys, a family of not specially close friends who still lived in their large, colonnaded house, standing hidden behind another big house, which had once brought them in a considerable income. Andronnikov, who lived there in the 1930s, wonderfully described the inhabitants of that big house in his book, *The Mystery of N.F.I.* In it he paints a hilarious portrait of the Lyuboshchinsky son-in-law, Anatoly Mikhailovich Fokin, a historian and the husband of their eldest daughter. But in the 1920s Anatoly was not there, he was locked up with other relatives of ours on the "workers' corridor" in Butyrka prison.

Once I got to the Lyuboshchinskys, I would timidly ask if I could borrow their gramophone for the evening, a request I never knew them to refuse. The gramophone was a large, heavy object in a carved wooden box with a trumpet speaker. I would tie it to my sledge and drag it along the snowdrifts and icy roads across Krymskaya Square and along Ostozhenka Street to our place. We had just two records;

one an English one, given to us by Sonia Witter, a foxtrot with a singer who bleated and made sounds like a donkey, which was labelled *Alleluya*; the other, an old one, with a march from *Faust* on one side, and on the other a march from *Aida*. We only danced to the foxtrot, guiding our partners to and fro across the room whilst engaging them in conversation. My sisters would urgently whisper to me to invite their friends who were standing bored against the wall. We danced until midnight and then in the morning I would load up the gramophone and drag it back to the Lyuboshchinskys. Once or twice I brought the same delivery to evening parties at Lyala Ilyinskaya's.

3

I come now to the subject of the railway station known as *Verst* 17. This was a little-used single platform on the Kiev line (then called the Bryansk line) close to the Samarin's village of Izmalkovo, where the Osorgin family were living at the time. This included Mikhail Mikhailovich (Uncle Misha), his wife, Elizeveta Nikolaievna (Aunt Liza), who was my mother's cousin, and their daughters, Maria and Tonya. Their daughter-in-law, my sister Lina, with her little girl Marina or Marinochka, lived with them, and there was also a simple country girl, their servant Polya. Shumilka, their faithful guard dog, lay dreaming in his kennel. My sisters and I went to see them all when Georgy Osorgin, my second cousin and brother-in-law was still there, but my most vivid memories of the Osorgin family date from the time when Georgy was already locked up in Butyrka prison.

On Sunday morning our whole lively group would catch the train to *Verst* 17, although sometimes I would go on my own so as to be able to have a frank talk with wise old Uncle Misha, or just sit and listen to others talking. Trains were very infrequent and totally unheated except by the breath of their passengers. We would leap out of the train and set off on snowy paths through the pine woods, circling the little village cemetery. Standing out above the trees one could see the cupola of the church in the ancient village of Lukin, which had once belonged to a famous family of boyars, the Kolychevi, but was now owned by a Baron Bode, who had a Russian-style house built there. In the 1920s and 1930s it stood roofless and gutted, the last Baroness Bode, an acquaintance of ours, having been condemned to exile in Kazakhstan.

From the path through the pines we would turn left, go downhill on a little track to some stepping stones over a stream, the Setun, and then after a few hundred paces reach a clapboard house painted in greenish-yellow. From a distance the banisters of its verandah gave the impression of a mansion with colonnade. A smaller house stood next to it and behind it, on the other side of a fence, were two or three more houses. This hamlet was so small it did not even have a name. Around it stretched unbroken forest of birch and fir, full of mushrooms and alive with grouse and other game birds. Wandering deep into the forest one day I came across a large badger set.

In the past fifty years this area has changed enormously. The platform is now called Peredelkino. Smart electric trains, whistling loudly, pass through one after another. The former Bode estate is now surrounded by a high stone wall and the elaborate Russian-style house has been restored as a boyar's mansion. It is now the summer residence of the Patriarch of Moscow and All-Russia. The little church has been renovated and is open. Its bells ring out, a rare sound in our country, summoning the faithful, who come by train from far and wide. The cemetery has expanded as far as the stream, the Setun. Here flowers are constantly laid on the grave of Russia's last great poet, Boris Pasternak. The forest has been broken up into separate plots and *dachas* built on them for Russian writers and top literary bureaucrats. A few hundred metres away from the house where the Osorgins used to live lies the piece of land belonging to the Union of Writers. There is a large Russian Empire-style house with a columned porch, surrounded by a number of fine cottages. More than a hundred writers can stay there by special permission, meet each other, play cards and chess, eat and drink and in between times get on with their creative writing, whether talented or not. Their wives can also stay there, likewise chattering to each other, walking about and no doubt gossiping about all those who have sinned against the seventh commandment.

When I returned many years later, I was pleased to find the pines along the road were still standing and had barely grown; only their foliage seemed somehow thicker. The Setun still flowed as before but its water was murky and there were no longer shoals of little fish darting about above its sandy bottom. The Osorgins' house had survived, though I had difficulty spotting it, such a muddle of conservatories and verandahs had been tacked on to it.

4

What a myriad of memories, happy and sad and poetic, the sight of the Osorgin house brought back to me. In the 1920s Uncle Misha

Osorgin was a sturdy, energetic old man, ever pulling at his long white beard and walking about in squeaky patent leather shoes. Once he had been deputy governor of Kharkov, then governor of Grodno and finally governor of Tula, a post he resigned from after some demonstrators were killed there in the disturbances of 1905. Following the revolution he started to dictate his memoirs to one of the family. Within a few years there were three thousand pages. Now they are stored in the Lenin Library. I made a request to have them photocopied in return for a large payment in dollars. It was refused, doubtless because the possibility of letting some sort of cat out of the bag was stronger than the lure of foreign currency.

All the Osorgins were intensely proud of the fact that their family tree included the sixteenth-century Russian saint, Yuliania Osorina. This was why Uncle Misha had named one of his daughters Yulyana. He was very fond of lecturing young men and women on morality, and would take them into the corner of the room to discuss their thoughts and behaviour, their love affairs and their doubts. He was also fond of handing out advice, and I can recall many good pieces of advice that he gave me, though unfortunately I did not always follow them. He insisted on being called Uncle Misha and being addressed in the intimate second person singular by even the most distant relatives of his wife.

The Osorgins survived by giving lessons to the local residents on any and every subject and also, like my sister Sonya, compiling medical statistical tables. They also received money from abroad from their two older sons, former White officers, and their eldest daughter, the wife of Nikolai Sergeievich Lopukhin – Uncle Kolya – my god-father. Uncle Misha's wife – Aunt Liza, the sister of the philosophers Sergei and Evgeny Trubetskoi – was a beautiful, well-bred lady, with fair hair turning white, fine features and a noble figure. She walked in a slow and dignified way and spoke slowly, with a drawl, all of which made her seem immensely important. Her daughter Yulyana, shortened to Liana, was married to the elderly Sergei Dimitrievich Samarin, her grandfather three times removed and uncle of Yusha Samarin. They lived at 36 Novinsky Boulevard, behind the famous Gagarin mansion that was later destroyed in the bombing. They were a very happy couple who, in six years of marriage, managed to produce five children. Their nanny later became a famous figure as the nanny of Svetlana Stalin. In 1929, Sergei Dimitrievich died – a timely death, as a man of such pure heart and soul would never have worked for the Soviets and would certainly have died under quite different circumstances. His grave in Vagankovsky cemetery, like the graves of so many of the people I am writing about, has now been wiped from the face of the earth.

The two younger Osorgin daughters, Maria and Tonya, persistently rejected the advances of the young and not-so-young men whose social standing was inferior to theirs. Yet among the many suitors who made the trip to *Verst* 17 in vain, many were worthy fellows, who eventually found themselves more obliging mates. The sisters remained spinsters to the end of their lives. Maria was artistic, painting pictures of flowers and silhouettes of her friends. One wall in the sisters' room was covered with these silhouettes, including all the members of our family. Whilst still living at Izmalkovo, Maria had filled an album with pencil portraits of her relatives. This album, a kind of historic document, found its way abroad, and then back to Russia; abroad it was of little interest, whereas my sisters and I saw it as a kind of relic that brought back countless memories. In order to earn a little money, Maria drew diagrams and figures commissioned by her admirers. Tonya was sickly from birth. She was well read and intelligent and occupied her time giving lessons to local children. She and I struck up a great friendship and spent many long, happy hours discussing literature and art. When summer came she found herself a position as tutor to a NEPman's family and so left home for a time.

The Osorgins were not simply religious, they were deeply and unshakeably so. In his youth Uncle Misha had dreamed of becoming a priest, a goal that he finally achieved in old age. The family went to church either out in the village church of Lukin, or in the church of Trinity on Krechetniky at the corner of Novinsky Boulevard in Moscow. They were all music lovers. Aunt Liza was a fine piano player. Artemy Rayevsky, with his rich baritone voice, was a regular visitor, along with his sister's husband, Misha Lesnov, a tenor. How well I remember their songs! Misha sang both of Lensky's arias from *Evgeny Onegin*. Artemy sang romantic songs, most successfully the song entitled *Alpukhara's Distant Golden Lands are Fading*. Whenever I now hear this serenade I think back to the warmth of emotions that were generated during those summer evenings. Artemy was the object of the love of both Maria and Tonya, his cousins thrice removed, but as he was much younger, did not respond to their feelings and came out to the Osorgins essentially to enjoy the wise counsel of Uncle Misha.

One of the visitors to the Osorgins was a well-known microbiologist, Professor Barykin. Before the revolution he had been a Menshevik and so under the Soviets was sent to serve a term of exile.

I enjoyed listening to him and Uncle Misha arguing. The one was profoundly, philosophically religious, the other profoundly, philosophically atheist. Uncle Misha would become very heated, whilst Barykin calmly and logically expounded his reasoning. Their disagreements in no way affected their respect for each other. Actually, Barykin came to *Verst* 17 in his capacity as a violinist. With Aunt Liza accompanying him, they tackled serious pieces of music such as the symphonies of Beethoven, Chopin, Liszt, and much else. We would all sit in meditative silence, without moving, even I, who understood little about music. Then the last train would take us all back to Moscow. Professor Barykin came to a sad end. For his work he needed live monkeys, but they cost a great deal, so instead he was offered the use of prisoners. He refused point blank, was arrested and what then happened to him I do not know.

We would return from an outing on our skis and all sit around the big table, eating the simple food that was on offer, usually plain noodles, a thin wheaten gruel and carrot tea. Then Uncle Misha would take his place on a soft divan and silence would fall as, for the benefit of us young people, he launched into his exposition of and discourses on theology. It must be remembered that at that time you could be prosecuted for doing this. We were excited by the romantic feeling of being part of a conspiracy. Uncle Misha spoke with fervour, trying to inculcate in us a belief in God, to make us convinced believers. It is entirely thanks to his teaching that I am familiar with the Old and New Testaments and that when I visit an art gallery I am able to understand paintings of biblical subjects and even explain them to others.

One thing about which they rarely spoke dominated the thoughts of the Osorgin family – Georgy Osorgin's imprisonment in Butyrka prison. This shared grief drew my sister Lina into a very close relationship with her husband's family, who had all come to love her dearly. Tonya, back from a concert to which she had been taken by some suitor, would be describing the music while criticising her partner, but would then suddenly fall silent, obviously remembering Georgy, or Uncle Misha, a better chess player than me, might make some foolish move, and I would realise that the thought of Georgy had crossed his mind, or Aunt Liza might be reminiscing about the past and suddenly cut short her story, remembering her son.

My sister Lina, once so lively, joyful and active, was now a much more serious person. She could not stop thinking of her husband, even when little Marinochka, the idol and consolation of the whole family, was ill. Uncle Misha's heartfelt prayers and Aunt Liza's more restrained ones were above all for Georgy's return. Meanwhile, their Sunday visits to the prison went on.

5

Quite unexpectedly an article appeared in *The Workers' Gazette* claiming that the industrial consortium where father worked was an inefficient, unnecessary concept. What had happened was that their patron and protector, Trotsky, had been thrown out of the leadership, and so now there would be reductions in staff. Before long, father came home in a state of despondency; he had been given two weeks notice. His intention was to register at the labour exchange, but he still had many acquaintances who remembered with appreciation his managerial skills before the revolution, and he was soon offered several options. He chose the Gosplan (the State planning organisation), the department dealing with chemistry, and took up a post there once again as economist and planner. His office in this prestigious institution, which was headed by Krzhizhanovsky, a colleague of Lenin's, was on Ilyinkaya Street in the district of Kitaygorod, so father did not have to travel far to work. His salary actually went up by two *chervontsy* to two hundred roubles.

The industrial consortium somehow managed to last a year longer before being closed down. Soon after, its former director, Kolegayev, who had been a Socialist Revolutionary, was arrested and perished, as did other colleagues of his. The *Financial Gazette* which father had written for was also closed down, but through Vladimir's influence he found other work writing pieces for the *Universal Pathfinder*. Father's brother, Alexander Vladimirovich Golitsyn, no longer sent him copies of financial journals, instead sending copies of the *Geographical Magazine* with their coloured photographs taken by correspondents who travelled to every country in the world, save our own. If ever the reader comes across copies of the *Universal Pathfinder* for the years 1926–29, he will certainly find on the last two pages short articles, no more than twenty or thirty lines, on a whole variety of subjects: for example, a description of a sperm whale thrown up on the beaches of the Falkland Islands, or archaeological finds in Mexico, or a tame tiger that had bitten off the head of its owner's daughter, and so on. The material for these notes came from those copies of the *Geographical Magazine*. Father found so many interesting things to write about that he didn't only sign them M.G. but was compelled to resort to a variety of initials.

6

Late one evening in the spring of 1926, there was a loud ring at the door. My brother, his wife and my sister Sonya had gone out to see the Norwegian minister, Mr Urbi. I opened the door and four men burst in, two of them in leather coats and two soldiers in the uniform of GPU trainees. Behind them came the house superintendent, half asleep. They held out the same kind of warrant as on the previous occasion, written in the same way and signed by the deputy head of the GPU, Yagoda. The warrant gave authority to carry out a complete search and to arrest one person, Vladimir. The leader ordered us to show them all the letters, journals and books that we had received from abroad. At that time we were getting many letters from our relatives in France, the USA and China. Fortunately, I had already soaked off all the stamps for my collection. My father attempted to explain why he needed American journals, but they did not listen to him and soon everything was piled up on the dining table. At this point Vladimir, Elena and Sonya returned, all dressed up and chattering about the happy evening they had just spent. Sonya remembered later how beautifully the Urbi's daughter, Anna-Liza, had sung that evening.

The intruders took a room each. The trainees were told to go through the back rooms. The room occupied by my sisters, Lelya Davydova, Aunt Sasha and Nanny Bush, was searched by a young trainee who tried to exchange jokey remarks with Masha. She responded coldly. The precious snuffbox with its portrait of Peter I had been given to Aunt Sasha for safekeeping by my father the previous autumn. She had filled it with pins and buttons and had put it into the bag where she kept her underwear. The trainee found it, exclaimed "Ah, Peter the Great!" and shoved it back into the bag. Apart from the letters, journals and newspapers from abroad they took nothing else away. Once more the police truck drove up and Vladimir, with his blanket, bowl, cup and spoon was taken away.

A few days later an elderly peasant came to visit us from the village of Orlovka, the former estate of the Pisarev family, close to our Bulchalki. He was due to marry our faithful under-nanny Lenya, who had been with us all the years of the revolution, although she had never set eyes on her future husband, the whole affair having been arranged by correspondence. The following Sunday father was supposed to lead her to the altar and then provide the wedding feast. The wedding actually did take place, but because of our misfortune, it was a quiet affair. The ceremony was held in the church of the

Trinity on Zubovo. The bride had only myself as a groom, while the brother of the bridegroom acted as his best man. Then we all went to a restaurant on the corner of Prechistenkaya Street and Zubovsky Square, where we were served some hors d'oeuvres and a bottle of wine, and that was all. The newlyweds left for Orlovka that same evening.

For three years Lenya exchanged letters with Aunt Sasha. Her husband was a good man, who did not drink and worked hard, but Lenya was treated as a stranger in the village, the people feeling she was somehow above their station as she was unable to milk the cows and did not know how to run a peasant holding. In addition, she had no children and was very homesick for her life with us. Then these letters stopped coming. Eventually, we found out from others that she and her husband had been labelled as *kulaks* and sent to Siberia. We never heard any more of them.

Vladimir was transferred from Lubyanka prison to Butyrka. A good friend, Sergei Kristy, was in the same cell, as well as the translator, Sergei Serpinsky. Both later described how Vladimir became the focus of that cell as the inmates listened with delight to his stories. He made playing cards for them illustrated with indecent pictures. Sergei Kristy was exiled to Archangelsk, later to Voronezh, then just before the war returned to Moscow, possibly helped by his cousin. Now and again my sisters and I met up with him and came to love him dearly. He died in 1984. As for Sergei Serpinsky, he was arrested five times, and every time emerged unscathed. Apart from his translations he also painted abstract pictures and wrote a history of Butyrka prison. I saw this bulky manuscript at his place, but did not look into it. He died in 1976 and I never knew what happened to that undoubtedly interesting manuscript.

Thanks to energetic intervention by Sonya Witter with commissar Enukidze, Vladimir was released after three weeks. Enukidze told her to advise Vladimir to stop having any relations at all with foreigners and to stop inviting them to his flat. It would be alright for him to visit the Witters, but only if no one else was there. The Urbis were very unhappy at this sudden break in relations. I would imagine the archives of the Norwegian Foreign Ministry hold many documents on Vladimir's relations with them.

Reginald and Sonya Witter decided to celebrate Vladimir's release by inviting him and his wife Elena to a meal in the Hotel National, a dinner that must have cost a fortune, at least a month's average salary, but the two Witters were exceptionally good people. It was natural, and taken for granted, that Aunt Vera and her youngest daughter, Elena, should be living with them. Reginald, as manager of an English shipping company, was very well paid. He sent money to his mother and also gave money to Uncle Vladimir Trubetskoi. Occasionally, he went to Sergiyev Posad, staying at the Trubetskois and going hunting with uncle. He loved the primitive life they led and the way they slept in heaps on the floor. Sometimes Sonya Witter would invite Aunt Eli to come and stay with her, and she would escape from her numerous hordes of children and live a life of ease and comfort with Sonya. On such occasions my sister Sonya, taking her medical charts with her, would replace Aunt Eli in Sergiyev Posad, washing and cleaning the flat, looking after the children, cooking the meals, putting everything in order before returning to Moscow.

In the spring of 1927, a series of new arrests occurred in Sergiyev Posad. It all began with an article in *The Workers' Gazette*. A correspondent from that paper visited the local museum and photographed the entire staff. They had no idea of the treachery he was planning. A full page of the paper was then devoted to a disgusting parody of the truth; photographs and some text about the staff of the museum, starting with the director, V.D. von Dervis, a former landowner. The main target was Yuri Alexandrovich Olsufyev, the scientific head of the museum, who was a major expert in Russian icons and early mouldings. He was blackened as a Count and a former landowner, and was alleged to be an enemy who had dug himself into this position. The rest of the staff were classified as priests' sons, former landowners and merchants, and it was also claimed that monks were guarding the collection. Olsufyev was arrested, and the other staff driven out. They were replaced by a motley bunch of people. Dervis survived, as although he had been a landowner, under the Tsars he had been sent into exile and so was considered a liberal. He probably also had high-level protection. So he remained director for a further three years but, in the end, even he was driven out.

7

In 1926, I completed Year 9 at school, or more accurately, my land surveyor's course. There were exams, including political knowledge, which we somehow avoided. Everyone was very nervous, but in fact the exams were not as bad as we expected and our teachers tried to help those who were borderline. The director of the school, Darsky, examined me in maths, trying at first to trip me up, but then softening his approach. I overheard a teacher ask him about me, and he replied, "Well, a three." That was all I needed, and no other marks other than "satisfactory" were given. I was awarded the diploma of graduate land surveyor and if I were to do a period of practice I would be entitled to call myself a "technical land assessor". No one organised this sort of practice for us, and anyway I was not in the least interested because that year there opened for me, not a door but more a little crack, into the bright realms of learning. A government decree had been enacted that very year allowing anyone to become a student after completing school and not just if you hailed from the proletarian working class. Some preference was given to the children of workers, but there was no mention in the decree that the children of land-owners, merchants, priests, officials or officers were forbidden entry. My parents decided that I could try to enter tertiary education.

When the programme of required exams was published, I was horrified. There were four; political knowledge, Russian language, mathematics and physics. I only felt confident in Russian. As for the rest, there was a yawning gulf between the teaching we had received in school and the list of subjects given in the programme. I felt that all I could do was to try my best. But what subject was I to choose? Already in school I had announced that I wanted to be a writer. My parents urged me to choose a specific subject, saying that to be a writer was not something you learned, it was a gift from God. As a child I had collected butterflies, so I went for advice to Nikolai Alexeievich Bobrinsky, the cousin of Alexei Bobrinsky and Sonya Witter, who was professor of zoology at the university. He warmly supported my idea and promised to take me on his expeditions. I dreamed of travelling through Central Asia and writing articles for the *Universal Pathfinder*.

I began preparing for my exams even before the end of school. I locked myself in and did nothing but swot. Following our final exams, we were all photographed in the school garden, after which we rushed off to break the flowerpots lined up on the school landings. Then we organised a final feast in Yuri Nevedomsky's flat. I was very sad to be sitting there for this last gathering of old friends. We drank vodka, but in moderation, and afterwards we wandered around Smolensk and Zubovsky Boulevards, before I took myself off home.

For the next three years that school, the former Alferov gymnasium, kept up its old traditions of respect and love for its teachers. But times were changing. Already while I was still a pupil there the younger classes began to be filled by local children, the school worked in two shifts and new, young teachers were taken on the staff who knew nothing of the awful fate that had befallen the school's founders. Darsky was replaced by a communist director, Reznik. In 1929 disaster fell on the old teaching staff. The new director decided to inspect the entire premises, discovering that on the first floor, in addition to the school boiler man, there also lived Elena Yegorevna Bekker, the geography teacher, and that on the second floor Antonina Nikolaievna Pashkova, the primary school teacher, occupied three entire rooms. Reznik had been led there by someone's denunciation, or perhaps just for reasons of good management, but when he entered these three rooms and saw the good furniture and large writing desk and over it the portraits of the two Alferovs, Alexandra Samsonovna and Alexander Danilovich, he was horrified. The room was kept as it had been in their lifetime as a sort of shrine. It was from here that they had been taken off to prison, and it was here that on every anniversary of their execution the few teachers who had been their friends gathered in secret to share a cup of tea. Immediately, Reznik rushed off to the local communist committee.

Some of the teachers, – Pashkova, Bekker and her sister, Olga Nikolaievna Maslova, Julia Fyodorovna Gertner and others, were sacked. A few were transferred to other schools. The three Zolotarev sisters survived as they described themselves in their files as citizens. The one who suffered most was Olga Nikolaievna, who although she had been a teacher her whole life, described herself as a noblewoman. No one would now take her on. For a couple of years she survived by giving private lessons and then, in 1931, she died. More than a hundred former pupils and teachers attended her funeral. I myself was not in Moscow at the time.

I want to say something about the fates of a number of my contemporaries at school. Zina Bekeer, Sima Gurevich and Kostya Krasilnikov became scientists and PhDs. The two latter are dead. Yura Gulenko, the only one of us to become a party member, was a factory manager. When after the war we dared to have a meeting of old classmates for the first time, he refused to join us. Misha Salmonov also refused, saying that he was an alcoholic and of no interest to any of us. Lenya Veselovskaya went out of her mind and died in a madhouse. Vasya Ganeshin was killed in the war. Mily Blagoveshchensky died young of unknown causes. Shura Sokolov died an alcoholic after the war. Seryozha Goryainov, formerly adjutant to General Karbyshev, was taken prisoner with him and spent four years in a German concentration camp. He then worked as a textile engineer for four years before once again serving time in a labour camp, this time Soviet. Seven years later he again worked as an engineer. I meet him on rare occasions. Vanya Talb died in the camps. Lelya Neiman, a German, was exiled to Kazakhstan in the war, returning to Moscow fifteen years later, where she died. I buried her. Leva Maklashevsky and his three brothers, as sons of a police officer, were deprived of their passports. Denounced by the husband of their beloved only sister, they all died in the camps. I know nothing of the fate of any others.

The Alferov school eventually became school No. 31, then later a court building. Much later, out of curiosity, I revisited it, but it had changed so much that only the worn steps at the entrance reminded me of the past. I was once asked to speak in the library opposite the school. I asked the librarian whether she knew what had been there before the revolution.

"I know," she said decisively, "a priests' seminary."

I did not try to contradict her, but my talk that evening was a rather distracted one.

8

I finished my schooldays and applied for entry to the biological faculty of the university, after which I went to Glinkovo to work for the exams. My sisters took over the tasks I had been used to doing, such as fetching water and going into Sergiyev Posad for the shopping. I felt myself to be in a privileged position and sat on the church steps from early morning, swotting up my books and only allowing myself a short walk when evening came. The main gap in my learning was political knowledge. I had to swot up Berdikov and Svetlov's massive textbook, as well as two thinner volumes, *A Communist ABC* by Bukharin, and *A Short History of the RCP* by Zinovyev. In none of these books was there any mention of Stalin. Over the decades tens of millions of students and other unfortunates have had to torture their brains over these books, fully aware what a complete waste of time it was, and yet having to take the exams, and if they failed them, to take them again the following year.

I got through the two small books in a couple of weeks, but could not face the big volume. I knew that before the exams I would never be able to master the mass of indigestible wisdom it contained. Incidentally, one of the pieces of wisdom it laid down was that socialism could not be built in one country alone. Later such statements were considered seditious, the authors vanished into oblivion and their works were taken out of the libraries and burned. This was the fate of all the works of Bukharin, Zinovyev and other authors.

In the early days of summer, Vladimir and Elena were not at Glinkovo as Elena was due to give birth. It was on the fifteenth of June that my nephew Mikhail came into the world. We had an amusing letter from Vladimir with a drawing entitled *Prince Mikhail Vladimirovich Golitsyn at the Age of Two Days*. The drawing has survived, but not the letter.

I had to go to Moscow to take my exams, but before that had to obtain an identity card. My details were sent on from the office in the village of Epiphany, and the militia handed me over a little red book that declared my identity. When I got home I discovered that they had written my name wrong as Galitsyn, born in Bugorky, so that ever since then I have been deprived of my birthplace. My father was given leave and went with mother down to Glinkovo. I was left alone with Nanny Bush in the Moscow flat and felt very proud to be looking after myself. Instead of going to the cheap eateries on Zubovskaya Square, I set my sights on the Prague restaurant, where I ordered a plate of green peas and a beer. It left me very hungry, but I really enjoyed sitting in that expensive restaurant and watching others having a good time.

My first exam was composition. We all sat in the very grand Assembly Hall of the old university building. In the hour allotted I had no difficulty in writing a colourful piece about the horrors of serfdom as conveyed by Turgenev's *Notes of a Hunter*. Three days later the Russian orals exams were held in this same hall. An ancient teacher in an old fashioned morning coat, decked out in white shirt and tie, pulled my composition out of a folder and pointed to two mistakes underlined in red. Then he began to ask me questions, to which I replied with confidence. When he asked me what genre *Dead Souls* by Gogol belonged to, I replied "The novel". He shamed me by pointing out that Gogol himself had called this work a poem. Still, he gave me a pass mark.

The next hurdle was political knowledge. I watched as those ahead of me went through this torture. Then came my turn. I marched up to the young man, who was wearing an open-collared Russian shirt, and sat down in front of him. I had only been able to swot up five hundred of the one thousand pages of the awful "Bible" of communism by Berdnikov and Svetlov. To my delight, all the questions were out of these first five hundred pages. I cannot remember the examiner's questions, but I answered without hesitation, except once when he interrupted me with a laugh, saying, "Actually, it's the opposite." I got another pass, and hurried off to the Prague, when I met Alexei Bobrinsky, who embraced me warmly and said, "I'm delighted to see you. I'm getting married on Sunday!" It became clear that none of his relatives were in Moscow and so there was no one to hold the crown above his head. Later I found out that Aunt Vera and her daughter Sonya Witter were very much against his marriage to the daughter of a merchant from Tambov. I only had time to ask for the name of the church before hurrying on. As my next exam, maths, was on the Monday, I thought I could allow myself a bit of entertainment.

The wedding took place in the seventeenth-century church of St Simeon Stolpnik on Povarskaya Street, which was later badly altered, then turned into a store where heating oil was sold, following which it was restored, the bell tower rebuilt, window frames carved again and gilt applied here and there, until one day some political bigwig passing by was annoyed by the golden crosses shining brightly in the sunshine and had them torn down. So the public was privileged to see these crosses for only one week before they were replaced by thin spires. Today, the building is the Museum of the Environment and stands out strangely, like a precious stone on a dirty cloth, against the massive, box-like skyscrapers behind it.

Alexei's bride, Alya, struck me as an ordinary but quite nice girl. The crown was held over Alexei's head by the older Kristy brother, Vladimir, and someone else from the bride's side. The bride's three brothers held the crown for her. We all repaired to her family's place on Yakimankaya Street to feast the couple. I should have made some excuse and left, after all, I had done my duty and had my exams to prepare. But I followed the others and we feasted and drank and shouted "*Gor'ko!*" (bitter) at the couple, and all that sort of thing. The punch seemed weak; in fact, I got horribly drunk.

"Can you manage to get home?" someone asked me as I was leaving. On Krymsky Bridge I stood for a long while staring into the murky water, feeling utterly sick. I barely made it home. Nanny Bush caught hold of me and helped me to bed. After fifteen hours sleep I woke up the next morning with a head like a stone and staggered off to my exam. I could not solve a single one of the three questions. We had done none of this work and the programme for the examination had not prepared us for anything like this. Afterwards I heard that the questions were supposed to test our initiative. I had never had much initiative and had not yet sobered up from the Tambov punch. I failed miserably, and as there was no point in my now trying to pass in physics, I got ready to go to Glinkovo.

I now think it was a good thing that I failed. I would probably not have lasted even two terms, would have flunked out like my sister Sonya two years earlier, so exposing myself to pointless torment. At the time, though, I was deeply ashamed of myself and very, very unhappy. It was a small consolation that Sergei Rayevsky had also failed; he had been caught out by questions from the second part of the "Bible" of communism.

9

On the eve of my departure for Glinkovo, my uncle, Nikolai Vladimirovich Golitsyn, suddenly emerged from Butyrka prison. He had served the whole of his three year sentence. When the warder shouted, "Golitsyn! And bring your things!" his cellmates lifted him high above their heads and bore him triumphantly out into the corridor. I went with him to Sergiyev Posad to guide him to the Krasyukovka district where Uncle Vladimir and his family, and grandfather with his dog Romochka, were living. Uncle Nikolai walked along the grass verge of the road, ecstatically exclaiming, "For three years I never breathed such air or walked on a single blade of grass!"

When I reached Glinkovo, Aunt Sasha, my sisters and Lyalya Ilyinskaya greeted me rather quietly and did not say a word about my exams. My parents were very distressed, but also said nothing. The next day, I was back to carrying water from the well and going shopping in Sergiyev.

In that summer of 1926, the papers printed a notice of the execution of twenty people, giving a short account of the accusations against them. The first on the list was Prince Pavel Dimitriyevich Dolgorukov, one of the founders of the Cadet Party and a prominent White emigrant, who had for some reason crossed back over the frontier and was caught in the Ukraine. He was the uncle of our friend, Vladimir Nikolaievich Dolgorukov. The second on the list was Elvengren, a former cavalry officer of Finnish nationality. He had moved to Petersburg to represent some Finnish company. Uncle Vladimir also knew him well. The third, Naryshkin, was a Hussar, living with his wife and son in Moscow. He had lost a leg, and was said to be a drinker and a man who loved telling funny stories. He was arrested only three days before that blood-soaked list was published. His wife had been about to see Peshkova, as well as to take him provisions in Butyrka prison, when she read the awful news. She came with her ten-year-old son Alyosha to Sergiyev Posad and was given shelter by the Trubetskois, who found her a nearby room. I saw mother and child in the street a couple of times until Peshkova obtained permission for them to leave the country. I know nothing of their later life.

The artist Favorsky was particularly fond of painting portraits of children. A great friend of the Trubetskois, he often drew their children, as well as Ksana Istomina and many others. Years later, after my book about Favorsky had already been published, I went to an exhibition of his work. There I saw a portrait, signed and dated 1926, of a child leaning forward on a chair, with strangely thin arms and sharp-pointed shoulders, his eyes wide open, gazing in astonishment, his mouth slightly open. I immediately recognized Alyosha Naryshkin. The artist has captured not so much the grief as the bewilderment of a boy telling his friends, "You know, my father's just been shot by the Bolsheviks." Had I known of this picture when I was writing the book, I would have included it among the illustrations, even though the reader might have wondered, "What a strange little boy the artist has drawn!"

I cannot recall the names of any of the others on the list. The OGPU announced that these executions were in response (but really, in revenge) to an act of terrorism, a bomb that had been planted in the headquarters on Lubyanka Square which had knocked out a piece of wall but injured no one. English Labour Party members who were making advances to our government at that time, sent a brief, three line telegram saying that their work in support of our country was damaged by these "executions without trial" and suggested they be stopped. In those days such telegrams were still published in our papers. A telegram in reply, signed by Rykov and justifying the executions, was also printed.

For three days, Lylya Ilyinskaya wandered about as if lost, muttering to herself and making notes. On the third day she read out to us in a loud voice the verses she had written, which struck me as excellent, and were entitled *On the Death of the Twenty*.

10

Andrei Kiselev came on a visit to Glinkovo. He was one of the few schoolmates whom I had invited to our house already, the previous winter. His father was a quarrying expert, his mother a teacher and his older brother later became an outstanding archaeologist and corresponding member of the Academy of Sciences. The family lived in Losinostrovskaya Street, but Andrei had a tiny room in Tyoplaya

Street in the home of the three Zolotarevy sisters, all teachers at our school. It was his enterprise and energy, his love of the past and the fact that he was very well read that drew me to him. What he saw in me I do not know. In time he became very interested in my sister Masha, and used to say that with her pert nose and curly hair she reminded him of a Roman cameo.

He came to us wearing a new cap, black with a green border and a gold badge, the uniform of a student of mechanics, which showed that he had just entered the MVTU, the Moscow Higher Technical School. That year not many of us had tried to take the university entrance exams. There was a trend in favour of taking a year off in preparation. Others, like myself, had tried and failed. Aside from Andrei, there were two or three who were starting university; one of our worst students, Lena Veselovskaya, who was so fat we called her "Tree Stump", managed to get in, but I imagine some strings were pulled to have her accepted into the faculty of medicine.

Andrei was immensely proud of his cap. Traditionally it was worn until graduation, when a new cap would signify that he had his diploma in engineering. Yet within two years, Andrei and all the other students had to give up their smart headgear for cloth caps, and a little later, when the very title of engineer was an object of contempt, many were sent off to the camps on trumped-up charges, and the old cap with its gold badge became a symbol of imagined sabotage.

As soon as he arrived at Glinkovo, Andrei immediately suggested we go on an excursion. We set off barefoot. Andrei removed his cap, covered his head with a paper hat and removed his boots. Led by him we all – Sonya and Masha, Lyalya and I – set off to the railway station at Buzhaninovo, which was the first stop after Sergiyev Posad. We made our way through the fields and woods and we delighted in the views of the countryside. In a little village we drank some milk and ate delicious rye bread. In those days the peasants still baked their own bread in their Russian stoves, laying the little loaves on cabbage or maple leaves; they came out with a rich golden crust, and were far tastier than bread today.

At the station we discovered that we would have to wait three hours for the next train. Seeing a freight train in the siding, Andrei urged us to climb up on the brake car, saying that he had often done this and that the Russian writer and populist, Zlatovratsky, always travelled that way. The locomotive gave a whistle and the cars began to move. We jumped aboard. As the train was gathering speed, a railway worker suddenly rushed in at us and, seizing me by the arm, tried to push me off the train, with my companions holding on to me and pulling in the other direction. As the train passed the signal box this man leaned out and shouted, "Call the OGPU!" He said that the girls would be set free but we lads would each get three years in gaol. Sonya and Masha begged and pleaded with him to have pity on us, and that we would never do this again, but he just went on shouting about the three years we would get, whilst Andrei tried to justify our action by referring to the writer Zlatovarsky.

Sonya, quite pertinently, observed that in Zlatovarsky's time there had been no OGPU. Meanwhile, the train was rolling on and we began to pass the magnificent architectural ensemble of Sergiyev Posad; but we were absolutely not in any mood for beautiful sights. Wheels squealing, the train now began to put on its brakes, and suddenly, without warning, our tormenter jumped off and disappeared from view. At first we did not realize that we were out of danger. When the train had slowed right down we all jumped off on the side away from the station and went our way talking over what had just happened. The girls, with one voice, announced that they were never ever again going to travel on freight trains.

The following day, Andrei suggested another expedition. The girls refused to join us, claiming they were tired, so only the two of us walked the eight *versts* to the little monastery of Paraclete, starting at Chernigovsky monastery and going along a straight metalled road that ran through unbroken forest. Whilst Gethsemane monastery was already under the sword of Damocles, threatened with eviction, its land confiscated and lying unused, thick with weeds, Paraclete was still safe. As we approached its high red walls we saw some monks with sickles harvesting the rye.

The rule at Paraclete was strict. Women were not allowed, the services were long and few pilgrims visited it. The guest monk let us in and showed us the way to the refectory, assuring us that we would certainly be fed. And so it was. A young, smiling monk served us hot cabbage soup topped with a lump of the special butter for fasting time and cut us huge pieces of bread, as well as placing a jug of *kvas* (ice-cold fruit drink) in front of us. We ate with relish and told each other that never in our lives had we enjoyed such delicious soup, bread and *kvas*. Many years later, I learned that Patriarch Pimen had once served in that monastery, which led me to wonder whether the young monk who had treated us so generously had been the future head of the Russian Orthodox church.

Andrei organised a third excursion, this time to a *pustyn* (hermitage) called Germogenovsky, about twenty *versts* to the northwest of Sergiyev Posad. It was founded by monks expelled from the Nikolo-Ugreshsky monastery in the years just after the revolution. We inquired about the way there and then the five of us – my sisters, Lyalya, Andrei Kiselev and I – set off. This excursion has remained one of the most lyrical memories of my adolescence. We were filled with a feeling of great well-being as we walked from village to village over fields, through copses, waded over streams and eventually took a little-used track through virgin forest until we were greeted by a sight that might have come straight out of a painting by Nesterov. In a clearing two horses were grazing, some monks were at work in the pasture, and on the edge of the forest stood newly-built wooden houses with straw roofs, the largest of them, roofed in plank, carrying a delicate cupola of aspen tiles topped by a wooden cross. A wooden fence surrounded the tiny settlement.

At first the monks were upset by our appearance, as they thought we were officials. Once they realised that we were pilgrims they gathered together to discuss how to accommodate us and what food to offer. We declined their food as we had brought a little with us and had drunk milk in the last village. The evening service was underway as we entered the little church, causing a stir as we hardly looked like pilgrims. At the end of the service we were invited into the Father Andrei's hut. He was trying unsuccessfully to heat the samovar, as the only pipe was ancient and riddled with holes so that the flames dispersed and the water just did not heat up. Father Andrei groaned and lamented the fact that he could not offer us tea made with strawberry leaves and honey. A disaster now occurred; Sonya, sitting down, banged her head against a hanging lamp, upsetting the oil which spilled all over her hair and the sheepskin that Father Andrei had laid on the floor for us to sit on. I thought he would scold her, but instead he crossed himself and then asked my embarrassed sister her name.

"Servant of God Sofia, don't be upset, it means God will send you happiness."

We all lay down in a heap for the night. I slept very badly as Sonya's oily hair was right in my face. In the morning we returned to Glinkovo. I must say that Andrei Kiselev showed great persistence. He assured his namesake elder that he would bring him a new samovar pipe as soon as possible, but only found an opportunity when the October celebrations came round, when all students, under threat of expulsion, were forced to march in the demonstration on Red Square. So Andrei marched in column under red banners and raised his fist as he passed the leaders on the Lenin's mausoleum, but all the time he was thinking about the samovar pipe. Finally, when he was free, he rushed to the Yaroslavsky station, caught a train to his home on Losinoostrovskaya Street, then another train to Sergiyev Posad and, carrying the pipe under his arm, tramped to the hermitage. It was night when he got there, and his unexpected arrival terrified the monks. Sadly, the pipe did not serve them for long. When, a year later, my sisters and Andrei repeated their walk to the Germogenovsky *pustin*, they were shocked to find the site deserted and despoiled; the local villagers had carried off the wood from the houses and the monks had dispersed in all directions. In the nettles lay the little cupola with its broken cross.

11. Into Adult Life

1

At the end of August 1926, I left Glinkovo with a heavy heart. I needed to get started in some way, in other words to decide what I should do. No longer a lad, I was now a youth who dreamed of the beautiful and the good, but saw only darkness around me, and was tormented by uncertainty. When I got to Moscow I discovered that, without my knowledge, father had entered me for a book-keeping course which one could join without taking any exams or coming from any particular institution. As father had a friend who was secretary to the director of studies, that got me admitted.

Father gave me ten roubles to pay for the course and so three times a week I went off in the evenings to the former school building in Tolmachevsky Lane, close to the Tretyakov Art Gallery. Commerce and bookkeeping were of no interest to me, even less than political studies. My parents tried to cheer me up by saying that the training would allow me to earn a living, and that I could write in my free time. So, I regularly crossed over on the ice of the frozen river Moskva. I made no friends on my course, but by the spring had successfully finished. In fact, I never worked as a bookkeeper, but much later, after the war, when I had earned quite a few thousand roubles, that training stood me in good stead. I could account for every last penny.

On the advice of Nikolai Alexeievich Bobrinsky, professor of natural sciences at the university, I began to attend lectures as an external, unregistered student. There was the slight hope that if I prepared myself well I might win a place the following year. Among the lecturers I remember the best was the professor of biology, Nikolai Konstantinovich Koltsov, a short, fair-haired bewhiskered man who wore a grey suit of plus fours. Using coloured chalks he nimbly leaped about in front of the blackboard drawing diagrams of the division of cells in all kinds of amoebas and other creatures. As the inventor of the science of eugenics, that laid down how to improve the human race in the same way as the breeding of sheep and cows, he achieved worldwide fame, including amongst fascist ideologists. This brought down on him the hatred of our proletarian leaders. Demyan Bedny poured out vitriolic verse about him so that Koltsov was reviled everywhere and had his work stopped, but he was too famous internationally to be arrested, which did not stop his students suffering that fate.

I remember the other professors who lectured simply as names, since I was able to go to only two or three lectures before being excluded by the system of admission tickets reserved for full-time students. The doors of the temple of learning closed in my face. For a time I forced myself to study the physics that I detested, but at this time articles were appearing in the newspapers calling for the purge of the sons and daughters of "former people". After reading that kind of article I glimpsed the humiliations I would face even if I could get into a university. This kind of reasoning provided an excuse to snap shut my textbooks.

2

Quite unexpectedly, father started to earn extra money. The publishing house Land and Factory decided to publish the complete works of Zola. Someone recommended my father as a translator. He came home one day wreathed in smiles with a volume of Zola under his arm – *Au Bonheur des Dames*. He had signed a contract and even received an advance. Suddenly this unexpected, heaven-sent good fortune was upon us.

That very day father and grandfather, armed with weighty dictionaries, got down to the work of translation. Grandfather was the first to begin on the text, knowing French "the way our ancestors knew and spoke French" (Leo Tolstoy), but his language was somewhat heavy and old-fashioned so father corrected it, but as he had no literary talent mother then improved it, after which it was polished up by brother Vladimir. After making a clean copy, father would deliver it chapter by chapter to the publisher. Every day, back from work, father would have his supper and then settle down at his table to work on the book until ten o'clock. Our entire family was caught up in the descriptions of elegant Parisian life, of the luxury-goods shop and the love of its owner, Octave Moureau, for the humble salesgirl, Denise.

Father said to me, "There, you see, if you know languages you can always get by." He passed me, together with a dictionary, another novel, *The Dream*. My knowledge of French had never been very good so I had to struggle to meet this challenge, but I stuck at it and within a year I had done four or five books and was more than familiar with the relationships of the Rougeon Makares. I moved on to Maupassant and loved his novels and stories, a love I have never lost.

Reginald Witter received the French newspaper, *Temps*, which he passed on to grandfather on the quiet. My brother and I used to read it and wonder at the colourful accounts of robberies and murders, which were so much more interesting than anything that appeared in our papers. When Cheka agents kidnapped the White general, Kutyopov, the French paper devoted long columns to describing this awful crime that I read avidly with the help of my dictionary.

As it turned out, father's work on *Au Bonheur des Dames* came to nothing. The decision was taken to set aside the collected works of Zola, since on closer examination it was found that in many of his writings capitalists were shown in a positive light and the proletarian girls shown as in love with them. According to Marx and Lenin such a thing could not happen, so only his writings that were saturated with the class struggle – *Germinal* and *The Trap* – were published. The advance father had received was not taken away from him, but he signed a new contract for Balzac's *Les Contes Drolatiques* and he and grandfather launched into this new translation. Grandfather's old-fashioned language was now very useful as the *Contes* is a work of pastiche in the sixteenth-century style. In recent translations the book is called *Daring Stories* but I think grandfather's title in Russian, *Amusing Tales* is more exact and much closer to the spirit of these witty tales by the great writer.

Father was very proud of the little book when finally it was published, printed on cheap paper.

3

In the autumn of 1927, the tenth anniversary of Soviet power was celebrated with great pomp, with red flags and red banners hanging everywhere. The procession down Prechistenkaya Street lasted for two hours, the demonstrators holding up red flags and banners, portraits of Lenin, caricatures of capitalists, NEPmen and White guards, and singing. One song began, "See how we've confounded the NEPmen!" The town of Sergiyev Posad was renamed Zagorsk in honour of a second-rank leader, Vladimir Zagorsk (real name Lubotsky) who was killed in an explosion in Leontiyevsky Lane in

1918. On this account many processions took place in the town. Eight-year-old Andrei, Uncle Vladimir's son, asked his father why people were carrying aloft the letter X; he had not yet learned Latin numbers. The authorities suddenly remembered that the town was full of priests and monks and "former people". Arrest them! A pretext was found when a bullet smashed a window in the regional secretary's house. The rumour was spread about that it was a jealous husband who had shot at the secretary for seducing his wife. Another story, however, was that it was a deliberate provocation organised by the authorities themselves to allow them to accuse clerics and "former people".

Thirty people were arrested – aristocrats, the clergy, rich merchants and also my friend Sergei Istomin. A major trial was expected. In those days, however, they had not yet begun to use torture during inter-rogation. No one confessed to the deed. In reply to the interrogator's question, "Where have you hidden the revolver?" Sergei Istomin replied, "I wouldn't have missed, I'd have got him." The interrogator was taken aback by this reply, which convinced him that Sergei was not guilty. But as Sergei had declared himself a monarchist, he was sentenced to "minus six". He chose the town of Tver. Some time later, Peshkova remarked with indignation to my father, "A seventeen-year-old and he says he's on the extreme right!"

In the end there was no trial. Those arrested were given "minus six" or exiled to distant places.

4

My brother Vladimir was now working very successfully as an illustrator for several magazines, but he was also a great help to many young artists. They would come to him and he would take them around the editorial offices, introducing them and saying a good word for them. No less than five young people were helped by Vladimir's benevolence. Maria Alexandrovna – Aunt Maritsa Kristi – brought him her fourth son, Fedya Glebov, and with Vladimir's help he became first an illustrator, then later a talented landscape painter. Petya Shipov, the grandson of one of grandfather's friends, the agrarian expert Dimitri Nikolaievich Shipov, brought some drawings to show Vladimir and also became an illustrator. Sadly, he did not have a long career, as he was arrested and, after his release, soon died of tuberculosis.

It was natural for Vladimir to try and help me, too. I was after all basically unemployed. First, however, he set me a stiff test. From the depths of Mongolia the famous explorer, Pyotr Konstantinovich Kozlov, who had discovered the dead city of Hara-Hoto, had arrived in Moscow. He handed in to the *Universal Pathfinder* his account of his expedition, and the editor asked Vladimir to quickly do some illustrations for the article. Vladimir needed to ask Kozlov some questions but the explorer had vanished somewhere in Moscow. Vladimir said to me, "Prove that you're not an idler. Find Kozlov for me by this evening." He suggested that I look for him in the old university buildings where at the time many professors were living.

Seeing me out of the door, mother said, "Don't fail! Be sure to find him!" I realised that I would have to put my heart and soul into this mission. I think I must have looked pitiful as I rang at the doors of the homes of all these professors, because the many husbands and wives who came to the door were very sympathetic, advising me where to go and making other suggestions. I walked about Moscow, hung on to the crowded trams, all in vain. By evening, tired and hungry and dispirited, I returned home. It turned out that I had done all this for nothing, as Kozlov himself came to the editorial office of the *Universal Pathfinder* at the same time as Vladimir was there so Vladimir got all the information that he needed for his pictures. In a sense though, I had passed the test he had set me.

Vladimir now decided to turn me into a sort of assistant artist. As the illustrator of travel stories, he was continually in need of maps. It was one thing to draw and paint men and animals and landscape, but quite another to have to leaf through atlases and then sketch maps with all their contours and place names. It bored him, and took up too much time. "You can draw the maps, and I'll pay you three roubles a piece," he said. I remembered how I had been held up to shame in class for my messy draughtsmanship, and how Shura Sokolov had helped me out; I really did not believe I could draw. Nevertheless, Vladimir supplied me with pens and pencils, ink and blotting paper, and set me to produce a simple map with only about ten place names and a compass sign in one corner. How I sweated and slaved over this challenge, with mother at my elbow saying, "Don't give up. Make sure you get it right!"

I took the finished product to Vladimir, who criticised my sketch and made me do it over and over again. Finally, he put the sketch in with his drawings, and the very next day handed me a green three rouble note. Within less than a month I began to be paid not by Vladimir, but at various publishing offices – *Pioneer, Knowledge is Power, Friends* – for the maps that I was directly commissioned to do. I also worked for magazines that rarely used Vladimir's work, such as *Vozhaty*, and the newspaper, *A Pioneer's Truth*. Mostly these publications were produced by two or three enthusiastic young *Konsomols*. I remember the large face of curly-headed Bob Ivanter, the editor of *Pioneer*, who was killed in the war. The editor of *A Pioneer's Truth* was a mature, unassuming lady, who had taken part in the civil war, Vera Nikolaievna Lyadova. She was very kind to me, occasionally asked about my plans for the future and gave me advice and encouragement. Like so many others, she and her husband perished during the years of the so-called "cult of personality".

I saw how well everyone got on with my brother, smiling when they met him, laughing at his jokes. Whenever he arrived with new pictures, they would hurry over to admire them as he laid them out on a table. I not only loved and cherished my Vladimir, I was also intensely proud of him.

5

The editorial set-up at the *Universal Pathfinder* was quite special. The editor, who was also director of the publishing house Zif, was the Bolshevik poet Vladimir Ivanovich Narbut, who walked with a limp and had lost one hand. However, he was never to be seen. The proofs of the magazine were taken in to his office for signature, and that was all. He too perished during the "cult of personality" years. The real heart and soul of the place was the executive editor, Vladimir Alexeievich Popov, "Vap" for short. I had heard a lot about how severe he was, so when Vladimir said Vap wanted to see me, my knees trembled, and continued to do so as I walked with my brother to the offices at No. 13 Kuznetsky Most (now No. 19). There were a number of people waiting to see Vap sitting on a bench along the walls of the outer office. At a small table sat the secretary and only other staff member, Alexander Zakharovich Sokolsky. There was silence in the room, the other visitors and even Vladimir looked nervous. Now and again glances were cast at the door on which one could read "Executive Editor". This outer room was called "Purgatory", the inner sanctum either "Heaven" or "Hell", according to the fate that befell the visitor.

Eventually, the door of the sanctum opened and someone, carrying a bulging briefcase, rushed out, leaving the office without a glance at anyone. Clearly, he had failed to sell his work. Behind him, on the threshold, stood a solid, middle-aged, bespectacled man, with a moustache above his tightly compressed lips, wearing a tight-fitting dark suit and dark tie against a white shirt. Vladimir had so frightened me with his description of this all-powerful editor that I looked at Vap as if he were a god. Without a word he gestured into his office a sad-looking cartoonist who very much resembled a character later depicted in Ilf and Petrov's comic novel, *The Twelve Chairs*. Soon this old man reappeared with a smile on his lips, saying, "He took them. Now my wife can have her shoes. The only thing is, he wants the trees changed, says they look like cabbages." With that he asked Sokolsky for some materials and began there and then working on his cartoons.

Once more the door opened and with the same silent gesture, Vladimir was summoned in. I was left to wait nervously, until after a few minutes the door opened again and Vladimir shouted, "Come on in". Vap's office was spacious, set about with a few chairs facing a massive writing desk, above which hung portraits of Jules Verne and Lenin. Vap himself sat enthroned behind the desk. He looked me up and down with a frown, and then his face cleared. I obviously pleased him. He called me Seryozha and shook my hand kindly. The interview concluded with unexpected success for me, as Vap decided that future numbers of the magazine should each have a map of the different continents and countries on their back covers, so that by the end of the year readers would have a little atlas consisting of twelve maps. I have to confess that this atlas was a pretty poor present, drawn as it was by me.

So I now began to earn quite good money, about seventy roubles a month, mostly from the *Universal Pathfinder*, but also from other journals. I bought myself a good suit and shoes and an overcoat. Once, and for the only time in my life, I took Lyalya Ilyinskaya for a long ride in a *likhachi* (fast sledge) all the way to the village of Vsekhsvatsky and back. I also was able to give mother the occasional gift of money when my earnings were particularly good. I quite gave up thinking of entering higher education, and went on reading Zola, now so well that I hardly ever used a dictionary.

This was how Vap paid for my work; silently sucking at his lips, he would look at the drawing, and in silence pull out of his drawer a cheque book, scratch something on it and hand it to me. Sometimes I noticed there was a bottle of brandy in that drawer. He would then close the drawer, and I would walk to the bank on the corner of Rozhdestvenskaya Street, cash the cheque, and that was that.

The editorial office was run by just two people, Vap and Sokolsky. When they started the journals *Around the World* and *Global Tourist*, they needed a third. Vap thought about taking me on, but then grew cautious. It was one thing to be feeding two former princes as freelances, quite another to have one on the staff whose appointment would have to be run past the watchful eyes of the staff committee. So Vap took on a humble young man, who did the work, though slowly, and was lacking in initiative. The three of them, however, coped with what was needed. Nowadays there would be twenty staff of one kind and another – editor, deputy-editor, head of the prose department, head of poetry, artistic director, technical director and several girls. And there they would all be, typing away, gossiping and chattering on the telephone from morning till night. At Vap's *Universal Pathfinder*, no one spoke as they got on with their work; the only disturbance was when the courier came in from the printing works.

6

Starting at the end of 1926, Vap began to help feed a third prince. This was Uncle Vladimir Trubetskoi. He was living with his large family in Sergiyev Posad but barely making ends meet. His work in the local cinema was badly paid; gifts of money from relatives abroad were irregular and insufficient for a family that now consisted of seven children who needed to be fed and clothed. Being very close to his uncle, my brother Vladimir decided to try to help him. Back in 1922, when Uncle Vladimir had joined us in Bogoroditsk, he had brought with him a great rarity, a pale, sandy-coloured rook that he had shot. Albino birds and animals are rare, but colour change is even rarer. This pale rook caused great excitement among biologists. The university museum of biology was going to buy the specimen for a large sum of money. Some important official was absent, however, and Uncle Vladimir was told to bring the bird back the following day. In the meantime, he visited us at Eropkinsky Street, and put his rook down on a trunk to greet us. As we were exchanging kisses and so on, a cat made off with his treasure.

Vladimir urged his uncle to write a funny story about this incident for the *Universal Pathfinder*. Uncle Vladimir took up the challenge and very soon came and read us what he had written, *A Billion for a Rook*. After a few corrections suggested by his nephew, the story was delivered to the journal signed V. Vetov. The story was accepted by Vap; he only changed the title to *The Precious Rook*. In Soviet literature, instructions from on high were never to refer to prices, especially such an astronomical one. Vladimir did the illustrations, portraying uncle very much as he was, tall and thin, wearing a cap, with a small head and a moustache, in a shabby black jacket and plus fours, with long legs in puttees that were unravelling over great big boots. Another picture showed three university professors peering at the bird – they were Kozhevnikov, Ognev and Bobrinsky, who were drawn as recognisable caricatures.

Popov had the gift of discovering talented writers and artists. My brother owed a lot to him. I have already mentioned the writers A. Grin, A. Belayev, V. Yan and others. Once the magazine ran a competition for the best short story, which was won by a geology student called Volodya Belousov. For the next three summers, Popov sent him off to remote and interesting parts of the country and printed the articles and tales of his adventures. Later this young man became an important scientist and corresponding member of the Academy of Sciences. He died in 1985.

Popov detected a hidden talent in Uncle Vladimir and asked him to write more humorous hunting stories. A second story by V. Vetov, *Shchadilov's Pond* soon appeared, this time featuring two unlucky hunters – the author with his long legs and trailing puttees, nicknamed Khvoshch, the other hunter, short and also thin, with glasses on his long nose, Semyon Semyonovich Bochonkin. Popov urged Uncle Vladimir to write a series around these two hunters, Khvoshch and Bochonkin. These duly began to appear, twelve of them being published over a period of two and a half years. Some were very good, some less so; Popov only rejected one. The setting for these tales was around "the old town of B. in the province of Tula" (obviously Bogoroditsk) at the beginning of the 1920s. The stories found a ready readership, and the inhabitants of Bogoroditsk quickly recognised the locality and delightedly tried to identify the many characters depicted in the stories.

Uncle Vladimir was now earning a useful additional income. In an editorial, Popov wrote that "the author is moving out into the mainstream of literature". At the same time, brother Vladimir was enhancing his reputation by his work as a comic illustrator. On his days off, Uncle Vladimir would come to us and in the evening we would all gather round the dining table, grandfather presiding, except for father who would go off to work on some writing task in his room. Uncle Vladimir would read aloud what he had written and there would begin a lengthy and detailed analysis and commentary, and suggestions for a change of word or a change of incident would come from the various members of the family. Uncle Vladimir, a little discouraged, yet inspired by the criticisms, would travel back to Sergiyev Posad to write the alterations into the story.

Now and again the idea for a plot would be born of our discussions around the table. My brother would ask, "What if a crocodile were to turn up in the lake at Bogoroditsk?". And everyone would start to fantasise about how it got there, what it would do, who it had eaten and how Khvoshch and Bochonkin would deal with it. And so would appear the story, *The Crocodile from the Mississippi*. I dared not say a word and sat modestly in a corner, but those lively and noisy discussions around the table were my first literary apprenticeship.

Uncle Vladimir, on his visits to us, talked more and more about the writer Mikhail Mikhailovich Prishvin, who in 1926 moved from Pereslavl-Zalesky to Sergiyev Posad, where he bought a house not far from the Trubetskoi family. In that same year he was becoming a well-known writer. His stories, *The Homeland of the Stork* were published in the journal *Novy Mir* and were read with delight. The character frequently depicted in them, the hunter Muzicant T, is Uncle Vladimir. The Prishvin home was a most hospitable one. It was not only hunters who foregathered there. The artist Favorsky was also a frequent guest. He and his wife and many others were extremely fond of Prishvin, a witty and generous person with an attractive character, who was always out front in the hunt and when entertaining at home, took the head of the table and loved telling fascinating stories and inventing splendid toasts. His wife, Ephrosina Pavlovna, large and voluptuous, was also a great favourite of their guests, and always generous with her hospitality. She was a simple peasant woman and took little part in the conversation around the table, but was very happy in the company of the wives. And as a true country woman, she ran her domestic economy efficiently, keeping a cow that she herself milked before driving it out into the grazing herd, as well as cultivating fruit trees and a vegetable garden with her own hands.

The Prishvin home was a cup of happiness that overflowed, with a loving wife and many friends. He could bask in their company, and spend much time hunting. What more could a man, who was receiving recognition as a writer, and whose subjects came to him from his surroundings and friends, ask of life? He had only to write his stories, filling them with poetry and love of Mother Russia's countryside. Every time Uncle Vladimir visited us he would have stories to tell us about Prishvin's life, about his hunting, his wife and the feasts she laid on. The only fly in the ointment was the two Prishvin sons who, it was said, were snobbish and ashamed of their mother.

Then, Prishvin was officially allocated a large flat on Lavrushin-skaya Street in Moscow, as well as a young lady secretary. And with that his idyllic life in Sergiyev Posad fell to pieces. He abandoned his wife in favour of the secretary, and this second wife, Valeria Dimitriyevna, ruthlessly did away with the record of his life, and particularly his time in Sergiyev Posad, with the result that in bio-graphical writings no mention is made of his hunting friends, nor is there any mention of his first wife, Ephrosina Pavlovna, with whom he had lived in warm intimacy for at least thirty years.

7

We spent the winter of 1926 very happily. Almost every Saturday we had guests of mine and Masha's around to our flat and danced the foxtrot to the music of the Lyuboshinksy's gramophone. We visited our friends, often went to the theatre, and at the weekends set off in a big group to see the Osorgins, where we would take to the woods on our skis. However, Uncle Misha's theology sessions no longer took place, arrest threatening any who indulged in such teachings.

Meantime the OGPU was still in action. There would be an arrest here, an arrest there. One early morning the doorbell rang and father, who was up early to go off to work, opened the door. I woke up and heard the following conversation in the hall:

"Is Osorgin, Alexandra Mikhailovna, staying with you?"

"Yes," replied father, "but she's still asleep. What is it?"

"We'll soon wake her up," said a loud, sharp voice.

A tall man in soldier's uniform strode down the corridor straight to the women's quarters. Everyone jumped out of bed. So did I. Our sister Lina had come to us the night before with her daughter, Marinochka, in order to take her to a doctor.

Lina pleaded, "But look, I've got a small daughter!"

"So what? There are plenty of people here to look after her!" the soldier said.

We soon discovered what had happened. A search had been carried out throughout the night at the Osorgins. Only Uncle Misha was there, but as a totally honest man he could not lie when the police asked for Lina's whereabouts. The police had gone straight back to the Lubyanka, sending one man to arrest Lina. As Lina was being taken away, all the Osorgins came over to our place – Uncle Misha, Aunt Liza, Maria and Tonya. Lina begged them to look after little Marinochka and managed to whisper something to her father-in-law.

Immediately, father rushed over to see Peshkova at the PRC and when she heard that Lina had been arrested, she immediately rang the Lubyanka and, in a tone that could not be refused, demanded to be put through to Yagoda himself. Even though a long queue of suffering people were waiting to see her, she walked past them and rode off.

This was the first Sunday ever that Georgy had not received a visit from his wife. Uncle Misha, with all the force of his Christian beliefs, tried to console his son. Later Georgy told us that those days when Lina was also under arrest had been the worst days of his imprisonment. Within three days Lina was freed. I thank that magnificent person, Ekaterina Pavlovna Peshkova. May she rest in peace!

Nadezhda Bogdanovna, our Aunt Nadya Rayevskaya, was also arrested. But her fate was quite different. Peshkova only acted decisively in exceptional cases, bypassing the whole Lubyanka hierarchy, as was the case with our sister Lina, who was released even before her interrogation. Aunt Nadya told her interrogators that she did not feel in the least guilty, and when asked about her attitude to Soviet power, replied that she was "loyal". When however they went on to ask her about other people, she replied very firmly that they could ask away, but she would say nothing at all about other people. So she remained in prison. Her three daughters were looked after by their nanny, but her poor husband, locked up in the same "workers' corridor" as Georgy, went through many agonising days. He must have envied Georgy who received visits from his wife, whilst he could only see his daughters.

8

I was frequently asked to be a groom at weddings. I held the crown over the head of our lodger Adamovich when he was wed to an empty-headed little blonde in the church of Ilya Obydenny on Ostozhenka Street. It was followed by an ample and tasty reception. Uncle Nikolai Vladimirovich Golitsyn married a Marquise Campanari, a middle-aged lady who we did not know. To put it more accurately, she proposed marriage to this lonely uncle who was then living in a tiny room in No. 26 Trubnikovsky Lane, and I held the crown above him in the church of Troitsa on Zubov. As the title of Marquise was not familiar to the authorities, she was considered of proletarian origin and given the job of house supervisor in the same building where he lived. However, their marriage only lasted a few years.

A friend of my sister Sonya, the young Countess Sofia Ribopierre, nicknamed "Cherry" for her large, dark eyes, also got married. I held the crown over her in the church of Pokrov on Levshin. Her betrothed was a Georgian prince, Archil Vanadze, who came to the ceremony dressed in exotic Caucasian costume, complete with golden cummerbund. With his black moustache and dark eyes, even larger than hers, he was a handsome man, but had lost a leg in the war and so limped around the lectern. His three grooms were also Georgians clad in their dark Circassian costumes. There was no wedding reception as the couple left immediately for the Caucasus. Two years later, with a two-year-old son and Archil's mother, after unbelievable adventures, they managed to escape through Kirghystan to China, and, eventually, to Europe. I know nothing of their later fate. All the Vanadze princes who remained in our country were arrested, some were shot. The only survivor was Archil's cousin, the well-known cinema actress, Nata Vanadze. Between 1923 and 1929, I was a groom nine times. Of these nine marriages, only one lasted any length of time, the rest ending either in divorce or when the husband died in prison.

Year by year, we continued to rent the *dacha* in Glinkovo. My younger sisters and Lyalya Ilyinskaya spent their summers there, visited by young men from either Moscow or Sergiyev Posad. I spent most of my time in Moscow, as I was eager to earn money drawing maps for publishers and acting as Vladimir's assistant.

Nearby on Volkhonka Street, in a garret opposite the church of the Saviour, there lived the artist Vatagin with his wife and little daughter. He did illustrations for children's books for a private publisher called Mirimanov, whose office was not far away on Prechistenky Boulevard, and I drew titles for these little books. I found it surprising that people who could hold a pencil in their hands had not discovered what a source of income publishing houses could provide. That they asked Vladimir to illustrate books was natural – he was a talented artist, but I, who had no such talent, was nonetheless in constant demand for my humble draughtsman's skill.

We now had a new occupant in our flat, the cousin of Vladimir's wife Elena, the twenty-two-year-old Yuri Saburov. Evicted from Vozdvizhenkaya Street, the Saburovs now lived outside Moscow in Tsaritsina. Yuri's mother and his sister, Ksenya, were not good at coping with life and only survived by teaching French to the daughter of some NEPman, while Yuri's older brother Boris was serving his sentence of exile in the north Urals. My brother was sorry for Yuri and managed to introduce him to my kind of work. Yuri in fact drew better than me and was a very conscientious worker. Orders were frequent, so every evening we three sat down round the table and worked until three or four in the morning, sometimes even later.

This was a time when the government was launching a policy of encouraging attention to the land and its agriculture, and planning to help hard-working peasants in all sorts of ways. A journal called *Be Your Own Agronomist* was founded in an office on Malaya Dimitrovka Street next to the church of Rozhdestvo on Putinky. Vladimir felt it was beneath him to illustrate a farming magazine, but Yuri and I set about extracting income from it by drawing maps and diagrams for the texts and titles for its covers. Whatever he earned Yuri handed over to his mother, himself going about Moscow in winter in a short fur coat, and in summer in a Russian blouse under a pea-coloured, ragged jacket. More than six foot four tall and very thin, with hair brushed back from his high forehead, he was a handsome young man, particularly thanks to his big eyes with long girlish lashes. Like a girl, he was timid and delicate. If my brother began to tell dirty stories – and he knew many – Yuri would lower his eyes and blush. He was also very peaceful; I never once saw him over-excited or heard him raise his voice. His delicacy meant that, apart from when he was with Vladimir and Elena, he used the formal "you" with everyone, even with me. If only one order came in, he would want me to do it, which of course, led to my conceding it back to him. He was shy with girls, usually avoiding them.

My sister Masha, used to the attentions of young men, was astonished to meet one who did not look at her or pay her any attention. She resolved to stir him up. As we worked late into the night, it was usual for us to sleep late. One day, Masha crept up to Yuri's bed as he slept and cut off a sizeable hank of the hair over his forehead. He seemed to be quite unconcerned, went to the barber's, who was intrigued to know how he had lost such an odd part of his hair, and was compelled to give him a very short cut. Masha did not give up. She sat down next to Yuri with a cup in her hand and asked, "Would you like me to smash this cup against your magnificent forehead?"

"I don't think you would do that," he answered, blushing.

She lifted the cup and – bang! broke it on his brow. The wound had to be treated with iodine. But this did not break through his shyness. When he saw her he still lowered his eyes and reddened.

Vladimir bought his son Mikhail an airgun, a useless gift for a one-year-old boy, so the adults took to amusing themselves with it. It was very simple to load and fire, just by putting little pellets down its barrel and then pulling the trigger – tsik! tsik! tsik! – until they were all gone. The three of us went on with our work until we were exhausted, when Vladimir would allow us to have a break for a smoke. An empty bottle was placed on the table and the challenge was for each of us to get three, four, five or more pellets into its neck from a distance of twelve paces. Our guests were astonished to see how we rarely missed. Then in the faint light of early morning, Vladimir would say, "Now let's go and tickle the old man!"

In the cold light of early morning, we would march out into the hallway and point the airgun through the little *fortochka* (window for winter ventilation). Below us was a row of sheds, then a garden and beyond the garden, on Mansurovskaya Street, a two-storey house about two hundred paces away. There was a particular window on the second floor at which we took aim, pointing the gun up so as to allow for trajectory. After a few shots the window would be flung open and an old man in his underwear would appear, look about cautiously before receiving a couple of pellets on his head or his chest, when he would jump back, slamming shut the window. We could see that he was still standing behind the window, we would fire again, and again he would open the window and hang out, completely unaware of where these shots were coming from. Once more we would open fire, and again he would jump back and close the window. We "tickled" the old man in this way for three years, until the gun broke, and in all that time he never spotted who were the guilty parties.

9

Vladimir and Elena, leaving their two little children with Nanny Katya and my mother at Glinkovo, set off on a long trip by train to Vologda, then by boat to Kirillov, Belozersk and some other place. They came back enthralled by their travels. Vladimir showed us his sketches and told us about all the interesting people they had met, while Elena read aloud to us from her diary.

I was also filled with a deep desire to travel. Father suggested I follow the route he had taken when he graduated from the gymnasium and was given a hundred roubles by his parents; by train from Moscow to Yaroslavl, then by boat down the Volga to Nizhny Novgorod, up the river Oka to Ryazan, then back by train to Moscow. Vladimir told Popov of my plans. One day, when I had brought Popov some work, he questioned me about my route, which he approved, and suggested that I pay the extra to travel second class, as he said I would see nothing from third class, which was usually very noisy and full of people being sick. Unexpectedly he paid me twice the usual amount for my drawings.

I left Sergiyev Posad with a small bundle and my savings, just fifty roubles. I got to Yaroslavl in the evening, spent the night in a hotel and the following day wandered from church to church and along the banks of the Volga. The ship was to sail at night. I bought my ticket and sat on the high bank gazing at the Volga in the sunset. Nowadays tourists go in their droves to Suzdal and gape in wonder at the beauty and variety of its many churches. But in my youth every town in Old Russia was filled with stone churches just as beautiful and just as different. Whenever our ship turned in to land at the next old town, all the passengers would cluster at the rail and gasp with wonder at its marvels.

Kostroma, with its many fine churches, was the first of these beautiful towns on my journey. Landing there in the early morning, the first sight I saw was the golden cupolas and high walls of the Ignatiev monastery. The town itself lay on the hills behind its fortress walls and towers, with the gilt domes of the cathedral at its centre. Bell towers seemed to hang in the air above every street, some with spires, some with tent roofs, some white, some yellow, some pink, and the churches themselves were crowned with gleaming domes.

Old Yaroslavl survived thanks to the love the then chairman of the city council felt for his home town. In Kostroma, which had fifty-seven churches, and where the Ipatiyevsky monastery still stands high above the Volga (and has become even more beautiful thanks to its renovation), everything from the past was mercilessly destroyed apart from the church of Nikola na Debryakh, now hidden behind high buildings. The *kremlin* (fort), with its towers and the monument to the peasant Ivan Susanin, was pulled down brick by brick.

Throughout the day our ship sailed along the Volga, passing village after village, each with its churches more beautiful than the next, rising high above the skyline. The ship sailed slowly and towards evening we tied up at Yurevets with its tall classical belltower that is still standing today. The story goes that they were frightened to destroy it in case the falling bricks would smash into the roofs of the houses below. Nor could they find anyone brave enough to climb to the top of the steeple to pull down the cross.

Next morning we reached Nizhny Novgorod. Girdled by the high walls of its fortress, the city that spread out before us resembled Moscow. Inside the fortress there rose high a white belltower very like the tower of Ivan the Terrible in the Moscow Kremlin, and alongside it the five massive golden domes of the cathedral. As for churches, there were scores of them; inside the fortress, along the banks of the river Oka, on the hillsides and in the little valleys, with their single cupolas and their many domes, their walls white, or blue, or pink. Even on the lower left bank of the river, where the market-place lay, there were four or five churches and a large cathedral. Today, the city has lost its medieval appearance. Almost all the churches have been pulled down. In the *kremlin* only the little church of the Archangel Michael has been preserved, though at the foot of the hill the beautiful Stroganov church is still standing. The fortress walls have been renovated, the tops of the towers covered by aspen tiling. But what barbarity led to the building of a huge concrete box, the city council building, in place of the lovely churches within the fortress!

There was not enough time for me to visit all the sights of Nizhny Novgorod before our Oka river steamer set sail. I sat on the deck gazing at the passing countryside until darkness fell, then went below. I found I had acquired a very unpleasant companion. He was accompanied by a bottle of vodka and various things to eat. Foolishly, I did not refuse his offer and drank half a glass of vodka. He was soon tipsy and told me how during the civil war he had been a commissar and had personally shot twenty captured and wounded White Guards, and how they had screamed and cursed him. Now he was having bad dreams.

I was unwise enough to reproach him. In his drunkenness he stared at me wildly

"So you want to defend the Whites, eh?" he shouted, shaking my shoulder.

I was really scared and angry with myself for sharing a drink with an executioner. I pulled away from him and said I wanted to go to sleep. To my great relief, by morning he had left the ship and I was alone in the cabin. It was nevertheless a useful lesson for me; to be wary, and above all to control my tongue.

We sailed on past towns with their many churches, just like Suzdal. No, actually better than Suzdal, which has only its little river Kamenka, whereas we were on the majestic Oka. These historic towns – Murom, Kasimov, Elatma, Ryazan – passed before my eyes in all their beauty. I returned to Moscow enthralled by what I had seen and found it difficult to settle back to drawing maps and plans. My mother said, "Why don't you try and write about it all?" I still wanted to become a writer, though after my first childish efforts I had not written a line. Now I sat down on the church porch in

Glinkovo and, laying out a sheet of paper, sat there chewing my pencil. I decided to write about how at Yaroslavl I had sat waiting on the banks of the Volga for the steamer to come into sight. But I could not find the words to convey my feelings. I would write something, scratch it out, tear my hair, write again, and again rub it out. Finally, I showed what I had written to my mother.

After reading it, she asked, "Why do you keep on repeating the verb 'was'?"

I was furious, and tore the paper up, but then thought again and wrote it all out once more, although this time I did not show my mother. I still had doubts about what I had written and seriously wondered whether I had the talent to become a writer.

12. The Kingdom of Learning

1

This chapter is on a subject that might be of interest to future historians. I want to describe how my younger sister Masha, her friend Lyalya Ilyinskaya and I entered into the "kingdom of learning" from autumn 1927 to spring 1929. How many times has some unexpected incident played a decisive role in my life? In August 1927, my parents went on a visit to father's cousin, Aunt Lelya Loseva, someone they rarely saw except at funerals. She told them about the fascinating higher education institute her daughter was attending, the interesting professors, and how her daughter was already in her second year. When my parents asked what sort of a course this was, the girl herself, my second cousin Alya, replied, "It's at the Higher State School of Literature, for short VGLK, and is a four year course to train writers and poets, critics and researchers." She spoke with such enthusiasm that my parents decided that both my sister Masha, who had just graduated after seven years of school, and I should be sent there.

A few days later Masha, Lyalya Ilyinskaya and I were sitting in the large vestibule of the former building No. 4 of the boys' gymnasium on Sadovaya-Kudrinskaya – now the site of the Higher Party College – writing out our application forms. The form was not very long, but of course included the most important question in those days: "What are your social origins?" They had not yet thought of adding the treacherous three words "Social origins of your parents", so we were able honestly to write "Father is an employee, mother a housewife".

I dreamed of becoming a writer, Lyalya a poet, and Masha was there to keep us company. There were four entry examinations; written Russian, oral Russian, a foreign language and political knowledge. We were relieved that there was no maths or physics. We were not frightened about written Russian and knew we could produce compositions on the decadent aristocracy as described by

Turgenev, or the decadent capitalists of Gorky's writings. We had read Jack London's *The Iron Heel*, Furmanov's *Chapayev* and even Seyfulina's *Virineya*, a book that was not supposed to be read by young girls.

The examination in political knowledge, however, we did fear. A year earlier I had swotted up that great volume of Berdinkov and Svetlov, and in the last few days had managed to learn the dates and places of the regular Party conferences and how the Bolsheviks fought with the Mensheviks. But Masha and Lyalya had been taught by their teacher, Elena Alexeievna Efimova, that communist ideology was a waste of time, and so were utterly ignorant of its theory.

We wrote our compositions conscientiously – whether they were good or bad, I do not know. They were handed in, but I rather doubt whether anyone actually perused them; we never saw them again. In oral Russian, we were examined by Professor Ivan Nikanorovich Rosanov, who later became a famous bibliophile, with the best collection of poetry in our country. I cannot recall what he asked me about. I was very struck by his wise face, his deep-seated eyes and prominent jaw. As for French, we probably knew that language better than the other students, so that our examination by an old "former person", Vorontsova-Velyaminova, was over quickly after she had questioned us on various forms of the past tense. In political knowledge we had to face a man called Granovsky, whose fierce, bespectacled gaze shone out of a face as thin as a carrot. He was long-bodied and long fingered, and unlike other professors wore a good suit. His appearance frightened us, and his lean features seemed to say, "I'm not going to pass anyone!" He questioned me for a long time, his glasses flashing contemptuously. I somehow managed to stammer out my answers.

Masha and Lyalya went in after me and I was sure they would fail resoundingly. After all, they did not know a thing. But they emerged smiling – they had passed. I am sure it was not what they knew that saved them, but their pretty young faces.

2

So there we were with our blue cards that certified us as students at the Higher School of Literature. I was now on the threshold of the kingdom of learning, and felt that I was the happiest person in the world, about to learn all about literature. Now there could be no doubts that I would really become a writer. We were told that we would have to attend four or five lectures an evening every day of the week, hours so arranged that working students could attend; only Sunday evenings were free. As our marks in the entry examination were "good", we did not have to spend any time on a preparatory course that was designed for those not yet ready to study properly. I was also very impressed by the word "lecture", which sounded so much better than "class" with its connotation of school. The lecture room was just like a regular schoolroom, but here it was called the "auditorium", which also made a quite different impression. There were three rows of desks with benches, and on each bench sat three students. I looked about for a free place. Had we come in ten minutes earlier we would have been able to choose where we sat, but now there were empty seats only in the front two rows. I picked a bench close to the window. Had we come in earlier the fate of my younger sisters, Masha and Katya, would have been utterly different – they would have married other men, and their progeny, now so numerous, would have been completely different people. But I see I have run on ahead by six years.

We took our seats, Lyalya by the window and Masha between us. Usually very lively girls, here they were quiet and sat with lowered eyes. Looking around the auditorium I saw that there were about a hundred young women, and wondered whether among them there were future Pushkins and Tolstoys. Behind us sat three young men. I have the bad habit on first meeting someone of comparing him or her to another person or thing. The one by the window was a plump, rosy-cheeked little lad in a cheap Moscow suit and tie; the one in the middle an extremely handsome lad with large, round eyes, curly hair and moustache, also wearing a Moscow suit and tie. He looked so sweet that he might have stepped off a pre-revolutionary chocolate box. The third boy was fair-haired and confident-looking, wearing a good quality suit of foreign cut. He was just saying something witty to his companions and I visualised him as a kind of Airedale dog, sniffing out the unknown.

A tall, bearded, middle-aged man now entered and introduced himself as Buslayev, who would be teaching us Old Russian literature. He was in fact the grandson of a famous nineteenth-century philologist, Fyodor Ivanovich Buslayev. He dictated the timetable of lectures to us. The names of the professors meant nothing to me, but I caught my breath when I wrote down the names of the disciplines we were to study – aesthetics, scansion, poetics, theory of prose, philology, psychology of creativity, history of literature – ancient Greek, German and Old Russian. I am sure, however, that the majority of the students groaned when they realised that we would have no less than three lectures in political knowledge; the history of the Party, political economy and economic policies, for which no less than ten hours a week were allotted.

Every evening, we attended these lectures, sitting on that same bench, while behind us there sat the three young men.

3

Not all the professors were good lecturers. Buslayev managed to drive all the poetry out of *The Tale of Igor's Campaign*, turning the immortal lines into things of such scholastic complexity that we nearly fell asleep. The three professors of political theory tried their best to make their subjects interesting, but failed utterly. One of the books was all pictures, but still remained boring, whilst Bukharin's textbook, *Dialectical Materialism*, was the most difficult political book I have ever come across in my life. Today, it has long been consigned to oblivion, but I remember with a shudder the long hours I wasted on it.

We had, however, some professors who before the revolution had been considered outstanding, and often by the end of a lecture I would be jumping with excitement at the brilliantly witty and inspired teaching and the many insights they were able to pass on to us out from their long lives of dedicated study. They were forced to start off their course by announcing that they would be teaching us the subject on the basis of dialectical and historical materialism and the teachings of Marx and Lenin, but from then on to the end of the year there would not be a single mention of materialism, as they taught us the subject as they understood and loved it. As a precaution, however, they did suggest we read some Marxist works; these were Trotsky's *Literature and Revolution*, Bukharin's *Dialectical Materialism*, works by Voronsky and Deborin and other Marxists, all of whose works were long ago burned by frightened citizens. Copies of them can now probably be found only in the Lenin Library.

I will name a few of our professors. Some I can even remember the intonation of their voices, so unforgettable were their lectures. German literature was taught by Grigory Alexeievich Rachinsky, who had previously been a disciple of the philosopher Vladimir Solovyev, whose complete works he had edited, and was close to the Symbolists, especially Valery Bryusov. In appearance, he resembled a Homer whom the gods had left with some sight, an old, widowed and therefore unkempt Homer in a crumpled jacket and trousers. He started us off by telling us something of old German mythology, then moved on to the Nibelungen, with whose exploits he got stuck for half the year. He spoke in a loud, lisping but inspired voice, enunciating very clearly, and at the end of his lectures we would often find our eyes were burning with enthusiasm. He lived very close to the school, in a tiny Empire-style house at the back of a courtyard, where the painter Polenov had once lived. After the war a plaque was put up on the house – "Ancient Monument" – but not long after that the house was pulled down.

I visited Rachinsky there once. He lived with his nephew, who had been a colleague of the Minister of Communications under the Kerensky government. This nephew was put in prison, and then, to everyone's surprise, the eighty-year-old uncle married. The last time I saw him he was wearing a good suit, was clean-shaven and did not look at all like Homer.

Ancient Greek literature was taught us by Sergei Mikhailovich Solovyev, grandson of the historian and nephew of the philosopher, who was a poet and friend of the poets Blok and Bely, and after the revolution became a Catholic Father. He resembled Christ as depicted in many nineteenth century icons, with a red beard and thoughtful, sad eyes that seemed to foresee the suffering that awaited him. In the summer of 1928, he was arrested. He went out of his mind in prison and soon died in a lunatic asylum. I had loved the ancient Greeks from childhood and Solovyev brought my love to even greater heights as he taught us the beauties of the *Iliad*. He would read aloud the timeless lines of Homer and those other poets whom I had known only by name, or the tragedies of Aeschylus, in a hollow, echoing voice like the rumble of distant thunder. Since then I have never heard anyone recite anything in such an enchanting way; it was just as the ancient Greeks must have read their poetry aloud.

The next year we were taught ancient Roman literature by a professor (whose name I cannot recall) in such a dry and boring manner that it put me off the Roman classics for the rest of my life.

Boris Nikolaievich Griftsov taught us French literature. He was a brilliant, witty man who loved to regale us with slightly salacious stories out of Rabelais and the minstrels, but also inspired in me a love of Villon and Ronsard. The great defect of all these professors was that they never completed the teaching programme, only partly covering the curriculum. Solovyev told us nothing about Euripides. Bruslayev did not even get as far as Zadonshchina. Griftsov got stuck on Corneille, and Rachinsky stopped with the Meistersingers. My knowledge of literature was therefore extremely partial, and I was stuck in the middle of the stated programme.

Alexei Alexeievich Sidorov, young, tall and elegant, taught us the history of art. After uttering a few sentences about Marxism-Leninism, he moved on to deliver each of his lectures as distinct, concise, finely chiselled and artistic entities. He lectured on Egypt, Assyria, Babylon and the Greeks, and then suddenly announced that the next lecture would deal with the art of Atlantis. Sceptics doubt whether such a continent has ever existed, but Sidorov spoke of Mexican, Egyptian and Etrurian art, finding in them common features, and before our enraptured attention drew a convincing picture of that legendary vanished continent. Under his flashing pince-nez, I learned to love Medieval and early Renaissance art. He had just returned from abroad and would often drop phrases such as "when I was walking along the Champs Elysées", or "as I stood at the foot of Cologne cathedral".

Dramaturgy was taught by Vladimir Mikhailovich Volkenstein. Small, with dark eyes and a lively manner, he would pace up and down in front of the first row of desks, then suddenly seize a chalk and draw a complicated design on the blackboard. At that time his play *Hussars and Doves* was being put on at the Maly Theatre, with some success. He said nothing about his own play but brilliantly analysed all the plays then running in Moscow and the different aims and methods of the directors at the Moscow Arts Theatre, the Vakhtangov, the Kamerny and the Meyerhold. His criticism of the theatre of that time was done with great delicacy, which made it difficult for the watchful guardians of Marxist orthodoxy to quarrel with him. He said nothing at all about Bulgakov as a playwright, doubtless because he wanted to avoid making himself vulnerable in terms of the dogmas of the time.

At the end of our course I was examined by him. Other examinees were in with him for some length of time, coming out looking defeated and frustrated. I came out after only three minutes, happily waving my report card. Volkenstein had asked me, "Who was in love with Desdemona?" "Othello," I replied. "Who else?" "Cassio." "And who else? Quick now!" I hesitated a moment and then took the plunge like a high diver, "Iago also loved Desdemona." "Yes, that's what I think too," he said, "although there's no evidence for it in Shakespeare. Give me your report card."

Fifty years later I ran into Volkenstein, now old and quite forgotten, in the House of Literature, where he had come to eat a meal. Playwrights of the next generation had been his pupils and it was decided to mark his eightieth birthday in the Maly Theatre. Hardly anyone came so the hall was nearly empty. I was attending another event, but I should really have gone to his celebration. I could have risen to my feet and recalled that examination of long ago, and added – "And in addition, Volkenstein loved Desdemona, although there is no evidence for that in Shakespeare!"

Poetry composition was taught by Ivan Sergeievich Rukavishnikov. He was one of the last of the Symbolist poets, had in his time donated money to the Bolshevik cause and was for some years highly regarded by officialdom. But he took to drink. His poetry was highly mannered, the lines arranged in strange shapes such as trapezoids, triangles, cubes and circles. He looked like a musketeer in his long cloak, floppy hat, high boots with turned-down tops; and his long hair, handlebar moustache and narrow beard were reminiscent of the style of Louis XIII. When lecturing he would stride up and down, his boots resounding on the floor, and explain to us the difference between iambs and dactyls, ancient Greek and Renaissance rhymes, and if he got close to the front row you could detect the smell of vodka on his breath. But we forgave him this weakness – perhaps the drink helped him to teach with such style and force. After teaching us about triolets and rondos, at the next lecture he would ask, "Well, who's written a rondo?"

Shyly a girl would stand up and hand him a sheet of paper. He would read it to himself and then set it aside, saying, "No, I won't read that out." On another occasion his eyes would light up, and he would exclaim, "Ah-ha!" and read it out, commenting on each line, picking out good adjectives and bad ones, appraising the whole effect. I shall never forget his lessons on the sonnet, when he quoted a dozen from memory, Italian and French, by Shakespeare and Pushkin, analysing them minutely, pointing out the way they scanned, where they needed masculine rhymes, where feminine. And again, at the next lesson, he asked, "Well, who's written a sonnet?"

A fair-haired girl got to her feet and handed him her paper. I cannot recall her name, only that she had a buxom figure. He read it to himself and exclaimed, "Oh!" and cried to the whole class, "You just listen to this." And he began to read the sonnet aloud. I can only remember the first couple of lines:

> *Like grandmother's dress, like orange blossom,*
> *So does the sonnet sing of love*

Waving the paper, Rukavishnikov appealed to us, "Do you see it's a masterpiece? It's a pearl! In fourteen lines she has managed to avoid using a single full stop, it's one long sentence. And what poetry!"

The girl's eyes shone as this old, drunken poet eulogised her work. I know nothing of her later life, never saw any work of hers in print, but then Soviet literature had little use for sonnets. Rukavishnikov's fate was a sad one. The following year he no longer taught at the School of Literature. One rainy, autumn evening I was travelling in a nearly empty tram. As the tram started away from its stop, I saw a figure in a soaked cap and torn cloak trying to climb on. By his long whiskers and beard I recognized Rukavishnikov and leaned down to try and help him. The conductress stopped me, and with the words, "No drunks! Get away!" pushed him in the chest so that he stumbled and fell down in the wet. The date of his death, given in the Encyclopaedia of Literature as 1930, is the very year that conductress pushed him off the tram.

The theory of prose was taught us by Professor Loks. He was the very opposite of Rukavishnikov. Small and bent, with the sharp-featured profile of a Dante and a little moustache, he delivered his words in a crisp and clear voice. He took apart the prose of Pushkin, Lermontov, Gogol and Chekhov like a surgeon wielding a scalpel. In doing this it might seem that all the impact and poetry of their writing would disappear, but this was not the case. His discerning analysis of structure was so exciting that ever since, when I read any writing I am seized not only by the content but also by the underlying composition. In my own writing, I have always remembered those lessons. After Chekhov he moved on to contemporary writers. He said nothing about Bulgakov, but he gave us Babel and the young Leonid Leonov, and from the minted phrasing of the former and the bright paragraphs of the latter he taught us how to structure a story, what epithets to look for, which metaphors to use and how to feel the innate rhythm of the prose. I remember once he asked us, "Take the adjective 'fantastic' – now give me a better one." "Magical," someone shouted out. "Fairy-tale," whispered Masha, not daring to speak up, but Lyalya did it for her. Loks gave her a kindly look. He died in his sleep a few years later.

Gustav Gustavovich Shpet would have counted as our most brilliant teacher, had we been wiser at the time. He was an imposing figure in his high, white collar under an old-fashioned morning coat. Clean-shaven and noble in appearance, he made one think of an English lord in an Oscar Wilde play. His official title was impressive – Vice-President of the State Academy of the Arts, which was housed in the former building of Polivanovsky Gymnasium on Prechistenkaya. Ethics was Shpet's subject. We students were proud and would never have admitted that his lectures were above our heads, but I could swear that not a single one of us could follow the wise things he tried to teach us. He spoke evenly and dispassionately, never raising his voice, without pause or hesitation, in long sentences full of subordinate clauses, and however hard I tried, I could not understand a single thing. Generally speaking I was good at taking notes, but in Shpet's case I would never have been able to repeat any of his thoughts.

He was a philosopher, and at another time and in another country might have achieved recognition. He had just published a book, *The Inner Form of Words*. Marxist critics instinctively sensed the hidden idealism in his long and complex phraseology, but in those days Marxists still did not go in for destroying their opponents, and in any case, just as for us, it was beyond their powers to understand him properly. Instead they silenced him, in the same way as they silenced Florensky and other Russian philosophers.

In 1933, when the Academy of the Arts, together with our courses in Literature, was abolished, Shpet took to translating German for a living. Another translator got to know a German diplomat who commissioned our scientists and translators to put together a Russian-German dictionary. As a result the OGPU discovered a "nest of spies" and arrested several of those who were working on the dictionary, including Shpet, who was sent into exile in some Siberian town. How he earned a living I do not know, but in 1937 he was arrested again. According to a friend of mine, Professor Alexei Vladimirovich Chicherin, a nephew of the People's Commissar who himself served time in the Gulag, he saw Shpet just before the war. He was standing with other prisoners, up to their knees in the river Yenisey as they struggled with floating timber. It may well be that a twenty-first century bibliophile will discover Shpet's work and explain it for the benefit of future generations. May my memories help to give a living picture of this martyred philosopher.

His dreadful fate was shared by two other professors at our institute. Boris Isaakovich Yarkho and his brother Grigoy Isaakovich tried unsuccessfully to flirt with my sister Sonya, occasionally visiting our place and sitting with us until two in the morning. When Rukavishnikov was sacked, Boris Yarkho took his place, teaching poetic composition to the junior year. Another unfortunate teacher was Mikhail Alexandrovich Petrovsky, who taught the optional subject of stylistics. His lectures were dry and boring and no one attended them. The poor man was eventually dismissed, and when he and Yarkho and Shpet got involved in the German dictionary project, he too was accused of spying and disappeared in the Gulag.

Professor Mikhail Stepanovich Grigoryev flourished. His subject was poetics and I do not remember much of what he said. He would walk from side to side like a mouse in a cage, which he resembled, talking without pause. I remember one of his lectures, which was on Freud, then the focus of worldwide interest. Later on our Marxists decided that Freud's teachings were too attractive and condemned him. The censors were told to blot out any reference to him. It was thanks to Grigoryev's teaching that I was able to read some of Freud's "seditious" writings. Grigoryev had a long life. I do not know what he published, but for many years he was deputy to Yablochkina in the Russian Theatrical Society.

Linguistics was taught us by Nikolai Mikhailovich Karinsky, a tall, bespectacled and bearded man who looked like my father. He lectured with a passion that revealed his deep love of his subject, as if for him no other science existed. Professor Pavel Sergeievich Popov, the husband of Tolstoy's granddaughter Anna Ilyinichny and biographer of Mikhail Bulgakov, lectured on the psychology of creativity in such a boring and colourless way that all I remember of him is his tall, dull figure. Zakharov-Mensky, the youngest of our teachers, taught us about folklore and preened himself before the girls. He published a little book of sub-standard poems, boasted about them and made a gift of them to Lyalya Ilyinskaya. I have no clear memory of him. Some time later he was arrested.

There were excellent professors on the other courses, but I never attended their classes and can only remember their physical appearance. Professor Dzhivelegov was a handsome Armenian who looked like an apostle out of a Spanish painting; his subject was Eastern literature. Italian literature was taught to the senior years by a Professor Gryshka, who resembled an ancient Roman. The president of the school, Pyotr Semenovich Kogan, gave occasional lectures; he was well known for his writings on art from the Marxist point of view. Sadly, I never heard Professor Mistislav Alexandrovich Tsyavlovsky, an imposing figure with a thick mane of white hair, who taught Russian literature to the junior year and who was said to lecture so magnificently that the students left his classroom burning with excitement.

Amongst Marxist literary scholars, Professor Pereversev was the acknowledged top man. In his writings he tried to crush all those who did not agree with him and led the battle against idealists, some of whom were our teachers. I must be fair to him, though; he did a lot to popularise Dostoyevsky. He himself was too grand to lecture to us, but sent four of his talented pupils to hold seminars with us, seminars in which they themselves became passionately involved. Pospelov led a seminar on Turgenev, Purishev on the age of Sturm und Drang, Focht on some other subject and Zeitlin on Dostoyevsky.

I wrote a semi-scientific paper on *Landscape in Turgenev*, while others wrote on other subjects which we discussed and argued about at length. I was struck by the indisputable tone of the judgements made by Pereversev's followers; for them there was only one wise man who had spoken the umblemished truth, and that was Pereversev; all the rest, Belinsky, Dobrolyubov, Dostoyevsky, Plekhanov and contemporary Literary-Idealists and Marxists were wrong. Later, when Dostoyevsky's work went out of favour, Pereversev fell from grace, but he was not arrested, merely consigned to the periphery of teaching, while his followers, sensing the tide had changed, shunned him to follow their own individual careers. Pereversev himself died of old age in Moscow in 1968.

4

When we started studying at the School of Literature there was no fourth year course. In the third year there were only four students, in the second, thirty, in our first year around a hundred and in the reception year two lots of a hundred students each. When Buslayev dictated our timetable to us on the first day, we had also to answer a roll call with our names. In the break one of the young men sitting behind us came up to me and asked, "Are you a Prince Golitsyn?" I had had this tedious question put to me scores of times, sometimes out of curiosity, sometimes in a more or less hostile tone. Even when it was put in a friendly way, I still could not get used to it.

This time I could tell that it was not just curiosity; his tone was quite friendly. When I answered in the affirmative he went on to ask whether I had been at a ball at the Sheremetyevs five years earlier. I answered in the affirmative, and he then said he remembered me from that evening, and introduced himself, "Andrei Durnovo." Then I remembered him, though he had been a youngster then. In turn, I asked whether he was a relative of a former Minister of Home Affairs, Pyotr Nikolaievich Durnovo. It turned out the minister had been his grandfather's cousin, and Andrei went on to say how bad that was for him. He told me his father, Nikolai Nikolaievich, lived in Czechoslovakia and was a linguist and a great authority on Slavonic languages. He was also a friend of the famous linguist Prince Nikolai Sergeievich Trubetskoi. Andrei himself had a room in

Trubnikovskaya Street in the wing of No. 26, below the flat where Nikolai Alexeievich Bobrinsky lived, while Andrei's mother and brother had two rooms in the other wing of the building. The occupant of the main house was Prince Nikolai Vladimirovich Golitsyn, who worked as a translator.

"That's my uncle," I said.

Durnovo spoke quickly and mentioned other names of princes, counts and other noble families. I had grown cautious in my conversations, always wondering whether I was talking to an informer. Even in conversation with a friend one had to be careful as there were certainly informers in the school, and all the more so with a new friend. Durnovo, however, talked mostly about himself and did not question me at all, which inclined me to trust him. To myself I thought, "Well, if he's so keen on the titled and noble, he must be friendly to me." At our next meeting he introduced me to his two companions on the bench. The short, plump one was Andrei Vnukov, the handsome one with big eyes and curly hair, Valery Pertsov. That month these two greeted me ceremonially every day. At the end of our lectures we discussed what we had heard, but we treated each other with caution, remained on formal "you" terms, and apart from our work, hardly asked each other any questions. With Andrei Durnovo, however, I was quickly on an informal footing, addressing him with the familiar form of "you". He was garrulous, with considerable style, but was also a good listener. Very quickly we became close friends. We had a mutual acquaintance in our year – Igor Daksergov, and also a second cousin of mine, Alya Loseva, but she looked down on us and barely condescended to greet us.

There was another friend in the reception year course, Kirill Pigarev, a great-grandson of the poet Tyutchev. His uncle, Nikolai Ivanovich Tyutchev, had served as special adviser to the Governor-General of Moscow, Sergei Alexandrovich, and was well known to my grandfather. After the revolution he established a museum on his estate of Muranovo with himself as director. He was dubbed "Russia's last landowner". At his death his successor at the museum was his nephew Kirill Vasilyevich Pigaryev.

Lyalya Ilyinskaya walked to school, usually accompanied by boyfriends. Andrei Durnovo lived only five minutes away. Poor Andrei Vnukov, however, lived out of town on the Kazan highway and spent a great deal of time commuting. Igor Daksergof lived in Denezhny Lane, Valery Pertsov quite a distance away near Serpukhovsky Square. They both took the "B" tram with Masha and myself. Igor paid a lot of attention to Masha, or rather, she flirted with him. Valery would probably also have liked to chat with her but he was shy, leaving the field to the more confident man and instead talking to me.

At the tram stop on Kudrinskaya Square, we would eagerly discuss the books we had read and historical personages. We were united in our love of Ancient Greece. Valery had read more than me and his conversation always interested me. He lived alone with his mother. His father had been a civil servant in the town of Vladimir, but committed suicide when Valery was quite small. The Pertsov family had their origins in the nobility of Kazan. Valery's grandfather had been one of eight brothers; the eldest, Erast, was acquainted with Pushkin and wrote obscene poetry, whilst Valery's grandfather and another brother had supplied defamatory news of the Tsar's government to the exiled writer, Herzen.

I became great friends with Valery, though we continued using the formal "you". It was a friendship that started merely because we sat close to each other and took the same tram home. Before coming to the School of Literature, Valery had trained as a pastry and candy cook. During the day he worked in the factory (the former Abrikosovykh plant) and often brought packets of sweet things to school. Masha and Lyalya were not worried how he obtained these goodies, but tucked into them, although this did not seem to make them fonder of him. One day Andrei told me with a laugh that he had visited Valery at home and seen that he, his mother and their dog, Funka, all looked like each other, with the same round faces, big eyes and short noses. When later I met them I also noticed a resemblance. The dog was a quiet animal and the mother received me in a very friendly manner, her voice touched by sadness. I was struck by their tiny room; the bed on one side, a cupboard on the other, and a pianino and a table between them. Valery slept under the bed. His mother earned a living by sewing, managing somehow in that tiny space to run a sewing machine.

Gradually, Lyalya Ilyinskaya drifted away from us. At break time, she was surrounded by her cavaliers, of whom only Yuri Veber has become a well-known writer. At that time he was a very tall, extremely thin and long-haired youth. Lyalya did however continue to sit next to Masha on our bench. Only Masha and I knew that her father was languishing in Solovki prison.

Yuri Galperin, a thick-lipped Jewish lad who wore a pince-nez on his long nose, made friends first with Valery, then with me. He was the cleverest and best read person on our course and the only one to begin to understand Professor Shpet. He was so proud, however, that he would never have admitted not understanding anything. At break time, Andrei Vnukov and others would surround Galperin and listen to him as he held forth with unstoppable verve on all kinds of humanitarian theories. He came to a sad end (in our country people with fine brains are not liked); he was exiled to Lake Kubensky, from where he exchanged a few letters with Valery, but then the correspondence ceased and he disappeared.

There was another Jewish youth, Victor Pevsner, small with curly hair, resembling the young Christ in a picture by Polenov. With his naïve, excited look he could only be a poet, and in fact he spent all his time writing verse. Once he showed me something he had written, but I was not impressed; he was far too free with his exclamation marks. I did not want to hurt his feelings, though, and kept silent. I have no idea what became of him.

Lyalya attracted girls as well as boys. Lydia Zuckerman, full of bounce, ended up in the Gulag. Zhenya Buromskaya was a very beautiful and mature woman who later captivated the old Shakespearean scholar, Mika Morozov, who abandoned his wife for her. There was Natasha Doroshevich, the fair-haired daughter of a well-known journalist, who later worked for the *Journal de Moscou* and was much appreciated for her work. Sadly, she died young. Another young woman was Tania Sikorskaya, who became a poet and during the war was evacuated together with Marina Tsvetaeva; rumour had it that she knew something about Tsvetaeva's death.

5

All these people I have been writing about were serious students who attended the lectures and spent their free time in the library, trying to learn as much as they could. There were, however, other students who wanted to become poets and writers right away, without waiting to graduate from the school. In those years there were many different literary groups and associations; there was RAPP, the Russian Association of Proletarian Poets, which was patronised by the authorities; there was "Kuznitsa" (Smithy), "Pereval", "Lef" and the "Serapion Brothers". Literary people could no doubt differentiate among these groups, but all I know is that they quarrelled violently amongst themselves, were even on terms of enmity, sometimes to the point of denouncing each other to the police. Some of our students went to their meetings and came back with their eyes shining, full of the excitement of those encounters and the violent speeches they had heard. The meetings were always in the evening, so most of us students did not get involved. Later the members of the group called "Pereval" were all arrested.

Also among us were activist-socialists, a few communists and many more *Konsomol* youth. There were also those who composed the wall-newspaper, or sat on various committees as well as on the main student committee. One man who stood out was Danilov, a Red commander with the rank of brigadier, who was much older than anyone else. He was chosen to be president of the student committee, so making him senior student. As he was on my course I had the opportunity to observe him closely. He had a wooden, clean-shaven face, small dark-blue eyes, thin lips that never smiled and he kept his military tunic tightly buttoned at the neck. No doubt this sort of wooden-faced man had shot White Guards and prisoners impassively during the civil war. Instinctively, I feared him and kept my distance from him, until one day, out of the blue, he came up to me and, looking away, said, "I want to talk to you."

My heart sank not just into my boots, but right down into the floor as I waited for the inevitable question – "Are you by any chance a prince?" But he asked me something quite different. It often happened that these activist-socialists could not get to their lectures, either because they were summoned over to the local committee meetings, or they were writing the wall-newspaper, or were sent off on Party missions, and so they fell behind in their studies. I had once been asked if I could lend my notebook to one of these people, who had then asked for it again and again. It was true that I was good at getting down the substance of our lectures, and in those days my handwriting was still fairly good. It had become a common practice for other students to borrow my notes over the weekend, and obviously one of them had recommended me to Danilov.

From that time on, every Saturday evening I handed him my copybook and every Monday evening, with a curt nod of his head, he would hand it back to me. I was very content to be on these terms with the most powerful student in the school, who could do what he liked with me, even to the extent of having me arrested. And as it happened, there was now talk of contamination of our student body by alien elements; there were not enough sons and daughters of the proletariat and the peasantry. I just hoped that Danilov would stand up for me and Masha if anything unpleasant were to happen.

A stupid incident now took place. Lylalya, who was a fine artist, sketched an angel in the back of my copybook without my noticing. It reproduced, detail for detail, the winged angel with a lily in its hand that one sees in pictures of the Annunciation. On Saturday, as usual,

I handed my copybook over to Danilov. On the Monday, returning the book, he remarked coldly, "Soviet students shouldn't even think about those things we've rejected for ever!" I stepped back, red with embarrassment and rushed to put the offending page down the toilet. The next Saturday, Danilov as usual took my copybook without comment and continued to do so to the end of the course.

There was another unpleasant incident. A student on our course called Zubkov came over to me and in a secretive voice asked whether I came from Bulchalki. I said I did, and he went on to say that he also came from there and remembered my father, the richest landowner in Epiphansky county. I denied that my father had ever owned any land or the big house.

"You're hiding the fact, you know," he replied in the same secretive voice. "I know your father was a great nobleman there." And he said this with a kind of smile. From that time he invariably came over to greet me and I had the unpleasant experience of responding to this greeting, even shaking his hand. His manner of showing complicity with me was absolutely repulsive. I felt he was aware of his power over me and was playing cat and mouse. This went on for almost half the year, until one day he took me aside, saying he had something very serious to tell me. He admitted that he had told Danilov that I was the son of a big landowner in the province of Tula, and that since then they had been keeping me under observation to see whether I attended the lectures and how I behaved myself. He now asked my forgiveness, and even promised always to defend me. The real truth behind his words I never discovered. Was he playing some sort of psychological game with me? Had Danilov intervened on my behalf? I never found out, but Zubkov continued with his greetings, which I found even harder to acknowledge than before; he became an odious figure in my life.

6

My father, a lawyer by training, believed that life should be lived according to the law. I personally paid the tuition fees out of my earnings, but Masha paid the twelve roubles a month out of my father's salary, which although it was a good one, nonetheless had to support a large number of dependants. My father concluded that on the basis of his support of a great many dependants he had a right to a reduction in Masha's fees.

It was not only Masha who claimed a reduction, but others too. Approval rested with a committee of students. However, at a later break in our lectures, a man from the second year course, a skinny bespectacled youth called Sipin, who had just had published a little book called *White Wolves* about the brutality and cruelty of the Whites and the great heroism of the Reds of which he was very proud, called out, "Comrades, don't go away! I have to tell you something very important." A few students remained standing, while others sat down and he announced – and I quote him verbatim – "You have demonstrated your lack of class consciousness. All sorts of princes and counts have managed to sneak in amongst us, and you've just reduced their fees."

It was a painful shock. My throat went dry with anger. I felt some unknown force had picked me up and pushed me against a wall. I clenched my fists and with difficulty stopped myself from hitting this Sipin. He stepped back and I took his place and blurted out with all my strength that my father had worked his whole life, had never owned anything, and that the only fault in our family was possession of a prince's title. Sipin muttered something and left, as did the others, not understanding what was going on, hardly interested in my tirade and really wanting to go out for a smoke or to the toilet. Valery, Andrei Durnovo, Andrei Vnukov and Yuri Galperin came over to me. Galperin expressed his feelings the most volubly, while the others showed their sympathy by shaking my hand. Also on our course was a Prince Gagarin, the son of the president of the law court in Dimitrov, who had not struck up a friendship with us, keeping himself to himself. But on this occasion he saw everything that had happened.

I was so upset and angry that for the first time I could only take very poor lecture notes. Two days later, Masha received back her claim for reduced fees marked "Rejected". From that day on we were noticed. Not so much myself, as Masha. I could not help but notice how someone would point her out to a companion, not in a spirit of enmity but in idle curiosity, and how it was clear that others were wondering how, ten years after the revolution, a real princess was studying in a Soviet college. An article appeared in the paper *Workers' Moscow* about our school describing how it aimed to produce poets and writers. The teachers were also referred to, and in general the tone of the article was friendly. At the end, however, describing the students it used the phrase "and next to a highness princess there sits the descendant of a Volga boatman."

A vicious article about the students in the reception year appeared in *Evening Moscow*. It mentioned Kira Zhukovskaya, the daughter of an important engineer in one of the ministries. She dressed elegantly, used lipstick and powder, manicured her nails and wore her hair in a fashionable, boyish style; in other words, she followed western fashion. The girls were fascinated by her, buzzing around her at every break. The rumour was that she taught them not only how to foxtrot, but also the dangerous Charleston. In those days public opinion on western dances was expressed by an obscenity, and those who danced them were considered idlers and parasites. Kira was taken to task not just for her appearance, but also for depraving other girls. The article ended calling for watchfulness, as well as for a purge of our School of Literature. It did not, however, make use of the phrase about "a highness princess". The topic was picked up by a music group called *The Blue Blouse*. They wrote a show and one of the singers was a girl made up and dressed like Kira, who sang the refrain "I'm a student of literature, and what a peach I am!" All these references to our school made me wince.

7

I continued to draw maps, and every day I also spent time in either the Lenin or university libraries reading the classics. How many wonderful books I got through! I read ancient Greek and Roman literature, Dante and Boccaccio, Rabelais and knightly tales, authors whom our present times barely know. I tried to read some philosophy, taking out something by Schopenhauer, but found his writing even more difficult than Professor Shpet's lectures. At our school twentieth-century literature was taught by Professor Fatov, but he read his lectures in such a monotonous voice that I now have no memory of what he looked like. However, he introduced us to the Symbolists, and it was through him that I came to know Balmont and Blok and other poets from the start of the century. In the vast reading room at the Lenin Library I soundlessly mouthed these poets in fine editions of *Apollon* and *The Golden Fleece*, read practically all of the works of Balmont, which prompted me to write an essay on "Landscape in the Poetry of Balmont". I did not take to Bryusov's poetry, but I enjoyed his novels *The Fiery Angel* and *The Altar of Victory*, though today I cannot remember anything about them. I became enthusiastic about Merezhkovsky, reading both his trilogies, but when I asked to have his pamphlet on Maxim Gorky, my slip was returned saying that it could be seen only with the permission of the director of the library.

I spent many happy hours in libraries. The absolute silence in the great reading rooms increased one's concentration. There was a line in one of the poets, whose verse was passed from hand to hand, about the "joys of study". Today, when I see young people who, after leaving school, do not want to study further but hang around the necks of their parents, I remember my own young years. Once mother asked me, "Are you happy with your life?" and I replied, "Yes, I feel that year after year I'm becoming wiser and wiser."

8

The authorities placed countless obstacles in the way of the sons and daughters of "former people" who not only wished to study but thirsted to do so. In our School of Literature the silver clouds of learning had a dark underside. Every time I set off to my lectures it was with a lurking fear of what might happen. The wall newspapers that were regularly put up echoed the hard line policy on higher education that appeared daily in the press, "Purge our schools of alien elements!" The condemnation of Western dances was a main feature. And yet Masha and Lyalya and I sometimes danced the foxtrot until seven o'clock in the morning. I imagine many of our classmates also surrendered to the "corrupting spirit of the West". The important thing was not to be discovered by the guardians of morality.

A purge of the students was finally ordered from on high. A general meeting was called, at which some disgusting speeches were pronounced, and I waited with a beating heart to hear my name and Masha's mentioned, but it was not. The representative of the local district committee spoke about watchfulness and urged us to root out secret enemies who had infiltrated our ranks, without naming names. Then the process started, with lectures postponed for four days while the purge was carried out. From a distance I watched how youths and girls, their faces grey with fear, went one by one into one of the auditoria. The questioning seemed friendly, then they were told, "You may go. Who's next?"

The fateful day for our course arrived. Andrei Durnovo went in before me and soon reappeared with a happy face. "It's nothing to worry about. They told me to get rid of my foreign tie, but they didn't ask a thing about my relative the minister." Then it was my turn. Three men sat behind the table; Karepatyan, the recently appointed director, the representative of the local authorities, a gloomy middle-aged man with a pointed beard, and a senior student, Victor Gusev, the representative of the student body.

"Sit down," said Gusev with a friendly smile. I did so with a feeling of sadness, inwardly fuming at this kind of pointless trial. Gusev put the questions, and they were all the usual ones; where and when was I born, who were my parents, what did I want to do at the end of my course? His friendly manner showed that he was entirely on my side. At that time his poetry was being printed in the papers, and a few years later his drama, *Glory*, was produced by the Maly Theatre. He was the only student from our school who immediately became quite famous. Sadly, he died young. I am still grateful to him for the way he inspired me with the courage to answer the questions concisely and confidently.

The director of the school said nothing and the representative of the local committee asked just one question, one that was always phrased the same way, "Are you a relative of Prince Golitsyn?" I replied that the elder brother of my grandfather had been a rich man, and my great-grandfather a Decembrist, and I repeated the sentence that I had uttered so often, that my father had never owned anything and had worked all his life. "You may go," the man said drily. Masha was next and I was just able to say, "Don't worry!" to her as she went in. We slept badly for the next three days. Would we be thrown out or allowed to stay? In the atmosphere of those days, a miracle now occurred; I cannot describe it any other way. We were not touched. Our student cards were returned with the stamp "Verified". Had Danilov been instrumental in saving us thanks to my notebook? Or had it been our Decembrist ancestor? I cannot tell, but in those days the fact that Masha and I were zealous students was totally irrelevant, although our orderly behaviour probably helped a little. Our modest appearance no doubt made it difficult to believe that we were given to such criminal acts as dancing the foxtrot. I also think Victor Gusev helped.

Kira Zhukovskaya was purged. Very soon her father was arrested for treachery. I do not know what became of them. Prince Gagarin was purged, and I do not know who else; no list was put up. Then our director Karepatyan left us as the result of an unbelievable scandal. In those times the student committee was not the submissive tool of the administration that it became later – on the contrary, it tried to flex its muscles. I cannot recall why the director and Danilov started a quarrel, but Karepatyan put up a notice on the board announcing Danilov's expulsion.

Someone rushed in to our auditorium with the cry, "Quick, everyone into the assembly hall!" The mass of students, stopping only briefly to read the notice on the board, crowded through the corridors from every part of the building, and filled the hall so that soon there was only standing room and the air was filled with the sound of indignant voices, fists were raised. None of the administration was present. Karepatyan had obviously taken fright, and indeed the angry crowd might have turned violently against him. Nor was Danilov there; it was his deputy who went up on the platform. Banging his fist on the table, he had difficulty quietening the students, who were all shouting, "Away with Karepatyan!" A resolution was unanimously adopted to re-admit Danilov, and drive the director out. Everyone was ready to sign but there was not enough paper, so only the leaders signed. We then all broke up, but many of us remained standing about in the street discussing this momentous event. So Karepatyan was dismissed. A few days later there were rumours that he had been arrested as a Trotskyist.

9

This account of my two years of study covers the years 1927 to 1929. I cannot always be certain of the exact date of events, but it was at the beginning of 1929 that our country began to experience great difficulties and disturbances as the first Five Year Plan of industrial-isation and collectivisation got under way. Our leaders hunted out the supposed guilty people, accusing "former people", saboteurs and Trotskyists of causing the troubles, but never, of course, blaming themselves. All resources were diverted into building industrial plant and factories. Culture had to be cut back. Fewer copies of fewer books were published, some newspapers were shut down, many museums closed, and these measures were also extended to the technical colleges and higher institutes of learning that were not directly related to industry or agriculture. It became an unnecessary luxury to teach people about poets and writers. The decision was taken to close our School of Literature. A resounding scandal was needed as a pretext for this action. Why a scandal? Well, such were the times; the papers were full of discovered plots and spies, of unmasked saboteurs and the like, though most of these stories were lies.

Occasionally well-known writers visited the school, usually after lectures, which finished at eleven at night. Members of the students' committee would remain behind to listen and put questions, but Masha and I rarely stayed on so late. I remember Vsevolod Ivanov, the author of an over-publicised play *Armoured Train*, which was put on at the Arts Theatre. He was a small man of modest appear-ance, wore glasses, and spoke in a boring low voice. Demyan Bedny came once, and on that occasion we all demonstratively kept away so that his audience filled only a quarter of the big hall, and I am sure the applause must have been very light and no questions were put to him. As he was a major socialist writer, used to huge ovations when he spoke to the massed workers, he went away highly offended and thereafter never lost any opportunity to defame the school.

I loved the poet Esenin, but had to keep that quiet. Masha and I and a few others used to read the poetry of Gumilov, who had been shot seven years earlier, and mention of whose name was considered a crime. But the true idol of the majority of students was the poet Mayakovsky. I have always felt he was a talented poet, while never really liking his work. Reading between the lines of articles in the papers and in journals, our students could tell that Demyan Bedny and Gorky both loathed Mayakovsky, indeed the gossip about their enmity was open, and was one of the reasons Bedny received such a bad reception.

Other literary figures also came, read their poetry and afterwards gathered a crowd of admirers around them. Sometimes they attended our lectures. Members of RAPP, headed by Altschuler, visited the school. He was a tall, athletic man and wore a blue silk Russian shirt belted at the waist. He had large, doe-like, typically Jewish eyes. Why a proletarian poet had to go about dressed like a member of a troupe of singers and dancers I do not know. He and his friends came to some of our lectures. Later it was realised that they did this so as to attract the girls in the lower courses.

Then came the disaster. A girl student, Islamova, had hung herself in a room in the Hotel National. Investigators with stern faces appeared among us and soon we learned that three members of the RAPP, Altschuler, Avrushchenko and Apokhin had been arrested. The accusation was that they had lured Islamova to the hotel, got her drunk and raped her. She was not just a good student and a Russian, but also the wife of one of the Uzbek leaders. The newspapers raised howls of fury. The "Altschuler Case" or "The Case of the Three A's" featured in every headline, and our school was deluged with insulting epithets; it was a vipers' nest, a focus of depravity, the professors were idealists, the students were gilded youth, Esenin was worshipped and there were foreign elements present. Nor did they miss out "the highness princess" and Kira Zhukovskaya. It also happened that some young people, caught dancing the foxtrot, were arrested about this same time, and the "Foxtrotters Case" was added to the other attacks on our school. The RAPP was never once mentioned in these articles – how could the proletarian ranks possibly include such vermin? Not a soul stood up for our school, no one spoke up to point out that these men were poets from the RAPP and not students.

The students held a noisy general meeting, at which there were loud calls for the death penalty for the guilty parties. I was not present, but Yuri Dombrovsky described the scene to us, and told us how he had been hissed from the room when he suggested it was not the job of students to sit in judgment. A short time later he was summoned to visit a certain establishment, where great interest was shown in his mother and father and also in Yuri's own views and convictions before they let him go. Some years after this he was arrested and during interrogation reminded of this past "crime". He was given three years exile in Alma Ata.

The judge sentenced Altschuler, as the instigator, to five years in prison, Avrushenko to three, and Anokhin to two, all without strict confinement. I cannot say what mitigating circumstances the judge adduced; probably the standard ones of proletarian origins and first offence, and no doubt there was a phone call from higher up. This was despite the evidence that they had deliberately made the girl drunk and taken it in turns to rape her, which were clearly aggravating circumstances. I imagine they enjoyed the fate of the ordinary criminal, that is, repented and earned remission and were released early. Of their later fate I know only that Anokhin disappeared, whilst the name Avrushenko figures on the marble slab commemorating the war dead in the Central House of Literature. I found the name Altschuler in a list of writers, where he is described as a poet living in Riga. Whether it is the same man, I cannot tell.

Igor Daksergof was rather a withdrawn student and appeared to attend lectures without much enthusiasm, but now he wrote a play about the crime in the Hotel National. I never read it, but it was said to be a talented effort. He sent it to some theatre directors and the play was accepted, but it was suggested that he change it to make the protagonist either an Armenian, or a Georgian, or a German or a Latvian – but under no circumstance a Jew. Igor refused to change anything and burned the manuscript.

10

The fate of our school was settled. The authorities could not let such a place continue to exist when they were launched on building our "bright future". They did, however, allow us to finish the year. It was with heavy hearts that we went to take our exams. Only four students had completed four years, and they received their graduation diplomas. Some of the students, after a meticulous process of sorting out, were allowed to go into the History-cum-Philosophy faculty of the university, or into the State Institute of Cinematography. But those who worked during the day, like Valery Pertsov, and could only study in the evening, had to give up their higher education. There were no correspondence courses in those days. Andrei Durnovo got into the university. Where Andrei Vnukov went, I do not know.

None of us became a Pushkin or a Tolstoy. Some of our students might have become well-known poets or writers, but in those years many, like Yuri Dombrovsky, were either exiled or sent to the Gulag. I heard it said that a Trotskyist organisation had been uncovered in our school. Today we know only too well how such plots were fabricated, so I cannot confirm anything. Before it was closed down, the school was moved to the Sadovaya-Sukharevskaya and I remember, after successfully sitting my last exam, how Valery Pertsov and I left the dark and gloomy building there. It was a warm June evening and we decided to walk along the Sadovaya Ring until we got bored and tired.

Thus, the gates of the kingdom of learning were shut in my face. Yet, I can say that those two years of study gave me a great deal. Our excellent professors had taught me to appreciate and love the arts and literature. Earlier, I had only talked of becoming a writer and when I wrote anything it was poor stuff. But those dedicated teachers had started me off on the road leading to creativity. Thanks to them, I took up my pen and began to write my first, hesitant pieces. As we walked along, Valery softly recited Blok's poetry, while I quoted Esenin. We walked in something of a dream. My future seemed very uncertain, and yet even in those dark times, I did not lose hope of a better tomorrow.

13. Travels to the Northern Lakes

1

My parents rented the Glinkovo *dacha* once again for the summer of 1928. Several families, including a number of youths and girls, were in residence, and many more young people came to visit from Moscow and Sergiyev Posad. I was hardly ever there as I had to stay in Moscow drawing my maps and plans. This was the year when an Italian expedition to reach the North Pole by airship, led by Nobile, went missing. After a Russian short-wave enthusiast picked up their distress signal there was enormous excitement as to whether we or the Europeans would save them. Our two icebreakers *Krasin* and *Malygin* sailed off on the search. Amundsen himself went to the rescue, but then he too went missing. It was a field day for the newspapers and magazines, and there was great demand for my maps.

The editors of the *Universal Pathfinder* made up their pages straight from the radio broadcasts. Popov ordered me to stay put in Moscow and doubled my fees. I had to redraw the *Krasin*'s route so as to keep up with the latest news. And there was a very good reason why I wanted to earn more money; I was planning to set off on my travels with my old school friend, Andrei Kiselev. The year before, on his own, he had wandered along the banks of Lake Seliger, returning with many sketches and full of impressions. He now suggested we go together. I was thrilled by his suggestion and flattered that he had chosen me. I agreed enthusiastically, especially as the Nobile drama had left me one hundred roubles richer.

Andrei showed me his maps of northern Russia. You could still buy large-scale, 1:420 000 pre-revolutionary military maps on Kuznetsky Most, very useful travellers' maps. Andrei proposed that he be the leader and I promised to follow his lead unquestioningly. We took very few things with us, just a blanket, a change of under-clothes, a cup and spoon and a cloak. Rucksacks were then a luxury, but we solved this problem by tying our things in a pillowcase.

Sergei, the survivor. In the fullness of time, he achieved maturity and fulfilment as a writer.

Coat of arms of the venerable Golitsyn family.

Grandfather Golitsyn when Mayor of Moscow. Civic-minded, liberal and generous, he encouraged artists and writers.

Sofia, "the beautiful Sonia", aged fourteen. She was only nineteen when she married Reginald Witter.

Reginald Witter, known to all as Reg.

Alexei Bobrinsky and his sister Sofia, the "beautiful cousin". Sergei believed he was an informer working for the Bolsheviks.

Count Leo Bobrinsky in prison, where he died in 1922. He was once rather a dandy.

The Osorgin family in better times. Father Osorgin, his wife Liza, Maria, Juliana, Tonia and Georgy.

31. Осоргин Георгий Михайлович. 1921. Карандаш

Georgy Osorgin playing chess. At his interrogation he swore loyalty to the Tsar.

Georgy at the time of his arrest in 1924. In love with life and sincerely devout, he paid for his loyalty to Old Russia with his life.

Happier days. Sergei's beloved older brother Vladimir, with his wife Elena. He died of starvation in the Gulag aged forty.

Grandparents' fiftieth wedding anniversary, Bogoroditsk, 1921.

Back Row: Lina, Sonia, Vladimir Golitsyn, Uncle Vladimir Trubetskoi, Alka and Sonia Bobrinsky.

Centre row: Alexandra Golitsyna, Uncle Misha and Katya, Golitsyn grandparents, Elena Bobrinskaya, Aunt Vera, Aunt Eli with Tatiana and Andrei.

Front row: Masha and Sergei Golitsyn, Grisha Trubetskoi, Alexei and Nikolai Bobrinsky, Varya Trubetskaya.

The author at Lyubets. In the background, the church where he is now buried.

The "Big House" at Bogoroditsk, built for Count Alexei Grigoriyevich Bobrinsky, Catherine the Great's illegitimate son by Grigory Orlov.

We packed two notebooks, one for our accounts, one for the diary of our travels. Andrei also brought a sketchbook. We did not plan any definite route, thinking we would go first to Vologda, then by steamer across Lake Kubensky, and then on foot, trying to get to all those monasteries that had not yet been broken up, and changing our plans in the light of the circumstances. My parents backed our expedition, realising that I was now nineteen-years-old, and well able to look after myself.

2

Early in July 1928, we left Sergiyev Posad by the night train.

Looking back, our travels now seem like a fairy tale. It was thanks to Andrei that I saw something of the untouched north of Russia when it was still living its old life, unaffected by civilization. That was the last year when it was still possible for the Russian peasantry to live autonomously, still scraping a meagre income from the harsh land. They built massive wooden houses with carved lintels and window frames, where whole clans, grandparents, fathers and mothers, sons and daughters with their spouses and their many children lived together, never quarrelling but obeying the grandfather, the unquestioned head of the household.

In a month and a half, we travelled one thousand five hundred *versts* by train, three thousand five hundred *versts* by boat and five hundred *versts* on foot. The rains soaked us, the mosquitoes ate us alive and our shoes fell to pieces. But all these hardships were forgotten and what remained were our memories of Old Russia, a beautiful, hard-working, sober and Orthodox land. Throughout the winter, I struggled with my first attempts at literary composition, which mother copied for me into a notebook. In spite of the many searches we have endured and our many removals, that copybook has survived, and is still in my possession. For literary and ideological reasons such a collection of short, poetic stories is quite unsuitable for publication. But as material for future historians of the twentieth century Russian peasantry, I hope it will be of some interest. I shall now, after a long life full of experiences, try to look back at that long past journey, relying both on memory and that little copybook.

We set off on the night train from Sergiyev Posad to Vologda, and I am sorry to say we were so anxious to start our journey on foot that we did not visit the old city's sights, not even the museum. That was a pity as forty years later, when I paid my second visit to that ancient city, there was little to see following the barbaric destruction of churches and old houses. On a little steamer we sailed along the Vologda and Sukhono rivers until we reached Lake Kubensky. It was sunny weather and the lake was a dark blue colour. We sailed past the little island with its monastery of Spas-Kamen and drank in the sight of the many old churches, few of which have survived. We disembarked at Novlenskoye on the south side of the lake, and from there we began our great journey on foot.

The banks were high and bare of trees, giving us exhilarating views over the broad blue lake with its many fishing boats and their white sails. After fifteen *versts* along the shore the landscape changed as we reached unbroken forest. Above the tops of the trees we could see many church bell-towers, standing out like white candles. We walked quickly, breathing in the wonderful fresh air of the lake, and although our bags pressed down on our shoulders, we hardly stopped for a break, wanting to cover as much distance as possible. Russia had many windmills in those days and we seemed to come on them at every turn, standing alone or in groups. I would imagine there is not a single windmill left now.

Our first night was spent in a newly-built log farmhouse by the lake. Farm settlements of this kind had been encouraged in the late nineteenth century under Stolypin, one of the Tsar's Prime Ministers, and also in the first years of Soviet rule. Then, with the horrors of the movement to destroy the private peasantry, and in particular the *kulaks*, farms like this one were the ones to suffer most. Our hosts were a young couple who questioned us eagerly and anxiously while their children watched us in silence. Their hospitality was wonderfully generous; we were served tea with honey, fish pie, eggs, milk and then more fish pie. The lake abounded with fish and there was as yet no law forbidding private fishing.

We rose early and breakfasted copiously. Our hosts adamantly refused to take any payment for their hospitality. So off we started. We were determined to reach the village of Kirillov that day. Andrei had set himself the goal of covering those fifty-five *versts* in one go and although I felt rather daunted, I was prepared to do my best. When the sun was slowly sinking towards the horizon, we came upon a peasant with a cart taking his goods – hoops and rings and suchlike – to market. He put our bags on top of his already full load and we walked with a lighter step, keeping pace with the cart and chatting with him about all sorts of country matters. Like the farmers of the previous night, he was full of anxiety; the authorities had already started to drive out the hardest working peasants and to smash their fine log houses, which they had built by themselves for their large families.

It was the time of year of the so-called "white nights". By now we were exhausted and could barely put one foot in front of the other when the carter pointed with his whip, saying, "There's Kirillov, shining white!" I have seen Kirillov twice since that day, but that first view of it, when I was young, has remained unforgettable. Actually, the town that lay ahead of us was not white, rather, in the strange light of the northern summer night, had a light with the quality of moonlight. It was a fairy-tale vision, all blue, with blue towers and walls and churches. It lay on the shores of a lake itself as pale as the sky, so that the town seemed to be suspended in the air.

The carter came to a halt outside a little house and banged on the door. It took some time for it to open. He then settled down to supper with his host, but we refused any food, all we could manage was to collapse on the floor in our clothes and fall straight asleep. In the morning, we discovered our legs were swollen like tree-stumps and our feet covered in blisters. Fifty-five *versts* in a day – that has remained my record, but I certainly do not recommend it to anyone. It left us utterly unable to walk that day, although after rubbing our legs and moving about a little we did manage to get them into some sort of shape, at which point we realised we would have to take a day off, and decided to look around the town.

The famous sixteenth-century Kirillo-Belozorsky monastery has survived, although today it looks slightly overdone in its picturesqueness. The water level of Lake Siversky has risen to lap its walls, which has certainly had a superficially beautifying effect, but the other churches that helped to set off the monastery have long been destroyed, with a consequent loss of beauty. Three years before we got there the monastery had been closed and was now empty and unattended, but at least the plunder and destruction of churches had not yet started. We sat down under one of the towers and Andrei set about sketching, I to writing up our diary.

As in other places, the monks who had been driven out of the monastery had found lodgings in local houses. Devout widows received the most ascetic monks into their homes where they lived in secrecy in any little space offered them, never going out. The ordinary monks became gardeners, carpenters, shoemakers or woodcutters, but they no longer wore their dark cassocks as in Nesterov's paintings, but pale cotton cloaks and dusty shoes. One could see them pacing slowly along, heads bowed, whispering their prayers. At that time the authorities had not yet started to send them into exile, or arrest them for vagrancy, as happened after a law was passed about "people who had no place to live or obvious occupation", which certainly applied to the monks.

On the steps of a church we came upon a young, bearded monk sitting deep in thought. People had not yet lost that very Russian trait – trustfulness. In our whole journey, we always referred to ourselves as students from Moscow and this was sufficient for doors to be opened to us and beds and food provided, usually without payment. We sat down next to this monk and he replied in simple trust to our questions. His name was Father Arkady, and he was able to give us a lot of useful information. All the monasteries in that area – the Kirillovo-Belozersky, Ferapontov, Goritsky, the *pustin* Nil-Sorsky, Spas.Kemensky, and others I cannot remember – had been closed down and the monks driven out to wander where they might. But beyond the town of Belozersk, some way into a thick forest on a little island in Lake Novoye, stood an ancient monastery untouched by the authorities. It was called Kirillovo-Novoezersk in honour of a St Kirill, a different Kirill who had lived a hundred years later than the local patron. The monks with their abbot, Ioann, lived holy lives there. Pilgrims could only reach the monastery through the nearly impenetrable surrounding marshland.

We were inspired by what we heard. Our plan had been to go north to the monastery of Ferapontov where the famous frescoes of Dionysus had just been opened to the public, and which my brother Vladimir had earnestly recommended that we see. After listening to Father Arkady we decided to change our plans and go west to the town of Belozersk, and from there south to Lake Novoye. Looking back now, after later twice visiting Ferapontov, I believe we should have made the trip to Ferapontov to see the Dionysus frescoes and then have come back to make our journey to Novoye and the monastery of Kirillovo-Novoezersk. But our youthful impatience dictated otherwise. We spent one more night in Kirillov and, although our legs were still tired, set off at dawn.

The road led up and up and after seven *versts* we were on top of the famous watershed, Mount Maura, between the Caspian Sea and the White Sea. Five hundred years earlier two monks had climbed up this mountain – Kirill and Ferapont. They had stopped to look out over the endless landscape, after which they stood in prayer together, and then Kirill set off to the east, Ferapont to the north. Thus, according to the hagiographers, were founded the two famous monasteries. As we were in a hurry to complete the more than forty *versts* to Belozersk, we stopped on this historic spot for only a few minutes without putting down our bags, then moved on.

When, after the war, I led a group of young tourists to this same place and we spent a whole day there, I was at last able to enjoy the truly marvellous view. To the east one sees the dazzlingly white complex of the Kirillo-Belozersky monastery with its towers and churches on the shores of the blue Lake Siversky, whose long arms stretch left and right. To the west, the top of Goritsky monastery peeps out above the forest. It was there that, on the orders of Ivan the Terrible, his pious aunt Princess Efrosinya Staritskaya was drowned in the river Sheksnya. And all around is unbroken forest, the same forest that those two saints gazed at five centuries before.

At Belozersk, the oldest town in the north of Russia, we were astonished by the number of churches, all dating back to the seventeenth century and later. They towered up over a mixture of wooden and stone houses. The belltowers raised their lofty classical steeples high into the sky. A high mound showed where the former fortress had stood. Most beautiful of all was the lake, forty *versts* wide, on which fishing boats under white sails furrowed the glassy water. Spotting a wooden church on the edge of the town, Andrei sat down to sketch it, while I sat beside him to write up our diary.

3

Forty years had passed before I again found myself in Belozersk. I have always been horrified at the truly satanic fury with which, starting in the 1930s, the beautiful past was torn down, broken up, despoiled. And doubtless among the destroyers were people who had grown up amid this beauty. Did they not have any feelings other than hatred? What I found now in Belozersk were a couple of five-domed churches, probably because their walls were too thick to allow them to be knocked down easily. The wooden church that Andrei had sketched was still standing, but all the other lovely churches and their tall bell-towers, as well as part of the colonnaded market buildings, had been wiped from the face of the earth, or rebuilt in such a way as to be unrecognisable. The classical villas stood abandoned, their stucco peeling off, their plaster decorations smashed, and around them had been built new, but already peeling, box-like blocks of flats without a single ornamental feature on them. Only the blue lake was still beautiful. A dam on the river Sheksna had raised the lake's level so that it now covered the water meadows and lapped the edge of the town. But there were no fishing boats with their white sails.

I went into the library. The librarian was excited to see me as my books were on her shelves and the children read them. She phoned the local paper and a reporter came to interview me. The town poet, an enthusiastic young man, also arrived. There would be a meeting in the club that very evening and "the writer from Moscow would give an address". The poet dragged me off to his house to listen to his poems. His mother cooked me dinner. I did not care for the poems, but I did not want to hurt him so I said nothing. But I did specially ask him to put a particular question to me that evening – "How does Belozersk today compare with the town you knew forty years ago?" It is taken as an indisputable truth that everything in today's world must be good, while everything under the Tsars was bad, so the poet saw nothing odd in my question.

The club filled up with both the young and old. I talked about my books and my writing. The lady reporter scribbled earnestly in her notebook, the photographer clicked away with his camera and flash. When I finished there were some questions, which I answered and then the young poet rose to his feet. It was now that I spoke the thoughts that had been burning in my mind. The reporter put away her notebook, some of the adults started to look at each other with bewilderment, others bowed their heads; only the children kept on staring at me as before. But there were no further questions. The meeting broke up.

As I was saying goodbye to the poet I asked him to send me a copy of the paper with the article about me, as the reporter had told me I would have an entire section to myself. It was only very much later that I heard from the poet; no article about me had ever appeared in the local paper. What can I say? For our times, for our system, it was to be expected.

4

And now back to our journey. It was with difficulty that we managed the forty *versts* from Belozersk to Novoye. It rained, was windy, and the path went along rotten planking through the bogs. We only reached the village on the shores of the lake in the evening, wet, tired, with sore legs, and spent the night in the hovel of a single elderly man. He promised that in the morning he would take us over to the monastery of Novoezersk, the silhouette of which we could just make out through the rain. The next day, barely awake, wet and cold, we boated across the lake, but the rain had stopped and the sunshine warmed us, reviving our spirits. Andrei did the rowing while the old man sat at the rudder.

The white walls of the monastery rose straight out of the water of the lake, with several domes and a bell-tower standing up behind the high walls. This scene, the walls with their towers and the church domes, was clearly reflected in the unruffled surface of the lake. The old man told us there were now only five monks left and that they survived by fishing and thanks to donations from pilgrims. Inside the monastery they had a small vegetable garden, and they used to grow cereals in a field across the water, but now the authorities had forbidden them to plough so their field lay fallow, overgrown with weeds. Their abbot, Father Ioann, led the life of a hermit. He used to receive those who came to see him or to seek advice, but now there were far fewer pilgrims and he was in his eighties, becoming infirm, and so only rarely received anyone. It was the cellarer, Father Vitaly, apparently a clever and efficient manager, who was in charge.

Our boat touched land at a little overgrown island from which a shaky wooden jetty led us to the gates of the monastery. We paid the ferryman his fare, and talking animatedly, walked along the jetty. Andrei proposed to give the monks all our food – bread, salted pork and some tinned meat.

"Won't they be offended if we tempt them away from their fasting?" I wondered. We decided to play it by ear but felt we should offer money to be allowed to see Father Ioann. An ancient blind monk in a faded cassock sat by the gates, quietly saying his prayers. We walked straight up to him but he did not change his position, nor respond to our questions. Was he really so concentrated in prayer? Later we discovered that he was deaf as well as blind. The open gates welcomed us into a quiet courtyard, where the only sound was the birds singing in the blackcurrant bushes. The white churches and their bell towers did not strike us as very old. A few little wooden and stone houses leaned up against the walls, their windows nailed up and their porches overgrown with weeds. Uncertainty halted us in our tracks, wondering where to go.

From somewhere there came a shout and a young monk emerged, smiling, who welcomed us and guided us to the cellarer, Father Vitaly. He was a stout, very lively man. We explained to him that we were travelling from monastery to monastery, and that we would very much like to see Father Ioann. Father Vitaly responded evasively to our mention of Father Ioann, saying, "Let's see about that this evening," and suggested we accompany him when he went to fish for the evening meal. The three of us returned to the wooden jetty. I have never fished like that again, one had only to cast the line and it was immediately taken by a fish; cast again, and again out would come a fish! Great shoals of them were visible in the crystal clear water.

Pulling fish off his line, Father Vitaly told us about the monastery's problems. In winter, hardly anyone visited them. But what was worse was that they all lived in fear of being driven out. And, he continued, who did they trouble, living in the depths of the forest, surrounded by the marshes? There were no other settlements anywhere near. But the worst thing was that the church had been sealed up, so that they could not hold their services. They could have set up a little chapel in Father Ioann's quarters, but without the antimins (a square of linen with a picture of Christ being laid in the grave) which was inside the sealed church, they could not celebrate. They met in the evenings, said their prayers and read the Bible; what they could not do was celebrate the Eucharist.

Andrei broke in to ask, "How can we see Father Ioann?"

"I'll ask him. Maybe he'll receive you," replied Father Vitaly, putting a worm on his hook.

In an hour we had filled a pail with perch and ruff, and were just packing up our rods when we saw a large boat with three sails approaching.

"Dear Lord God, what trouble is this coming?" cried Father Vitaly, crossing himself with a shaking hand.

In the monastery they had also noticed the boat. Two monks joined us: the young one with a black beard who had first welcomed us, Father Nikander, and a short elderly one whose name I cannot recall. The three monks talked to each other in great excitement, wondering who it could be and why they were coming. They kept repeating, "Oh God, oh God!" They went out along the jetty to the islet to meet their guests, and Andrei and I followed. There were five men; three rowers, the fourth our ferryman of the morning, and the fifth a tall man in an oilskin coat. Except for the tall man, the monks knew them all – they were local people, one of them the chairman of the village Soviet.

"Oh, God, that's the man who sealed up our church!" whispered Father Vitaly. "Lord, Lord!"

The tall man disembarked. The three monks drew closer together, as if to protect each other.

"Good day to you, holy fathers!" said the chairman of the village Soviet, an ordinary-looking peasant, for some reason carrying a briefcase bulging with papers, "I've brought you a visitor." The three monks bowed low. The tall man gave them a slight nod and immediately turned to us.

"Well, lads, on your travels? Interested in old things, eh?"

The rowers stayed in the boat while the rest of us went into the monastery. Father Vitaly stayed close to the man, trying to say something to him, but the man ignored him, telling us that he was a scientific worker at the Cherepovetsk Museum and had come to the monastery to "remove", as he put it, the old icons and books. He asked us where we had been and where we were heading, and was astonished to learn that we had not visited the monastery of Ferapont.

"Heavens, they've just opened up such beautiful frescoes, the wonder of the world," he said with much force.

We were silent. The thought crossed my mind that we should have gone to Ferapont after all, but now there was no question of turning back.

"Yes, you absolutely must go to Ferapont," he insisted, "but now you can help me."

We passed in front of the old blind and deaf monk, who was still muttering his prayers, and went up to the iron doors of the church. The man from the museum pulled off the seal, the village chairman turned a big key in the lock and the door opened with a groan. Taking off our caps, we all went in, the visitors first, then Andrei and I, the monks last. In the half-light, we were met with a wave of cold, mouldy air. Spiders' webs hung from the ceiling and, the carved gilt screens were covered in dust, as were all flat surfaces. The man from the museum advanced to examine the iconostasis and said, "This doesn't interest me, but these . . ." and he quickly went around the church collecting all the icons from the window ledges, the lectern and small tables. At the altar he opened a cupboard and began to leaf through the thick, leather-bound books that were either printed or manuscripts. Father Vitaly, silently standing behind him, suddenly stepped forward.

"Citizen-comrade, we've a tiny favour to ask – give us this back," and he pointed to a small mat lying on the altar, its embroidery hidden by a thick layer of dust. "To you it's just a worthless rag, but for us it's the antimins. We really need it." These last words he spoke with a quaver.

"Oh, Father Vitaly, you can't ask such a thing," answered the man, not turning from the books he was examining. "I haven't the authority to give you even that," and he pointed at a pile of candle stubs. "Everything that's of artistic interest we'll hand over to the museum, with a receipt of course. The church will be sealed up again by the distinguished village chairman." And he smiled with all the complacency of his authority, full of the importance of his task. We went out into the fresh air. The man from the museum sat down to leaf through a thick volume.

"Come here," he beckoned us over, "look at this marvellous miniature. What fine lines, what expressiveness. It's fifteenth century. What a find!" I looked and saw in the tiny miniature a group of figures raising sticks and in their midst the bowed, half-naked Christ. In a few simple lines the unknown artist had been able to portray in Christ's face the extremes of suffering.

"The scourging of Christ, a well-known gospel legend," the man said, turning the page. "Now here's another interesting miniature."

Andrei suddenly interrupted with deliberate rudeness. "We've got to cook something up, we haven't eaten since the early morning. Let's go," he added in a loud whisper to me. The man was clearly taken aback, about to become angry, but instead turned back to the book. Without saying goodbye Andrei walked to the gates, with me hurrying behind. On the jetty the pail of fish were waiting for us. We sat down by the water and started to clean them.

"I couldn't stand there and listen a moment longer!" said Andrei. I said nothing. We went onto the little island, built a fire and in a bucket put some of the fish to cook. As we waited, we were both silent. The landing stage was on the other side of the island, so the departing uninvited guests did not see us as they embarked with their bundles of confiscated goods. Father Vitaly accompanied them to the last, and when they had set off, returned along the path muttering sadly. We called him over and invited him to share our fish soup. He sat down, pulling out a wooden spoon from under his habit.

"So they came, opened the church, took our precious things, closed it up again and put a seal on the door," he said with great sadness, and repeated what he had said in the church, "For them it's only a bit of rag, but for us it's holy." Andrei expressed his compassion with great heat, but these were only words. We had been able to do nothing. After our satisfying meal, we were shown to a small cell where we lay down on soft hay. Father Vitaly promised he would arrange for us to see Father Ioann that evening.

Later he came for us and took us to a little house overgrown with lilac. We entered a tiny room with a low ceiling. The window was obscured by the branches of a lilac bush, so the room was very dark. Behind a table sat a very old, bearded monk in his cassock under a black cloak. Two old ladies were fussing about him. The samovar bubbled away, surrounded by cups and a saucer full of honey and a plate of little cakes. The holy corner was crowded with icons, many icons, some in frames, some not, some in folding brass triptychs, all lit by an oil lamp.

First Andrei, then I went up to the old monk for his blessing and kissed his hand. He rose, said a short prayer and then we all sat around the table, Father Vitaly on one side, Andrei and I at the ends. The old ladies came and went, or just stood against the wall. Father Ioann smiled warmly at us and asked us where we had been and what we had seen. I said nothing, leaving Andrei to do all the talking. He began hesitantly but was soon talking enthusiastically about our journey , about the monasteries and churches, and our future plans. Father Ioann listened with his eyes fixed on Andrei. Afterwards Andrei told me how conscious he had been of the old man's eyes, sunk in their deep sockets, looking deep into his soul.

"And we, we go on praying as long as we live," said Father Ioann, sitting back in his chair. He closed his eyes and fell silent.

"Something will happen – something will," added Father Vitaly, continuing to drink his tea.

Father Ioann began to talk again. He came from Simbirsk, loved to go to church, as a youth sang in the choir. His father served as an accountant in the civil service and was able to send his son to gymnasium. And God ordered things so that Father Ioann was in the same class as Alexander Ulyanov, who was top of the class. His father, Ilyich Nikolaevich, was a pious, much respected man. Ioann had visited their home on several occasions. He remembered there was another son, a bright lad, Vladimir Ilyich.[19] He never thought he would become the sort of man . . . and here old Father Ioann broke off, obviously finding no words to express his thoughts.

The older of the ladies poured out more tea. Seeing me stretch out for another little cake, Andrei turned reproachful eyes on me. Father Ioann noticed the look. "Never mind, never mind, eat your fill!"

The talk turned to Moscow. Father Vitaly rose and we understood we must leave. Father Ioann got to his feet with difficulty, clutching the arms of the chair. We wanted to go up to him for his blessing. "Wait a moment," he said. "I want to say something to you as a farewell. You have set off on a journey to seek the Holy Spirit. That's wonderful. I see the spark of God in you, and I believe that perhaps after many years this spark will turn into a flame that will set others on fire. Goodbye. I will pray for you."

---

19. *Lenin.*

Father Vitaly wrote our names in a little notebook, we went up to Father Ioann for his blessing and took our leave, deeply moved. More than fifty years have elapsed since that visit. I have never forgotten his words, even through the most unhappy and difficult times. We went outside and, dangling our legs in the water, sat beside the old, blind monk. The lake was rosy pink in the light of the setting sun, and we watched him sit there, face raised to the heavens, muttering his prayers, oblivious of our presence.

I started to write in our diary, but Andrei took it from me. "I want to write up today." He sat in thought for a while before he gave up. "I can't get started. I'll do it tomorrow." We continued to sit by the old monk, listening to the murmur of his prayers.

"Have you ever heard the word *peshestvovat?*" Andrei asked me.[20]

"Never."

"What a lovely word," he said.

We fell silent again, watching evening turning to night.

5

The next morning we said farewell to Father Vitaly after making a donation of a rouble. The cheerful, black-bearded young monk rowed us across the lake, so once more we were off on our travels through marsh and forest. About a year later, Andrei learned that the Kirillo-Novoezersk monastery had been shut down. What was the fate of the monks? It is not difficult to guess. They would either have died due to old age, or perished behind barbed wire. I visited Kirillov and Belozersk after the war and by making enquiries, found out that the little island in the lake had been turned into a prison camp. Yes, they chose a fine spot for it, a lake surrounded by marsh and forest, a land without roads, and on top of that the high walls of the monastery. Who could escape from such a place?

I also made enquiries about the man from the museum, and discovered that such a man from Cherepovets was remembered. It seemed that when the authorities wanted to pull down a seventeenth-century church, he had opposed their decision, wrote around trying to enlist support, and was arrested for sticking his nose in where it was not wanted. How or where he perished, no one knew. Whether that was the man who had removed the icons and books from the

---

20. *Unknown verb, conceivably invented by the monks. Pesh relates to "foot',*
shest to walking or progressing, but also connotes the number six. Andrei's point
is that the word is lovely yet mysterious.

church when we were there, I do not know. One does meet such people here and there, lovers of old things; but they only admire these objects as artistic, and not miraculous, works.

Some years later I read an essay by the late Alexander Yashin about how he and his wife and two little sons spent a summer on Lake Novoye, far away from civilisation. He described how they fished, swam and went boating. He only mentioned in passing some rotting posts of what he called a "stockade" on another island – these were the remains of the jetty by the monastery. It was a fine essay; Yashin was a poet and prose-writer with a lot of talent, but his observations were limited to the beauties of nature. He seemed not to have intuited the lives that had once graced the little monastery; or perhaps he had guessed at them, but then kept silent, knowing it would prevent publication if he wrote of the despoiled, ruined monastery.

6

We reached the landing stage of Kustovo on the Marinskaya river system by evening, soaked and shivering. Learning that the ship was due in a couple of hours, we hung our wet clothes on the railings to dry, but then discovered that the nearby shop was closed. We ate our last tin of meat without heating it up; we had no more bread at all. We should have gone to any of the houses in the village, where I am sure they would have helped us, but we were too diffident.

The wait for the steamer seemed endless and we were getting hungrier and hungrier. The other people waiting seemed unconcerned, no doubt quite accustomed to the unpredictable sailing times of these river steamers. Finally, paddle wheels churning, our boat arrived. We went down to fourth class and found ourselves a place by the bow. Sheltered by a cloth curtain, we lay down on the deck among all the other adults and children. In the morning, we made the nasty discovery that the buffet was not operating, all that was on offer was boiling water. Our situation was unenviable; it was two days sailing to Lake Onega, and it was not at all clear whether we would manage to find any food during that time. Surrounded by the chatter of the people around us, we lay there nursing our hunger.

The conversations around us were indeed lively, mostly about soaring prices and the policy of creating collectives to work the land. Someone said that the priest had been arrested in their village and there was now no one to hold the services. Someone else said the father and two eldest sons of the most important family in their village had been arrested, the wife and children driven out, the cattle taken, and their house was now a club. They talked about shortages and how there were now no nails to be had anywhere. In those days people talked of Soviet rule without fear. We heard voices saying, "Why do they come and cause trouble? We've done nothing to them! What are they after? And what's happened to the nails?" One man tried to defend the authorities, but he got it in the neck. The women attacked him as fiercely as if he had tried to steal their possessions. Suddenly, somehow, they found out that Andrei and I were totally without supplies of food, which was of course entirely our own fault, but this discovery roused our neighbours to noisy concern. They surrounded us and forced upon us bread, meat pies, ham, fish and sugar, and all this for not a kopek of payment. The focus of attention switched to us and our plight and seemed to serve to stoke up their indignation against the authorities.

"Look at that! Here's these lads without any bread, having to travel all hungry."

Even the man who had tried to stand up for the authorities gave us some bread. Their heated discussions went on rising and falling. Passengers embarked and disembarked and at once fell into lively exchanges. Having eaten our fill, thoroughly grateful that we had been saved by the compassion of the "common people", Andrei and I rolled ourselves up in our blankets and went to sleep to the sound their voices.

I cannot describe our travels day by day. The daily diary so diligently transcribed by my mother is often silent, and I have forgotten much. We sailed along the Marinskaya river network, at first rising through many locks, then sailing along the canal south of Lake Onega. We were told that in Tsarist times there had been a great deal of trading in these parts. Rows of barges would wait in turn to get through the locks as Mother Russia sent her products to St Petersburg and abroad, feeding her capital and the whole of Western Europe. But now we hardly saw a single loaded barge.

At Vosnesenye at the mouth of the river Svirya we transferred to another steamer and sailed on the blue waters of Lake Onega to Petrozavodsk, where we changed boats once more to sail to Sennaya Bay, the station for Klimetsko Island opposite Petrozavodsk, which was the end of our travels by water. It was from this village that we intended to start our expedition on foot through the region of Lake Onega. I had a letter of introduction to the local priest written by the curator of the Museum of Ethnography, a good friend of Yusha Samarin's. A year earlier, Yusha had come to this untouched part of the world to record its songs, tales and poetry, and had lodged with the priest and his two daughters. He had spoken of the unmatched beauty of the lake's shore, of the fine, artistically carved houses, and above all, of the hospitality of the people. It was unthinkable for us not to visit the region.

On deck we sat next to two deeply sunburned women teachers and got into conversation with them. We discovered they were the daughters of the priest in Sennaya Bay, who spent the winters in snowy countryside around Lake Onega as schoolteachers, saving up their money to travel to the Crimea, from where they were now returning for another winter of teaching in preparation for the following summer. We fell into animated conversation, discussing the merits of Yusha Samarin and the members of last year's expedition. They had been particularly impressed by the director of the Moscow Museum of History, and leader of the expedition, Yura Matveyevich Sokolov. So the time passed until our vessel tied up at the landing stage.

From time immemorial crowds have gathered to greet the arrival of Russian river steamers. It was no different here. A big crowd in their best clothes was waiting at the landing stage. A harmonica was playing, the children were fooling about, the young people smiling and waving, the old watching silent and motionless. But I was not looking at the crowd as we tied up, but at the line of houses on the top of the steep banks of the shore. These houses were of one or two storeys, obviously fairly newly built, with carved and painted window frames and eaves, all a beautiful sight. Nearby stood what looked also like a newly built, three-domed wooden church. I must repeat what I wrote earlier, that 1928 was a year of great plenty for the peasantry. Bukharin's much-repeated slogan, "Enrich yourselves", was clearly being lived out. And although there were rumours and stories everywhere, and vicious articles about getting rid of the *kulaks*, the people still worked the land without straightening their backs. Even in the depths of their severe winters they still had plenty to do clearing the land of stones, which they piled along the edges of their holdings. In the spring they had to manure, plough and harvest as provision for the next winter. They were a determined and self-reliant people. Half a century later a friend of mine landed at this same landing stage and was met by a crowd, but not at all a cheerful crowd and no harmonica was playing. He too saw the line of beautiful houses above the landing stage, but many of them were nailed up, their walls sagging, their roofs falling in.

The priest's daughters now led us to a big, two-storey house beside the church. We were shown into the main room on the first floor and left alone under the gaze of many icons. After a little while the double doors swung open and a procession entered. In front was the elder daughter with a steaming samovar, followed by her sister, then their mother with a tray of cups and plates and a variety of things to eat, and last of all the priest, a tall, sturdy figure with a long beard, wearing a fine cassock, and making a very majestic impression. Many priests in those days emanated this sense of authority in the exercise of their pastoral duties to their flock.

A great feast now began. Later Andrei reproached me again for reaching for a third slice of fish pie. The priest himself ate very little. He answered very fully our many questions about the region's tales and legends, about the fate of the monasteries, and he named the villages where there still were ancient churches. He advised us first to go fifteen kilometres to the south end of Klimetsk Island to look at a monastery that had recently been closed down, then to return, when he would organise a trip by boat to Kizhi, and at Kizhi the local priest could help us further.

We slept soundly on a feather mattress laid out for us in the main room under the icons. After a good breakfast we set off to see Klimetsk monastery. It had become a home for the aged, which meant we could not go inside, so we sat on the stony beach watching the waves rolling in, and staring out over the boundless expanse of Lake Onega. I also remember a little chapel that we passed on the road, a simply decorated wooden structure; on entering it we discovered that the iconostasis had been smashed and the interior despoiled. This sort of vandalism was only just becoming common at that time. Later, it is sad to record, we all became accustomed to the savage vandalism of holy places. On occasion I would find myself with others in a ruined church, a sight that would move me to sad thoughts, whereas the others would be completely indifferent to the sight, it was so common.

We spent a second night at the priest's home and in the morning parted on warm and grateful terms. He spoke a blessing over us as we left. Eighteen months later Yusha Samarin told me that Professor Sokolov had received a letter from one of the priest's daughters, saying that her father had been arrested and was being kept in the Petrozavodsk prison, and asking for him to intervene. But what could anyone, even a great scholar, do in those times?

8

I cannot remember how many *versts* we covered on the way to Kizhi, passing many little wooded islands. Two lads rowed the boat, with Andrei sometimes taking a turn. I was considered incompetent for this task. As for Kizhi, much has been written about it, and does not need to be repeated. At that time the two churches were faced with thick planks. I have not seen what they look like today. Having seen pictures of them in Grabar's book, we were prepared to be hypercritical, but their size and their many domes and cupolas certainly created a grandiose effect. The priest was at least twenty years younger than our host of the night before, but just as hospitable. After a good meal, he took us first into the church with twenty-two domes, then into the twelve-domed one. In the lobby of the first church we read a piece of paper pinned up behind glass which announced that the church could only be used for the celebration of holy services, not for any other purpose. The signature at the bottom was Professor Sokolov's. I later realized that apart from being a famous man in the field of folklore, he was also a good man.

When the churches were closed down for services, I do not know, nor do I know the subsequent fate of the priest. What I do remember is how he prised off a tiny sliver of wood off one of the pillars to show us the fine white pine underneath, still as healthy and sound as if the church were newly built and not two-hundred-years-old. Dark and sad, the faces of the saints looked down on us from the iconostasis; Andrei crossed himself and murmured some prayers. I also made the sign of the cross. I wonder how many future generations will visit these churches to admire the work of the icon and fresco painters, and how many of them will cross themselves. Actually, I believe no one is allowed inside the churches today.

Some time later, when again sailing along the Marinskaya river system, we saw another church very much in the style of the churches at Kizhi, no doubt built by the same master builders, only with seventeen domes. Soon after the war, it suffered an awful fate when some hooligans set fire to it. Why did they do it? Well, just because. The glow of the fire was visible thirty *versts* away. One is not supposed to remember such wickedness.

We spent the night in the Kizhi priest's house and then set off further, first by boat, then on foot. We went north, then turned west, cutting across the Onega peninsula, passing waters full of fish and forests full of wild game, going ever deeper into the wild countryside. We were hospitably received, even joyfully, but also with a touch of caution. We felt the people were anxious, but what they were anxious about they did not know, nor did we when they questioned us; all we knew was that there was something looming ahead of us, something threatening the whole of Russia.

We reached the Murmansk railway at Kondonog, where a huge paper pulp factory was being built. Nearby stood a beautiful, tall church, as usual in the north made entirely of wood. There is no photograph of this seventeenth-century church in Grabar's book, so we were surprised to come upon it. It has not been destroyed and its picture now features in all books on Russia's artistic past, though the photos show it standing alone, whereas we saw a fine, although smaller, bell tower next to it. Art experts now say there never was such a belltower, and that the bells hung on a special beam. During our travels Andrei was very thorough about making sketches of all the lovely churches and houses we saw. I do not know whether that album is still in existence; if it were it would be invaluable, as much of what Andrei sketched has been lost, just like the belltower in Kondonog.

We went up the river Suna, saw the famous Kivatch waterfall, the rapids of Girvas and Porporog, continued through wild and beautiful places till we almost reached the Finnish border, where for the first time our papers were checked by a Red Army guard. This area was inhabited by Karelians, who greeted us coldly and made us pay for accommodation. Finally, we made it to Medvyezhya Gora, the most northerly point of Lake Onega, where there was a railway station. We had walked about five hundred kilometres. In our marches we saw wonderful forests, lakes and mountains, and especially the beautiful wooden carvings of the local people. The area of Medvyezhya Gora, a great sweep around the north of the lake, was especially picturesque.

The White Sea to Baltic canal had not yet been planned and there were only a few labour camps whose inmates were set to logging in the pine forests for export. Solovki on the White Sea was the principal prison camp. But when the building of the canal began a year later a large labour camp was established to supply manpower. Behind its barbed wire hundreds of thousands of innocent and hopeless people went through dreadful sufferings, and now lie buried, not in graves but in hastily dug trenches. Andrei and I had no presentiment of this fearful future as we waited for a train, gazing about us with interest.

We went north to the station at Soroka, the future town of Belomorsk, that was to be built on the bones of prisoners. There, in the delta of the turbulent river Vyg, were some forty small islands, each settled with several houses, and behind each house its own cemetery. The graves, however, were marked not by crosses, but by tall planks with carved and painted designs. For centuries Old Believers had lived and died here. From Soroka we sailed along the shores of the White Sea, stopping at ancient settlements by the sea before landing up at the little town of Onega. We travelled in second class, in a communal cabin for ten people. We were aboard for three days, and watched how at every stop grain and sugar and flour was unloaded and salted fish taken on board. At night the vessel lay at anchor.

In Archangelsk at that time there were many churches, all on the right bank of the river Dvina. The stone-built cathedral of the Archangel Michael impressed by its enormous bulk and five domes. Next to it was an equally grand eighteenth-century building, the Customs House. In the mist one could hardly see the other bank of the Dvina. The river was full of vessels of all kinds, from sailing boats to large foreign freighters, and there was a great bustle of loading and unloading as the stevedores, calling and shouting, but without swear-words, carried drums and barrels and bales up and down the narrow gangplank. The air reeked of fish. Our vessel docked and we walked along the wooden sidewalks past two-storey wooden houses and stone churches.

9

I had carefully kept two letters throughout our journey. One was from my brother Vladimir to his friend, Boris Victorovich Shergin, who later became quite a well-known writer. I wrote about him when I described Vladimir's wedding. The other letter was written by Vasily Sergeievich Arsenyev, a relative of my parents, who had once been an official in Tula, and after the revolution busied himself with the genealogy of noble families. His mother and his two sisters were living in Archangelsk, exiled there for enjoying too many contacts with foreigners, and in particular, indulging in western dances, behaviour that was then considered a worse sin than today's drunkenness at work.

The Arsenyev girls Alexandra (Alexa), and Anna (Atata), were five years older than us, but were pleased to see us. The family probably survived on dollars sent them by their older brother, Nikolai, a professor at the University of Koenigsberg. They eventually left Russia after he had paid a large sum of money to secure their exit visas. The sisters showed us round the town, and we bought them ice creams, though ourselves refraining out of a need to economise. They were not just lighthearted and jolly, but also pious. We were taken to meet a very holy old monk, as well as a very holy old nun, both of whom treated Andrei and me with a certain reserve, no doubt taking us to be atheists.

The famous Archangelsk artist, Pisakhov, was not in town, but we called on Shergin several times, though without the two sisters. I wrote a memoir of him for an anthology half a century later, but the collection has not yet been published. He was then still dreaming of becoming a writer. His appearance and his fluid Northern voice as he told us about the former life of the people of that region, made a great impression upon Andrei and me. I have given a detailed account of his difficult career as a writer, and how he was viciously attacked in the press. Our intention was to sail from Archangelsk up the river Dvina, so when we came to say goodbye, Shergin gave us a long scroll that recorded the names of all the villages and churches along the Dvina, with the dates of their construction; unforgivably, we lost that carefully-made scroll somewhere along the way.

We spent a day in Veliky Ustyug, where the churches stood in a crowded row along the river bank, and the ethnographic museum was packed with interesting items from olden times. To judge by today's photographs, only a little of all that has survived. In Vologda we boarded a train for Rostov Veliky, to which I have returned many times since then, but I shall never forget that first time and the beauties of the ancient town as they unfolded before us.

We arrived back in Moscow hungry and penniless. We could not even afford a tram ticket. I walked home all the way from Kalanchevskaya Square.

10

The very next day Andrei and I went to Glinkovo, where we were received like heroes. "And you never quarrelled?" asked my sisters. "Never," we replied with honesty. The real reason for this was not that there had been little cause to quarrel, but that I had been so flattered to be asked to join Andrei that I had blindly obeyed him in everything, whether cutting wood, lighting the fire or being sent off to find bread. During the month and a half of our travels, I had also been in a mood of poetic excitement, hungrily absorbing the myriad impressions of the beauty of nature, the rich artistry of the old churches, the wonderful carvings on the houses and everyday objects of peasant life, the unhurried conversations with the priests and country folk. I was too much in the clouds to resent any slights or hurts.

Summer came to an end. I was spending more time in Moscow, drawing my maps, than in Glinkovo. I was also still in a state of inspired excitement. I copied out the diary of our journey, resolving to write some essays, not for publication, but for myself. The whole of that winter, I sat chewing on my pencil in rare periods of solitude, writing, crossing out, rewriting. Mother copied these efforts into a notebook, which despite removals, searches and arrests, was never lost and is still in my possession. I recently re-read this collection of essays, entitled *Among Northern Lakes*, and was quite surprised at those vivid memories in what was otherwise a dark time of my youth. Their style is naïve and exalted – but then I was far from being a mature writer.

To complete my story of northern Russia, I will describe the amazing journey on skis made by Andrei in the winter holidays of 1930. He was unable to persuade anyone, including me, to accompany him on this adventure, which was to ski from Konosho on the northern railway line westwards to the Murmansk line. But he was a determined person – if he decided to do something, he did it. Equipped with tinned meat and apparently impeccable documents, he set off alone and, in spite of the intense cold, covered thirty kilometres a day and was able to sketch the churches he passed. The nights he spent in priests' homes where he was struck by their deeply anxious thoughts for the future.

Collectivisation was then in its early stages. All over the countryside people were in a fearful mood as inexplicable changes took place. The hardest working peasants were arrested and exiled with their families, as were all those who refused to enter the *kolhozy* (collective farms). And now here, in regions where outsiders hardly ever penetrated, a man who called himself a student from Moscow was travelling on skis, sketching the churches and sheltering with priests. The watchful authorities were alerted; who was this man? Was he a runaway prisoner, a White Guard, a spy, a snowman, a man from Mars? He must be caught, tied up and brought in. The young *Konsomol*s were diverted from their main mission of driving out the *kulaks* and, together with the head of the local OGPU, set off on the chase.

They would never have caught up with him, had it not been for a thaw. Andrei could only manage ten kilometres a day in the heavy snow that stuck to his skis. Nevertheless, he managed to get from Vologda to Karelia where, exhausted, he was welcomed into a priest's house and, rolling himself up in his blanket, fell into a deep sleep. He was awakened by vicious kicks in the ribs to find three frightened youths covering him with their hunting guns. Next to them was a soldier with a revolver and behind him the terrified priest and his wife. After a thorough search the brave lads took their prisoner to Konosho and threw him into the former church building. There Andrei found more than a hundred prisoners of all ages – peasants, schoolteachers, priests, amongst whom Andrei, to his horror, recognised his earlier hosts. One of them told him with bitterness, "You've done for me!"

The food was dreadful. A few lucky people received provisions from their relatives. Everyone lay about in a dispirited mass, simply not comprehending why they had been arrested. Some walked up and down, others talked to each other. Later Andrei described the scene as being exactly like a Dantean circle of hell. Every day he was taken off for questioning. The interrogators and their chiefs simply could not grasp the notion of a student from Moscow who travelled on skis, sketched churches and spent the night with priests. To them this meant that his documents were false, even though in addition to his student card Andrei had a paper certifying that he was a student of the Moscow Technical College of Chemistry, on a sporting trip on skis to such-and-such places and requesting whom it might concern to give him what assistance he needed. They suspected a plot, a traitor, heaven knows what else.

One of the superiors, showing Andrei the compass they had taken from him, asked him, "What's this?"

"A compass."

"No, it's a hellish machine, a very dangerous thing!"

Andrei managed to get a letter to his parents. His father arrived and found to his horror an bearded and emaciated son, but somehow managed to get him released. I do not know what excuse for lateness Andrei gave his director of studies. He finished his studies and became an outstanding chemist, professor and doctor of sciences. He was not fond of recalling this particular youthful adventure.

14. Calamities Loom

1

The Urusov family lived in a big house on Bolshoy Znamenskaya Street. Most of the family was going to celebrate the New Year away from home, thus leaving the large flat at the disposal of their son, Kirill, and daughter, Lenya, who invited their friends to club together in arranging a party. Kirill dreamed of becoming a geologist, but as the son of a princely line obstacles kept being put in his way. Lenya was the friend of my youngest sister, Katya, both of whom were in Year 8. Together with another friend of hers, Lenochka Zheltukhina, Lenya earned money by working in a private café on Prechistenky Boulevard behind the Church of the Holy Spirit, where there now stands the building that is the entrance of the Metro station, Kropotinskaya.

It is only in France, and there not always, that I have ever seen such swift, attractive and happy waitresses as those two girls, nimbly carrying their loaded trays between the tables and even finding time to flirt with the clients. It was in that café that Lenochka met the handsome student, Pyotr Alexandrovich Rebinder, who was to become a famous academician-chemist, and her husband. When I reminded her of this some fifty years later, my sisters jumped on me; the wife of an important scientist does not always like to be reminded of the adventures of her youth. Lenya Urusova's fate turned out quite differently; I will write of that further on. In any event, the owner of the café was driven out of business by heavy taxes and had to shut up shop, after which Lenya went to work taking round books in the library of the Institute of Teaching.

At that New Year's party were my two younger sisters, Masha and Katya, and our cousins, Sasha and Olechka, the children of Vladimir Vladimirovich Golitsyn; Sasha had a job somewhere, Olechka was still at school. The three Rayevsky brothers, our distant cousins, also came. Sergei, the eldest, worked as a photographer in

311

an electro-technical institute under the famous Pavel Florensky. The second son, Mikhail, my contemporary, was a student in the faculty of mathematics and was expected to have a bright future; he was also studying singing. The youngest, Andrei, was a student in the studio of the painter Khmelev and hoped to become an artist. Lyalya Ilyinskaya, with whom my sister Masha and I had studied in the Institute of Literature, came as well. There was also my cousin, Lelya Davidova. Her mother, my Aunt Katya, was my mother's sister. Her father, Alexander Vasilieyevich (Uncle Alda) had been driven out with his whole family from their estate of Kulevatovo, and who was now a legal counsel of the Tambov market committee. This meant that he defended the interests of the lower-middle-class market traders – a career to be condemned by definition. The president of the market committee was a certain Paleolog, a descendant of the Byzantine emperors. Another guest was a friend of Lyalya's, Marina Cheltsova, the granddaughter of the last tsarist Minister of the Interior Protopopov. She was a very affected young lady and, in my opinion, not a very nice one.

Around midnight our family friend Yusha Samarin arrived, bearing a bottle of champagne. Although much older than the rest of us, he preferred our young and lively crowd to the rather stiff company at the party being given by my cousin, Sonya Witter, the wife of the Englishman Reginald Witter, in their apartment in the Gerye house on Gagarin Street. My brother Vladimir, together with his wife Elena and my sister Sonya, had gone to that party.

Compared to present times, we feasted very simply; a vinaigrette salad, potatoes, cranberry juice, homemade ice cream and pastries. The only moderately alcoholic drink was a jug of wine punch with sliced apples in it. But we really enjoyed ourselves, dancing the forbidden foxtrot untiringly to the one and only record, whose singer bleated out what sounded like a long-drawn out "Alleluya-a-a-a-a". When we sat down to rest, Mikhail Rayevsky would entertain the girls by singing his invariable aria in a piercing baritone, "I sing to the God Hymen, and to all newly-weds". My youngest sister, the fifteen-year-old Katenka, enjoyed herself most of all; it was the first time she had been allowed to join the "grown-ups". Incidentally, the writer Anatoly Rybakov in his novel *The Children of the Arbat* paints a picture in those years of easygoing sexual relations among the young, regarded with tolerance by their parents, but when I look back, although there were couples who fell in love, these relationships were always quite chaste.

The Urusov parents came home at four in the morning – Yury Dimitrevich, at one time Comrade-Prosecutor of Moscow, and his wife Evdokia Evgenyevna, the daughter of a one-time famous novelist, Count Salias. Her father's books have never been reprinted, doubtless because of his title. Following the parents came their oldest son, Nikita, and their daughter, Eda, with her husband Mikhail Unkovsky, a cousin of the Rayevskys. The couple were both art students, working in Khmelev's studio and both promising to become fine artists.

It was time for us to leave. We went our different ways. I walked with my sisters up Prechistenkaya Boulevard dreaming of a wonderful and happy future, trying out in my head various titles for my next essay on *Northern Lakes* and imagining myself an established writer. That was my dream. Yet what a cruel fate was subsequently to befall many of those I have just named.

2

When I think back sixty years, what I first remember is the hatred that radiated persistently and viciously from on high. It came from Stalin – not then yet called "Great" – and his entourage. This hatred was picked up on and spread by a servile press; the papers screamed with hatred of capitalism. They also poured even greater hate on class enemies, who were supposedly concealed in every corner of our vast and long-suffering country. Was the engine of State creaking and barely making progress? It was the class enemies who were responsible. Be on your guard! Be watchful! Those words were all over the newspapers. Who were the enemies? First of all the *kulaks*, those hard-working peasants building a life for themselves and their families, but not building socialism. Then engineers, scientists and civil servants were enemies, deliberately wrecking factories, construction sites and scientific institutes. Other enemies were the "popes" – that was the only term used for the clergy – preaching an alien and hostile ideology. The "popes" must be arrested, the churches destroyed!

Other irreconcilable enemies were the "former people" – landowners, officers, officials, industrialists, both tsarist and "White". They had all lost their privileges and their benefits and so they hated Soviet rule. It was especially all those with titles, whether princes, barons or counts, who hated the Soviets. Sometimes counts might be "pardoned". Prince Urusov, who survived by a miracle, even though he was a former governor and friend of a tsarist Minister of the Interior, remarked with some irony in his interesting memoirs that the title of prince never enjoyed such high esteem before the revolution as after it.

The main perpetrator of this hatred was the Secretary of the Moscow Party Committee, Lazar Moiseyevich Kaganovich. His principal executive agent was Emelyan Yaroslavsky – or to give him his real name, Minya Israilovich Gubelman. The writer Nadia Ginsberg recalls Yaroslavsky in her amazing memoir of the Gulag, *The Steep Journey*. She turned to him for help, but he not only did not help her, he betrayed her. Not long ago I looked in on the Museum of the Revolution, and saw there a memorial exhibition on Yaroslavsky, depicted as "the greatest Leninist". The museum guide, leading a group of school children, was heaping praises on this man who had shown such dreadful hatred of Russia, of Russian history, of everything Russian. The school children were listening and, I suppose, taking it all in.

It was Yaroslavsky who launched the wholesale destruction of monuments, but that was later. In 1928, he introduced laws to deprive people of their right to vote and to carry out purges of institutions. The law on the loss of the right to vote was at first met with feelings of hurt rather than of fear, especially in the countryside, where people who were not allowed vote felt they were objects of humiliation and shame. Later, the loss of this right became a terrible instrument that punished people who had committed no crime, and more than that, punished their children, even those underage.

The basis for these purges was a short quote from Karl Marx – "your way of life determines your consciousness", which was then reformulated as follows: "You, your son and your grandchildren come of the formerly privileged classes, namely, the nobility, the merchants, the priesthood, and since you have lost these privileges you feel yourself wounded by Soviet rule, therefore you hate it, which means you are its enemies, so you must be persecuted." In 1928, the authorities began the so-called "cleansing", that is, purges of the institutions. The primary target was not qualifications, honesty or zeal, but social origin. At first the forms to be filled out did not go into great detail. There were questions such as, "Who were your parents? Had they served in the tsar's army, or the White Guard? Were they prosecuted, and if so, on what charge? Did they own property?" In the early period one could answer the question about one's parents with "Son of an employee", or "Doctor's daughter". It was only in the 1930s that the watchful authorities began to ask about the social origins of one's parents.

3

What did the purges of 1928 and 1929 mean in practice? The very same Emelyan Yaroslavsky invented three categories of punishment. The first category meant that you could not be employed anywhere. The second that you were driven out of work in the capital, but could find work on the periphery. The third that you could stay where you were, but at a lower level. These purges were carried out in public; you were judged by your own colleagues, under the pressure of the chairman of the committee on purges and its other members.

Let us take the example of my father's brother, Nikolai Vladimirovich Golitsyn – Uncle Niks – a historian by profession, working as a translator in the Marx and Engels Institute. The committee had him up, but his colleagues defended him, saying he was irreplaceable, and could translate both from and into three languages quickly and proficiently. Yet he was a former prince, and had been in prison for three years on a political charge. This was not all, however. He had translated an article about how Henry Ford trained his workers like horses. So, a former prince was comparing the proletariat to animals! The chairman delivered an angry speech, and then gave the floor to the unfortunate Uncle Niks. He justified himself, saying that he had translated quite literally and that the word in the original was "trained". But this only added oil to the flames. "So you continue to compare the proletariat to animals?" stormed the chairman. And the poor prince was purged in the first category. A brave journalist reported all this in his newspaper. The family tried to help him to survive. Mother's brother, Uncle Alyosha Lopukhin, was making a living knitting socks on his special machine so he thought he could teach Uncle Niks how to work it, but Uncle Niks was all fingers and thumbs. It was clear the historian could not be turned into a knitter. Fortunately, he was saved by his skills as a translator; he was taken on by the French newspaper *Journal de Moscou* and worked there contentedly until his death in 1942.

Another example was Nikolai Vissarionovich Nekrasov, a former Minister of Transport in the Provisional government and a highly qualified professional. From the first days of the revolution he served under Soviet rule, and was held in high esteem by Lenin, but then was purged from his important job in the Commissary of the Economy. Denunciations of him were published in the papers, and an artist sketched him defending himself before the committee and the assembled employees: an upright, noble-looking man with an eagle's gaze. He worked on the White Sea canal project, then the

Moscow-Volga canal, where for a time he was superintendent of works before being downgraded. His tall figure as he walked among the workers was pointed out to me on one occasion. Once the canal was built many people were sent to prison, including Nekrasov. He disappeared.

These purges did not affect everyone in the State institutions. Victims were chosen selectively. Kirill Urusov, still a young geologist, was one of these. A colleague of his described the scene to me. Kirill stepped up to the platform, a tall young man with fair hair and a handsome face, and said, yes, my father was once a prince, but he worked his whole life, never owned any property, and I, his son, know of no other fault of his than that. The hall fell utterly silent, save for a girl who gave a scream and was led out. Kirill survived this purge. Some years later he married a woman called Volkovaya and under the law of those days was allowed to take the surname of his wife. So Prince Urusov became Citizen Volkovoy and under that name lived out the rest of his life in safety.

4

What of our family? In that year, 1929, our large family seemed to be living happily on the second floor of a two-storey house at No. 16 Eropkinsky Street. Grandfather Vladimir Mikhailovich continued to receive ten dollars a month from his son, who was prospering as a surgeon in Los Angeles, and a further ten dollars a month from Italy, from the wealthy Moina Abamelek-Lazareva. Every day grandfather wrote up his diary and occasionally set out his patience game with me and Vladimir.

Father was working as an economist and planner in the chemical division of Gosplan for a salary of two hundred roubles a month, a fairly decent amount, though not for the number of his dependants. He had not studied chemistry at school, so what exactly he did at work I do not know, but I know he would have done his job conscientiously and thoroughly. For the sake of the exercise, he always walked to his office on Ilyinkaya Street and anyway he would never have been able to board the tram at our stop, Maly Levshinksy – in the peak hours it was always packed to the buffers.

I have already written about my brother Vladimir and his work as an illustrator of journals and books. As for my mother, and how her earnings suddenly collapsed, I will write later. I have also described my own life, drawing maps and plans, writing away at night at my essays on the Northern Lakes, constantly in a state of inspired excitement. I was happy. My sister Masha continued to study with me in the School of Literature. She had not grown up a classic beauty, but with delicate features under a cloud of curly hair she still attracted many young men and was constantly being taken out to the theatre or cinema. My youngest sister Katya attended, together with her friend Olya Sheremetyeva (not the countess), a private class organised by the former head of the girls' gymnasium, Vera Nikolaievna Velichkina, in her own flat in Serebryanaya Street. This kind of private establishment was eventually condemned by the authorities, and Katya then moved to a regular school.

My sister Sonya was still working at those medical statistics, a job which was helping several "former" families to survive. The statistics they catalogued helped the medical profession to monitor the general health of the country and if necessary to raise the alarm. Today such data is classified secret, and it is only recently that we have been able to learn that infant mortality in our country is higher than in many African countries.

Sonya's long-drawn out affair with the former officer, Prince Vladimir Nikolaievich Dolgoruky, finally came to an end. He was undoubtedly a man of great intelligence and culture, but a cold egotist. Thanks perhaps to his wound in the First World War he was never arrested or imprisoned and in due course became a writer. He lived not far from us in Maly Levshinsky Lane, and was constantly in and out of our house until Sonya and he parted, when he stopped coming. I do not know much of this love affair. Sonya and mother would sit together whispering, and Sonya obviously suffered greatly from the break, after which her character altered, she took to religion, continually visiting churches and holy old men. She was already twenty-five-years-old by then.

Suddenly a not-so-young ichthyologist, Victor Alexandrovich Meien, appeared on the scene. Up until then he had been a visitor to the Osorgins out at their *dacha*, where he commissioned their artist daughter, Maria, to paint signs and vainly attempted to court her. Knowing that he lived not far from us, the Osorgins had asked him to see us on some errand. He appeared, saw Sonya and, as he later confessed, fell in love with her at first sight. He resolved, however, to proceed with caution. We were always a hospitable family. We sat Victor Alexandrovich down next to grandfather and offered him tea. Vladimir, hearing our talk, broke off his work and joined us. Soon a lively conversation was in progress. It turned out that our guest needed a translation done from English, and also drawings for his scientific writings. Father received an order for the translation and

I began to draw various diagrams for Victor. He invited Sonya to the theatre, which she refused, but she accompanied him to church to some special evening mass and together they also went to see some holy old man.

Victor invited us all to Lake Biserovo, near Chernaya station on the railway line to Nizhny Novgorod, to take part in a massive fishing excursion. Vladimir and Elena, Yusha Samarin, my sister Masha and Sasha Golitsyn all went, but Sonya refused. Of course this whole occasion was organised so as to see Sonya again, not for us. The lake had once belonged to the Donskoy Monastery, but was at that time rented by a private Belorussian on condition that the catch was handed over to the state. The Belorussian way of fishing was quite strange. Nets were lowered through holes in the ice and dragged along to a much bigger hole. When pulled up they were full of fish, the small fry being thrown back in. After this had been done three times, we were invited into a little house the man had just built on the river bank, where a feast was on offer, washed down by plenty of vodka. We went home rather unsteadily, carrying bags full of carp and bream. A few months later the man was imprisoned and his family sent into exile. The cooperative ceased to exist.

I know that during that excursion Victor Alexandrovich had hoped to further his relationship with Sonya. I told Sonya, "Don't be so hard on him, or he'll stop ordering my drawings."

This was our life at the beginning of 1929 – a contented, hard-working and fortunate family. But then everything changed.

5

Two months after that happy fishing excursion, father came home early from work, his face pale and his eyes tense. Mother immediately sensed something was wrong. Father slowly hung up his coat, and without a word they retired to their bedroom. Much later father was able to tell us what had happened. His immediate boss at the chemical factory was an engineer, Kamsolkin, about whom father writes in his memoirs – a man of absolute integrity. Years before he had visited our estate at Bulchalki to advise on ways of improving its management. Kamsolkin warned father that purges were planned at Gosplan and that he, father, was to be the first victim. He would be purged under the first category. Father asked him whether he should appeal to Professor Osadchy, senior deputy chairman to Krizhanovsky, the head of the Gosplan.

"Osadchy is also fearful for his position," objected Kamsolkin. "What you should do is resign of your own free will at once, and so leave without a blemish on your papers. Then you can find a more modest job elsewhere."

Father remembered how his own brother had been humiliated and expelled from his job for just translating the words "trained like horses". There and then he sat down in Komsalkin's office and wrote out his letter of resignation. Only a year later the entire upper echelons of Gosplan, including Osadchy and Kamsolkin, were arrested and accused of sabotage and polluting the staff with class enemies. Some were shot, others sent to the Gulag. Krizhanovsky, once a close colleague of Lenin's, was made an academician and pushed aside, Kuibyshev taking his place.

At first father remained quite cheerful. He registered as un-employed at the labour office and at the recommendation of that office and also of his old friends from pre-revolutionary times, he set off every morning, as if to the office, in search of work. This was the first year of the first Five Year Plan. Staff were being taken on everywhere. At first the managers greeted father warmly, talked of the work he would do, even showed him where he would sit. Father filled out all the necessary forms in a very positive mood. He had always been a completely honest person, never hiding anything. So he wrote: former prince, former nobleman, former president of the district assembly of the nobility, former member of the Moscow Council, then listed the Soviet organisations in which he had worked from the first days after the revolution for the last eleven years. Seeing this, the managers, with embarrassment or fear in their voices, would say, "Come back in three days." One of them even shouted, "What are you sticking your nose in here for? We'll build socialism without you!"

The newspapers were full of the purges, screaming abuse at "former people", calling them class enemies, and, after picking on a particular organisation, listing all the officers and princes and officials and landowners who worked there, the very people who were probably working the hardest and most zealously out of conscientiousness and fear. I know of no man who worked harder than my father. The effect of all this was that his spirits gradually sank. All his life he had been used to working behind a desk. At home he was always busy, not going out much, but now he wandered about lost in thought, stopping and gazing around, then resuming his pacing. Once he even stopped by my desk and said, "Look, why don't you teach me to be a draughtsman?"

"Oh, Daddy, that needs a lot of training," I replied.

He suffered terribly from inactivity. Used to being the main bread-winner, he would ask my mother, "How are we going to exist?"

"Things will sort themselves out," my mother would reply, using the very words she had heard Steve Obolensky's servant use.

In fact, the occasional translations he did for the newspapers only earned a pittance, but father had been used to working since his days as a student and so continued to do them. One day Sonya came home from her public health institute to announce that there would be no further work for her. The statistics she had been compiling were now considered a waste of time, almost an act of sabotage. I do not know whether the doctors responsible for that work were arrested or not, but it is very likely they were. This meant that not only Sonya, but also my sister Lina and several other families of "former people" lost their livelihood.

Vladimir and I were still working and earning normally, mother was also making some money, and grandfather went on receiving his dollars, so all in all we could still just make ends meet.

6

One day in March, Vladimir's wife Elena came home from shopping and announced, "There's a crowd downstairs. Something's stuck up on the wall by the main door." I immediately went down to where people were stopping to read a notice. The writing was in the hand of our house superintendent, who was not hostile to us, but who always scrupulously carried out orders. I read (quoting from memory, but I believe accurately) as follows:

A list of all those deprived of their voting rights in No. 16 Eropkinsky Street:

1 *Golitsyn Vladimir Mikhailovich (the elder) – former prince, former governor, former head of the Moscow Council, former landowner, former house owner.*
2 *Golitsyn Mikhail Vladimirovich – former prince, former president of the assembly of nobles, former member of the Moscow Council, former landowner, former house owner, presently not working anywhere.*
3 *Golitsyn Anna Sergeievna – former princess, dependant of a former prince.*

4   *Golitsyn Vladimir Mikhailovich (the younger) – son of a former prince, not working anywhere.*
5   *Golitsyn Sophia Mikhailovna – daughter of a former prince, not working anywhere.*
6   *Golitsyn Elena Petrovna – dependant of a former prince.*
7   *Golitsyn Sergei Mikhailovich – son of a former prince, not working anywhere.*

My sisters Masha and Katya were not on the list as they were not yet eighteen-years-old. The list continued:

8   *Rosset Alexandra Nikolaievna – dependant of a former prince.*
9   *Babynina Elizaveta Alexandrovna – former landowner.*

These were the only names listed for our house. The whole thing was full of inaccuracies and deliberate distortions. Only grandfather was described correctly. My father had never been a landowner or owned any property. And did not his eleven years of employment since the revolution count for something? He had only been unemployed for the last two months, and was registered with the labour office. What about Vladimir, working successfully as an artist all these years? And myself, a student and draughtsman. It was true that Sonya was no longer working, but she had laboured over medical statistics with great dedication. Our poor Aunt Sasha, after leaving the Smolny Institute, had spent forty years earning her living as a governess to a number of families. Our neighbour, Babynina, was only included because she lived with us: had she lived with ordinary citizens, she would never have appeared on that list, as many former but untitled landowners managed to live in Moscow undisturbed.

Father sent me off to see whether similar lists had been put up on other houses. I walked down our street, along Ostozhenka, down Mansurovskaya and back home. Lists had been put up on some doorways, but not everywhere as there had not yet been time. It was surprising how many former titled people, former generals, former officials, landowners, officers, policemen, priests, deacons, NEPmen and industrialists still lived in Moscow. And their sons and daughters! In the papers such people were invariably described as the dregs, as class enemies.

Amongst our relatives and friends who had lost their voting rights were: my father's brothers, Nikolai and Vladimir and their families, the Urusovs, the Osorgins, the Samarins, many old people; and in Sergiyev Posad, both my uncles, Alyosha Lopukhin and Vladimir

Trubetskoi and their wives, the Istomins, and many monks. Some famous citizens were also deprived of the vote – Stanislavsky, Ostroukhov, the director of the Tretyakov Gallery, and Abrikosov, a professor of medicine, because he was the son of an industrialist.

There followed a lull, as if the authorities had had second thoughts. An article suggested that it was an error to include so many young people. The story was that an official came to Stanislavsky to apologise. "Write in a request," said the official "and we'll restore your rights at once." Stanislavsky refused, saying "You took them away, you restore them!" I do not know how it ended. In his autobiography, *My Life in Art* he does not mention this episode. Abrikosov did make a claim and his rights were immediately restored. But Ostroukhov's fate was tragic. In the late 1960s, I was working on my book about the artist Polenov, *A Sunny Palette*. In the library of the Writers' Guild I was given a thick file marked "I.S. Ostroukhov's Archive". It contained the rough drafts of many of his appeals to have his voting right restored, taken away because he had been an industrialist, together with his letters to Lunacharsky and to many other influential people. I was horrified to find this evidence of the insulting and demeaning attitude the authorities had adopted against this talented man who had achieved so much for Russian art. He had been driven out of the Tretyakov Gallery and had soon died. To judge by this documentation, his death had been brought on by that cruel experience.

Our literary course did not escape this scourge. A list went up, and the students approached and read it. There were seven names; a priest's son, a policeman's son, the daughter of a NEPman and the daughter of a former general. My name was also on that list – a former prince's son. So I was twice deprived. This fate did not, however, prevent me from attending lectures as before.

Father reproached Vladimir with failing to establish his legal status earlier and not paying attention to the question of union membership, thinking it would sort itself out. He also blamed Sonya for not claiming an official document while working at her medical statistics; now it was too late. It was clear, however, that apart from grandfather, now eighty-two-years-old, we had all been deprived of our rights unlawfully. This was how my father, a trained lawyer, assessed the situation. It was not how the authorities saw it.

"We must all put in our claims," said father. "We must get together all the papers that relate to our work."

"To the devil with them," said Vladimir. "I'm working and will go on working. I'm in demand everywhere."

"No, we must put in our claims," insisted father. "Otherwise there's the danger . . ." But what that danger was, he could not say. It was the same all over the country; people were not concerned at their loss of voting rights. "The devil take them," people said – meaning the authorities.

I wonder whether historians will ever be able to discover how many people were rejected in this way. Perhaps several million. Many abandoned their native villages and towns so as to conceal their situation in fresh documents and applications, and managed to continue to work and be paid. It was said of the famous Stakhanov that he had run away from being unmasked as a rich *kulak*.[21] But there were no hiding places for the princes Golitsyn. The burden of our origins was something we had to endure throughout our youth.

In Ozhegov's dictionary the word *lishenets* is defined as "a person deprived of their voting rights". But in the 1955 edition the word has disappeared – our venerable linguists have excluded it from the language. So only my contemporaries and people a little younger than me can remember what tears, suffering, lost hopes, insults, prison and death resulted from that word. Today, happy are the young who have no notion of the random cruelty and callousness that was perpetrated by human beings on other human beings in those dark days.

7

From the beginning of 1929 my relationship with Lyalya Ilyinskaya became close. It was not a matter of anything romantic between us (she had a succession of suitors), but a platonic friendship, growing out of her delight in my writings about the Northern Lakes. I went frequently to her house on Povarskaya Street and we talked endlessly, working ourselves up into exalted states of mind, and she would read me her poetry, or the poems of the Symbolists. Together we went to our course on literature. Her mother, the medical doctor in their district, was very kind to me, sometimes inviting me to their meals. I collected information in our library for her husband's literary studies, as he was in exile somewhere along the river Vychegda.

---

21. *A.G. Stakhanov (1906-77) was widely and vigorously publicised by the Soviet authorities as a super-productive miner who regularly cut many times his quota of coal. His record of two hundred and twenty-five tons of coal in one shift was certainly a fabrication. Still, the term "stakhanovite" became familiar worldwide, while he himself rose to high rank in the industry.*

One day I was paid a hefty sum of money for my maps and invited Lyalya for a ride in a *likhach* (fast sledge). It is the only time in my life that I have experienced that thrilling pleasure. We sat pressed together on a narrow seat, our legs covered by a bearskin rug, and the sledge raced along, bouncing and tilting on the rutted, uneven snow. Our route went from Arbat Square, where these fast sledge drivers waited outside the Prague restaurant, along Sadovaya-Kudrinskaya and Bretskaya, past Alexandrovsky station and right out to the park at Petrovskoye, then turned at the church in the village of Vsevsyatsko and returned by the same route to Arbat Square. That was the last year that there were such special sledges in Moscow.

Lyalya and I were entranced by the story of the invisible city of Kityezh, lost in the waters of Lake Svetloyar, and read everything that had been written about that poetic and religious legend by those who had been there – Korolenko, Merezhkovsky, Durylin and Prishvin. Lyalya suggested that we should make the journey there together, and we set about planning our route, first by train to Nizhny Novgorod, where I had been two years before and could show her all the sights, and then on to the little town of Semenov, from which we would finish our journey to the lake on foot. Pilgrims made a point of arriving there by the feast day of the Mother of God of Vladimir, the twenty-third of June (Old Style), which meant we had enough time ahead of us to take our exams at the School of Literature and set off in early June. There were persistent rumours that our course was to be closed down, but I hoped the decision would be reversed. We intended, after Svetloyar, to wander around the area of Melnikov-Pechersko with its Old Believers' hermitages, before ending up in Kerzhenets, extolled by the writer Korolenko.

I told my mother of our dream. I was now twenty-years-old and felt I did not need to ask my parents for their permission. To my surprise, mother was aghast. "What are you thinking of?" she cried out.

"The two of us are setting off on a journey. What's so wrong with that?" I replied.

"You know how your trip will end up?"

"End up? It'll end up with me writing stories and Lyalya poems, or even an epic."

"It'll end up with a little baby."

Lyalya's mother, Sophia Grigorevnya, was also upset by our plans, but her eighteen-year-old daughter was used to being independent. She probably told her mother, "Don't interfere in my life. We've decided, and that's it."

Our happy lives continued the while, even though some of us became "deprived" people. We danced the foxtrot in the largest available homes; at the Ilyinskys on Povarskaya Street and in our flat on Eropkinsky. The Nikulichevy invited us to their place on Myertvaya Street; they were a very hospitable family, the father a former capitalist and NEPman, and there were two daughters and a son. We also went to the luxurious apartment of Alexandra Lvovna Tolstaya on Merslyakovsky Street. She was away in Japan lecturing about her famous father, so it was her secretary, a young-looking and energetic lady, who received us. Much later, when it was clear that Tolstoy's daughter was critical of the Soviet Union, the secretary was put in prison, and the apartment allocated to some Party bigwig.

The Nikulichevy sisters decided to put on a play. They chose Goldoni's *The Hotel Manageress*. The actors were the two sisters, with Mikhail and Andrei Rayevsky, Lena Urusova and someone else. The director was Yusha Samarin. The rehearsals went famously, but then suddenly stopped and the play cancelled. I imagine the Nikulichevys, as people who had lost their voting rights, were worried about possible consequences. My cousin, Alexei Bobrinsky, was a frequent member of our crowd. We all knew that for the past four years he had been a secret agent of the OGPU, and warned everybody of this, but we assumed that his main task was to keep an eye on the guests received by his sister, Sonya, and her English husband, Reginald Witter. Alexei was also working as a secretary to an American journalist. In short, he had plenty to do elsewhere. Nevertheless, we were careful what we said in front of him.

We were playing charades one day. In the course of the game someone piled chair upon chair to make a tower, which suddenly collapsed. Lyalya shouted out, "That's like building Socialism!", then bit her tongue. There was a sudden silence. Out of the corner of my eye I watched Alexei. After all, in those days you could be arrested for such words.

One day Alexei Bobrinsky turned up when our Golitsyn cousins, Sasha and Olechka, Lelya Davydova, my sister Masha and one or two others were together in the Ilyinsky's flat. He said, "Why don't we agree to meet once a week and make a list of the members of our little company?" Names were mentioned, which Alexei wrote down. Lyala named her cousin, Vera Bernadskaya, who did not belong to our little group. We had studied together at school, but in parallel classes, and when school finished we never saw her. When the list was finished, Alexei proposed we should all sign; he held out the list and his American fountain pen – at that time, a marvellously rare object.

Lyalya made to sign, when Sasha, with a grimace, dug me in the ribs.

"There's no need to sign," he said loudly.

"No, there's no need to sign," I said also, sensing something fishy about all this.

Shrugging his shoulders, Alexei said, "Alright, as you wish," and put the list in his pocket. I invite the reader not to forget this seemingly insignificant episode.

15. Eleven Days in Prison

1

I concluded my chapter on the School of Literature with a scene where two friends are walking along the Sadovoye ring road, reciting poetry, their heads full of dreams, and where the one says to the other, "Shall we address each other with the familiar form of 'you'?" And the other replies, "Yes, let's." The first was Valery Pertsov; I was the other.

We arrived at Zubovsky Square. My way home was along Prechistenkaya, whilst Valery needed to catch a tram. He remembered, however, a book of ours that he wanted, and although it was midnight I asked him up to our flat. Masha opened the door for us and started to chat to Valery, who looked embarrassed, while I went to get the book. Vladimir came out of his room, happy to see a guest and have an excuse for a smoke. And then the bell rang – once, twice, three times.

Vladimir opened the door, and in burst a man in glasses and a leather jacket, with a soldier behind him wearing the hated blue cap with a red border and, lastly, the sleepy house superintendent. The man in glasses marched up to me, training his revolver on my chest, and shouted, "Hands up!"

I was so shocked I just stared at him with my arms by my side.

"Hands up! Hands up!" he roared. The soldier began to pull out his revolver. I got my hands awkwardly into the air. The man in glasses frisked me roughly on both sides, then stepped back and held out to me a piece of paper, on which I read "Order to search and arrest Golitsyn, Sergei Mikhailovich", signed "Deputy Chairman of the OGPU, G. Yagoda." My immediate thought was, thank God, it's only me.

Vladimir took the paper and read it. Mother came out of her bedroom, read the paper and looked at me with sorrow. Other relatives did the same. Finally, father read it and laid it down on the table. There was total silence. Only later did it occur to us to wonder

327

how the man in glasses had pointed his revolver at me. How had he known what I looked like?

"Where's your work table?" he asked. I showed him. He went up to it, as did all our family. "Get further away!" he ordered them, and pointed at me, "You stand there!" My heart missed a beat when I saw that the notebook with my stories about the Northern lakes, lovingly copied out by my mother, lay for all to see on the left hand side of the desk. But now a miracle happened – I cannot describe it otherwise. The man in glasses seized the notebooks on the right hand side; these were my lecture notes. And mother, with uncharacteristic swiftness, grabbed my precious notebook and laid it on the windowsill.

I began to explain to the man the contents of the different notebooks. This one was the history of art, that one the history of German literature. I said how interesting the Nibelungen were – I wonder whether he had ever heard of them? I talked about the Renaissance and the Reformation. He listened, picking up the notebooks one by one and leafing through them. Finding the diary of my journey with Andrei Kiselev, he was clearly pleased and laid it aside separately. He opened the drawer and found letters, and a blank sheet headed "Pioneer's Truth" with the printed signature "With the Committee's Greetings". I explained that I was not only a student, but also earned a living doing drawings for magazines. This whole scene took place under the reproachful eyes of our ancestors' portraits from the reigns of Peter, Anna, Elizabeth and Catherine.

A piece of paper covered with rows of figures and criss-crossing lines now appeared in the official's hand. My sister Sonya was on flirtatious terms with the two brothers Yarkho. The elder, Boris Isaakovich or Bobochka, was a scholar of literature. Spectacled and plump, he was a lecturer at the school, while his younger brother, Grigory Isaakovich or Grisha, was tall and thin and worked as a translator. They visited us on occasion, and Bobochka, for the purpose of his academic studies into rhyming couplets, had commissioned me to lay out the complex notations that he had computed in diagrammatic form.

The man now put Bobochka's sheets of paper to one side. I realised that he intended to remove these, and was aghast at the thought of all that work being lost. I tried to persuade him, explaining what those figures meant, telling him how Russian rhyming couplets were constructed. He clearly found my explanations suspicious, and had obviously decided these papers were the work of a spy.

328

When the search was over there began the depressing time of waiting for the police van to arrive. Still keeping my diary, one or two letters, and those pages of Bobochka's computations, the man sat down to write his report. The sleepy house superintendent signed his name as witness and was ordered to leave. We all waited, standing in silence. Only the samovar made a noise. Mother looked at me with unspeakable sadness. My sisters gathered a spoon, a bowl, sugar, sandwiches, cigarettes and a blanket together in a pillowcase. Our family knew all too well what an arrested person needed.

The van arrived; the time had come for our sad farewells. Each member of the family hugged and kissed me. Sonya and Masha whispered the same words to me, "Reply only to the questions, nothing else." Father and mother signed me with the cross. Mother afterwards told me that at that moment I had looked like a martyred St Sebastian. My youthful immaturity made me oddly proud of being arrested, but I did not feel like a martyr. I visualised martyrs as early Christians going to their death in the Coliseum or, in Russia, Old Believers setting fire to themselves, or Decembrists facing execution and exile for their revolutionary ideals. Then there were martyrs like Uncle Misha Lopukhin, refusing to swear an oath against his conscience, or my brother-in-law, Georgy Osorgin, a loving husband and father, asserting his fidelity to monarchy, for which he was sentenced to ten years in prison. Or even my friend Sergei Istomin, declaring himself a monarchist at the age of seventeen.

And I? I had expected to be arrested sooner or later, and at any time, simply because I was the son of a prince. I was prepared for an interrogation and had decided that in reply to the question about my political views I would say "loyal". This was the reply my father and brother and many others had given, and had been set free, though something was also owed to outside intervention. Many others, however, had signed statements of loyalty to the Soviet Union and still received sentences of imprisonment. And others, like Alexei Bobrinsky, sold themselves for their freedom. I was prepared for my awful fate. I knew that no threats would make me undertake anything shameful and that therefore all my hopes would be dashed when I did not sign. It was with such thoughts that I went down into the street.

St Sebastian had died from the arrows shot at him, inspiring artists by his martyrdom. Later in life when I saw pictures of the young man with the blood gushing from his wounds, I could not help remembering, with some irony, my mother's words that night.

2

Dawn had risen when I climbed into the canvas-topped lorry. A sullen old man and a woman with tear-stained cheeks were sitting on the benches, together with several guards. We drove along Prechisten-kaya, Volkhonko, Mokhovaya and across Teatralnaya Square. At that hour the streets were deserted except for a group of drunken revellers who paid no attention to our lorry. We reached the most feared building in our country, the Lubyanka prison, not the main building but the one on the corner of Myasnitsky Street. Today, both these buildings are joined up. I was put with the old man into a tiny, windowless cell. There were two stools, a table with pens and an inkwell, and a bare electric bulb in the ceiling. We were given forms to fill out with our names and dates of birth and so on. On the second, blank page we were supposed to write a detailed autobiography.

The old man wrote for a time, then dropped the pen. "I can't understand why they've arrested me."

"I also don't know why they've arrested me," I echoed.

His name was Mazurov. I know nothing more about him. He was taken away and I sat alone until a soldier came in, made me undress, searched me all over, felt through all my clothes and then left me alone again. After two hours I was taken out, put into a lorry alone and driven to the dreaded No. 14 Lubyanka, the original head-quarters of the Cheka and notorious for the horrors that took place there. (Today the building looks very attractive, painted blue with plaster decorations, and serving as the reception area for the Moscow section of the KGB). I was put in cell No. 11 on the first floor, a small windowless room with a light bulb in the ceiling, protected by a wire cover so that nobody could throw a boot at it. There were ten men lying about, wearing nothing but their underwear; in those days the rule that you could not sleep during the day but must sit quietly "repenting of your crimes", had not yet been introduced.

Most were asleep, others were talking. I was asked for the latest news in the newspapers. I remember an old German, a NEPman from Kaluga. He had been arrested for owning a sausage factory and had been awaiting interrogation for more than two months. He had lost half his weight and kept showing everyone his loose trousers. I also remember a handsome, long-bearded Jewish money changer who was taken for interrogation two or three times a day. On his return he would lie groaning and crying on his mattress. They were trying to get him to reveal where he had hidden his gold and valuables. His groans prevented us sleeping.

The following night I was woken by a shout, "You Golitsyn?"

I leapt up. A soldier with a list in his hand stood before me. "Name and patronymic? Get dressed, you're off for questioning!"

I was escorted along the corridor and as we went, I counted the numbers on the doors. Around the corner I was put into a small room furnished with a desk, on which were a lamp in a green shade, a few files and some pieces of paper. Behind the desk sat a young, slightly-built soldier.

3

Sixty years later I still have a crystal-clear memory of that interrogation. The officer had a handsome, broad-browed face, with fair hair swept back. His dark eyes looked me over keenly. He was wearing a cloak with a single thick red bar on the lapels, which meant he had the rank of brigadier. My immediate thought was that I must be considered to be a serious criminal, but then I remembered someone telling me that in order to frighten prisoners, they often used the trick of dressing their interrogators in high-ranking uniforms. I could see the cloak was too big for him. My fear vanished. I even smiled to myself.

"Sit down!" he said.

I sat down on the stool. The lamp shone brightly on me, leaving his face in the shadows. For some minutes his large, dark eyes stared out at me from this half-light. Leaning forward, he kept his eyes fixed on me, as if he wanted to see right into me. I could not stop my eyes from lowering, but at the same time I knew this was all a masquerade to frighten me.

"Have a smoke," he said suddenly, and held out his packet. He lit his own and then mine. I dragged on my cigarette as he continued to watch me from the shadows. What I thought was, "Devil take it, when are you going to stop staring at me!" Then abruptly he began to fire disconnected phrases at me:

"So that's what you look like! We've heard a lot about you. They all say you're an arch monarchist, and not just a monarchist but also a declared fascist! A prince – a descendant of Ryurik – a class enemy of Soviet rule!"

"I'm not a descendant of Ryurik but of Gedymin," I managed to interrupt his flow of words.

He fell silent, continuing to fix me with his fine eyes, and then asked in a quiet voice, "Who's Gedymin?"

I started to explain in detail that this was the name of a fourteenth-century Lithuanian grand-prince. His great-great-grandson, the warrior Mikhail Ivanovich Bulgakov, had been given the nickname "Golitsa" in the time of Ivan the Terrible, because in battle he had lost a hand and wore a prosthetic iron gauntlet, a *golitsa*. I told him how the Golitsyns had produced many boyars and warriors, including two field marshals, who had died for the Motherland.

The interrogator shouted, "And with such ancestors, you're not a monarchist!"

"I've never been one. I've always been loyal to Soviet rule, always."

"Prove it!"

"I will prove it!" I began to outline my father's views. In conversations with me, father had often explained that he was against the autocracy of the imperial throne, that he thought it was an evil influence in Russian life, and that we should have a republic like in France, or if not, as the lesser of two evils, a monarchy like the British. My father's views turned out to be very appropriate to my situation, and I outlined them so clearly and fully that they seemed to produce a favourable impression on my interlocutor, who stopped talking about the monarchy.

I cannot now recall the order in which he questioned me, but I do remember every single question. He persistently asked about Lyalya Ilyinskaya's cousin, Vera Bernadskaya; who was she? What were her political views? I replied that since leaving school three years ago I had not seen her, and had no idea at all about her political opinions. I found out later that she had been arrested at that same time as me, and at her interrogation had been asked the same questions, and had replied more or less as I did.

"We know all about you. You've only to start thinking something and we already know all about it."

Such statements might have a frightened an inexperienced youth, but I was prepared and knew they were all a piece of acting. The man kept asking me why the play at the Nikulichevys had been cancelled. I had no idea, and even today do not know, but he kept coming back to this point. He showed me a paper on which was typed a well-known poem by Maximilian Voloshin, "Suzdal and Moscow are not for you . . ."

"You see the sort of counter-revolutionary doggerel your friends are spreading about?"

"They're not at all counter-revolutionary. The author is living a quiet life in the Crimea."

"And who's this?" he held out a photograph of General Annenkov of the White Guards.

"But that was printed on the cover of the magazine *Ogonyok*."

He said, "By the way, I read your diary with great interest. I see you're a traveller."

He questioned me about the political views held by Yusha Samarin, Artemi Rayevsky and others. I said I had no idea about them, and that when we met together we never talked politics; our interests were literature, the theatre and the cinema. I kept quiet about our pleasure in dancing the foxtrot.

"I've never heard of anyone having literary convictions!" laughed my questioner.

Sitting opposite him, I tried hard to remember anything incriminating that might have been said in our conversations. All I could think of was how the tower of chairs had collapsed, and Lyalya's remark about building socialism. I could think of nothing else. Many of us were religious, some going regularly to church, others, like myself, going only rarely. My religious feelings were that I believed in God but did not put Him first in my life. I was frightened the man would ask whether I believed in God. I knew I could never deny my faith, and was preparing to enter into a detailed explanation of how I could be a Christian, whilst at the same time being loyal to Soviet rule.

Thank God, he did not ask that question. Unexpectedly, he commented that I was still an adolescent and so not considered sufficiently adult to be invited to the Witters. I realised that, thanks to our childhood friendship, and wishing to defend me, this version of my supposed adolescent status must have reached the interrogator from Alexei Bobrinsky. I suppose I should have thanked him later, but there were too many weighty reasons why I could never have done that.

I pretended to be offended, and replied, "That's not true, I'm a grown-up. Nobody's ever thought me an adolescent."

My interrogator smiled. I think I had once again made a favourable impression on him. He held out a piece of paper. I began to read it and froze. It was the very same list that Alexei Bobrinsky had written out in Lyala's apartment, written in fountain-pen ink. Now I understood why my interrogator was so interested in Vera Bernadskaya – her name was on that list. And at the bottom were also the names of my sister-in-law Elena's four cousins – Dimitri and Andrei Gudovich, Boris and Yura Saburov.

"Look at that, all those princes and counts and courtiers, that's your circle of friends!"

I replied that Elena's cousins had never been part of our circle of friends. I could have offered some much less famous names – for instance, my sister Masha's cavaliers, Igor Daksergof, Valery Pertsov, Andrei Kiselev and Kolya Davydov, but why get them mixed up in this?

"You've been left untouched too long," said the officer, "and you've become brazen. Look at the smart set you frequent, and dance your little foxtrot and tell anti-Soviet jokes."

I cried out, "We never tell such jokes!"

It was true that in the first years after the revolution stories about our leaders had circulated widely; but now people held their tongues, knowing that such jokes could lead to ten years in the Gulag.

"How have we become brazen?" I asked angrily.

The officer raised his voice, "I warn you, I ask the questions, you answer them."

He began to write out his report. I cannot now remember exactly what he wrote. I had said nothing that could possibly incriminate Vera Bernadskaya, or Yusha Samarin, or Artemi Rayevsky or Lyalya Ilyinskaya. The words "I do not remember" featured extensively. I did not remember political discussion, or anti-Soviet jokes, or anti-Soviet organisations. There was no reference to anybody's criminal activities. I objected to the words "I do not remember" and wanted him to write "I never heard".

"It's all the same," he said. "Do you really think I'm going to rewrite the report just for that?" I read it through and signed it. He handed me another form, on which was already written – "Investigator Gorbunov Nikolai Ivanovich accuses the following person under article 58.10 of the Penal Code". He asked, "Do you know what that article is?"

"I know," I cried. "It's not true! Not true! I have never been involved in anything anti-Soviet." And I added indignantly, "You've not proved that I'm guilty of anything!"

"And you've not proved that the accusation against you is unfounded."

Article 58 was a merciless article in the penal code. It covered all counter-revolutionary activities in about fifteen points. Point 10 was considered the "lightest" and was the most frequently invoked, and yet it carried a sentence of ten years. All in all, this article 58, according to Western historians, caused the death of some twenty million innocent people.

The interrogation was over. I stood up and had the impertinence to ask him for a cigarette. He laughed, and held out the packet; for a second I thought of taking five, but refrained. I said, "Goodbye." He laughed again and responded, "Goodbye."

As I write now, I realise that my interrogation was nothing compared to the horrible tortures that were to start up only a year or two later in the cellars of the OGPU and the NKVD. Indeed, I can say that the man interrogated me in quite an objective manner. But now my life was suddenly confined to the walls of a cell. Only a day earlier I would have been thinking of delivering a diagram to Bobochka, and then going to the editorial office of the *Universal Pathfinder* or *Pioneer's Truth* for new orders. I would have gone on to the cinema to see the next reel of a Douglas Fairbanks film. I would also be dreaming of my journey with Lyalya to the city of Kityezh. All this had now been taken away. Where would I be exiled? Would I be able to go on with my writing?

I woke after a poor night. Breakfast was brought in – porridge, a piece of bread, some sugar and a can of hot water for tea. I had just gone back to sleep when the door open and I was shaken awake. The guard was looking at his piece of paper, "Golitsyn?"

I sat up and gave my name and patronymic.

"You, and your things."

4

"Your things" meant freedom. With trembling hands I tied up my clothes in the pillowcase and set off down the corridor, the guard at my heels. We went down the stairs into the courtyard, where some other men with their things were already standing. A black police van, known as the "black crow", with two tiny openings fore and aft, drew up. So it was not going to be freedom after all. Someone said, "Probably it's Butyrka."

My name was one of the first called. I climbed in and sat on a bench right in the front, very close to one of the tiny openings behind the driver. The benches filled up, leaving the last on board to stand jammed together in the middle. They were ordered to squeeze up, and pushed each other until they were like sardines in a tin. The door was slammed shut, the air became foul-smelling. Someone cried out, "We must protest. We're going to be suffocated!" But nobody responded; they were like a flock of sheep.

The vehicle went along Bolshaya Dimitrovka, then Malaya. That meant we were going to Butyrka prison. A man fainted but could not fall, remaining jammed between others. Someone else was sick on his neighbour. At Novoslobodskaya we turned into a courtyard and stopped. The door was opened, we all hustled to get out, sucking in air like fish hauled out of water. I looked with curiosity at the high walls and ancient round towers, very like the Kremlin, that rose around us. In the eighteenth century, one of these towers had held Pugachov, the peasant rebel leader, in solitary confinement as he awaited execution. I wondered whether some poor man was sharing that fate today.

Iron gates opened with a screech. I remembered the lines from Dante, "Abandon hope, all ye that enter here", and the contemporary saying, "Who's not been in, will be put in; and who's been in, will never forget". We were lined up in fours and led into a large room, where we signed up for ration cards and were searched, though rather superficially. A couple of hours later I went with two other unfortunates to cell No. 55 on the second floor. It was a large room, with two grated windows on one side and a row of bunks along the opposite wall on which were sitting a number of prisoners, most of them only in their underwear. In the middle was a low table. Later, when Ezhov replaced Yagoda, the windows were covered with so-called "muzzles", but at this time they still gave a view onto the exercise courtyard and other buildings, behind whose windows one could see more prisoners. A tiny patch of sky was visible, but not a trace of green – neither the tops of trees, hidden by the high walls, nor a blade of grass between the cobblestones of the exercise yard. I was shown a bunk close to the large zinc toilet bucket.

I will describe some of the people I met there. The bunk on the far left, close to the window, was occupied by Fyodorov, a professor of metallurgy, a teacher at the Moscow Higher Technical Institute and a consultant in the building of metallurgical factories. He was a bearded, solid man of imposing aspect, invariably dressed in a good suit. He had been arrested two months earlier and asked to write out a long autobiography, but had never been taken for questioning, nor accused of anything. Later he suddenly got ten years in the Gulag. Much later I read a book by Alexander Bek about the famous steelmaker, Kurako, and found Professor Fyodorov referred to as the son of an admiral and a vicious "saboteur".

Next to Fyodorov was a civil engineer, Drozdov, a little old man with white hair and glasses. He had taken part in the building of the railway line to Khabarovsk and other places, and was charged with sabotage. Then came two NEPmen, one a heavy-built Russian, the other a delicate Jew. Whilst I was there they were both exiled – one to Vyatka, the other to Ufa. The Russian was pleased as he had feared it would be the Gulag and his property would be confiscated, whereas now he would at least travel by passenger train to his appointed place of exile. The Jew, however, was very upset, stating that he had done nothing wrong, and appealing to us, "All my life I've been a merchant. My father was a merchant. What on earth will I do in a place like Ufa?"

There was a member of the Znamenye church choir. The church, a building in the Naryshkin baroque style, still stands behind the old university building. I do not know what the accusation was against the choir. Another prisoner, who I saw in the distance exercising, was the church elder Pribytkov, who had paid for Vladimir and Elena's wedding. He still had the full figure that gave him a resemblance to the hero of Gogol's tale *Taras Bulba*. At his interrogation the singer in our cell justified himself by saying that he did not believe in God and only went to church because he loved the music. Later on, all the members of that church choir were sent into exile.

There was also a tailor, a Tartar who repaired old clothes, mostly for other Tartars. Despite the lack of space he managed to bow as he said his prayers every day. There was a youth, the nephew of the late Commissioner of Justice, Kursky. In the building opposite was another nephew; both lads contrived to exchange signals with each other.

Victor Kholoptsev was a member of the *Konsomol* from Chernigov. All the *Konsomol* youth had been arrested there for an offence that was treated as a major crime, namely "nationalism". They had been brought to Moscow for questioning. Kholoptsev was a well-read, cultivated fellow, very thin and weary-looking. He had already been in prison for a long time and his pale face made him look like a corpse, but his spirit was strong and manly.

In a bunk to the right of the door lay a tall, athletic man with a long blond beard, the head of the depot at one of the stations on the Ryazan-Urals railway. He spent a lot of time caring for and comforting his neighbour, Kalyapin, an engineer, also one of the bosses on that railway, who was suffering from extreme anxiety about his fate. All the managers of the railway had been arrested and the case, under investigation in Moscow, was being treated as a very serious one.

Nearby I saw a middle-aged monk, whose name was, I think, Father Georgy Belayev from the monastery of Golutvin near Kolomna. Very much later I learned that he was he was held in great respect by the faithful. In the cell he was mostly silent, and was sometimes even mocked by the others. He got into conversation with me, rather cautiously at first, but then more openly. In a low voice he advised me to pray, and told me that he was praying for me. There were many clergy in Butyrka. Looking at the prisoners out in the exercise yard, there would always be three or four priests among them, walking about in pairs, heads bowed, just as in Nesterov's paintings. It was a welcome distraction to gaze down on the yard and recognise other prisoners, which was why the windows were later sealed off.

We also had in our cell a very pleasant agronomist who turned out to be an artist by the name of Staronosov. He was exiled to Kazakhstan that year, and my brother Vladimir made efforts to get him commissions from various magazines. Then there were six Chinese. The Chinese general, Chan Dsao Lin, had just expropriated a branch of the Trans-Siberian railway, built under the Tsars, that ran through Manchuria. Our authorities had swallowed the insult, but in return arrested all the Chinese in Moscow and the rest of the country. Among these six in our cell were a tailor, a merchant and a student of the Sun Yat Sen Communist University, who had difficulty understanding why he had been arrested.

I am sure that none of those I have been describing were in any way guilty. There were, however, also genuinely guilty people. A major court case was taking place at that time, to do with an organisation called Mologoles, where a group of managers had been expropriating its funds. We had the deputy chief accountant in our cell. He was escorted every day to the court, telling us about it on his return. In the end the authorities took into consideration his proletarian origins and sentenced him to a mere three years in exile; he was very pleased with that. There were also six restless, noisy young thieves in with us, but as they were in the minority, they behaved perfectly well. One day they were all very excited on seeing a stately, white-bearded and dignified man being escorted across the yard; it seemed he was more or less the King of Moscow thieves.

There were no members of the opposition to Bolshevism amongst us. This was a period when such people were being rounded up, but were held in the Lubyanka, or if in Butyrka, in separate cells. We saw them exercising in the yard, where they walked in twos, looking just like a picture by Van Gogh. Once we found a message written in pencil on the wall of the toilets – "Leninists – they are beginning to sentence us to the Gulag. Be strong!"

More and more prisoners were put into our cell until it was so full people were having to sleep on the floor. These new prisoners would arrive, confused and miserable, and be shown to a bunk by the elder of the cell. The bunks now mostly held two men; you had to lie on your side, then at the word of command, both of you would turn over on to the other side. Amongst the newcomers was a pilot in training, his epaulettes torn off, who was convinced he would be released at any moment. There was a ragged, barefoot, silent little man who had been picked up at Yarolslavsky station, and a well-dressed man wearing American glasses, deputy director of one of the hospitals in Moscow. He had doubtless seemed a god to his hospital staff, but here lay silent, huddled up in the foetal position. There was a peasant from Kolomensk, a black-bearded man who, the moment he lay down on his bunk, covered his face with his hands and prayed. Later he told us that he, his brother, his father and grandfather were all market gardeners, supplying vegetables to Moscow. Living all together with their families, they were Old Believers, and had all been arrested – why?

Parcels of provisions were allowed once a week. Some of them were very splendid, containing rich dishes and pies, bread rolls and ham. Monday was the day for the letter "G". I was surprised when my name was called out; I had only just been transferred to Butyrka and here was a parcel, like a message from home. The list of contents was in my mother's handwriting. I was only allowed to write the words "Received in full" and sign, and not a word more, but I dared to add the letter "k" for kiss.

The prison routine was organised around three distributions of food; breakfast was a can of tea, some bread and three lumps of sugar to last the whole day; in the middle of the day there was soup and weak porridge, then in the evening something else. Once a day we were taken to the toilet and for exercise. There was no peace at night as the door kept opening for people to be taken out for questioning.

5

One night it was my turn. To my great surprise, the warder was a young woman, fairly pretty, who looked good in her uniform and shoulder belt. Our eyes met briefly and I thought I detected a flash of pity in her eyes: "So young and already a criminal!" I went ahead of her down the corridor, turning now left, now right. Normally the guards looked at one with cold, glassy eyes, as if looking at a wall rather than a human being. Whereas she . . . I turned and winked at her, as I never did to girls of my acquaintance.

"Don't look round!" she said loudly, but her voice did not ring out as a command. Going down the stairs I again looked round and gave her a wink. "Don't look round!" she ordered again, but her voice expressed both annoyance and weakness. Had I turned and winked again she might well have started crying.

She led me into a large room with a stone floor. Under a naked bulb in the ceiling, sitting behind a scratched old desk in an old chair that probably dated back to tsarist times, was the same interrogator, Gorbunov. Now he was not wearing a brigadier's cloak, only a plain blue shirt. "So," I thought, "that's his real uniform." He began by saying that loyalty was not enough, that I should show dedication by helping the Soviet Union. I realised what was coming, but pretended not to understand. He came to the point:

"In a moment I'm going to ask you to sign a piece of paper. By signing it, you will be agreeing to help us and, what's more, help us in certain tasks."

"No," I said quietly, lowering my eyes.

"Either you are free tomorrow, or I send you to rot in Turukhansk."

I stiffened, looking straight into his fine, dark eyes. "Then Turukhansk." I was proud of this answer for the rest of my life, though I did not like to talk about it.

The man looked at me for a long time in silence, and I thought he was preparing to cajole or threaten me. Unexpectedly he said, "I won't insist. I thought you would not sign. Anyway, help from people like you isn't worth a thing." He began to write, then handed me the result. Even after sixty years I can remember that text almost word for word:

> I, the undersigned, swear that I will never speak to anyone, not even my nearest and dearest, about what was discussed at my interrogation in June 1929. If ever I speak of these matters I will be guilty of revealing state secrets and will be liable to prosecution under Soviet Law.

I signed. Gorbunov stood up and in a quite different voice, such as he would use when speaking to his wife, said, "The interrogation is over. Let me give you a personal piece of advice. Major projects are under construction now in our country, yet you're dancing the foxtrot. You should join the creative efforts of the masses. My advice is, leave Moscow, get out of Moscow to work on one of the big projects, and show your loyalty to Soviet rule by your hard and zealous work."

His words struck me as coming from the heart. I said sadly, "But no one would give me a job – without my rights, and with my origins."

"You'll get your right to vote back again," he said confidently.

"If only you knew how important it is for me to live in Moscow. I want to be a writer."

"Drop silly dreams," he said. "Take my advice, get out of Moscow."

He pressed a button, the guard came in and escorted me away. I was so worked up I did not look back at her; my thoughts were far from girls. Would I really be freed? Gorbunov had not said so directly, only hinted. I was torn between hope and despair.

6

The next day I spent in a state of excitement, quietly talking to Father Georgy about what, I cannot recall, but not of course about my interrogation. Suddenly he said, "But they're going to release you."

In the afternoon of the next day the door of our cell was opened with a screech. The guard read from a piece of paper, "Golitsyn!" I got to my feet and gave my name and patronymic. He said, "With your things, and hurry!" I was so nervous my hands were trembling uncontrollably, causing me to fumble with my things. A Tartar came over, helped me get everything into the pillowcase. Father Georgy whispered in my ear, "God bless you."

The guard was getting impatient. A dozen pairs of very sad eyes followed me to the door. As I went out I said, "May everything go well with you all!" I was escorted along endless corridors until we reached a room where an officer, sitting behind a partition, said, "You're released," and put a paper on front of me for signature. It turned out that I was signing a pledge not to leave Moscow. At the time I was thinking only of my freedom. I had been in prison a mere eleven days, three in the Lubyanka, eight in Butyrka, but those were days I shall never forget. What a lot of ink I've used describing them!

Feeling totally confused I stood on the corner of Novoslobodskaya and Lesnaya streets with my pillowcase under my arm. The sun was shining. I had not a penny in my pocket. Should I ride on the buffers of a tram? I saw a cab, hailed it and drove, bumping and rattling along Moscow's cobbles, talking to the cabbie, who happened to be a fellow countryman from Tula. He told me he was frightened of going back there. The country was now suffering massive collectivisation of the peasantry, with the richer families being driven out, exiled or arrested. Here in Moscow, it was impossible to buy oats for the horse. I suggested that he sell his cab and get himself a job on a construction project. Finally, we reached our street. I leaped out, took the stairs two at a time, rang the doorbell and fell into my parents' arms. One of my sisters ran down to pay the cabbie. Then we all sat down around the table and I was given a plate of soup. As I ate, and was talking in a disjointed sort of way, mother suddenly interrupted me and asked, "And did they make you an offer?"

There was total silence as they awaited my answer. What could I say? Only the day before I had signed a paper saying that I would never ever, even to my nearest family, say anything about my interrogation. I said nothing, but looked at my father, mother and brother in turn. Mother saved the situation by saying, "And what a good friend you have. He came round three times to ask about you and see if he could be of any help." She was referring to Valery Pertsov, with whom I had agreed to be on terms of the familiar "you" just an hour before my arrest.

Then the bell rang; it was Uncle Koka – Nikolai Mikhailovich Matveyev – a relative of the Davydovs and a descendant of the well-known eighteenth-century public figure Artamon Matveyev, a connection of which he was very proud. He was a solitary old bachelor, once a legal official, on living goodness knows what resources. He knew seven families, each of which he visited once a week. At our place he would eat with us and then be put to sit with grandfather to talk quietly about the good old days. On this day, however, it was I who was the centre of attention and the one who did all the talking. I knew that Yusha Samarin had been the only other person arrested. Father told me that he had been to see Peshkova and that she had shown a great interest in my case. Then I was interrupted by Uncle Koka.

"And when the Cheka arrested me in 1918," he began in a sad voice, and out of politeness we all sat listening to his boring story. Then I was able to resume my own story, but was once again interrupted by, "And when in 1922 the OGPU in Tambov again arrested me . . ."

Mother could not stand this. Without any ceremony, she cut him off, saying, "I want to hear my son's story, not yours!"

The bell rang. This time it was Valery Pertsov. We embraced each other with great joy. I went on with my story and they all listened eagerly, sometimes laughing, sometimes looking serious, as I told them my adventures and how I had taken a second cigarette from the interrogator and about his blue shirt. Valery put in, "Seryozha feels like the birthday boy!" and everybody laughed.

Now, sixty years on, I must try to answer the question my reader must be wanting to put: that is, why was I released so quickly? I think there were three reasons. I have no doubt that my answers made a favourable impression on my interrogator. Secondly, my mother prayed fervently for me. Thirdly, Ekaterina Pavlovna Peshkova intervened on my behalf, which was probably the most important reason. Two days after my release, father went to see Peshkova on some business of his own. When she heard I had been released, she said she would like to see me. At her modest office, she received me straight away, sitting me down to face her at her desk. This was the first time I had been so close to her; she was strikingly beautiful, with a beauty that one simply could not ignore. Looking at me with her wonderful, deep blue eyes, she asked me that same fateful question, "And did they make you an offer?"

I was silent. What could I say, after signing that paper?

She said, "I understand. And what did you reply?"

"I replied, Turukhansk."

"That's what you said? Turukhansk?" She went on fixing me with her piercing gaze.

I said, "Yes, that's what I said."

"Do you give me your word that you said that?"

"I do," I said firmly.

She believed me. Learning that I had signed a pledge not to leave Moscow, she said that meant my case was not finished. I could go to our *dacha* or to Sergiyev Posad, but if summoned would have to return to Moscow immediately. When I asked whether I could travel through the region of Nizhny Novgorod, she replied categorically – no! Thus, my cherished dream of journeying with Lyalya to the invisible city of Kityezh dissolved.

7

Following my release, I went back to drawing maps and diagrams for the magazines as if nothing had happened, but feeling I had matured by many years. The middle Rayevsky brother came to see me and, leading me out into the hall, asked in a whisper, "Did they make you the offer?" I was quite angry. He was the fifth person to ask me, and I simply could not say anything in reply. It turned out that Mikhail had been sent by his cousin, Artemi Rayevsky, to find me and ask me to meet him urgently at their *dacha*. Artemi was one of our frequent visitors, so I was surprised that he had not himself come, but anyway the following day I went out to the station, *Verst* 17, where the Rayevskys had a *dacha* next to the Osorgins. As ever, the Osorgins greeted me warmly and said how much they had been saddened by my arrest. But I read in their eyes, including those of my sister Lina, the sad thought, "They released you, but our poor Georgy is now in his fourth year of imprisonment."

Uncle Misha took me aside and asked me, "Did they make you the offer?"

"Uncle Misha, I can't answer that."

"Well, as if you were confessing it to a priest."

"No, no, I can't. I beg you, don't ask me."

I hurried over to the Rayevsky *dacha*. Their sister Katya ran the household. With her I found Yusha Samarin, who had also just been released. At that time they were courting. Artemi had not yet come back from the shipping office where he worked for Reginald Witter. In a chair on the verandah sat Ivan Ivanovich, Artemi's father, a handsome, imposing man with grey hair and a strong resemblance to Rabindranath Tagore. He was in the middle of composing riddles and rebuses for the papers, by which he earned a living.

I discovered from Yusha that he too had been in the Lubyanka and then Butyrka and had been taken to the same interrogator, who had worn a brigadier's cloak on one occasion and a simple blue shirt on the next. He had asked him the same questions about the same people, with emphasis on Vera Bernadskaya. Yusha had said he had never heard the name. I told him she was Lyalya's cousin. Neither of us asked each other whether we had been made the notorious offer.

Artemi finally arrived. He said he had been held up at the office. The last train was imminent, so he walked with me to the station after dissuading the others who also wanted to come. I had known Artemi from childhood as the Rayevskys had been our neighbours in the country and he was a close friend of my brother Vladimir. We walked in silence, holding hands. He was a tall, broad-browed, fair-haired man with well-formed features, but his eyes expressed hopeless sadness. He confessed that he had arrived late because he had been summoned to the Lubyanka, and this for the second time. He was being urged, coaxed and threatened, as he put it, to "collect information" about foreigners as well as about his family and friends.

He had refused, but as he lived with, and also supported his not-quite-normal father in Bolshoy Afanasiyeva Street, the officers at the Lyubanka had said, "And if we arrest you, how will your father survive? For his sake you have to agree."

Artemi begged for my advice. I decided to break my oath, and after swearing Artemi to keep it secret, I described how they had proposed the same to me and I had refused, despite all threats, and yet been released. My advice to him was to refuse under any circumstances such a shameful course of action. The train arrived and we embraced. A few days later Artemi was arrested. It was just before Yusha Samarin's marriage to Katya Rayevskaya. They were wed in the nearby church at the village of Lukin. The church has now been restored and is close to the summer residence of the Patriarch. I was one of Yusha's grooms. There was a huge crowd of guests, and a rather modest reception, but without Artemi, it was a sad occasion. He was not released. He was given five years in labour camp, felling trees near Kemi in the region of the White Sea, where he became psychologically ill. Under circumstances that were never clarified, and which he himself could not remember, he lost a leg and was let out after two years.

Peshkova, that wonderfully charitable lady, intervened to get him permission to leave the country for his relatives in France. Quite by chance I was on leave in Moscow just before his departure. I discovered that I could see Artemi where he was living with his sister Lelya – Elena Ivanovna, the wife of A.A. Gvozdev, an important designer and engineer. I went to their flat in Georgyyevsky Street, and saw sitting in an armchair a middle-aged man, physically and morally broken, with one leg missing. He had aged by fifteen years. When we embraced I could not stop myself bursting into tears. I never saw him again.

Artemi joined his family in France, but as he was not needed by anyone, lived alone in some kind of charity home, where he died twenty years later.[22] I cannot leave the subject of Artemi without remembering him at the Osorgins' *dacha*. A tall, elegant man standing by the piano, with Aunt Liza, delicate, with beautiful features and

---

22. *Translator's note: This shows, not surprisingly, that Sergei Golitsyn's knowledge, or memory, is not infallible. I personally knew Artemi in his English years, from ca. 1940 to 1960, and far from sitting alone in a charity home in France, he was a clerical employee of British European Airways in the Haymarket, London. He was living with his sister, Anna Shuvalov, in Earl's Court, and leading a very normal life. He eventually died of cancer, though where and exactly when I do not know.*

white hair, accompanying him as he sings his favourite songs in his velvety baritone: *Now Fade the Golden Vistas of Distant Alpukhara*, Delvig's *Elegy* and the *Song of the Varangian Guest*. The two Osorgin daughters, both in love with him, are sitting nearby on the divan, rapturously attentive. Uncle Misha Osorgin is stroking his long white beard as he too listens, whilst their daughter-in-law, my sister Lina, sits next to him with her little daughter Marinochka on her knees. How many such evenings I enjoyed, even though I am not musical, and how long ago it all seems now!

16. Justice and Love

I mentioned that father was going to see Peshkova on business of his own, which was to consult her about the loss of our voting rights. Father was not concerned about grandfather, who had firmly asked to be left in peace, but about the rest of the family. He believed that we had been unlawfully deprived, and although the PRC dealt only with political prisoners, Peshkova, out of long friendship, had agreed to send our papers off somewhere.

So one day father sent me to the flat that Peshkova shared with Maxim Gorky. It was on Mashkov Lane. The door was opened by a pretty maid and then Ekaterina Pavlovna herself appeared, wearing a beautiful patterned silk robe. She recognised me and asked about my life. I told her I was still working as a draughtsman. I could have told her that I was also now disenfranchised, but missed that opportunity, and simply handed over father's papers. She asked me to wait in the hall. A man in glasses walked past, sizing me up suspiciously; that was Gorky's secretary, Kryuchkov, who was shot after Gorky's death. In the distance I heard the voice of the classic of Soviet literature growling, "My shoes have gone missing again!"

Ekaterina Pavlovna brought me father's request for the restoration of his voting rights, with Gorky's writing in the top right hand corner: "Citizen Golitsyn's request supported, M. Gorky". Father tried every avenue with his case. Everywhere he was told, "As you were president of the assembly of nobles, in other words you were a landowner, and since you were a member of the Moscow city council, in other words a homeowner, and on top of that, a prince . . ."

Father pointed out that Schlippe, the governor of Tula, had refused to appoint him to a third term of office because of his liberalism, that he was under police surveillance in Tula, and that he had only filled the two other offices as a proxy for his uncle, Alexander Mikhailovich Golitsyn. Unfortunately, he could not produce the proxy paper, it had disappeared during one of the searches and vanished into the maw of the GPU. None of these assertions convinced the authorities. A joke was circulating at that time – "Prove that you are not a camel". Father had to prove that he was neither a landowner nor a homeowner, but where could he find such documents? He had friends everywhere who sincerely felt for him. A lady who worked in the Rumyantsev (now Lenin) Library managed to get a copy of the appropriate pages from the document *The Moscow Nobility in 1916* and from A. Chernopyatov's *Genealogy of the Tula Nobility*. Father pointed at these copies and said, "Look at all these Golitsyns, and not one of them has the initials M.V." He also added to his petitions the fact that his grandfather Mikhail Fyodorovich had been a Decembrist, Gorky's supporting paper, and his eleven years of unblemished work in various Soviet organisations. Alas, none of this impressed the stoney-faced authorities. All they said was – "You and your family are all former princes, it is unclear on what resources you survive, therefore you are 'non-working elements', therefore your demand is rejected."

Father's youngest brother, Uncle Vovik – Vladimir Vladimirovich – was more fortunate. At their first attempt, despite their titles, he and his son Sasha and daughter Elena were restored to their voting rights. But then he had a trump card; he had been an ordinary civil servant in the Livensk town council, had never owned any property, and above all, was married to an orphaned peasant woman (she died in 1923). This fact impressed the Soviet officials, and Uncle Vovik kept his job in the fashionable Bank for Foreign Trade for many years without ever been arrested. Ironically, his late wife's brother, a genuine Livensk peasant, was arrested and sent into remote exile with his whole family simply because he was related to a prince by marriage!

There were four levels of appeal against loss of voting rights in those days: the local district electoral committee, the city committee, then the RSFSR and finally the USSR. All these bodies were greatly overburdened with appeals and they had to handle them with the greatest degree of "watchfulness", the key word of the day. After months of waiting, people would be brought up before a panel of three people, who would see in the appellants only class enemies, and would subject them to insulting, or even just stupid questions.

After receiving a rejection from the district body, father was summoned, after a long wait, to the Moscow City committee. He was advised to go with Vladimir. Of all of us, brother Vladimir hated answering questions or filling out forms. Despite all the blows of fate, he remained proud of his prince's title. He suffered deeply, but kept this to himself and always maintained an outward appearance of light-hearted spirits, even jollity. During the more liberal years, 1925–1928, he had not bothered to join the Artists' Union, which would have established his legal status, as it would have meant facing a general meeting and both friendly and hostile questions. So when the summons to the City committee came, he said, "I'm not going. To hell with them!" It took all the entreaties of mother and father to persuade him.

Later, to our great amusement, he described the interview at the committee, which met in the corner of the largest room of the Moscow City Council, the building on Skobolev Square that had been the Governor-General's palace. Vladimir regretted that he had not been able to sketch the faces of the committee members when he showed them some of his illustrations for books and magazines, trying to prove that to them his artistic talents.

He was asked, "Why were you not in the Red Army?"

"Good heavens, they never asked me that in the GPU, but here they ask me!"

I have already written of how Vladimir was enlisted as a sailor in expeditions to the Arctic. Now the committee accused him of dodging military service during the civil war, in fact of being a deserter.

They also asked him, "Have you danced in this room?" To which Vladimir quite rightly replied that children were not invited to balls by the Governor-General. Our father, always totally honest, had of course answered that same question affirmatively.

So the City committee rejected our petition. Father tried to appeal elsewhere and was everywhere refused. As a lawyer by training, he could not accept this injustice. Finally, he appealed to Molotov. Long periods of time elapsed between appeals, until the hypocritical Stalin Constitution of 1935 was promulgated, which stated that the only persons deprived of their rights were prisoners and mad people. Even after the war the same tricky question was still to be found on application forms, "Were you ever deprived of your right to vote, and if so, when and under what circumstances?"

During all these legal struggles father was greatly encouraged by an old friend, the well-known Moscow advocate Nikolai Adrianovich Silversvan, who gave his help cost-free. Silversvan lived in an old, stuccoed house on Sobachaya Square, once the home of the poet Khomyakov. It had been visited by Turgenev, and Slavophiles had foregathered there for their meetings. After the revolution three rooms were arranged as a museum to reproduce the style and atmosphere of the 1840s. The daughter of the poet Olga Alexeievna Chelishcheva was still living there in my time. The museum was dissolved in 1930, and eventually, on the orders of Khrushchev, the Khomyakov house, the entire square and Bolshaya Molchanovka Street were barbarously destroyed.

By what right the Silversvans lived there, I do not know. His wife, Elena Vladimirovna, was a scientific official at the Tretyakov Gallery. Occassionaly, I was given free entry tickets. Sometimes father sent me to the Silversvan's house with drafts of his appeals, or to collect corrected versions. On a couple of occasions I was asked to stay to tea. Nikolai Adrianovich lived a long life; even after the war, when he was already retired, I would visit him and seek his advice. Then, as if by a bolt of lightning, his prosperity was swept away. In 1952, he was asked by the famous singer Obukhova to take up the case of the brother of her maid, who had been accused of setting fire to a barn in the province of Bryansk, killing an entire herd of cattle. Silversvan went down to Bryansk and proved that the man had been miles away at the time of the fire. The court accepted this verdict, but the local authorities were furious and denounced Silversvan to Moscow. He was arrested as an "enemy of the people" and sent to the a labour camp, and his wife, who had worked more than forty years at the Tretyakov Gallery, was summarily dismissed from her job. I heard this tragic story from S.N. Durylin.

Father was both physically and morally wounded at being classified as a disenfranchised person. People said he was upset by the revolution, but it was not that at all. In fact, he was only fifty-six-years old and hated being idle. He began to suffer from urological problems, then cardiac symptoms and was thought to be suffering from psychological stress. He became an insomniac, preventing mother from sleeping and constantly crying out, "How are we going to survive?" Mother did her best to comfort him and raise his spirits. Silversvan suggested he should go before a medical board. Being deprived of voting rights meant he could not receive a pension, but a certificate of incapacity to work would give him a certain legal standing.

Father had many medical friends; Professor Shervinsky, who was sentenced to twenty-five years in the Gulag after Gorky's death, and Fyodor Alexandrovich Getye, a fine man who had been Lenin's personal physician. Either would have certified him unable to work, but there existed a medical commission that was made up not only of doctors, but also officials, and these officials were hostile to him, picking on his loss of voting rights and his title of prince. They sent him off for investigation to a mental asylum. Father said the institution was exactly as later described by the writers Ilf and Petrov. Quite normal people were in hiding there, officials with a dubious past, NEPmen, people fearful of the purges, and traders. One man sang "O Lord, save the Tsar!" every morning. When father asked him if he was mad, he replied, "It's only in here that I can sing what I like."

In the end, father was judged psychologically normal and fit to work. So once more he was condemned to a state of idleness. Victor Alexandrovich Meien got him some English translation work and father spent time collecting information for his legal appeals, but none of this was real work. He yearned for regular employment.

2

We rented the *dacha* at Glinkovo for the sixth time in 1929. Vegetables and milk were extremely cheap there, and the owner, the widow Annushka, charged so little for a room that it was cheaper to live there than in Moscow. In retrospect, I regret having spent so much time working at my draughting in Moscow, rather than enjoying the fresh air and natural beauty of the countryside. My parents also spent most of their time in Moscow, where mother was bolstering father's spirits as he went to humiliating medical commissions.

Lyalya Ilyinskaya did not come to Glinkovo that year. She was very disappointed that, because of the prohibition on my leaving Moscow, I could not make the journey to the city of Kityezh. Together with Alexandra Tolstaya's secretary, she set off for the Caucasus, where the young women met three students from Leningrad, one of whom, the biologist Ganya Strelin, Lyalya later married. Our friendship was never resumed.

As in previous years, there were far more young women than young men at Glinkovo. Boyfriends came out from Moscow, and all of them were fed, mostly with potatoes and watery gruel. Vladimir and Elena, who now had three little children, together with their maid, Katya, rented a newly built cottage. Valery Pertsov and Victor Alexandrovich Meien rented places for their mothers, saying that they were attracted by the beautiful countryside, but we suspected their attraction had more to do with Cupid's arrows. A close friend of ours, young Nikolai Khramtsov, worked as a truck driver in Sergiyev Posad. One day he offered to drive us all to Pereslavl-Zalessky. A huge group assembled, but because of the restriction on movements I decided to play safe and not go, though I was full of envy. They all came back delighted by the lake and its many lovely churches.

Uncle Vovik Golitsyn's daughter, Elena, was not one of our company in Moscow, but when she came to Glinkovo she was followed by her suitor, Nikolai Sokolov. He was a handsome young aviator with the blue lapels of a flyer and two gold bars, the rank of division commander – today the rank of general. He charmed us all and took part in all our games, which were mostly played on the church square in the evenings. One incident I recall was when we were all playing a card game on a train to Moscow. The conductor came by and said, "No gambling is allowed on the train!" Nikolai Sokolov, who was sitting to one side, told him coldly, "I allowed it!" The conductor looked abashed and went his way.

In general, many who had fought in the civil war found it difficult to adapt to peacetime life, and now and again would break out with some act of folly. Nikolai sometimes shot into the air with his revolver. One day Elena announced that she was going to marry the handsome aviator. We were all delighted. He was, however, a communist, whereas Elena wanted to be wed in church, so it was decided to have a quiet wedding in Glinkovo. The priest, Alexei Zagorsky, celebrated with great spirit. Elena's brother was her first groom, I the second. Father Alexei's sermon was an inspired one, and we all went to Vladimir's *dacha*, the biggest one, for the wedding feast. The young couple left for Moscow that evening, but Nikolai had now retired and was appointed head of customs in Kyatka, so the newlyweds soon took the train again. They alerted the Trubetskois to the fact that their train would be passing through Sergiyev Posad; the whole Trubetskoi family assembled to wave them through, receiving from the happy couple a box of chocolates thrown out of the moving carriage.

Not long after, Nikolai's tendency to act anarchically led to his appropriating thirty thousand roubles of government money. He fled into hiding with Elena, where he was caught and tried. Elena, now a peroxide blonde, returned to Moscow, but I know little of the details of this intriguing story, as she refused to speak about her adventures. When, in 1932, I was due to travel to Novosibirsk, Elena gave me Nikolai's address. He was delighted to see me, but I could not help being intimidated by his OGPU uniform. He now taught marksmanship to the guards in Siberian labour camps – in other words, those who would shoot prisoners. Whether he himself was a prisoner I do not know, but they probably trusted him, as he was no class enemy. I had no desire to meet him again, and I do not know what became of him. Elena had divorced him in the meantime.

I remember that summer as a time of happiness. I seemed able to forget that I was a non-person, that the course in literature had been shut down, slamming the door on my progress to learning, and that I was earning very little. Masha's suitors kept turning up with cookies and chocolates, without her favouring any particular one. Sonya's suitor, Igor Daksergof, who was younger than her, had made way for Victor Meien, who was seen as a sounder prospect. He and Sonya went on more and more walks alone, although when we remembered how she had refused to go to church at Easter so as not to have to exchange the Easter kiss with him, we failed to understand the significance of these walks. So our reaction was astonishment when Sonya came in from one of these walks, her face shining with happiness, and Victor, normally an impassive man, literally skipping along. Clearly, Cupid had hit his target. We all kissed Sonya and felt on our cheeks the sharp bristles of Victor's whiskers, whilst Katya tried hard to get out of Sonya the precise words with which Victor had proposed. It was of course high time for Sonya, now twenty-five, to be married and for Victor, thirty-six, to surround himself with a family. It so happened that this engagement took place on the feast day of Ivan Kupala, when it was the custom to indulge in water pranks. My younger sisters succeeded in creeping up on Victor and pouring a bucket of water over him.

Victor told my parents that he was as happy as a teenager and would care for and look after Sonya just like any hero in a novel. They were pleased that their older daughters were now settled in life, and I was content because I imagined Victor, now a member of the family, giving me many commissions. Masha said she winced when she imagined Sonya's beautiful young head on a pillow next to Victor's avuncular whiskers. Vladimir only frowned; Victor was a nice man, but not an aristocrat, an important factor for Vladimir. Victor's father, Alexander Genrikovich Meien, came of the merchant class. He had once been co-owner of two blocks of flats familiar to Muscovites, located on either side of the monument to Yuri Dolgorukov. Both have since been redeveloped; in one there is a bookshop, in the other the Aragvi restaurant. Victor said that his ancestor, a specialist in shipbuilding, had been brought from Holland by Peter the Great, and he was proud of the extra "e" in his name, which showed that it was of Dutch, not German, origin.

It was decided to hold the wedding without delay in Glinkovo. First Sonya and Victor went to Moscow to fast, confess and receive communion from Father Vladimir Vorobyev of the church of Nikola Plotnik on the Arbat. He was a greatly respected figure among believers, and had been our family's spiritual elder for many years. With his luxuriant white hair and beard he resembled Karl Marx, but his eyes were full of goodness and he celebrated services with great conviction. How well I remember the measured clarity with which he delivered the words, "In the name of the Father, the Son and the Holy Spirit!" In the 1920s he was arrested, then released, then rearrested and exiled to Vasilsursk. Whether he died a natural death there, or in the Gulag, I do not know. The authorities would hardly have allowed such an outstanding priest to gather around him a flock of the faithful.

The church of Nikola Plotnik, the very one painted by Polenov in his *A Moscow Courtyard*, was destroyed in the 1930s along with two others on the Arbat – Trinity church on the corner of Denezhny Lane, and the seventeenth-century Nikola Yavlenny church on the corner of Serebryanny Lane. The date of the wedding was fixed, the feast prepared and guests began to arrive the day before, including the grooms. Much gaiety lay ahead. But a piece of bad news came with them. The four cousins of our sister-in-law, Elena, had been arrested; Boris and Yuri Saburov, Dimitri and Andrei Gudovich. They had been living with their mother in Tsaritsin, which was near Moscow. The wedding was overshadowed by this disturbing news. Yuri Saburov was a great favourite of our family. He had lived with us on Eropkinsky Street for two years, sleeping in the same room as me. Earlier in these memoirs I wrote how Masha flirted outrageously with him. Hearing of his arrest, she burst into tears, revealing to us the strength of her feelings for this tall, handsome, very shy young man. Only just aroused, these warm feelings were now lost hopes.

The subsequent fate of the Saburov brothers was tragic. They were exiled for some years to Siberia, returning at the end of their term to live with their mother and unmarried sister, Ksenya, in the town of Vladimir. This did not last long; in 1937 they were again arrested and disappeared for good. As for Dimitri Gudovich, he was sentenced to five years in the labour camps, ending up on the building of the White Sea to Baltic canal. Like many other prisoners he was released before his time was up and sent to the construction site of the Moscow-Volga canal, where he managed to persuade the bosses to have his younger brother, Andrei, join him from exile.

To revert to Sonya's wedding, Father Vladimir Vorobyev, helped by the local priest, Father Alexei, wed them. Sonya went into the church on father's arm. He looked particularly smart in a rather old-fashioned suit and starched white shirt, and made a gallant attempt to look happy, though his eyes revealed his deep sadness. Sonya was radiant and beautiful in her white bridal veil. Victor beamed with happiness. I was No. 1 groom, then Sasha Golitsyn, and I cannot remember who was third. Victor's first best man was his younger brother, Vadim, a student at the Conservatory, followed by Masha's admirers. The church was filled to overflowing with family, friends, local people and peasants from neighbouring villages. An abundant feast followed – as on many other occasions, the potato under various guises saved the day. The two priests were placed in the corner under the icons, tables were brought in from neighbouring houses, but even so there was not enough room for everyone. When the meal was over, the place was cleared and everyone danced to the music of a harmonica. The two priests also took to the floor, solid and dignified men, and as they moved to and fro, we all clapped in time. The dancing overflowed into the street, and here Victor showed the stuff he was made of; he danced like a young man, first with Sonya, then with another woman, then with a second, then with a third, who all danced around him, waving their kerchiefs and singing flirtatious couplets. I have never seen Victor dance again.

We all made merry at that wedding feast with sincere, unconcerned happiness. It never crossed our minds that the church would not see such another wedding, and that such merriment would disappear from Glinkovo for ever. A few days after this Sonya lost her wedding ring when swimming in a deep pool on the river Torgosha. She and Victor and the rest of the family took this as a very bad omen. Victor and several youths from Glinkovo spent hours diving for the ring, but they never found it. So the happy couple left for Moscow with feelings of anxiety for the future.

3

It will be the historian's job to dispassionately study and explain the unexpected and unforeseen calamities that fell on the long-suffering Russian people, and above all the peasantry, in the autumn of 1929. The newspapers raged hysterically, using disgusting words like watchfulness, class enemies, *kulaks*, disenfranchised people, purge, eliminate, liquidate, along with unrestrained praise for the great and wise Stalin. The classic Soviet writer, Maxim Gorky, for ever shamed himself before posterity with his slogan, "If the enemy does not surrender, liquidate him!" Nor should one forget Lenin's earlier catchword "Who is not with us is against us".

My brother Vladimir's opinion was that all this was monstrous provocation by a group of sadists who hated humanity and, having seized power, wanted to cause as much harm as possible to the people and to Russia herself. Who, in actual fact, carried out these evil acts? The authorities used young people aged sixteen and up – *Konsomols* and others, the so-called "light cavalry" – to go out into the villages. A target for "de-*kulakisation*" of a specified number of homes was set in advance by agreement with the village Soviet. And the "light cavalry" helped the local authorities to liquidate whole families or force them into the collective farms.

The writer Vasily Grossman, in his largely autobiographical story *Everything Flows*, describes how he himself as a young *Konsomol* mocked and insulted helpless, terrified peasants. In the Khrushchev years, an old peasant told me how he had been chairman of the village Soviet in the Kolomensk district when the representative of the OGPU and a group of youths came to him. They demanded that he select for them which and how many farms were to be broken up. When he said that there were no *kulaks* in the village they threatened him with the same fate. Forced to lead the ruffians into the biggest house in the village, he saw how one of the men thrust a revolver into a bag of nails, which was then discovered as incriminating evidence. The owner was arrested and led away. Later the local paper described him as a terrorist.

Whilst we were still in Glinkovo, the authorities from Sergiyev Posad arrived and explained to a gathering of villagers how they would have to go into the collective farms, and that if they did not they would be driven from their homes as enemies – the notorious sayings of Gorky and Lenin were shouted at them. The peasants listened, scratching their heads. They simply could not understand why they had to give up everything they had worked for with their hands and the sweat of their brows. After all, their fathers and grandfathers had worked the land for generations and never complained.

How was it decided that someone was a *kulak*? Quite simply – by the appearance of his house. For two years, I had watched some local people building themselves a pair of fine houses, decorated by craftsmen carpenters with carved lintels and window frames. They spent so much money on these houses that they had perforce in summer to rent them as summer *dachas* to people like us. My brother Vladimir and his family had rented one of these. Then came that black day when both owners with their wives and children were sent to Siberia, and all their property taken away from them. What tragically little time they had been granted to live in their lovely houses, built with their own hands.

The remaining inhabitants of Glinkovo, witnessing the tragedy of their neighbours, were ready to go into the collective farms just so as to continue living in their own homes. They lay low in their houses in fear of that nighttime knock at the door. Once they had spent the evenings in the street dancing to the music of the harmonica – now that dreadful autumn of 1929 silenced the music. Meanwhile the local authorities, in order to demonstrate to the district bosses how zealous they were, thought up something for the people of Glinkovo, which I will now describe.

Two kilometres away from the village was the monastery of Vifaniya, once the late eighteenth- or nineteenth-century summer residence of Platon, then Metropolitan of Moscow. He had ordered the little river to be dammed to create a string of picturesque lakes, and had a domed white church built on one shore and a single-storied house as his residence. The monastery, a long, two-storey building, was built after his death. After the revolution the monastery was shut down and Platon's house became a little museum in his memory, the monastery building now being used as a teacher training institute. In one unobtrusive corner of this building lived a holy man, Father Valery, who my sisters used to visit.

The brilliant idea that came into the minds of the authorities of Sergiyev Posad was to get rid of the teacher training school and house the inhabitants of Glinkovo and neighbouring hamlets in the monastery building, with its rows of cells on either side of long corridors. This would create the first ever commune, be a material manifestation of the dreams of Marx, Engels, Lenin and Stalin and nothing less than a leap straight into communism.

"Everything will be owned in common," asserted the authorities at a meeting of horrified Glinkovo people, "there'll be a communal kitchen at the end of the corridor, tools and animals and even the chickens all owned in common."

"Will the women be in common, too?" someone foolishly asked. He was accused of being a class enemy and a *kulak*, and arrested two days later. The terrified peasants waited to see what would happen, while the local papers whipped up fear as they trumpeted the paradise that was being planned for the people of Glinkovo. I know all this at first hand, as petitioners from the village tried in vain to get to see Kalinin and consulted Vladimir and our brother-in-law Victor. Unexpectedly Lunacharsky himself, the Commissar of Education, heard of the plan to break up an institute of education and intervened to stop it. The dispute lasted all winter, and the people would certainly have had to abandon their birthplaces had it not been for Stalin's famous article "Dizzy with Success" – but more of that later.

It is easy to imagine the emotions felt by Father Alexei at all these events in Glinkovo. He had served the community for forty years, celebrating mass on Saturdays and Sundays, marrying couples, christening their children and taking funerals. Now calamity was looming on the horizon. He had three unmarried daughters, no longer in their first youth, all three teachers in various local schools. They were summoned to Sergiyev Posad and given an ultimatum, more or less in the following words: "Go back to your father and tell him to give up his priesthood. The villagers have organised a commune and he is causing trouble about that. If he doesn't agree, we don't know what measures we'll take with him, but you will have to give up your teaching. The daughters of priests can't be entrusted with the education of Soviet children in the spirit of communism."

The daughters put up an argument that had doubtless helped on earlier occasions. They said, "Our name is Zagorsky and we are cousins of the famous fiery Bolshevik who died in the revolution and whose name has now been given to Sergiyev Posad."

"That's no help," was the reply. "A dead man can't defend you. Get back to your father!"

What could they do? They had taught the schoolchildren for years and were no doubt on good terms with their superiors, but the memory of their cousin was of no help. They cried for a little and then returned to Glinkovo to persuade their father to take this unholy step. He was senior priest over a dozen parishes, and a greatly respected man. But now – when pilgrims arrived for the late night Christmas service, they found the church closed. It has never again been open for religious services. In due course the lock on the door was broken open by the authorities, the iconostasis removed and the icons burned. Now this church, built in the 1840s, is a mere skeleton. Yet how beautiful it was once, high on the banks of the little river Torgosha. In the book devoted do my brother, *Vladimir Golitsyn: Some pages from the life of the artist, inventor and sailor,* there is on page seventy-four a delicate pencil drawing of the church done by him in 1927.

Father Alexei's story was told me by Uncle Vladimir Trubetskoi. That same winter he had been walking along a street in Sergiyev Posad when he passed an old man in a short fur jacket, patched trousers and felt boots, unshaven, and with a mass of grey hair coming out from under his wool cap. The old man cried out,

"Vladimir Sergeievich, don't you know me?" My startled uncle replied, "Father Alexei, is it you?" Father Alexei lowered his gaze and said sadly, "I've changed." And he told the story I have just written above. In the end, he and his wife had been evicted from their home and their land and animals taken from them. They were living with their youngest daughter, the two older, God forgive them, fearing to take them in. I know nothing of their eventual fate.

4

I must now go back seven years to write about mother's life. The reader will remember how whilst still in Bogoroditsk she trained herself to be a shoemaker. On arrival in Moscow, she decided try to open a shoe repair shop, but was dissuaded on the grounds that too many shoemakers were coming into the capital and the competition would be too great. An energetic woman, mother was not about to give up, so that when peasants from Bulchalki sought her out and reminded her of the extra money they had once earned sewing linen, she saw an opening.

In those days of the NEP, the gap between peasant earnings and the price of industrial commodities was widening, so that the countryside was suffering from what was called "Trotsky's Scissors". The Buchalki womenfolk believed that if they organised a workshop to sew and embroider linen for export, bringing in hard currency, they could narrow the gap. Remembering how mother had helped them in pre-revolutionary times, they asked her to be their Moscow representative. Not just a friendly, but a delighted welcome greeted her at the Museum of Country Crafts, where they knew her to be a specialist. It was also a time when these crafts had begun to flourish in all parts of the country, and were approved by the authorities. But the officials in Epifansky district thought otherwise. "What!" they said, "after three hundred years of having the blood sucked out of you, you want to go under the yoke of your former mistress again?" Which meant that the womenfolk of Buchalki lost their chance to earn extra money.

Mother was not discouraged. The staff at the Museum of Crafts advised her not to set up her workshop on a former Golitsyn estate, but somewhere else. She wrote to her good friend, Anna Vasilyevna Bibikova in Bogoroditsk, an equally enterprising lady. And things went well. Window dressing, they picked as chairman Nikolai Vasilyev Soustov, a member of the staff of the Agricultural Institute. Anna Vasilyevna became vice-chairman, and mother merely the agent. From then on she and I would regularly go to the post office to send off parcels of cloth, and in return would receive the finished articles for delivery to the Museum. Every month she would despatch money orders to Bogoroditsk together with her accounts.

Everyone was happy with this arrangement; Soustov, Anna Vasilyevna, the Bogoroditsk sewing ladies, the Crafts' Museum, the government in receipt of hard currency from exports to a number of countries. And, of course, mother, who at first earned ten roubles, which later rose to twenty-five a month. The workshop flourished for three years, until the officials in Bogoroditsk became aware that Soustov did not know a thing about sewing, that a former landowner, Anna Vasilyevna Bibikova, was the manager, and that, horror of horrors, the Moscow end was run by a former princess. So it was all a pseudo-workshop, and the result was that mother and everyone else stopped earning anything.

At the Crafts' Museum, however, they had other views. Yes, Anna Sergeievna was a former princess, but she was also a top expert in Russian crafts, and her products were being exported all over the world, including to America, for dollars. So they must defend her. They urged mother to organise a new workshop in Moscow, not embroidering blouses and dresses, but cushions. This was the time when the prosperity of the so-called NEPman was coming to an end as the authorities imposed ever higher taxes on them. Up until then they had thrived on buying and selling the property of all those old ladies whose husbands had been shot or imprisoned, and who had no other means of subsistence than selling, at a tenth of their real price, their ancestral portraits, their gold and silver, their china and objets d'art, and their precious furniture. As this world of vampire-like exploitation came to an end the old ladies were facing destitution, so the news of mother's new initiative led to a rush of willing volunteers.

Made wise by experience, mother knew that the head of such an enterprise must have some touch of the proletariat, so she chose Sofia Nikolaievna Davydov, the daughter of a well-known lawyer friend of Leo Tolstoy's, Professor Davydov. The workshop took on two princesses Obolensky who were distant relatives of ours, Princess Christyna Golitsyna, not related to us, and Countess Uvarova, who had sheltered on her estate the future administrator of the Moscow Arts Theatre, Fyodor Mikhailovich Mikhalsky. Some other penniless ladies, titled and untitled, were reunited, including Elizabeth Alexandrovna Babynina, who lived in our flat and had been a land-owner in Kashiria. The only young woman to join the workshop was someone who had just married another tenant of ours, the amiable but stupid accountant, Dimitri Nikolaievich Adamovich.

The new enterprise flourished. Mother inspected their work carefully, rejecting some pieces, then, making up a bundle, would walk with me to the Museum in Leontyevsky Street. As agent, mother received twenty-five roubles a month. The workshop was registered with the local financial office to which it paid a reasonable percentage of tax.

5

In the autumn of 1929, the watchful goddess Themis decided there was something fishy about mother's workshop. An officious young man came to our flat, showed his warrant and demanded that mother bring out the records of this pseudo-workshop, as he called it, together with all its products and cash. Mother laid out the various papers and notebooks that were the record of the work done and accounts paid, fifteen roubles in cash, together with some embroidered cases and reels of cotton destined for future work. The impudent lad treated all this with contempt, saying this could not be anything but a fake set-up, there were no savings books, only a few articles, and mother was a former princess, and so on and so forth. At this point the young wife of Adamovich raised her voice at him. Furiously, he asked her what her social origins were and learning that she was the daughter of a former official, announced that clearly this was a nest of class enemies.

He left, taking with him all the documentation and some of the pieces of cloth. Mother refused to sign his report. Thus began the case of the alleged fake workshop, the 'Embroidered Cushion'; she was accused of being, the actual owner of a business that was exploiting its workers under the cover of calling herself the agent. The changing fortunes of this case continued for three years; from the point of view of today's lawyers it was an astonishing case, so I will try and describe what I remember of it, and what I heard from my relatives.

The investigator into the case was a Latvian called Parum. To the militia station, tucked away in the lanes of Ostozhenka district, he summoned many of the old ladies, as well as Adamovich's newly-wed young wife, whose honeymoon was thus completely spoiled. He also summoned Sofia Nikolaievna Davydova. He did not call in my mother. His tactic was to question the others about her, frightening them with threats that if they did not confess, he would punish them, and so on. And what were they to confess? Quite simply, that the princess, head of this fake workshop, had been exploiting them.

The old ladies, by this time no longer well-dressed but clad in worn-out and old-fashioned clothes, endured these interrogations with dignity, defended my mother in every imaginable way and refused to sign the records of their questioning. Only Adamovich's wife signed everything that was put before her by the investigator. Finally, he summoned mother. I do not know the questions he asked, or how he bullied her, but I know that she put up a skilful defence and refused to sign the papers she was handed with their inflated, false accusations. Still, it was clear that this case was no joking matter.

We set out to enlist help. Peshkova did not handle criminal cases. Smidovich was an old communist with excellent credentials, but said he would not exert influence at the lower levels, only if the case went to the Supreme Court. When the case was finally sent on to the district court, we were helped by our relative, Nastenka Baranova, who was teaching foreign languages to the children of a lawyer called Orlovsky. Nastenka referred to him as her "tame" Bolshevik and a decent man. He undertook the case, refusing any fee. He called in the old ladies and gave them a lesson in being witnesses. "Don't sit there all crumpled up and miserable, hold your heads high. When the judge asks, 'Did you kill him?' don't start saying, 'Well, ten years ago someone told us that . . .' stand up straight and say clearly, 'No, I did not kill him!'"

Initially, they wanted both my mother and Sofia Nikolaievna Davydova, as nominal chairman of the workshop, to appear in the dock. Then they remembered that Sofia Nikolaievna was the daughter of a close friend of Tolstoy's, and although Tolstoy was a count and a landowner he was admired by Lenin, and doubtless also by Stalin. So, it was my mother who was tried. The old ladies were witnesses and, as taught by Orlovsky, they answered clearly and briefly and said not one word that could harm my mother. The prosecutor based his whole case on Adamovich's wife, who mumbled confused words about how mother exploited her.

Orlovsky questioned her closely. She answered first one way, then another, then was on the verge of tears. He asked her a final question:

"How long have you been married?"

"Soon it'll be two months."

"Well, that explains your answers," he said, turning with a smile to the judges.

The prosecutor repeated his charge about a pseudo-workshop, the title of princess and her status as a non-voter.

Then it was Orlovsky's turn. He spoke brilliantly, stressing the great utility of the products of the 'Embroidered Cushion' in the building of socialism. He read out an affirming statement from the Crafts' Museum, including the statement that bringing my mother to court meant the loss of hard currency earnings to the value of two tractors. He described the charitable works my mother had been engaged in before the revolution, the orphanage she had founded at Bulchalki, the crafts' workshop, her membership of the organisation for the protection of mothers and children and the many orphaned children she had saved from death during the German War. He finished his oration with these words:

"She should be given an award, not sent to trial!"

The judges retired, returning after half an hour to announce their decision in favour of mother. The crowd applauded. At the exit the prosecutor hissed at mother, "I'll have you arrested again." Overhearing these words, Orlovsky said, "And she'll be cleared again." Some months later mother was called in to the investigator's office. The prosecutor had protested against the acquittal; the case was being reviewed. The prosecutor accused Orlovsky of being one-sided in his handling of the serious crime committed by my mother, thus misleading the court.

At this stage, I was no longer in Moscow, but can tell the story from the accounts given by my family. A different interrogator summoned the old ladies. Once again they stood firm and defended mother, and once again, Adamovich's young wife signed whatever was put in front of her. Mother was put under provisional arrest by the militia. She was in a cell with all sorts of women – prostitutes, peasant women with children fleeing from collectivisation, specu-lators, nuns, thieves and many who simply did not know why they had been arrested. I was living far away and the family hid mother's sufferings from me. But during those days of her incarceration I had a terrible dream about her, which made me insist in a letter home that they tell me how she was. Father's letter of reply made every effort to console me.

The lawyer Orlovsky was outraged by mother's arrest and did everything he could to have her freed. She was in prison for two weeks. He himself, however, having been criticised for one-sidedness in her earlier defence, could not take her case again. He turned to a lawyer friend of his, Otsep. This lawyer's name is now forgotten, but in his day he was the best-known advocate in Russia. In the widely reported trial of the Promparty – a party of technocrats who were alleged to want to take over the government – Otsep defended the principally accused person, Professor Ramzin, and it was he who suggested that Ramzin should finish his declaration to the court with the words, "What is more useful for the country, my work or my corpse?" It seems that these words so pleased Stalin that he ordered that the death penalty should not be pronounced. All the accused – professors, engineers, scientists – were still given ten year sentences and sent to the just-created *sharashki* (penal scientific laboratories).

Otsep undertook to defend my mother and, like Orlovsky, refused any fee. I imagine his appearance in the court must have surprised many. First the major Promparty case, and now the 'Embroidered Cushion'. Unlike Orlovsky's fiery oratorical style, Otsep spoke slowly, calmly and strictly logically. The court once again acquitted my mother, and once again the prosecutor appealed. The case was now considered without any witnesses and without my mother, first in the city court, then at the level of the Russian Federation, where my mother was again acquitted thanks to Otsep, but again the prosecutors appealed. The case went to the Supreme Court where it was finally settled. The prosecutors were reprimanded for wasting time on such a minor case when all around were class enemies, saboteurs, *kulaks* and agents of capitalism.

So in those days justice could prevail. But Orlovsky himself, who had done so much to ensure that justice, was arrested and disappeared forever.

6

Another case involving our family, this time without the favour of the goddess Themis, started in the autumn of 1929. Father received a summons, initiated by some organisation, to attend the People's Court in the district of Frunze. The purpose was to have us exiled from Moscow. Father called on Silversvan for advice, and as mother was worried by father's state of mind, I went with him. Silversvan showed father a supplement to the paper *Evening Moscow* containing the decree that all persons who had lost their voting rights and were not in employment would be exiled from Moscow. These supplements to the newspapers were the cunning way the authorities concealed any news they did not want the world to know, which also meant that the ordinary public remained in ignorance.

Silversvan undertook to defend father, and instructed him to attach to his documentation the certificates of his eleven years of employment in various Soviet institutes, photocopies of the statistics in *All Moscow* and the pages on the nobility of the province of Tula from Chernopyatov's book, which proved that he had never been either a landowner or owned any property, and most important of all, the paper showing that he was registered at the labour office. My brother Vladimir and I were told to collect information about our work and earnings. But Silversvan warned us that as persons without the vote we must be prepared for the worst. He added that one of the reasons we were picked out was that we lived in a spacious flat with high ceilings. There would have been no case if we had been crowded into a cellar.

I did no drawing in the next few days, but ran from office to office collecting certified statements of my work, including from private individuals such as Bobochka Yarkho. I collected ten such statements. Vladimir cursed and swore, and only managed a couple. At his main clients' offices he was refused – I will explain why later on. Father took all this material to the court and personally saw it included in the file of the case. Silversvan picked Varvara, a former servant from the Golitsyn house on Pokrovka Street, to witness that father had no links with that house and its former income.

The hearing finally took place, attended by all of us and many friends. Before the session Varvara walked up and down with the judge, "working him over" as she put it. Then the court sat; the judge was flanked by two deputies, a secretary sat in front and below them. Varvara spoke at length of the kindness of the Golitsyns to the poor, how much they had helped them, and how good they had been to their peasants and servants at Bulchalki. At one point she said, "The Golitsyns always lived as one family." The judge interrupted her and told the secretary to write down those very words. Varvara was very upset that she had blurted that out.

When father testified his voice quavered and he gave the impression of a dray horse being asked to pull too great a load. He kept repeating that he had worked for eleven years, that he had never owned land or any property, that he hoped to have his voting rights restored and was now registered at the labour office. The judge in a deliberately loud voice told the secretary, "Put down that the labour office has a man deprived of the vote on their list."

Silversvan took the floor. He said that our family was hard working, that all its members would undoubtedly be restored their full rights. He mentioned my talented brother, the artist, and his three children. The court did not adjourn. The judge took up the file of the case, turned a few pages and showed his two colleagues the last sheet, which was Bobochka Yarkho's statement about my work for him. The two colleagues never said a word, simply nodded their heads. The judge began to write his report. When after five minutes he handed it to each of them to sign, we saw that the second man refused. The judge rose to his feet and asked us all to do the same. He began to read out all the injurious opinions of our family that I have already noted. The only new point he made was that we had produced statements of earnings for totally insignificant sums of money, so that we obviously lived off some other unknown resources. He concluded by reading out that the court had decided to exile the family of the former Princes Golitsyn from Moscow on the grounds of their loss of voting rights. An appeal against the decision must be made to the city court within two weeks.

The next decision was the eviction of our neighbour Elizabeth Alexandrovna Babynina, as a person without voting rights and a former landowner. The only reason for this was that she had occupied a room in our flat. Later her daughter and her son-in-law, Professor A.B. Mlodzeyevsky, took her in. As a lawyer by training, father was indignant that the court had not withdrawn before coming to its decision. Silversvan agreed that this was good reason for an appeal; a second reason was that one of the three judges had refused to sign the decision. But still, he advised us to look for new living quarters somewhere outside Moscow. All this was happening at the same time as mother was involved in her court case over the 'Embroidered Cushion'; so the most practical and energetic member of our family was out of action. How would we find new quarters?

7

In the spring of 1929, the destinies of my sister Masha and our cousin. Lelya Davydova, who had lived with us during her university term time, changed abruptly. When the literary courses were wound up, Masha was left high and dry. Lelya, however, who had done two successful years at the Higher Technical Institute, was suddenly and unceremoniously expelled.

This was typical of the age, when enthusiasm and hate went hand in hand. Lelya was a good student, but a campaign to uncover class enemies, hiding themselves behind false declarations of their origins, was raging. Letters were written by our active young communists to local authorities, asking questions about particular people, trying to discover if they had lied about their origins. Most of these queries remained unanswered, but occasionally the reply would come that so-and-so was the daughter or son of an officer, a *kulak*, a nobleman, thus trapping the poor person who had claimed they were the offspring of humble workers. In Lelya's case, a letter arrived that declared that her father was a miller. It was true that Uncle Alda had for a time rented a mill on the Davydov family's former estate of Kulevatovo, but, worse than that, at the time of this denunciation he had lost his right to vote and been exiled to the province of Vologda.

Lelya rushed to try and pull strings. Her trump card was that the name of Davydov linked her with her father's uncle, Nikolai Vasilyevich Davydov, about whom I wrote earlier. A friend of this uncle's, Professor Chichibabin of the Higher Technical Institute, a world-famous chemist and contemporary of Academician Zilbermunz, was willing to help. But the active communist cadres won the day. Lelya remained expelled.

Thus, both my sister Masha and Lelya were at a loss what to do. Just at that time, Kirill Urusov came to see us and mentioned that the Moscow Geological Committee was moving premises and needed people to load up its collection for transfer. The pay offered was low, but the work promised to be interesting. The very next day the three of them went to the old villa by Yauzky Gate, where they immediately set to work with great spirit. The geologist Yablokov, supervisor of their work, was more than satisfied. Then came the time for pay and the three of them were asked to write down their names. It was over thirty years later, now a corresponding member of the Academy of Science, that Yablokov confessed with what horror he had seen those three names – Princess Golitysna, Prince Urusov and Davydova was doutbless of the same ilk.

It was too late to abandon the work of sorting the specimens, so he hired three other people without even asking their names. However, the whole affair ended happily. That summer Kirill and Lelya set off on their first geological expedition, and Masha won over the professor of geology, Alexei Pavlovich Ivanov. Learning that we were being driven out of Moscow, this man took a great interest in our fate. He had a *dacha* near the station of Khlebnikovo on the Savelovskaya line; in the neighbouring village of Kotovo was another *dacha*, owned by a friend, which he recommended Masha to rent. Father went to see the owner in Moscow and signed a one-year lease at a moderate rent.

Still we delayed any move, hoping for the best. But the city court rejected our appeal and set a deadline for our eviction. In the early years after the revolution, if evicted one was offered alternative accommodation, usually poor but nonetheless a roof over one's head. Now the authorities' merciless position was, "Go where you please!" Three days before the deadline, two people, accompanied by the house manager, knocked at our door. I opened and when they saw all our furniture still in place, they started to shout and threaten that they would throw it all out into the street, saying that now people without the vote were being evicted all over Moscow.

Our eighty-year-old grandfather, once governor of the city, who had done much for the poor and needy in his time, took our eviction very badly. When these people arrived he was sitting playing patience, but now he cried out, "I can't take this, I really can't take any more!" and slumped in his chair. The house manager and I took hold of him and gave him some water; the two unknown men just laughed. My mother came running out of her room and while comforting grandfather, assured the men that we would move out within the next three days.

We distributed the heavier pieces of furniture, that we had been left by mother's cousin, amongst our friends. Fortunately, we had not far to move that furniture, which included some books. What we burned in the courtyard were old letters, mainly our great-grandfather Mikhail Fyodorovich's correspondence with his wife, Anna Trofimovna, together with Aunt Sasha's diaries and accounts. Historians today would find Aunt Sasha's papers invaluable as the basis for a learned dissertation.

Early on Sunday morning, four or five commercial carriers came to our door, as well as many of our young friends. Furniture, trunks, boxes, bundles, suitcases, books and portraits were loaded up, covered with tarpaulins and tied down. Vladimir paid special attention to the loading of the portraits. From the windows opposite, curious onlookers stared down at our eviction; whether they were sorry for us or gloated, I do not know. The horses began to move, and Vladimir and I walked beside them.

We had lived on Eropkinsky Lane for seven years. In those years we had seen four weddings, five arrests and the birth of three children. We had celebrated many a birthday, name days and other joyful occasions. These had been the years of my and my sisters' youth, years of hard work and the joys of learning. What cares and sorrows there had been had been quickly forgotten, even though now I have been mostly writing about unpleasant events. There had been no deaths – our grandmother had died in Sergiyev Posad. Always we had lived together in love and friendship.

Our carts rumbled across the whole of Moscow. When we passed the prison of Butyrka, Vladimir and I looked up at its high walls, remembering our experience of it. We went out of Moscow on the

Dimitrovsky highway and came to the village of Likhobory, where – as was always the case on the roads into Moscow – there stood a tavern that was patronised by carriers bringing supplies into the city. We ordered a dish of food, Vladimir ordered vodka, and we talked to the carriers, who turned out to be from Tula province, and indeed very close to our Bulchalki. They all had the same story as I had heard from my cab driver when I was released from Butyrka, that it was dangerous to return home, that people were being driven out of their farms, their cattle confiscated, and that there was no mercy even for small children. The drivers said you could not buy hay in Moscow, nor oats. How were they to feed their horses?

Vladimir advised them to sell up and find work on the big construction projects. As it happened, a few days earlier the papers had issued a stern ultimatum – horses were being fed bread, it was written, whilst the people were going short of bread. So rationing was having to be introduced, yet another example of our incompetent rulers placing the blame for their failures on others – this time, on horses. Within a very short time there were no horses on the streets, so nothing could be transported. Trams were of no use, and in those days taxis were undreamed-of luxuries. The poor horses went under the knife; butchers now sold horsemeat, as well as horsemeat sausages. A joke sprang up: "Why do Muscovites now walk in the roadway, not on the pavement? Because they have replaced the horses they've eaten".

Our cavalcade moved on from Likhobory. A fine, autumn rain began to fall; the wind got up, blowing piercingly. We tramped on through the mud alongside the carts. Vladimir was anxious about the portraits and kept checking their covering. It was evening when we reached Kotovo, to find the house only just beginning to warm up. Masha and her cavaliers, Igor Daksergof and Valery Pertsov, were awaiting our arrival. We unloaded and paid off the carters, parting from them with warmth and sincere gratitude. Vladimir hastened to unpack the pictures, to find that the uppermost one of our great-grandmother, Varvara Ivanovna Golitsyna, was badly damaged by rain, but the rest unaffected. Thus, in October 1929, did our life in Kotovo begin.

Many people who had lost the vote were being driven out of Moscow at this time. Some of the old ladies involved in the case of the 'Embroidered Cushion' were among them, including Princess Chrystina Golitsyna. After her death Irakly Andronnikov discovered in her suitcase on Perkhushkovo station the portrait of N.F.I, the beloved lady of the poet Lermontov. Priests were being exiled, as well as NEPmen who, despite cruel taxation at two or three times the proper rate, still persisted in trying to operate their factories or their trading activities. The well-known family of the Nikulichevys tried to hold out in their spacious apartment to the very last moment. People marched in and began to throw out their furniture. They pulled a beautiful chandelier out of the ceiling by its roots, breaking most of its crystal pendants. The family moved to their *dacha* in Ilyinskoye, whilst their son went to Sandunovsky baths, and after paying for a separate room, slashed his wrists in the bath.

I have already mentioned Alexander Alexandrovich Rayevsky – Uncle Shurik – married to Baroness Nadezhda Bogadnovna Meiendorf – Aunt Nadya – who was our Elena's aunt. Uncle Shurik was serving his ten year sentence in the "workers' corridor" in Butyrka. Then Aunt Nadya was arrested and sent to the Gulag in Karelia, leaving their three young daughters in the care of their faithful nanny in the flat on the Arbat. They too were evicted and I was one of the friends who helped them move out to Losino-Ostrovsky, where they joined an already expelled Uvarov relative in a winter *dacha* she had rented. Aunt Nadya did not stay long in the Gulag, thanks to the help of the wonderful Peshkova, who found her, her daughters and their faithful nanny a couple of rooms on Starokonyushnaya Street.

After ten years in Butyrka, Uncle Shurik was sent into exile in the Ural town of Mias, returning to Moscow on the eve of the war. There he was arrested again and disappeared for ever. Aunt Nadya died twenty years later. All those "former people" who had survived the horrors of the thirties and forties attending her funeral service. At first, we did not recognise each other, but on the way to the cemetery fell into endless reminiscences of our youth.

17. A Time of Tragedy

1

The Osorgins, Uncle Misha and Aunt Liza, who was my mother's cousin, their daughters Maria and Tonya, and my sister Lina with her little daughter, continued to live in their little house near *Verst* 17 Station on the Bryansk (now Kiev) railway line. There were no more concerts, the piano was shut, and those whom Aunt Liza had once accompanied on the piano were now languishing in various prisons. Maria was arrested, and released with a "minus six" sentence of exile; she chose the not very distant town of Maloyaroslavets. I visited the Osorgins from time to time and had heart-to-heart talks with Uncle Misha about our family misfortunes. When it came to our legal battles he was deeply sympathetic.

The Osorgins no longer went to Butyrka prison to visit Georgy. He had been sent to Solovki after some kind of incident. Lina managed somehow to find out where the prison train was standing in the yards at Nikolaievsky Station. Lina, Masha and I went there and stood next to the sealed carriage waving our handkerchiefs. After a while Georgy's head appeared in a tiny window. It was the first time I had seen him with a long beard. He said how good it was to breathe the pure spring air. A guard came and told us it was forbidden to talk to the prisoners. Lina begged him to allow her just ten minutes. The guard withdrew a little distance, keeping an eye on us. I cannot recall what Georgy talked about. Masha stood by, crying. Then the guard came up again and insisted we left. Neither Masha nor I ever saw Georgy again.

Lina saw him twice. I was travelling in the north when, thanks to Peshkova's intervention, she went to Solovki with Sonya, the wife of Oleg Volkov, who was the grand-daughter of the wealthy capitalist and philanthropist Sava Ivanovich Mamontov. Lina also managed a second trip to Solovki in the autumn of 1929, again thanks to Peshkova. By this time the OGPU were making it very difficult for relatives to come to Solovki to visit the prisoners. Lina's trip was paid for by the entire family, and even people outside the family, and so she was able to set off with valid documents and supplies of provisions. While waiting for her connecting train in Kemi she met Artemi Rayevsky and Dimitri Gudovich, who were just starting their spell in the Gulag, and were unloading timber for export. Lina said that Artemi looked very sad and kept repeating "It's absolute hell!" whilst Dimitri seemed cheerful, jokingly encouraging Artemi.

The number of prisoners had gone up tenfold; they were no longer on the island of Solovki alone, but also on the mainland. The station was quite different from before. The churches were closed, there were no services, and the monks either lived on the mainland if they were still free, or had been arrested. The prisoners lived in anxiety and fear, the guards were vicious. Lina's arrival was greeted by the prisoners as an unprecedented sensation. The prison authorities, following their orders from Moscow, allotted the couple a separate little house. By day Georgy went to his work, returning to Lina in the evening. Later, Lina told us how that time was the happiest time in their short marriage. Their dream was that, since it was now four years since his arrest, he would be free after six more. Even with Peshkova's help, they would not be allowed to live in Moscow, so they would find a place in exile where they could live a happy life. Lina returned to Moscow radiantly happy, telling everyone about those wonderful ten days. She sent off a telegram, and waited for an answer. Then there arrived two letters, one from Dimitri Gudovich to his mother and sister, and one from Artemi Rayevsky to his sisters. Both letters contained the same words, "Please give Lina our heartfelt condolences on her tragic news".

These letters came when we had already moved to Kotovo, but I was constantly in Moscow. I heard about those words quite by chance, but some kind of intuition made me uneasy. I went to Tsaritsino, where the Gudovichs lived in exile, and Maria Sergeievna, Dimitri's mother, showed me the letter. I immediately went to the Novinsky market where, behind the magnificent Gagarin mansion built by the architect Giliardi, the Rayevskys, Osorgins and Samarins were all living in one flat. Tonya showed me Artemi's letter, which indeed had more or less the same phrase in it. Tonya, too, was alarmed, but we decided not to tell Lina.

I hunted down my mother, who was at that time deeply involved in the case of the 'Embroidered Cushion', finding her at prayer in the church of Pokrov in Levshin. I called her out and told her my fears. "Oh, my God, how terrible!" she cried. By the next day, so many people had heard of this phrase that it inevitably came to Lina's ears.

She went to Kuznetsky Most to the PRC, where she would in any event have gone to thank Peshkova for making her trip to Solovki possible, and told Ekaterina Pavlovna of the letters. Peshkova tried to calm Lina's fears, but suggested she come back. Two days later, I was coming out of the Meien's flat on Bolshoy Levshinsky Lane when I met Lina, as white as a sheet and with sightless eyes.

"It's true," she said in a whisper.

We went up. My sister Sonya looked at us questioningly. We took off our coats, went into the room and sat down.

Lina repeated, "It's true," and slowly, in a calm voice, told us what Peshkova had told her. No one cried, we just sat there stony-faced, but that grief without tears was worse than anything. Yagoda had told Peshkova that Georgy was executed on the tenth of October, three days after Lina's departure. Much later, Lina remembered something that had happened during her stay with Georgy. They had been on the point of going to bed when someone knocked at the door. Georgy went out and for a long time was engaged in conversation with the visitors. Coming back in, he told her it was nothing, something to do with his work. Lina had paid no attention to the incident, but now she realised that they had come to take him away for execution, and he had managed to persuade them to wait until she had left.

Fearful of the authorities, we wanted to hold the requiem service for Georgy in secret, but news of his fate spread far and wide. The church of Saints Boris and Gleb where he and Lina had been wed was now closed, so we held the service in the church of the Mother of God of Rzhev, later also destroyed, in the same street, Povarskaya. There was a big crowd, many of them in tears. Lina and the Osorgins stood with frozen faces. The service was led most movingly by Father Mikhail Shpik, though for the sake of prudence he did not preach. His reputation was that of a fine preacher and thoughtful philosopher. Jewish by birth, he was married to Princess Natalya Dimitriyevna Shakhovskaya, the daughter of a prominent member of the Kadet Party and minister in the Provisional Government, Dimitri Ivanovich Shakhovsky. Both Father Mikhail and his wife perished in the Gulag. Their children were adopted by their mother's sister, Anna Dimitriyevna, and given the name of Shakhovsky. Dimitri Ivanovich himself survived a series of OGPU chiefs – Dzerzhinsky, Menzhinsky, Yagoda, Ezhov – only to be arrested in 1939 at the age of seventy-eight, when he perished.

I brooded a great deal about Georgy's fate. I wondered whether I could be a man like him, but felt this was not very likely. I compared

Georgy to Uncle Misha Lopukhin. In my fantasy I likened him to the heroes in *War and Peace*. How would they have behaved if they had lived in our time? Georgy would have been like Prince Andrei, never betraying his principles and convictions, and would, of course, have perished. In the autumn of 1930, when I was setting off to work in the northern Caucasus and was being seen off by several people, Lina came up to me and discreetly showed me six red-covered passports for foreign travel that she had just received. She begged me to try to find out how her husband had died. I promised, and also said that I would name my first-born son in honour of Georgy.

It was very difficult to question people, and former inmates of Solovki were frightened to talk. Boris Akerman, a Crimean Tartar and former officer, had known Georgy well in Solovki and did tell me a little of what happened when I met him on the building site of the Moscow-Volga canal seven years later. There had been several attempts to escape from the island, but the escapees had always been caught, either on the shore or at the frontier. But one attempt had succeeded. Three naval officers reached the mainland on a boat and, going west, crossed the Finnish border. The authorities, thinking they had drowned, had abandoned the chase.

This caused a sensation in the West. These exhausted men in rags had arrived as if from a distant planet, and told stories of their life as prisoners that seemed beyond belief. One of the men still had tokens in his pocket that showed how work in the camps was rewarded by proportionate amounts of food. Photographs were printed in all the Western press. When I was in Paris in 1968 I asked to see these, but they could not be found. English workers in the timber business now began to find pencilled messages on the logs they received, revealing to the Western world how this timber was felled by slave labour. The journalists took up the cry, "Look where this timber comes from!" The world became aware that behind our closed frontiers there were tens, even perhaps hundreds of thousands of prisoners. In fact, they numbered in the millions.

Yagoda got it in the neck from a furious Stalin. Articles with Molotov's by-line appeared in the press, denying the stories. The stories of forced labour in the USSR were described as total fabrications, pure slander put out by the enemies of socialism. Yagoda raged and sent a commission to Solovki to find out how the breakout had been organised, who had known about it, and to shoot them all. That is how forty men were executed, including Georgy. (In his memoirs, Oleg Volkov, quoting a female prisoner, Putilova, gives the figure as four hundred executed. I do not know which is right.)

I quote here in full Lina's letter to her second cousin, Sergei Grigorevich Trubetskoi, written forty years later after the appearance of Solzhenitsin's *Gulag Archipelago*:

There are many errors in this book. In 1929 my visit was not for three days, but for two weeks. I left there on the thirteenth of October (old style) and the forty men were shot on the sixteenth. Georgy was not involved in any attempt to escape by sea. He told me this himself. He was called as a witness, as he had known these naval officers. But after my departure it would seem that someone (and there were such people) decided to liquidate the officers condemned for counter-revolutionary activities, which is why Georgy and Sivers were shot, even though they had no involvement in the escape. So the sentence that "he was shot immediately" is untrue. I remember that walk to Glubokaya Bay, and not to Svyatoye Ozero.

I was told how Georgy went with the other condemned men singing "Christ is Risen"' and other prayers as they passed under the monastery gates. I well remember those gates. They faced out on the bay where an old steamship lay at anchor, where Georgy and I had been given a cabin for four weeks when I visited him for the first time in August 1928. I was at all the wondrous services held in the cemetery church of Holy Onufry, where no less than three bishops celebrated – there were sixteen bishops and many priests in Solovki at that time. The singing was especially beautiful, with on one side the local monks and clergy from the still-functioning Solovetsky monastery, and on the other side the prisoners, including many clergy and monks. I still have a large photograph of Bishop Ilarion of Moscow and others.

My second visit to Solovki was in October 1929, after our son Misha was born. For a long time I was tortured by the thought that if I had not paid that visit, Georgy might have survived. From spring of that year he had been transferred to the little island of Anzer, north of Solovki, as punishment for sending communion and the holy robe to the dying Father Pyotr Zverev of Voronezh. Georgy was even put in the punishment cells, but Maxim Gorky came on a visit, so all the prisoners in the punishment cells were released. If only he had stayed there and not come into the field of vision of the infuriated leadership!

When I learned all the truth from Peshkova, I begged her to obtain passports allowing us to emigrate so that my children would not have to become young pioneers. Let me add to this letter something told to Solzhenitsyn by Academician D.S. Likhachev, himself once a prisoner in Solovki, about Georgy. It may not be totally accurate, as Solzhenitsyn took no notes. Georgy's mysterious death had given me no peace both before and after the war. I felt that Likhachev could clarify a lot for me. Three times I travelled to Leningrad to try and see him. On two of these occasions he was not there and on the third I learned that he had just lost his daughter, so it was not the time to approach him. I also tried to reach him in Moscow, when he was there on a visit, but again without success. He sent me his books, signed by himself, but I never dared write to him about what I really wanted to know.

Sixty years after Georgy's death, my son had a two hour long conversation with Likhachev, which he recorded as follows:

Interview with Academician D.S. Likhachev:

Dimitri Sergeievich received me in his sitting room for two hours, after which I hurried off to catch the train to Moscow. I made written notes of what he said.

From the autumn of 1928, he was an inmate in the fortress building of Solovki Monastery, founded in the fifteenth century by the most reverend monks Zosima and Savaty. The camp held around forty thousand prisoners. There were many orphaned, homeless adolescents in the camp. Likhachev was involved with them, recording their details and listening to their stories, working at educating and re-training them. He was acquainted with Georgy Osorgin, though not closely, probably because of their age difference – he was 23 and Georgy 35. Georgy worked as a clerk in the health section, establishing the findings of the medical committee and acting as witness for the prisoners. The chairman of the committee was a former professor of medicine, Zhizhelenko, who had become a priest and was arrested in Leningrad when he was already a bishop. The third member was a volunteer who invariably tried to countermand the professor's decisions to let prisoners off physical work. Likhachev had been put in that category when he arrived in the camp weak and exhausted, and the professor did the same for Likhachev's former teacher, Andriyevsky.

Georgy Osorgin was of medium height, with fair hair, and walked with an energetic soldier's step. He wore a short coat and went bareheaded until it got very cold, when he jauntily sported a round cap. He was given to joking, and was on a special list of those allowed to attend church. In those days, Onufria church was not yet shut and there were still seven monks. These monks were skilled in catching a particular kind of tender-fleshed herring, so tasty that much of their catch was sent direct to the Kremlin. When in 1929 the church was closed and the monks scattered, no more fish were caught, and the knowledge of the currents and places to fish was lost forever.

At the end of September, the camp authorities received orders to shoot four hundred inmates so as to rid themselves of dangerous prisoners, such as officers who were held in esteem by the other prisoners, and to tighten camp discipline. The arrests began in early October. The men were packed into the cells on Sekirnaya Hill; Georgy, his friend Sivers, Baron Fitztaun, Lozina-Lozinsky, who had been warden of the university church in Leningrad, Pokrovsky, the one-legged teacher of ballistics in the Artillery Academy, who always introduced himself as "White-bandit Pokrovsky", and Gatsuk, an officer from Kiev who headed the sports unit that was located on the shores of Svyatoye Ozero. Gatsuk had a devoted German Shepherd dog called Black.

The prisoners were held in the cells for about a month. The regime in the camp was still quite liberal. Relatives were allowed to visit, though such visits required a great deal of influence. Likhachev's parents came in early October, as well as Georgy Osorgin's wife, Lina. Georgy was allowed out of his cell on his word of honour that he would not tell his wife anything – he kept his word. (Sixty years later, Aunt Lina wanted me to find out the reason for his death, as she still wondered whether her visit had been the cause.) Likhachev saw Georgy walking with his wife near the fosse on the north side of the monastery fortress, and noted that she was taller than her husband. "I wanted to tell you that detail so that your aunt knows that I really did see him," Likhachev told me.

On the twenty-ninth of October, the prisoners were not allowed out of their cells and were taken in batches for execution. The dog called Black howled miserably. All the dogs were shot, but Black escaped. Some members of the escort became hysterical.

The men went to their deaths in sad powerlessness; only a certain Pokrovsky put up a fight with his wooden leg as they filed out through the main gate of the monastery, and was shot on the spot. The executions took place on the edge of the cemetery, close to the women's barracks. In command was Dimitri Uspensky, head of the cultural-educational side of the camp. He was a volunteer and had come to Solovki after shooting his father, a deacon. At his trial he had explained that his father was a class enemy. He was sent to Solovki, where he became a Chekist. He is said to be still alive. He himself used his revolver to shoot those prisoners who were still alive. The executions went on by day and by night. In the morning, the pit was still moving, as it had been only lightly covered over. On the morning of the twenty-ninth, Likhachev had seen Uspensky come into the medical section and go to the toilet to wash his boots clean of dirt and blood. Julia Nikolaievna Danzas worked in the same office; she told Likhachev of the panic and hysteria in the women's barracks the evening before. Later, she showed him the site of the burials.

Julia Nikolaievna had had an extraordinary life. In her youth she had been a lady-in-waiting to the Empress Alexandra. When the German war began she joined a regiment of Ural Cossacks, Old Believers with very strict morals, and fought courageously at the front, being promoted to officer's rank. In 1917, just before the revolution, she was offered command of a women's battalion, but refused. Likhachev did not know what she had done during the civil war. Before being sent to Solovki she had been imprisoned in the staging camp at Alexandrovsk in Siberia. She was set free in 1932, and he remembered how she had visited him at his parents' flat on Lakhtinskaya Street in Leningrad. With Gorky's help she managed to leave the USSR in 1933. Gorky, before the revolution, had been imprisoned for political crimes in the Peter-Paul Fortress. Julia Nikolaievna got the minister of the interior of the time, Prince Svyiatopolk-Mirsky, to intercede on his behalf. After his visit to the White Sea – Baltic canal, Gorky no longer intervened on anyone's behalf, but remembering how Julia had once helped him, he made an exception, and pulled strings to obtain an exit visa for her on condition that she gave her word of honour, once abroad, not to say anything or write about the camps she had been in. In France, Julia Nikolaievna became a nun, and then, a few years later, Pope Pius XI released her from her oath, and she published a book of her memoirs ("If only I could get hold of that book," exclaimed Likhachev).

In the summer of 1988, Likhachev went back to Solovki. On the site of the executions there now stands a little blue house. When building its foundations, many bones and skulls were dug up, mostly at a depth of only eighty centimetres. The occupants calmly told Likhachev that when planting their potatoes they often came across bones.

Dimitri Sergeievich mentioned other witnesses, S.N. Antsiferov, and the memoirs already mentioned of Julia N. Danzas, about which he had read in Antsiferov's book. It was when he was in Paris that he had seen that book and the date given as October the twenty-eighth, though he himself only remembered it was at the end of the month. So in the end the question remains, can one know, sixty years on, the exact date of the death of one single person? I think the answer is, yes, if one tries hard enough, and bearing in mind that Georgy Mikhailovich Osorgin was an outstanding man.

Georgy Sergeievich Golitsyn

How many were actually executed in Solovki at the end of October 1929? Was it forty as Peshkova had told Lina and Boris Akkerman had told me, or four hundred as Oleg Volkov and Academician Likhachev claimed? It was very likely around four hundred. I am sure Yagoda hid the true figure from Peshkova, and Akkerman could not bring himself to tell me the truth. The figure of four hundred was also given in the documentary film *The Rulers of Solovki*. The archives of the OGPU/NKVD have the truth, hidden away.

With this comment I could bring my account of this terrible chapter to an end, but there is still something more to add – I actually met one of the people mentioned by Likhachev, namely Uspensky, the man who commanded the execution squad at Solovki, the man who killed his own father, the deacon. A book was published that described the journey of a group of Soviet writers along the newly opened White Sea – Baltic canal in 1933. They were accompanied by Uspensky. He is much praised; there is even a verse about his smiling face together with a sketch of a round-faced young man, grinning happily. It was a glorious trip as the writers talked, ate and drank, and viewed the canal and its locks and sluices from the deck before returning to Moscow. They were not shown the prisoners.

I came across Uspensky when he was deputy head of construction on the Moscow-Volga canal; he was now a puffed out, plump man with three gold bars on his shoulder, driven about in his personal car. His story now was slightly different from Likhachev's account – the father he had killed had been a priest, not a deacon. I do not know how he managed to be the sole survivor of all the Chekists who had been on the building of the canal, but later on he was provisional deputy head of the building of the Kuibyshev hydro-electric plant. What Gulag camps he headed during and after the war, I simply do not know.

The documentary film *The Rulers of Solovki* had a great emotional impact on me. It shows a former leading Chekist, stating that he began his career by killing his own father, and one sees an old man, his chest decorated with six rows of medal ribbons, holding a string bag, limping along a Moscow street. When I saw this scene I cried, "Look, that's the man who killed my sister Lina's husband, Georgy Osorgin!"

18. The Struggle for Existence

1

Until they bought the village of Archangelsk, Kotovo had been the home of the Yusupov family. When we moved there all that remained of their property was a few old lime trees and the ruins of the stone foundations of their mansion. There was a small church with one dome, with memorial tablets of various members of the family. I do not know whether any of the lime trees have survived, but now the church has been turned into a garage and is so altered and disfigured that nothing of its old character remains. The village is not mentioned in any guidebook.

It was a struggle to adapt to our new life. Instead of electricity we had paraffin; instead of running water, trips to the well. Journeys to Moscow took several hours and the trains were infrequent. The house was also not big enough for us. Nonetheless, Vladimir hung the portraits of our ancestors on the walls and had his own work table. The rest of us had to make do with the dining table. Grandfather was found a room close to Uncle Vladimir and Aunt Ely Trubetskoi and their family in Sergiyev Posad.

Our life was also made harder by the introduction of ration cards. Workers, office staff and dependants received varying amounts of bread, but people without the vote received nothing at all – you had to survive as best you could. This system had been introduced while we were still in Eropkinsky Street, but we had been saved by the kindness of two workers' families who, although they should have hated us, in fact made sure we had both black and white bread every day. When we moved to Kotovo we had neither bread, nor flour, nor lard.

It may seem incredible, but we were saved by dogs. The frontiers of the country were not then fenced with thousands of kilometres of electrified wire, not even barbed wire. People fleeing collectivisation were managing to escape into the capitalist world. With the slogan "Close the Borders!" our authorities decided to encourage the breeding of fierce Doberman dogs, and for this issued ration cards for their supply of food. There were plenty of volunteers, even though it was not easy work looking after the dogs; they had to be walked every day and regularly taken for training. The poor dogs could not complain that most of the food destined for them was diverted to our needs, especially the horsemeat. We had no qualms about eating it. Several families that we knew also acquired dogs, but did not want to eat the meat, and gave it to us instead.

One of Masha's suitors was an elegant, rather listless young man, Nikolai Dimitriyevich Kuchin. He used to visit us in Kotovo, bringing Masha little editions of Russian poets like Gumilev, that were printed in Berlin, and for us packets of horsemeat obtained by his parents with dogs' ration cards. We all thought this combination of gifts made him an exemplary suitor. Then his visits stopped, and we discovered that he had been arrested – it could have been for passing around Gumilev's poetry. Years later, now released from the camps, I met him on the construction of the Moscow-Volga canal. We reminisced about those distant years of our youth. After the war, I bumped into him again, now a sick and lonely old man.

A decree was published allowing the under-age children of people deprived of their voting rights to be issued ration cards for groceries and bread. So for the eleven members of our family we now had five cards: those for Masha and Katya and the three children of Vladimir and Elena. At this time there was a sharp increase in the price of food sold in the markets. A hue and cry had gone up over the idea that markets were manifestations of the petit bourgeois spirit and should be shut down. Manufactured goods also disappeared from the shops. I do not know what happened to the textile factories. A joke made the rounds: "A peasant woman demands to see President Kalinin to complain that there are neither textiles nor ready-made dresses to be bought anywhere. He reassures her by saying that in Africa the people go about naked. She replies, 'So they've had socialism in Africa for the last fifty years?'" There was another joke about disappearing foodstuffs. "So the letter M has vanished from our alphabet – there's no milk, no meat, no macaroni, no milled flour. All we're left with is Minister of Trade Mikoyan . . ." Here the joke becomes obscene, so I cannot repeat it.

We had to let our servant Katya go. She wept as she said goodbye to the little ones she had come to love. Now only family members were left. Mother did the cooking unless she was away, when Elena took over. Father's job was to look after the grandchildren.

2

Superficially my brother Vladimir had not changed. He was still energetic and good-humoured, but I sensed that he suffered most from our status as *lishenets* (citizens deprived of the vote). He was earning good money and was much liked by publishers and editors. Then the position began to change. At first Popov at the *Universal Pathfinder* concealed from Vladimir the fact that attempts that were being made to drive out their best artist. Of the first six covers of the magazine in 1929, four were by Vladimir. Then a new editor, Yakovlev, put an embargo on Vladimir's work. Yakovlev was a communist who had moved up from the printing side and knew nothing about editing, but could sniff out class enemies. When he discovered that the magazine was feeding a prince and a deprived voter, Yakovlev stopped giving him any commissions, despite Popov's protests that Vladimir was their best artist. Popov not only valued Vladimir the artist, he also loved the man. Some of the artists decided to help Vladimir by having him do the work, presenting it as theirs but giving him the payments. This stratagem only worked for a short time, as Vladimir's work was so clearly his and no one else's.

The *Pathfinder* was still printing Uncle Vladimir Trubetskoi's stories under the pseudonym V. Vetov, but in the autumn of 1929 his last, and I think best story in the series *The Strange Adventures of Bochonkin and Khvoshch* was published – *The Rosy Black Skewbald*. With that his work for the magazine came to an end.

I was sacked as well, another draughtsman taking my place. I did, however, visit the office one more time. For an article about polar exploration, Popov needed a map of Wrangel Island. I had not been able to track one down anywhere, not even in the Lenin Library, and then by chance a copy of an American magazine that Uncle Alexander Vladimirovich sent us regularly turned out to have a fully detailed map of the island. On Vladimir's advice I copied it out, putting all the names into Russian, and took it to Popov. He was alone in the office and, seeing me, sat up in surprise. I said hello and handed over the map. For a long time he sat looking at it, then pulled out his wallet and gave me a ten rouble note. It was obvious he was paying me out of his own pocket. In a sad voice he said, "Give your brother my warmest, most sincere greetings." I never saw him again.

The comparison between the magazine under Popov and later is like the comparison between heaven and earth. The adventure stories of foreign writers, as well as Russian writers like Alexander Belyaev, were no longer published; instead came stories of the civil war, usually written by authors without any talent. Popov either resigned or was sacked. Later the magazine itself shut down, partly thanks to Maxim Gorky's influence, as he considered adventure stories were harmful to young proletarians. Popov left Moscow and was able to resurrect his magazine in Sverdlovsk under the title of the *Urals' Pathfinder*, and invited Vladimir to contribute, but Vladimir only finished two or three commissions. Probably the watchful officials in Sverdlovsk had sniffed out his prince's title.

The editors of *Young Guard* continued to use Vladimir for another two years. They valued him greatly and I can remember how whenever he came into the office they would greet him with smiles, say nothing at all about his being a prince and a non-citizen, and hand over their commissions, begging him to do the work as quickly as possible.

The *Pioneer* supported Vladimir in the person of its editor, Boris Ivanter, a tall, handsome man who died in the war. At the magazine *Knowledge is Power* Vladimir was given work by the engineer Nikolai Bulatov, and the philologist Nikolai Solntsev. Then there was the newspaper *Friendly Lads*, edited by an old Bolshevik, Gvosdikova, the wife of Frumkin, commissar of finances for the RSFSR; later both perished in the Gulag. When I went to her with my maps or Vladimir's work, she would sit me down, ask me all about my life and doings, and then urge me to leave Moscow and find work on the big construction sites. I would thank her for her advice, but with my status, how could I leave? She did not know that I had lost the right to vote.

Vladimir continued to illustrate the sea stories of writers such as V.S. Zhitkov and A.S. Novikov-Priboy. One day he went to Alexei Silych as he was engaged in writing his novel *Tsusim*. Silyich confessed that, when thinking of Admiral Rozhestvensky, who had stubbornly led his fleet to sure annihilation by the enemy, he could not helping thinking of Stalin leading our country God knows where.

3

On that terrible day for our family in 1929, I had just had my twentieth birthday. Up until then I had led a fairly carefree and light-hearted life, had read and studied a great deal and danced the foxtrot with real pleasure. Now I was a changed person; the eleven days in prison and our expulsion from Moscow, as well as the other blows of fate, were a turning point. I withdrew into myself, rarely going to the theatre or to evening parties. More than that, I lived with the knowledge that as a person deprived of the vote, existing on random earnings and still a titular prince, I was inevitably going to end up in prison, and neither the goddess Themis nor Peshkova would be able to help me. People were constantly being arrested and either exiled or sent to the Gulag. Only a few were ever released. Why were they arrested? There was a saying: "Give me a man and I'll soon find a law to fit him".

Father worried about me, fearing that I would miss out on my higher education. After the course in literature was closed down, many students found other places for themselves. Andrei Durnovo got a place at Moscow University, Lyalya Ilyinskaya at Leningrad University, whilst Valery Pertsov and Igor Daksergof still had jobs in their institutes. Since the committee that decided on these issues required a full biographical form to be filled out, I was convinced it was hopeless for me to apply. I did not want to face the humiliation of being rejected.

An advertisement then appeared in the papers, announcing that students with middle school education could join a course in philosophy without taking a preliminary examination. Father was enthusiastic, "Of course it'll include lessons in Soviet political literacy, but you'll study humanitarian subjects, as well as Kant, Fichte, Schelling – you'll get a higher education." I went to Volkhonka Street, asked to join the course and was accepted. A delighted lady handed me a thick folder of papers, and, equally delighted, I left. On the train home I opened the folder and was horrified; I was going to have to study a whole series of works on Marxism-Leninism, on the history of the Party, on historical and dialectical materialism, political economy and economic politics. Incidentally, practically all the authors of these works, starting with Bukharin and Zinovyev, were eventually unmasked as enemies of the people. What thousands of students have had endlessly to swot up on such useless, boring, pointless writings and so graduate from their studies at a professionally mediocre level – doctors who cannot heal, teachers who cannot teach.

Taking time off from my draughtsmanship, I forced myself to begin studying this indigestible literature until, after about two weeks, a packet arrived with all the usual application forms on which you had to describe your social origins, what your parents did and whether you had ever been deprived of your voting rights. I hung all the papers from my folder up for use in the toilet, and so ended my attempts to get a higher education. Father then encouraged me to study a language. "You'll never be in need with a knowledge of languages," he said. But which one? French, of course, since in

Eropkinsky Lane I had been keen on Zola and Maupassant. I did most of my French reading on the train, or waiting for one. One day a man sitting next to me on the station bench went on at me about reading the works of an author from a decaying capitalist country. Why did I not read the writings of our great Soviet authors? He quoted to me some of their names. Thanks to having heard about them, or read reviews of their books in the papers, I was able to think up some sort of comment. I still do not know whether my interlocutor was manifesting social watchfulness or was just curious, but the incident frightened me. There is an old saying, "A scared crow fears even a bush".

The attitudes of people towards me were varied but were never indifferent. Some tried secretly to do me harm, others were sorry for me. My earnings were steadily declining, while prices were rising; my contribution to the family's housekeeping became less and less. One day I went to the editorial office of *Knowledge is Power* in the hope of getting a commission and was bluntly told, "Don't come here any more." To avoid further hurt, I did not personally go to the offices of the *Pioneer* and *Pioneer's Truth*. At the magazine *Be Your Own Agronomist* they suspected nothing about me and actually asked me to become a staff member, giving me a form to fill out. I was aghast at the questions and said I would fill it out at home. That was the last they saw of me.

There were also people who wished me well. A remote friend of our family, the philologist and landowner Anatoly Mikhalovich Fokin, had become a geologist during his time in the Gulag. Irakly Andronnikov, in his story *The Riddle of N.F.I*, has portrayed this extraordinary man, though when Andronnikov approached Fokin's relatives for material about him, he was received with mistrust; life in the Gulag made people suspicious of everything. This Anatoly Fokin ordered geological charts from me on condition that my invoices were in some other name. I chose Valery Pertsov to be my intermediary. My brother-in-law, Victor Meien, also commissioned me, again on condition that it was through a third party, and he recommended me to Professor Sergei Nikolaievich Stroganov, the head of the Moscow sewage system. Stroganov said of himself, "I'm the head of Moscow's back passage." Victor must have said something about me to him, as he treated me as though I were a close member of his family. He and his wife often asked me to stay for a meal, and I had some big, well-paid commissions from him. I billed this work in my own name, and these invoices were the only ones I could show to prove that I was not a social parasite. Today, when

I walk along Trekhprudny Lane, I never fail to look up at that three-story house where my benefactor once lived.

Frequently, I had to spend the night in Moscow. There were three homes where I was always welcome – at Lyalya Ilyinskaya's mother's flat on Povarskaya Street, at the Daksergof parents' home in Denezhny Lane and at Valery Pertsov's mother's place in Molochny Lane near Ostozhenka. I felt most at home at the latter, where we usually played a game of cards – though the watchful house manager always demanded that I hand over my documents. At all these places I simply slept on the floor, lying on some old mat. My only shoes had reached a state of total decomposition. They were fine for dancing, but worse than useless for the muddy, waterlogged streets of Kotovo. I could not buy new ones; shoes had simply disappeared from the shops. Sofia Grigoryevna Ilyinskaya, noticing my distress, gave me a pair of her husband's good boots. He had been exiled to the river Vychegda. In addition, she often slipped me packets of grain or macaroni.

I had also to feed myself as I went about Moscow. I could not impose on my friends. This was a time when public eating places were being progressively closed down to be replaced by canteens where only workers and employees with passes were allowed. In the markets one could sometimes buy a pie or a glass of thick sour cream, but the militia went about driving out these individual traders. Often it was with an empty stomach that I trudged along the streets of Moscow. One day I noticed a crowd of young people pushing into a restaurant and, made bold by hunger, joined in with them. At the cash desk, however, it turned out that they had special tokens, which of course I did not have. I was grabbed and someone called out, "Get the militia". The manager appeared and in a threatening voice demanded to know who I was. I replied that I lived outside Moscow and that I had come in because I was hungry and showed him my valid identity card with its Kotovo stamp. The manager, without asking me what my occupation was, thought for a moment and then allowed me to eat, though without any bread. I never again tried to enter that kind of eatery.

Another incident was more serious. I was travelling on the platform of a tram when a man boarded who was clearly quite drunk. Suddenly, he fixed his gaze on me and in a loud voice said, "So you're still around? Or have you run away? I know this ***"and he used a curse word. The woman next to him turned to her neighbour. "D'you hear what he's saying about this young man?" All the people on the platform began to look at me suspiciously. My heart began to thump and I edged towards the exit, even though I was far from my destination. The man continued to mutter threats and, even though it was obvious that he was drunk, the people must have half-suspected I was a thief or an escaped convict, or whatever. I got off at the next stop, knocking into the people trying to get on. Someone shouted "Grab him!" The tram moved off and, trying not to run, I walked swiftly into a side street and stopped in a doorway. Once I was sure nobody was following I went back to the tram station. I have no idea who that drunkard was, or how he knew me, but he clearly recognised in me a class enemy.

Yet another incident happened one November night when the streets of Kotovo were as black as pitch and we had all gone to bed to save our paraffin. At ten o'clock there was a loud knock at the door. My heart jumped. Who was it they wanted, me or Vladimir, or both of us? Vladimir went to the door, "Who's there?" he asked.

In answer there came a soft, feminine voice, "The chairman of the village Soviet."

The young woman, who held this quite important position in those cruel times, came in, followed by a large man in a long coat and an older woman carrying a lantern.

"Hand over your gold!" the man shouted from the threshold.

Trying to keep calm, Vladimir asked, "Show us your authorisation."

"What do you mean by authorisation," snarled the man, pointing at the young woman, "here's your authorisation!"

She was in fact a modest young woman, who when we went to her for information was polite and helpful. Now she looked as alarmed as the rest of us.

"Give me your gold and valuables!" said the man again. His eyes were red with hatred for all of us, even the little sleeping children. He was ready to liquidate, crush, torture these class enemies. Mother said as calmly as she could, "We do not have any gold or valuables. All we have is a few silver teaspoons."

She was not telling all the truth. We had one valuable piece, the gold snuffbox with Peter the Great's portrait, given to our ancestors. She had long before sewn it into the head of a fox fur that used to keep grandmother's feet warm when she sat at her card table. Now it served the same purpose for my father's feet, laid out under his desk.

"I don't care about your teaspoons," said the man contemptuously. He took off his overcoat and we could see the strap of his revolver holster. "Hand over your gold and valuables. It's a decree from the Moscow Soviet – all persons without voting rights must give up their valuables. If they don't do it voluntarily, we can carry out a search. I warn you, if I find anything, you're under arrest."

He did not say who that might be. Instead he began to pull open the sideboard, the cupboard, our trunks, the box with the children's toys. He only cast a glance at our books and the portraits on the walls, which were in fact our real valuables. All of us, including the young woman from the village Soviet, stood watching him in fearful silence. Suddenly, he caught sight of the fox fur under the desk, and seeming to intuit something, picked it up. "Ah ha, something heavy here," he exclaimed. We all froze. Whether he really suspected something, I do not know. But at this point he also froze. Standing before him was an entrancing young woman, holding out her hands towards him. It seemed as though he was looking at a mirage and, forgetting all his feelings of hatred towards class enemies, he also put out a hand towards this enchanting girl, my sister Masha. Smiling, she uttered a couple of enticing phrases; he stepped towards her, she stepped back; he repeated his movement towards her, she slipped further away. She had never behaved like this with her admirers. The man forgot about the fox fur. For form's sake he glanced fleetingly around our three rooms, seeking out Masha with his eyes all the while. She was now standing by the stove, aloof and unattainable,.

"Lead me on to the next house," he said to the others. The uninvited guests left.

That same night, searches and confiscations took place all over the region of Moscow among people like us, those who had lost the right to vote. They searched the house of Princess Maria Evgenyevna Lvova, the spinster sister of prince Lvov, who had been Prime Minister in the Provisional Government. Some friends of our friends, the Nikulichevy, saw their father arrested and only released after he had revealed where a box of valuables was buried in the garden. This one night was clearly chosen so as to catch people by surprise, and as they were not enough OGPU men, they enlisted workers and others who were known to have good "class consciousness". It was just such a man who had come to us.

That same fox fur moved from home to home with us. It was only after the war that we cut the head open to remove the precious snuffbox. I will not say where it is now, but when I visit that house I always ask to see it, and I love to tell its story, how it was ordered by Peter the Great from a Parisian craftsman and the adventures that happened to it up to the night of that search, when Masha diverted it from the grasp of that insufficiently class conscious searcher and saved at least one of us from certain arrest.

4

That first winter in Kotovo I spent a lot of my time in thought, whether waiting for a train, or sitting on a train, or walking about the gloomy streets of Moscow, or going off to sleep at home or on the floor of my hospitable friends. My thoughts were focussed on my unfulfilled and rather vague desire to become a writer. I was not going to write for the press, but only for myself. What was then being published was full of hate for the enemies of socialism and unstinting praise for the existing regime; it was not for me. Today nearly all the writings of that time have sunk into oblivion.

The subject I had chosen was a great friend of Vladimir's, Pavel Dimitriyevich Korin. I never discovered how they met, but from what Vladimir told me, Korin and his wife, Praskovya, and brother, Alexander, lived in utter poverty in the attic of a tall house on No. 23, the Arbat. Pavel Korin was more than Vladimir's friend, he was an idol, unattainable and god-like. From what Vladimir told me, Korin had conceived such a grandiose idea for a picture that he intended to devote his entire life to painting it. He also painted portraits of monks and priests. I was fascinated by this amazing fact, that in these cruel times there was living among us a great, selfless and inspired artist. I implored Vladimir to introduce me to him, but my brother refused, saying that Korin, like writers with their rough drafts, never showed anything to strangers. I stopped bothering Vladimir, but could not stop thinking of Pavel Korin. I had met many artists and illustrators in my rounds of the editorial offices; they were good fellows, jolly and kindly, but I knew that they were primarily interested in their earnings, not their art. I also saw that Vladimir tried to earn as much money as he could. I therefore classed illustrators as second-class artists, needing only a bold pen and bright colours, working without much inspiration, concerned above all as to whether their work would be accepted. The artist Favorsky's wonderful illustrations of course prove how wrong I was to have this attitude.

In my imagination, however, I conceived a story that I entitled *Town and City. Town* meant my experience of the north with its lakes and forests, old wooden houses and churches, its peasant carvings and songs, and my dream of the undiscovered city of

Kityezh. *City* would be where my other hero lived, a lively, witty artist-illustrator, who inevitably flowed from the tip of my pen as a caricature of my brother Vladimir at his best. The third part of my story described the lively illustrator conducting his friend, the true artist, around the editorial offices in an attempt to find him work. Here I described, successfully, I think, Popov in his editorial office, and someone similar to Boris Ivanter at a magazine like *Konsomol*. In the fourth part, I showed how the true artist refused the temptations of his illustrator friend, and continued to work on his creation in a damp basement outside Moscow. The story was to end with the arrest and death of my hero.

Korin in fact survived thanks to Gorky, and survived to prosper and become famous. But how many true artists, writers and musicians, known and unknown, perished in the camps, their work turned to ash. We do not know, and never shall know. God alone knows.

I abandoned my story, realising that I lacked the scope to bring it to completion, and also that it would not be kind to portray Vladimir in such a negative light. But my hands still itched to write up all the impressions I had received on my travels, stirring my imagination and clamouring to be put down in words and phrases. The trouble was, I had nowhere to write. My stories of the northern lakes I had written when we were still in Eropkinsky Street. Now, I was sleeping on the floor in my parents' room, and could only draw my maps and plans at the family table in the communal family room. Vladimir was able to work in his room by night, when nobody disturbed him, but nothing like that was on offer to me. Drawing at the family table was one thing; it was quite another to be able to sit over my writing, struggling with words and thoughts, writing and rewriting.

Yet my desire to write was very strong. The effect of my eleven days in prison, together with the knowledge of the cowardly behaviour of my cousin Alexei Bobrinsky, informing on his own friends and relatives, gave me a new idea. My future fictional hero would be like Alexei, but would suffer torments of guilt, in the end throwing himself under the wheels of a train. Planning the story in my head, I gave it the title of *The Scoundrel*.

I was becoming more and more solitary, living within myself. I hardly ever feature in the family photos in our old albums. The unofficial poetry of those times, with its themes of lovelessness, the blows of fate, the absence of true learning, and with its atmosphere of random violence and the horrors of imprisonment, entirely reflected the mood of young people. Only in one respect was it wide of the mark; we did still manage to find love. But I will write about that later.

One day I called on my sister Sonya in Bolshoy Levshinsky Lane. She was living with a loving and considerate husband, and had been spared our misfortunes, though of course she suffered for us. She was not entirely without difficulties of her own, as her title of princess prevented her from finding work. I told her all my problems and she tried to comfort me, suggesting that I might go to a highly respected old priest, Father Serafim, who might help me to deal with my depression. I went to his church between the two morning services. Father Serafim, an emaciated figure with fanatically shining eyes, was blessing the communicants as they left – rather perfunctorily, I thought. When it was my turn, I knelt before him and started with the words Sonya had suggested, "Father, I've come to you because my soul is suffering." I was going to say something more, but he interrupted me with, "Have you been breaking your fast?"

His question startled me, and I mumbled something about how I barely managed to have enough to eat.

"So are you breaking the fast?" he asked, almost angrily.

I said in a low voice, "Look, I'm disenfranchised. I don't know where to go."

Immediately, he adopted a softer tone, but the line waiting for his blessing was very long so he dismissed me rather quickly. I stood in a corner of the church, waiting to take communion. He had not comforted or encouraged me one whit. Heavy-hearted, I left the church, and although I remained a steadfast believer, for some years I did not go to confession.

5

The whole of Russia was struggling to feed itself in those difficult times. The eleven of us, with only five ration cards, managed to eat slightly better than most thanks to *torgsin* (trade with foreigners). This name will be quite unfamiliar to the reader of today. As our country had now been launched on Stalin's policy of heavy industrialisation, it needed foreign currency to pay for its imports of machinery and equipment, as well as experts, which we lacked. There were various ways of earning this currency. One way was to rob the peasants of not only their seed-corn, but even of the corn they needed to feed themselves. The Secretary of the Central Committee of the Ukraine, Kosior, himself subsequently shot, created a horrific famine by adopting such measures. During the war an officer described to me how he used to work loading Ukrainian wheat for export on to English ships for a crust of bread.

Another method, which I mentioned earlier, was to sell timber abroad. Yet another was by selling our art treasures, especially those in the Hermitage Museum in Leningrad and the Museum of Figurative Arts in Moscow. Anyone who – well, not exactly protested, but expressed surprise – was consoled by our Commissar for Trade, Mikoyan. He offered the thought that we need not be worried that American millionaires were buying up Rembrandt, Rubens, Van Dyck and Breughel since, once world revolution had happened, all these treasures would be returned to us.

Hard currency could be earned by organisations such as the 'Embroidered Cushion', although as "former people" had "infiltrated" into these, they had to be liquidated. Later on, realising their usefulness, similar workshops came into existence. Palekh, Mstera and Holuy, though they employed trusted proletarians, used to manufacture quality artistic objects for export. These enterprises are still earning us hard currency today.

Then there were the shops, the *torgsins*, where foreigners could buy what they needed, including the caviar and sturgeon that had vanished after the NEP was crushed. A special antiquarian *torgsin* was opened near the Moscow Conservatory. Here antiques were on sale that had been sold to the shop by "former people" in exchange for so-called "*torgsin* coupons". I myself, on behalf of Countess Uvarov, once came here with a fine eighteenth-century wall clock. It was here, too, that a Frenchman bought the beautiful Shubin marble bust of Catherine the Great that had been buried in the grounds of Petrovskoye by my father's brother, Alexander Vladimirovich, in 1917. How much my uncle's valet got in return for this dishonest sale, I do not know. On the death of the Frenchman, the bust went to the Victoria and Albert Museum in London.

There were *torgsin* restaurants – the Prague, the Metropole and the Sava – where foreigners with dollars could have a good time, and even Russians could come along with their gold watches or other items, have them weighed at the cash desk, and then make merry with the proceeds. *Torgsins* selling food were everywhere, even in small towns from which the last foreigner, usually some old maid who had been governess to the local landowner's children, had long since departed. So why did they set them up in places where there were no foreigners? The thinking was simple; to extract all the gold and silver still hoarded everywhere. A hungry old lady could bring in her gold wedding ring, have it weighed on the very accurate scales, and thus be able to buy what were then considered luxuries: sausage and cheese and butter. If you were a poor, disenfranchised person, you could get black and white bread.

These were times when emigrants were still sending foreign currency, which was changed into *torgsin* coupons, to their relatives who had remained behind. From California, Uncle Alexander Vladimirovich still sent grandfather ten dollars a month, which went towards feeding Vladimir Trubetskoi and his wife and their seven children. Moina Abamelek-Lazareva, about whom I wrote earlier, continued to send us ten dollars a month, with which we bought grain and flour and margarine at the *torgsin*. Sausage, cheese and butter were beyond our means.

6

The scourge of our titled origins was particularly felt by my younger sisters, Masha and Katya. They themselves, because of their age, were not officially disenfranchised, but their parents were. In later years, Masha said that in overcoming all her difficulties she had always felt as if she were hanging upside-down by the heels. I will not describe the number of times she was driven out of the Institute of Geology then readmitted. Her main advantage was that she was always a hard-working, cheerful and indefatigable person, and an attractive girl with her curly hair and frank, open gaze. Colleagues liked her, and somehow it seemed inconceivable that one could expel such a nice girl. Many young men paid her court, taking her out to the theatre and cinema; she was friendly with them all, without any particular favourite.

In this same year, 1929, Katya turned fifteen and had completed seven years of school. She now had, to register for senior school together with her friend Olga Sheremetyeva. When the director saw the registration forms, she exclaimed, "Oh, what grand names!" It then turned out that Olga, though a Sheremetyeva, was not a countess, and also her mother was a teacher, so she was admitted. But Katya, a princess, and the daughter of a disenfranchised man – how dare she! – there was no way she could be admitted. So Katya was forced into doing odd jobs and attending various courses, sometimes being thrown out, sometimes being allowed back in.

At this time, during the first Five Year Plan, there was still a wide range of personalities in leading positions in addition to those ideologically watchful and zealous managers and directors of enterprises and schools. In the sons and daughters of former people they found that they had keen, conscientious and intelligent employees or students. So they defended them, or were simply sorry for them. I am sure my sisters were greatly helped in all their difficulties and handicaps by their attractive appearance. How could such nice girls be thrown out?

Among the guests who visited us in Kotovo were the younger Urusovs, Kirill and Lyona, and the three Rayevsky brothers, Sergei, Mikhail and Andrei. Masha and Katya, and sometimes I, would join in with this noisy bunch as they rushed off on their skis. Lyona Urusova was a year older than Katya, also a princess, but she was managing to continue her education in Year Eight. Lyona had started a romantic affair with Sergei Rayevsky, who was seven years her senior. Her parents did not approve and forbid them to meet, so they came to us in Kotovo in secret. Once they came to us not in order to ski but to invite us back to Moscow to a concert that was to be held in Vladimir Ivanovich Mordvinov's flat. He was professor of singing at the Conservatory and one of his pupils was his nephew, Mikhail Rayevsky. At first I refused to go as I had no decent shoes to go with my only good suit, but Vladimir talked me into it. "You can hide your feet under your chair," he said. So we set off for Moscow, Vladimir and his wife Elena, myself and Masha. Katya was too young to be invited.

The Mordvinovs apartment was a large one in Leontyev Lane, with fine furniture and pictures by well-known artists. The three Rayevsky brothers were there, as well as Kirill and Lyona Urusov, Yusha Samarin and his wife Katya, two other married couples and Mikhail's girlfriend, Tamara Pridvorova, a shy young woman quite unlike her father Demyan Bedny, the Kremlin court poet and fellow-travelling scoundrel. Mikhail sang arias and romances, and his famous *I Sing to you, Hymen, God of Newly-weds*. He had a very loud voice, more suited to the concert hall than a private room, and he seemed also to lack feeling. I could not help remembering the fine passion with which his cousin Artemi, now a convict in Siberia, used to sing. Vladimir Ivanovich, a lively middle-aged man, was the accompanist. Mikhail got enthusiastic applause for his performance. In fact, his singing was more like a hobby; his real talent lay in mathematics. After the music, we all moved into an adjoining room where a spread of food and drink had been prepared, modest by today's standards, but for those times a positive feast. Vladimir Ivanovich and my brother Vladimir tried to outrival each other in witty repartee. As the glasses were refilled, laughter became louder, and some of the other guests were even able to get a word in edgeways. I listened quietly, laughing with the others, and did not forget to fill my plate or refill my glass.

Yusha Samarin interrupted this flow of wit to announce that the following summer he was being sent by the State Academy of the Arts to the Nizhegorodsky region to collect folklore. He said he would go to Vetluga and Kerzhenets and would certainly also go to the famous lake of Svetloyar. My heart beat faster and my slight intoxication melted away. That was the lake I had intended to travel to that summer, where the city of Kityezh lay deep under its waters. Was Yusha going alone, or in a team? I tried to hypnotise him across the room with the thought, "Take me with you!"

The food and drink was followed by tea and rich pastries. Suddenly, rather red in the face, our host sprang to his feet and said in a loud voice, "Now I shall sing to you!" This was greeted with delight, we all trooped back into the music room, and Vladimir Ivanovich sat at the piano, announcing, "I shall sing you some Neapolitan songs." He had a light, slightly unsteady voice, but he sang the songs, the words of which we could not understand, with great expression so that we could feel the lyrical tone of one and the cheeky, impudent tone of the next. His audience listened raptly, as did I, though I could not help wondering to myself how I could manage to talk to Yusha before he left. Suddenly, our host banged the piano lid shut and got to his feet. "You can't understand a thing!" he said angrily. "It isn't getting through to you. And yet every song is a jewel. I shan't play any more." Someone tried to persuade him to continue. It might just have been that he was tired, but his words expressed the sadness of a great, ageing singer who felt his passion was not getting through to his listeners.

It was time to go. I was finding it impossible to get to Yusha through the crowd in the hall, when he himself came over to me and asked, "Where are you spending the night?" I had intended to go to the Ilyinskys, whose place was within walking distance and who did not mind me turning up after midnight. Yusha said, "Come to our place." I was overjoyed, but resolved not to talk about Kityezh as we walked. Yusha and Katya lived in a huge eighteenth-century house right by Kamenny bridge, the very house where a plague had once started. Their room was tiny and I was given a blanket on the floor alongside their bed. Before we went to sleep I learned all I needed to know about Yusha's summer expedition. He was going to record the songs, poetry, folk and fairy tales of the Nizhegorodsky region, Katya was going with him, and he would take me along with pleasure, but only as an unpaid helper, living from hand to mouth. I was of course willing to agree to any conditions if only I could fulfil my dream of standing on the shores of Lake Svetloyar, looking down into its depths, on the feast day of the Mother of God of Vladimir.

Before leaving for his work at the institute of ethnography in the morning, Yusha said, "I forgot to ask you this last night, but what of your right to vote?" My heart tightened, but I blurted out, "By the summer I'll certainly have that back."

All Yusha said was, "Well, well."

7

New Year's Day 1929 was approaching. I could have joined friends for the celebration, but did not feel like it. Nor did Vladimir and Elena want to go anywhere. In general, my brother preferred people to visit him than himself to go visiting. Igor Daksergof and Valery Pertsov arrived. The latter had by now accepted the fact that Masha did not welcome his advances, but still came to have what he called intelligent conversation with Vladimir. Igor also enjoyed talking with Vladimir but had not given up courting Masha; he must have been sad not to find her at home, as she and Katya had flitted off to Moscow.

Our parents eventually went off to bed. Elena was busy making a few modest titbits whilst Vladimir was engaged in telling a story. As Elena put the dishes on the table, Vladimir reached for the one remaining half-litre bottle of vodka. He treasured an old crystal beaker engraved with the imperial two-headed eagle, which he used to fill either up to the bird's feet, or its wings, or its beak, or even right up to the rim. In my story *Forty Explorers* I have included a description of this glass, which is now preserved as an almost holy relic by Vladimir's descendants.

Midnight was still a long way off. With the precision of an apothecary, Vladimir poured us all out a measure of vodka, leaving just enough for us to toast the New Year at midnight. We clinked glasses and forked up the not-very-enticing titbits. My mind was dwelling on the past year and so I listened to Vladimir with only half an ear. Recently, I had been writing out some of my thoughts in pieces that I entitled *Poetry in Prose*. Later, when the times were dangerous, I burnt these, but on the last page I had been composing before this New Year's Eve, I had written "I still hoped for and trusted in a better future!"

19. Keeping Up our Spirits

1

I had meant it when I told Yusha Samarin that I would have my voting rights restored. While involved in the case of the 'Embroidered Cushion' mother had told her lawyer, Orlovsky, about my difficulties and had received this advice from him: "The local electoral committees are overwhelmed with such cases. Even though the people on them are watchful guardians of the new Soviet order, they can't handle the mountain of work and there is terrible confusion. What you must do is separate your son's case from your own appeals. Let him put himself forward as if he had never been refused. The OGPU are also snowed under with cases and he can forget about his promise not to leave Moscow – they'll never notice." Mother passed on this advice to me, but at first I flatly refused to go before yet another committee to answer their offensive questions. Then mother came to me and said, "Your father couldn't sleep a wink last night because of your attitude." At that moment, Vladimir came out of his room; and said sternly, "Get going, and no more waffling!"

I had first to call on Professor Stroganov to get him to certify my work there. He was friendliness itself, sitting down at once to write me a recommendation that was full of kind phrases about the high quality of my work as his personal assistant. A few days later I received this paper typed, stamped and signed. Father, in the meantime, had put together a file of documents recording my working life. It was January 1930 when I set off with my papers to present my appeal to the authorities at the Frunzensky district offices on Prechistenka Street.

My heart was heavy. I expected to be asked sneering and demeaning questions. But when I entered the building I was comforted to find the entrance guarded by an amiable elderly lady of the kind usually to be seen in churches, not in government buildings. Following her directions, I climbed the stairs with a lighter heart. There was no need to knock at any office door as on the landing there stood a small table, three chairs, and along the wall a couple of benches on which were seated several petitioners. I can remember a young man in a padded jacket who looked like a worker's son, a slender, pale-faced girl, and a heavy-built, middle-aged man whose features had a marked Asiatic cast. I immediately recognised him as Miromanov.

During the period of the NEP, there flourished in Moscow and Petersburg small publishers who made a good living out of supplying the market for cheap, educational books. Miromanov was one of these. His little illustrated children's books, mostly abridged classics for which he paid no royalties, were published in great numbers at considerable profit. The illustrator V.A.Vatagin often drew their covers, while I was sometimes commissioned to do the letterwork. I once saw Miromanov and his plump wife drive out of the gates of their residence on the corner of Prechistenkaya and Gagarin streets in a fine coach-and-four, a scene that was drawn by Vladimir and was reproduced in the book *V. Golitsyn: Pages From the Life of the Artist*.

After a few years, crushed by taxes, Miromanov was forced to close down his business. His residence was confiscated and he was driven out of Moscow. And now here he sat with bowed head on the petitioners' bench, and I was asking him, "Are you the last in line?" As I sat next to him, I remembered how not long before his books were to be found in every peasant house in the country. He had published children's books by Marshak and Chukovsky, authors who were now under attack in the press for their work. Chukovsky in particular was a target for these attacks. Miromanov was paying the price for having published such "harmful" literature.

The entry of a lady interrupted my thoughts. Tall, elegant and with almost aristocratic features, she in no way resembled the typical Soviet women of the day, cloned imitations of Lenin's wife Krupskaya, with their plain clothes and dowdy look. This figure was followed by a bold-looking girl, a typical *Konsomol* activist of the time, carrying a stack of files. They both sat down at the table and the elegant lady picked up the files, called out the names, and as the person named came up to her, stated, in a voice that brooked no appeal, "Rights restored", or "Refused". Some left with radiant faces, others with heads bowed. Finally, the only people left on the benches were the young factory worker, the pale-faced girl, Miromanov, myself and after me, two other women. The lady began to call us forward.

The factory worker took his place in front of her and I could partly overhear how she questioned him about his work and his parents. It was clear from his answers that he was trying to justify himself. She put his file to one side, and called out, "Next!" The young girl, with a terrified look, took her place in front of the table. I could see under the chair how her legs were trembling. Once more came the questions as the girl's papers was read. Her file, too, was set aside and she returned to her seat. It was now Miromanov's turn. The chair creaked as he set his great weight down on it, laying a bulky file in front of his questioner. She read only one or two of the papers before the questions and answers began. The interview seemed to drag on, and I was now feeling very nervous. Miromanov spoke heatedly, but all I could hear was the phrase, spoken at least twice, "But I've spent my whole life working!" After a while the lady looked up from her writing and said sharply, "That's enough. The interview's over." Miromanov started to say something, but she was not listening to him. He returned to his place on the bench.

"Next," said the lady.

Jumping to my feet, I went up to the table, sat down without being invited and put my file in front of her. She began to examine the papers. I had to clench my fists to control my nervousness. Today, sixty years later, I cannot remember the order in which she conducted the interview, but I clearly remember the substance. In particular, Vladimir and I were often asked one question that not very historically literate people invariably asked, "What is your relationship to Prince Golitsyn?" as though there existed one individual, rich beyond belief, master of vast lands, owner of many palaces, an intimate of the Tsar, bearing this name. Vladimir and I, after consulting each other, had come to the conclusion that the only answer to this question was to refer to the book *The Golitsyn Family Line*, published the year before, in which all living Golitsyns were listed, roughly a hundred or so, not one of whom was considered to be "The Prince Golitsyn". I was trying to explain this somewhat complex idea to the lady, but she interrupted me to ask about my father. How many times in my life have I had to describe my father's life and work to the authorities, from their point of view a catalogue of sins, from my point of view, his wonderful personal qualities. The lady soon got tired of my account and said, "Let's talk about your own life."

I began to describe my work as a draughtsman. She asked me who Professor Stroganov was. I was about to repeat his own flippant description of himself as the head of Moscow's back passage, but caught myself in time and gave her a straightforward answer. Halfway through this, she suddenly asked, "Do you pay income tax? Do you have a professional licence?" The questions took me aback. I was able to say that when the cashiers paid me, tax had already been deducted, but going through my mind was the undeniable fact that Stroganov paid me in cash out of his own pocket. I tried to excuse myself, but all she said was, "Anyway, that's the business of the tax people. Our job is to discover by what means you earn a living. Clearly, you are an artisan. You should get an artisan's licence."

I was sent back to the bench. The remaining women had their interviews. The lady swept out of the room with all our files and we sat anxiously waiting, not saying a word to each other. Eventually she and her assistant returned. The worker and the pale-faced girl had their rights restored and left with happy faces. Miromanov was refused; probably the members of the committee had seen in him nothing but a man trying to recover his position and make huge profits. Head bowed, he went slowly out. The *Konsomol* girl now handed the lady my file.

"You're restored," she said tonelessly, handing me my file. Clipped to the file was an extraordinarily narrow slip, no more than three centimetres wide. I opened it, but could hardly read the officialese, my eyes were jumping about so much. Finally the news sank in; I was restored to my rights! I was no longer a despised individual! And so quickly. I had thought I would have to wait for months, and here it had happened in a couple of minutes. I still have this tiny slip of tape.

My circumstances did not immediately change for the better. I went on working as before, both for Stroganov and others. But it freed me from fear of the militia who stopped and questioned you in the streets, and above all, it released me from anxiety before the perfidious question so often put to one, "Were you ever a disenfranchised person?"

2

For historians, and indeed the ordinary citizens of today, 1937 is considered to have been the most terrible year in the history of our country. And it is certainly true that no little blood and tears were shed in that year. But for the majority of the people, namely the peasantry, the worst period was the last few months of 1929 and the beginning of 1930. It was then that disaster struck that age-old institution, the Russian village, sweeping away its centuries-old customs and traditions. I have already quoted Vladimir's outburst, characterising the age as one when a circle of sadists had seized power and were driving the country over the precipice. There was no one to save it. The authorities took out their rage on the peasants of Glinkovo, and all over the country hatred was vented against Russians, Ukrainians and Belorussians; for the time being other nationalities were spared. The majority of the peasants were driven into the *kolkhozy* out of fear of being "de-*kulakised*", in other words, evicted and stripped of their possessions. I know of no novel that has truly described the horrors of those times.

The widespread slaughter of cattle and a mass exodus from the villages began. People fled to the so-called "great" Soviet construction sites, where at that time there were no checks on your papers or your origins, and where if you came along with a horse you were more than welcome. People fled in all directions; to the nearest village, or far away, or to the towns where they struggled to establish themselves as best they could. Some of those who fled their homes ended up in the *kolkhozy* of neighbouring villages, where they became "activists", causing trouble and mischief in their new surroundings. I remember how such activists tore down the iconostasis in the village church of Lyubets in Vladimirsky *oblast*, where I now live and where I am writing these memoirs, and burned the wooden frame together with the icons and manuscript books whilst the local residents looked on in horror. The soot from the fire can still be seen in the church.

The Old Believer and bibliophile, Mikhail Ivanovich Chuvanov, has told me the amazing story of his own home.[23] He and his five brothers were factory workers in Moscow in those days, returning to their home at the weekends. One such weekend, they learned that their parents were going to be "de-*kulakised*". They realized that the catastrophe would affect not just their parents, but all of them, so in just one night they dismantled their house and loaded it lock, stock and barrel on to sledges and drove it to Lyubertsy, where the father was friendly with the village chairman. They could not find him, so they picked a quiet lane abutting the forest edge and there, in just one night, rebuilt their house. It is still standing. I have visited Mikhail Ivanovich there and heard his account of that miraculous

---

23. *In 1666, when Archbishop Nikon reformed old Orthodox practices, many believers refused to accept these, and were called Old Believers. A minority, they withdrew to remote villages around Moscow, and have remained in existence to this day.*

escape, and in particular, how puzzled the authorities were when they found nothing but a hole in the ground where the house had once stood.

The army was not exempt from this wave of denunciations, evictions and arrests. Commanders had to inquire into the social origins of their officers and soldiers, driving out all those who were considered sons of *kulaks*, sometimes even stripping them of their greatcoats and boots. The situation caused Voroshilov to bring it up at a Politburo meeting; the brave Red Army was losing its strength! Then in March, the "great leader", Stalin himself, wrote his article *Dizzy with Success*. This article, historians consider, was the watershed between the two stages of collectivisation. The article began with a resounding list of successes, followed by vicious criticism of the village authorities. The Politburo never made mistakes, so it is "you fools and idiots in the countryside who are failing to apply our wise counsels". All the blame for the failures of collectivisation was laid at the door of the local leaders. They were not carrying out their orders properly; the people had to join the collective farms voluntarily. So all these reports by the local authorities of the great numbers driven into the *kolkhozy* were a mistake; this was the "dizziness".

Following Stalin's article, people streamed out of the collective farms. In some cases only the chairman remained, in other cases the whole collective disappeared. Some remained in existence thanks to the "zealous class-consciousness" of a few members, usually lay-abouts, rogues and drunkards, who had nowhere else to go. In my village of Luybets, the *kolkhoz* survived thanks to four families who had fled from their home village to avoid "de-*kulakisation*". In Kotovo, which is where I was living at that time, the collective ceased to exist. In Glinkovo, the peasants were so frightened by the threat to move them all into the abandoned monastery that they did not abandon the collective farm. A former chairman from the region of Tula described to me how, not having read the paper, he had stood up at a meeting and ordered people to enter the *kolkhoz* without further ado, until someone shoved the article under his nose. The peasants mocked him, shouting back at him, "Why are you threatening us? Stalin himself says it's all voluntary."

3

In the spring, a letter arrived from Uncle Alyosha announcing the birth of a daughter, Tania, and inviting Vladimir to be her godfather. As this would mean Vladimir travelling to Tver, and he was in the middle of an urgent and profitable commission, the family proposed that I should go in his place. I was always fond of travelling, and accepted with pleasure. Also, I had been a wedding groom thirteen times, but never a godfather. So mother packed me a little bit of food and I set off.

Uncle Alyosha and his family had moved from Khilkovo, where he had rented a fruit orchard, to Sergiyev Posad, where he had set up the knitting machine that made the socks that my sisters sold in Moscow. In 1927 an act of provocation against the regional secretary in that town, which was followed by a wave of arrests, led to Uncle Alyosha and his family being exiled to a "minus six" town. In Tver, he continued for a while to knit socks, but after the arrest of all the Chinese and so the end of supplies of wool, he was forced to look for other work. He was hired by the town administration as their water sampler, which involved taking samples from eight places. His wife, Aunt Tyosya, made him a special belt with eight bottle holders; it was a considerable weight to carry about, as he had also to carry a heavy spike with which to pierce the ice in winter. In winter, his body heat kept the samples from freezing.

"Seryozha, I'm delighted you've come!" cried Uncle Alyosha, embracing me warmly, when I appeared on the threshold of their room. The eyes of their many children, all seven of them, stared at me as we all sat down to a meal. The family was surviving thanks to the ration cards that went with his job, and also the help they received from Sandra Meiendorf, Aunt Tyosya's sister, who was secretary to Mr Steed, the representative of the millionaire Harriman, owner of manganese concessions in the Caucasus. In 1929, however, the Soviet government cancelled the concessions. Mr Steed left the country and his secretary, Sandra, was imprisoned, which meant an end to her financial help.

Uncle Alyosha and I set off to visit the local priest. Along the road were large posters depicting various types of undesirable disenfranchised people; there was the fat NEPman, the priest and the former general, copied from caricatures in the magazine *Krokodil*. As for the type of the person exiled for administrative reasons, for which no caricature existed, the artist had simply used Douglas Fairbanks' face. At the priest's house we were first met by a row of frightened children, then the frightened face of his wife appeared, finally followed by the priest himself. After we had explained the reason for our visit, and he had agreed to come and christen Tania, he said, "How you scared us!" This was a typical reaction to unknown callers in those dark years.

There were many guests at the christening; two pairs of neighbours, and the rest "minus" people from Moscow and Petersburg,
who were managing to survive by finding the sort of jobs that did
not require proven working-class origins. Many friendships had
formed among these exiled people, and a christening was an excuse
for a happy party. I had known some of the guests in earlier years
and was joyfully welcomed. After the ceremony had finished, we all
sat down to a modest feast, mostly potatoes. There was a tiny bit of
vodka, which Uncle Alyosha measured out in minute amounts, but
this did not prevent everyone making merry. Only the priest sat
gloomy and silent; his church had just been shut down, he still had
young children, and he had no idea how he was going to survive.
There is a portrait by Korin of just such a sad, seated priest.

I went visiting the next day. I called on Vladimir Vladimirovich
Wulfert, one of Elena Sergeievna Petukhova's four brothers-in-law.
Short, slim and vivacious, with whiskers and sideburns, he had once
been an officer in the Lifeguards, but had been forced to resign when
his wife became the mistress of Archduke Mikhail Aleksandrovich,
the Tsar's brother. Wulfert divorced her, then married the beautiful
Vera Grigorevna Petukhova. The couple welcomed me with open
arms, after which Vladimir Vladimirovich led me into his little
garden and showed me the different flowers he was growing there.
His ambition was to create a blue camellia blossom. When I wrote
my story *Forty Explorers*, I remembered the man who had dreamed
of producing blue camellias, and included him. In 1937, all four
brothers-in-law of Elena Sergeievna were sent to the Gulag, dying
either in Vorkuta or Kolyma.

I also visited the Istomins, Petya and his sister Natasha. Petya, two
metres tall and a languid, haughty youth, was a friend of Vladimir's
and had once worked with the Nansen mission when that famous
explorer organised aid to the famine-struck lands across the Volga.
When the mission was over, Petya was arrested and spent three
years in the "workers'corridor" in Butyrka before being exiled to
Tver, where he worked as a simple labourer with a group of
geophysical prospectors. How his sister came to be exiled to Tver, I
do not know. While at the Istomins, their cousin and my great friend,
Sergei Istomin, rushed in. He had been looking for me all over town.
He, too, had been sentenced to "minus six". We embraced joyfully,
and he dragged me off to see his parents, who were living on the left
bank of the Volga.

Sergei's father, Pyotr Vladimirovich, was one of the most
honourable men I have ever met. He considered that as he had sworn

the oath to the Tsar, he could not serve Soviet rule, nor send his children to godless schools. He personally taught his children up to the ninth grade, after which they took and passed external entry exams – at that time this was still allowed. During the period of NEP, Pyotr Vladimirovich earned his living selling the property of "former people" to the newly rich, keeping a percentage of these sales as his commission. When the NEP ended, he bought himself a knitting machine like Uncle Alyosha and he and his wife made a better living out of it than my uncle. When the Chinese supply of wool dried up, they found an alternative source of wool from a rather shady elderly lady. The totally honourable and honest Pyotr Vladimirovich never knew that in fact this lady was selling wool that had been stolen.

I was invited to spend the night with the Istomins. Pyotr Vladimirovich told me many fascinating things about Solovki, where he had spent three years before being exiled to Tver. Life at Solovki had been relatively free until 1929. He showed me some quite unique photographs of the prison-monastery. In one of them he is sitting between three orthodox Metropolitans, who were supposed to be church leaders, but in fact lived their lives remote from church affairs.

In the morning, Sergei went off to work and his sister Ksana was delegated to show me the town. It was a fine day and the churches and white houses were dazzling in the sunshine. I saw before me the ancient and beautiful town with its many golden-domed churches by the broad Volga and the narrower river Tvertsa. At the confluence of the two rivers stood the famous monastery of Otroch, where once upon a time Malyuta Skuratov had with his own hands strangled Metropolitan Filipp. I was lucky to have the opportunity of seeing the beauty of this town. Ksana and I crossed the bridge to the right bank of the Volga and the main street, called Millionaya. It was so named because Catherine the Great had given the town a million roubles for rebuilding after a fire. There stood the massive, five-domed cathedral of the Archangel Michael, which had only just been stripped of the relics of Prince Mikhail Yaroslavich of Tver, martyred by the Golden Horde. There too stood the many-domed church of the White Trinity, as well as the gleaming white, colonnaded market row. Alongside Millionaya was a double crescent of elegant residences and amongst these the local picture gallery and ethnographic museum, to which Ksana took me. My heart is sad when I think of all that ancient beauty. How fortunate I was to have the chance to see it all. Now only the church of the White Trinity has, by a miracle, remained intact. The colonnaded market place was pulled down under

Khrushchev, and the rest has vanished, not at the hands of the Germans, but in the dark and sinister 1930s. Tver and Kostroma were the two cities that suffered most from the vandals, Tver even being deprived of its historic name. I returned to Uncle Alyosha's late that evening to find them deeply anxious about me. Such were those times that someone could leave home quite normally and then never come back.

In 1934 the Meiendorf brothers, in return for a considerable payment in hard currency, arranged the departure from Russia of their two sisters, one of them my Aunt Tyosya, her husband Uncle Alyosha and their seven children. They went to the Meiendorf family castle in Estonia. Just before leaving, Uncle Alyosha, looking sad and fearful of the future, paid us a farewell visit. When our troops occupied Estonia, there was an agreement between Hitler and Stalin that all inhabitants with German blood could leave for Germany, so Uncle Alyosha with his German wife and all their children resettled there. His eldest son, Sergei, served in the German army on the western front. I have no idea what my uncle felt through all those years; I hope he empathised with our victories. The family were living in Berlin when we occupied the city. Oddly enough, I was in Berlin at that time, but had no idea they were living there. Eventually, they emigrated to America. From the time of their departure, my mother only ever received one communication from Uncle Alyosha. It was a long letter that started with a rambling passage about the Antichrist and the end of the world, after which he recalled the poverty in which he and his family had lived in Russia before describing their present comfortable lives. They all had large homes, two cars each, and many children, and he was the patriarch of this numerous family. Sadly, none of us know our cousins, or they us.

As for Petya Istomin, he got tired of his labourer's job in Tver and left for distant Yakutia, where he became an accountant and eventually head of a large enterprise. His uncle, Pyotr Vladimirovich, spent several more years in Tver making stockings for the inhabitants of the town, but in 1934 the "minus" people there faced further persecution. Many, including Wulfert, vanished in the Gulag, others were exiled to remote places. Pyotr Vladimirovich and his family were first in Orel, then in Kokchetav in Kazakhstan, where he was arrested and perished. His son Sergei became a physical training teacher in Kokchetav, but caught typhus and died. I am sure that if he had survived he would have shared his father's fate.

4

Our family continued to live in Kotovo. Vladimir, despite being disenfranchised and no longer able to work for the journal the *Universal
Pathfinder*, still managed to do paid work through friendship with
a man called Gilgendorf, a wildly unconventional editor of a
magazine that published adventure stories. Gilgendorf even arranged
an official mission to the Black Sea for Vladimir. Together with
Elena, leaving the children in the care of my parents, Vladimir was
able to visit this part of the world where once the ancient Greeks
had ruled. They got to Olvia, Khersoness and Kerch, and Vladimir
returned with many watercolours of ruined temples and romantic
views of the Black Sea coast. Masha, too, was able to travel, setting
off with Elena Alexeievna Ivanova, the daughter of the professor who
had helped us settle in Kotovo, as a collector of samples on her first
geological expedition to the region of Orlov.

My father meanwhile went on with his translation work and
helped look after the grandchildren. Mother ran the home, but was
constantly forced to go to Moscow in connection with the intermin-
able case of the 'Embroidered Cushion'. As for provisions, we bought
milk and vegetables from the neighbours, with our five ration cards
got our bread, and as for cooking oil, flour and sugar, we bought
these thanks to the few dollars, convertible into '*torgsin* coupons',
that could be used in hard-currency shops.

5

I was in seventh heaven, my dream of seeing the enchanted city of
Kityezh about to come true. Yusha Samarin and I were to travel in
the province Nizhny Novgorod, to research and record the local
songs, poems and fairy tales. I was only sad that I would not be able
to help with our household expenses for a time. But this was a unique
opportunity. Yusha went ahead to arrange things with the local
authorities; his wife Katya – the Rayevsky brothers' sister – and I
would follow. Soon there came a telegram, "Come. Semenov Yusha"
and I went to Kursk station to buy our tickets.

Poor, poor Russians. What trials and troubles they have had to
endure whenever they have had to travel any distance throughout
these seventy years of the building of socialism. And why did most
of them travel? Only a few went on holiday or on business; the great
majority travelled in search of provisions and goods. On the first day
that I stood in line, I got no tickets, so I had to go again during the

night when I did manage to get two tickets on the evening train. Katya and I secured space on two shelves, one above the other. The train rolled slowly along through the night. At dawn the entire carriage was woken up by wild screams. A woman on a lower shelf was grappling with a man, whose head and shoulders were thrust through a window and who was pulling her kitbag from under her. He managed to tear the bag away from her, jumped down on to the track and slowly disappeared into a copse of birch trees. Today, I often pass this spot where development has led to the building of little houses and the disappearance of the birch trees, and I remember the screams of that woman as she was robbed.

We reached Nizhny Novgorod by midday, took a tram through the city to the riverside quays and crossed the Volga in a large rowing boat. The view of Nizhny with its high fortress and domed churches, its tall belltower similar to the tower of Ivan the Terrible in the Kremlin in Moscow, and its white walls, was splendid. Unfortunately a squall of rain struck us, soaking us to the skin, and my enthusiasm for the view went down badly with Katya, "To the devil with your beautiful Nizhny!" she shouted as the water dripped off her straw hat. Safely on shore, we set off to walk three *versts* to the station at Mokhovy Gory, the beginning of the line to the northeast, to Kerzhenets and Vetluga and the forested countryside where the Old Believers had settled and which has been described so well in the writings of Melnikov-Pechersky.

I had packed a light cloth bag, easy to sling over my shoulders; Katya had filled an ordinary suitcase with I do not know what manner of goods, but it was heavy and I had to change hands frequently as we trudged along; but at least our clothes soon dried out in the sunshine. At Mokhovy Gory we got tickets surprisingly quickly, only half an hour's waiting in line, and the little train took us north to Semenov. Katya was very much on edge about whether we would find Yusha. In fact, he was waiting for us at the station, having come to meet the same train three days running. We were soon installed in the local guest house.

Semenov was a pretty little village of mostly wooden houses; the only stone houses were by the church. In the morning we went to watch wooden spoons being made. In the garden of one of the houses a group of both young and old people were seated in a circle. We watched from the sidelines as an old man took a rough piece of aspen and with a little axe chopped at the piece with seven strokes, neither more nor less. This piece he then passed to his eldest son who, with the same type of little axe, shaped the piece into something vaguely resembling a spoon. The second son then worked on this with a knife before passing it to yet another lad for further refining. So the piece went round the circle, the women finishing it off by smoothing and painting. The circle was closed by a young lad with a pot of paint and a split twig, which he dipped into the pot, applying several silver stars on the spoon and then setting it aside to dry. Yusha made notes, whilst Katya and I marvelled at the speed and dexterity with which this original kind of production line worked. In those days, half the population of Russia ate their cabbage soup with wooden spoons made in Semenov and the surrounding villages.

When I woke up the next morning I was bursting with impatience. We were due to cover forty *versts* to the village of Vladimirskoye on the river Lyunda, not very far from Lake Svetloyar, which I had dreamed of seeing for so long. We would be there on the eve of the feast day of the Holy Mother of Vladimir, when orthodox believers make the pilgrimage to see the holy city of Kityezh rise from the depths of the lake. Yusha went off to arrange our transport, but came back rather embarrassed, saying that they could only give us a little willow-plaited two-seater trap, so only two of us could make the journey. I at once volunteered to walk, saying I was used to covering long distances on foot, but Yusha decided that, as I was his assistant on this expedition, I must accompany him. Katya was left behind to pass the time as best she could.

We set off, squashed tightly in the little basket, the driver in front of us. The road went through woods and across fields and past villages, from which women and girls, in black with white head-scarves, came out to join others like them on the high road. There were few men. All walked in silence, heads bowed. When we lit up cigarettes, one old woman looked up and scolded us.

"It's a sin to smoke on a day like this!"

We immediately put out our cigarettes. Yusha and I were wary of our driver, so we kept silent as we overtook more and more Old Believer pilgrims, but we were thinking how all over the country the authorities were persecuting, imprisoning and executing the faithful of all religions – Orthodox, Baptist, Old Believers, Judaic and Muslim – shutting down churches, arresting priests, preachers and the ordinary faithful. Yet here the Old Believers were on their pilgrimage to see the drowned holy city.

By evening we had reached the village of Vladimirskoye. We paid off the driver and went into the village office to present our papers. Behind the desk sat a mature man with a revolver in his belt, surrounded by a group of young "activists". Whether because he was illiterate or over-watchful, the chairman of the village soviet studied our documents for a long time. Then he looked suspiciously at me, so Yusha quickly said, "That's my assistant, Galchin," deliberately distorting my name. Then he explained what we were here to do. The men listened to us with evident suspicion, quite unable to understand why recording popular poetry and songs could advance the cause of socialism. In the end, Yusha's documents inspired respect and we were taken by one of the young men to our lodging.

Our hosts welcomed us with obvious distrust, but did light the samovar and offered us some pastries. Chatting to them, we learned they were what were called *tverdozadantsi*, an example of one of those contemporary words that no one would understand today. It meant you were better than a *kulak* but worse than a normal citizen, on whom hard tasks (hence the name) could be laid; producing bread for the State at short notice, contributing sums of money, working so many days. You were quite defenceless in the face of the State; you might accomplish the tasks and still be stripped of your possessions and imprisoned. You were at the mercy of the activists. Our hosts said, "We were forgiven. They took away our voice, then they gave it back." Yusha tried to comfort him. As it was the eve of the feast day, our host put a half bottle of homebrew on the table.

Despite feeling very tired, we now set off to walk the three kilometres to our destination. The road was full of pilgrims in their black and white headscarves, heads bowed, moving along in silence. We were joined by a couple of young "activists" who talked about the opiate of the people and confided in us that they had been ordered to take someone in for "examination", as they called it. Yusha said that their presence with us would inhibit us in our conversations with the pilgrims, so mercifully they left us.

The sun was setting. It was clear that all these pilgrims intended to spend the night on the banks of the lake. "Soon, soon," I said to myself, "up that little hill and we shall see it!" And see it we did. In a green vale lay the "blue eye with white birch eyelashes", as the writer Prishvin called it. In the evening light the birches along one bank were pink, while on the other bank rose small hills covered with pine trees, already crowded with people. Coming closer, we found that on the first hill enterprising traders had set up stalls selling little buns, pumpkin seeds and dried fish. Young girls, clearly not pilgrims since they wore brightly coloured scarves, stood around, as well as more young "activists", but rather than taking anyone in, they were chatting up the girls.

"Let's move on," said Yusha, "this is no place for us."

We climbed the second hill. Here a group of people were singing, one or two of them jumping about in a kind of dance. Conscientiously, I was about to open my notebook and write down the verses – after all, that was what we were here for – when I realised with disappointment that this was nothing more than an ordinary village fete. Yusha said, "Let's go on." Next we came across a crowd of men gathered round an old man with the appearance of an Old Testament prophet, who was locked in argument with a much younger man. They were disputing the existence of God, the old man raising his eyes and hands to heaven as he asserted the certainty of God, the young man trying to shout him down. Finally, the young man said, "Lenin doesn't believe in God, which means that all you believers are enemies of Soviet rule. You should all be arrested!" Nonetheless, the argument seemed to go the way of his opponent; eventually the defeated man turning away with a scornful face. "You'll be rounded up soon enough!" was his parting shot. And that was to be the fate of the Church, mocked and accused. The believers, forbidden to defend it, were arrested, exiled and imprisoned, while the Church lived on, persecuted and humiliated.

Finally, on the third hill, we came to a gathering of women singing spiritual and liturgical prayers. Their singing was slow and sad. Below them on the shore were more pilgrims wearing black and white. It was impossible to see how many. These were the pilgrims who came here on this special day, hoping that as true believers only they would hear the bells of the drowned city and see its white walls rising out of the depths. As we stood there watching, I heard a watery rustling and saw a faint light rising from the surface of the water. To my amazement, the figure of a woman wading along the edge of the lake came into sight, followed by others. These were people who had made a vow to wade round the whole lake.

It was a warm and starry night, so we lay down to catch a few hours sleep. I intended to recall everything that had happened to us that day, but had no sooner had I lain down than I fell fast asleep. When Yusha woke me, dawn had already broken. The lake was shrouded in mist, the far bank with its birch trees barely discernible. We went back up the hill. Everywhere people were waking up, lighting fires and cooking breakfast. On the hill where the women had been singing their prayers there were scores of sleeping forms. As we walked back towards our village, I looked for the last time at Lake Svetloyar, the "blue eye in pale eyelashes", and its hidden city of Kityezh. To me, a sinner, it had not revealed itself. We trudged along, sunk in our own thoughts.

I heard that the following year the militia were out on the roads to the lake, not letting any pilgrims through, even arresting some. When the war broke out and there was no one to police the area, wives and mothers made the pilgrimage to pray for the safe return of their husbands and sons. After the war, with the idea that a drink of the lake's water would bring good luck, schoolchildren started to make the journey.

Yusha and I spent a week walking from village to village, gathering together young and old and prompting them to tell us their songs and tales, which we carefully wrote down in our notebooks. The young girls fell to Yusha's lot, while I gathered the young men around me. It was often difficult to get them to remember their songs; it usually required one, bolder than the rest, to start things off. I can only remember a few of the hundreds of verses that we collected. Some of them were bordering on the indecent. The villages we covered were all inhabited by Old Believers and are colourfully described in the writings of Melnikov-Pechersky. We were careful to smoke out of sight of the people. We drank from "peace" cups, and ate from "peace" plates. The forests around Kerzhenets, great stands of ancient pines, have been wonderfully painted by the artist Shishkin. I understand they have since been mercilessly felled and the landscape is covered with small secondary growth. In one village, Khakhala, we spent three days sitting next to an old lady as she sang us her songs of weddings and funerals and other themes.

In that same village I nearly bought a small boat, with the intention of rowing down the river Kerzhentsa to the point where it joins the Volga. The boat was cheap and the villagers told me I would be able to sell it on for ten times its price. It was not fear of the trip that decided me against it, but the thought that along the way some busybody militiaman would ask me what I was doing in those parts, and then a watchful superior would put that inevitable question, "What is your relationship to Prince Golitsyn?" So I went back to Semenov with Yusha, where Katya, who had been dying of boredom, met us with delight. In Nizhny Novgorod, we parted company, Yusha and Katya catching the train back to Moscow, while I, in whom there had always lived a little devil urging me to go on expeditions, took a ship up the river Oka to the town of Vladimir, on the way stopping to visit Murom. I even had enough money to pay for a first class ticket, and what is more, for the first and last time in my life I ordered caviar in the ship's restaurant.

I spent a day walking around Murom, taking in its fine seventeenth-century churches and only regretted that I had no one with whom to share my impressions. I gazed with pleasure on the endless open views of the countryside along the river Oka, and delighted in the town's picture gallery with its collection put together by generations of Counts Uvarov, whose nearby estate, Kacharovo, was where Ilya Muromets was born. That evening I boarded another ship, this time sleeping in third class. In the middle of the night I woke to the infernal noise of passengers boarding and passengers disembarking. I cursed the noise and rolled over to try to get to sleep again. This was the town of Kovrov. Little did I realize at the time that half my life was to be spent in that little town on the river Klyasma.

I arrived in Vladimir in the early morning and took myself to the local militia office to discover the address of a friend of my parents, Fyodor Alexeievich Chelishchev. On the card I had to fill in I wrote, under profession, "Teacher". When the official came back with the address he began asking me why I wanted to visit these people. I was alarmed and muttered some sort of reply, but the militiaman was not listening and with ill-concealed hostility handed back the card, saying that Chelishchev was a disenfranchised and administratively exiled person, and a *Konsomol* like me had no business being involved with such a man. I have no idea why he thought I was a *Konsomol*.

The Chelishchevs received me with open arms. He was a delightful and original man, deeply religious, a philosophical idealist, a former landowner and a jurist by profession. I do not know how he managed to survive, as he had no love of the Soviet system. I think he had various jobs at different times, one of them teaching local children, but he never lost heart. Tall, with glasses and a black beard, he secretly wrote poetry and loved to talk about literature and history. He was recently married and seemed boundlessly happy. His wife, Olga Alexandrovna, was just like him. I could write a lot about her, but it would be too great a diversion. She was born Gresser, the daughter of a senior official in Odessa. Her father, brother and sister were all doing terms in prison, whilst she, already getting on in years, had married a similarly not-so-young Fyodor Alexeievich.

Staying with them was Alyosha Bobrinsky, the thirteen-year-old son of the biologist Nikolai Nikolaievich Bobrinsky, who despite being a count and a former tsarist officer, was never imprisoned. He was married to Maria Alexeievna Chelishcheva, and so Alyosha was the nephew of my hosts.

Fyodor Alexeievich led me enthusiastically around the town of Vladimir. We went from church to church, but we could not visit the Rozhdestvensky cathedral as it stood inside the monastery which was then being used by the OGPU as a prison. We met many of Fyodor Alekseyevich's friends as we walked about the town; some I knew, most of them were exiles, "minus people", who had chosen Vladimir, just as other "minus people" had chosen Tver. The next morning we took the train to Bogolyubovo, where the church was still open and we were able to marvel at the finely carved gilded wooden iconostasis. We then crossed the railway line and reached the world-famous church of Pokrov on the river Nerly. I had long dreamed of visiting it, rather as I had dreamed of reaching Lake Svetloyar. Since then I have been back to this church many times, but I shall always remember the joy I experienced as I saw its beautiful architecture for the first time. I also took a bus, actually a tarpaulin-covered lorry, to Suzdal, but it rained heavily all day and I only remember that I briefly saw the barbarously damaged Trinity Church in the Risopolozhensky monastery before returning, soaking wet, to Vladimir. The delightful Fyodor Alexeievich then saw me off on my way to Moscow.

I never saw him again. The couple had a son, Nikolai, and then Chelishchev was arrested and exiled to the distant river Vychegda. On his return he worked on one of the NKVD construction sites. He died relatively young. As for the young Alyosha Bobrinsky, his fate was a very sad one. He fell under a tram in Moscow, severing his leg, and before the ambulance could reach him, he died from loss of blood.

To conclude my account of these travels, I have to say that all the notes Yusha and I made of songs and verses were badly received by the Academy of the Arts. We had not recorded a single paean of praise for the building of socialism or the joys of the collective farm. A collection of songs had just been published, with texts such as the following:

> To live prosperously in the kolkhoz
> Is something within our power;
> So said Comrade Stalin,
> Our beloved friend and leader

After our expedition together, I never met up with Yusha again. The eighteenth-century Moscow house he had been living in was pulled down. He and Katya moved to Frunze, where he helped to organise the Kirghyz Academy of Science and became its scientific secretary. After the war he taught in the Kirovogradsky teacher training college and on retirement, settled in Yaroslavl. He died in Moscow. I was at his funeral.

6

As an artisan-draughtsman I might now be enfranchised, but that still did not give me the full protection that a proper job would bring with it. I remembered the words of my interrogator, Gorbunov, who had advised me to leave Moscow and to find work on the construction sites. My parents saw the wisdom of this, too, and mother encouraged me, saying, "You'll avoid arrest for a few years, then things will be back to normal and you can return to Moscow and become a writer." She did not turn out to be a good prophetess. Various friends suggested the names of enterprises that needed educated and conscientious staff without any speciality. I was almost taken on by one institute, but when the watchful official heard my name he was frankly astonished that a person like me was still allowed to move freely in Moscow. From there I fled down the stairs, terrified of being chased, and from then on I could not bring myself to try to find work for fear of arrest.

It was not only the disenfranchised, it was the whole of Russia that lived in great fear. At night people waited in expectation of the knock on the door and their doom. One constantly heard "So-and-so has been picked up," and if the arrests were happening in another town, the letter-writer would put the words "So-and-so has fallen ill." I shared this fearful expectation, and was daily surprised to find myself free to go about, even to enjoy myself. Yet I knew my fate was inevitable.

Now a wonderful thing happened. I had a friend from my schooldays, Shura Sokolov, the son of a former lieutenant-colonel. Whenever Shura had to describe his social origins he would write, "Son of a military intendant", a phrase that seemed not to arouse the suspicions of our watchful officials. Shura worked as a line surveyor for the Ministry of Petroleum, and was usually away on prospecting missions. When I told Shura that I was now restored to my voting rights and that I needed to find work outside Moscow, he looked carefully at the thin slip of paper attached to my documents and enthusiastically suggested I should join his outfit. "What about the application form?" I asked. "Oh, forget about that. My chief will only ask you if you've passed your practical exam. You just say, yes, I've passed."

I had indeed been to a school where surveying was taught, and my diploma stated that I had done my fieldwork and could call myself a technician-surveyor, but in fact I had never been out into the field and had only seen geodesic instruments in pictures. Shura put me through a series of lessons about the work, gave me text books to study, and said I would be working in Glavneft and we would be going on survey to the northern Caucasus, where they had found oil.

"The boss is an old man, very strict and if you do anything wrong, gets into a terrible rage."

I assured my friend that I would be extra zealous and super-conscientious. The process happened as he had predicted. The "old man", as he was nicknamed, who was in his seventies, had been an important manager in the Commissariat of Communications and Transport. When rumours of so-called sabotage began to circulate, he decided it would be safer to retire, but, the idle life didn't suit him and he got a job with Glavneft as a survey party leader. When I finally met him on my first day at work, he did indeed put the question to me, "Have you passed your practical?" to which, looking him in the eye, I boldly answered, "Yes, I've passed."

Taking my already prepared form, he quickly wrote something on it and passed it to Shura, who carried the paper into an adjoining office. In no time at all, he was back to tell me that I was now a member of prospecting party No. 3, with a salary of a hundred and seventy-five roubles plus sixty percent field allowance. That was two hundred and eighty roubles, a truly princely sum. I went home in a daze of happiness. Rushing into the house, I told them the exciting news, "You know who I am now? I'm a prospector-linesman with Glavneft!"

Father tried to make a joke of it, "Ah, so you're a prospective live man now, eh?"

It did not occur to me that I was placing a yoke around my neck, becoming a regular employee with regular working hours and saying goodbye to my dreams of becoming a writer. I happily reported to work and was immediately assigned to a group of four other young men. Our job was to collect and pack up for the expedition all the instruments, steel tapes, poles and other materials. For the first time I was in my life given an advance of a hundred roubles, and also for the first time in my life, a pair of boots. Hurrah – I was a working man!

That Sunday, I travelled out to station *Verst* 17 for the last time to say farewell to the Osorgins. The family were preparing to leave the country. Liana Osorgin's husband, Sergei Dmitriyevich Samarin – Uncle Yusha – had died, and with the death in Solovki of Georgy there was nothing to keep the family in Russia. Georgy's wife, my sister Lina, also went with them. There were thirteen of them, including Aunt Liza and Uncle Misha, and they were only waiting for their passports and the French visas. Men aged between sixteen and fifty were not allowed leave the country, but anyone else could do so without difficulty, if their relatives invited them; passports cost a mere trifle. It was only later, after 1931, that the authorities demanded considerable sums in hard currency for permission to leave.

On my visit I saw that the grand piano, at which I had so often seen Aunt Liza playing, was gone. I learnt that a cart had come from the village and some officials had removed the instrument on the pretext that they were allowed by law to requisition it from "people who were not working" in order to teach music to the country youth. The piano had belonged to Nikolai Petrovich Trubetskoi, one of the founders of the Moscow Conservatory. The famous pianist Nikolai Rubenstein had played on it. At the village club, the priest's former house, the children hammered away on it so that it quickly deteriorated and fell to pieces.

The day of my departure arrived and my parents saw me off at Khlebnikovo station, whilst at Kursk station in Moscow I was seen off by Masha, who came with a girlfriend of hers. My sister Lina arrived at the very last minute. I embraced my sisters and shook the girl's hand, thanking her for coming to see me off. The train started to move. It was farewell, Moscow, and welcome to my new life!

7

The reader may well be wondering whether I ever intend to introduce the subject of love, but I have deliberately left this to the end of the story of my youth. Going back to 1924, when I was fifteen-years-old and our family spent the summers in Glinkovo, I was often sent to Sergiyev Posad to do the shopping. I would meet my friend Sergei Istomin and his sister Ksana in the suburb of Krasyukovka, where they lived with their parents. On one of these visits, Sergei told me that some neighbouring children were going to put on a play in their garden, to which he had not been invited. Hurt and annoyed by being left out, Sergei proposed that we climb up on their fence and from that viewpoint spy down on them.

They were doing Gogol's *The Engagement*, and three of the parts were played by the Nersesovy daughters, Rina, Masha and Zina. Knowing that I could draw caricatures, Sergei had equipped me with a notebook and encouraged me to make some sketches. After the show was over, he kept the notebook, which then somehow came into the hands of the Nersesovy family, who asked if they could keep it as a souvenir. It also happened that my sisters often met the family at church services in the monastery of Gethsiman, which lay equidistant from both Krasyukovka and Glinkovo. So we all became friends. Masha and I visited them in their house, and on one occasion we made up a small party and walked some five *versts* to the seventeenth-century wooden church in the village of Blagoveshchenye.

Back in Moscow my parents exchanged visits with the Nersesovys. My sister Masha, Lyalya Ilyinskaya and the eldest Nersesovy, Rina, were part of a study group run by a former teacher, Elena Alexeievna Efimova. In this way we began to know each other better. Kirill Urusov and the three Rayevsky brothers were part of the company, but my Golitsyn cousins Sasha and Olechka were never invited, nor was Lyalya. The family lived behind the main post office in a large house, of which they occupied three or four rooms. They were what one might term a patriarchal family. The kind of wild parties that we organised in those days, where we danced the foxtrot and grandmother's furiously fast galop and were not worried if some of the furniture got damaged, simply did not happen at the Nersesovys.

The father, a short man with strong, slightly Armenian features, was a jurist with the rank of professor and head of the University of Moscow library. I remember later, when working in the reading room there, seeing him emerge rather grandly from his office and move about the great hall, looking carefully at the rows of readers at their desks. He was too busy to pay much attention to his daughters, leaving their upbringing to his wife, Evgeniya Aleksandrovna. She was a strict yet passionate woman, and deeply religious. It was she who chose the boys and girls, and later the youths and young women, with whom her daughters were allowed to mix. Anybody at all rough or vulgar was not allowed in their home. I remember the occasion when a youth, for some small slip, was told, "Please don't visit us any more."

Among the young men who were part of our company, I remember Nikolai Khromtsov, not at all brilliant or witty, but by his quietness and modesty very much loved. Sadly he was quite lame, and so did not take part in our dancing. Another youth was Kirill Voskresensky, studious, serious and bespectacled, who had had a part in *The Engagement*. In later life he became a well-known biologist. Then there was Brilling, the son of a professor, who was paying court to Rina, and whom I therefore detested. Why did I detest him? Quite simply because I had by then realised that I was in love with her. I was in love with her, but it was from a distance – an abstract love. I watched her from afar, but was too timid to make a move. On one occasion I plucked up my courage to invite her to the Arts Theatre where they were playing *The Marriage of Figaro*. We had seats on the steps of the gangway, and although I was engrossed in the performance, Batalov playing Figaro, and Zavadsky the Count, I was also very conscious of sitting beside my beloved. On the way home, full of impressions of the play and sharing our thoughts and ideas, I still could not bring myself to hold her hand.

Her mother was very fond of me, especially after I had described my travels with Andrei Kiselev around the northern monasteries. She learnt of my writings and got me to read aloud to them my essays *Round Northern Lakes*. I can still see the little circle of mother and daughters listening to me in attentive silence. When we were expelled from Moscow to Kotovo, I continued to visit them and was always warmly welcomed. Mother and Rina interrupted whatever they were doing, listened to my stories and pressed me to stay to dinner, but they never asked me to spend the night – they had no spare bed, and felt it was not proper for me to sleep on the floor.

Eventually Rina entered university to study mathematics, at which she excelled. As a top student, she was always being urged to join the *Konsomol*s, which eventually led to her admitting that she was a believing Christian. There was a terrible reaction from the university "activists" and an article denouncing her appeared in the student wall-newspaper. She was expelled from her course. Later she managed to complete her studies as an external student. As for me, I was in love with her, but I also knew that I had no right to be so. Who was I in comparison with the brilliant Brilling? I was then still a citizen without rights, and could be arrested and exiled or imprisoned any day. I had seen how much my sister Lina suffered with a husband far away in the Gulag. I simply did not have the right to condemn a beautiful and intelligent young woman to that kind of torment. I had no right to love her. My visits to their place in Telegraph Street became fewer, though my heart still beat faster when I saw her.

Through the Nersesovy I was offered a job by an Armenian friend of theirs to work on the road that was planned in Asian Russia, near the Pamir and Hindu Kush mountains. I was thrilled with romantic expectations, but the job never materialised; when I filled in the application form and put down that I had done nine grades at school, the office turned me down for lack of experience. As it turned out, I was fortunate – not much later, the Armenian and all his engineering colleagues were accused of sabotage and arrested. I would have been among them.

In the summer of 1930, I learned that the Nersesovy had taken a *dacha* in Vereya. Rina wrote to Masha inviting her down there, adding a footnote that read, "Perhaps Sergei Mikhailovich would like to come, too?" Masha could not go as she was just off on her first geological expedition, but I was absolutely free and decided to accept the invitation. On arrival at the station called Dorokhovo, I expected to finish the journey on horseback, but was astonished to find a colossal landau, drawn by four horses, waiting outside the station. It was the kind of vehicle that Pushkin might have travelled in. Twelve adults, with small children on their knees, could fit into such a carriage. Everyone piled in and settled themselves as best they could, and eventually this strange anachronism set off.

At Vereya I had great difficulty finding the address. No one seemed to know the name of the street. I must have walked about the entire small town for about two hours before it occurred to me to ask people, not for the name of the street, but for a house where three beautiful, dark-haired girls were staying with their mother. I was immediately shown where they lived, and was joyfully greeted by Nina and Masha. Rina and a friend were away swimming in the river, but soon appeared. Wearing a loose dressing gown, Rina looked somewhat embarrassed at seeing me and ran off to dress, only greeting me when she reappeared.

During my two-day stay, Rina and I had the opportunity to go on walks together. I told her of my hopes and plans for the future, and chatted of all sorts of other things. She listened very attentively – after all, we had not seen each other for several months. I spent three days with the family, and much of that time alone with Rina, but when I finally returned to Moscow I made the firm decision not to see her again. That visit has remained a delightful memory, and was the reason why I was so touched to be seen off by her at Kursk station that autumn.

After I joined Glavneft, I occasionally exchanged letters with her mother. In one of her replies she enclosed a note from Rina; I cannot remember the contents, she said nothing special. Her mother wrote that sometimes, when Rina visited her, she would read her my letters. I replied, and half-expected a second note from Rina, but nothing came. Many years later, when I was already married, my sister Masha told Rina that I had been in love with her. Rina was utterly surprised and questioned Masha further, who repeated that I had been madly in love with her; Rina protested that she had had never guessed for a moment.

Years later she married an older man. I was in Moscow on leave and quite by chance bumped into her father, looking very much older, on Pokrovka Street. He invited me back for tea. Rina's husband was away on a mission. We sat side by side drinking tea, when she suddenly said, "Let me show you my little boy." We went into the adjoining room and stood on either side of the cot. I bent down to look at the crumpled little face. When I straightened up, Rina lifted her face and looked into my eyes. We looked at each other for a long while. What her thoughts were I do not know, but I know what mine were – this child could have been ours.

After the war we rarely met. Her marriage was a happy one. She was a person of deep faith and brought up her children as believers, always taking them with her to church. The years passed and her husband died and then, in 1975, so did she. I was at her funeral service in Ilya Obydenny church near Ostozhenka Street. As it happened, I was on the other side of her coffin from Nikolai Khromtsov, both of us thinking our own thoughts. Had she loved me? It seems that she had. Would we have been happy together? I cannot tell. We might have been, or evil times might have destroyed our love.

20. The Prospectors

1

Speeding south, our train was leaving the cold winds and rains of Moscow behind. Our leader, Vyacheslav Viktorovich Sakharov – "the old man" – and his deputy were in the sleeping car, while the rest of the prospecting party occupied reserved seats. When morning came we woke to blue skies and sunlight, and the sight of people not wearing overcoats. At a station called Lozovaya, where the train was to stop for a while, my friend Shura Sokolov and I went off for a walk. Instead of going in the direction of the station building, we set off along a siding. The warmth of the sun raised my spirits, and I felt full of the joys of this new life. Here I was, a prospector, on the way to new adventures. The future seemed to brim with romance.

Then I saw a sight that I have never forgotten. In the siding stood a freight train, all its doors wide open. Inside those cars, packed tightly together, were men and women and masses of children of all ages, some standing, others lying against each other in the depths of the cars. Red Army guards with rifles walked up and down the ballast alongside the train. I did not immediately understand what was happening and then the people in the train began to shout at us, "Look at them! That's the proletariat! Cursed people!" I suddenly realised that they were shouting at us. As we passed the second car, more people began shouting angrily.

"Let's go back," I begged Shura.

"Don't pay any attention," he said, unmoved, "it's just *kulaks* being transported."

The dreadful train started up, carrying away those unhappy people still shouting abuse at us. As it accelerated away, we went on with our walk, chatting of this and that, seemingly indifferent to their fate. I have never again seen such a train.

At our final destination, Belogrechenskaya, we had to unload all our heavy equipment and wait while Sakharov and his deputy went off somewhere in a trap. Sunning myself in the unfamiliar warmth,

I looked out on the white huts of the Cossack village of Apsheron-skaya, just visible in a sea of green, lying along the banks of the river Tukha. On the far side of the village I could just make out a wider river, the Pshekha, with low, forest-clad hills above it that rose to higher hills, and behind those the white of snow-capped mountains.

Eventually our foreman, Fyodor, returned with several carts. After loading up, we set off to the settlement where we were to live. A self-confident young village official, against the wishes of the owners, allotted us three little white huts. The engineers were given a small room in the hut that was to be the office, the "old man", Sakharov, took the second hut for himself, and we technicians bunked down in the third. The earlier tradition of generously equipping prospecting parties was still observed. We had come with pots and pans, plates and cutlery, cups and bowls as well as all the basic foodstuffs – flour, salt, sugar and canned meats. We also had tents, but they stayed rolled up. As for our clothes, we were proud of our special khaki outfits, not so different from the uniforms worn by young *Konsomols* who in those days spread fear among the ordinary people.

As we were undressing that evening, Shura whispered urgently, "Your cross – take your cross off!" Carefully, so that no one noticed, I took off the silver cross on a silver chain that I had worn since my earliest childhood and hid it in my suitcase. It was to be forty years before I wore it again.

At six o'clock in the morning, Shura woke me, carried out the surveyor's bag and instruments on to the grass, and gave me a thorough grounding in how to use them. I applied myself very seriously to following his instructions and made a great effort to remember everything he told me. It was the first time I had handled a theodolite. At the end of his instruction, Shura said, "Well, let's hope the old man doesn't notice that you're a bit of a novice."

After breakfast, and having collected together a group of young people to help with holding the surveyors' rods, drawing out the steel tapes and driving in the pickets, our entire party set off, climbing higher and higher to the site of the future settlement. I was very nervous about my work and could only give half my attention to the magnificent view that opened out at our feet. When we stopped, half a day was spent training the young people we had hired, so it was only the next day that the engineer finally indicated the general direction and we set to work.

I will not describe these working days in detail, as we followed each other with our instruments, sighting the striped poles, shouting to our rod holders to move this way and that, to lift the marker, or lower it, then moving on. I was aware that, hovering in the background, the "old man" was watching me and judging my work. I sweated profusely as I worked with my eye to the theodolite and waved my arms at my helpers. Sakharov never said a word. At the end of the day the measurements had to be calculated out, and there was usually an error of a few millimetres that crept into even the best work. We all did this job in the office. I completed my calculation, checked my figures over and over, and was so pleased with the result I could not stop myself shouting out, "Four millimetres!" The "old man" looked up, "Sergei Mikhailovich, don't disturb the others at their work!"

2

I also witnessed his legendary anger. One day a tape got caught on a rock, and instead of carefully releasing it, the young man jerked it, causing it to break. Sakharov called the man over and, in the most thunderous tones, poured out a torrent of reproach, which only redoubled when the fellow tried to excuse himself. Some time later, it was my turn to experience this rage; I was charting some points on a plan, when I discovered one was missing. Turning to Shura, I said, "Look, there's a point missing here, so I'll have to invent something with this horizontal."

The "old man" pushed back his chair with a screech, stood up with the alacrity of an athlete, and shouted "Sergei Mikhailovich, stand here in front of me!" I remembered that Shura had warned me never to try to justify myself, so I hung my head and tried to look repentant. How Sakharov scolded me! "Remember once and for all, never talk about inventing anything in any kind of technical work! Technique means absolute accuracy at all times! You may go back to your work."

3

This village of Asperonsk, in the Kuban region, was home to the famous Cossack regiment of that name. In the autumn of 1930, the villagers still managed to live well off their smallholdings. They kept horses and cows, sheep, chicken and geese, and for heavy work, an animal I had never seen before, the buffalo. Their pigs grazed freely on fallen fruit in their orchards. They grew wheat and maize, the latter growing so high that our three-metre-high rods were barely visible. In their gardens were apples, pears, cherries and plums. Grapes wound themselves round tall trellises and there was also tobacco, which I smoked in my pipe, delighting in its aroma. Up till then only the most important Cossacks had been dispossessed and driven out of their homes as *kulaks*. But the people lived in fear of what the future might bring, and our presence there, walking over their land with our measuring equipment, and helping ourselves without asking to the fruit on their trees, made them anxious. They would ask us why we were measuring, offer us milk or even the new wine and invite us into their homes. Their little white houses, even with floors of beaten earth, were clean and neat. In the holy corner would hang icons and the ever-burning little lamp. On the walls would be portraits of their family and ancestors in their tall Cossack hats, embroidered jackets, with daggers stuck into their waistbands. It was obvious they were proud of their warrior past, but they never ventured an opinion about Soviet rule. Only once, when I was alone with a driver, he pointed at the wooded hills and said, "That's where some men hid for two years."

"They were Red partisans?" I asked.

"No," he said, "White."

Our surveying took us close to the recently built settlement of Neftegorsk, where oil had recently been found. Unfortunately, one well had caught fire, and we saw the enormous column of burning oil and gas, millions of tons of fuel, rushing skywards out of an eight-metre-wide pit. The black smoke could be seen for miles around, and the flames lit up the sky to such a height that the glare was visible much further away. Nothing was said about this catastrophe in the national press; only when it was finally put out was there a mention of awards made to the firefighters.

Among the members of our expedition I became quite friendly with another linesman, Little Seryozha (I was Big Seryozha). He confided in me that his father, a priest in a village in Tula province, was languishing in the Gulag near Archangelsk. He showed me a photograph he kept carefully hidden in his suitcase; a family group, the priest and his wife in the middle, surrounded by no less than ten children, all of them smiling. I urged Seryozha to write home, advising his sister to visit Peshkova at the International Red Cross. Two months later, Seryozha tore open a letter from home; immediately his face lit up with joy. That evening he whispered to me that his father had been released. Whether this was thanks to Peshkova or was an act of good fortune, he did not know, but his mother had written that Peshkova had received her daughter with great sympathy and had promised to do all she could about the father's case.

Later Seryozha told me that his father had abandoned the priesthood, and the family had all moved to Tula. And then, as the children grew up, one by one they had left the family nest. Seven years later the father was arrested again and disappeared for ever. Much later he was posthumously rehabilitated. I saw Seryozha from time to time until his death in 1988.

Another member of our team was Fyodor Kolesnikov. His main job was to serve the "old man", essentially by supplying him with his daily vodka intake – Sakharov was never drunk, but every evening he would drink half a small bottle of vodka in the solitude of his little room, followed, after dinner, by the second half. Fyodor wore a smart short jacket, polished shoes and loved to talk about his parents, peasants living near Tula. He used to boast about the fine bed with brass knobs, the sprung mattress and dressing table and other things they had bought with the money he sent home. The fate of these luxuries was a sad one; the local authorities confiscated them. Hearing this news, Fyodor lost his cheerfulness and became less communicative about his family misfortune. I met him in Moscow three years later, when he told me that he was trying to find work, that his family had been expropriated as *kulaks*. Seryozha's gifts had given them the appearance of being rich, and rich peasants were *kulaks*.

When my first salary came through, after deductions and necessary spending money, I was still able to send my parents two hundred roubles. Mother wrote how needed the gift had been. She added, "Papa and I are so proud of you!" From then on, I faithfully transferred the same sum every month.

I had been forced to give up reading. Not only were there no books, and very rarely papers, there was no leisure time for reading. Often we had to sit up late transferring our day's measurements to paper. My life now was spent amongst people; solitude was non-existent. And yet, deep inside me, the plot and first chapters of my book , *The Rogue*, were slowly developing. So although my literary ambitions were bottled up, I was happy in my work, happy that I could send money to my parents, and above all, happy in that I was living an existence free of the fear that had hung over me for years. Working far out in the field, we were liberated from the inquisitive probings of watchful officials. Sakharov was of the old school and applied strict discipline, but that was in respect of our work.

I experienced none of the sense of persecution of a "former person", and only Shura and Sakharov knew of my prince's title. I can think of several young people who saved themselves by working in prospecting parties far out in the field.

Once, however, I nearly fell foul of officialdom. I had been sent off with two assistants and all our instruments to plot a piece of land below the pumping station on the river Pshekha. After we had crossed the river on a rope bridge, I told my men to wait for me as I went to the village council to ask for accommodation. I found a keen young man, the village chairman, wearing a tall Cossack cap, with a revolver in his sash.

"Documents!" he ordered.

I showed him my identity card and began to explain why we were there. Just as abruptly he said, "Your travel authorisation!" I began to explain that we were here as a survey party and surely did not need a travel authorisation from the next village.

"Suppose you're a secret agent of imperialism, I'll have to arrest you and send you in to Mykop!"

My heart sank into my boots. Luckily, through the window he could see my two workers with all the equipment, and must have realised that he was overstepping the mark. "Show me your papers tomorrow," he said, and then himself led us to a large house, warning us that he was putting us in with a family of *kulaks*.

The family consisted of mother and daughter. They bowed humbly and showed us to our quarters, but they were obviously terrified by our arrival. Meanwhile, I sent off a messenger to collect some kind of official authorisation from Apsheronskaya. As we settled in, I could not help but notice the tear-swollen faces of mother and daughter. I explained why we were here and eventually their fears were dispelled. The mother then told me of the tragedy that had befallen them; the father and son had been arrested only two days earlier, a couple of horses had been confiscated and they were under threat of being evicted from the village. I tried to comfort them as best I could; I was particularly sorry for the not-very-pretty daughter. The mother was touched by my concern, laid out a feather mattresses and blankets for us, and cooked us ample meals for the three days we were there.

The next day, my messenger came back with a stamped, official-looking travel warrant, and the village chairman graciously shook my hand, adding that he had always to exercise great watchfulness. I have described this incident only because it was the only time that I ever came into contact with local people; as prospectors we lived our own, separate lives. Only once did a local paper come into our hands; sadly, it was bursting with articles full of hatred and indignation.

There was a prison camp not far from Apsherovskaya, with barbed wire fences and watch towers. The prisoners were marched out every morning to work on the construction site of a factory for making lamp-black, a petroleum by-product. We often walked past the area of the camp and the factory, but no one ever talked about the camp, or wondered how many inmates were there, or asked why they were imprisoned. In those days, it was inconceivable for us to talk about such forbidden topics. The factory's output was to be sold to the USA, and the expert in charge of its assembly was an American, who went about in the only private car in the area. We speculated about his comfortable life-style, his diet, and his pretty interpreter – was she also his mistress? We were great gossips.

4

New Year 1931, came round, but it was now forbidden to celebrate this much-loved day. The authorities had decided that New Year was a throwback to capitalism and had nothing to do with the revolution, so our expedition could not celebrate either. It was now a typical Apsheronskaya winter – rain, wet snow, slush and mud, so for the next few months we usually returned from work wet through, tired and hungry.

When March came round we had been in the field for six months. The unions were active in those days and made sure that our entitlement to leave was actually granted. Shura Sokolov and I applied for leave and after some delay, Sakharov let us go, although without any salary, which he promised to send on by telegraphic transfer. We found ourselves at the Belorechenskaya station in a huge crowd of families with small children and all sorts of other travellers crowding around the shut ticket window. It was the day of my birthday; over the years my birthday invariably seems to have fallen on awful days of cold or wet. This day was no exception. Contemplating the crowd of jostling people, I wondered how we were ever going to get away, even though we had been given very authoritative travel documents. Shura, however, headed straight for the door marked OGPU – unlike me, he felt no awe for that service – and within an hour, beaming in triumph, reappeared with two tickets for Moscow, and what is more, in reserved seats.

On arrival I went straight to Savelovsky station for the train out to my parents, who had been forced to move out of Kotovo to a place near Khlebnikovo station. The new landlord had done well during the NEP growing flowers for the wholesale market and had built a large brick house, but by the time my parents moved in he was in prison. They only saw him once, from a distance, when he was brought back to his garden by the police in order to show them where he had hidden his gold and silver. After they had dug up his treasure, he was taken away for good.

I found my family in a happy mood. Mother had finally been cleared in the long-running case of the 'Embroidered Cushion'. They had hidden from me the fact that she had at one time sat in prison for a whole fortnight. Her bitter experience in this case discouraged her from ever again trying to set up her own business. My brother Vladimir was still getting some work from the journal *Young Guard*; it would seem that their attitude was "He may be a former prince and disenfranchised, but he is talented and hard working". Masha was working hard on the Moscow geological committee, and only came home in the late evening. Katya had work on an experimental farm at Dolgoprudnaya. As for poor father, he was noticeably sicker as well as worn down by lack of employment. Now and again kind friends would give him something to translate, but mostly he looked after the grandchildren.

Vladimir was fascinated by my account of the terrible well-head fire that had been raging so long, and tried to think of ways to put it out, sketching out his ideas and even thinking of sending his drawings somewhere or other. I had come home without any money, though I did have a suitcase full of aromatic tobacco for him, but he only wanted to keep a kilo and sell the rest. This he did through his sister-in-law, the actress Mansurova, who indulged in a quick piece of speculation. I later received a ticket to Schiller's *Cunning in Love* as a mark of gratitude.

The transfer of salary that Sakharov had promised never arrived. It turned out that it had been lost in the post. He eventually sent Shura and me an authorisation to receive the money at our Moscow offices, which we managed to do, though with difficulty and delays. This whole process took two months, and during that time I stayed at home and even began to write the first chapters of my novel *The Rogue*. No one seemed to consider this long absence from my work of peering through my theodolite a problem. Had it had happened only a year later, I would probably have got three years in a labour camp for parasitism.

5

How often in my life has some insignificant event altered its whole course. I was back at Apsheronskaya when I began to suffer from severe toothache. Sakharov ordered me to report to the medical section, saying, "In our kind of work, the only solution is to get the tooth pulled out!" Once this was done, he told me to man the office as he was going off somewhere. Before long, an elegant carriage drawn by two fine bays drew up, and out jumped a heavy-built, middle-aged man – the chief engineer, Sergei Sergeievich Zelenin. I went out to meet him and when he learned that Sakharov was away, asked me to show him the work we were doing. With the confidence of youth, I laid out the plans we had been drawing and gave him a full explanation of what we were doing. I think I made a favourable impression on him.

The summer season drew to a close. One day, Sakharov called us all together and announced that the prospecting party was recalled to Moscow, but that the organisation Myneftestroy needed two technicians to remain behind. "Who wants to stay?" he asked. A terrible question – of course we all wanted to return to Moscow! Sakharov went off to the offices of the requesting organisation and returned, saying that Zelenin wanted to see us all. The very next day he arrived in his elegant carriage, spoke to us about the building of socialism, mentioned the speeches of "the great Stalin" in which he asserted that it was the cadres who were the key people, and then pointed at me.

"I want him to stay," he ordered and, looking around, pointed at Kostya Masharov, a fellow a couple of years older than the rest of us and a solid-looking man. "And him, too." A law had just come into force that individuals had no right to resign from a job – it was the organisation that made the decision to hire or fire an employee. This was called "the strengthening of cadres". So neither Kostya nor I dared refuse. If I had not had toothache, how differently things would have turned out.

Kostya and I reported to the main offices in Sotsgorodok and were registered as technicians. The form I had to fill out asked the usual question about social origins, but without the rider "former status of parents", so I could confidently write down "son of an employee". We were taken into the project room and introduced to the chief, Mouseya Gursky. Curious eyes were turned upon us, as we were still dressed in our worn and muddy field clothes and so looked rather wild. However, everyone was very welcoming. After a couple of days we were issued with a shirt, trousers and leather shoes. A less happy development was when we saw the bookkeeper and learned that we now had no right to any field allowance; our salaries dropped from three hundred roubles to a hundred and seventy-five, which meant that I could only send my parents fifty roubles, and sometimes not even that.

Kostya and I were the only unmarried men in the section, so the three young women draughtsmen looked at us with unconcealed interest. We soon got to know them. Kostya went out with fair-haired Lyusya, whilst dark-haired Tasya fell to my lot. Today, I can only remember that she wore shoes with little ribbons on the toes. Whenever I accompanied her to the cinema, I would remind myself that my heart belonged to Rina Nersesova. The third girl was an attractive, sixteen-year-old Jewish girl, Mousenka, to whom I was attracted, but we could only chat to her at lunch-time, as when work finished her strict father led her off home.

The majority of the staff came from a town called Tuapse. Conversation was nearly always about the families and homes they had left behind, with nostalgic memories of the beautiful town it was and how, when they built new communal housing, they would all have their own rooms. But the order now came for us all to move nearer to Apsheronskaya, further away from Tuapse. No one dared to discuss the decision, far less protest about it; in those days, orders had to be obeyed without question.

For living quarters Kostya Masharov and I shared a tent, which naturally brought us closer together. I liked to quote the poet Esenin aloud and as Kostya had never heard his poetry, it made a great impression on him. He wanted to hear these verses again and again, and even recited them himself. Gradually, we communicated more openly with each other. I confessed my princely origins and described my hard-working father; I told him of the anxieties I had to face in life, of the fear I so often experienced. I even told him of my dream of becoming a writer. Pulling the first pages of my novel out of my suitcase, I read them aloud. There was only one subject on which I remained silent, and that was my hatred of Stalin. During the whole of my life I have lived with that hatred, considering him the main culprit for the terrible fate that befell Russia, but I have never given voice to that hatred – punishment without mercy would have fallen upon me.

Kostya also became frank with me. Generations of merchants of Tobolsk were his ancestors. After the revolution, the town was occupied first by the Reds, then by the Whites, then by the Reds again.

Then the reprisals started; prominent merchants, civil servants and clergy were shot. Kostya and his mother went to the site of the executions themselves and hunted among the bodies, finally finding the corpse of Kostya's father and taking it away for a decent burial. Kostya was one of three brothers, all of them hiding their origins for fear of what might befall them. One brother was on an expedition in the Far East; the other had found work in a secret institution in Moscow, but lived in fear that the application form he had filled out, in which he had detailed a fictitious account of his family, might lead to his unmasking. Their mother, deprived of her voting rights, evicted from her home, lived in desperate fear of arrest. Kostya wanted to bring her to Apsheronskaya, and since he asked for my advice, I of course agreed that it would be a good idea.

In our outfit there were two older men, Bergman and Krokos, who kept to themselves, spoke to no one and did not eat with us. They were always followed discreetly by a young soldier. Nothing was said to us, but it was obvious these two engineers were prisoners. One day we were ordered to inspect a site, riding there on horseback. I used any excuse to ride out for my work. Krokos and I started to gallop, leaving the escort bumping along behind, and soon lost sight of him. Unexpectedly, Krokos asked me whether I was a prince. In response to my affirmative, he promised never to reveal this to anyone. He then asked if I would do him a favour, which was to post a letter, not in Sotsgorodok, but in Apsheronskaya. From that time on, I committed this minor crime for him several times.

All that summer Kostya and I worked and lived together, until one day we were both simultaneously struck down by tropical malaria. This was a scourge that affected at least one third of all non-local staff; the locals had built up immunity. I will not describe in detail the course of this unpleasant disease, as it must be familiar to the reader. Suffice to say that we were laid low with high fever, and when Kostya's mother arrived – once a plump merchant's wife, but now fearful and emaciated – she also went down with malaria. No special treatment was on offer – we were given sick leave and lay motionless, hardly talking, as the fever came and went. Then a fine thing happened; Lyusya and Tasya arrived at our tent with various food supplies, and after one look at the accumulated junk and dirt, energetically got down to scrubbing and carting away our rubbish and making our quarters shipshape.

We had now reached the age to be called up into the army. There were three categories – those with a clean record were taken into the regular army. Those with dubious social origins were assigned to non-military duties and could continue to work or study, only being called up for a month or so now and again. The third category, the sons of merchants, *kulaks*, disenfranchised parents or "enemies of the people", were classified as rearguard material and sent to the Gulag as prisoners.

The twenty of us in our organisation who were due for call-up were sent by truck to the examining commission. The weather was fine and all around was the beauty of nature, but my knees were shaking with fear. As it turned out, I need not have worried. I appeared stark naked in front of the panel (which included two young women) and was asked, "Where did you study?" Before I could answer, the examining doctor said, "Let's weigh him first." I was six foot tall – my weight was fifty-five kilos! "He needs feeding up," said the doctor, and I was given a year's postponement of service, which meant I could return to my work. However, it was not long before the malaria struck again. A rule had now been introduced not to give sick leave to sufferers from malaria, so we had to struggle to work, weakened and feverish as we were. Our chief Nasarov was an old Bolshevik, totally committed to the cause of the revolution. He had languished in tsarist prisons as well as been a captive of the Whites, and was later to end his life in the Gulag. He now ordered us to report to a medical board, where we received a certificate authorising us to go for extended therapy and also never again to work in malaria-infected areas. Once our fever had gone, and equipped with impressive-looking travel documents, we were allowed to leave Apsheronskaya, heading for the station of Belorechenskaya.

6

The station was teeming with the usual crowd of hopeful travellers. Watchful OGPU agents spotted us and hauled us into their office, but were fully satisfied by our papers. Kostya had the confidence to ask them for three tickets to Moscow, and not only did they issue them to us but we were able to catch the next train. At Kazansky station we parted company after exchanging addresses; I wrote to him once, but received no reply. I am sure he must have ended up in the camps – he was a tall, unusually distinguished-looking figure, the sort the authorities automatically distrusted.

My parents had once again been forced to move home and were now living in Dmitrov. On seeing me, mother was horrified and called in the local doctor, Ekaterina Mikhailovna Lionovich, who expressed the opinion that I should go into hospital. This would have been no easy thing to arrange, and in any case I definitely wanted to stay at home. In the end I was sent to the central medical board in Moscow, where the doctors at once recognised my condition and gave me a letter to certify that I was not fit to work in malaria-infested areas. This I sent on to my organisation in Apsheronsk, only to receive a cryptic message from the deputy head, a certain Pandov, "Finish your cure and return immediately to work." Obviously, I was taken to be some sort of malingerer. I showed this telegram to our old lawyer friend, Nikolai Adrianovich Silversan. "Totally arbitrary," he said, and without more ado, wrote me out a petition to the Office of Complaints of the Central Committee of the Party. Where there once had been the beautiful church of Nicola of the Great Cross in the Kitaigorod district of Moscow, there now stood a modern building housing the Central Committee. The lawyer there, to judge by his appearance a veteran Bolshevik, asked only a few questions, which did not include the dreaded question, and I was given a document with the impressive stamp of the Central Committee, stating that I was released from my job for medical reasons. I was now free to look for work elsewhere and, remembering the advice of my Lyubyanka interrogator, I remained determined to find work away from Moscow.

Later, my artist friend Dimitri Dimitriyevich Zhilinsky, who had grown up in Apsheronskaya, told me of the vicious pogrom that had been organised against its inhabitants in 1933. Their cattle, fowl and grain were taken from them; they were forbidden to sow any crops, even potatoes. A dreadful, artificial famine set in, and whole families died of hunger or were wiped out by malaria. Zhilinsky's family were spared only because his father worked in the forest, but in 1937, he too was arrested and disappeared for good. His son painted a picture of the moment of his arrest. I saw a crowd gathered around this picture when it was exhibited for the first time in the post-Brezhnev years. Years later, now myself an established writer, I returned to visit the places of my youth. The town, clearly a thriving community, was now called Ashperonsk. The oil fields had closed down, malaria was a thing of the past, and no one remembered the burning oil well. There were no photographs of gallant Cossack fighters – indeed, there were very few descendants of the Kuban Cossacks anywhere to be seen. People from elsewhere had moved in and settled the area. Only the forest-covered mountains and the distant snowy peaks were the same as when I was there, and as they will be long after I am gone.

21. Destruction of the Old

1

Before going on with my own story of adventure and misadventure, I want to write about events that are now spoken of freely, though with much pain, but about which in those times not a word was said.

Under Lenin no ancient buildings or churches were destroyed; in fact, he called for their preservation or restoration. It all began after he died. The vandals moved in on Russian art and sculpture, attacking the history of my country. Instead of history, what was now taught in the schools was "Political Literacy". The leader of the new ideology was the deputy commissar for education, M.N. Pokrovsky. In his brief history of Russia, reissued once a year, he wrote much about class warfare, about the peasant rebels Razin and Pugachov, and referred with scorn to General Suvorov and the war of 1812. This was the beginning of the constant brainwashing of public opinion.

The first buildings to be destroyed were not churches, but public buildings. It was a deliberate policy, a cunning approach to what was to follow. Articles were written in the daily papers saying that the Krasniye Vorota (Beautiful Gate), built by the architect Ukhtomsky in the time of empress Elizabeth in the early eighteenth century, was a serious obstacle to the proper running of the trams. The controversy did not rage without there also being letters praising the beauty of the structure, but the polemical struggle was won by the vandals. In 1927, this ancient and beautiful tower gate was pulled down.

In 1930, the authorities declared war on the churches. Their first target was the Simonov monastery, similar in style to the Novodevichy monastery, standing on a hill above the river Moskva, visible for miles around, an object of admiration for all who saw it. It included sixteenth-century buildings and was encircled by a strong wall and towers. The papers screamed, "A nest of bigotry and superstition!" adding that its location would be perfect for a "Palace of Culture" for the nearby Stalin truck plant. It was nonsense to talk

436

of bigotry and superstition when the monks had long ago been driven out; in fact, it had become a fine museum with wonderful medieval armour, a record of Russian military prowess. But the voices of protest were drowned in the hysteria of the press. I still have a copy of the *Workers' Gazette* from the twentieth of January 1930, with its notice from the City Council calling for volunteers to turn up with spades and shovels and pickaxes, outlining the plans for feeding them and organizing first-aid, and alongside this announcement a triumphant article trumpeting the coming act of destruction.

Subsequent destruction was carried out without prior warning. Churches were closed one after another, enclosed in corrugated iron fences, after which men would go in with ropes and hooks, removing and destroying their interior decoration. The iconostases were torn down and burned, metal objects were sent off to be melted down and the song books sent off to the archives of the Novospassky monastery located, like the Simonov, on the left bank of the river Moskva, but two kilometres further upstream. This monastery has survived and been restored, and is now the pride and joy of Muscovites, but the Simonov was grander and more impressive.

I actually watched the destruction of the seventeenth-century church of Trinity on Zubov on Prechistenkaya Street. With its five domes and tent-roofed bell tower it was considered the tallest church in Moscow. Its downfall started with agile young men throwing ropes around its crosses, tearing them off by their roots, then with crowbars smashing in the domes before attacking the walls. It was no easy job to destroy those walls, built as they had been with medieval plaster made of lime mixed with egg white and sour milk. Explosives could not be used because of the nearby buildings. At this time, the poet P. Grigoriyev wrote some verse that Samuel Pokras set to music:

> *We're setting the world on fire,*
> *Levelling churches and prisons*

As history demonstrated, only a third part of this prophecy came true; the churches were destroyed, but the world fire went out, whilst the number of prisons multiplied many times over. There were also two lines that went:

> *From the taiga to the British Isles*
> *The Red Army is the mightiest*

Where once again the poet was a poor prophet.

Nineteenth-century churches were easier to pull down. On occasion the broken bricks were piled up for re-use – this was dubbed "the Lenin system for producing bricks", even though Lenin himself had never encouraged such destruction. Some of the churches that survived were the least interesting, such as Bogoyavleniye in Elokhov, or Ioann Bogoslov under the Elms, which is now the Moscow Museum of History. The many that were destroyed include: Nikola of the Great Cross in Kitaygorod, Uspeniye na Pokrovke, Nikola Yavlenny on Arbat, Grebnevsky Mother of God and the belltower of the Vladimirsky Mother of God on Lyubyanka Square. New buildings were built on these sites, or they were turned into rather mean little squares. On Myasnitsky was the church of St Evplo, the only church that had celebrated services throughout Napoleon's occupation of Moscow. The church of the Mother of God of Kazan, on the corner of Red Square, was also destroyed and a public toilet erected in its place. In the district of Zamoskvorechye, a similar public toilet was built against the walls of the Rastrelli's church of Pope Clement. As a matter of fact, this toilet was removed recently.

People's attitudes to all this destruction varied, and some, whom one might have expected to love and cherish Russia's past, thought quite otherwise. My brother's friend, the writer Leonid Leonov, once said to him, "At first I was upset by what was happening, but now I realise that a new age has dawned." The main inspirer and ideologist behind this vandalism was Lazar Moyseyevich Kaganovich, and the chief executor was Minya Israilevich Gubelman, better known by his pseudonym Emelyan Yaroslavsky. Evgenia Ginsburg has painted the definitive portrait of this monster in her book about the Kolyma Gulag, *The Steep Journey*.

Today young people often ask me, "Were there no lovers of old Moscow to protest against what was being done?" Yes, there were those who tried to protest. Before the Krasniye Vorota was pulled down, letters for and against appeared in the papers. Later, the authors of letters of protest were called saboteurs, and so were frightened into silence. There was an "Old Moscow Society", of which Pyotr Nikolaievich Miller was president, and its members included many enthusiastic young people. On hearing of a planned demolition of a church or another old building, they would hurry out to measure, sketch and photograph it. Miller, as well as most of his young followers, were soon taken off to the prisons. I know of one girl who, ended up in exile after prison, and is now an old woman with a broken life behind her. I want to pay tribute to the memory of those defenders of the past whose bones now lie in the damp ground of the camps of Pechora, the Urals, Kolyma and other places of martyrdom.

After the Society was broken up in 1930, who could dare to protest? Muscovites walked past, horrified but silent. I, too, went my way with bowed head.

2

Present generations can have no idea of the scale and grandeur of the Church of Christ the Saviour, standing above the river near the Kremlin. It was even bigger than the already immensely impressive Cathedral of St Isaac in Petersburg. It was dedicated in 1883 after more than forty years in the building. On a foundation of red granite, forty-five million bricks went into its construction, and it was faced in white marble, with forty-eight sculptures by famous Russian artists around its exterior walls. Its five golden domes could be seen for miles around. Magnificence was the keynote of the interior, with its decoration of marble and bronze and silver and gold, whilst the iconostasis radiated the vivid, freshly created figures of the saints, the Mother of God and Christ. Massive bronze candelabra hung down everywhere and if one looked up into the dizzying height of the main dome, the awesome face of the Pancrator looked down. In fact, the taste of many of Moscow's inhabitants was more inclined towards smaller, more intimate churches such as the church of the Mother of God "Soothe my Sorrow", standing very near Christ the Saviour, a delicate, limestone building with finely carved windows and figured exterior balustrade. I once heard my parents say that Christ the Saviour was too big for the Moscow skyline.

But future generations were not destined to see this great building. In 1931, to the horror of Muscovites, disaster loomed; news spread that the church was to be demolished. Only one man was bold enough to protest publicly; the artist Vasnetsov, who treasured the history of the city and had painted many pictures of its streets and buildings. He wrote a letter to Molotov, then Chairman of the Council of People's Commissars, probably hoping to appeal to Molotov's sense of patriotism as one of the few Russians on the Politburo. He never received a reply. In the 1970s I decided to write an essay on Vasnetsov and, thanks to his son, was able to study the artist's personal papers; amongst them was a copy of his letter to Molotov, and I was bowled over by the passion and style of his pleading for the great church, that exemplar of Russian art and culture. When I wanted to include this letter in my essay, the editor of the series, M.I. Seleznev, made it clear that such a letter could never be published. My enthusiasm cooled, and I did not pursue my project.

The city awoke one day to see little figures like flies, suspended on ropes, climbing all over the main dome – they were stripping the gold leaf. I do not know how many kilos of gold they removed. Then they destroyed the dome by hand. I passed by one day and, behind a high fence, could see the jagged walls of the roofless building. All Moscow was horrified, not so much at the religious impiety of the destroyers, as at their trampling on this glorious symbol of Russian history. The final stage was the demolition all that remained standing with explosives of. The little white stone church I mentioned earlier was also pulled down.

Articles began to be written with monotonous frequency about the grandiose tower of Babel that was to be erected on the site. It was to be called the Palace of the Soviets. Sketches and plans were published of what indeed would have been a remarkable structure, twice the height of the destroyed church. It was to be crowned with an eighty-metre-high bronze statue of Lenin, though rumour had it that actually it would not be Lenin, but our great and wise leader Stalin who desired to immortalise himself in the clouds. The project was touted as the symbol of the imminent age of socialism. The artist Korin was commissioned to do the internal decoration; his designs can be seen in his memorial museum – marching lines of muscular lads and bosomy girls. The metro station built on the site of the adjoining little church was named "Palace of the Soviets".

I will not go into the reasons why the project was never started. Suffice to say, a swimming pool now occupies the site. The metro station was quietly renamed "Kropotkinskaya". Nothing is now said about the Palace of the Soviets. The symbol we are left with is – a swimming pool.[24]

This wave of destruction of churches swept over the whole country, its intensity subject to the zeal or, conversely, patriotism of the local authorities. In Yaroslavl, a hotel now stands on the site of the cathedral. The fine ensemble of Ilya Prorok (the Prophet Elijah), a five-domed church with adjacent tent-roofed campaniles, was threatened with demolition, but thanks to a word from some official was spared, so that now the people of Yaroslavl can admire the many seventeenth-century churches on both sides of the river Kotoroslya,

---

24. *In the 1990s, under President Yeltsin, Christ the Saviour was rebuilt on its former site in a very short time.*

a tributary of the Volga. But in nearby Kostroma more than fifty churches were pulled down, as well as the walls and towers of its fortress. Also destroyed was the only monument to a peasant leader, Ivan Susanin. The seventeenth-century church of Nikola na Debryakh, it is true, was left standing, and the Ipatievsky monastery on the banks of the Volga, some distance from the town, has also survived untouched. I have already written of the fate of the churches in Nizhny Novgorod and Tver.

After the war, under Khrushchev, churches were again the target of vandalism. This time it was village and country ones, and instead of human hands, bulldozers and tractors tore them down. In the museum in Kolomna one can see a tiny fraction of the beauty that was destroyed; the gilt wooden carving of several principal altar doors, a sophisticated clock-tower mechanism, wrought iron church decorations. In the Donskoy monastery in Moscow, beyond the graveyard, one comes upon a large piece of sculpture, the sole surviving item from the Church of our Saviour, some pieces of carved window embrasures and lintels from the seventeenth-century church of Uspenye na Pokrovke, considered one of the finest churches in Moscow, and a number of other fragments of stonework from other churches. There is talk of the restoration, for example, of the Sukharyovaya tower, but I cannot believe that the skills of those medieval masons and carvers, who worked in the spirit of the love of God, can ever be equalled by today's restoration.

22. A Year in the Taiga

1

My recovery from malaria was slow but sure. I now had to look to my future again. This time I could not expect any help from my friend Shura Sokolov as he had gone off to the Far East to work on a second Trans-Siberian railway line from Chita to Vladivostok. There were regular announcements in the papers looking for surveyor-technicians to work on the opening up of the shores of the Sea of Okhotsk and the regions of Kolyma and Chukhotka. This sort of Jack London life, as I imagined it, attracted me, but my mother dissuaded me from applying, pointing out that I would have to sign up for too long a period. I did not at that time know that these regions were to be developed using prison camp labour.

I saw an advertisement for specialists of all kinds to work in the Siberian mining region known as Kusbas. Considering that to be closer to Moscow, I went to the recruitment office just off Prechisten-kaya. I was asked just one question, "Are you a young *Konsomol*?" and then handed a form to fill out. But as I went away I began to hesitate; after all, I could see that I would have to sign up for a long period. So I went on looking for work closer to home.

One evening my good friend Valery Pertsov arrived at our place and said he must have a serious talk with me. He had long ago abandoned his hopes towards my sister Masha, who was in any case in Moscow. Vladimir, with whom Pertsov loved to have passionate discussions, was working in the next room, my parents had gone to sleep and only Katya was left in our living room. Valery chatted in a friendly way with her and then rather abruptly asked her to be good enough to leave us alone. Offended, Katya left; she naturally wanted to know what secret conversation we were going to have.

He then told me that at work the day before an OGPU agent had come and taken him off to the Lyubanka. Valery thought he would never return, but in fact the military interrogator was not in the least

interested in Valery himself, but only asked about me. Why I had
come to Dmitrov? What were my plans? He repeatedly asked questions about my political views and my character. Valery answered
the truth – that I had caught malaria, had been released from my
work, and that I intended to find other work. He tried to describe
my favourable political views. Finally, they made him sign a statement
saying he would never reveal a word of what had happened, and
let him go.

I went cold with fear, feeling like a hare cornered by dogs. For a
year and a half I had lived without fear, lived like an ordinary citizen,
and now it looked as though calamity was about to fall upon me,
a calamity that I could not avoid. We called Vladimir in and Valery
repeated his story. Vladimir recalled that he had recently spent the
night at our cousin's, Alexei Bobrinsky, who was then working as
secretary to the American journalist, Walter Duranti. We all knew
that Alexei was a secret agent for the OGPU, but we assumed that
his mission was to report on foreigners. Now Vladimir recalled
that he had mentioned my return from the Caucasus, and that I was
recovering from illness and looking for other work. Had Alexei
denounced me – me, his own cousin? The very next day I returned
with Valery to Moscow, went straight to the offices of Kusbasugol
and signed a one year contract to work as highways technician at a
salary of 175 roubles a month. Two days later, seen off at the station
by Masha and our cousin Lalya Davydova, I was on the train to
Novosibirsk.

2

Novosibirsk was then only a fraction of the size it is now, with a
small wooden railway station. I was put up by some friends of the
Neresovys, and spent my first three days reporting to the office. There
did not seem to be much need for a highway technician with only
one year's experience behind him. Finally, the Forestry Division
posted me to their most distant area of operations, a region I had
never heard of called Gornoy Shorii. I arrived in the ancient town of
Kuznetsk, not yet renamed Stalinsk, where I spent two days at the
forestry representative's house waiting for my onward journey by
sledge. I had the leisure to observe the early stages of the construction
of the new town to be called Sad-Gorod (Garden City) and also of
some blast furnaces. The forestry accountant was also waiting to
travel with me. He told me the indigenous inhabitants of Gornoy

Shorii were called Shortsi and were hunters and fishermen, but that there were many Russians who had moved in to mine coal and iron ore and exploit the forests. He explained that the forestry area being exploited was a huge region to the south of Kuznetsk, that the timber was taken out on the river Toma and its tributaries, and that the office was in the settlement of Balbyn, some fifty kilometres away. One thing he did not mention was who actually did the work in the forests.

Eventually, before sunrise, we set off in our small sledge. The accountant wore *valenki* (felt boots) and a fur coat over a sheepskin jacket. I was wearing only a felt coat and ordinary shoes. Fortunately, the frost was not too severe. We drove through the forest, here called the *taiga*, though it hardly corresponded to the *taiga* any more; there were sickly looking birch trees here and there, and some small fir tree growth, and the occasional massive cedar standing alone with black capercaillie sitting in rows on the branches. We came across a group of hunters on short skis, guns slung over their shoulders, wearing embroidered fur jackets, skin boots, knives in their coloured belts and carrying decorated sacks tied to their wrists. They had slit eyes and rosy cheeks and greeted us with big smiles, waving their ski sticks, whose tips were like little children's spades. We stopped to talk to them and I offered them cigarettes, which they refused, instead pulling out curved pipes trimmed with silver that they lit with flint and steel. Our driver spoke to them in their language; then we went our ways.

It was still light when we reached Balbyn. I was shown into the manager's office, denoted in pencilled writing on a torn piece of card, and found a heavily-built middle age man who greeted me with a grunt. He was slowly perusing my documents when the secretary rushed in, saying "Novosibirsk is on the line!" Left alone, I could hear the manager trying to justify himself to the person on the other end of the line. Suddenly I noticed a paper on his desk marked "Top Secret" and was overcome with curiosity. I cannot now recall the exact words, but it was an order from Comrade Eiche, chief secretary of the West Siberian Party, instructing all organisations, on account of the prevailing shortage of food, to recruit single men, and to cease the recruitment of families. This was my first encounter with the name of Eiche, the all-powerful boss of the huge region of West Siberia. At the notorious XXth Session of the Communist Party, at which Khrushchev revealed Stalin's crimes, he lamented the fate of this same Eiche, a dedicated communist who had, poor man, suffered torture. But I knew Eiche as one of the nastiest perpetrators of the torture of hundreds of thousands of innocent people. This document alone –

"cease to recruit families" – for how many had that spelt poverty and starvation?

Incidentally, this was a time when one saw everywhere a picture of the great leader holding a little girl in his arms and smiling, with the caption "Thank you, Comrade Stalin, for our happy childhood!"

3

This gloomy general manager sent me over to see his technical supervisor, a rather young, fair-haired man called Pyotr Spiridonovich Meshalkin, who had me sit me down next to himself, asked me a few questions and then said, "I'm going to send you off to build my roller-transporter." It transpired that he had designed an improved version of the log rolling system by which timber was brought out of the forest by sliding it down a bed of rollers on a slope. Filled with enthusiasm, I completed all the usual formalities, visiting the staff office, the payroll section and the general manager. To my surprise, all my details were written down on torn pieces of wallpaper, and to my great chagrin, my request for some writing paper revealed the fact that there simply was no ordinary paper around; I could not get even a single sheet to write to my parents. Moreover, I had expected to be able to get on with my first novel, the first pages of which were at the bottom of my suitcase.

So I set off the next day without having written to my parents. It was a bitterly cold day and in my inadequate clothes I was forced to jump down from the sledge every so often, run alongside it until I felt a little warmer, then leap back up on to the sacks of flour we were carrying. Even so, when we reached the timber-felling station of Mzas, and I stepped inside, I could hardly move a limb. The men gathered there took one look at me, and after telling me that I would freeze to death if I did the final twenty kilometres to my destination of Shodrovo, their chief showed me into a little room where a stove blazed and the samovar was boiling. We got into conversation. Petrov – I have forgotten his name and patronymic – had a very low opinion of Meshalkin's design for the roller-transporter. He said it was a silly invention, and would be a failure, whilst he, Petrov, was desperately in need of a sensible young fellow who could pick out new stands of trees for felling; I was to stay here with him. Rather timidly, I objected, but he said he would sort things out with Meshalkin. Thus began my work in Siberia, living with Petrov in the guest room, sleeping on a straw mattress under a prickly blanket and eating my privileged rations in the communal dining room.

4

Petrov and I got on very well. He arranged for me to be issued with a fur-lined jacket and felt boots. We spent the evenings together, when he unburdened his soul to me. He told me of his wife and children living in Balbyn, and how, although he was an engineer in buildings' joinery by training, here he was made to be the destroyer of forests that were being felled without care – there were millions of cubic metres of timber rotting on the ground. My days were spent going about on skis, crossing the frozen river Mras-su and its tributary, the Mzas-su, selecting stands of trees for felling, calculating their yield and planning the approach road for the woodcutters. I loved being alone in the *taiga*, startling the large grouse and seeing the tracks of wild animals. One day I spotted a gulley-shaped valley that would be suitable for Meshalkin's roller-transporter system; I had not been discouraged from this scheme by Petrov's scorn, and continued in the belief that one day it would be built.

It was at this time that I discovered the existence of an entire class of people, not just groups but an entire class, who had no rights whatsoever – the "special exiled people", about whom the average Russian has only just found out about through the writings of Ivan Tvardovsky, the poet Tvardovsky's younger brother. Before the revolution, the Altai region along the rivers Katun and Biya and their tributaries was famous for its fertility, its rich meadows, its herds of cattle and, above all, its hard working people. Their fathers and grandfathers, settlers from Russia, had cleared the forest, ploughed the fields and built their wooden houses. Then, as they formed communities and communal workshops, they built their churches of wood or stone. The Altai, with its towns of Barnaul and Biisk, was known as the granary of Russia.

Then collectivisation began. On the orders of Eiche, overlord of the region, a wave of "de-*kulakisation*" swept the land. All those who hid their bread, refused to go into the collective farms, lived in spacious houses or had more than two cows or more than one horse, were driven out, their goods confiscated and their cattle seized. Driven where? To the major construction sites, especially around Kuznetsk. In freight cars and on open platforms the crowds of men, women and children were brought to the stations and then taken into the forests where, in wind and rain, in heat and in cold, they built what shelters they could for themselves. Along came foremen on horses to select, as if they were cattle, the best and fittest young men, ignoring if possible men with large families, and led them off, bowed under the weight of their remaining possessions. Many ended up in Gornoy Shorii as coal and iron ore miners or forest workers. They built themselves barracks, houses for the bosses, an office, underground storage pits and a punishment cell. This was how, over a year before my arrival, the forestry settlement of Mzas had come into existence. I learned all this from the unhappy deputy head of the local school, Natasha Poltavets, who had ended up in this region with her father, mother and younger brothers.

5

In the evening, I would occasionally look into the barracks of these "specially-exiled" people. Double bunk beds stretched in a long line down either side. Each family occupied a separate section, the older folk sleeping below, the younger on top. Stoves at each end of the barrack burned day and night; in the evening lanterns hung from the rafters gave a feeble light. There were no ceilings and the inside of the roof was white with frost. I would sit down and talk to the older people. It was both stuffy and yet damp, with a cold draught at one's feet, and too much heat at one's head. There was a strong smell from the clothes drying around the stoves. Children crawled about everywhere, the adults ate the gruel brought in from the kitchen and shared their ration of bread. One could hear voices raised in argument in one section, children crying in another. No one ever laughed. Sickness was endemic and the first-aid orderly had neither medicine nor bandages. Little children often died, deprived of milk, as did old people. The graveyard was on the banks of the river Mras-su, but the management would not allow coffins to be made; bodies were simply laid in the open grave.

In a friendly enough way, I was advised by Petrov not to go into the barracks and talk to these people. They were *kulaks* and contact was not allowed; I could only speak to them in connection with work. The entire management and volunteer workers kept away from these "special exiles". Some of the bosses openly despised them and swore at them at work. In a word, we were the masters, they the slaves, as in ancient Rome or in the USA a century and a half earlier. And I belonged to the masters. The Commandant of the camp went about in his white fur jacket, a revolver at his waist. With his staff and a secretary from among the exiles, he lived in his own quarters in the same building as I did. When in our company he was a jolly fellow and a joker, and in the evenings would accompany himself in song on the harmonica. But if someone from the barracks came to see him

447

his hackles would bristle like an angry dog and he would answer abruptly and scornfully, without hiding his contempt. For the people in the barracks he was a menace and a danger.

Once he told us how, in some other place, he and his men had been herding along a large crowd of former *kulaks* and their families. The frost was severe and he and his men, even in their fur jackets and felt boots, had suffered from frostbite. He said nothing about the people – old men, women and children – and how they had fared in that cold. Nor did we ask what had happened to those without warm clothing or boots. And it was this murderer I met every evening, and politely poured him tea. He, on occasion, did likewise for me.

In the mornings, still in darkness, the dull thuds of an axe on a piece of steel rail would announce the time to rise. From all sides dark shadows of figures would hurry to the canteen with their tea-cans. One hour later, everyone would assemble on the open square. The free volunteers rushed about giving orders for this party to go this way, that party that way. Drivers harnessed their horses. Incidentally, these horses had also come from the Altai, where once they had been cherished, cared for and well fed; now they were overworked, whipped into hauling excessive loads and poorly fed with a minimal basic ration.

Once in the forest, the woodcutters felled the trees with their crosscut saws, then sawed them into different lengths. The women dealt with the branches and foliage. Then the men, with ropes and belts, dragged the logs out to the forest road where the drivers loaded the horse-drawn sledges. The more logs per load, the higher the quota that would be ascribed to their team. As for whether the horses could cope – well, a good piece of branch would see to that. Pay was entirely dependent on production, and the call for higher and higher production kept on coming, and from the very highest levels, so that everyone along the line was always calling for greater effort from their underlings. The call was – get as much timber as possible as quickly as possible down to the rafts of logs that were being put together on the banks of the river. Measurement of the volume of timber was done by the foreman, holding a tape against the upper end of the log and recording the figure. There was always the temptation to add a couple of centimetres to the figure, though if caught out, the punishment was severe. The free volunteer workers were paid according to the foreman's figure for cubic metres. One third of what the "special exiles" earned went to the OGPU.

Money, however, was not the special exiles' priority. There was nothing to buy with it except for coarse tobacco and salt. It was bread that was crucial. Bread could not be bought, only earned. If a team fulfilled its quota the ration would be eight hundred grams a person. If it exceeded its quota, it might receive up to a kilo and a half. If the weather were bad, the roads impassable, or the foreman in a bad mood, that would mean less bread. Women who did not work, or feeble old people, received no bread, only the gruel distributed by the canteen. So the able-bodied men always had to work their guts out, striving to earn as much bread as they could to feed themselves and their children.

Attempts to escape from these settlements were not unknown; Ivan Tvardovsky has described the several attempts he and others made to get away from similar places in the Urals. Yet during my time in Gornoy Shorii I never heard of anyone trying to escape, even though conditions were unlike the prison camps themselves, with their barbed wire and watchtowers. But at the regular assemblies conducted by the commandant, he always, following the teaching of the great leader, addressed the "special exiles" with these words: "You are people without rights, you have no papers or documents. Even your sons are refused service in the army. No one would ever give you a job. Where would you end up if you escaped? What could you possibly do?" He would then hold out to them the hope that if they worked hard and conscientiously they could redeem their sins (sins against whom?) and be freed. If he was asked when, he would reply vaguely, sometimes saying three years, sometimes five.

Petrov finally gave me a small piece of wallpaper and I was able to write to my parents. There were no envelopes, so I simply sewed the edges together and wrote the address across a row of yellow flowers. My parents guessed my lack of paper and sent me what they could, but it was only one or two pieces at a time. Communication between us was necessarily short and laconic; it was risky to write about real conditions, as we could all see that the mail was being opened and read. So I knew nothing of the shortages and difficulties that they were enduring.

Meshalkin now arrived at our camp and began to encourage me to build his roller-transporter in the sloping valley I had picked out. He was full of optimism and infected the management with his enthusiasm. They promised to help me set up a lathe to make the rounded end of the sections of tree trunk that would form the bed of rollers along which logs would have to slide. Some way of making grease would also have to be conceived and put into operation. I had no idea how to do either of these tasks, but to my great good fortune we discovered among the special exiles men who had experience of making and using wood lathes. We also set an elderly man to work to refine tar out of birchwood and for this task the Commandant gave permission for us to build a small hut, which became known as the "clever little *izba*" (peasant house). So the work on Meshalkin's invention proceeded.

In the evenings, I had no scruples about visiting the man in the little hut, as I could always say it was to discuss the work. So I would sit with him and listen to the stories he told of his ancestors – how his grandfather and father had left their birthplace in Poltava to settle on the banks of the river Katun, where they founded their village and built its church. All three generations were smiths, and all three had suffered the same fate. When the first of May holiday came round that year, it coincided with Easter Day. The old man produced some white bread – it was made from flour he had saved from when he was still a free man – and we ate it, officially to mark the official holiday, although in reality we were celebrating the wonderful Resurrection of Jesus Christ.

At this time, whilst we were struggling to build our lathe ready for the construction of Meshlkin's project when the spring thaw came, the general manager Petrov was dismissed, He had failed to meet production targets. His replacement, Lebedev, took Petrov's bed in my room. Massive and morose, in his previous post he had received an official reprimand and now had to expiate that failure by putting our house in order. For a few days he did nothing but observe the work of the camp, saying nothing but making the occasional note on a piece of wallpaper. When he came to our workshop and stood watching the lathe cutting the tips of the roller logs, he made no comment in response to my explanation, just sighed and walked away.

Then a general meeting of all the foremen and voluntary workers, including me, was convened. Looking down at his notes, Lebedev spared no one in his criticisms, naming the foremen or volunteers who were not working hard enough, accusing them of insufficient class-consciousness, of going too easy on the "special exiles", these former *kulaks*. If someone was not working hard enough, his bread ration must be reduced. Suddenly, he praised one foreman, and, to my surprise, myself. After this, there were one or two speakers who tried to justify their performance, but Lebedev interrupted them, renewing his criticisms. When he returned to our room, gloomy and silent, he refused any tea and in silence we lay down to sleep.

Production rose. The foremen with their tally boards seemed to move faster, to be more cheerful. Even the horses hauled their loads more speedily. This lasted a week or two, until the drivers who had gone to Balbyn for fodder returned with empty sledges. Thanks to Petrov's carelessness, too little hay for the winter had been cut. Lebedev sent the weaker members of the camp off to the marshes to cut what dried sedge there was. For three days the horses were able to haul the heavy sledges on a diet of some hay and sedge, then one after another, regardless of the lash, they collapsed and died from exhaustion. Production plummeted.

The horsemeat was put into the food stores, though some individuals managed to swiftly cut pieces off the dead animal before it was dragged away. Lebedev called another meeting; he announced that all the horses could not be allowed to die and so the few remaining would be left in their stables. It was the people who would now haul the heavy sledges, ten to a load for the three kilometres to the river. So now human beasts of burden strained under the yoke, looking fearfully over their shoulders for the arrival of Lebedev's threatening, accusing figure. Good fortune, however, smiled on him. Over the silent *taiga* a warm wind began to blow; the sun shone down from clear skies. I had never seen spring come so suddenly and so completely, turning the ground soft, making it impossible to move any timber, and just as impossible for any big boss to reach our camp. The people who had been hauling sledges now joined the wood-cutters but, as nothing could be brought out, the felled trees were left to rot. Quickly the snow melted, streams ran everywhere, the ice on the river turned blue and was covered with pools of water. Our work on the roller-transporter would have to wait until the spring floods were over.

6

Now for the first time I watched the grandiose spectacle of rivers thawing, first the narrow Mzas-su, and then the bigger Mras-su. As the ice broke up, its blue-white floes joined the growing tide of ice flowing swiftly past. The power of nature was an awesome sight. At the camp, preparations for floating our log-rafts were begun. Rafts of pine, fir and spruce of different lengths and thicknesses had been assembled along the steep river bank. It was vital not to miss the exact moment when, the ice having passed or melted, the waters had risen to their highest level. At that crucial time, all the timber would have to be rolled down the banks. If it was left too late, the waters would fall, and the timber would have to wait for the following year.

Equipped with grappling irons, hooks and axes, we waited for the first raft to be released, and when it started to roll our work began. The river now reached high up the bank. Once the first logs rolled into the water we had to grapple and haul the remaining ones into the stream, straighten out any that had caught on the bank or got stuck on a sand bar. This was no time to stand idly by; everyone was involved in dragging the timber into the current – the volunteer workers, the "special exiles", women and old men. There was no distinction of status now, all were focused on the same goal – to get the entire winter's production of logs into the waters before they receded.

Lebedev was in charge of our team. He was the first to plunge into the water. "Get hold of that one, and that one. Come on!" he was shouting.

I pointed at a particularly thick trunk. "Let's get that one, that old auntie!" I cried. Everyone laughed, Lebedev most of all.

"That's it, Seryozha! Now you're really in the drink," yelled Kuzmin, our union man, as he swung at a log and began to haul on it. He was a slight but virile and sure-footed man.

It was sunset before we finished, and the first chance we had to have a smoke. The crowd dispersed back to the camp, everyone talking animatedly, exchanging impressions of the day. A good meal of horsemeat and spiced millet was awaiting them. Our team sat down to a feast of salmon trout and an individual ration of vodka. The dinner was a jolly event. My cry of "old auntie" was recalled with much laughter, and people slapped me on the back. This was the first time in Gornoy Shorii that I had had a drink. As a matter of fact, in those days drinking was a rare occurrence, and then only in exceptional circumstances. Today, people find that fact astonishing.

When I walked out in the morning I found the river full to the brim with logs, just as a few days earlier it had been full of ice floes, as the forestry gangs upstream had also pushed their tree trunks into the water. Logs were jostling each other, bumping and giving way, carried inexorably downstream on the flooded river. Below Balbyn the Mras-su joined the river Tom, and I knew that a little way down the Tom a barrier of chained logs was in place to stop the timber floating any further. Men would be manning this barrier to divert the timber into a quiet side-channel, from which it would go to Sad Gorod for construction and mining purposes.

But a disturbing rumour began to go the rounds – that the steel barrier, though calculated to withstand some incredible force, had failed to hold, that the dam had burst and all that timber had floated on down the Tom into the great river Ob, and from there into the distant Arctic Ocean. So all that work, that incalculable work, was irretrievably lost. I know we were all saddened by this futile loss of so much effort.

7

The OGPU was ordered by Eiche, the overlord of West Siberia, to investigate the failure of the Tom river barrier and arrest those responsible, but the OGPU's investigation did not affect us. What did happen, however, was that our union representative, Kuzmin, a nice, lively fellow, good at organizing competitions between the various teams of woodcutters, and who often spoke up at our meetings, was discovered to be no Party man at all, but an escaped prisoner. So he was an "enemy of the people"! I was on the bank of the river when, with hands tied behind his back, he was taken down to a boat. I can still see his sad face looking back at us as he was rowed away by the Party and *Konsomol* officials. This event greatly upset our Mzas settlement, particularly the "special exiles". They foresaw worse ahead, though they could not say what. It was just a feeling, an intuition of imminent troubles, which I also shared.

This year, I was again due to report for army service. With two other lads, we set off on horseback to the local registration centre at Myska, riding slowly to conserve the energy of our emaciated mounts. My fear that I would asked tricky questions was quite unfounded. I simply gave name, qualifications, place of work and that was all that was required. The two others stayed on in Myska, so I set off on the return journey alone. It was a delight to ride along the banks of the river, enjoying the beauties of nature. On one side of the river were steep hills, on the other a flat plain before the hills rose again. I reached a place where I had to circumvent a cliff, in doing which I lost the path and found myself riding down towards the river. I decided that this was probably a ford and, urged my horse into the water, but soon found that we were being carried away by a strong current. I tried to steer my mount, but she thrashed about in a panic and I was suddenly unseated, with one foot caught in the stirrup.

I struggled to control the horse but she kept turning her head and trying to bite me. I forced myself to feel brave, but was quickly running out of strength, when my foot came out of the stirrup and I began to be carried along with the current. I was sure I was going to drown, and my last thought was, "What beauty all round, and I'm going to die." Suddenly, my feet touched ground and I was standing only waist-deep. Very slowly I got myself to the bank. I was too exhausted to undress and ring out my soaking clothes; I could not even remove my boots. After a long while I got myself back to the camp. As for the horse, she floated down the river a long way and was only brought back the next day.

Once again in my eventful life, I had survived, and by a miracle.

8

We began to build Meshalkin's invention, the transporter-roller, which was designed to accelerate the transfer of timber out of the forest. I was given a team of ten "special exiles", strong young men led by Smetannikov, who had been promised his freedom if the transporter was a success, and who was therefore particularly keen to get on with the work. The men cleared away the brushwood and other small growth in the sloping valley I had chosen. I took two men and marked out the places where the supports for the cross-logs would be driven into the ground. After a few days, we installed the pointed pieces in their greased sockets and were ready for testing. We were all happy to see the work done, and the men were pleased, too, because they had earned over a kilo of bread a day on this project.

I tried to turn one of the special pointed logs by hand to see how it moved, and was surprised to find it very hard to shift. We laid a log across several of these rollers – it failed to move. We gave it a shove, but nothing happened, the rollers simply refused to revolve. We threw a rope around the end of the log and pulled it across the rollers; they turned with a screech. Adding more grease to the sockets, we tried again, but there was no difference in the reluctance of Meshalkin's invention to function as expected. I was in a terrible state at this total failure. Was the project doomed? Across the way the leading *Konsomol* was observing our efforts in silence. After a while, he walked away without comment. We tried a second log, with the same result as before.

Evening was upon us. We returned to camp in depressed silence. Smetannikov looked miserable – he knew his chance of freedom had melted away. Some weeks before Lebedev and the Party man, Maslov, had moved into a small house and asked me to share it with them. Wanting to be alone, I had chosen to install myself in their attic, which gave me solitude, although not peace and quiet, as the floor of my attic was the ceiling of their two rooms, through which I could hear everything they did or said. Now I crawled up into my attic, without saying anything to Lebedev. Later that evening I heard the *Konsomol* who had observed our work.

"A technician – and he can't calculate! It's pure sabotage."

"No, hold on," said Lebedev, "inventions don't always work straight away. Wait till Meshalkin comes, he'll sort things out!"

The man went out, leaving me feeling very frightened. I imagined how I would be accused of sabotage. The next day I was back at the site with my men. There did not seem any point in testing the rollers again, so I sent them into the forest to trim beams. Quite unexpectedly, Meshalkin appeared, accompanied by Lebedev and the leading *Konsomol*. The workers once again dragged a log over the rollers. Meshalkin ordered them to drag another one, then a third, then said sharply, "This project is closed down."

We returned in gloomy silence to the office. Meshalkin asked me to calculate the cost of the experiment, and to send him the figure. To my query as to further work he simply told me to await his orders. It was obvious that his thoughts were elsewhere. As for my thoughts, they went something like this – "So much money has been wasted on this work, so of course I'll be considered a saboteur! As for Meshalkin, he's a bright young thing, a member of the Party, he'll get out of this somehow. But I'll be investigated and all the blame will fall on me."

I suffered acutely from the failure of the project, and not just because I might be punished for it, but from wounded pride. The whole settlement would know what had happened. I reported sick, took to my bed and lay there for several days. On the second day, I suddenly thought of the few pages of the story I was writing, hidden in my suitcase. I imagined with horror what an interrogator could make of those writings. Early in the morning, I hid the manuscript under my jacket, crept out of the house, found a quiet spot in the *taiga* and burned every page. Then I went back to my straw mattress.

One evening, Lebedev had invited over the general manager of the neighbouring settlement. They sat below drinking and talking. After a while I heard this man ask Lebedev about the transporter-roller, and when he heard of its failure, he said, "Of course, it's no surprise that a Prince Golitsyn is a saboteur." Up to this time, no one had asked me about my princely origins. My family name was a familiar one in European Russia, but in Siberia there had never been big landowners and ancient families – even the term *barin* (master) was unknown. Lebedev asked, "What? Is he some sort of Tartar?"

"What do you mean, Tartar!" exclaimed the other. "He's a relative of the Tsar."

Lebedev clearly failed to grasp this implication. The two went on drinking and talking of other things.

Cold with fear, I thought to myself – so I'm a relative of the Tsar! Neither before nor after had I been accused of such a "crime" (in fact, I suppose by stretching a point I could be considered a relative, inasmuch as the daughter of my uncle in America, Alexander Vladimirovich, was married to a nephew of the Tsar – Vasily Alexandrovich Romanov, son of the Tsar's sister, Ksenya). Anyway, the two men got quite drunk that evening, with the result that Lebedev must have forgotten the whole conversation. Not having seen me for a few days, he came up to the attic, slapped me on the back and told me not to be downhearted. I imagine the discovery that the union man Kuzmin was an escaped prisoner was more of a shock to Lebedev than the failure of the transporter-roller. After all, people were used to seeing huge sums of money wasted, for instance, the millions of cubic meters of timber that had floated out into the Arctic Ocean.

9

A far worse disaster than the failure of Meshalkin's invention, or Kuzmin's unmasking, now fell upon us. Earlier the horses had gone without oats, but had survived. Now the team that had gone to collect our supplies of flour came back with empty hands. There was no flour, and we could expect none. So all of us – "special exiles", voluntary workers and the management – were left without bread. We began to exist on gruel made of fish heads and sorrel.

All work stopped. Not a soul went out with saw and axe, and no one tried to persuade them to do so. Along the river bank men, women and children sat with fishing lines – I do not recall that they caught a great deal. Others collected a kind of wild garlic plant that had a small, soft bulb, as well as other edible plants such as nettles and sorrel. I received a parcel from home; it contained two small tins of some kind of sprat, which I swallowed in secret. Then I wrote home asking them to send me dried bread, but my parents never received the letter with that request, which would have instantly alerted them to our desperate situation.

Lebedev and Maslov's wives cooked up various things from their personal store. I had eaten nothing for two days. On the third day, I went downstairs and found Lebedev's little daughter at table, sucking on a bun. I sat her on my knee and drew pictures for her on a piece of wallpaper. After a while she put her bun down and in a flash I had slipped it into my pocket. I waited a while before putting her down. Then I went to my attic and swallowed the bun. "After all, she's pretty well fed," was my thought.

I continued to starve, lying in my attic. I felt a terrible apathy, an indifference to everything. I just lay there, floating in and out of consciousness. I realised that this was the beginning of dystrophy, the very same condition that had killed millions of prisoners, and was now decimating our settlement. The volunteer workers had been sent off to work elsewhere, where they were fed, but the "special exiles" were left to their fate. Men, women and children were dying every day. Every day boatloads of corpses were taken across the river for burial.

One day Lebedev came up to my attic and said, "Seryozha, get up. I'm sending you to hospital. There's a boat setting off for Myska." So I found myself in a hospital bed, surrounded by many others in the same condition. The doctors prescribed some kind of medicine, and we were fed with millet soup and a little bread. After a week, they told us there were no more provisions; we could go wherever we liked. I stood outside the hospital building with my suitcase. Where could I go? I walked to the market and bought a bun for an outrageous price, which I ate on the spot. But fortune was on my side; walking about in the market was our accountant, who said he was about to set off to the Balbyn forestry project and I should go with him.

Meshalkin was delighted to see me and put me to work compiling some huge series of figures. I was able to feed myself up and recover my strength in the special canteen that served the bureaucrats. Then Meshalkin said he was going to Moscow and if I liked, he could deliver a letter to my family. I later found out that this good-natured gesture was not a disinterested one. His suspicions had been aroused by a letter from the military authorities reporting that when they wrote to the village of my birthplace, Bulchalki, they had received the answer that nothing was known of my person or character, but that I was a prince's son. So he began to wonder about my presence here; what sort of fish was I? On delivering the letter he found my sister Sonya at home, who sat him down to tea and told him the story of my working life. This completely reassured him of my trustworthiness. It also happened at this same time that three young men on the point of call-up into the army were revealed as sons of *kulaks*. The poor fellows were arrested and removed, an event that was far more alarming to the forestry management than my humble self, the technician who had failed with the transporter-roller.

10

The time came for my call up into the army. Together with some fifty others I sat in a hall and had to listen to a long diatribe about our great and glorious leader. The speaker was suddenly interrupted by an officer rushing up to him in a rage. "Someone has written insulting verse about our great leaders on the washroom wall!" he shouted. He quoted the verse, which satirized Voroshilov. Everyone burst out laughing.

"Ah!" he shouted, "so you're laughing! You're all class enemies!"

Instantly, the hall was as silent as the grave.

Just like the year before, I had to go before a commission in my costume of Adam that included two young *Konsomol* girl-activists. They either kept their eyes modestly lowered or glanced furtively at me. Then the interrogation began. A tough-looking peasant, probably a former Red partisan, looked at me menacingly – "Well, out with it, who's your father?"

I was, of course, ready for this question. Yes, my father was a prince, but he had never owned anything. Yes, he had been a civil servant before the revolution, but after 1918 he had worked for Soviet organisations. Yes, he had lost his voting rights, but he had applied for them to be restored and hoped they soon would be. He was now a translator of foreign languages. As for my mother, she had always been a housewife.

At this point the chairman asked me an unexpected question. "Are you a relative of Golitsyn the artist?"

"Yes, he's my older brother," I said with relief, and launched into an account of Vladimir's life, how he had been a sailor on Arctic expeditions and how he painted and illustrated books and magazines. The chairman livened up, told us how he had enjoyed the *Universal Pathfinder*, recalled the Bochonkin and Khvoshch stories and was about to say more in the same spirit when he remembered where he was, looked round at the other members of the commission and said drily, "I categorize him for non-military duties." My papers were stamped and I went off to get dressed. Until the war I remained classified as an unskilled soldier and was never once called for duty. All through my life I have been blessed by such instances of good fortune. Supposing the chairman of that commission had never read that magazine, would I not have been sent to the Gulag, just like those three unfortunates, the sons of *kulaks*?

11

Back in Balbyn, I sat down again to my work on long lists of figures. Then one day I was told to report urgently to the office of personnel. I went there quaking in my shoes. Next to this office, which was staffed by only one man, was the office used by the local OGPU.

"We've looked through your papers," said the personnel man.

I felt my knees shaking.

"We've looked through your papers," he repeated, "and see that you finished nine years of school on the technical side. We're just starting a Year 10 class. Would you be willing to teach Russian language and maths to that class?"

Of course, I agreed – and with relief. And so I found myself standing in front of about twenty young men. There were no books, no paper and not even any rolls of wallpaper. I realised I would have to be adopt a different approach to this kind of teaching. The class was eager to learn; they wanted very much to exchange their axes and saws for the measuring tape, the pencil, and the tally book. I picked out two of the names in the class, Ivanov and Sidorov, and put the question – "If Ivanov has cut such and such an amount of cubic metres, and Sidorov such and such an amount, what percentage of the plan has Ivanov filled, what percentage Sidorov?" When it came to Russian grammar I said, to general laughter, "Ivanov is to marry soon, whilst Sidorov does not want to get married." Sadly, it turned out that this class had come into being because there was no logging to be done. When a new lot of timber was floated down the river, the men were sent off to deal with it with the promise that once that job was done, they could return to the classroom. In that the authorities deceived them; the class was not re-started.

A long, descriptive letter arrived from my parents. My youngest sister Katya, had married my old school friend, Valery Pertsov. He had started out being keen on Masha, but when she rejected him, turned his attentions to Katya, and this was the happy outcome. The wedding had taken place in a village close to Dmitrov, Podlipechya. Our old benefactress, Moina Abamelek-Lazareva, who for years had been sending us ten dollars a month from Italy, sent a hundred dollars, so the wedding had been a luxurious one for those times. My parents wrote that Katya had looked lovely in her white wedding dress, but I was sad not to have been a groom for the fourteenth time.

The other astonishing news in that letter was that a Party decree had been signed ordering the construction of a canal between the Volga and Moskva rivers, and that it would run through Dmitrov. Notices were out calling for all manner of technical and other personnel to apply. Why should I not live closer to home, my parents wrote. I immediately went to see Meshalkin, but he told me I had signed a one-year contract and would have to wait until the following January, when it might be possible to release me.

12

I was sent to the Abashevo forestry operation. What a pleasure it was to float down the river Mras-su and then the river Tom. It was autumn and the forest on the hills around had turned yellow, orange and red, dotted with dark patches of cedar, spruce and fir. In the village of Abashevo the church rose high into the sky and there were solid, well-built log houses on either bank of the little stream, but the church had been turned into a warehouse, and one of the fine houses had become the offices of the forestry operation. Upriver were three settlements of workers.

I do not wish to repeat my description of life in these parts – but once again I saw those long barracks with their tiers of bunks, and heard the bitter stories of the people who had been rounded up and sent into this life of "special exile". I heard of the terrible effects of that summer's famine, how old and young had died of starvation, and how supplies of flour and other provisions only began to arrive in the autumn. Later, I wrote a story about the life such people lived. Mother managed to hide the manuscript – it would have been condemned as seditious – until after the war. When I showed it to another writer, his only comment was, "Rather a gloomy piece of naturalism." I do not know if it will ever be published.

I referred earlier to the "Top Secret" paper that I had surreptitiously read, signed by the first-secretary of the whole region, Eiche, ordering the dispersal or dismissal of families with too many children. In my time in Abashevo I heard many tragic stories of the merciless way such families were left to fend for themselves, and how they had been forced into labour in the far north or in the distant gold mines in desperation. The room I slept in was also occupied by a foreman,

Rosanov, and his family. Once he had been a member of the militia in Kuznetsk, well provided with provisions and living in a comfortable room with wife and children. He was treated as a trusty official, did his job of catching thieves, as well as arresting completely innocent people. Then suddenly, he and five other militiamen, families with too many children, were dismissed without notice. Rosanov himself was fortunate – he found work in Abashevo thanks to his brother-in-law, who was in forestry.

The reader may be surprised that I have written nothing about the indigenous people, the Shortsi, but we had little contact with them. We would see them on the river in summer in their dugouts, hunting chipmunk and squirrels, which they shot with great accuracy from ancient guns, economising their shot. In the winter, on their short skis, they would be out hunting for sable. We would sail past their little settlements without visiting them, even though they were reputed to be friendly and hospitable. Our forestry operations destroyed the habitat of the wild life that supported the Shortsi and so gradually their lives became more difficult, forcing them to move deeper into the forest.

13

My work at Abashevo came to an end in January 1933. I returned to Balbyn and asked to be released. As I was waiting in the office for these formalities to be completed, which included a fairly large accumulation of salary, a commission arrived to investigate the whole operation, and in particular why the goals set had not been achieved (what in Soviet terms was called "fulfilling the plan"). I was in the office on the very day when the chairman of the commission read out the conclusions of their investigation; there were far too many people sitting around in the offices, and of these, one was a priest's son, another's father was a *kulak*, the third came of a family of tsarist officers. The chairman said, "It's clear that these people are saboteurs, and that's why the plan is not being implemented!" My name did not feature – I was already counted as having resigned. Whether those people were arrested or not, I do not know. But once again, good fortune had saved me.

The commission departed. Finally, I was able to leave. Having said farewell to everyone, and with all my back pay, I set off saying to myself, "Thanks be to God!" and inwardly crossing myself.

The station in Kuznetsk was overflowing with people. Whole families, who had been removed from their villages and had come to the town to hire themselves out on the big projects of that time, were crowded into every inch of space. Because of their many children they had failed to be accepted, and were now desperate to go anywhere where they might be able to survive. Those who had nowhere to lay their heads stayed in the station. It was a moving, frightening sight. In those days it was the custom to get your ticket through the intermediary of a porter. The one I spoke to said, "First go into that office." I did so and faced the familiar and unpleasant sight of an OGPU soldier with his blue-trimmed cap. After long consideration of my papers he said, "Permission granted." As I waited on the platform with my ticket in my pocket, I noticed how the porters went about the crowds, picking out suspicious-looking people and directing them to that little office. The Kuznetsk-Moscow train eventually pulled in. I had a place reserved in a compartment with people on their way to some other big project and as we progressed slowly towards Moscow across our suffering country I got to know them a little. Amongst other things, they spoke warmly of their general manager, Frankfurt, a friend of Commissar Ordzhonikidze. Little did any of us guess how short a life lay ahead of that important personage.

It was the last days of January 1933. The loudspeakers were everywhere, repeating the angry denunciations of the Politburo at the burning down of the Reichstag in Berlin and the seizure of power by Hitler. I had no conception then of the tremendous effect this would have on our lives. We reached Kazansky station in Moscow at four o'clock in the morning. I sat waiting for the first tram, thinking back over my year, of the amazing number of people I had met, the tragic things I had seen, the events I had taken part in. Not just a chapter, but a whole book would be needed to do justice to all that I had experienced.

23. The Blessed City

1

Before travelling out to my family in Dmitrov, I called on my sister Sonya, who was living with her husband, Viktor Meien, her little daughter and her mother-in-law in Bolshoy Levshinsky Lane. After our joyful reunion and embraces, Sonya told me their most important news: that they had all been issued with passports.

"What's a passport?" I asked.

Astonished, she exclaimed, "You don't know what a passport is?"

In Gornoy Shorii, I had hardly ever read the newspapers as they were always quickly torn up for cigarette paper. Now I learned about Vladimir Fyodorovich Dzhunkovsky, who was considered to be the creator of this new system of passports for every citizen, and who had been head of police under the Tsar before being dismissed after he dared to have Rasputin arrested in the Yar restaurant for drunken and turbulent behaviour. In 1920, Dzhunkovsky himself was arrested together with a group of church officials, including Alexander Dmitrievich Samarin and Grigory Alexeievich Rachinsky. The prosecutor, Krylenko, called for the death sentence for some of the members of this group – Samarin was one – but the court sentenced them to various terms in prison. Dzhunkovsky, however, was acquitted. There was general surprise that a former head of the police had been set free. Dzhunkovsky himself explained that Dzerzhinsky had called him in and asked him, "Tell me how you organised security for the Tsar," in response to which Dzhunkovsky wrote him out a full account and from then on acted as a consultant, first to the *Cheka*, then to the OGPU.

I know nothing of his work, except that he was reputed to have survived because he never said a harmful word about anyone. My father pointed him out to me in the street one day; I saw a well-dressed, stately old man with a fine white beard, his head held high. At this time he was giving English lessons. Father asserted later that it was this man who had developed the passport system that every

Soviet citizen has had to endure. Incidentally, in the 1928 edition of the *Small Soviet Encyclopedia*, the entry under "Passport" states that this is a police measure introduced by the Tsarist regime and that Soviet citizens, being free people, know nothing of such a system. In fact, they know all too much about it. Initially, it was introduced in order to limit access to the big cities by the millions of people leaving the land during collectivisation. Then the system of registration was introduced not only for the big cities but for any place within a hundred kilometres radius of Moscow, Leningrad, Kiev and Odessa.

There were few entries between the covers of this little grey booklet and the question about social origins was absent, but the fate and indeed very life of all citizens was, and still is governed by what is written in there. So when I reached Dmitrov and threw myself into the arms of the family, the first thing I heard was a joyous, "We've all been given passports!"

2

I must go back a year and a half now, to the time when my family was still living in Khlebnikovo, before coming back to the subject of Dmitrov, the city saved by God, which played such an important role in their lives. What caused us to move to Dmitrov? It started with a seemingly insignificant incident, when my brother Vladimir fell asleep in the train returning from Moscow and missed our stop, Khlebnikovo. On waking at the next station, he discovered there were no trains back, so he stretched out on a bench to wait for the morning. The first train in the morning was for Dmitrov, and having heard a little about this ancient city, Vladimir hopped aboard and soon found himself discovering the beauty of its monastery, churches and old houses, none of that yet barbarously destroyed. It was then a small town of low wooden houses, a dozen stone buildings, eleven churches and the large monastery complex of Saints Boris and Gleb. The only industry was a few craft workshops. Inside the citadel stood a five-domed sixteenth-century church, then still in service. Vladimir returned home full enthusiasm for the place. As our landlord had just had his house impounded, compelling us to move, Vladimir suggested Dmitrov. The family objected on the grounds that it was too far from Moscow, but then Masha's patron and protector, Professor Alexei Pavlovich Ivanov, became involved. His sister lived in Dmitrov; he wrote to her asking her to look out for available lodgings, but instead she decided to rent us three rooms in her own house on Kropotkin Street.

When I arrived in Dmitrov following my bout of malaria, the family had already settled into these new quarters. Using a large cupboard as partition, Vladimir and Elena had arranged themselves a sort of bedroom and study in one large room. The communal table was in the main room. Their three little children, Elenka, Mishka and Laryushka, slept in one of the small rooms, and my parents and grandfather in the other. Aunt Sasha, Masha and Katya shared a room in a neighbouring house. The family portraits that Vladimir was so attached to were hung around the walls, surprising visitors by their rich appearance in these modest surroundings.

For whatever reason, Dmitrov had been spared the usual fierce onslaught of collectivisation. There had been a drive to get people into the *kolkhoz*, but many individual farm holdings still existed, and this was the reason why there was still a wonderful Sunday bazaar, when the peasants drove in on their carts with a great variety of produce at amazingly low prices. Sadly, the authorities eventually considered the market a manifestation of the capitalist spirit and closed it down. From then on the peasants came into town surreptitiously, and on foot, to sell their goods.

3

I want to write something here for the sake of my descendants and as a last tribute to my grandfather, Prince Vladimir Mikhailovich Golitsyn. The reader will recall my earlier references to his long and active life. When we moved to Dmitrov, grandfather was still living in Sergiyev Posad with his daughter, Aunt Eli, the wife of Vladimir Sergeievich Trubetskoi, and her family. Now father and Vladimir brought him to be with our family.

A fairly robust eighty-four-year-old, short, but distinguished-looking, with a narrow, somewhat wrinkled face, grandfather was head of the family, the person to whom we all deferred. He was the picture of a pure aristocrat in everything he did, whether eating or writing or playing patience, as he often did with Vladimir. I loved to watch his delicate hands that had never known physical labour laying the cards out for patience, or lifting a spoon to his mouth, or moving over the pages as he wrote his diary, which he did unfailingly every day of his life. We never quarrelled with him, and indulged him as much as we could. The dollars that his son sent from California went to purchasing our oil and flour supplies, but also a special supply of little cakes or candies, one of which he would consume every day after the evening meal; the children were never offered these. Sitting under the portraits of our ancestors, he made a great impression on visitors.

His memory was outstanding. Just before my arrival in Dmitrov, he had received a considerable sum of money from Vladimir Dmitriyevich Bonch-Bruyevich, the director of the Literary Museum and one of Lenin's contemporaries, in payment for identifying all the figures in a large album of photographs from the 1860s that had come into the possession of the museum. Grandfather could name every single one by name, patronymic and family name. Only three figures did he fail to name, and he decided that they must have been foreigners. One of the identifications, later confirmed by another old lady, was of the photograph of Pushkin's wife in old age, seated in an armchair, a picture one often sees in writings about the poet.

Pneumonia struck him down in the middle of February 1932. As I was on the point of leaving for a long time, I went in to say my farewells to him. He embraced me and blessed me, saying, "My friend, I doubt we shall meet again." He died in my absence, on the twenty-ninth of February, and in his diary there was a slip of paper, not yet entered, on which was written, "Seryozha left today. I shall never see him again". He was buried in the nearby village of Podlipechye. Vladimir made a simple white cross for the grave, on which he wrote his name in full, including his title of prince. Two years later, the entire cemetery was bulldozed to make way for construction, and his grave was no more. May his memory live for ever.

4

In the years 1933–34, truly revolutionary changes took place in Dmitrov. The White Sea to Baltic canal was complete, so now attention was turned to building the Volga-Moscow canal. Thousands of prisoners, who in the exultant triumph of the earlier canal had been freed, were now urged to transfer their labour to this new project. A horde of "former" people – professors, tsarist officers, priests, White Guards, titled and untitled nobles, members of the intelligentsia, students, peasants and workers – arrived in Dmitrov. Only those described as "Trotskyists" were not freed. The Boris and Gleb monastery was adapted to house the offices, whilst a trainload of two-storied wooden houses arrived for the workers from the Baltic. Curiously, these turned out to be infested by bedbugs.

Some of the freed workers were friends of ours, and given my brother's gregarious and hospitable nature, our lodgings became a meeting place for many interesting people. Dmitry Gudovich, our Elena's cousin, was one of them; another was Nikolai Dimitriyevich Kuchin, once a suitor of Masha's. Then there was Alexander Petrovich Preklonsky, a former officer in the famous Preobrazhensky regiment and regimental contemporary of my mother's brother, Raphael Sergeievich Lopukhin, killed in the First World War.

Preklonsky was a tall, imposing figure. He told us a story of the 1905 uprising in St Petersburg. His was the regiment that had been ordered to fire on the huge crowd demonstrating peacefully outside the Winter Palace that ninth of January, but Preklonsky swore that he had ordered his men to fire at a group of agitators who were standing to one side, and not on the peasants and workers. Preklonsky fancied himself as a dramatist, and I remember him reading us his tragedy about Ivan the Terrible and the savagery of Ivan's special militia, the *Oprichniki*. It was an uninspired piece of work, but Preklonsky made it quite clear that he saw it as a reflection of Stalin and his gang of criminals. He must certainly have read it to other audiences, as two years later he was arrested. Also arrested, three days after his wedding, was his brother-in-law, Baron Taube. Both men disappeared for good.

There was Sergei Sergeievich Baranov, head of an engineering works, who had been serving a sentence for alleged sabotage. He was an inventor, a poet and a great storyteller. I remember him describing how they had threatened him with execution if he did not confess. He was taken down to a cell, ordered to take off his jacket, trousers and shoes and, forbidden to look left or right, led in his underpants along a stone-flagged corridor. He was sure he was going to his death and wondered whether he would hear the whistle of the bullet but when they reached a certain door, it opened and there stood his interrogator. During the war he worked in one of the special prison *sharashka* (technical institutions), where the talents and experience of scientists and engineers were exploited by the State. After the war I met him once or twice at my sisters' places and found he was as witty and interesting as ever. Then he was arrested for the second time, and disappeared for good; it was said his wife denounced him so as to get hold of their flat for herself. Such things did happen.

Another visitor was Nikolai Lebedev, the son of the well-known soil scientist Professor Alexander Fyodorovich Lebedev. Professor Lebedev was arrested, sentenced to ten years and sent to take part in the building of the White Sea to Baltic canal. His son, then aged sixteen, set off for Petersburg to enlist support for his father from the leading scientists Joffe and Vavilov. When he knocked on Joffe's door and explained his father's situation, Joffe said, "I do not know anything of your father's scientific writings, so I'm afraid I cannot help you." Vavilov, however, received Nikolai in a friendly manner, took him into his study and wrote an eloquent letter to one of the top commissars. Hearing that Nikolai was staying with friends, he invited him to dinner and showed a great interest in his hopes and plans for the future. Vavilov's intervention on behalf of Nikolai's father did not help; Lebedev worked on the canal for a year and a half, and then he and his whole family turned up in Dmitrov for the construction of the Volga-Moscow river project. We all became great friends, and I formed a special bond with Nikolai, who also had literary ambitions.

Tall and awkward, Nikolai had upset his parents by announcing that he had no intention of going further with his studies or of taking a job. He was a great reader, loved the symbolist poets, and wrote verse himself. I recall his poem about my sister Masha, which had lines where Mary rhymed with prairie, Maria with Evangelia and Masha with Daughter.[25] He had a line about the full moon shining as we went to the all-night service before Easter Day, yet when my mother pointed out that it was always a new moon at such times, Nikolai firmly refused to change his line.

His father, Professor Lebedev, worked as a consultant to the canal project, and after two years was completely rehabilitated and moved to Moscow to work in some scientific institute. He was allocated an apartment on Pyatnitskaya Street, where I visited the family. Nikolai's room was distinguished by a long line of pictures of philosophers, from Socrates to Lenin. The father soon died, and Nikolai, no doubt having recited his poems to too many people, was arrested and sent to the Gulag. Some years later, just before the war, we received his greetings from one of the camps, brought by a recently freed inmate.

I also remember with pleasure another young man, my namesake, Sergei Mikhailovich Obolensky, who was a year younger than me. His father, Prince Mikhail Fyodorovich Obolensky, with his wife, son and daughter Irina, all lived on a small farm at Peredelkino in the first years after the revolution. They had a horse, a cow and chickens, and survived by ploughing the land and growing their own food. They were then denounced as *kulaks,* but were not evicted, as they were protected by the scientists working at the Timiryazevsky Academy, who were using the Obolensky land to plant experimental

---

25. *In Russian, dochka. It is an allusion to the title of Pushkins' novel,*
Kapitanskaya Dochka.

crops. Thus, ironically, this former prince was serving the needs of Soviet agriculture. In the end, however, the farm was liquidated, and Mikhail Fydorovich, his wife and his son were arrested. The son was soon released and went to work as a bibliographer in the Lenin Library. He loved the work and was full of praise for the director, Vladimir Ivanovich Nevsky, who stoutly defended Seryozha from the attacks of young activist communists. In the end, however, Nevsky was forced to dismiss him.

Seryozha Obolensky then arrived in Dmitrov to try and find a job on the canal, but was not taken on as a bibliographer or a veterinarian, even though he had long experience with horses. It was perhaps because he was the son of an "enemy of the people" that they dared not hire him. One of the managers of the project was a lady called Tolskaya, who suggested Seryozha should apply for the job of veterinarian in a distant prison camp. He did not pursue that idea. Instead, meeting Masha at a concert in Moscow, he fell in love with her and thus formed a strong bond with me – which lasted two weeks. Incidentally, he told Masha he wanted me to marry his sister Irina, as otherwise she would marry just anybody. Masha told him I had no intention of marrying and so putting some young woman into danger. I did, however, meet Irina, and for a moment felt an attraction to her, but my heart was under lock and key; I said a few words and turned on my heel. She eventually married the composer Peyko, and had a happy married life until she died in 1988.

Seryozha found no employment and was arrested a second time. My friend Sergei Konshin, who had been in the camp with him, told me that Seryozha was always cheerful, always trying to encourage others, but that one day he was called out of the ranks, led off under escort and never came back. In 1988, in an interview in the magazine *Ogonyok*, a former communist woman said that a female prisoner who had been in the camp with her had become pregnant by Prince Obolensky. The interviewer asked what crime Obolensky had committed. She replied, "He was a prince". It seemed perfectly natural to her that anyone who was a prince should be sitting in the Gulag. Poor Seryozha.

5

My sister Masha was continuing her successful work in the Moscow geological commission, going on expeditions in the summer months, and just as successfully studying for a higher qualification as an external student. Her time was divided between Moscow and

Dmitrov. Then one day she was called in and told that if she wanted to continue as a student she would have to sign a paper renouncing any relationship with her parents. In giving her this paper the staff assured her that this was just a formality, she could continue to see her parents as she liked and no one would spy on her. But she must sign, as otherwise, "regretfully" she would be expelled from the course. She was allowed three days to think it over.

With a shaking voice father said, "Please, just sign the paper." Mother sat with her face in her hands. I could think of nothing to say. Then Vladimir appeared from his room and said firmly, "There's no way you can sign that." It ended with father writing an eloquent letter to Peshkova, which Masha took to her at Kuznetsky Most. I do not know what happened, whether that truly extraordinary and courageous woman wrote or telephoned to someone, but the result was that Masha never heard a thing more, continued her studies and passed her exams. Meanwhile, the evening papers were full of announcements that X or Y had broken off relations with their parents, who were priests, tsarist officers, *kulaks* or nobles. I knew several such renouncers, but will refrain from naming them.

Masha was an entrancing figure in those days; with her fine features and curly fair hair over a wide brow, and she drew all eyes when she arrived at the theatre or a concert. And how many young men fell for her without success! Igor Daksergof continued to court her, ostensibly visiting Vladimir, with whom he had endless discussions, but we all knew he really came to be near Masha. This Igor was a pilot and in fact became quite famous for being the first man to parachute with a radio transmitter, broadcasting live his impressions and sensations as he floated down. Thereafter we applied the term "parachutist" to all of Masha's admirers. In fact, the term is still current in our family, only now it denotes suitors of the next generation in our numerous family.

6

After grandfather's death, my father should have become head of the family, but because of his poor health and generally depressed state of mind, he preferred to hand this duty on to Vladimir. All these years later, I still vividly remember everything to do with my beloved brother. His life was a difficult one and fate dealt him many blows. The editor of the *Pioneer*, Ivanter, was forced to stop commissioning work from Vladimir. Until 1934, he continued as the illustrator of new editions of Novikov-Priboy's writings, but was then dismissed.

The commissariat of the navy at first welcomed Vladimir with open arms; he drew pictures of ships and several posters for them, before they too, were forced to dismiss him. After this, he found some work doing technical drawings, but these were simply draughtsmanship. In Dmitrov he was asked to do some sketches for the museum, for which he received very little pay. He also turned his hand to writing, composing sketches of some of the strange and eccentric people who were to be found in Dmitrov, writings that I still hope may be published one day.

Our landlady, Praskovya Pavlovna, was summoned to the local OGPU office, and when she returned, confided to my mother that she had been warned that we should receive fewer friends and guests in her home. Thus our social life, which Vladimir had done so much to encourage, and which, more than any of us, he enjoyed, had perforce to be curtailed. On top of all this, he was now suffering constant pain in one knee. Some time before he had fallen on the railway track at Khlebnikov; the knee had seemed to get better, and the X-rays showed no damage, but the pain gradually became more and more acute. He went about with a stick, and this also restricted his trips to Moscow in search of work. He took to devising, novel board games with his growing sons Misha and Laryusha, and produced some really interesting ones. But there was little financial reward in such inventiveness. Obstacles to production and sale were invariably put up by petty officials wherever Vladimir tried to have his games accepted.

On my occasional free evenings, once the children were in bed, I would tell them stories, usually historical tales or re-tellings of Shakespeare's plays. Some forty years later, Misha told me what a shocking and lasting impression my account of Macduff's birth had made on him, not born of woman but "from his mother's womb untimely ripp'd". Misha was seven at the time.

We lived as economically as possible, rarely had any meat to eat and cooked with the vegetable oil that we were able to buy with the few dollars we received from abroad. Our state of neediness grew worse as Vladimir's health deteriorated. Father still managed to earn a little money giving English lessons to two little girls, who we nicknamed the two little mice. He also did translations of technical articles from English, French and German for the canal journal so that our designers and builders should know what the West and America were doing in that field. Dashing forward two years, I must record how father translated an article about a German canal called the Hitler canal. Mere mention of this name in the bulletin led to a scandal and publication was stopped, which meant that father lost a useful little income.

7

My own life was turning out badly at this time. I had counted on finding work in Dmitrov, living with my parents, receiving a ration card as well as helping them with my earnings. However, the completion of the White Sea to Baltic canal resulted in the arrival in Dmitrov of hundreds of well-qualified ex-prisoners – engineers and technicians and the like, and when I put my head in to the recruiting offices, they did not even ask who I was, or what I could do, I was simply told that they were not taking anyone on, although they did add that this was only a temporary situation.

I now had to get hold of a passport. The family had feared that they would be refused, but had all received theirs without any complication. The same happened with me – I put in my papers and was issued with the document without any questions being asked. I then set off for Moscow to look for work, going first to look up Shura Sokolov, but he was not in town. His mother told me how Shura had expected to be in the Far East planning the second line for the Trans-Siberian railway during the summer, then returning to Moscow to work over the plans in the office, but that once out there, the authorities had taken away their papers and forced them to stay on site during the winter, telling them, "You're here till the line has been built!" He wrote that they were living crowded into poorly heated barracks. This action was typical of the times, when even regular citizens could be lured into a project like fish into a net, and then treated like prisoners.

I could have taken work in the Far East as a volunteer, but I really wanted to stay nearer home, so I began my attempts to find a job in Moscow. At the construction offices of the underground system, the Metro, I was immediately shown the door. In another institution, the technical head said, "Heavens, why didn't you come earlier! You'll have to catch up our expedition." But I never did catch up any expedition. The personnel officer took one look at my papers, asked me if I was a prince and returned my papers, saying I was wasting his time. In yet another place I was again told how much they needed technicians like me, but the personnel man said, "I'm surprised you're still wandering round Moscow."

What was I to do? It was obvious that I was wasting my time looking for work in Moscow. So I wrote to two people; one was

Uncle Alyosha, then living in Tver, and the other was Valery Pertsov's uncle in Kaluga. Both invited me to come. I opted for Kaluga, where the Moscow to Kiev highway was then under construction. Pertsov's uncle, Nikolai Nikolaievich Khaimin and his wife, turned out to be wonderful people who received me with open arms and invited me to stay in their house. Nikolai Nikolaievich was the county land surveyor, a short man with untidy hair, a little grey beard, and a general air of being as untidy as his hair. He looked after the geodesic instruments used on the highway, but his real income came from breeding ducks, of which there were about thirty. He proudly showed me the electric fence he had built around them to keep off robbers.

In the morning he set off for work, saying that he would set things in motion for me, so I spent the time wandering around the old city of Kaluga, visiting the many churches and also the local picture gallery. In there I saw portraits of my Armenian ancestors, the Lazarevy, and realised that they came from the small estate that belonged to my aunt, Sofia Nikolaievna Golitsyna. It was called Zhelezniky and was not far from Kaluga.

After lunch, Nikolai Nikolaievich and I set off for the offices. He assured me they were keen to recruit me and that there were many "former people" working on the project. But once again I had to endure my Calvary – the technical department wanted to take me on, but the head of personnel drew out of me all kinds of unpleasant facts. The technical manager still insisted that I was needed, whilst I just stood there hanging my head. In the end, we went to a little office where the OGPU man, after looking at me for a moment, asked me only one question – did I have any relationship to Zhelezniky? I had to admit it belonged to my aunt, and although it was a tiny estate of only four hectares, he pronounced that I could not be taken on. Nikolai Nikolaievich was very upset, saying that there were scores of priests who had been in prison working there, and yet they refused to take on a prince's son with good qualifications and no criminal record.

I left Kaluga for Tver, where Uncle Alyosha Lopukhin and his family, as well as the Istomin family and many other "minus six" exiles were living and working. Surely I could find work there? Spring was upon us, streams were flowing everywhere, the sun was shining. On arrival I really wanted to go to the Istomins to see my old friend Sergei once again, but they lived beyond the Volga, whereas Uncle Alyosha's place was close to the station. So I chose him. Little did I know that this choice was to determine my future.

I have described my uncle and his family in earlier chapters. The family now consisted of seven children. Uncle Alyosha assured me that I could get a job in a certain organisation, I cannot now remember which, where he himself had once worked. They knew who I was and would make no difficulties about my origins. And thus it was; I was greeted with, "Ah, so this is the prince's son!" and told that I would be sent off about a hundred kilometres down the highway to work as a surveyor. A young woman took my papers and handed me a form to fill out. Since they knew all about my circumstances, I boldly wrote "nobleman" in the space for social origins; despite everything, I was still proud of my birth. I left the office with joy in my heart. I had work at last. I would find a lodging with some old grandmother and be able to get on with my stories of Gornoy Shorii. But when I got back to uncle Alyosha's place, a telegram was waiting for me: "return to Dmitrov at once work here your parents". So that was that! I guessed that someone had used influence to find me a job on the canal. I hurried back to the highway offices, somehow managed to convince them to give me back my papers, called briefly at the Lopukhins to collect my suitcase, and was off and away. I never managed to visit the Istomins.

8

Our landlady in Dmitrov, Praskovya Pavlovna, who was a dentist, had always taken an interest in my career and it was she who had talked to the foreman of a nearby sand quarry when he was having his teeth attended to, and persuaded him to offer me a job. When I went to see him on my return, however, it turned out badly, as what he needed was a technician in quarrying. Praskovya Pavlovna had confused road surveying with mining. I fell into despair. My situation was truly desperate. Going back to seek work in Moscow, I was once again treated with anger or contempt. I thought of moving to Vladimir, where I knew many "minus six" exiled families who might help me to find work. Praskovya Pavlovna continued to worry about my situation. Apart from dentistry, she also read people's fortunes in the cards, and now she decided to lay them out for me. Mother watched as she turned up cards and on my card, the king of diamonds. No six came up, so she exclaimed, "He won't be going anywhere – he'll stay here." The next card was the queen of diamonds. Mother gasped. "Your son will marry," said Praskovya firmly.

When mother told me this I was furious. "What, you believe that sort of rubbish?"

In Dmitrov there lived a professor, Vladimir Romanovich Riedeger, an expert in draining marshes as well as an obsessive inventor. He was a nobleman, the great-grandson of that General von Riedeger who had been sent by Tsar Nicholas I to put down a Hungarian uprising, which he did savagely. The present Riedeger had managed to lose the "von" in his name, and was later also able to drop his German nationality. Praskovya Pavlovna knew him and suggested he might have work for me. Father called on him first, having heard that the professor had need of a translator. While discussing the article to be translated, father mentioned my situation, to which Riedeger responded that he did not give a fig about my social origins, but that he could only take me on as a simple workman. I was unhappy at the thought of slipping from the level of technician to that of a poorly-paid labourer, but had little choice. The family encouraged me to accept. I went to visit the professor's office. Riedeger was a tall, vigorous older man. There were no application forms to complete; his sister-in-law, who was secretary, bookkeeper and personnel officer all in one, she simply wrote my name and date of birth in a register. I had become a labourer in the Moscow Experimental Marshland Station of the Belorussian Institute of Melioration. Why Belorussian? Riedeger firmly believed that the further away one kept from the Moscow top brass, the less they could interfere.

The next morning, with my bag over my shoulder, I set off through the town and across the river Yakhroma. Riedeger passed me on his bicycle, waving cheerily at me and telling me there were still seven kilometres to go. I walked happily along on this mild, May day, delighting in the countryside. Eventually, I came over a rise and saw before me a curious structure shaped like a can of beans. I was taken by the professor to the second floor of this round building and shown an empty room, No. 16, which was to be mine. Down below he instructed the carpenter to make me a trestle bed and table, and then, turning to a young man with fair hair and freckles, introduced me, saying, "Semyon, this fellow's your assistant. Now get to work."

Professor Riedeger was an awkward, uncompromising man in his relations with authority, but to those under him he was invariably considerate. On top of being a passionate inventor, he was also surprisingly good at making money. His energy and enterprise alone were responsible for the round building, with its rooms like pieces of cake, narrow at the centre, broad on the circumference. It was also equipped with a novel heating system, the boiler being located on the ground floor from which the heat travelled along ducts to the rest of the building. The walls too were of a curious design – double wood panels filled with clay. I only mention these details because somehow this kind of curious inventiveness was typical of the disturbed times we were living through.

9

Semyon took me out into a wet, turfy area some three hundred metres from the building. A contraption stood there, composed of a beam, a windlass and a cable attached to an object rather like an artillery shell. We were able to lower the cable into a pit and from there drag the shell-like piece through to another pit so as to make a drainage tunnel. The work was very hard and Semyon did not seem to think of stopping for a smoke. I found my hands beginning to blister, my shoulders to ache unbearably. Finally, I pleaded for a break – after all, I came from a long line of men who had not had to do physical work. At the end of this arduous day, Semyon and I climbed up to the main room, where Riedeger was sitting at a long table. I could see that Semyon wanted to talk to the professor, no doubt to tell him that I was no good at the job, when two barefoot young women burst into the room, saying that their enemies had ploughed up their plot of experimental plants. Riedeger sprang to his feet and set off on his bicycle to the village that could be seen about a kilometre away.

I ate the provisions my mother had packed up for me, then lay down on my mattress. For the first time in my life I had a room to myself; I would be able to get on with my writing. But would I pass my probationary period in this job? My hands were blistered, my arms and shoulders ached. The next day Semyon and I were back digging holes and dragging the cable. The technician, Fyodor Ivanovich Kuznetsov, a small, lean fair-haired man, who I had met the day before, now came along with the surveying instruments, accompanied by his linesman, Masha. His task was to establish the level for the drainage tunnels to follow. He set up his instrument with difficulty and was occupied with it for some twenty minutes, obviously finding it difficult to adjust. After a while I could not restrain myself, jumped up and went over to him, saying, "Here, let me have a try." Although I had not handled an instrument for some time, I was able to fix the point in a few moments, and then shout to Masha, "Let's move on to the next point!" Masha told me later on what a sensation my sudden intervention had caused. Fyodor Ivanovich was a good technician-meliorator, but had no training in survey work. From that day on I ceased to dig holes, and was entrusted with the surveying work and any draughtsmanship that was needed.

For meals we went over to the village, the one that Riedeger had hurried to on his bicycle. There was another organisation there, also an experimental marshland station, but subordinate to Moscow, not Minsk as in our case. As often happens in our country, the two bodies lived in an atmosphere of mutual rivalry and hatred. It was Konstantin Shishkov, the director of the other station, who had allowed his men to plough over our experimental plot. His staff numbered forty, whereas Riedeger only had ten. Shishkov actively undermined Riedeger's work, at which Riedeger just shrugged his shoulders. It was soon known that he had hired a former prince, so Shishkov wanted to create a scandal, but Riedeger defended his choice, saying there was no reason not to hire the man for the job if he had previous work experience and a valid passport.

Our chiefs might have been on terms of enmity, but this was not true of the rest of us. We got on very well with Shishkov's people. Occasionally the botanist, Nikanor Lozhkin, his wife Sima and their laboratory assistant and sister-in-law, Marusya, would visit us in the round house, as did the meteorologist, Pantaleymon Pyatikrestovsky. Visiting us meant being hosted by our technician Fyodor Kuznetsov, his wife Klavdia, a botanist, and another botanist, Klavdia Bavykina. Marusya would sing, accompanied by Fyodor on his guitar. I became a close friend of Petya Pyatikrestovsky, a cheerful, quick-witted and well-read youth. There's an old saying, "One fisherman can spot another from far away". Petya lived under a slightly less threatening cloud than I did; he was the son of the priest of the church of Vvedenye in Dmitrov. After seeing off our guests, we would stay talking, opening our hearts to each other. If there were no guests I would go off to my room and, under the light of an oil lamp that my parents had sent me, wrote stories under the general title of *Taiga*. I believe I was happy.

One thing did make me unhappy, and that was my low pay. I was classified as a labourer, came last on the payroll, and was barely able to meet my own expenses, let alone send my parents any money. Yet I was doing the work of a technician, and knew that Riedeger valued my quick understanding and conscientious work. One day the rest of the staff were given the little red books that were awarded to *udarniki* (outstanding communist workers), but I was refused one. So I could be an exemplary worker, but as a prince be denied recognition! My brother Vladimir noted this sarcastically in his diary.

10

When I began writing these memoirs I did so in the expectation that they would perhaps be read in the twenty-second century. But events in our country have now moved so quickly in the right direction that I must revise my assumption. Perhaps I shall be published even in my own lifetime? And another thing, all sorts of extraordinary pieces of writing appear every day about the horrors of life under Stalin; in comparison, my own account may well strike the reader as pretty mild. So much has changed.

At this stage, the reader must be wondering about the second half of Praskovya Pavlovna's prophecy. And indeed, the story of my love life is unusual, although it all started in a banal enough way. After I had become established in my job, Fyodor Kuznetsov and his wife, Klavdia, who lived with their baby daughter on the same floor as me, hatched an intrigue to matchmake me with Klavdia Bavykina, the second of the young botanists, who also had a room on our floor. Mother had sent me a primus stove and some vegetable oil so that I could cook my own meals, rather than going over to the nearby village. Klavdia Bavykina had a frying pan, but no cooker, so it was natural for us to share our resources; we would fry up potatoes for breakfast and dinner. Also Fyodor, who was in charge of us, contrived to send Klavdia and me off together to hunt in the fields for rare specimens of plants. On our expeditions we were naturally drawn into conversation. More loquacious than me, Klavdia told me a great deal about her large family and her childhood in Voronezh.

One day Fyodor whispered in my ear the great secret that Klavdia liked me. At the time this news did not strike me as anything special. However, one evening when we were together alone, I asked her, "You do know who I am?" She said she did, and that everyone in the organisation knew, but Riedeger had forbidden them ever to raise the subject with me. She added that the director of the rival outfit, Shishkov, intended to write off somewhere about me, but Riedeger was defending me.

One day, out on a plant collecting expedition, we came across a flooded field and in a deep pool discovered a multitude of tiny fish, which we collected and that evening organised a tasty meal for our friends. We even managed to get hold of some vodka. Fyodor played his guitar, Marusya sang. One of the songs had the line, "It is not the one who kisses, but the one who is silent, who loves." When Fyodor and I were about to accompany our guests out, Klavdia turned to me and said, "Please, stay here with me." So we sat down together. She told me that of all Marusya's songs, there was one that she specially liked, and in the song, one line in particular.

"Do you mean 'he who loves is silent'?" I whispered.

Working together, meeting every day for breakfast and supper, we had become close to each other. It was my opportunity to declare my love that evening, but instead I talked about my outcast status, about how astonished I was to be still free when so many of my friends and relatives were sitting in the Gulag or in exile. It was very possible that I would only be free for another month. I simply did not have the right to destroy a young woman's life. Having said all that, I did not wait for her answer, but got up and left. We breakfasted together as usual the next day. I could see that she had been crying. We hardly said a word to each other, and she announced she would not be coming with me into the fields. In the evening, after our shared meal, she again asked me to stay with her. Embarrassed and excited, she blurted out that she did not mind if it was only a month, that if she had a son she would bring him up, and in loving him, remember me. I said, "Alright, for a month then!" We kissed for the first time, and stayed together until past midnight.

11

We now faced the daunting task of breaking the news to our parents. I have always tried to write as honestly as I can, so I cannot now hide the bitter truth of their reactions. Having seen Klavdia off on her train, I went home and first told my mother of my engagement. She could not believe her ears: this step was totally contrary to my principle that I did not have the right to marry. As to the idea of it turning out to be only for a month, mother declared that that was foolish nonsense and one did not get married on such a basis. When father, who was teaching one of the little girls, came in, mother told him, as she saw it, of my childish aberration. His comment was brief: "There's absolutely no question of such a thing!"

I stood my ground, citing the fact, which I thought would impress my parents, that Klavdia was a deeply believing person and regularly attended church. My parents continued to argue with me; it was nonsense to talk of a one-month marriage, and did I not feel attracted to any of the girls among our circle of friends? Besides, I earned far too little money, and Klavdia was two years older than me; and on top of all that, she had the wrong sort of name. Another reason why they were so strongly opposed was because she was a railwayman's daughter, though I sensed that this would not be a decisive element in their thinking. I had to promise to delay the wedding until the autumn, which I thought was far too long a postponement; on the other hand, I did recognise that such an important decision could not be taken on the spur of the moment. It was also decided that nothing would be said to my brother or sisters.

When Klavdia and I were together again I learned that her parents, too, had been distraught at the news. On the one hand, they realised that she was getting older – she was twenty-six – and her previous affairs had led to nothing. On the other hand, connection with me would show up badly on all their papers, would perhaps cause them a great deal of trouble. One relative even said, "Listen, Klavochka, one phone call from me and your fiancé will disappear." Her parents made him promise never to make that phone call. Her family was a large one; there were five sisters and their husbands, two brothers and their wives, and a multitude of children. They were all good Soviet citizens, doing a variety of jobs, drawing ample rations, believing in the collective farms, the Five Year Plan and the wise leadership of our great leader. None of their family or friends had been arrested, so they firmly believed that only enemies of the people, crooks and saboteurs were imprisoned. They lived happily together, admittedly in communal accommodation, but in those days quarrels amongst neighbours were much rarer. It was only in subsequent years that they began to understand the illusory nature of their existence. At that time they had no idea of what was happening in our country, or of how the ordinary peasants were living. As for religion, they were indifferent to it, and would hide the fact if one of theirs was a believer in "those old superstitions".

I had already met Klavdia's parents when they visited her at the round house. It even seems that her mother, looking at me, had told her daughter, "There's the man for you!" Now I was shown off to the many members of her family, starting with the most important, Sergei Davidovich Golochevsky, the husband of Klavdia's third sister and the manager of a perfume plant. He turned out to be the first member of the Party for whom I never felt any fear. He had fought in the civil war, was a deeply convinced communist, a Leninist, and had joined the Party in 1917, but withal his good nature shone through; he told me openly that he approved of me. The next most important person was Efum Mikhailovich Bavykin, the oldest member of the family, who was an accountant in the commissariat of defence. To him, too, I was presented for approval.

Klavdia and I usually slept on the floor at these various relatives' homes, and had to run for the early morning train at Savelovsky station. When I described to my parents the hospitable welcome I had received, it was decided after all to break the news to my sisters and to Elena, Vladimir's wife. After this, Klavdia came with me to meet the family. It was of course a frightful experience for Klavdia to sit at our family table and endure all the looks turned on her. I took her next door to where she was going to sleep in Aunt Sasha's room, and returned to the family. What critical, even bitter words I had to listen to; they said she had a stubby nose, had nothing to say, and wondered aloud what on earth I could see in her. I knew that it was Vladimir who was most unhappy about me but in his diary he only wrote – "Seryozha has lived a virgin until the age of twenty-five and now wants to marry. Nothing special about the girl. She is fond of her food." As a matter of fact, both my father and Vladimir had been chaste until they married, and as for the remark about food – well, we had come from the round house and were jolly hungry.

Thus did the second half of the prophecy about me come true.

At this time there was an exhibition of pictures by Rembrandt in Moscow, to which I took Klavdia. One of them was *The Man in a Helmet*, later sold to an American millionaire, or, as the story went, "sold for forty tractors". I was surprised and somewhat dismayed to discover that Klavdia had never heard of Rembrandt. I decided little by little to correct this ignorance; in the evenings at the round house I took to reading Russian history and the classics of our literature to her.

My sister Sonya, a deeply believing Christian, welcomed us warmly and blessed us. Her husband, Viktor Meien, was absent, but I heard that he was unhappy about my forthcoming marriage. I do not remember how Masha felt about us, but Katya, who was then living happily with her husband, Valery Pertsov, and a newborn baby in Molochny street, kissed me very warmly. Valery, however, disapproved of my intentions and wrote a sixteen-page letter to my parents and brother urging them to talk me out of what he saw as my lighthearted commitment. That autumn and winter of 1933–34 we kept our promise to my parents and lived in our separate rooms in the round house. Slowly my parents began to unbend towards Klavdia.

A decisive change was brought about by my Uncle Alda – Alexander Vasiliyevich Davydov – and his wife, my mother's sister Katya, when they returned from exile and settled near my parents in Dmitrov. They spoke of Klavdia in approving terms and urged father and mother to make an effort to love their future daughter-in-law. In his youth uncle Alda had sown many wild oats. Many evenings in Dmitrov he played the guitar and Elena sang. He now worked as an archivist at the Literary Museum, whose director was the old communist, Bonch-Bruyevich. One day the director called my uncle into his office and asked, "Do you know that you're a descendant of the poet Lermontov?"

"Of course I do," replied my uncle, "mother was his cousin thrice removed on the Stolypin side."

"Why have you kept it quiet?" Bonch exclaimed, and proceeded to arrange a pension of six hundred roubles for him, thanks to which he was allocated a room in Moscow during the war. The pension continued until his death in 1963.

12

Two events happened around this time. The first concerned my sister Masha, still working in the Moscow Geological Commission. She was called in by the OGPU and asked to inform on her professors. They had done nothing wrong, so there was nothing Masha could say about them, even had she wanted to harm them. Summoned a second time, she was asked to spy on them and write down whatever they said amongst themselves. Masha refused, even though they threatened her with arrest. She came down to Dmitrov to seek advice; should she resign? But this would only excite suspicion. At this point, one of the professors was arrested, and it was clear the authorities were going to cook up a case of sabotage against the Geological Commission.

Late one evening, Vera Nikolskaya, one of Masha's colleagues, arrived in Dmitrov to announce that Masha had been arrested, together with six professors and Anna Dmitriyevna Shakhovskaya, the secretary of Academician Vernadsky. Two men had come to the offices just when Masha had slipped out to change one of the dollar transfers that we received from abroad. Masha's chief, a woman known in the office as "the witch", had rushed about hunting for Masha and getting more and more furious at not finding her. Then Masha had appeared and been ordered into the waiting van. Anna Shakhovskaya, who was already inside, afterwards said, "She got in all smiles, just as if she were going to a ball."

Father immediately sat down to write one of his eloquent pleading letters to Peshkova, whilst Academician Vernadksy wrote to one of the Communist leaders. The OGPU realised that they had blundered in arresting such small fry, and freed both girls. When we saw Masha, she described the women who had been in her cell; one was

a prostitute who worked the foreigners' pitch, the other an agronomist called Bezobrazova. Masha described them both as wonderfully
open and honest people. At her interrogation Masha had been asked
to sign a series of accusations against the professors, but had flatly
refused, even though threatened with the camps. Not a single question
was put about our family or any other relatives and she remained in
the Lubyanka for three weeks. As for the professors, they were forced
to sign false confessions, then sentenced to various prison terms.
Two of these professors subsequently turned up on the Volga canal
project.

Vladimir, despite his painful knee, continued to canvas work in
Moscow. He spent a night at the home of the writer, Leonid
Leonov, who told him that he had seen Stalin in real life for the first
time. The fearsome dictator was not at all as he was portrayed all
over the country; he was short, his face heavily marked by smallpox
and his forehead so low he resembled a Neanderthal man. Leonov
also claimed that in travelling by train across the Ukraine he had
seen no sign at all of famine, that it had all been the invention of
enemies of the Soviet Union. How little this talented writer respected
the truth!

Then one day Vladimir did not return. On the third day, Elena
went off in search of him. She discovered that he had been arrested
together with Alexei Bobrinsky, at whose place Vladimir had spent
the night. That same night they arrested another cousin of ours,
Sasha Golitsyn, the son of our Uncle Vovik, as well as Petya Urusov,
the husband of Sasha's sister Olyechka. When Elena turned to the
artist Korin, a very old friend of Vladimir's, for assistance, Korin
exclaimed, "Goodness, why didn't he sleep here?" Korin and his wife
were then still living in an attic on the Arbat – he was later to be
privileged with a beautiful apartment on Devichy Polye after the
famous visit by Maxim Gorky, and to become well-known among
the Party leaders. He promised to intervene energetically for Vladimir,
and it so happened that he was in the middle of painting Yagoda
himself, the head of the OGPU. Yagoda had become interested in
Korin's work and had visited his studio several times incognito and
in plain clothes, later commissioning the portrait of himself. He and
Korin occasionally discussed art in Yagoda's office. At one of these
meetings, the artist took the bull by the horns and mentioned his
friend Vladimir's arrest. Yagoda promised to look into it.

Why were three cousins and one brother-in-law arrested that
night? It seems that Alexei Bobrinsky called in on Uncle Vovik
Golitsyn one evening and asked him to look after his revolver as he

was going to the theatre. Uncle Vovik assumed the revolver had been issued for Alexei to protect his foreign boss, the journalist Duranti, and readily agreed to look after it. The very next day a search was carried out and the revolver, of course, found. At their interrogation, this revolver was the principle evidence in the accusation of an assassination attempt on Stalin. Torture was not practised in those years, pressure being applied by depriving victims of their sleep, so that strong-willed individuals were sometimes able to resist confessing to trumped-up crimes. Papers were put before Vladimir for signature, which he categorically refused to do. His final interrogation was conducted in a different room and by a very senior officer, no doubt at Yagoda's instigation. He was then released. As for the fate of Sasha Golitsyn, Petya Urusov and his wife, I will come to that later. Alexei Bobrinsky was sentenced to ten years in a labour camp in Vorkuta, thus bringing to an end his career as a traitor to his class. His boss, Duranti, was honoured with a personal interview with Stalin, which was published in all the newspapers, but one question he raised did not feature anywhere – why had they arrested his personal secretary? Perhaps one day historians will discover the answer.

Alexei was freed at the beginning of the war, fought on the front line and returned from the war with the rank of sergeant and a row of medals. He became head of a sanatorium in the Crimea. In 1949, he was re-arrested and sent to a camp in Dzheskaskan, from where he was freed seven years later. He settled with his second wife in Rostov on the Don. When, later on, he came to Moscow on a visit, the wife of his cousin, Professor Nikolai Alexeievich Bobrinsky, phoned me up and asked me to come and see him. I refused. For me he remained a traitor, and responsible for the death of many people. He died in 1986. Incidentally Count Nikolai Bobrinsky, the naturalist, was one of the few titled people to survive these times, thanks to a happy combination of circumstances. He is the subject of an entry in the big *Soviet Encyclopedia*.

13

My Klavdia suffered the news of these arrests vicariously; she had never known that people were rounded up for no reason at all, and then imprisoned. This was her first contact with the atmosphere of fear in which my family had lived since the revolution. Masha put her overcoat under Klavdia's nose so that she could smell the carbolic used as disinfectant in all the prisons and camps of the Soviet Union.

"Perhaps we should split up?" I asked Klavdia.

"No, never!" she cried. We embraced fiercely.

We patiently endured the months of waiting that we had promised my parents. During the winter it turned out that the heating system invented for the round house was totally inadequate; we suffered from the cold at night, and in an attempt to improve matters we took to sleeping in the corridor that formed an inner circle. I continued to read the classics to Klavdia when I came in after work; we would sit together, fully dressed against the cold, on her bed. Why on her bed? There was no other furniture.

When spring came I told my parents that we could wait no longer to be married. They gave their agreement. In those days there were no tricky formalities to complete; one simply came to the village chairman's office and in five minutes it was all done, so we decided against Moscow, instead registering for marriage in Konchinino, a nearby village. On the day, heavy snow had fallen. With difficulty we managed to trudge the two kilometres through deep snow. The chairman failed to appear, so we went to his house, where he came to the door, covered in blood, and apologised – a pig had been unable to give birth and had had to be killed. After a long wait, and in this strange atmosphere, our marriage was finally signed and sealed.

We had decided in advance that Klavdia would keep the name of Bavykina. It would have been foolish to become a princess seventeen years after the revolution, and a former princess at that. As for me, in those days I could have chosen to become simply "citizen Bavykin", and at a stroke do away with all fears and humiliations. This was her family's advice, but I refused to do this; I was born a prince, a prince I would stay, whatever happened. This was how my cousin, Kirill Golitsyn, had acted, and it cost him seventeen years in the Gulag. Whereas Kirill Urusov, on his marriage, had changed his name to Volkov, and was the only member of his family to survive.

On the eighteenth of April we were married in the church of St Vlasy between Prechistenkaya Street and the Arbat. The church is still there and has recently been restored. Few church weddings took place in those years, as people were fearful of the consequences. Mother and my sister Sonya were present, but Masha could not come as she was now working in the geological section of the canal project and her day off was not on the Sunday. On Klavdia's side were her parents and her eldest brother, Efim Mikhailovich, and his wife. The ceremony was performed by the old priest, Pavel Levashov, who had married Vladimir and Elena eleven years earlier. Klavdia wore a simple dress and a muslin headdress, and contrary to church custom, the crown was held above her head by her married brother. I, who had acted as groom thirteen times, had no groom, and had to hold my own crown. This was awkward when the priest led us around the lectern, but the old Orthodox custom, when the priest holds out the cup of wine for both bride and groom to drink from, was wonderful and moving.

We walked to the flat of Klavdia's eldest sister, married to the aircraft designer, Georgy Mironovich Mozharovsky, on Malaya Nikitskaya Street, where we were greeted not with bread and salt, but sweet pie and salt, a much tastier offering. The entire Bavykin family were present, but of our family, only mother and Sonya. Katya had not been allowed to come by her husband Valery Pertsov, even though he was my best friend. Nor was my brother Vladimir present. As for my father, he was chronically unwell and never went anywhere. The only Party member present was Sergei Davydovich Golochevsky; he made a wise and tactful speech, wishing us health and happiness and participation in the great creative processes that were taking place in the country. I replied that I would always work for the benefit of our homeland and if necessary take up arms to defend it, a speech that I believe was well-received.

Klavdia's fourth sister and husband, an actor with the Red Army troupe, had offered us for our wedding night their simple room in the barracks where they lived. The elderly lady guard who sat on a stool at the end of the corridor, noticing a strange couple going into Serafima's room, raised the alert. In the middle of the night, we were woken by a loud knocking. Klavdia went over to the door and then with a frightened face came back to tell me, "It's the militia!" I went cold with fear; had they come for me already? But the other actors on the corridor, who had known that we would be using the room that night, defended us, including Ranevskaya (not yet the famous person she was to become), and so the incident passed off happily.

That summer, and indeed the whole of 1934, remains for me the happiest year of my life. Mother and Masha came to see us in the round house. Mother was delighted about the beauty of the countryside on their way over and the picturesque landscape around us. On another occasion Nikolai Lebedev came, though he rather alarmed the others with his great height and impressive appearance. In the evening he recited his poetry to us in dramatic style; happening to open our door, we discovered some of our colleagues standing outside listening.

14

About this time a high level celebratory meeting was organised between the leadership of the Party and young people from the collective farms who had received awards for their work. Adulatory speeches from the floor were made in praise of the great leader. Then one young tractor driver rose to his feet and said that since he had been given the floor he would like to confess that he was the son of a *kulak*, a fact he had managed to hide. Stalin interrupted him, saying, "A son is not responsible for his father." The papers naturally printed Stalin's words. First father showed me the cutting, then Klavdia's parents. They were all delighted. Sergei Davydovich slapped me on the shoulder, saying these words were completely unexpected, and that now I could rest easy about my origins. Soon a long article of analysis and commentary signed by some bigwig appeared in a leading paper. My father rejoiced for all his children, and I was happy that in future I would not be reproached for bearing the title of prince. How little I knew of the disillusion that lay ahead.

The cold weather had set in. We no longer went off to the fields. Klavdia continued her work making bouquets of dried flowers. She was pregnant and not feeling well. I occupied myself drawing and reading. The cold became more and more intense and we realised that once our child was born we could not continue to live in the inadequately heated round house. Then a miracle happened; the architect who had designed the house arrived and announced that the heating system had not been built according to plan. He set to work to rebuild it. We made ourselves responsible for feeding him and enjoyed his company in the evenings. He was a dedicated Leninist, but we could tell he was not happy with much of what was happening in the country. The day came when the new heating system was put back into operation. Anxiously we awaited the result and were overjoyed when warm air began pumping through the vents in our room; so we could continue to live here. Together with the architect we had just sat down to supper, when there was a knock at the door. It was fair-haired Semyon, all covered in frost, having walked over from the village. "Listen, the radio's blaring all over the place. The big man in Leningrad's been killed."

The architect jumped to his feet. "Who's been killed? Not Kirov?"

"Yes, some sort of name like that," replied Semyon indifferently. "The radio says he was killed by a Party man."

The architect sat in silence for a long while, then said he must get back to Moscow urgently. We tried to get him to stay the night –

there would be a cart to take him to the station in the morning – but he refused and set off on foot. We never saw him again, and I have the feeling he was one of those who only had a few years left to live.

1934 was a year when many historic events took place. The icebreaker *Chelyuskin* sank in the Arctic Ocean, but the crew were saved by the heroic deeds of the aviators who had flown to their rescue. The whole country held its breath while this disaster was unfolding. In March, sodomy was declared punishable by eight years in prison. In April, the award "Hero of the Soviet Union" was created. In May, a tenth year in school was introduced. In June, a law on treachery to the homeland came into force, decreeing capital punishment for anyone who tried to flee the country and ten years exile for the members of his family. In July, the OGPU was renamed the NKVD, headed by Yagoda, and *troikas* (tribunals of three judges) were created, with the power to pronounce a sentence in a matter of minutes. A law on giving false weight in the shops, punishable by ten years in prison, was introduced. At the end of November, ration cards were abolished. All these laws were brought into force by Kalinin and Enukidze.

Klavdia and I were in the great crowd that gathered, voluntarily, without any orders from above, to greet the returning aviators and crew of the *Chelyuskin* in their procession through the streets of Moscow. With everyone else we joined in the hurrahs. Two volumes of articles and photographs of the rescue were published, although these were soon withdrawn from the libraries; some of the rescuers had turned out to be enemies of the people.

24. Harsher Times

1

The murder of Kirov in Leningrad marked a turning point in the history of our country. The very next day a new law came out – those accused of terrorism must be tried without delay, sentence must be pronounced within ten days after the trial, there could be no appeal, and execution must be immediate. The list of the accused was published; there were thirty each from Leningrad, Moscow and the Ukraine, fifteen from Belorussia. What hysterical outpourings appeared in the papers! Fury was directed at the leaders in Leningrad for not maintaining proper watchfulness, and at all kinds of enemies, from *kulaks* to saboteurs, former nobles to priests, class enemies of every kind. Many of the secret police of Leningrad were sent off to the camps in Siberia, though not as prisoners, but as guards. A joke circulated at that time – what is the difference between a forest and the OGPU? In a forest a *medved* (bear) eats *yagoda* (berries), whereas in the OGPU Yagoda eats Medved, the name of the then head of the Leningrad secret police.

Kirov had been a popular leader, controlling Leningrad with a relatively light touch, even tolerating opponents. Access to him had been easy, and his style of collectivisation aimed only at the richest peasants. His successor was Zhdanov, one of the cruellest of the leaders, but a clever, well-educated executioner, which made him even more dangerous. He is remembered now as the persecutor of the poet Akhmatova, the writer Zoschenko and the composers Prokofiev and Shostakovich, but he also sent thousands of others to their deaths. Up to this time few Party members had been arrested and even fewer shot. It was Zhdanov who started to arrest middle rank and worker members of the Party. He started reprisals against all those who had shown any trace of opposition in Leningrad, or even those who had sympathised with such opponents. Kirov had respected such people; Zhdanov began to liquidate them. This was one aspect of the persecution that now raged; another can be gathered from an order published in the papers on 25 March 1935:

> In Leningrad the following were arrested and exiled to the eastern regions of the USSR for violation of the law on residence and of the passport system: 41 former princes, 32 former counts, 76 former barons, 35 former industrialists, 68 former landowners, 19 former rich merchants, 142 former tsarist officials, 547 former tsarist generals and officers and members of the White Army, 113 former gendarmes. Some of these were guilty of espionage.

An accountant of my acquaintance added up these figures to make a total of one thousand and seventy-four, to which must be added their wives and children, which would quadruple the number. In fact, it was said that many times this number were driven out of the city. The writer, Constantin Leonov, has written of his two Obolensky aunts, exiled to Kazakhstan. The four Lvov brothers, nephews of the Prime Minister of the Provisional Government, with their children and very old father, ended up in exile in Samara and Saratov.

How were these expulsions into exile carried out? You were called in by the militia, where your passport was taken from you and you were ordered to appear at a railway station on a set date and time with only hand baggage. Thus did the columns of exiles form up and depart for the east. There is an account of Anna Akhmatova going to a station to see off some friends, seeing old folk and children proudly mounting into the crowded carriages as they said farewell to the people seeing them off, and farewell to their beloved city. The very lifeblood and culture of the city were being sent into exile. This was followed by a fabulous sale of the accumulated possessions of the dispossessed – pictures of ancestors, entire libraries, furniture, ceramics and glass. Some people made a fortune in this trade. For a time Moscow was spared these purges, until word got about that the capital should also be cleansed of its class enemies. Soon the whole country was plunged into purges. People went about their lives in fear, praying to themselves, "Not me, anyone else, but not me!" In our family we thanked providence that Alexei Bobrinsky had deposited his revolver with our uncle in the beginning of 1934, not at the end; prison camp, or worse, would have been the outcome, and my brother Vladimir would not have returned home.

2

Klavdia was with her parents in Moscow awaiting the birth of our first child. Thanks to Professor Riedeger's kindness I was often sent on errands to Dmitrov or Moscow, so my time alone at work was not difficult to bear. I remember being in Moscow at the time of a major art exhibition. This was held in the Manege building near the Kremlin. The only picture from that show that I recall was by the now-forgotten painter, Alexander Gerasimov, a huge portrait of Stalin entitled *Comrade Stalin Making his Report to the 17th Congress of the CP*. The great leader's face was high-browed and on such a scale it must have measured the size of a beer-barrel; he is looking majestically across a table, hands resting on the red baize, the ring on his middle finger the size of a horse's hoof. A crowd of admiring viewers stood gazing in adulation. Oddly enough, not one of my present artist friends has ever seen or heard of that picture.

Nikolai Lebedev and I persuaded Vladimir to take us to see the artist Korin in his studio on the Arbat. The artist, fine-featured and lean in body, received us in his black Russian shirt, the same as the one in his portrait by Nesterov; his wife was welcoming and sat us down to tea. We were bowled over by the marvellous pictures of beggars and persecuted priests that Korin showed us. I have never since seen such honest pictures. Over tea I sat in thoughtful silence, going over the impression of those works. Nikolai Lebedev sat scribbling in his notebook, then rose to his feet and said he had written a poem about Korin and would like to read it to us. He called Korin a great painter, at which the artist protested, saying there was only one great painter in Russia and that was Alexander Ivanov. Since that visit I have often been in Korin's house where, after his death, the curator would show his work, and each time I think back to the joy I felt on first seeing his paintings.

3

The authorities created a new holiday at the beginning of 1935, namely New Year, until then considered to be alien to the proletariat. An article appeared over the name of P.P. Postyshev suggesting that on that holiday a tree be decorated for the sake of the children. So this was a complete U-turn; the Christmas tree, mocked in the press and forbidden, was back. In the satirical magazine *Krokodil*, Postyshev was depicted as a smiling Santa Klaus with a decorated fir tree full of presents over his shoulder.

I spent New Year with the Bavykin family, returned to the round house, did some writing and returned to Moscow one Saturday evening. That very night Klavdia began to have contractions. I took her to the maternity home in Leontyevsky Lane. In the afternoon of the next day, the twenty-third of January, I saw the list of newborn infants pinned up on the wall. I read the name, K. Bavykina and jumped to the conclusion that the feminine form of the word must indicate a girl. I felt some disappointment as we had both so much wanted a boy. Then my father-in-law stepped up, put on his glasses, and read out "born to K. Bavykina, a boy".

"Don't you see, it's a boy," he cried.

I jumped for joy. So our glorious princely name would be perpetuated. That same evening I went to Dmitrov to announce the birth of our son, and from there to the round house, where everyone congratulated me, and where I worked in something of a daze, all the time dreaming of how I would bring up my son and consequently doing my work very badly. When I got back to Moscow in my state of happy excitement I was in for a sad disappointment. My father-in-law had gone to the local office to register the birth and had been asked for the passport of the father of the child. On replying that I was away and would bring in the passport in seven days, the official scared him by saying that under the law the registration had to be done within three days, otherwise there would be a massive fine. My father-in-law therefore registered his grandson under the name of Bavykin. Only after the war was it possible, after a great deal of fuss and bother, finally to give my son his true name, Golitsyn.

We christened him in the huge church of Vasily Keserisky on Tverskaya-Yamskaya Street, where the Children's Bookstore now stands. His godparents were Efim Mikhailovich, Klavdia's elder brother, and my mother. From the round house we returned every weekend either to Dmitrov or Moscow, carrying Goga slung over our shoulders in a sling that I had sewn together. Even in the hardest frosts we carried him this way. Though Klavdia had returned to work, she found it hard to keep up with her colleague as Goga cried a lot and needed constant soothing. It was just then that a party of inspectors came to the round house and, amongst other deficiencies, discovered that we were too many staff. They asked Riedeger, why do you need so many staff in winter; hire them as temporaries in the spring. And why do you need two botanists? The result was that Klavdia was fired, together with two labourers, Marusia and me.

Still we went on living in the round house. We had just bought a sack of potatoes and felt it would be easier to wait until we had consumed it than to move with it. We spent our times reading and looking after our son. I did some writing on my opus, *Taiga*. We were confident that in due course, like many other "former" people, I would find work on the canal project. But then one of those unexpected incidents occurred that change the course of a life. On the first floor of the round house stood a huge old carved walnut cupboard. How it had come there from some landowner's mansion no one knew, but there it stood, completely unused. One day men came from the rival experimental organisation and began to carry it down the stairs. Fyodor Ivanovich and I stood by, but as the cupboard was enormously heavy, we moved in to lend a hand. Just as I had grasped one corner, one of the men stumbled and I was suddenly pinned against the wall with the whole weight of the cupboard pressing on my chest. They pulled the cupboard away, but I was unable to straighten up. Somehow or other I managed to crawl to my room and fall on my bed. By evening I had a soaring temperature.

The local medical orderly came to see me, and after sounding my chest said that there were no broken ribs and that my pleuritis would heal itself. Three days later my temperature was back to normal, but I still felt a terrible weight in my chest and could only breathe with great difficulty. I stopped smoking, and since that day have never once wanted to start smoking again. But my breathlessness did not go away and I found it almost impossible to bring in the four or five pails of water that we needed every day. It was clearly out of the question for us to stay on, so we sold off the sack of potatoes and moved to Klavdia's parents in Moscow. It was goodbye to the round house.

4

We left just in time. A political section was set up at the experimental farm, supposedly to help the collective, but in fact to pick out "class enemies". My friend Petya Pyatikrestovsky, who had just married and had worked there with all his heart and soul for a number of years, was expelled – he was a priest's son. I am sure they would have done the same to me. The priest of the village of Konchinin was arrested. As a hobby he collected old coins and had quite a collection, including silver Tsarist roubles and other small denominations. He was sent to the Gulag for "undermining the finances of the State" – I read this in the local paper. In Dmitrov, the OGPU initiated a kind of Bartholomew's Night massacre, arresting fourteen priests and deacons of the local cathedral. The churches in thirteen surrounding villages were nailed up.

Father Konstantin Pyatikrestovsky of the church of the village of Vvedenye was arrested, but the faithful were able to keep the church open, and it is still open and serving today. After the war, his son Petya told me how when he and his mother took a food parcel to the prison they were told that all the priests had been transported away. They returned home to hear the radio blaring:

Is there any country in the world
Where man can breathe so freely?

Much later on they received in the post a folded triangle of paper with just a few words saying that the priests were being taken to the east – it must have been thrown from the train and some kind soul had put a stamp on it and sent it on. In Khrushchev's time, a single one of the fifteen, a deacon, returned from the Gulag and told how that fateful night the priests had been taken in by the militia, and, to mockery and jeers, had had their robes torn off, their heads and beards brutally shaved. There was no trial, they were simply sent off to the terrible Mariinsky camps to slave in the forests. Only this one man had survived.

Petya showed me the paper declaring his father completely rehabilitated for "absence of substance to the accusation". But Petya had had a hard time in those years, having to frequently change jobs to avoid trouble. He served in the war, reaching Vienna and returning a hero. I could write much more about our friendship until his death in 1985, but that would divert me from the main theme of these writings.

5

Vladimir had become a close friend of the writer Zhitkov, the partner of Vera Arnold, one of the daughters of the director of the agricultural institution in Bogoroditsk where we had lived in 1919. Zhitkov helped Vladimir enormously by commissioning him to illustrate his sea stories. One day Vladimir told him about me and my desire to become a writer. Zhitkov asked to see me. With much diffidence, I visited his flat near Devichy Pole, and was warmly received by him and invited by Vera to share their meal. This was the first of several visits, at which I took him a couple of my stories. He not only helped me to revise them but even added some ideas of his own, and finally, with a smile, rolled them up and said, "Well, I'm off to Leningrad and will personally hand them in to the journal *Chizh*" (Goldfinch).

I waited and waited for a response. Then I learned that the editor of this journal had been arrested, so assumed my stories were lost. Very much later I received a letter addressed to my parents in Dmitrov, saying that my stories had been discovered in the archives of the journal and asking who I was; eventually both stories were printed in 1940.

Vladimir was helped by Lazar Berman, the editor of ONTI – a scientific and technical publishing organisation – with commissions to do technical drawings, which Vladimir found tedious, but had to accept so as to feed himself and family. One day Berman talked to him about a series of technical books for children. Vladimir's eye was caught by the title of one *Topography for School Children* and asked who was going to write it. Berman said he could find no one to write it.

"Why, my brother's a topographer!" Vladimir exclaimed. Berman was delighted and asked him to send me along.

In general, I was not a very self-confident person, nor did I know much about topography. I had been a highway surveyor for some time and then a simple workman, and now here I was being asked to teach young people about topography. Taking me to see Berman, Vladimir said, "Look, don't be diffident. Bluff a bit. Above all, don't let me down!"

Berman's office was on Ostozhenka Street by Prechistenkaya Gate. He met me with a warmth that no other editor has ever shown me, and I found myself agreeing to write the text for the little book, some eight pages. I would in due course receive the contract and my advance, Berman said. I then went for advice to Zhitkov. He fully approved of my bold presumption and offered me some technical advice as well as counsel on how to write a lively text for what he termed "Geodesics for Idiots".

I went away rejoicing, but the leaden weight in my chest still oppressed me. It was not painful, but when I had to walk uphill or upstairs, I could only do so very slowly. I knew that I was unwell, even though the medical orderly, and later the doctor in Dmitrov had found nothing wrong with me. Father gave me a letter of introduction to his old friend, Dr Fyodor Alexandrovich Getye, who had once been Lenin's doctor. I got through to him with some difficulty at Botkinsky hospital. After greeting me affectionately and asking after my parents, he examined me carefully, and then led me through to the X-ray room. I had no sooner put myself behind the big X-ray screen when Dr Getye cried to an orderly, "Get all the students in from next door!"

Some thirty students, nurses and doctors in their white coats burst into the room to look at my chest on the fluorescent screen with oh's and ah's and general expressions of astonishment, such as "the first time in my life!" or "I can't believe it!" I did not know the medical terms, but gathered that I was seriously ill of a very rare condition. Dr Getye took me back into his office where he explained that I was suffering from spontaneous pneumothorax, a condition that more usually affected players of wind instruments. I would have to stay in bed, moving about as little as possible, until the air that had entered the cavity next to my lungs had escaped, a process that might take several months.

I walked back to Klavdia's parents' place in a far from cheerful mood. It was only one room, and we had to move the table back to make space for Klavdia and me to sleep on the floor. It was hard to imagine how I would write a book and get better under such conditions. Our situation, however, suddenly began to look a lot brighter. One of her brothers-in-law, Alexander Kubatovich, a geneticist who specialised in pig breeding and worked at an animal research institute, offered me work compiling statistics on the genetic characteristics of animals from several collective farms, work that was aimed at improving the breeding quality of the pig. I would be paid ten roubles a pig, or rather, as they could not be on record as paying a former prince, Klavdia would receive the money. So there I was with two jobs – writing a book and counting pigs. Just then Masha came hurrying to tell me that a money order for four hundred roubles, which only I could cash, was waiting for me in Dmitrov.

Limping along on two sticks, I managed to get myself to Dmitrov, collected the four hundred roubles, and found us a lodging, or to be more accurate, a summer house in the garden of a lady, Dr.Sedovaya. There was plenty of time before the autumn to find a proper flat. I would finish writing the book on topography, get better and find work on the canal project. That was my plan. So I lay in bed in the little summer house reading whatever I could find on geodesics and topography, dictated some of the future book to Klavdia, and corrected my father's efforts on the pig statistics. He had offered to help, but his mathematics left much to be desired. Sadly, I could not read aloud to Klavdia, as I had been doing; if I tried the pain in my chest flared up.

Now and again my parents or a sister came to visit us. Vladimir never came. I was reproached with my action in helping with the cupboard. What need had I to assist? No longer on the staff, I could perfectly well have stood by with my hands in my pockets. And as an unemployed person, not even a member of a union, I had no right to compensation of any kind.

6

No matter how carefully Vladimir and his family and my parents lived, there was never enough money. He was finding it harder and harder to get work as an illustrator and his ideas for board games, though promising, had yet to yield any return. My father's earnings were tiny, and Masha, who had lost her job at the geological committee and was now working as a geologist-collector on the canal, also earned very little, although her generous food rations were a great help. Moina Abamelek-Lazareva's monthly ten dollars, exchanged for special coupons, made it possible to buy some of the basic food items, such as cooking oil, in the foreign currency store. Ironically, there were no foreigners at all in Dmitrov.

Father's brother, Nikolai Vladimirovich, still worked at the *Journal de Moscou*, but on a low salary. His son, Kirill, had returned from exile and thanks to his marriage was allowed to live in Moscow, but he worked only as a draughtsman, or not even that, and the couple had begun to have children. Another of father's brothers, Vladimir Vladimirovich, had to everyone's surprise got a job in the Foreign Trade Bank, but again the salary was very modest. The worst affected, though, was father's sister, Aunt Eli, married to Vladimir Sergeievich Trubetskoi, living in Sergiyev Posad with their seven children. In 1934, her husband and their eldest daughter, eighteen-year-old Varya, were arrested and exiled to Andizhan. The rest of the family was preparing to join them there. So all four families were in need of money, but above all Aunt Eli.

The main Golitsyn possessions were the ancestral portraits that father and Vladimir had saved from the house on Pokrovka Street in 1923, as well as a small painting by Rembrandt, *The Circumcision of Christ* and the marble bust by Shubin of Fyodor Nikolaievich Golitsyn. The question of selling these came up, and although they had been saved in our family, father considered that whatever money they raised belonged to all four families. First the Rembrandt was sold to the Museum of Figurative Arts. Acquired in the eighteenth century by Ivan Ivanovich Shuvalov, and left at his death to the Golitsyns, the family had always thought it to be a genuine Rembrandt, but sadly it was decided by the art experts that it was by a pupil, and so fetched half the amount we had expected. As for the bust by Shubin, the nose was damaged and so it, too, was bought for a lower figure by the Tretyakov Gallery.

Vladimir had preserved and guarded our ancestral portraits out of his love of them. While other "former" people might own one or two pictures of their family, we had more than a score, the sight of which, carefully hung in a particular order by Vladimir wherever we lodged, and however cramped our quarters, never failed to astonish our visitors. The first in line was always Andrei Matveyev's portrait, painted in 1728, of Prince Ivan Alexeievich and his wife, born Princess Prozorovskaya; this couple were quite undistinguished, and only familiar to us thanks to their portrait. Then came their son's picture, followed by his son's, and so on right through the eighteenth and into the nineteenth centuries. It amounted to a sizeable collection.

However little we wished it, circumstances now forced us to start selling off our ancestors. A picture of Lomonosov was the first sold. He was the eighteenth-century founder of Moscow University but no ancestor, though it was still a picture we were sorry to see go. Moscow University bought it for a sizeable sum. Next we sold the young Emperor Paul and his wife, followed by a wonderful picture by Lebrun of Ivan Ivanovich Shuvalov, who was not a direct ancestor but the uncle of our great-great-grandfather, Prince Fyodor Nikolaievich, and so we were not too miserable at seeing it go. Then we parted with Fyodor Ivanovich himself as a lad, followed by his wife, the daughter of Field Marshal Prince Repnin. We descended from his second wife, born Shipovaya. The Tretyakov Gallery made fools of us with these two purchases, sold as by unknown artists; in fact, the first was by Vishnyakov, the second by Rokotov. In later years we sold off small watercolour portraits, two by Sokolov, one by Bryullov, others by unknown artists, largely because Vladimir had by then been forced to stop work and was preparing to go into hospital with his bad knee. As a legally unregistered and disenfranchised person, he was not entitled to any financial help from his union.

7

Misfortune continued to dog our family. Following the assassination of Kirov in Leningrad, a pogrom was whipped up against the city's intelligentsia, while in Moscow a number of families were sent into exile beyond the hundred kilometre zone. Our passports had been issued in 1932 with a validity of three years. When father and Vladimir took them to the militia for renewal, they kept the passports, ordering the whole family to remove to beyond the hundred kilometre line. Vladimir fumed, "Why does it make any difference whether we are sixty or a hundred kilometres away?" Help had to be sought. Should we turn to Peshkova? No, it would be more effective to ask Korin, who was in direct contact with Yagoda, and who had once before helped Vladimir to be released after arrest. So my brother wrote the following letter:

Dear Pavel Dmitrovich,

Misfortunes are piling up on us. Two days ago I fell ill with the flu and have a high temperature. Yesterday my daughter, suffering from scarlet fever, was taken into hospital, and today my passport was taken away from me and I was ordered to move from Dmitrov into the 100 km zone within 24 hours. Tomorrow I hope to get a certificate from the doctor allowing me to postpone this for two or three days. In addition, on 5 December I am due to enter the orthopaedic hospital for an operation. I have 400 roubles worth of work lying on my desk, which I am unable to hand in, as my wife and children are in quarantine because of the scarlet fever. My parents have not yet had their passports taken away, but I imagine that will happen without delay. It would appear that instructions about me have come from Moscow. If you were able to help us in this very difficult situation we would be eternally grateful to you. If you do help, you could mention the games I've devised to Gorky and to Bubnov of the Committee on Games, and also my bad leg. If you find you are not in a position to plead for our passports, then at least please ask for an extension of 10 days for our move.

Should any intervention on our behalf in any way affect your own position or in particular interfere with your creative work, then forget this whole affair. After all, this is not such a disaster – it's the 10th time we've had to move on. We are all already very much obliged to you and your family for help. Your main purpose now, and in the future, is your creative work; the rest is insignificant. Greetings to Praskovya Tikhonovna. My sister Masha can give your more details if needed.

V. Golitsyn

Korin was not the man to remain indifferent to the fate of a friend. As it happened, some priests and a deacon, Kholmogorov, whose portrait he was painting, were being sent into exile beyond the one hundred kilometre limit at this very time. He went to see Yagoda.

"So you're trying to help your prince again, eh?" were Yagoda's exact words.

In the event, our parents were allowed to remain in Dmitrov and were all issued with new passports, whilst Vladimir entered the hospital for his operation. The problem was that his knee was unable to bend. Inventive by nature, Vladimir devised a contraption, approved by the doctors, to help his knee recover its flexibility, but this failed to have the right effect. In the end, the doctors suggested he move to the coast of the Black Sea where the warm climate might effect a cure. Early in 1936, he and his wife Elena and the two boys, Misha and Laryusha, settled in Gudauty, leaving their daughter Elena behind to continue her schooling. Vladimir wrote interesting letters home, and in the summer of 1938, Korin and his wife visited them, staying for a month. Korin did some landscapes, whilst Vladimir continued with his book illustration. The diary he wrote of Korin's visit appeared in the book *Memories of the Artist V. Golitsyn* and was also was included in a collection of memorial essays on Korin.

8

My youngest sister, Katya, had been refused school attendance beyond Year 7. After first finding work on an experimental farm in Dolgoprudnaya, she then moved from one organisation to another, teaching herself to be a laboratory assistant and then also a draughts-man. In 1932, she married my friend Valery Pertsov and the couple lived with his mother at No. 7 Molochnaya Street near Ostozhenka, where Katya put up with the capricious nature of her mother-in-law and gave birth to two sons, Volodya and Kolya.

In 1935, she found a job in the laboratory of the Physical Institute of the Academy of Sciences, which had just moved from Leningrad. In filling out the usual personnel forms, Katya had written, under the question "social origins", "daughter of a civil servant", and had left blank the space for her answer to the give-away question "social origins of your parents". Her married name, Pertsov, was not likely to attract any special interest. Eventually, however, the union representative discovered that she was not a member. Questioning her, he asked what her maiden name had been. When she told him, he asked whether she had anything to do with the village of Bulchalki, to which she replied that she had spent the first three years of her life there.

"Ah, so you're a former princess!" he exclaimed, and blushing a little, said that he had been a child in the orphanage there. He rushed off to see the scientific secretary, Vul, and the two of them hurried to the personnel officer, where they saw that Katya had failed to answer the infamous question. This caused a great scandal and that very day a notice went up announcing that Katya was dismissed for "hiding her social origins". But this was not the end of the affair. An extraordinary Party meeting was convened, at which Vul delivered a blistering speech about the unmasking of a class enemy. He attacked the negligence of the personnel officer and alluded to the fall and disgrace of Enukidse, in whose office there had likewise been discovered a former princess. Now see what had happened in their own institute! Fortunately, the class enemy in Enukidse's office had been arrested; they must do the same with their own.

The next day Katya, quite unsuspecting, went to the office to sign off. She was told to go and see Vul, who received her with ill-concealed contempt. He had obviously already been in touch with the organisation that half the population of the country feared. He told Katya to go to Kuznetsky Most, house number such-and-such, office number such-and-such, to have her pass signed. She went there quite innocently, though sad at losing her post, and no doubt thinking tenderly of her two little boys. At Kuznetsky Most she was briefly questioned by a surprisingly correct-mannered NKVD officer, who then, to Katya's bewilderment, uttered the following words – "No, you're not the one we're looking for," and stamped her pass.

At this difficult point in time, my old friend Andrei Kiselev, now a professor, turned up trumps. He gave Katya work in his Institute of Textiles, even though she had earned a black mark on her work record. She did not, however, remain there for long. She became a freelance draughtsman, undertaking all manner of graphic work, from labels for industry to museum displays. I have never known anyone who could work so fast and accurately. Thanks to her freelance status not once, neither before the war, nor after it, did she have to fill in any form with that infamous question.

9

By the autumn of 1935 my lung had healed. Dr Getye looked at my X-ray and congratulated me on a good recovery. I finished the little book *I Want to be a Topographer* and posted it to Berman, who promised to send for me. Patiently I awaited his call, meanwhile going on counting and logging pigs. I did not abandon my hopes of becoming a true writer, but I did wonder whether I should perhaps think of continuing to write popular technical and scientific texts. Meanwhile Klavdia and I had found a separate, though tiny, house for us alone. As we settled in there happily, it came to me that we had now been married not just for a month, but a whole year and a half. Although I was earning good money, still I worried about the general uncertainty of my position, and kept wondering whether I could make a living as a writer.

Finally the telegram from Berman arrived. When I got to his office he was in conversation with an officer, a short, lean, bearded man with two pips on his shoulder. Berman signed me to sit down. I could not help overhearing them, and after a little while realised they were talking about my manuscript. The officer was full of praise for it, saying that when it was in print he would recommend it to his pupils. Berman now introduced us and I was startled to discover that the officer was no less than Professor Kazachkov, the author of *Military Topography*, from which I had unashamedly stolen whole paragraphs. It was he who had reviewed my book. There and then we made a few minor corrections to my text, publication was approved, and I was paid.

At my request Berman wrote me out a paper stating that I was working for his publishing organisation on a contract. On the basis of that paper, without any questions being asked, I was issued a passport in Dmitrov. At last I could count myself a complete and lawful citizen of my country. Kazachkov invited me to join the circle of topographers that he led in his ministry. I went several times but now remember only the tasty fish-roe and ham sandwiches that were served at their meetings.

I had an idea for another text, *The History of Road Building*, but now learned that Berman's outfit had been liquidated and Berman himself moved to other work. I put the idea to the magazine *Young Guard* but they said the subject was not topical. I do not know that I could have brought it off, anyway. The book on topography was published and although it was nothing much to be proud of, it marked the beginning of my literary life. After the war it was twice reissued, and was a key element in my obtaining a pension. Poor Kazachkov, however, was arrested and his book declared an act of sabotage. The director of the publishing house, an old Bolshevik called Meshcheryakov, was also arrested. Kazachkov's erstwhile and daring pupils had his book published once more, more or less unchanged, but under their names.

The writer Zhitkov now recommended that the two stories of mine he had sent to the magazine the *Goldfinch* be published by Detgiz, the publishers of children's literature. I added a couple more to make up a small book. While awaiting publication, I happened to see on the back cover of an earlier book the names of the authors they planned to publish in the future – these included Pushkin, Krylov and Nekrasov, as well as other, now forgotten contemporary authors. It was quite a thrill for me to see at the bottom of the list, "S. Golitsyn – Short Stories". But when I went along to Detgiz to check on the situation, I was told the book would not be printed after all, as there was no paper. Later I discovered that the editors, Obolenskaya, Sher and Botkin, had all been arrested. That was the end of my literary career before the war.

I saw Zhitkov only once more when he came to Dmitrov to attempt to organise the transfer to the canal project of those writers and artists who were languishing in the distant prison camps of Siberia. He even hoped to plead for their release. I led Zhitkov to the office of the head of the canal camp, Firin, but there he was told that he could only see Firin in two hours' time. I left Zhitkov there, and was told how afterwards he went straight to the station, having achieved nothing. He died of cancer of the throat in 1938. Before he died, mother saw him and convinced him to make his confession and take final communion. With tears in his eyes he agreed and so she sent for the priest. Vladimir and I were far away from Moscow when, with a huge crowd of friends and relatives, together with mother and my sisters, he was taken to be buried. A requiem mass was said for him later, in secret.

10

Feeling that my attempts to become a writer were not getting anywhere, I knew that I must find work, and where else could I find work but on the building of the Volga-Moscow canal? A friend of Vladimir's, Sergei Sergeievich Baranov, who was head of a mechanical workshop, agreed to help me and took me to the office of the manager of the department dealing with stress in the concrete of the dams and locks that were being built, where he thought I might fit in. This man, Uginchus, questioned me thoroughly about my work, asked about my book on geodesy, then sent me on with my application form marked, "OK, recruit this man as a technician."

The personnel office was in the former monastery of Boris and Gleb. There, in what had been the refectory, I came face to face with a fair-haired, grim-faced NKVD man in a uniform without any badges of rank. Without a word, he handed me an eight-page form to fill in. As I sat there writing, I was treated to the spectacle of three technical institute graduates who were becoming ever more irritated as this official rejected their applications just because they had missed a line or crossed something out. Their protests evoked from him nothing more than a stony look and, grumbling to themselves, they were forced to start again.

A whole line of people, newly arrived from the train, waited in front of the NKVD man. I joined the back of the line. The three graduates went to the head of the queue, but once again their forms were rejected. They had obviously never come into contact with anyone from the NKVD and began to argue with him. He responded coldly and indifferently. They threatened to leave, at which he simply shrugged his shoulders. Complaining loudly, they marched out. I am sure young men with their training were desperately needed. I later heard a great deal about how intolerably that inveterate bureaucrat had always behaved. His name was Osipov.

My application was taken in to the head of the office. A lieutenant came out and called me in. He subjected me to a thorough grilling about myself, my parents, my relatives, my ancestors, what they had done, who had been arrested, and so on. He told me to go out and write everything down on a separate sheet and attach it to my application. "Don't leave anything out! We want the whole truth." Once again I sat at the table and saw and heard Osipov tormenting the applicants, who alternately went red, or pale, the sweat standing out on their faces, until they were told they had been accepted, when they went away greatly relieved.

My papers went in to the office. Again I had to wait. Then Osipov called my name. When I stood before him he said, with unconcealed contempt, "You're rejected. We can build the canal without you. You're just wasting our time." I saw that on my papers was written in big blue letters, "Rejected". Later Klavdia told me that on my return my face was the colour of ivory. Well, my situation was worse than two years before, when I had not been married or had a little son. And Kirov had not been assassinated. I could not understand why I had been rejected when so many former prisoners, former nobles and people of that sort were all working on the canal. Why me?

11

I knew that it would be a total waste of time to try and find work in Moscow. So I went on counting pigs, for which Klavdia received the payment, expecting to be listed as a man without rights – what today they call a "parasite". Father suggested writing to Peshkova and so, once again, I found myself at the office of the PRC on Kuznetsky Most, hoping to see that truly great woman of our times. Penetrating with difficulty past the waiting crowd, I asked the receptionist to announce my name, then continued through the waiting rooms where the mothers and fathers of prisoners waited their turn to plead their case with Peshkova. She greeted me warmly, asked about my sister Lina and her family in France, about my parents, my brother and sisters, learned that I now had a little son, and promised to help. She told me to come back in a week.

A week later I went through the same waiting rooms and the same crowd of petitioners. Peshkova told me she had raised my case "up there" and they had promised to help. I was to go to the secretary of Firin, the head of the Dmitrov camp, and say that Bulanov had telephoned about me.

"Who's Bulanov?" I asked.

"It doesn't matter," said Peshkova, smiling. "Just don't forget the name!" And she added that if things did not work out, I should come and see her again. It was only fifty years later that I read in the paper the name of Pavel Petrovich Bulanov. He had been the secretary of the OGPU and had been posthumously rehabilitated after being supposedly involved in the deliberate poisoning of Maxim Gorky.

I saw Peshkova only once more. It was 1962 at the birthday party given for Marshak, the children's writer and translator of Shakespeare's sonnets. Peshkova was now an old lady, but her skin was as clear as fine china and she was as dazzlingly beautiful as ever. Marshak was kissing her hand as she handed him a bouquet of flowers. She was then invited up on the stage. I waited with impatience for the end of the ceremony to have the chance to greet her, but she was surrounded by such a dense crowd, I simply could not reach her. I wrote a little note with my name and telephone number, eventually managing to put it directly into her hand as she was talking to someone. She took it without looking at me. I went away. For a whole month I waited in vain for her call. Then I decided to go to the museum in memory of Gorky on Malaya Nikitskaya Street. I was told that Ekaterina Pavlovna was not well. Not long afterwards, I read of her death, aged 84. May these few lines convey some little token of my gratitude; twice she saved me, once from prison, once when she helped me find work. I say nothing of the many thousands of unhappy people she saved from death. May her spirit rest in eternal peace.

25. The Moscow to Volga Canal

1

On my arrival in Dmitrov I already knew that I would have to present myself in person to Firin, the head of the canal project. I walked up the hill to the monastery of Boris and Gleb and entered an office out of which two doors led, the left one marked "Chief of Construction Moscow-Volga Canal, L.I. Kogan", the right one "Chief of Dmitlag and Deputy Head of Gulag, S.G. Firin". An NKVD man sat behind a table and considered me with the cold gaze that interrogators turn on prisoners. When I mentioned the name of Bulanov, his expression changed, he wrote down my name and disappeared into Firin's office. He was back in a moment and said briefly, "Go in!"

The inner office was a large room that struck me then as luxurious, with soft chairs and divans and a large conference table. Today, of course, most bosses have far better rooms. Behind a huge desk sat a stout general officer, dark-haired, with strong Jewish features. Not saying a word, he let his large and attractive eyes fix on me intently, like an adder hypnotising a frog. At first I met his gaze, but then was forced to lower my eyes. He held out his soft hand, which felt like a stick of bread. Then he said, and I quote the words of this all-powerful secret policeman literally, "So Prince Golitsyn has expressed the desire to work on the Moscow-Volga Canal?"

"Yes," I stammered, "I've nowhere else to go, and my parents live in Dmitrov."

"Why did you not, when you were rejected by the personnel office, come directly to me, instead of doing it in a roundabout way?"

"I thought my case was hopeless," I replied.

He stretched out his hand to a curious metal contraption with a tube on one end such as I had never seen, and never saw again – no doubt the work of a prisoner who was a self-taught engineer. He said, "The chief of personnel!" After a moment he continued, "Prince Golitsyn will be with you right away. Sign him on as a technician."

There was a sound of speech in the instrument. Firin raised his voice, "I repeat, sign Prince Golitsyn on at once!"

He pushed back the device, held out his soft hand again and said in a gracious voice, like a magnate addressing a serf, "I wish you success."

I uttered my thanks and raced over to the admissions' office, from there with a paper marked "OK, recruit" to the personnel section where Osipov caught sight of me and over the heads of the waiting applicants and shouted, "Golitsyn, bring me your application and documents!" Half an hour later I was on the staff of the canal project and had signed the "Top Secret" document that every employee had to sign, promising never to reveal, not even to one's nearest and dearest, anything of the work one was engaged in upon pain of a severe prison sentence pursuant to article such-and-such of the penal code.

2

Before continuing with my personal story, I want to describe the Gulag system, by which whole armies of prisoners worked on the massive construction projects of those years. At that time, the majority of the population had only the faintest awareness of this system; my wife's relatives had just about heard of the Dmitlag at Dmitrov, but nothing else. The thousands of eager young volunteers who were recruited had all signed the "Top Secret" document and were careful to hold their tongues. All this time the number of prisoners was rapidly increasing. Today, few people have ever heard of one of the cruellest laws of those times, the law of 7 August 1932, by which anyone caught taking any state property at all, whether a handful of hay, or a few ears of wheat, or some youths shaking an apple tree on a collective farm, was to be arrested. If the "criminal" was over twelve years of age, the sentence was ten years. The camps were full of such youngsters.

The legendary former currency trader, Frankel, who became a general in the NKVD, had developed a system of sweated forced labour on the White Sea canal project. If the worker worked his quota, he got his rations; if not, tough luck, he went without. Firin, however, who had been one of the chiefs on that same site, had developed a system by which prisoners could shorten their sentences by good work, a system known as *perekovka* (re-forging). The prisoners had the hope, if they worked well, of having their sentences reduced. Firin, both at the White Sea canal and in Dmitlag, also produced a weekly camp bulletin called *Perekovka*, in which the prisoners were referred to as "canal soldiers", a term which did not, however, catch on.

Compared to other camps, Dmitlag was relatively privileged. The special clothing issued was always of the best quality, the daily gruel more nutritious. Horrors such as occurred in Vorkuta, Kolyma and other camps were, so far as I know, unknown in Dmitlag. The prisoners did not look like the exhausted living skeletons described by Varlam Shalamov, Anatoly Zhigulin and other ex-prisoners. The camp commanders doubtless realised that it was not far to Moscow, which meant that one of the top leaders might pay a visit at any time.

The fact that prisoners were working on many other construction sites was kept secret. The only sites ever mentioned in the press in this connection were the White Sea project and, later, the Moscow-Volga canal. Actually, Firin himself often visited the prisoners' barracks. He could talk with their slang, and was popular. In general, Firin was a cultured man who visited the theatre in Moscow, knew Gorky and vied with other NKVD men in paying court to Nadezhda Alexeievna, Gorky's daughter-in-law. It was also on Firin's initiative that troupes of prisoner-actors were organised in the camps. He had presumably wanted to see me out of pure curiosity.

The life of the prisoners was one long Calvary of work. In a hod called a *marusya* they would carry earth from one place to another, doubtless dreaming of the reduction in their sentence they might earn. Free workers, such as myself, were strictly forbidden to talk to them except about work, though I sometimes did snatch a conversation with them and, cautiously looking over my shoulder, would take a letter to post for them. All work sites were surrounded by two rows of barbed wire, with watchtowers at regular intervals. The sentries who lurked there were contemptuously called *popki* (parrots) and entry to the "zone" was through a guarded gate where everyone, including the truck drivers, had to undergo a document check. Incidentally, it was only much later that one saw any trucks; at this time it was horses that were harnessed to the diggers. The truth is it was the prisoners who dug the bulk of the canal, laboriously hauling their *maryusas* up the slopes as fast as they could in their pairs, desperate to fulfil their quotas and so earn a remission in their sentence.

How many prisoners worked on the canal? The figure was a state secret known only to a few, but it was whispered that there were fifty thousand at first, then one hundred and fifty thousand. The true figure will only be found in the archives. In 1987, on the fiftieth anniversary of the project, many articles appeared in the press which made me grind my teeth in anger – they wrote of the early heroes of technology, the captains of science, the marvellous seamen and communications experts, of the first chief engineer Fiedman and his deputy Semyonov, of the number of excavators and diggers, the total mechanisation of the project. As I said, mechanisation only came in very late; in fact, the canal was dug by hand, the hands of prisoners. There was not a single article that dared mention those prisoners, even though the commemoration was taking place at the height of *perestroika*. Such a passing over in silence of the memory of all those who laboured on the project, many of whose bones lie there in the cold earth, is a piece of contempt and mockery that I hope these few lines will remedy, if only a little.

Since those anniversary articles made no mention of the prisoners, they naturally passed over in silence the existence of the huge NKVD apparatus of the camp of Dmitlag. I have already described the chief commander, Firin. In comparison with him and his like, the head of construction, Kogan, was a puny figure. Then there were all the NKVD officers who headed up the various sections in charge of both free workers and prisoners. These prisoners were known as *pridurki* (foolish ones). There was also a special section, a sort of NKVD within the NKVD, responsible for watching the others; it was they who sought out and persuaded prisoners to become informers.

For some reason, no mention was made of an outstanding leader, who was called "the soul of the Canal", Sergei Yakovlevich Zhuk, the chief engineer, a man who had never been imprisoned, had been deputy on the White Sea project and came to Dmitrov when only a few volunteer workers had started construction. I shall write of him later.

3

The superintendent's office consisted of two rooms in a little white house some way away from the management building, near the village of Podlipechya. Wooden buildings had been brought over from the White Sea canal to set up the club and canteen, as well as an entire settlement of barracks and associated buildings for the prisoners' camp, which was ringed by a barbed wire fence. But these were privileged prisoners with special passes that allowed them to move about the centre by day, only having to return to their barracks to sleep. Many of them wore jackets and ties and you would never have guessed they were serving sentences; others held important positions. Professor Sokolov, for example, had been deputy head of the geology section and before that on the staff of the Geological Institute in Moscow. As I described earlier, both he and my sister Masha had been arrested, but whereas she was released, he got ten years. Once, during his time on the canal, he decided to risk travelling to Moscow to attend his mother's funeral, trusting that in good clothes and wearing a hat he would not be noticed on the train by the ever-watchful NKVD. On the way back, however, he was picked up, and had to spend two weeks alternating between his management job by day and the dank and freezing punishment cell by night.

On site the prescribed working day was ten hours, with a free day every tenth. In the superintendent's office it was eight hours, followed by a three hour break and then back to the office until released by your chief. If there was urgent work to be done, you were sometimes there until midnight, or later. In the geology section, paradoxically, free workers who were *Konsomols* or members of the Party had to ask permission to finish their work from Professor Sokolov, a prisoner.

The evening before the day off was always a free evening and greatly treasured. A happy party of former prisoners, together with my brother Vladimir, his wife Elena and my sister Masha, would come together at Sergei Sergeievich Baranov's house in Dmitrov to sing and drink. Elena and Masha looked lovely, and the men were divided into two groups of admirers of either Masha or Elena. I only went to one of these jolly evenings, as I did not want to leave Klavdia and our little son Goga alone, and I did not like to forego my reading aloud, which we both much enjoyed. There was also another reason why I avoided Baranov's place; it was rumoured that there was an informer among them, and this turned out to be true, as two ex-workers on the White Sea project, Pokrovsky, the son of a priest, and the aviation designer Rayevsky, were soon arrested.

It was now the autumn of 1935. I had a pass that gave me access to the entire site. My boss, Uginchus, had sent me off to lock No. 3, which was close to the Yakhroma station. There was mud everywhere and the rain was pouring down, but I had been issued with a new trench coat and rubber boots. Up till now in my work I had usually been in a vehicle of some kind. Now, for the first time in my life, I came face to face with the great masses of prisoners, dragging their loaded *maryusas* with exhausted grey faces, indifferent to the world around them. And there was I in a new coat and new boots!

Suddenly a lieutenant came running up, shouting, "Get out of the way, get to one side!" I froze. Coming towards me was a group of overweight, high-ranking NKVD officers in their red-rimmed blue caps and impressive insignias of rank, led by a tall, lean man in uniform without insignias. I froze because I immediately recognised, from his huge portrait that hung on one of the lock gates, that this was none other than Yagoda himself. There is a painting by Serov of Peter the Great swaggering ahead of a group of overweight magnates who, jostling each other, struggle to keep up with him. This was just such a sight, with the great man striding ahead of his jostling generals, with the same angry expression as Tsar Peter's. I was staring at this man, who held the fate of millions in his hands, when I heard a voice crying, "Good morning, Golitsyn!" Turning, I saw that Firin was among the group of followers. I put my hand to my cap. The procession passed me only a few yards away.

When the canal was completed in 1937, my sister Masha was witness to the sight of a similar suite of leaders visiting the Yakhroma station, only this time it was Stalin himself at its head. What really struck her was the dark colour of his face and his small stature. She had eyes only for him and so did not notice who the others were. It was from the time of this visit by the great leader that A.N. Komarovsky, a young engineer, began his dizzying climb to the heights. Stalin had arrived unannounced and the head of engineering, Afanasyev, was absent, so Komarovsky accompanied him on his tour of inspection. After inspecting lock gate No. 3, Stalin took the young engineer on to gate No.4 and was so impressed by his comprehensive explanations that he recommended his promotion. After the war, Komarovsky was chief engineer for the entire NKVD program of works. He ended up as deputy minister of defence.

4

In 1935 bread rationing, which had been such a problem for my parents and Vladimir and his wife and children, was abolished. Stalin spoke the exalted phrase, "Life is better, life is happier!" which was of course picked up by all the papers. Actually, more and more people were being arrested. 1936 saw the promulgation of a new constitution guaranteeing all manner of freedoms, which changed nothing in people's lives. Voting rights were given back to the disenfranchised, but the catch question, "Have you or your relatives ever been deprived of voting rights – if so, where and when?" only disappeared a long time after the war. Children went on suffering for the "sins" of their parents.

Do people need that much? Klavdia and I were happy in our little house on Semenuka Street, not far from my parents flat. She had access to the canal food shop, which was off limits to ordinary citizens. Chopped wood was delivered to our door for our heating, and every day an elderly prisoner carried in our supply of water. Then she discovered that she was pregnant again, and what a torrent of indignant advice poured down on us from her five sisters. We had no proper home, my salary was miserable, we would find it impossible to manage and Klavdia should have an immediate abortion. But we were both believers, so we replied, "We cannot murder our unborn child. We'll have a second son."

My work was extremely tiring and I began to realise that my dream of becoming a writer would have to wait, for how many years I did not know. Every day I was out in the field with my assistants. Some were trusted prisoners, some of them priests, others former members of the *Konsomol*. In the evenings I had to stay in the office to do the calculations and draw the charts. This work was over-shadowed by our mistrust of each other, as none of us had any idea who might be the informer among us. A prisoner who had been condemned for raping an under-age girl, who we regarded with barely concealed disgust, once dropped a copy of the Gospels on my desk; I immediately put it away on the common bookshelf as it was clearly an act of provocation. I could not become close to anyone, and conversation was limited to "Please pass me that ruler!" or "Do you know what's happened to my pencil?"

Forty years on I met one of my colleagues from that office, Nikolai Petrovich Bulayevsky, now a professor in Tver, who had sat at the desk next to mine. We talked about our youth. I had not known that he was the son of a prisoner, an outstanding hydro-electric power technologist, and so the son of an "enemy of the people". He told me how he also had had a copy of the Gospels laid on his desk. This sort of provocation could be fatal. During the war Mikhail Rayevsky, my cousin twice removed, a doctor of mathematics and favourite pupil of academician Luzin, with a wife and newborn child and a brilliant career ahead of him, found a copy of Hitler's *Mein Kampf* on his desk. Some envious colleague must have deliberately placed it there. Casually he started to look through it and when his colleagues came in they were interested to know what he was reading. A few days later he was arrested and perished in the Gulag. His mother and sister were exiled to Siberia, where they too soon died.

5

Occasionally on our days off, Klavdia and I, carrying our son slung in the cloth bag I had sewn, managed to get to Moscow to visit her parents. If we stayed in Dmitrov on our day off, then we would have my parents to dinner, which they really loved. Father would have a glass of vodka tempered with St John's Wort. I preferred *zubrovka*, a vodka steeped in sweet grass. Mother would have only the tiniest taste. Klavdia was able to treat them to various delicacies. In Moscow we would stay with Klavdia's parents. Her father, Mikhail Vasiliyevich, a railway conductor, was an impressive old man with a slight resemblance to Bismarck. Until 1931, they lived in Voronezh in a house they had built with their own hands. One by one their children moved to Moscow, so they too followed, buying a tiny ten square metre room for the money they received for their five-roomed house in Voronezh. In Moscow, he had a job as doorman at one of the foreign exchange shops; he wore a braided uniform and kept at bay those naïve people who had neither vouchers nor foreign currency. He loved telling stories of his forty years as a train conductor. He was once, thanks to his imposing appearance, detailed to accompany Tsar Alexander III on his special train. The Tsar came out to go to the toilet and, meeting Klavdia's father in the corridor, asked him at some length about his work and his family. As he left, he gave Mikhail Vasiliyevich a gold ten rouble coin. In the 1930s the family, who were proud of this incident, kept very quiet about it and only told me under strict oath of secrecy.

Sergei Davydovich Golochevsky, the husband of one of Klavdia's sisters – Eudochia – and director of an organisation in Moscow, was summoned to the district Party headquarters. He was told that he had been in Moscow too long and must now go as supply manager to then little-known Kemerovo district in the Altai region of the country, where a large chemical plant was under construction. His letters from there were full of interest, and in particular he talked of one of the old Bolsheviks he had met there, Drobnis, who had been in the underground in the time of Kolchak and three times managed to escape being shot.

Within a year both Golochevsky and Drobnis returned to Moscow – the former to take up his old job, Drobnis to work in the Sovnarkom (Soviet People's Commissary). Then suddenly, Drobnis was arrested – it would seem he had been involved in some sort of opposition in Lenin's lifetime. A well-publicised trial, was organised also accusing him of sabotage in Kemerovo. Sergei Davydovich had strong communist principles and reported to the district Party office that he knew Drobnis. The secretary reproached him with lacking "communist watchfulness" and on the spot took away his Party card. Sergei Davydovich lived for some months in expectation of the disaster that was bound to strike him; he was arrested on the second of April 1937.

For the entire Bavykin family it was as if the house had collapsed on them. They had, up until then, believed everything they read in the papers and knew nothing of what was really happening in the country – that, to quote the great leader, "when you chop wood, the chips fly". Golochevsky was sentenced to five years. At first he was a privileged prisoner in one of the Siberian camps, allowed to write letters to his wife and receive food parcels. He wrote that he felt himself to be totally innocent, that he had sent a personal appeal to Yezhov himself (the new head of the NKVD) and was hoping to be freed. What in fact happened was that he was sentenced to twenty-five more years, and disappeared. The Bavykin family had been planning a massive celebration for the golden wedding anniversary of their parents, with a reception for a hundred guests in an expensive restaurant. With the arrest of Sergei Davydovich, all talk of celebration ceased. Fear had entered their lives.

A new calamity struck them in the autumn. Golochevsky's wife Eudochia, as the spouse of an enemy of the people, was summoned to report to the militia, who took away her passport and ordered her to depart into exile in Omsk within three days. She would be directed further on arrival there. She took her eight-year-old daughter with her, even though her sisters half-felt they ought to offer to look after the girl. Klavdia and I even thought about taking in little Valechka, but my own position was very shaky. In those days the relatives of disgraced persons were fearful of their connection with such individuals. Children were consequently often abandoned, ending up, if they were fortunate, in an orphanage. So Eudochia, who took Valechka with her, was sent on to a place called Cherlak, where she found work in the post office. Mother and daughter lived in a hovel.

During the war the Bavykins suffered another tragedy. Boris Alexandrov, the husband of Klavdia's fourth sister, an actor with the Red Army theatre and a man of considerable talent and character, was arrested just because he and a couple of colleagues had let slip an idle comment which was overheard by an informer. The three of them died in the Gulag.

6

The summer came, and with it, instead of Yagoda, came a new commissar for internal security, Yezhov. The huge portrait on the lock gate was replaced, but everyone felt utterly indifferent to the change. New slogans appeared on the canal sites, exhorting everyone to greater achievement. Days off were cancelled. An order was issued forbidding the voluntary workers from leaving the site of lock gate No. 5. We became prisoners of our work. Thanks to Uginchus, I was spared this separation from Klavdia, but many others languished away from their families.

Robbery was common around Dmitrov. Someone climbed into my quarters and stole the leather jacket that I had acquired in Gornoy Shorii. Then our house in Dmitrov was broken into by escaped prisoners, desperate to acquire civilian clothes. A murder occurred nearby; we went in fear of violence. In the autumn, I was still working on lock gate No. 5 when Klavdia began her contractions; I took her off to the maternity hospital, returning to my work in the evening. I was called in by Uginchus, who asked me how many children we had. I said I did not know. He looked at me with astonishment, and I explained about Klavdia's state. He then told me he wanted to promote me to senior technician, which would mean a raise of one hundred roubles a month. So on the day of the birth of our second son, Mikhail, it was not only my family that was added to, but also my salary.

Mikhail was christened in Moscow by my sister Sonya and brother-in-law Mikhail Vasiliyevich in the beautiful, five-domed eighteenth-century church of the Birth of Christ in the district of Palashy. The church of Vasily Kesariisk on Tverskaya-Yamskaya Street, where Goga (Georgy) had been christened a year and a half before, had been pulled down. The christening was done very quietly – in those days you could be arrested for such an act.

7

The year 1937 became known as the year of Yezhov, the head of the NKVD, and is usually now considered to have been the worst year of terror in the history of our country. I do not think that is true. For the peasantry, 1929 was the worst year, when the foundations of country life were destroyed by the collectivisation, exile and imprisonment of millions of innocent people. 1932 was also a terrible year for the peasants when the pernicious law called "seven-to-eight", by which petty pilfering was ruthlessly punished, came into force; knocking apples off a communal tree could be treated as a crime, with anyone over twelve years of age sent to prison for ten years for such insignificant peccadilloes. We, "former" people, had suffered arrest from the very beginning of the revolution; then from 1926 on, supposed "sabotage" was a common pretext for arrests. Mass arrests of Party members began after the murder of Kirov. There was the ugly slogan invented by Gorky: "If your enemy doesn't give himself up, liquidate him!" Then Stalin whipped up the concept of increasing class enmity. Arrests went in waves, with peaks and troughs. Our family had lived in fear of arrest from 1917; the Bavykin family only learned about fear in 1936.

Under Yagoda prisoners had often been released thanks to the intervention of so-called tame communists who protected certain families. Enukidze helped many, and Peshkova acted very energetically in the same way. Under Yezhov, however, intervention was fruitless. The PRC was shut down. Vinaver and other employees were arrested, but Yezhov did not dare to make a move against Peshkova, so she was left to remain idle, without outlet for her considerable talents and energy.

For "former people", 1937 started out quietly – that is, relatively. So many had already been sent to the camps or exiled. Then a new wave began; the exiled, who had served out their terms, were re-arrested. The fate suffered by my relatives in the Gulag is something hard to describe. The Bavykins also lived in fear, for them a new and unexpected experience. Golochevsky was arrested, and then even the relative who had once said to Klavdia , "One phone call from me, and your Sergei disappears for ever". The Bavykins had made friends with a family called Tomlenov, whose father had worked with my father-in-law on the railways. Their eldest son, a deputy commissar for communications, was arrested, so that up until the war his family lived in fear of further arrests. A friend of my father-in-law's, Colonel Polkovnik, a professor in the academy for armoured vehicles, was arrested. Klavdia's eldest sister's husband, Mozharovsky, an aircraft designer, quaked in his shoes as other staff in his office, including even the famous Tupolev, were put in prison. He was not arrested, continued to design fighter aircraft and ended up with the medal of the award of the Red Star.

We all lived in fear, but none of my family was arrested. On the canal project arrests took place from time to time, which of course meant that I lived under continual stress. One evening there were loud knocks at the door. I looked around at my family, thinking "this is the last time I'll see them". I went to the door and asked, "Who's there?" No answer. I asked again "Who's there?" Silence. I opened the door, but there was no one outside. There were footprints in the untouched snow. Who had knocked? Why? I never knew.

8

Construction of the canal was completed by the spring of 1937. The architecture of the different buildings, locks and pumping stations was outstanding. Little is now known about the talented architects and sculptors who were responsible for the design. No. 3 lock was the most original, its four towers topped by golden sculptures of Columbus's caravelles. The principal architect was a young and reputedly sympathetic expert, Friedland, who was no less than Yagoda's son-in-law. When his father-in-law was demoted to Commissar for Communications, Friedland's reputation became clouded over, and when Yagoda was liquidated, things looked very black for him. One morning the staff arrived to find their chief's door wide open, papers lying everywhere, and no sign of the occupant. The next day a brief announcement was posted, signed by the head of the whole project, informed them that the post of chief architect had been abolished, and Perlin, the head of section, was now in charge.

Under Friedland the top man in the department of architecture was Pyotr Dmitriyevich Kozyrev. A tall, bald man with large eyes and a lively expression, he liked to visit my brother Vladimir and his wife Elena and sometimes brought other young architects with him. They had lively discussions about art. He was considered the heart and soul of the canal and the fact that he saw and approved all proposed designs ensured a high degree of unity in the overall architectural design. In other countries and at other times he would have been a major figure. Instead, together with a good half of the section, he was arrested, never to be seen again. Perlin, who had certainly spread slander about him, rose to great heights, even to the extent of being awarded a Lenin prize.

Kozyrev's secretary was our cousin twice removed, Ekaterina Vladimirovna Davydova, whose beauty made people's heads turn and had given rise to her nickname, Beautiful Katya. Her life, however, turned out tragically. As early as the late 1920s her betrothed was shot, following which she married Anatoly Alexandrovich Zagryazhsky, only for him to be imprisoned. He worked on the canal as a prisoner and was released when it was completed, but the couple only enjoyed married life for a short time. Now Katya herself was arrested; she disappeared. Zagryazhsky became a successful engineer on the Ryabinsky hydro-electric project; he was also an accomplished poet, and I can attest to the quality of his poems. Sadly, after the war, when dark clouds were gathering over his career, his wife burnt all his poems, so that now there is not a single copy extant.

How much tragedy flowed from Yagoda and his likes.

9

The great day arrived when the very first steamer could navigate the canal. On the first of May 1937 a splendid new vessel sailed up from the Volga, all white and yellow. It proudly bore the name *Josef Stalin* on its bow, its lifeboats and lifebuoys. We all rushed down to the quay, where there was such a crowd that even chief engineer Zhuk, who had just come up in his car, could not elbow his way through. The people on board waved and cheered; we waved and cheered back at them. The programme was for some of the passengers to disembark here and others to embark for the trip to Moscow. Just then one of my colleagues in the superintendent's office appeared but, far from looking thrilled with the occasion, he looked quite worried.

He whispered, "Firin has been arrested, And Puzitsky. They were taken off the ship at Tempy this morning."

I can't believe it, I said to myself. Only yesterday the papers had been full of photographs of Kogan, Firin and Zhuk – respectively head of construction, of Dmitlag and of engineering, whilst Puzitsky was Firin's right hand man and in charge of the ultra-secret section of the NKVD. But our country was capable of the most arbitrary actions. My colleague moved on to spread the news and it was soon obvious how much less cheerfully we regarded the great day. That evening a celebratory concert took place in the Park of Culture and Leisure in Moscow. Stalin and other leaders, although expected, did not deign to attend. The concert was a long one; during it the black vans of the NKVD were lurking in the shadows; as they left, many were picked up in those "black crows". They were basically rounding up close and high ranking colleagues of Yagoda. I have already written of the arrests made amongst the architects, and of our Elena's cousin, Dmitry Gudovich, a former count, already twice sentenced. They took Polivanov, a former Tsarist officer and son of a minister of the Tsar. I could name many others. It was whispered that the arrested had already been executed in Dmitrov. So our celebration was poisoned by fear.

Some people, however, received medals. A contemporary joke said you could tell medal-bearers from behind by the fact that in the baking hot weather, when everyone else was in shirtsleeves, they wore their jackets. Commemorative lapel badges were given out, but I was not included on the list, probably deliberately. I did, however, receive a bonus of five hundred roubles in Dmitrov and three hundred and fifty in Iksha. As for the prisoners, they all expected a major amnesty to be declared, but in this they were bitterly disappointed. Those who had worked particularly hard, hoping for a reduction in their terms, received nothing. Only those who had served their time were freed.

One man, who had worked with me on No. 5 lock, begged me to get him civilian clothes as he intended to run away. I refused to go along with this plan, begging him to sit out his term. He ignored my advice and made his escape. I was closely questioned by the secret police and blamed for lack of watchfulness, but that was all. I suffered only an acute bout of fear.

10

The fact that the first vessel had sailed along the canal did not mean that it was completely finished. Secondary construction remained to be done. Half-finished buildings out of view of the waterway needed to be completed and the banks were to be planted with trees. The canal had now been handed over to the Commissariat of water transport. All volunteer workers were divided into sheep and goats. The goats, that is ex-prisoners, were sent on to other construction work; the sheep, who had no prison record, stayed to operate the canal. Which was I – a goat or a sheep? The superintendent's office remained in place, as it was needed to deal with the inevitable cracks and subsidence that would occur. Uginchus called me in and asked whether I would like to stay; my answer was obvious; my parents lived here in Dmitrov, and it was not far from Moscow.

A few days later he told me he had talked to the general manager, who was willing to keep me on despite my title. So I moved from NKVD employment to working for the commissariat of water transport. My working day became a standard one of eight hours, with no evening shifts and Sundays free. I was able to be with my children at bedtime and to take up again the pleasant habit of reading aloud to Klavdia. A month passed. Uginchus was away on some trip and our office was being managed by his deputy, Tsyplakov, a Party member and engineer by training but someone who understood nothing about technical matters. I feared him instinctively . Unexpectedly I was called into the personnel office. Behind a desk sat a puny little man in sailor's uniform. He asked me to sit down and I could see my file in front of him. Without any preliminaries, he said he wanted me to write out and sign my voluntary resignation.

I asked for three days to think about this; I could not decide my fate so quickly. He began to reproach me with the palaces I had lived in, the peasantry I had exploited, the life of luxury I had always enjoyed. I countered that there had never been any palaces, that my father had spent his whole life working in ordinary jobs, and I referred to the newly promulgated constitution and to Stalin's words – sons are not responsible for their fathers. He got up and, going to the door, locked it, saying that I would not be allowed to leave until I had signed the paper. I could have killed that puny man with a single blow, but all I could do was sit in front of him, hanging my head. He said there were other ways of getting rid of me, and crossed his ten fingers in a crude representation of prison bars. He pushed forward paper and pen, but my hands trembled so that he himself wrote out the text of my resignation. After I had signed, without a word he got up and opened the door for me. I stumbled back to the office.

There was no point in my going to Uginchus's deputy, Tsyplakov. I dealt with a couple of routine matters first, then went to see my immediate chief, an engineer called Martsinovsky. What I told him about my situation aroused his sympathy. Knowing the secretary of the chief engineer of the entire canal project, he without delay rang him up and arranged for me an appointment with Zhuk, chief engineer of the whole project, who was still in Dmitrov. Stalin had recently ordered all managers to work at night, so I was not surprised when he told me my appointment was for four in the morning. I went home. Klavdia of course immediately saw how upset I was, as were my parents when I told them the story. My father was particularly distressed and, as usual, took all the blame on himself; he saw himself as the source of all the troubles that fell on our family.

Zhuk was a man of great ability and quickness of mind. At my early morning interview, after asking me a couple of questions – and incidentally, saying that he knew Riedeger and had seen Riedeger's strange round house from a distance – he advised me not to try to hang on at Dmitrov, pointing out that from now on the work would be monotonous, but that I should transfer to Kuibyshev, where a major hydro-electric project was about to start under his direction. As he showed me out, he said that if I had any other difficulties, I should let him know.

11

At this time, Masha was still working in the geological section of the canal project. She had been studying in the evenings and so gradually improving her qualifications and achieving promotion. Her superiors valued her as a hard-working and cheerful person. The prisoners loved her, too, calling her simply Masha. With great discretion she was able to take their letters to the post. In my work I often had to discuss things with the geologists and had got to know the deputy head of the section, Elena Konstantinovna Kozlovskaya. I now asked Masha to see if she could arrange for me to work in her section. I was taken to see Kozlovskaya, an impressive figure in her military uniform; she was not so much beautiful as striking in appearance. In turn she took me in to see her boss, Valerian Alexeievich Sementsov, who was Zhuk's deputy. Semenstov had a large, pockmarked face and little pigs' eyes. He fixed me with a sharp, searching gaze, and after a while announced that he could take me on for the Kuibyshev hydroelectric project as senior technician-geodecist.

With that began a lengthy process of recruitment. The weather was baking hot. In those days there was little ventilation, so people had to sit for long hours in stifling heat as the bureaucratic procedures were gone through. There were queues at every office. Staff were being taken on for Rybinsk, others for Uglich, as well as for Kuibyshev. I discovered that Sementsov had written on my papers, "Recruit as a new member of staff", which meant that I did not receive a month's salary as an allowance for my transfer.

I was not, however, in any hurry to move. I had the money from my two bonuses and wanted to remain with my family as long as possible. And there was another, more important reason to linger; my sister Masha was about to marry. She was now twenty-six-years old, and had always said that she would only marry a man who was more intelligent than herself. The many suitors who clustered around her, some attractive, some not, she kept at a distance, enjoying herself in their company but never encouraging them to hope for more. Finally, she did meet an intelligent man, eleven years her senior, someone with a philosophic turn of mind. I had already met Vsevolod

Stepanovich Veselovsky four years earlier when he was head of the mineral laboratory where Valery Pertsov, my sister Katya's husband, worked. Vsevolod came from an old, noble family of Polish origin. His forefathers had been academics under the Tsars, and his father, the historian Stepan Borisovich, had managed to escape arrest with other historians in the early 1930s thanks to posting himself to work on the archives of the monasteries of Kostroma, deep in the forests beyond the Volga. He only returned to Moscow when the danger was past.

Katya and Valery Pertsov, with their two little children, had rented a *dacha* near Dmitrov in 1936. Vsevolod visited them there, and it was there that he first met Masha. She hurried in straight from work in her special clothing. After she left, Vsevolod asked to know more about this attractive, fair-haired girl. That winter they met again at some concerts in Moscow, and from the following spring of 1937, he began to court her seriously, coming specially to see her in Dmitrov on his days off, walking out with her, and one day making her a gift of Goethe's *Faust* inscribed to Masha with the words "From Dr Faust". Masha recognised that he was more intelligent than her, slowly developed warm feelings for him and, in due course, accepted his hand.

It was decided not to delay the wedding. We were all very happy for Masha, although my parents were disturbed by the fact that Svevolod was a declared atheist. They got him to promise that he would not prevent Masha from attending church. To the sadness of her colleagues at work, Masha resigned her job, but she told them she was being replaced by her brother, "an even better worker". The church we chose for the wedding was the Sretenskaya, as the Tukhvinskaya had been closed down and the church in Podlipechya was too close to the canal workers' village.

Not very many people came, and those that did made a point of arriving by twos and threes, not in a large crowd. Masha only put on her veil at the entrance to the church. The couple had one groom each – Vsevolod had his younger brother and Masha had her cousin, Alyosha Komarovsky, the son of our second cousin, once a count and also a recently released prisoner. Masha's prayerful face reflected the joy and dedication she felt, whilst Vsevolod stood tall and handsome by her side, accepting the necessity of this ritual occasion. There was a joyful reception at our parents' place, which was suddenly cast into gloom when beautiful Katya's mother began asking why her daughter, although invited, had not come to the wedding. It was immediately obvious that she had been arrested.

The happy couple were seen off at the station. They stood waving to us on the steps of the carriage. All I could think was, "Get going, get going as fast as possible, or they'll arrest you!" In those days, a timely departure had saved many an individual from that calamity.

26. Work in the Sok Valley

1

I was not at all happy at leaving my wife and sons, but I had no choice and immediately after Masha's wedding set off for Kuibyshev. I spent the first night there at the home of a distant cousin of ours, Sofia Medem, whose brother Fedya had been at college with Vladimir, and who herself had been a pupil with my sister Sonya at the Alferov gymnasium. She greeted me warmly. She was living alone. Her mother had died of typhus just after the revolution, her brother had joined up in Kolchak's army and then escaped to Germany, where he was employed as an estate manager on lands belonging to the Bismarcks. Her younger sister, Dina, was working in some other town.

Sofia Medem was a highly qualified specialist in the selection of wheat, oats and barley seed and much appreciated in her post at the local seed production farm, but when I arrived she had just been sacked quite unexpectedly and was in the process of collecting testimonies to help her get her job back. She told me how meanwhile she had a job in the town library sorting out books by "enemies of the people"; these were taken away to be burned; she had also to black out the names of "enemy" publishers and tear out introductions by now-disgraced people.

The two Lvov brothers, nephews of the Prince Lvov who had been Prime Minister in 1917, also lived in Kuibyshev, to which they had been exiled after the death of Kirov in Leningrad. Sofia said she would take me to see them shortly. In the morning, she accompanied me to the offices of the hydroelectric project and I never saw her again. When I went back to her place a few days later to collect a suit I had left there, I found the door sealed. The owner of the house told me Sofia had been arrested the evening before, as had the two Lvov brothers. I was too scared to visit their wives. Thus Yuri and Sergei Lvov, and Sofia Medem, disappeared for ever. I recovered my suit only a year and a half later.

2

The actual construction of the Kuibyshev hydroelectric plant had not yet begun. Local geologists and surveyors were still prospecting the area. When Zhuk and Sementsov and the other chiefs arrived, they were determined to speed things up, familiar as they were with pressures on the part of the NKVD.

Sementsov sent me off to work forty kilometres away in the village of Staro-Semeykino on the banks of the river Sok, a tributary of the Volga. I got to within six kilometres on a local bus, walking the last stretch. Two geologists who had worked on the Volga-Moscow canal were there to meet me. Neither had good reputation – Fedotov had been in the camps, whilst Troitsky was the son of a priest. After looking at my documents, Fedotov exclaimed, "It's taken you a long time to get here!" It was true that it was a good two weeks; I made some excuse or other; I could not say that I had stayed for Masha's wedding.

Waiting for the arrival of my surveying instruments, I reconnoitred the area. Primarily I was looking for somewhere for my family to come and join me. This turned out to be out of the question. The village was quite a large one, with perhaps a hundred and fifty houses, but the inhabitants, who were Mordvinians, were poor and lived poorly. Most houses were thatched; many had no floor. I lodged in a big, one-roomed house with a family that consisted of mother and father, three children, the father's brother, some young lad and the grandmother, who stank of urine. She had the only bed, and there was a table and some benches. The rest of us slept on the floor. I realised I could not bring Klavdia and our sons here; we would have to live apart, for how long I could not tell. Barracks for the team were supposed to be built, but no one could tell when. My letters home were sad ones.

My geodesic instruments arrived. I hired three local girls to assist me. I had to get them to sign the usual paper about never breathing a word about their work; the sight of this paper frightened them and it took me a lot of persuasion to get them to sign. I covered a lot of the local territory. That year the harvest was abundant but could not be adequately gathered in, and I came across fields of overgrown wheat and rotting stokes of corn that were being eaten by wild geese. The river Sok, rather overgrown by bushes, was a swift-flowing, bendy river that formed small lakes where the land was flat. Hills covered by dense bushes rose directly behind the village.

One day, I was doing some surveying work with my level when I noticed the arrival of a sedan car. I trained my instrument on it and watched as a heavy-built man got out and began slowly walking through the uncut wheat towards me. It was Zhuk, head of the whole project.

"Greetings, Golitsyn!" he cried, holding out his hand. "What are you doing here?"

I was proud that he had recognised me and answered him briskly, knowing that he liked brevity of speech.

"What's the reading we're standing at?" he suddenly asked.

Large-scale maps were not then considered top secret. I had been given a map of the area of Staro-Semeykino and had studied it thoroughly. So now, instead of muttering some sort of rough figure, as a less experienced surveyor might have done, I was able to rap out the exact figure. Zhuk bent to peer through the lens, swivelling the instrument around the whole plain. He was clearly trying to picture how high the future reservoir would reach. When he straightened up, he asked me how I was faring and whether I was happy in my work. I replied that I was very content; I could not say that I was miserable about being away from my family. In fact, I was very happy with my work; I felt I was able to show initiative – in other words, I had a degree of independence. I watched Zhuk leave with gratitude in my heart. That was the kind of leader he was, remembering the names of his staff, concerned for their welfare, even for small fry like me. Not like today's big bosses.

Staff and workers now began arriving at the site. Drilling and sampling got under way. I staked out my survey lines, showing where drilling was to be done. Prisoners arrived and built themselves the "zone", in other words barracks surrounded by barbed wire, as well as a separate barrack for free workers. Masha had alerted me about Tsarev, head of the geological team. "Try not to end up under his command," she had warned me. "He's not only a nasty piece of work, but also an informer." And it was Tsarev who arrived as boss of the geologists, and he was exactly as Masha had described him: a coarse, rude and illiterate man who could only manifest his leadership by shouting, cursing and banging his fist on the table. He was in charge for a whole year before the combined complaints of his staff became so vociferous that Sementsov was forced to move him. Sementsov had been given the ultimatum – it's either him or us!

The geologists were a fine group of intelligent and likeable people. I made a special friend of Vsevolod Sakharov, the son of the stern Vyacheslav Sakharov who had been my boss in Gornoy Shorii. His son had studied as an external student, and was now the senior geologist on site. With his strong Armenian features, large nose, heavy eyebrows and big, dark eyes, he must have been a very handsome youth. He was cultured and had read a great deal. Our conversations were always lively and interesting. He could sense that I was sad about living away from my family, especially as he, too, was separated from his wife, who was in Moscow. We talked of art and literature and life, but there were certain subjects that we avoided, a boundary that we never crossed. If by chance we mentioned politics, the failure of the Five Year Plan, the arrests, we quickly passed on to other topics. We were never a hundred percent sure of each other; I had learned by bitter experience to be very careful about trusting anybody; whilst Vsevolod, just like many others, must have asked himself how it was that this prince had survived.

The geologist, Boris Leonov, and his wife, Katya Apasovaya, arrived in Staro-Semeykino. Both had been students at Leningrad University. In the early 1930s, Boris was sent to the camps as one of the group of so-called "Gilded Youth". I would, of course, have liked to ask him about this group, but did not. Once, when we were sitting together over a glass of vodka, he revealed that he had been in the same camp as Father Pavel Florensky, the famous philosopher, and that Florensky, whilst in prison, occupied himself by studying the nature of permafrost. When I asked how he had died, I got no answer. Thereafter Boris never spoke about Florensky to me. Today, researchers have remained incapable of ascertaining how Florensky died.

3

The old Bolshevik, Postyshev, is nowadays described as a loyal and orthodox Party member who, amongst other things, re-established our New Year's holiday. In the 1930s, he was Party Secretary of the Central Volga *obkom* (regional government) and was as bloodthirsty an executioner as Eiche in Western Siberia and Sheboldayeth in the Northern Caucasus. I could mention others. I have already written about Eiche, whilst as for Sheboldayeth, I have read about him in the writings devoted to the author, Sholokhov. Those three bigwigs died under torture, but that was only later when it was suddenly remembered how many people they had killed, including practically half the communists in their own regions.

The regional newspaper, *The Volga Commune*, carried angry articles about the arrest of wreckers and saboteurs in the factories and the villages. Court cases similar to the trials in Moscow were organised in Kuibyshev. One or other district would be selected and the entire Party apparatus, from the Secretary down, arrested. There were whole articles about the crimes that had been exposed. In court the accused confessed to giving poison to their cows or horses, throwing nails into the thresher and dropping dead mice into bread dough. And the accusers never failed to be present and make heated statements. Articles appeared describing factory and village meetings where everyone cried out: "death to the enemies of the people!" Our district central office was in Krasny Yar some twelve kilometres away; there the entire staff were arrested and the local newspaper printed their confessions and the angry speeches of denunciation that were delivered. It was whispered that two members of our hydroelectric personnel had been arrested – NKVD men, not ex-prisoners. A huge investigation was started when a swastika drawn in chalk was discovered on Zhuk's car.

Even simple citizens were arrested. One morning our rodswoman, Tanya, arrived in tears. Her seventeen-year-old brother had stood by the roadside trying to hitch a lift to Kuibyshev. He put out his hand, and a car with only the driver in it stopped and picked him up. He sat in the back, as happy as can be. Then the driver took him straight to the NKVD office and he was accused of political hooliganism and given a five year sentence. I do not know who committed this vicious deed.

Here is another story. Our survey party was sent two girl technical students for a period of practical training. The geologists had no work for them so they passed them on to me. I had little use for them either; I explained some of the tricks of my trade to them, and in general was rather distracted by their presence. One day I noticed that they showed signs of being upset; thinking I might have caused this, I asked them what was disturbing them. They told me that one of their fellow students, a friendly lad, top of his class, a good sportsman and a *Konsomol*, had been arrested one night and taken away. It was said that he had said something to someone, but nobody knew what or to whom. The girls remained under my supervision for two months; I made every effort to raise their spirits. I can only imagine the student ended up in the Gulag.

And a third story: this happened when I was no longer working in Staro-Semeykino. I was spending the night in Kuiybyshev at the home of the parents of a young school-leaver, Sasha Grebenshchikov, who had started to work on my team. The father was a Party member, the director of a psychiatric home and, incidentally, a very

plump man. Suddenly, he was arrested. It was most likely his subordinates had denounced him. Two months later he was back home,
and so thin that he had to wear his son's trousers. This happened at
the end of 1938, when Yezhov was moved to the Commissariat for
Water Transport, and Beria took his place at the NKVD. At first Beria
wanted to play the good, humane leader, so he released a very
limited number of prisoners, which is how Grebenshchikov got out.

Very soon the press reported that the Commissariat for Water
Transport had been divided into two; inland waters and the high seas,
and named the two chiefs; there was no mention of Yezhov at all.
People joked that Yezhov had been divided into two, and were
delighted. This kind of secret, silent liquidation of Stalin's henchmen began in 1938. The ordinary citizen only got to know of these
disappearances from the photographs of the leaders on the stage at
anniversaries, or when their photos were surreptitiously removed
from window displays. Thus did Marshal Blucher, Politburo member
Rudzutak and the bloodthirsty Postyshev, Sheboldayev and Eiche
meet their ends; first they were imprisoned, then executed.

4

I go back to the beginning of 1937. Klavdia and I were miserable at
being separated. Our letters to each other were full of sadness. She
wrote that she would be happy to sleep on the floor with the children
if it meant we could be together. Finally, a barrack for free workers
was built, and a room allotted to me off the long corridor that ran
down the middle, with the kitchen at one end. I immediately moved
in, even though I had not a stick of furniture. I planned to beg for
some wood and have a local carpenter build me beds, a table and
chairs; Klavdia would bring the plates and cutlery. My dream did
not materialise. The hard frosts started. I shared a stove in the
corridor with my neighbour, but however much wood we burned,
we were frozen. Lying on my straw mattress I shivered uncontrollably
through the nights. By morning the water in our buckets was solid
ice. It was out of the question for my family to move in. I got a heart-
rending letter from Klavdia.

The geologist Igor Bonch-Osmolovsky, a lively, self-assured, snub-
nosed man, and very good company, who had earlier been
incarcerated for belonging to the "Gilded Youth" group of Leningrad
students, was in the same situation. Together, by promising to come
to work in whatever weather and at any time, we got permission from
Tsarev to lodge six kilometres away in Novo-Semeykino where there

were well-built houses. I rented space in a *kulak's* house, occupied by a widow and her two children. It was the best house in the village, but there was one snag, which I only discovered later. That was that the widow ran an illegal pub. I found that my colleagues at work who lived in Kuybyshev would stop off in the widow's house on their way back to Staro-Semeykino, eat and drink and then stumble off into the night for the rest of their journey. Once or twice they got me to join them, but I was not keen on such drinking bouts, preferring to drop in on Bonch for a chat.

Finally, we received telegrams announcing the arrival of our families. We were assigned a truck, collected our wives and children at the station and after work, tired and frozen, I had a tasty meal, played with the children and rejoiced in Klavdia's presence. Our landlady continued to operate her illegal inn, which did not bother us too much as she carried on this operation in her kitchen, but I was worried that the militia would suddenly raid her and I would be pulled in for failing to denounce her. I was always very much aware of my vulnerability.

What actually happened was quite different. Klavdia was away in Kuiybyshev to visit the dentist, leaving me looking after the children on my day off. In the evening a large group of drillers and other workmen had a jolly evening drinking in our landlady's kitchen, myself among them. When it was over, I put the children to bed and went to sleep. In the morning the landlady told me that after we had all left another man had turned up; he had had some drinks and then walked off into the night. I thought nothing of this, went to work with my girl assistants and at the end of the day turned in my instruments in the office. There I was shocked to be told that a driller, Simonov, who had been to our landlady's the evening before, had been found with a battered head lying in the snow that morning. He was in the hospital, and might even now be dead. An investigator had arrived and questioned some of my colleagues; now he wanted to see me.

A plump man, with an apparently friendly manner, was sitting behind a desk in our office. Hearing my name, he brightened up. The questioning began; where was I born, where christened, and so on. To my surprise, the blank form he was filling in did not include any question about my social origins. When he had finished, he leaned back in his chair and stared at me in silence for a long time, just as my interrogator had done in the Lubyanka nine years before. I felt fear in my stomach.

"Tell me," he began in a gentle, sweet voice, "what did you hit Simonov with? A knife, or was it an axe?"

I jumped up and heatedly replied that I had not seen Simonov. He had arrived at the landlady's when I was already in bed.

"The landlady has told me you and Simonov sat drinking and fell to quarrelling. She heard it all from her kitchen. Then Simonov left." All this the man uttered in a soft voice, with a smile on his face.

I realised that he had already been to my house and had managed to get the woman to tell these lies.

The investigator went on, "Your colleagues all describe you as hot-tempered."

I plainly denied all this, including my hot temper. I had never raised my voice or quarrelled with anyone. I was worried that he would start asking about my title, but above all, I was frightened that he would arrest me on the spot. However, this did not happen. I returned home to Novo-Semeykino. The investigator then went to the hospital and questioned Simonov, and it turned out that it was two men who had attacked him on the road. He had got away from them. That same day we all learned that two prisoners had escaped the day before. So all suspicion was lifted from me. And yet I could easily have been arrested and sentenced.

Tsarev called a meeting and forbade further drinking at my landlady's; in any event, the investigator had frightened her out of her wits so that she shut down her illicit operations. Later, she told me that when the man had questioned her about me, she had done nothing but speak praise of me. I was glad that Klavdia only learned of this affair long after it was all cleared up. Only Bonch was amused, saying, "You've managed to avoid prison under article 58, but you nearly got it for attempted murder!"

5

Many events occurred in that winter of 1937, whether in our country, in the central Volga region, or just in our reconnaissance party. Sakharov and Leonov went to work elsewhere and our new senior geologist, Serafim Grigoriyevich Sokolov, nicknamed Sixwinged Seraphim, arrived. He also settled in Novo-Semyekino, so naturally we came to know him well. In the evenings he played with our children, drank tea with us and we talked a lot. He had worked on the Moscow-Volga canal, in the southern sector, where I had got to know him. He had never been in prison, but I instinctively knew that he had joined the canal because other organisations would not take him. Although his name was ordinary, he was clearly of noble origin; doubtless his father had been some sort of high official before the revolution.

Sixwinged Seraphim was a completely honourable man. He became an outstanding geologist. Thanks to his strength of character he managed to get the arrogant Tsarev transferred somewhere and in his place hired a resident of Kuibyshev, Ivan Anashkin, after which our work went along happily and efficiently.

In the summer of 1938, our geological prospecting showed that the left bank of the river Sok was undermined by cavities, a phenomenon scientifically known as karst. The managers were worried. Water would leak under and behind any dam built there. Special drills were imported from Sweden, regardless of the cost in foreign exchange, but they gave the same results.

Eventually a special commission was sent. We had in the meantime collected all relevant cores from our drilling, drawn charts and plans of everything we had discovered about the situation. The commission consisted of Zhuk and Sementsov, academician Arkhangelsky, and others. They arrived with colleagues in a string of vehicles, quickly ate sandwiches and drank mineral water straight off the bonnets of their cars, then held this most important meeting.

Sixwinged Seraphim reported on our case with great skill. We were immensely proud of his performance. He replied to every question firmly and clearly. When the consultation was over, the big bosses shook hands only with him, disregarding we mere mortals gathered around. The convoy roared off. Klavdia, leading away our sons heard Georgy, say "When I grow up I'll be an academician!"[26]

The decision was taken that, to prevent leakage, a thick, tamped stratum of heavy clay would be layed along the bed of the Sok up against the natural rock formation on the left bank.

6

In the summer of 1938, work began on the branch railway line that would run up to the hydroelectric power plant. The workers digging the line were prisoners from Central Asia, so-called *basmachi* who had opposed Soviet rule. They were a mixture of young and old and wore multi-coloured robes; many of them had fine features and were very handsome.

---

26. *Forty-nine years later he was made a member of the Academy of Sciences of the USSR.*

Walking past them one day, their guard came towards me shouting, "Stop! Lie down!" I stopped in astonishment. He again shouted, "Lie down!"

"Are you mad?" I asked. "I'm returning from my work. I'm a free worker."

"Show me your papers!"

All I had in my bag was a notebook covered with figures. I showed them to the guard. "Show me your passport!" he ordered.

I did not have it on me. I did not lie down, but I did sit. It was the stupidest of incidents. He accused me of being a runaway prisoner. My girl assistants came by and tried to talk sense into the guard, at which he began to threaten them. They treated him with scorn, which only made him furious. I begged them to get my wife to bring my passport. The prisoners, the Uzbeks, Tadjiks and Turkmens, watched all this with complete indifference from under their long eyelashes.

Klavdia arrived in a panic, handing my passport to the guard. He refused to look at it. Klavdia left to raise the alarm in the office. The commander of the guards and my boss, Anashkin, came running up. The guard tried to justify himself, saying I had resisted and cursed him. I denied this and nodded in the direction of the prisoners, saying they could confirm what I said. But it turned out prisoners could not bear witness at all. As Anashkin, the commander and I walked away, the latter defended his man's actions, saying he could have shot me and it would have been justified. It was necessary always to be watchful. Watchfulness – next to the name "Stalin", that was the word most beloved of journalists and political agitators.

The commandant of the prison camp was a certain Kolbasyuk who lived with his wife, child and a nanny in our barracks building. Klavdia made friends with his wife and taught her how to prepare tasty meals, how to sew dresses and how to look after her child. I told Klavdia to break off this friendship with the wife of such a man, but Klavdia insisted that the woman was a poor creature who lived in fear of her husband. One day our little son fell ill with terrible stomach cramps; his temperature went up alarmingly. He would neither eat nor drink and was clearly failing fast. We managed to get the camp paramedic to come and see him, but it was soon clear he had little medical knowledge and no medicines of any kind. Then the Kolbasyuks' nanny appeared, muttered something over the child and told us to give him a distillation of the bark of the oak tree with a little sugar. Whether it was the words muttered by the nanny, or the distillate, but within two days little Misha was totally recovered. Klavdia was enormously grateful and asked the nanny whether we could do anything for her. The woman then revealed to my wife that she was not a real nanny, but had got herself the job so as to be near her husband, who was one of the prisoners in that camp. Everyday she would go out with her little charge to stand by the place where the prisoners were led past and she and her husband could exchange imperceptible nods. In reply to my wife's question, she asked us to get a note to her husband. I felt pity for the woman, but had to refuse this request, as we were strictly forbidden to talk to any of the prisoners. Later that year, Kolbasyuk discovered her stratagem and sacked her.

7

Klavdia was pregnant with our third child, and as conditions were difficult where we were, I reluctantly sent her away to Dmitrov to live with my parents, who were delighted with the prospect of their little grandchildren coming under their care. There was space for Klavdia and our two sons as Vladimir, together with his family, was at this time curing his bad knee in Gaudaty, Abkhazia, while painting the landscape of the Black Sea coast. A wave of arrests was taking place all over this southern land, including their much-loved leader Lakoba, but a sick Moscow artist did not attract the attention of the secret police.

Father and I exchanged letters. It was crystal clear to him that war was inevitable, but he could only say, this safely in proverbs, as all letters were then being opened. When I read "Two beggars can sleep soundly in one bed, but the world is too small for two potentates", I knew exactly what he meant.

In December 1938, I learned that Klavdia had given birth to a healthy son, our third child, who we named Sergei. Unexpectedly, Vladimir and family returned to Dmitrov. A professor of medicine on leave in the Caucasus, Dimitri Yazykov, had examined Vladimir's knee and arranged for it to be operated on in Moscow. The operation was successful, but Klavdia had perforce to move to her parents' tiny room in Moscow. Taking leave a month later, I found my wife and children crammed into these inadequate quarters, and Klavdia in tears, telling me that both our younger sons were dying. A lady doctor examined them and declared their condition to be serious, and indeed, three days later, little Seryozha died. My father-in-law and I knocked a tiny coffin together, wrapped it in a blanket and took it by tram to the Dorogomilovskoye cemetery. There we borrowed a spade, dug a hole alongside the grave of my Golitsyn grandmother and laid the infant beside her. Not long after, the order came to do away with the cemetery; my sister Sonya managed to collect the remains of our grandmother and my little son, reburying them in the Vostryakovskoye cemetery, which in turn was destroyed during the war.

My sad furlough came to an end. I had to return to Kuibyshev. I decided that we could live as a family in my one room providing we managed to heat the place properly, so I sent for them. Our very decent head of surveying, Anashkin, allowed me to use a truck to collect Klavdia and the boys, and we settled in to a happy family life, even though we had practically no furniture. Such poverty did not frighten us so long as we were together.

8

So as to tighten up on workplace discipline, a law was passed to the effect that any worker who reported to work more than twenty minutes late would be dismissed without recourse. This had little effect; people said, who cares, if you lose your job, you can find a better one elsewhere. The authorities then tightened up the law; the sentence would now be from one to three years in prison. I had to make the journey to the market in Kuibyshev to buy food for the family – my allocation of black bread at the time was just six hundred grams of black bread a day, with nothing for the family, and the only way we could survive was by buying, at a price, whatever the market offered. Officially the whole country was supposed to have plenty to eat, but these were the empty words of the newspapers.

Anashkin gave me permission, but warned me, "Don't be late!" I set off before dawn, easily walking the six kilometres to Novo-Semeykino with my empty rucksack on my back. At dawn, I caught the first bus to Kuibyshev, going straight to the Tsigansky bazaar and filling my rucksack with bread and other food products. I was due to return by the early afternoon bus, but it occurred to me to visit the wife of an arrested man, a lady who was born Gudovich and was a cousin of Vladimir's wife, Elena. I had been living so near to her and yet had never once tried to see her. But just then the sky went very dark, heavy snow began to fall and I took fright. Hurriedly I made for the bus stop but it was too late, the bus had already left. I would have to wait for the next one, which was two hours later.

As the later bus set off, snow was falling thick and heavy. After fifteen kilometres the driver stopped and announced that he could go no further and was turning back. Some of us decided to continue our journey on foot. I shouldered my heavy pack and off we went through the warm, wet snow that lay in heavy layers on our heads and shoulders and pulled our feet back with each tread. Soon I found myself alone as the others gave up. Night was now upon me; I groped my way forward from marker post to marker post, the rucksack pulling ever more painfully at my shoulders. But I had to go on, I had to deliver my provisions, above all I had not to be late. To my great joy, I overtook a cart. Horse, driver and cart were enveloped in the heavy snow and were moving very slowly, but I was allowed to place my pack on top of the load, and so slowly we continued the journey, the horse knowing his way homewards without any hesitation. I do not know how many kilometres we covered or how many hours it took, but in the end we reached the first house in Novo-Semeykino. We hammered on the door of the house where I had once lodged, the lady opened up and, refusing her offer of tea, I dropped to the floor and went straight off to sleep.

Meanwhile, in Staro-Semeykino, concern about my fate had been growing. Anashkin had looked for me at least three times that evening, and Klavdia never slept a wink. I slept the night through and at dawn set off in good humour to walk the last stretch as the low sun lighted my way. I was going to deliver my provisions, and I would be in time for work. I was received like a hero by Klavdia and my colleagues, who had been imagining all kinds of disasters. Anashkin, sleepily, shook a reproachful finger at me.

This was not the end of the story. A few days later, I heard a light knock on my door and there stood an unknown elderly man looking confused and even a little fearful. He introduced himself as the father of Ninnochka, one of my girl assistants, who had gone home to her parents in Kuibyshev on her day off and then failed, because of the heavy snowfall, to return to work on time. Her boss had refused to accept her excuse, had forbidden her to return to work and was taking her to court. The poor girl was sitting at home, crying her eyes out. The prosecutor had promised she would be condemned to three years in prison. The only hope the family had was if I appeared as witness and described how hard I had found it to get home through the storm. The father promised me a rich reward if I could get Ninochka off.

I flatly refused any reward, but promised I would deliver a strong testimony. The father spent the night with us and left in the morning. A few days later, the summons arrived and I set off happily, thinking to buy food supplies before the court sessions. In the court I saw Ninochka, still tearful, a nice young girl with pigtails; I felt great compassion for such a young person about to serve three years in jail. The hall was full of young people, her classmates.

I spoke at length, tried to be as convincing as possible, waving my arms about and got so involved that I never did buy any food supplies. I was heard in silence. Her lawyer was just as eloquent and the meteorological record was also important. The court acquitted Ninochka. Her mother practically suffocated me in her embrace and wanted to haul me back to their house. But hungry though I was, and I knew a hot meal awaited me there, I refused. I had my bus to catch and could not risk taking a later one.

Those were the terrible laws of the time!

9

New work now opened up for me on the right bank of the Volga in an area known as Gavrilov's Field, but it meant leaving the family behind until I could secure accommodation for them. Klavdia was very unhappy to see me go, even though her neighbours promised to help her with carrying water and stoking the fire. Her anxieties were well founded, as our party of surveyors and geologists were treated very shabbily at the new site. One communal building was already fully occupied, and the second, that in principle would be allocated to us, was still being built, but very slowly.

I suffered a professional setback when Sixwinged Seraphim told me that I should have been made head of the surveyors, "but you know . . ." and he did not need to elaborate the reasons why I was passed over. My new boss was to be a young aviator, at present on leave. I swallowed my pride and went on laying out my instruments.

Others managed to find time to travel to Kuibyshev to visit their families, but there was far too much work for me to even think of trying to visit Klavdia. Her letters were heartbreaking; she was sick with waiting for me to call for the family and wondered whether she should not return to Moscow. The second communal house was still not finished, and my new boss seemed in no hurry to return from leave to shoulder some of the heavy burden of surveying for the intensive borehole drilling campaign that was under way.

27. Gavrilov's Field

1

Spring came early. One night we were all woken by the sound of thunderous explosions, as if hundreds of cannons and machine-guns were being fired. It was the ice on the Volga breaking up. Ignoring breakfast, we all raced to the river bank to watch the spectacle. Russians today know the Volga only as a river controlled by dams and hydro-electric installations and will never see the awesome sight of the spring break-up. For several days we all went down after work to watch the sight of the ice floes, whitish-blue or gleaming grey, bumping and crunching together and sliding under each other as they floated majestically past. Local people explained that first came the Volga's ice, then the ice of the river Oka, then the Kama. As the ice came past, melting as it went, the river banks started to flood, the water gradually rising higher and higher, covering the tributaries and piling up tons of ice floes, while great flocks of seagulls swooped down, plunging into the water for their catch of small fish.

For several days we were cut off from our administration. When the first vessel could finally safely make the crossing, however, I was unexpectedly allowed by Anashkin to join it. He said I should go to Staro-Semeykino to collect Klavdia and the boys. He would be coming there himself, and would bring us back on his cutter. The last part of my journey was on foot through flooded fields and forests still deep in snow; it was heavy going, but at the end of it I was able to enjoy three days of rest with the family. The weather was sunny and warm, the grass growing swiftly; I took the boys on walks, telling them the names of flowers and birds. Anashkin and Sokolov arrived and we spent more days catching fish that Klavdia cooked into succulent fry-ups for us all. Then we all sailed back to the Volga down the flooded river Sok between steep banks of yellow reeds, a journey that our son Goga, then three-years-old, has never forgotten.

539

2

On our return, we had to fight for our accommodation. An order from on high had forbidden the survey party from occupying the second communal building that had been completed. Some of us decided to defy this order, moving into several of the rooms and adamantly refusing to budge. Neither commands nor pleadings had any effect on us. We had been promised somewhere to live, and intended to force the issue. In the end we won, and even the infamous "blue caps" failed to shift us. One unpleasant result of our victory with accommodation was that our field allowances were cut, someone higher up having decided that since we were now "comfortably" lodged we did not deserve this extra salary. I was at this time doing drawings and caricatures for our office wall newspaper. I produced a picture of our team holding hands and under it a short satirical verse about our loss of privilege. My colleagues and others laughed and congratulated me, but our party activist, normally a peaceful soul, felt it went a bit too far and pulled it off the wall. Years later I read the novel *The Children of the Arbat* by Rybakov, where the author describes how a character is sent into exile for posting up a careless piece of writing on the wall newspaper, and I remembered my own action. Such were the times that I could, indeed, have suffered a similar fate. All that happened to me was that I was replaced by a less proficient artist, but a man with a clean record.

3

My new boss, Pyotr Constantinovich Tyurin, finally arrived. Clearly, Sokolov had already warned him who I was and what I was. Pyotr never touched on this delicate subject and never gave me orders, on the contrary, he consulted me and learned from my experience. We split the work, he doing all the drawing and paper work, I doing the fieldwork. So I sweated or shivered as I took my measurements and moved my equipment about, while he sat inside at his desk. We never became friends, but I remember him as a completely honourable man.

Here is another tale of the times. One day, I was forced indoors by heavy rain. Tyurin and the others had all gone into Kuibyshev to attend a meeting. Sitting myself down at his desk, I drew out his folder of coordinates and began to busy myself doing the calculations. These were considered top secret and instructions were that they should never be left in one's desk, but locked away in the safe. Yet here was this fatal file in his desk drawer.

Just then someone shouted, "*Smetana!*" (a sort of thick yoghurt.) All of us still in the office seized whatever receptacle we could find and rushed downstairs. There were already about thirty people crowding around the cart with its drums of *smetana*, but after half an hour I was back in the office with my tin mug full of the creamy yoghurt, and as all the chiefs were away, no one made a fuss.

A few days later, however, a great scandal blew up. Someone had come into the office to look for Tyurin, had not found him but had sat down at his desk before leaving. The scandal arose because the man was the inspector appointed to verify that the proper procedures were being followed on the construction site, and secret documents were not being left lying around. He had detected a clear violation of official instructions.

Tyurin was called into Kuibyshev. He took all the blame on himself. He was asked who worked with him. He said I had never been condemned for anything and that his other two staff were *Konsomols*, so by definition beyond suspicion. The authorities then asked us all to fill out personal biographies. I had already filled out a long form and had no desire to repeat the exercise; my original must already be in Kuibyshev, so why another? It also worried me. But then Anashkin and Tyurin came to a wise decision; why not wait and see if the whole thing blew over. And that is what happened. There was no repeat demand for our biographies.

4

I have always wanted to travel. Gavrilov's Field was close to the Zhigulev Heights, low hills within the curve of the Volga. In my daily expeditions, I had often looked at these through my theodolite. On the pretext of prospecting for a borehole that would one day be needed in that area, I obtained permission to absent myself for two days, taking with me a young student called Dima, as well as an armed soldier detailed from the prison camp. The long climb into the hills discouraged the soldier; he turned back, leaving Dima and me to continue happily striding up with a sense of new-found freedom as we moved away from the camp and our routine cares. We ate our provisions, camped for the night and in the morning continued our march. There was no path now, just spiky bushes and rough terrain. We began to look about for a spring to quench our thirst, without success.

"Let's keep going on and down, we're bound to find a spring lower down. And in twenty kilometres we'll reach the river station anyway," I said.

In the middle of an expanse of prickly growth we were surprised to come across a field of melons. We collected a heap of these small globes and began to enjoy their sweet, succulent flesh that satisfied both thirst and hunger. When we had finished, Dima filled his rucksack and I took two ripe ones in my hands and we set off. Suddenly we heard, "Stop! Or I'll shoot!" A bearded man, pointing his rifle at us, jumped out of the bushes. Dima dropped his rucksack, but I froze, still holding the two melons. The man fired a shot over our heads and ordered us to go ahead of him; Dima tried to get rid of his load, but the man ordered us both to keep this evidence of our crime. We were taken to a straw-roofed hut where workers were cooking potatoes on an open fire. They looked at us with indifferent eyes. A portly woman seemed to be their leader. I explained who we were and what we were doing there. I showed her our papers and tried to justify our action. None of this had any effect. As far as she was concerned we were just ordinary thieves, stealing government property. With evident satisfaction, she told us how they had just caught three lads in the same field, taken them down to the militia post, where they had been sentenced immediately to ten years in prison. Our situation was desperate. Young Dima burst into tears. We were told that a truck would come for the workers that evening and would take them and us down to the ferry, from where we would be sent to Kuibyshev. We sat to one side of the fire. The woman took away our melons. One of the workers offered us some fried potatoes, but we refused and sat in mournful silence, suffering.

I thought about how cruel these people were in depriving three young lads of their freedom for so petty a crime. Listening to the workers talking, I could tell that there was little likelihood of the whole melon harvest being transported; so most of the crop would in any case rot in the fields. What then was the point of punishing people so viciously under such a harsh law? My gloomy thoughts were interrupted by the arrival of a mounted, armed man. The woman boastfully told him about our capture. I realised that he was her chief and stood up to explain to him our circumstances, showing him our documents and the technical sketches that we had made. He asked me a few questions and then told the woman that he would himself escort us to the ferry station and hand us over to someone. The woman protested, saying she had caught us and it was her duty to hand us over to the militia. The man raised his voice, repeating his decision. Dima tipped the melons out and shouldered his rucksack, and we set off with the mounted man behind. A little farther on, when the workers' camp was out of sight, the man stopped, pointed to the path leading down to the ferry, and went off in another direction. We thanked him and continued our way.

The next day I described to Bonch, in colourful terms, what had happened to us. He took me aside and whispered, "You've managed to avoid Article 58 so far, and now you nearly got ten years for a couple of melons!"

5

Let me tell another story of those times. We were joined by a nice young couple of geologists, fresh from their studies at the university of Kazan, Rafael Musin and his wife, Katya. In their building, the first floor was also the prison camp office. We would exchange brief nods with the two officers, but their job had to do with prisoners, not with us.

One day, Katya, who was a little bit empty-headed, arrived looking rather puzzled and asked, "What do those officers actually do?" Somebody replied that they dealt with the prisoners. Then Katya asked why had one of the men had asked her to write down what Bonch said to Kumanin and his wife, and to me.

There was total silence for a bit, broken by my direct boss, Tyurin, who asked "Did he mention me?"

"No."

"Then I'll give you a special notebook for your observations!" Everyone laughed before going on with their work.

Kumanin perished in the war, but Bonch I sometimes met after the war, though he lived in Leningrad and I in Moscow. We talked a lot about our time at Gavrilov's Field. He confessed to me that he had had to hide his origins; his father had been a general before the revolution. He also acknowledged that he had at first believed me to be an informer, though a deeply concealed one, as he could not believe a prince could have survived that long. It was only after a year of working with me that he had begun to trust me.

Recalling our lives in those times, we both agreed that despite the poverty in which we lived, with no furniture or other comforts, and with the feeling of being constantly under watch, and the ever-present risk of being fired or arrested, we and our wives had nonetheless been happy, and that this was due to our youth and energy, and the hope of a better future.

6

Finally, in November 1939, my long-awaited leave was granted and I travelled to Moscow. It was a leave spent in pure joy. We lived on Zhivoderk, Klavdia's parents slept in the only bed and we four bunked down on the floor. Every evening Klavdia and I went either on visits or to the theatre. Klavdia's sister's husband was an actor at the Red Army theatre, so we saw all the productions staged there. Shakespeare's *Othello* was on at the Maly Theatre, with Ostuzhev in the main role, but there was not a single ticket to be had.

I remembered how, thanks to Yuzhin, I had seen so many shows in the 1920s, and took myself to call on his widow, Maria Nikolaievna. She welcomed me with great pleasure in her apartment, now a sort of museum of the Maly, hung with photos of all the famous actors. She gladly gave me two of the best seats at the theatre and so we were able to delight in the great artistry of the famous Ostuzhev. Next to us sat a man I recognised – he was General Pavlov, who a year and a half later was to be blamed by Stalin for all the defeats our army suffered in the first days of the war.

Visiting Dmitrov on leave, I found Vladimir in better spirits. His knee was cured and he was receiving commissions for illustrations once more. Father, too, was busily engaged in writing his memoirs, which had lifted him out of his long period of morose depression as he remembered his youth, student days and active adult life. Incidentally, we have become so used to hearing that the aristocracy was an "enemy of the people" that we have been blinded to the lives of the likes of my father. Before the revolution, in his position as Leader of the Assembly of Nobles of his district, Epiphania, in the province of Tula, he strove for more and better hospitals and clinics to be opened, for schools to be built, for bridges and roads to be properly maintained. He struggled with the bureaucracy and although his position was considered to be a public office, received no salary and was often forced to use his own resources. He was considered to be a dangerous liberal, never received any award and was secretly under police surveillance; the governor of the province, Schlippe, refused to endorse his fourth term of office. I mention this public service of his because it was precisely his title of prince and position as Leader of the Assembly of Nobles that led to his and his children's continual persecution after the revolution. I cherish the two precious volumes of his memoirs, and occasionally allow friends to read them.

7

My leave came to an end. I returned to Kuibyshev alone. Klavdia's sisters, horrified by the poor conditions of our family life, persuaded Klavdia and the boys to remain in Moscow. I went back to a sad and lonely life. Then finally spring arrived and for the second time I watched the grandeur of the Volga as its winter ice cracked and broke. As soon as navigation was possible, Klavdia and the children arrived. Once again we were settled in our poor accommodation, but a camp of pioneers was opened next to our barrack and the camp cook generously brought us their leftovers, whilst my girl assistants helped us with bread rations.

Most of us also grew vegetables on little plots that we cultivated not too far away. One evening, as we were working there, we heard a shout, "The second building is burning!"

We raced back that kilometre, which was also uphill, at top speed. Our children were in there, fast asleep; my feelings can be imagined. A crowd had gathered, and we saw that it was the storehouse part, which was our part, that was on fire. But then the firemen came and some of the prisoners also helped. The fire was soon out. Later, it was rumoured that the storekeeper had deliberately started the fire to conceal his pilfering of the stock.

That summer Sixwinged Seraphim's family joined him. His wife confided to my wife that her father had been the famous Cadet leader, N.N. Astrov, shot during the early years of Soviet power. My father and he had worked together in the city administration.

Learning about her father, I guessed that Seraphim Sokolov must be a nobleman. After the war, his name became famous all over the country, as it was due to his initiative that the Kuibyshev hydroelectric plant was moved upriver, so saving the fruitful and beautiful valley of the Sok. He was first on the list of awards for a Stalin prize.

I was now given a new assistant, an older man from Kuibyshev. He was not very well educated but adaptable and resourceful. He noticed a brick ruin on the banks of the Volga, got permission from Anashkin, and then repaired it with his own hands. His wife and young daughter came to live there, acquired a cow, and supplied his family and also me with milk.

At work he talked endlessly about Samara (the real name of Kuibyshev) before the revolution.[27] Huge fortunes were made by

---

27. *Many towns were re-named after Communist figures, but have now been given back their names after the collapse of the USSR.*

those who traded in grains, and these fortunes were carelessly spent in wild orgies. He himself was a billiard marker and one of his roles had been to hunt out young women, even under-age girls, luring them into to taking part in these orgies, where cognac would be poured on to the lids of grand pianos, set alight, and hundred-rouble notes tossed into the flames. Then, with drunken shouts and hoots and slaps, the half-naked girls would be urged to try and snatch the notes out of the flames. He also told me of the brothels and what disgusting scenes of revelry, drunkenness and immorality were common.

The country homes of these wealthy merchants, each one grander than the next, stood in a line along the banks of the river. The last and grandest was flanked by two gigantic alabaster elephants, clearly visible from the boat. When I asked him about the fate of these rich merchants, he told me most of them had managed to get away with their possessions, but that some had been executed.

He told me the story of an amazing merchant, whose life and work was utterly different from his debauched colleagues. A tall, austere man with a long black beard, who took no part in their carousing and never touched alcohol. He was elected president of the All-Russian Temperance society, created reading rooms and other charitable organisations aimed at weaning people away from drink, and was elected a deputy to the Duma. This outstanding man was shot in the first year after the revolution, without any investigation or court process.

8

It was September 1940. We continued to work with great zeal. Every morning lines of prisoners were led past our office, guarded by armed soldiers and dogs. The construction of the dam had not yet started, as the geologists had not settled on the best site for the curtain of the dam. The prisoners worked on auxiliary sites, roads and so forth.

One day, a man sent in to collect fuel for the drilling machines returned empty-handed, saying they would not supply him any as the construction was being closed down. "What rubbish are you talking?" he was asked. He went back to the city and immediately afterwards the news was confirmed. We were alarmed at the prospect of changed lives; for the prisoners, of course, nothing would really change.

The drills and hammers fell silent, trucks began to remove materials to storage. I bade farewell to colleagues, helped pack up our instruments, and we gathered to finalise our work. We found out how this historic decision had been taken. Our chief engineer, Zhuk, was summoned to Moscow. He reported to the Kremlin, where he met Stalin and his suite of henchmen. Stalin shook his hand, and apparently said, "Come to the cinema with us. They say it's an interesting film." They talked of this and that, when suddenly Stalin said, "By the way, we've decided to shut down your project."

I have no idea whether this is fact or legend. But it is true that to continue that gigantic project at a time of grave national concerns would have been inappropriate. War had broken out in the West. Hitler had crushed France and conquered half of Europe. Although Stalin had agreed on friendship with Hitler, there was little doubt in most minds that this friendship was fragile. One could not of course say this aloud. In my correspondence with my father, he expressed himself so vaguely and in such euphemistic language that I could often not understand a word.

We awaited our fate, and then in October came the government order. Instead of one enormous hydroelectric plant, we were to build many smaller ones on the lesser rivers of our country – the Oka, Klyasma, Upper Kama, upper Volga and others. Tyurin and Anashkin remained in Kuibyshev. I wanted to be nearer Moscow, in Vladimir or Rzhev. Kumanin, Bonch and I sent in our requests to our superiors, even though in those times subordinates were expected to bow to orders from on high and not express any personal wishes. Kumanin and Bonch were called to Moscow. I nervously waited for my orders; soon the cold weather would be on us. Finally, a telegramme arrived – "Send Golitsyn to Moscow." I collected my family and with a few possessions we left Gavrilov's Field for good.

28. On the River Klyasma

1

The hydro project's offices were on Matrosskaya Tishina Street, and there I was overjoyed to find Vsevolod Sakharov. He had got his external degree and was now the head of the geology section. I started to exchange news with him, but he took me aside and said in a low voice, "There's a strict rule only to talk business here. Look, we're located between a prison and a madhouse; we could be candidates for either!"

At lunch he told me that the plans now were to flood whole areas for hydroelectric plants, and this had been decided by the administration, so there was nothing we lower orders could do about such mad schemes.

I was posted to the Klyazma project. Discipline was so tight that I was sent off that very evening. On arrival in the town of Vladimir at three in the morning, I was told to report to a room in the local hotel, an old-fashioned building on the main street. To my surprise, the door was opened by Osipov, that inveterate bureaucrat, who I had seen giving such a hard time to recruits to the Moscow-Volga . I was surprised that he even seemed delighted to see me, putting both hands on my shoulders.

"Golitsyn, fancy seeing you!"

I was given a coupon with which to collect my sugar ration and assigned a room. On waking, I collected my ration of sugar, then headed for the militia office to inquire about a certain address. I had a family duty to fulfil; our Elena's aunt, Anna Sergeievna Saburova, was living in Vladimir.

I found the house and on opening the door of her room saw an old woman poking at a dying fire. It was an awful scene; the room was freezing cold, the bed was a heap of old rags and there was rubbish everywhere. Turning, she recognized me, smiled and invited me to sit down. I saw that her once-beautiful face, with the big Sheremetyev eyes, was unhealthily puffy and jaundiced. As I sat there

I could not help thinking of how once upon a time this beautiful lady, in a low cut dress and fine lace shawl, like a portrait by Rokotov, would have entered the ballroom of the Winter Palace as a close friend of the Empress Alexandra.

Icons hung in the corner of the room and on the walls were watercolour portraits of her ancestors, gallant officers in dress uniform, fine ladies in their silks. There were a few books; a Bible, Karamzin's *History of the Russian State* with an ex libris of her father's, Count Sergei Dimitriyevich Sheremetyev, and a few other old books. These family relics had followed her after her eviction from Moscow to Tsaritsina, then to Kaluga, then finally to Vladimir. There were three photographs on the wall; her daughter Ksenya, living in exile in Kazakhstan, and her two sons, arrested in Vladimir, the elder for the third time, the younger for the second time, both now dead. Here was their mother, all alone, unwanted, with all her relics and memories. She offered me tea, apologising that she had no sugar and that the bread was stale. I refused and instead sat for a while talking about family. Then I left, quietly placing my packet of sugar on her window sill. She died in 1949.

2

I knew the head of the geological section, Bonitenko, slightly from my time at Kuibyshev. At some stage he had been something in the synagogue, then he was arrested. At Dmitrov it was noticed that he was an energetic leader and he was promoted. At Kuibyshev something went wrong and he was demoted. Now he had been noticed again and made head of the geology party.

He greeted me in a cold, official tone. I was to be assigned work by the senior geologist, Fedotov, but as he had not yet arrived, I was free to do what I liked for a while. Once again I had time to examine the ancient monuments of Vladimir. In the end, I was sent to Kovrov to draw a plan as to how to reach Pogost, from where we would start our prospecting. Little did I think, when I jumped down to the platform at Kovrov, that I would spend more than half my life in these parts.

I was found a place to sleep in a room where only a partition separated me from the family of four who already lived there. I wrote to Klavdia, asking her to come alone at first and we would see how things worked out. She was horrified by the lodging, but at least brought with her my last salary and also my allowances from Kuibyshev, so we had a welcome sum of cash.

3

One day a tall, very smart officer, accompanied by several civilians, came into our office.

"Zhulenev, Ivan Vladimirovich!" he introduced himself. "Head of the Kovrov plant."

He wanted at once to know where the curtain of the dam was to be located. When he was told it had not yet been decided, he was angry. He mentioned Beria's name, the leader he had to report to, and announced something that startled us; columns of prisoners were already on their way to us and we had no work for them.

Our deputy head, Nikolai Vladimirovich Alshansky, a former tsarist officer as well as agronomist but also an ex-prisoner, took it on himself to say that we would determine the location of the dam within three days. With that, Zhulenov calmed down and asked us how we were faring. We explained about the miserable accommodation we had been offered. He promised to make the locals give us better housing. He also arranged for decent food supplies to be brought in.

Now we had to race to settle the location of the dam, get the first poles indicating the line of the dam in place and draw up our plans. Luckily the lake we chose nearby was frozen, so we could put our drills on the ice. We drilled down a hundred metres – the bottom was soft limestone, with cavitation. Later, drilling on another bank of the Klyasma revealed hard rock. But we had taken our decision and could not go back. To admit a mistake would have been fatal – it would have been labelled sabotage, and we all knew the consequences. We had somehow to strengthen the ground beneath the dam. Day and night we poured cement but it just disappeared, so now the geologists knew they could build nothing on the bed of the lake. At that stage, an order came from Zhulenev to build two bulkheads across the lake and from these to drill holes, filling them with concrete. This work went on all winter and into the spring of 1941.

Meantime, a rather sad Klavia was waiting to join me.

4

My brother Vladimir had a very old friend, dating back to the 1920s. Sergei Nikolaievich Durylin, an "intelligent-*narodnik*",[28] who

---

28. *The narodniks were members of the educated intelligentsia who thought social progress could be made if they went out to teach the people (narod in Russian). The movement was at its height in the second half of the nineteenth century.*

after the revolution gave up his literary activities and became a priest. I mentioned him earlier as the producer of the play *The Wedding* at the home of the Nersesovys.

He was exiled to the Tomsk region and on his return settled in the town of Ivanov and there produced plays in the local theatre, including *Anna Karenina* in his own adaptation for the stage. In 1937, when so many people were being sent to the Gulag, he was rehabilitated. His energetic wife, a former nun, built in those difficult times a country house in Bolshevo, near Moscow, and Durylin made a career from there, becoming a well-known theatre critic and writing articles for many journals and papers. He was close to Igor Ilyinsk, Obukhova, Nezhdanova, Grabar and a friend of Nesterov, who painted his portrait – a bearded monk with glasses, in a black robe against a dark background, with hands laid on a thick book. The portrait is called *Heavy Thoughts* and is now in the Theological Academy in Zagorsk.

Vladimir told him about my ambitions and Durylin got quite excited, saying, "Tell him to write a play on a contemporary theme and with a role for Igor Ilyinsk. If it's good I'll help him get it put on at the Maly Theatre." When my mother passed this news on to me, my ambitions were fired up again. A subject occurred to me at once: Sixwinged Seraphim working on the grandiose construction project while his wife remained in their little Moscow flat. I wanted to sit down and write without a moment's delay, but how and where?

I soon hit on a solution. I would use our office, for which paraffin for the lamps, unlike in our quarters, was available at all times. I got up early and worked until my colleagues arrived for their work at eight in the morning. In two months I had written *The Moscow Apartment*, not only about an enthusiastic geologist and his wife, but with other characters, including a comical man based on the billiard marker from Samara.

To cut a long story short, I eventually showed the play to Durylin; he suggested many changes, the addition of other characters, a secondary plot. He looked upon me with kindliness, never hinting that the play was no good. He approved of the subject and said that the plot was genuinely contemporary. It just needed further work. I left, feeling newly inspired. I would improve the play and then it would be shown at the best theatre in the country, the Maly.

Six years later, back from the war, I was still determined to become a writer. Once again, Durylin promised to help me. I re-worked the play, took it to Igor Ilyinsk himself at the Maly. But theatre in general had now entered a phase of drama without conflict.

In 1954, Durylin died. So I had wasted eight fruitless years; I burned the manuscript.

5

War was imminent. We voluntary workers were sent west to build defensive fortifications. My wife and children and sister-in-law, Dusya, settled in a village with the poetic name of Lyubets, close to Vladimir.[29] Both women found work in the local *kolkhoz*, remaining there for the duration of the war. At the time, little did I realise that I would spend nearly half a lifetime building a life in that village, finally becoming a writer, publishing many books, and, of course, writing these memoirs.

I served in the army engineers for the whole war. As the war turned in our favour, we advanced with our forces, building bridges and roads. I reached Berlin and was never wounded, seeing death only out of the corner of my eye. I survived.

---

29. *Lyblyu tibya in Russian means "I love you".*

This is a list of my close relatives, that is, only including first cousins, born between 1893 and 1920, who either perished in the camps or were eventually released.

Lopukhin, Mikhail Sergeievich – my mother's brother – shot in 1918.

Osorgin, Georgy Mikhailovich – husband of my sister Lina – shot in 1929.

Golitsyn, Vladimir Mikhailovich – my older brother, a talented artist who illustrated around forty books between 1925–1941, worked for the magazines the *Universal Pathfinder*, *Pioneer* and others. In November 1941, he was arrested in Dmitrov on the denunciation of a neighbour for allegedly "waiting for the Germans". But as a lame man, with seven dependants, he could hardly have escaped, and Dmitrov was never captured by the Germans. He died from exhaustion and under-nourishment in the Sviyazhska camp on 6 February 1943. In 1974, an exhibition of his work was held in the Central House of Literature, which was then shown in 48 other cities with great success.

Meien, Viktor Alexandrovich – husband of my sister Sofia. He was arrested for his allegedly German name (his ancestors were Dutch) in November 1941. He perished in the Dzhezkazgansky camps.

Pertsov, Valery Nikolaievich – husband of my sister Ekaterina. He was recruited into the Moscow defence forces in 1941, from which he never returned.

Trubetskaya, Elizaveta Vladimirovna – my father's sister. In the autumn of 1942, she was arrested in Taldom, Province of Moscow, and soon died in prison of typhus.

Trubetskoi, Vladimir Sergeievich – her husband. Was arrested for the seventh time in 1934 and sent to into exile in Andizhan, where he was arrested for the eighth time and disappeared.

Trubetskoi, Grigory Vladimirovich – their son and my cousin. Was arrested in Uzbekistan in 1937, held in camps in the Tomsk region but not made to work because of his chronic asthma. He was released in 1947 and died in 1975.

Trubetskaya, Varvara Vladimirovna – their daughter and my cousin. At the age of eighteen was arrested in 1934, exiled with her father to Andizhan, there arrested again and disappeared.

Trubetskaya, Alexandra Vladimirovna – their daughter and my cousin. Was arrested at the age of nineteen in Andizhan in 1937, from which she wrote letters. She took part in prison theatricals under the well-known director, A. Dikii (who was not long in prison). She died of heart failure in the camp in 1943.

Trubetskoi, Andrei Vladimirovich – their son and my cousin. Was drafted into the army at the beginning of the war, taken prisoner, escaped to join the partisans, was demobilised and then in 1949 was arrested and sent to the Dzhezkazgansky camps. He returned from there in 1955, and is now a doctor of biology, married to my niece, Elena Vladimirovna Golitsyna. They have four sons; their one daughter died at the age of twenty-three.

Golitsyn, Alexander Vladimirovich – son of my uncle and my cousin. In 1934, he was arrested and exiled to Tomsk. There he was arrested again in 1937 and disappeared.

Golitsyn-Urusova, Olga Vladimirovna – my cousin. Arrested in 1937, disappeared.

Urusov, Pyotr Petrovich – husband of the above. Arrested and exiled to Pavlodar in 1934, where he was arrested again and disappeared.

Golitsyn, Kirill Nikolaievich – son of my uncle and my cousin. In 1925, he was arrested and held for 5 years in Butyrka prison. In 1929, he was given "minus six", went to live in Yasnaya Polyana, married and returned to Moscow, where he was arrested again in August 1941 and held in various secret prison laboratories. He was released in 1956, now lives in Moscow and is writing his memoirs.

Bobrinsky, Alexei Lvovich – my cousin. Was arrested in 1934, held in various camps in Vorkuta, then went to the war, was rearrested in 1949, freed in 1956 and died in 1985. I have written about him at length in my memoirs.

To sum up: twelve of my close relatives perished, only one of them, Valery Pertsov, in action. Four relatives returned from the camps.

I could go on and on with the list. The terrible fate of more remote relatives and friends I have already mentioned in these memoirs, and there are many more I know of, but have not mentioned. I will try to draw up a list of perhaps a hundred or so for submission to the Memorial foundation.

POSTSCRIPT

Sergei was demobilised in 1946 and without delay set himself to write up his war experiences, "before I forget them". Employed as a land surveyor, he pursued his literary ambitions, and although he wrote a play that was never staged, over the years a number of his articles and stories were published. These were mainly about the history, the churches and people around Lyubets, the hamlet near Moscow where the family spent their summers. He also produced short books on Russian painters, in particular Polenov and Favorsky.

By 1959 he was able to give up his job and earn his living by writing alone, but he also devoted a lot of time to being among the children on holiday in the three nearby summer camps, telling them about their country's past and passing on to them something of the values by which he lived. His love of country life and of Lyubets was what his children most remember about their father. It was in the last ten years of his life that he wrote his *Memoirs of a Survivor*.

N.W

DONATION

A part of the proceeds of this book will be donated to the Bogoroditsk Museum, the restored Big House on the Bobrinsky estate as featured in the first part of this book.

The estate was neglected in Soviet times, burned down at the end of the Second World War, then lovingly rebuilt by local residents in the 1960s. It is now a cultural centre for the town, serving as a venue for concerts, lectures and receptions. The interior, partially restored, offers a view into Russia's past.